THE BILLY THE KID'S BAD BUCKS HOAX

FAKING BILLY BONNEY AS A WILLIAM BROCKWAY GANG COUNTERFEITER

Gale Cooper

GELCOUR BOOKS

COVER AND BOOK DESIGN BY GALE COOPER

THE TITLE, *Billy the Kid's Bad Bucks Hoax*, is derived from one of that hoax's articles appearing in June, 2015's *True West* magazine, titled: "Billy Bonney's Bad Bucks: Did the Kid Travel the Counterfeit Trail?"

THE SOURCE OF COUNTERFEIT BILLS is the National Archives at College Park, Maryland, Secret Service Library, archivist, Michael Sampson

OTHER BILLY THE KID BOOKS BY GALE COOPER

THE HISTORY

BILLY AND PAULITA: THE SAGA OF BILLY THE KID, PAULITA MAXWELL, AND THE SANTA FE RING

BILLY THE KID'S WRITINGS, WORDS, AND WIT

THE LOST PARDON OF BILLY THE KID: AN ANALYSIS FACTORING IN THE SANTA FE RING, GOVERNOR LEW WALLACE'S DILEMMA, AND A TERRITORY IN REBELLION

THE SANTA FE RING VERSUS BILLY THE KID: THE MAKING OF AN AMERICAN MONSTER

THE CORONER'S JURY REPORT OF BILLY THE KID: THE INQUEST THAT SEALED THE FAME OF BILLY BONNEY AND PAT GARRETT

THE HOAXES

CRACKING THE BILLY THE KID CASE HOAX: THE STRANGE PLOT TO EXHUME BILLY THE KID, CONVICT SHERIFF PAT GARRETT OF MURDER, AND BECOME PRESIDENT OF THE UNITED STATES

THE COLD CASE BILLY THE KID MEGAHOAX: THE PLOT TO STEAL BILLY THE KID'S IDENTITY AND DEFAME PAT GARRETT AS A MURDERER

CRACKING THE BILLY THE KID IMPOSTER HOAX OF BRUSHY BILL ROBERTS

BILLY THE KID'S PRETENDER JOHN MILLER

BLANDINA SEGALE, THE NUN WHO RODE ON BILLY THE KID: SLEUTHING A FOISTED FRONTIER FABLE

For the real Billy Bonney

"*I noticed in the Las Vegas Gazette a piece which stated that, Billy 'the' Kid, the name by which I am known in the Country was the captain of a Band of Outlaws who hold Forth at the Portales. There is no such Organization in Existence. So the Gentleman must have drawn very heavily on his Imagination.*"
    BILLY BONNEY, December 12, 1880 letter to Governor Lew Wallace

COPYRIGHT © 2019 Gale Cooper

FIRST EDITION

*Reproductions, excerpts, or transmittals
of the author's original text or art in this book
are prohibited in any form whatsoever
without written permission of the author.
Infringers will be prosecuted
to the fullest extent of the law.*

ISBN: 978-1-949626 -26-1 HARDCOVER
ISBN: 978-1-949626- 27-8 PAPERBACK
LIBRARY OF CONGRESS CONTROL NUMBER:
2019914268

GELCOUR BOOKS
ALBUQUERQUE, NEW MEXICO

ORDERING THIS BOOK:
Amazon.com, BarnesandNoble.com, bookstores

WEBSITE:
GaleCooperBillytheKidBooks.com

YOUTUBE
"Gale Cooper's Real Billy the Kid"

Printed in the United States of America
on acid free paper

CONTENTS

PREFACE xvii
AUTHOR'S FOREWORD xix
METHODOLOGY xxi
ACKNOWLEDGMENTS xxiii

PART I:
THE REAL HISTORY
OF BILLY BONNEY

CHAPTER 1:
MURKY MYTH AND TALL TALES

BURIED HISTORY 3
A FOUNDATION OF FAKERY 3
THE SANTA FE RING'S OUTLAW MYTH
   OF BILLY THE KID 5
LEW WALLACE'S OUTLAW MYTH
   OF BILLY THE KID 20
PAT GARRETT'S OUTLAW MYTH
   OF BILLY THE KID 41
THE ANTIQUE FOUNDATION 43

CHAPTER 2:
REAL HISTORY

REALITY VERSUS FICTION 45
SALVATION BY PUBLIC IGNORANCE 46
REAL HISTORY 47

CHAPTER 3:
BILLY BONNEY IN HIS OWN WORDS

SPEAKING THROUGH TIME 67
AFFIDAVIT AND DEPUTIZING 68
DEPOSITION TO FRANK WARNER ANGEL 69
"REGULATOR MANIFESTO" 74
HOYT BILL OF SALE 75
LETTER OF MARCH 13, 1879 TO LEW WALLACE 76
LETTER OF MARCH 20, 1879 TO "SQUIRE" WILSON 77
LETTER OF MARCH 20, 1879 TO LEW WALLACE 77
THE LEW WALLACE INTERVIEW 78
THE "BILLIE" LETTER TO LEW WALLACE 81

LOST GRAND JURY TESTIMONY 82
TESTIMONY AGAINST N.A.M. DUDLEY 82
LETTER OF DECEMBER 12, 1880 TO LEW WALLACE 87
SANTA FE JAIL LETTER: JANUARY 1, 1881 89
SANTA FE JAIL LETTER: MARCH 2, 1881 90
SANTA FE JAIL LETTER: MARCH 4, 1881 90
SANTA FE JAIL LETTER: MARCH 27, 1881 91
LETTER TO ATTORNEY EDGAR CAYPLESS 92
NEWSPAPER INTERVIEWS 93
CONCLUSION 98

CHAPTER 4:
BILLY BONNEY'S CHAMPIONS

RESPECT FOR A FREEDOM FIGHTER 99
FRANK AND GEORGE COE 99
YGENIO SALAZAR 101
GOTTFRIED GAUSS 101
IRA LEONARD 103
HENRY HOYT 103
JOHN P. MEADOWS 104
E.C. "TEDDY BLUE" ABBOTT 104

CHAPTER 5:
THE CORONER'S JURY REPORT
OF JULY 15, 1881

PROVING BILLY'S DEATH SCENE 105
PAT GARRETT'S LETTER TO THE ACTING GOVERNOR 107
ISSUES COMPLICATING REWARD COLLECTION 109
REWARD NEEDING LEGISLATIVE INTERVENTION 110
REWARD GRANTED TO GARRETT
    BY THE LEGISLATURE 113
LATER FINDING OF THE REPORT 114

PART II:
A HISTORY OF HOAXING HISTORY

CHAPTER 1:
OLD HOAXERS DOING NEW TRICKS

OVERVIEW 121
THE "BRUSHY BILL" ROBERTS IMPOSTER HOAX 122
THE "BILLY THE KID CASE" HOAX
    ADDING FAKED DNA 124

THE "COLD CASE BILLY THE KID" MEGAHOAX 134
THE FOUNDATION OF FAKERY 134

CHAPTER 2:
W.C. JAMESON'S HOAXING
OF "BRUSHY BILL'S" MOON ERROR

A TRUE-BELIEVER TURNED HOAXER 135
ALIAS BILLY THE KID'S DEATH SCENE'S
    BRIGHT MOON 136
THE RETURN OF THE OUTLAW BILLY THE KID'S
    DEATH SCENE'S DARK MOON 137
RETURN OF THE DARK MOON IN
    BILLY THE KID: BEYOND THE GRAVE 139
THE RETURN OF THE BRIGHT MOON IN
    BILLY THE KID: THE LOST INTERVIEWS 141
PAT GARRETT: THE MAN BEHIND THE BADGE
    AND THE MOON 146
HEADING TO A MEGAHOAX 146

CHAPTER 3:
STEVE SEDERWALL'S
"BILLY THE KID CASE" HOAXES

A PROLIFIC HOAXER 147
HOAXING "BRUSHY" AS BILLY 148
HOAXING PAT GARRETT AS
    MURDERING AN INNOCENT VICTIM 150
HOAXING THE JAILBREAK SUB-INVESTIGATION
    WITH DR. HENRY LEE 174
HOAXING THE BELL KILLING SUB-INVESTIGATION
    HOAX AS HIS OWN INVESTIGATION 179
HOAXING CARPENTER'S BENCH "BLOOD DNA
    OF BILLY THE KID" 180
HOAXING CARPENTER'S BENCH "BLOOD DNA"
    RESULTS FOR MY OPEN RECORDS
    ACT LITIGATION 193
RECYCLING THE BENCH BLOOD DNA HOAX
    AS HIS PRIVATE INVESTIGATION 195
HOAXING A CRIME SCENE FOR THE
    "BILLY THE KID CASE" 196
RECYCLING DR. HENRY LEE'S FAKE
    CRIME SCENE FOR *PAT GARRETT:*
    THE MAN BEHIND THE BADGE 201

RECYCLING DR. HENRY LEE'S FAKE
   CRIME SCENE FOR *COLD CASE BILLY THE KID* 202
HOAXING JOHN MILLER AS BILLY THE KID 204
RECYCLING THE JOHN MILLER
   PILTDOWN MAN-STYLE HOAX..212
HOAXING THE "BILLY THE KID CASE" AS ONLY ABOUT
   THE BELL MURDER TO HIDE ITS RECORDS 214
HOAXING THE "BILLY THE KID CASE" AS A
   PRIVATE HOBBY TO HIDE ITS RECORDS..............................216
HOAXING THE OMI AS DENYING BILLY THE KID'S
   BEING BURIED IN FORT SUMNER......................................223
THE "MEMORANDUM" HOAXING THE "BILLY THE KID
   CASE'S" FAILURE AS A CONSPIRACY AGAINST
   HIMSELF AND TOM SULLIVAN 228
THE RETURN OF THE "MEMORANDUM" AS A
   CONSPIRACY AGAINST HIMSELF 240
FORGING DR. HENRY LEE REPORTS 247
THE RETURN OF MY LITIGATION AS
   MERELY AN ATTACK ON SEDERWALL............................263

CHAPTER 4:
STEVE SEDERWALL'S OTHER
BILLY THE KID HISTORY HOAXES

HOAXED "INVESTIGATIONS" 265
HOAXING THE TUNSTALL MURDER 265
HOAXING THE MORTON AND BAKER KILLING..................270
HOAXING THE SHERIFF BRADY KILLING 271
HOAXING THE "BUCKSHOT" ROBERTS KILLING 275
HOAXING THE LINCOLN COUNTY WAR BATTLE................277
HOAXING PAT GARRETT AS LACKING AUTHORITY...........284
ATTACKING PAT GARRETT BY THE "BRUSHY BILL"
   AND "BILLY THE KID CASE" HOAXES 287
HOAXING DEATH SCENE DOUBTS 290
HOAXING NO CORONER'S JURY REPORT 307
HOAXING DISCOVERY OF "BILLY THE KID" MONIKER 308
HOAXING DISCOVERY OF TOM O'FOLLIARD
   BEING TOM "FOLLIARD" 309

CHAPTER 5:
DAVID TURK AS A
"BILLY THE KID CASE" HOAXER

U.S. MARSHALS SERVICE HISTORIAN DAVID TURK..........315

IN THE "BILLY THE KID CASE" HOAX	315
POISED FOR THE "BILLY THE KID'S BAD BUCKS" HOAX	325

CHAPTER 6:
BOB BOZE BELL AS A HOAXER

FAKING THE OLD WEST	327
TRUE WEST MAGAZINE HOAX COVER-UP	328
HOAXING WITH W.C. JAMESON	330
HOAXING WITH STEVE SEDERWALL	331
READY AND WILLING FOR THE "BILLY THE KID'S BAD BUCKS" HOAX	332

CHAPTER 7:
AN ARMORY OF SMOKING GUNS

NOTHING BUT HOAXING	333

PART III:
HOAXING BILLY BONNEY AS A COUNTERFEITER

CHAPTER 1:
FRAMING THE KID AS A COUNTERFEITER

A NEW DIRECTION IN HOAXING	337
RECYCLING A SEDERWALL HOAX	338
OVERVIEW OF THE COUNTERFEITING HOAX	338

CHAPTER 2:
REALITY OF BILLY BONNEY AND WILLIAM BROCKWAY

BILLY BONNEY AS A RUSTLER"	343
THE SECRET SERVICE AND BILLY BONNEY	344
WILLIAM BROCKWAY AND HIS COUNTERFEITING GANG	371

CHAPTER 3:
STEVE SEDERWALL'S COUNTERFEITING HOAX ARTICLES

A BACK-UP BY FELLOW "BILLY THE KID" CASE HOAXERS	375
HOAXING ARTICLE: "COUNTERFEIT BANK NOTE REWRITES CHAPTER OF BILLY THE KID"	375

HOAXING ARTICLE: "BILLY BONNEY'S BAD BUCKS" 379

CHAPTER 4:
THE RETURN OF THE COUNTERFEITING HOAX IN A BOOK

PARTNERING WITH W.C. JAMESON 383
PULP FICTION INSPIRATION 383
HOAXING A LINK TO A COUNTERFEIT BILL......................384
HOAXING SOURCES AS EVIDENCE FOR
   A BROCKWAY LINK 385
HOAXING A LINK TO BILLY BONNEY'S RUSTLING 386
HOAXING BILLY IN BROCKWAY'S GANG 390
HOAXING A LINK TO JESSE JAMES
   AND COUNTERFEITING 400
HOAXING A LINK OF BILLY BONNEY
   TO BILLY WILSON FOR COUNTERFEITING..................404
HOAXING BILLY AS A SECRET SERVICE
   "SNITCH," INFORMER MURDERER, AND
   CONSPIRATOR TO ROB MAIL 414
HOAXING BILLY AS A COUNTERFEITER DOING
   WITNESS INTIMIDATION 420
HOAXING A LINK TO A.P. ANAYA'S
   COUNTERFEITING CLAIM" 420
HOAXING A COUNTERFEITING LINK
   TO STINKING SPRINGS..421

CHAPTER 5:
HOAXING JAMES DOLAN AS A COLLUDING COUNTERFEITER

ADDING ANOTHER CHARACTER TO THE FICTION 427

CHAPTER 6:
A NON-EXISTENT CASE

SMOKE AND MIRRORS AND THE WILLIAMS
   BONNEY AND BROCKWAY 431

PART IV:
SUMMARY AND CONCLUSIONS

CHAPTER 1:
A RETURN TO ANTIQUE MALARKEY

MASQUERADE 435

ANNOTATED APPENDIX 437

ANNOTATED BIBLIOGRAPHY

RELEVANT 19TH CENTURY HISTORY....................................463
HISTORICAL ORGANIZATIONS 463
   SANTA FE RING..463
   SECRET SERVICE, 19TH CENTURY..................................466
NEW MEXICO TERRITORY REBELLIONS AGAINST
   THE SANTA FE RING..467
HISTORY OF WILLIAM HENRY BONNEY 471
OTHER HISTORICAL FIGURES (PERIOD) 479
OLIVER "BRUSHY BILL" ROBERTS
   BILLY THE KID IMPOSTER HOAX 505
JOHN MILLER BILLY THE KID IMPOSTER HOAX...............509
"BILLY THE KID CASE" HOAX, LINCOLN COUNTY
SHERIFFS DEPARTMENT CASE NO. 2003-274......................509
COLD CASE BILLY THE KID MEGAHOAX OF
   W.C. JAMESON'S 21ST CENTURY BOOKS..........................542

INDEX..551

PREFACE

I tell you what: Just when I was figering on being put out to pasture like some old-timer - being what I am, cept for being fictional - there come galloping back some of the varmints who'd tried to rustle Billy Bonney's history back in the early 2000's as their "Billy the Kid Case," saying Sheriff Pat Garrett never did kill Billy the Kid - Billy's nickname from his Santa Fe Ring enemies. And they was saying that Billy didn't push up no daisies till he dropped dead on his own from old age. Course, the truth is that Billy was killed by Sheriff Pat Garrett on July 14, 1881 when he was 21. And them varmints was just seeking suckers dumb enough to line their pockets by buying hogwash.

Well, this here author stopped them shenanigans back then, but the same fellas come up with a new angle to pat theirselves on the back for nothing. They was always taking shots at Garrett as lying bout killing Billy, and killing some other kid instead, and trying to bring down Garrett's repatation. But seems they got tired of repeating theirselves, so they went after Billy hisself.

So they said Billy was some counterfeiter, in cahoots with Jesse James and some famous counterfeiter by the name of William Brockway. And if that wasn't bad enough, they said Billy was also a low-down highwayman, who robbed the mails and murdered some freight carrier who gave away his crimes. Now, Billy was no counterfeiter, and the rest was fake too. And Jesse James was no counterfeiter neither. So, like Billy hisself wrote to Governor Lew Wallace when he was seeking a pardon but was being called some outlaw in the papers: "The Gentleman must have drawn very heavily on his Imagination."

Truth is, back then, Billy was being set-up by the low-down, land-grabbing politicians of the Santa Fe Ring, who wanted him dead for fighting them in the Lincoln County War, and then for not hightailing it out of the Territory. And they got them some Secret Service agent to frame him as a counterfeiter to give Garrett the chance to track him down. So if Billy's looking down from some fluffy cloud, he might say: Dang, they's doing it again."

And I'd say, "Rest easy, Billy. They ain't gonna do nothing when this here author's around."

Vern Blanton Johnson, Jr.
Lincoln, Lincoln County, New Mexico

AUTHOR'S FOREWORD

This book exposes a bizarre hoax created by well-practiced Billy the Kid history fabricators, whose original fakery was rooted in mid-20th century hoaxes of Billy the Kid impersonators: Oliver "Brushy Bill" Roberts and John Miller. The hoaxers had been empowered, in 2003, by publicity-seeking New Mexico Governor Bill Richardson for his huge forensic DNA hoax, which they all named the "Billy the Kid Case." Its intent was to fake DNA matchings from exhumations to declare "Brushy Bill" as having been Billy the Kid. I stopped and exposed them. But corrupt New Mexico judges shielded the hoaxers from deserved penalties for grave-robbing, and for hiding and forging of public records.

For their rerun, the hoaxers changed direction, now attacking Billy the Kid himself in contradiction to the imposter hoaxes they originally promulgated, in which Billy was a good guy, deserving of a gubernatorial pardon. For this profiteering stunt, they reverted to earliest outlaw mythology of Billy the Kid, generated by the Santa Fe Ring to cover-up its own crimes and the Lincoln County War freedom fight against it, in which Billy was the people's hero. That myth was taken up by Lew Wallace too, who disreputably betrayed his pardon bargain with Billy; and by Pat Garrett, who killed him, and portrayed himself as on the side of law-and-order to conceal that he had been a Ring pawn.

This antiquated return to dime novel-style evil Billy the Kid left open any heinous accusations the hoaxers could fabricate. So their pseudo-Billy was a member of William Brockway's national counterfeiting gang, a wanton murderer of a freight carrier who exposed Billy's counterfeiting criminality, a slimy snitch against his counterfeiter cohorts, and an intimidator of anyone who would dare testify against him.

The imposter hoaxes had been destructive to Pat Garrett by claiming he murdered an innocent victim instead of Billy, and then covering it up. This new counterfeiting hoax is as destructive to Billy Bonney in its fictional portrayal which buries the magnificence of his actual anti-Santa Fe Ring fighting and testifying, and his Robin Hood idealism that would have made cheating local citizens with bad money an anathema. This insult to history demands debunking.

Gale Cooper, M.D.
Sandia Park, New Mexico

METHODOLOGY

PRIMARY DOCUMENTS: For readers' reference, primary documents are presented; with italics for handwriting, two column newsprint for articles, and in distinctive font for books.

COMMENTARY: Author's responses are in boldface and brackets. Boldface also highlights important claims by hoaxers. Underlings and italics are added for emphasis. Page numbers are given for cited text in books, or to refer back to pages in this book itself. And the "Appendix" and "Bibliography" are annotated.

ACKNOWLEDGMENTS

Overriding is my debt to Billy Bonney, whose cause, courage, intelligence, and joie de vivre are my inspiration.

Special thanks goes to archivist, Michael Sampson, at the National Archives Secret Service Library Counterfeit Division, for clarifying the bogus claims made in the "Billy the Kid's Bad Bucks" hoax about a random counterfeit bill in the National Archives, and for providing extensive Secret Service records to help in debunking its other claims.

Historical bedrock is from books by Frederick Nolan on Billy the Kid, the Lincoln County War, and John Henry Tunstall. As valuable is Leon Metz's Pat Garrett biography and Jerry (Richard) Weddle's book on Billy Bonney's early adolescence.

In addition to the Secret Service archives, other National Archives divisions used were the Civilian Records Branch, the Justice Department, and the Department of Interior. Collections used were at the Las Cruces, New Mexico State University Library's Rio Grande Historical Collections' Herman B. Weisner Papers, ca. 1957-1992; the Albuquerque, University of New Mexico Center for Southwest Studies, University Library, Catron Papers; the State of New Mexico Office of Cultural Affairs Historic Preservation Division; the Office of the New Mexico State Historian; the Silver City Museum and Library; the Midland, Texas Nita Stewart and J. Evetts Haley Memorial Library and Historical Center. Collections used for William Bonney's and Lew Wallace's documents were the Santa Fe, New Mexico, Fray Angélico Chávez Historical Library; and the Indianapolis, Indiana Historical Society's Lew and Wallace Collection.

PART I

THE REAL HISTORY OF BILLY BONNEY

CHAPTER 1
MURKY MYTH AND TALL TALES

BURIED HISTORY

From the time Billy Bonney aka Billy the Kid could comment on his own history, it had been obscured by fakery ranging from cover-up to profiteering.

On December 12, 1880, to New Mexico Territory's Governor Lew Wallace, Billy objected about a December 3, 1880 *Las Vegas Gazette* article by its owner, J.H. Koogler, titled "Desperadoe's Stronghold." Declaring himself not an outlaw, he wrote: *"I noticed in the Las Vegas Gazette a piece which stated that, Billy 'the' Kid, the name by which I am known in the Country was the captain of a Band of Outlaws who hold Forth at the Portales. There is no such Organization in Existence. So the Gentleman must have drawn very heavily on his Imagination."*

And that problem only got worse after Billy's dramatic fatal shooting by Sheriff Pat Garrett in Fort Sumner on July 14, 1881. The outlaw mythology of Billy the Kid has continued to flood the media and public consciousness with lurid lies, leaving the real history masked, and the actual freedom fight of the Lincoln County War, with its hero Billy Bonney, lost in its sea of ignorance and obfuscation.

A FOUNDATION OF FAKERY

The history hoaxing that will be discussed in this book, harks back to the original, antiquated, outlaw mythology, which culminated in old-timer Billy the Kid imposter hoaxes of the mid-20th century, and their re-run in the 21st century with the "Billy the Kid Case" forensic DNA hoax. The motives of all were the promulgators' self-aggrandizement and profiteering.

But arguably the strangest hoax to be spawned by this continuum of historical hijacking is the recent "Billy the Kid's Bad Bucks" hoax, about a ruthless, despicable, informer-murdering, counterfeiting Billy the Kid, in cahoots with his day's worst criminals - robber-murderer, Jesse James, and diabolically clever counterfeiter, William Brockway.

This travesty, like the past Billy the Kid imposter hoaxes, relies on public acceptance of Billy's outlaw myth, since knowing the real history easily reveals it as preposterous.

Its savage Billy character brings to mind odd-ball Billy the Kid hoaxer, Sister Blandina Segale, a frontier missionary nun who faked a relationship with a "Billy the Kid" who was a horrific, murderous Colorado highwayman, terrorizing by scalping victims. I exposed her in my 2017 book: *Blandina Segale: The Nun Who Rode on Billy the Kid*. Her 1932 book, *At the End of the Santa Fe Trial*, attained multiple reprints - and even helped put her in the running for sainthood - because of her claim of her holy powers subduing Billy's devil. She wrote:

> Saturday, 2 P.M. came, and I went to meet Billy and his gang ...
>
> **The leader, Billy, has steel-blue eyes, peach complexion, is young, one would take him to be seventeen – innocent-looking, save for the corners of his eyes, which tell a set purpose, good or bad** ... My glance took this description in while "Billy" was saying: "We are all glad to see you, Sister, and I want to say, it would give me pleasure to do you a favor." ...
>
> I took the hand saying: "I understand you have come to scalp our Trinidad physicians, which act I ask you to cancel." ...
>
> "Not only [do I grant] that, Sister, but at any time my pals and I can serve you, you will find us ready."
>
> I thanked him and left the room. (*At the End of the Santa Fe* Trail, 1948 edition, Pages 74-75)

Blandina's malarkey was no different in its wild historical fakery from the "Billy the Kid's Bad Bucks" hoax, 78 years later.

An overview of the growth of the outlaw myth gives an idea of how 19th century dime-novel tales got entangled with real history in a manner arguably unique in its resistance to reality.

THE SANTA FE RING'S
OUTLAW MYTH OF BILLY THE KID

New Mexico Territory's real history of the 1870's featured freedom fights against the land-grabbing, political cabal of the Santa Fe Ring; with its Territorial "boss" being Thomas Benton Catron, and his Washington, D.C. "co-boss" being Stephen Benton Elkins. Not until my books, has the Ring been put in perspective, as it rapaciously infiltrated Territorial executive, legislative, and judicial branches, reducing the populace to its fiefdom.

In 1872 was the Legislature Revolt attempting to stem the Ring's judicial control by beholden judges shielding corrupt members and doing malicious prosecutions of opponents. It was crushed by the Ring-controlled Governor's use of the military. In 1876, was the Grant County Rebellion, with intent to escape Ring domination by seceding to Arizona Territory, as proclaimed in its "Declaration of Independence," but deflated by lack of leadership. The Colfax County War, peaking in 1877, with exposés and pleas for aid to secretly Ring-backing President Rutherford B. Hayes, resulted from the Ring's descent to murder, suppression by troops, removal of courts, and malicious prosecutions to subjugate settlers of the original Maxwell Land Grant, which it now controlled. Though continuing into the 1880's, those Colfax County uprisings resulted only in futile deaths of its freedom fighters.

The most famous was the Lincoln County War of 1878. Emboldened by its success and obvious immunity to presidential sanctions, the Ring had escalated to assassination of T.B. Catron's local mercantile and ranching competitor, John Tunstall; outlawing, by Proclamation of the Ringite Governor, of the self-named Regulators, seeking to arrest Tunstall's murderers; and massacre of freedom fighting Hispanic residents of San Patricio by the Ringite Sheriff using Ring rustlers. It culminated on the July 19, 1878 last day of its six day battle in Lincoln, in which the military was treasonously used to enable arson and murdering of the resistance fighters. That barbaric brutality, unmitigated by bringing to justice a single Ringite, effectively ended Territorial resistance. And the Ring hid its heinous crimes by the victor's option of writing the history: calling the Lincoln County War local mercantile competition by outlaws.

But the Ring encountered an unforeseen problem: the rise of the charismatic, brilliant, literate teenager, Billy Bonney: a multi-cultural hero of Anglo homestead farmers and oppressed Hispanic residents. His militant zeal foreshadowed his potential to instigate a future uprising, as, refusing to flee like other Regulators, he began retaliative rustling against Ring targets, like he had threatened in a pre-battle letter to T.B. Catron's brother-in-law: *"We are all aware that your brother-in-law, T.B. Catron sustains the Murphy-Kinney party ... Steal from the poorest or richest American or Mexican, and the full measure of the injury you do, shall be visited upon the property of Mr. Catron."* And Billy was willing to risk his life to testify against Ringites.

The Ring's response was creating the outlaw myth and moniker, Billy the Kid, to label him for their next assassination.

BILLY BONNEY'S FEDERAL INDICTMENT

When Billy was just one of the Regulators, he had been included in the federal indictment against them made by then U.S. Attorney T.B. Catron to insure his control over the case, and to prevent a Territorial pardon by any Governor. Filed June 21, 1878 as "Case Number 411, the United States versus Charles Bowdre, Josiah Scurlock, Henry Brown, William Bonney alias Henry Antrim alias the Kid, John Middleton, Steven Stevens, John Scroggins, Frederick Waite, and George Coe," it was for the Regulators' killing of a possemen involved in Tunstall's murder: Andrew "Buckshot" Roberts. It was quashed three years later in Billy's Mesilla hanging trials by his loyal attorney, Ira Leonard, as erroneously claiming the murder site as the federally controlled Mescalero Indian Reservation, when it was actually on the private property of Blazer's Mill, making it a Territorial case. It stated:

The United States of America)
Territory of New Mexico   )
Third Judicial District   )

In the United States District Court for the Third Judicial District of the June Term of 1878.
The Grand Jury of the United States of America from the body of the good and lawful men of the Third Judicial District aforesaid – duly empanneled sworn and charged to the Term of aforesaid to inquire in and for the body of the Third Judicial District aforesaid upon their oaths do present that Charles Bowdry [sic - Bowdre throughout], Doc Scurlock, Henry Brown, **Henry**

Antrim – alias Kid – John Middleton, Stephen Stevens, John Scroggins, George Coe and Frederick Waite, late of the Third Judicial District in the Territory of New Mexico on the fifth [sic - fourth] day of April in the year of our Lord Eighteen hundred and Seventy-eight **at and in this reservation of the Mescalero Apache Indians in the Said Third Judicial District, Said Reservation then and there being a part of the Indian country,** *with force and armed in and upon one Andrew Roberts then and there being in the Said Reservation feloniously, willfully, unlawfully of this malice aforethought and from a premeditated design to effect the death of the Said Andrew Roberts, did make an assault, and that the Said Charles Bowdry, Doc Scurlock, Henry Brown,* **Henry Antrim – alias Kid** *– John Middleton, Stephen Stevens, John Scroggins, George Coe and Frederick Waite certain guns then and there loaded and charged with gunpowder and divers leaden bullets, which said guns the Said Charles Bowdry, Doc Scurlock, Henry Brown,* **Henry Antrim (alias Kid)** *John Middleton, Stephen Stevens, John Scroggins, George Coe and Frederick Waite in their hands then and there had and held to, against and upon the Said Andrew Roberts there and then within the Said Reservation feloniously, willfully, unlawfully of this malice aforethought and from a premeditated design to effect the death of the Said Andrew Roberts – did shoot and discharge, and that the Said Charles Bowdry, Doc Scurlock, Henry Brown,* **Henry Antrim – alias Kid** *– John Middleton, Stephen Stevens, John Scroggins, George Coe and Frederick Waite, with the leaden Bullets aforesaid, out of the guns aforesaid, then and there by force of the gunpowder that discharged and sent forth as aforesaid and on Roberts in and upon the right side of the belly of him the Said Andrew Roberts then and there within the Said Reservation feloniously, willfully, unlawfully of this malice aforethought and from a premeditated design to effect the death of the Said Andrew Roberts, did strike, penetrate and wound, giving to the said Andrew Roberts then and there and within the said Reservation and with the leaden Bullets aforesaid, that discharged and sent forth out of the guns aforesaid by the said Andrew [Charles] Bowdry, Doc Scurlock, Henry Brown,* **Henry Antrim – alias Kid** *– John Middleton, Stephen Stevens, John Scroggins, George Coe and Frederick Waite in and upon the right side of the belly of him the said Andrew Roberts one mortal wound of the depth of ten inches and of breadth of one half of an inch of which said mortal wound the Said Andrew Roberts then and there at the said*

Reservation instantly died and so the Jury aforesaid upon their oaths as aforesaid do say that the Said Charles Bowdry, Doc Scurlock, Henry Brown, **Henry Antrim – alias Kid** *– John Middleton, Stephen Stevens, John Scroggins, George Coe and Frederick Waite the Said Andrew Roberts in manner and form aforesaid feloniously, willfully, unlawfully of this malice aforethought and from a premeditated design to effect the death of the Said Andrew Roberts, did kill and murder against the form of the Statute in such case made and provided against the Peace & dignity of the United States. And the Jurors aforesaid upon their oaths aforesaid do further present that Charles Bowdry late of the Third Judicial District in the Territory of New Mexico on the fifth day of April in the year AD Eighteen hundred and Seventy-eight at and within the Reservation of the Mescalero Apache Indians said Reservation being then and there situate in the Third Judicial District aforesaid and then and there being Indian Country in and upon Andrew Roberts then and there being in the Said Reservation in the Said District, feloniously, willfully, unlawfully of his malice aforethought and from a premeditated design to effect the death of the Said Andrew Roberts did make an assault and that the Said Charles Bowdry a certain gun then and there loaded and charged with gunpowder and one leaden Bullet which gun he the Said Charles Bowdry in his right hand then and there had and held to at against and upon the Said Andrew Roberts then and there within the Said Reservation feloniously, willfully, unlawfully of his malice aforethought and from a premeditated design to effect the death of the Said Andrew Roberts, did shoot and discharge and that the Said Charles Bowdry with the leaden Bullet aforesaid out of the gun aforesaid then and there by force of the gunpowder aforesaid shot and sent forth as aforesaid the Said Andrew Roberts in and from the right side of the belly of him the Said Andrew Roberts then and there and in the Said Reservation feloniously, willfully, unlawfully of his malice aforethought and from a premeditated design to effect the death of the Said Andrew Roberts, did strike, penetrate and wound, giving to the Said Andrew Roberts then and there with the leaden Bullet aforesaid so as aforesaid that discharged and sent forth out of the gun aforesaid by the Said Charles Bowdry in and upon the right side of the belly of the Said Andrew Roberts one mortal wound of ten inches and of breadth of one half of an inch of which said mortal wound the Said Andrew Roberts then and there at the said Reservation instantly died and the Jury aforesaid upon their oaths aforesaid do further* *present that Doc Scurlock, Henry Brown,* **Henry Antrim – alias Kid** *– John Middleton, Stephen Stevens, John Scroggins, George Coe and Frederick Waite of the Third Judicial District aforesaid and on the day and year aforesaid with force and arms at the Said Reservation in the Said District aforesaid* **feloniously was present aiding and abetting and assisting the [Said] Charles Bowdry the felony and murder aforesaid to do and commit against the form of the Statute in such case made and provided against the Peace & dignity of the United States and the Jurors aforesaid upon their oaths aforesaid do say that the Said Charles Bowdry Doc Scurlock, Henry Brown, Henry Antrim – alias Kid – John Middleton, Stephen Stevens, John Scroggins, George Coe and Frederick Waite in manner and form aforesaid feloniously, willfully, unlawfully of his malice aforethought and from a premeditated design to effect the death of him the Said Andrew Roberts, him the Said Roberts did kill and murder against the form of the Statute in such case made and provided and against the peace and dignity of the United States.**

Thomas B. Catron
United States Attorney
for New Mexico

<u>411</u>

The United States
vs)
)
Charles Bowdry, Doc Scurlock, Henry Brown, **Henry Antrim alias "Kid,"** *John Middleton, Stephen Stevens, John Scroggins, George Coe and Frederick Waite*
A true bill
   C.P. Crawford
   Foreman of the Grand Jury

Witnesses
Aurelius Wilson, John Pallen, John Watts, J.H. Blazer, Sam F. Mills, [missing first name] Howe, William Gentry

Filed in my Office
the 21 day of June 1878
   John S. Crouch, Clerk

THE PARDON REQUEST

A tenacious Ring adversary, Billy realized that his only hope of avoiding the Ring's preferred method of killing - the legal guise of hanging - was to get a pardon for his Lincoln County War indictments for the Regulator killings of Lincoln County Sheriff William Brady; his Deputy, George Hindman; and his posseman, Andrew "Buckshot" Roberts.

Having witnessed the Ring's Lincoln murder of Attorney Huston Chapman, there to litigate against the Commander who illegally intervened in the Lincoln County War Battle, Billy offered then Governor, Lew Wallace, a bargain, consisting of his testifying for the prosecution in exchange for that pardon.

Wallace ultimately betrayed the bargain - which Billy had fulfilled - because Ring retaliation that would have destroyed him politically. As Wallace had secretly written to his Civil War friend, Absalom Markland, on November 14, 1878: *"I came here, and found a "Ring" with a hand on the throat of the Territory. I refused to join them, and now they are proposing to fight me in the Senate. Ex Delegate Elkins is head-center in Washington."*

MAKING THE MONIKER FOR MURDERING

As Billy had stated to Lew Wallace, he did not use the "Billy the Kid" moniker himself. It first appeared in the May 23, 1879 military Court of Inquiry testimony by Susan McSween against Commander N.A.M. Dudley's Lincoln County War Battle intervention, which enabled the arson of her home and murder of her husband. It was used by Dudley himself, proving its being bandied about by his Ringite associates - like his defense attorney, Henry Waldo, T.B. Catron's law firm member.

Describing Dudley's treasonous action, and refusal of his duty to protect women and children, Susan McSween stated:

> *I then asked [the men setting fire to her house] what they were doing, they said ... [t]hat Peppin and Col. Dudley had sent them to carry lumber to our house to set it on fire ... I then begged them not to do so ... I then started again for Col. Dudley's camp and met Mr. Peppin ... He then said that if I did not want my house burned down I must make those men who were in the house get out of it, that he was bound to have these men ... dead or alive ... I then started again for Col*

Dudley's camp. Arriving there I told him ... that these men and [Sheriff] Peppin intend to burn down the house, and to ask him if he would give me some protection and save our house from being burned. He said he ... did not intend to have anything to do with either party ... I then said it looked strange to me to see his men, or his soldiers I should say, guarding Peppin back and forth through town and sending soldiers around our house ... if he had nothing to do with it. ***He then got very angry and said it was none of my business, that he would send his soldiers where he pleased, that I have no such business to have such men as Billy the Kid, Jim French, and others of like character in my house*** *... He said I have no business, or we had no business, to be in that house, that he would not give us [women and children in the house] protection."*

THE SECRET SERVICE FOR MURDERING BILLY

By late 1880, the Santa Fe Ring had been unable to capture or kill Billy Bonney. So it added high-powered help.

It used its Washington, D.C. influence to contact the head of the Secret Service: an organization founded by Abraham Lincoln in the Civil War to address counterfeiting, but with broad powers to take the law into its own hands, as well as to pay local informants and posses. Sent to New Mexico Territory was one of its 40 Special Operatives, Azariah Wild, with alleged mission of addressing local counterfeiting, but with covert purpose of achieving the killing of Billy Bonney and the few Regulators who had remained with him.

By empowering a past buffalo hunter named Pat Garrett, first for election as Lincoln County Sheriff in November of 1880, then by appointment as a Deputy U.S. Marshal, Azariah Wild created the man to hunt down Billy. Garrett twice tried to kill Billy outright: first by ambush in Fort Sumner on December 19, 1880, killing Tom O'Folliard instead; then by trapping him at a line cabin at Stinking Springs, but killing Charlie Bowdre when he mistook him for Billy. Garrett then settled on capture and a hanging trial, with himself as intended to carry out that legalized killing. But Billy's escape from Garrett's Lincoln jail on April 28, 1881, ended that solution. It took till July 14, 1881 for Garrett to fulfill his directive by his ambush killing of Billy at Fort Sumner's Maxwell family mansion.

SANTA FE RING OUTLAW MYTH PRESS

By December 3, 1880, the Ring began its press campaign against Billy using leaked "secret" reports of Azariah Wild about a fictional "Kid gang" as the biggest counterfeiting-rustling group in America, with Fort Sumner as headquarters. That day, Ringite John H. Koogler, published in his *Las Vegas Gazette* an editorial titled "Desperadoe's Stronghold, An Organized Gang Assisted by Nature and Defiantly Reckless, Who Terrorize the Country to the East of Us." It encouraged a lynch mob for "the army of vengeance." And Billy Bonney was now publicly "Billy the Kid."

Billy's reasonable response should have been to leave the Territory. However, nine days later, on December 12th, he would defiantly choose instead to write his corrective letter to Governor Lew Wallace. The article stated:

DESPERADOE'S STRONGHOLD.

An Organized Gang Assisted by Nature and Defiantly Reckless.

Who Terrorize the Country to the East of Us.

There is a duty which the people of San Miguel county should immediately discharge in the busting of a powerful gang of outlaws, who are continuously harassing the stock men in the Pecos and Panhandle country and terrorizing the people of Ft. Sumner and vicinity.

Between thirty and forty miles from Sumner is a place called the Portales, a lake on the edge of the Staked Plains, the shore of which is fringed with rocks, and is by nature and situation one of the wildest places in the country. When the storms come, the herds are driven there for shelter, and no matter what direction the storm blows it is sue to carry with it a rich bovine tide.

Taking advantage of this, a gang of outlaws have made it their *rendezvous*, and building dugouts, have made for themselves a little camp, which with the natural advantages of the locality, they consider well nigh impregnable.

The gang includes forty to fifty men, all hard characters, the off scouring of society, fugitives from justice, and desperados by profession. Among them are men, with whose names and deeds the people of Las Vegas are perfectly familiar, such as "Billy the Kid," Dave Ruterbaugh [sic], Charles Bowdre, and others of equally unsavory reputation ...

The band is well armed and have plenty of ammunition,

and as they have no hankering to be "pulled in" are very determined ...

Although the band has been organized for some time, it never was so strong as it is to-day, and the party of old offenders who have been obligated to change their quarters many times are the nucleus of the present organization ....

Lincoln county people who have been made the victim of their depredations, at last rose in their might and making it too hot for them, flatly and forever drove them from their territory.

[AUTHOR'S NOTE: Faking the Lincoln County War.]

The gang is under the leadership of "Billy the Kid," a desperate cuss, who is eligible for the post of captain of any crowd, no matter how mean and lawless. They spend considerable time in enjoying themselves at the Portales, keeping guards out and scouting the country for miles around before turning in for the night. Whenever there is a good opportunity to make a haul they split up in gangs and scour the country, always leaving behind a detachment to guard their roost and whatever plunder they may have stored there ...

Whenever the caprice seizes them, they flock to Ft. Sumner and take possession, running things to suit themselves, drinking, carousing, rowing and giving balls.

They run stock from the Panhandle country into the White Oaks and from the Pecos country into the Panhandle, equalizing the herds, but true middle-men style always make heavily by the transaction ...

Are the people of San Miguel county to stand this any longer? Shall we suffer this hoard of outcasts and the scum of society, who are outlawed by a multitude of crimes, to continue their way to the very border of our county?

We believe the citizens of San Miguel County to be order loving people, and call upon them to unite with little bands, scattered to the east of us, in forever wiping out this band. Now is the time to act, for every storm enriches them by driving to their *rendezvous* large herds from which they make their selection. If anything is done, reinforcements in plenty could be secured from the Panhandle country, and resolute men from the association of stockmen could **be drafted into the army of vengeance.**

By December 22, 1880, again using leaked Azariah Wild Secret Service reports as a jumping-off point for fabrication to achieve Billy's capture or killing, the Santa Fe Ring released its first national Billy the Kid outlaw myth propaganda in a *New York Sun* article titled "Outlaws of New Mexico, The Exploits of a Band Headed by a New York Youth, The Mountain Fastness of the Kid and His Followers, War Against a Gang of Cattle Thieves and Murderers, The Frontier Confederates of Brockway, the Counterfeiter." It made Billy nationally famous.

For the readers, it added the hook of already famous counterfeiter, William Brockway, who had just been captured in the publication's site of New York. So the unnamed reporter joined Billy's tale to Brockway's. This fakery would later inspire the modern "Billy the Kid's Bad Bucks" hoaxers to the same end.

The article stated:

OUTLAWS OF NEW MEXICO.
THE EXPLOITS OF A BAND HEADED BY A NEW YORK YOUTH.

The Mountain fastness of the Kid and his Followers— War against a Gang of Cattle Thieves and Murderers — The Frontier Confederates of Brockway, the Counterfeiter.

LAS VEGAS, New Mexico, Dec. 20.—One hundred and twenty-seven miles southeast of Las Vegas, New Mexico, is Fort Sumner, once the base of operations against the Indians who committed depredations against the stockmen. The fort was abandoned some ten or twelve years ago, owing to the removal of troops further south, toward the border of Mexico. The property was condemned and sold to Pete Maxwell, a well-known ranchman of the section. Since then it has been a depot of supplies for stockmen and a stage station on the postal route to the Pecos Valley and Panhandle, Texas.

Until recently, on almost any fair day, there might have been seen lounging about the store or engaged in target practice four men, all of them young, neatly dressed, and of good appearance. A stranger riding in the little hamlet would have taken them to be a party of Eastern gentlemen who had come into that sparsely settled region in search of sport. Many who have gone into that country have struck up an acquaintance with these men and found them agreeable fellows. These men are the worst desperadoes in the West, and large parties of armed men are now scouring the country in pursuit of them.

For a number of years the people of eastern New Mexico and Panhandle, Texas, have been harassed by a gang who have run off stock, burned ranches, and committed acts of violence and murder. It was only recently that the leaders and organization of the band were discovered. The leaders are Billy the Kid, so called from his youth; Dave Rudabaugh, **Billy Wilson**, and Tom O'Phallier, the four loungers about Fort Sumner. The Kid is the captain of the gang.

[AUTHOR'S NOTE: Billy Wilson, actually passing counterfeit bills, would also be used in the "Billy the Kid's Bad Buck's" hoax.]

Their fastness is about thirty-five miles nearly due east from Fort Sumner, on the edge of the great Staked Plain. In that region there is a small lake called Las Portales. It is surrounded by steep hills, from which flow numerous streams that feed the little lake. This place the robbers selected for their resort partly on account of its hiding places, but mainly on account of the opportunities it afforded them for stock thieving. No matter from what direction the storm came, it drove to the lake the herds of cattle which roam at large in the rich grazing country. There the band built for themselves one of those rude dugouts so common on the Western frontier, two sides formed by the side of the hill, the other two constructed of sod and dirt plastered together, and the whole covered by a thatched roof. Stockades or corrals were built near by in which to put stolen stock. During pleasant weather the members of the gang lounged about Fort Sumner or other stations in that section. When the storm sent cattle scudding over the plains to the haven afforded by the hill-protected lake basin, the gang would hurry to their rendezvous and cut out from the herds the best cattle, driving them into their corral, whence they were later sent to market. Their booty was large, for they had a vast stock to select from, the whole country for a distance of one hundred and fifty miles either way being a rich, continuous pasture. Besides the active members of the band, there were many who had apparently some settled occupation and made themselves useful in disposing of the stolen cattle. In every town of any size within a radius of 150 miles there were butchers who dealt regularly in this stolen stock. When supplies from roving herds ran short the desperadoes would make a raid on herds that were guarded, attacking ranches and killing or diving off the inmates. Besides their station at Las Portales, they had one at Bosque Grande, fifty miles to the southwest, and another at Greathouse's rancho, fifty miles to the north. Whenever they were pursued when running of stock, they had the choice of three places to which to resort.

The people of the surrounding country finally found the existence of this band unendurable. After repeated searches, which failed, owing to the smallness of the pursuing parties, it was resolved to organize several bands, who should cooperate in a campaign, which should end only when the outlaws were driven out of the country, or their capture, dead or alive, was effected. The authorities of the several counties which bordered on the country ranged over by **the Kid's gang** had been repeatedly petitioned to send out a posse of men to hunt them down, but, as Las Portales was on disputed territory, the authorities were never able to settle upon any plan of action. At last the ranchmen took the matter into their own hands, and the first party they sent out succeeded in getting on the track of a detachment of the gang who were hauling material to Las Portales, where they were building large stock yards. Although the party was not successful in capturing the outlaws, they made the outlaws flit about the country in a more lively manner than had been their wont. This showed that nothing could be done by a small force. A guard was always kept out on the numerous peaks about Las Portales, from which outlook; the country for twenty miles either way could be scanned by the outlaws, so that they could easily elude a small party!

The Panhandle Transportation Company, an association of stockmen of western Texas, banded together for mutual protection, commissioned their superintendent, Frank Stewart, a brave fellow, who was just the man for such work, to organize an expedition against the outlaws. The White Oaks, a flourishing mining camp, organized a band of rangers. Still another party of picked men, under the lead of Sheriff Pat Garrett of Lincoln County, who is considered one of the bravest and coolest men in the whole region, joined in the campaign. In the latter part of November Garrett, with a force of fourteen men, made a dash for Bosque Grande, riding all night, and there succeeded in capturing five of the outlaws. One of them was a condemned murderer who had escaped from jail; another of them was a murderer for whose arrest $1,500 had been offered. These are the sort of men who reinforce the band. Las Portales has long been an asylum for fugitives from justice. Bosque Grande (Great Forest) is situated in one of the most fertile regions of the West, and as the rich lands bordering on the Pecos River are the objective point of many who intend to settle in the Territory, it was thought best to rid that region of the outlaws first, in order that none might be deterred from settling there. Precautions have been taken which will prevent this refuge of the band from ever sheltering them again.

It was expected that the two other parties would work with Garrett's band, but the Panhandle party were delayed, owing to scarcity of feed, and the White Oaks Rangers had their hands full in another quarter. The latter party had a brush with the Kid, Rudabaugh, Wilson, and several others at Coyote Spring, near the Oaks camp, and the outlaws succeeded in escaping, although two had their horses shot from under them. The rangers started back for reinforcements and supplies, and then pressed on after the outlaws, coming upon them at their other station at Greathouse's ranch. It was night when the rangers reached the ranch. They threw up earthworks a few hundred yards from the stockade of the ranch, and when the outlaws rose up in the morning they found themselves hemmed in. The rangers sent a messenger to Jim Greathouse, the owner of this ranch, demanding the surrender of the outlaws. Greathouse replied in person. He came out to the camp of the rangers and stoutly asserted that the outlaws had taken possession of his ranch and that he had no power over them nor anything to do with them. It was considered best to hold Greathouse as a hostage, while Jim Carlyle, the leader of the rangers, heeded to the Kid's request for a conference. A long time elapsed and Carlyle did not return. His men began to feel uneasy about him, and dispatched a note to the renegade chief saying that unless Carlyle was given up in less than five minutes they would kill Greathouse. No reply was received. Soon after the rangers saw Carlyle leap from the window and dash down the hill toward their entrenchments. He had not gone far, however, when they saw the Kid throw half his body through the window, and, taking deliberate aim, brought down poor Carlyle, killing him instantly. A sharp fight followed, but the outlaws succeeded in making their escape, Greathouse also getting away during the confusion. Before leaving for home with the dead body of their leader, the rangers fired everything about the place, and Greathouse concealed some miles away, saw the smoke of his burning property.

The three parties are now engaged in scouting the country, and will not give up the chase till the country is rid of every one of the outlaws. Money and outfits have been freely offered by men who have large interests in that section. **Government officials are now interested in the campaign, for, in addition to their other crimes, the outlaws have put in circulation a large quantity of the counterfeit money manufactured by William Brockway, the forger. The bills were obtained by one of the gang named Doyle who formerly operated in Chicago, and counterfeit $100 bills in large numbers have been put in circulation among the stockmen and merchants in all that region.**

[AUTHOR'S NOTE: This was the fake news that inspired the "Billy the Kid's Bad Bucks" hoax.]

The information that enabled the Government officers to discover the handling of counterfeit money by the Kid's gang came from a freighter named Smith. Soon afterward, while Smith was on his way from Las Vegas to Fort Sumner with a load of freight, he was waylaid and murdered by some of the gang.

[AUTHOR'S NOTE: This fake news was also in the "Billy the Kid's Bad Bucks" hoax.]

William Bonney, alias the Kid, the leader of the band, is scarcely over 20 years of age. He is handsome and dresses well. He has a fair complexion, smooth face, blue eyes, and light brown hair. He is about six feet tall and deceptively handsome. A beautiful bay mare, that he has carefully trained, is all that he seems to care for, unless he reserves some affection for his brace of six-shooters and Winchester rifle, which have helped him out of many a tight place. His care of the beautiful mare is well deserved, for many a time has her fleetness which surpasses that of any other horse in the Territory, saved his life. The Kid is an admirable rider, and as he is always expected to be obliged to take flight, he usually rides another horse, leading his pet behind, in order to make the best time possible on a fresh horse. He is considered a dead shot and much of his time is spent in target practice. He was born in New York State, but his parents removed to Indiana when he was quite small, and thence to Arizona. There in the Tombstone District the Kid killed his first man when he was only 17 years old, and was obliged to leave the country. He came to New Mexico, where he has since lived.

About three years ago a difficulty arose in Lincoln County, New Mexico, between the stockmen and the Indian agent on the reservation. The trouble arose in regard to some cattle that had been purchased for the Indians. Nearly every man in the county was under arms, and the troops were called out by Gov. Wallace to quell the disturbance. The Kid was mixed up in the affair, and had some narrow escapes. On one occasion he was hotly pursued and was obliged to take refuge in a house in Lincoln, which was surrounded by sixty solders. To the demand to surrender, he only laughed and shot down a soldier just to show that he was game. The house was set on fire, when the Kid, after loading up his Winchester Rifle, leaped from the burning building and made a dash for liberty. All the while he was running he kept firing from his Winchester, bringing down a number of his pursuers. Bullets whistled over his head, but he made his escape, and leaping on a horse was soon laughing at his pursuers. There is no telling how many men he has killed. He sets no value on human life, and has never hesitated at murder when it would serve his purpose. Gov. Wallace a few days ago offered a reward of $500 for his capture, and prominent citizens would make up a handsome purse in addition.

Billy Wilson is much the same sort of good looking fellow as his chief. He is about the same build, with dark hair and a slight moustache. He left the Ohio home where his people, who are all highly esteemed, still reside, several years ago. After being engaged in the cattle business in Texas for some

time, he came to New Mexico. When the excitement broke out over the new camp at White Oaks, he went there and was engaged in the butchering business. He was always considered a smart, energetic fellow, and was well thought of. In some way the Kid persuaded him to join his party, and it was by him that much of the forged paper was put into circulation.

[AUTHOR'S NOTE: This linking of Billy Bonney and Billy Wilson was used by the "Billy the Kid's Bad Bucks" hoax; with reality being that Wilson was a possible bill pusher for the actual local counterfeiters.]

Tom O'Phallier is a Texan and is also a man of good appearance. He has a ruddy, face, and can be an exceedingly agreeable companion. He has been with the band from the first, and has committed many crimes.

Dave Rudabaugh is 36 years old, and was born in New York city, where he lived until about eight years ago. He has raided over southern Kansas, the Indian nations, Texas, southern Colorado, and New Mexico. It would not be difficult to establish charges of murder against him in any or all of those States and Territories. In Colorado, a few years ago he ran off some Government stock, and, while pursued by a detachment of soldiers, he killed a Sergeant and two privates. He once headed an attack on the Las Vegas jail, in order to liberate one of his friends, and shot down a guard who interfered. He is a thorough desperado in look, word, and action, ready at all times for a fight. He thinks no more of putting a bullet through a human brain than through the bull's eyes of the target before which he is continually practicing. He is 5 feet 8 inches tall, and weighs about 180 pounds. He has a swarthy complexion, black hair and beard, and hazel eyes, whose cruel, defiant expression has often been noted.

The career of the band is about run, for they are hotly pursued, and the chances are that before long they will be killed or captured. It is not expected that the Kid or Rudabaugh will be taken alive, as they will fight to the last.

LEW WALLACE'S OUTLAW MYTH OF BILLY THE KID

New Mexico Territory Governor, Lew Wallace made a bargain, proposed by Billy Bonney, to issue him a pardon for his Lincoln County War Regulator group murderers in exchange for his testifying against the 1879 Ringite murderers of Attorney Huston Chapman. Though Billy kept to his side of the bargain, Wallace reneged under Ring pressure.

Knowing he was the cause of Billy's tracking down and death, to assuage his guilty conscience, for the rest of his life, Lew Wallace obsessively published outlaw myth articles about "Billy the Kid," in which he reversed the betrayal of the bargain as Billy's, and fabricated him as an incorrigible outlaw.

This had the additional benefit to Wallace of tacitly placating the Ring, by backing its own outlaw myth-making, as well as hiding its role in the Lincoln County War, which Billy's pardon would have exposed as grounds for clemency.

ARTICLE OF JUNE 18, 1881

On June 13, 1881, back home in Crawfordsville, Indiana only 11 days after leaving his hated New Mexico Territory Governorship early, Lew Wallace was already obsessively reworking his pardon betrayal of Billy Bonney for a Crawfordsville *Saturday Evening Journal* interview, published on June 18, 1881 as "Billy the Kid, General Wallace Tells Why the Young Desperado of New Mexico Wanted to Kill Him. A Dashing and Daring Career in the Land of the Petulant Pistol."

This version had Wallace's despicable formulation of his pardon promise as being broken by Billy the Kid's refusal to abandon outlawry. Wallace embellished his lying by faking Billy as being a serial murderer and rapist, and himself as being both the hero and the Kid's potential victim of revenge. And the pardon bargain, with its proposal and Billy's sham arrest, are reversed as devised by him, not Billy. Sprinkled are facts, like Attorney Huston Chapman's murder, obfuscated by attention-grabbing fiction of adding famous Jesse James, instead of actual Jessie Evans - as later lifted by the "Billy the Kid's Bad Bucks" hoax.

The article stated:

BILLY THE KID.

General Wallace Tells Why the Young Desperado of New Mexico Wanted to Kill Him.

A Dashing and Daring Career in the Land of the Petulant Pistol.

Late newspaper accounts of the exploits of "Billy the Kid," the New Mexico outlaw, have made him the chief among frontier desperados and familiarized readers with his depredations and murdering. In Crawfordsville additional interest in him is created by the fact that he is the same who swore to kill General Wallace, late Governor of New Mexico. His real name is William Bonne [sic], and he was born in New York, which place he left when a small boy with his widowed mother, for Indiana. He lived for a while in Indianapolis, and then Terre Haute, and four years ago went to the Territory of New Mexico. He had been a close reader of blood-and-thunder literature, and soon succeeded in out doing any of the desperate thugs he had ever read of. He now belongs to Silver City where his mother resides, but lives in the mountains to evade the edicts of the law, he now being under sentence for death for murder. He has killed in all, thirty-nine men, and is still not satisfied. He worked for John Chisum, the cattle dealer, in the late Lincoln county trouble, and **claiming he has never received the promised $5 per day for his services, he is hunting down and killing Chisum's herdsmen, and giving their employer credit for $5 for each man killed.**

[AUTHOR'S NOTE: Hiding Ring issues, Wallace uses anger at Chisum as Billy's motive for killings.]

It is only recently that he killed two guards of the Lincoln county jail, compelled one man to file off his irons, and another to furnish him with a horse and rode away before the eyes of the whole town. It was during this confinement that he swore to kill Governor Wallace. Given in the following narrative which a reporter of THE JOURNAL got from General Wallace, last Monday, is the cause of Billy's anger at the that Governor: **A young lawyer named Chapman was murdered in Lincoln county, and for this were arrested four men, among whom was the notorious Jesse James, under one of his many names**. The witnesses against the murderers all lied, and the latter were about to be liberated on a writ of habeas corpus. Governor Wallace heard that the "kid" saw the murder, and finding a man who could find Billy, sent him a note requesting a conference with him at midnight at a certain house which was designated. **The note assured the "kid" that if the conference proved that he did not have the necessary information about the murder he would be permitted to leave the city, but if he did and** would testify before the grand jury, the note implied that the Governor would pardon him for crimes for which he had been indicted, provided he would leave the Territory for good.

[AUTHOR'S NOTE: This admits reality of pardon promise letters which Billy referred in his jail letter of March 2, 1881. And Wallace admits to a pardon bargain; though adding a condition of leaving the Territory.]

Governor Wallace repaired to the meeting place early, and promptly at midnight, a slight knock was heard at the door and upon response in the inside, "Billy the Kid" opened the door and walked in. The Governor found Billy to be a mild-faced young man, 19 years old, small, slender, sloping shoulders, manly head, and an open expression of the face, and a deliberate and pleasant voice. After taking a cigar apiece, and talking over matters in Indiana, (for Billy was proud to say that he was once a Hoosier), Governor Wallace asked Billy to tell what he knew. He proceeded in good language to slowly tell what he knew, which proved to be what the authorities wanted. The Governor asked him if he would go before the grand jury and tell the same thing. Billy's reply was that he would not dare to do it voluntarily, as the criminals' friends would kill him. The Governor suggested that the difficulty might be surmounted by the "kid" permitting himself to be captured.

[AUTHOR'S NOTE: Lying Wallace, in his decades of reworking this tale, would always undo Billy's courage in contacting him and in suggesting the sham arrest, by claiming he himself instigated both.]

This was agreed upon, and accordingly and by arrangement Billy was surprised at a safe place in the mountains, while asleep, captured, and taken to jail. **He went before the grand jury and by his evidence the criminals were indicted for murder.** But before the trial in which he was to appear as a witness for the prosecution, he tired of jail life, and one day at dinner, he left his guards and took to the mountains.

[AUTHOR'S NOTE: Wallace, in this jumbled version, admits Billy testified for the pardon bargain. But to hide his own betrayal, he fabricates that Billy absconded before testifying in a another fabricated trial. In later articles, Wallace used the absconding story to make Billy the bargain betrayer. Omitted here, and forever after, is that Billy stayed in jail until June of 1879 to testify in the Dudley Court of Inquiry.]

He then resumed robbing raids and stealing cattle ... until two years later, Pat Garrett, Sheriff of Lincoln County, and the only man now in New Mexico who is not afraid of Billy, got on his track and effected his capture. **During this imprisonment** the "kid," who had constantly carried the Governor's note about the convicting of Chapman's murderers, wrote twice to Governor Wallace, threatening to publish the proposition to pardon if he was not liberated. No attention was paid to these and Billy's lawyer then came before the Governor with the same threat. The reply from the executive was that Billy might publish as much as he chose, as the matter had been reported in Washington and there approved.

[AUTHOR'S NOTE: Here is evidence of a lost pardon promise letter; further implied by Wallace's made-up tale of standing up to Ira Leonard ("Billy's lawyer") by reporting to Washington about "the matter."]

Billy was further informed that he had not complied with all the conditions of the promise. This greatly enraged the young outlaw and he said he would take the life of the Governor. While under sentence of death he swore to kill three men before he died – Governor Wallace, John Chisum, the cattle dealer, and Pat Garrett, the Lincoln County Sheriff. In a short time he gained liberty by killing his two guards as before stated. Although Bonne [sic] was a desperate character, Governor Wallace felt no particular alarm and was more anxious to find Billy than Billy was to find him. He had it so arranged that he would have heard of the young desperado's approach 150 miles from Santa Fe, and other precautions were taken at the Governor's office.

[AUTHOR'S NOTE: This fabricated tale of Billy's murderous vendetta against him, is Wallace's projection of his own murderous feelings against Billy. It might have also been his real fear of retaliation for his dastardly betrayal. For this fiction, "threat" by Billy also puts Wallace in the center of Billy's jailbreak tale, when, in fact, he was irrelevant by then. But Wallace recycled this fakery it in all his future outlaw myth articles after Billy's killing.]

Billy was sentenced to be hung, and took desperate chances to escape. He was successful and was in no hurry to come in the way of the law. His success had in his great amount of nerve. He never allowed himself to become excited, and never missed the object he shot at. **Before Billy became involved in so many crimes he had one day showing Governor Wallace a specimen of his workmanship. He explained his perfection thus: He never took aim with the revolver, but placed his index finger along the barrel, and as if pointing at the object pulled the trigger with his second finger** ... Nevertheless he is ever on the alert guarding against the other fellows getting the "drop."

[AUTHOR'S NOTE: When Billy was jailed in Lincoln, Wallace likely requested a shooting demonstration. But his preposterous pointing finger for aiming seems to be Wallace's fabrication; and it was repeated in his later articles.]

There was once a three day siege of a house in which were Billy and a party. **General Wallace had a report of the maneuvering on the outside and when Billy was a prisoner had him to tell of the workings on the inside.** The besieging party finally succeeded in firing the house and those inside were driven from room to room, and finally to the kitchen. Then, there was but one door of exit and the outside men kept a continual storm of bullets pouring into it. One by one those attacked "took chances" and ran out the door rather than to be burned. Each fell with from four to fourteen bullets in the bodies until the "kid" who was the last to go rushed out and escaped without a scratch, though his clothing was completely riddled with bullets, and even his necktie was cut at his throat.

[AUTHOR'S NOTE: Though Wallace was fully aware of Lincoln County War issues, and himself testified in the military Court of Inquiry against Commander N.A.M. Dudley, he gave this fictionalized version to hide it as a rebellion against the Santa Fe Ring, with Billy as its hero. It is also an admission that, in his interviewing of Billy during the sham arrest for the pardon bargain, that he heard Billy "tell of the workings on the inside" [of the besieged and burning McSween house. This further confirms that Billy's larger agenda in the pardon bargain had also been to elicit Wallace's aid in his anti-Ring agenda, as implied in his March 24, 1881 "Billie" letter (see page 81 below). If so, one can assume that Billy also told Wallace about Dudley's soldiers firing a volley at those escaping, meaning giving treasonous orders to kill civilians. But it should not be missed that Wallace inserted himself into this mangled version of the Lincoln County War Battle as being on the "outside."]

The "Kid" is a great favorite with Mexican women and does not want for friends, but as hard, bold, and daring as he is, he will doubtless soon meet death at the rope end of the gun's muzzle.

[AUTHOR'S NOTE: Wallace revealed that his agenda matched the Ring's: ensure the death of this dangerous political gadfly, Billy.]

ARTICLE OF DECEMBER 10, 1893

Lew Wallace's December 10, 1893 *San Francisco Chronicle* article titled "Lew Wallace's Foe, Threatened by "Billy the Kid," The Writing of "Ben-Hur" Interrupted, An Incident of the Soldier-Author's Career in New Mexico," was to make himself the hero.

It can also be contemplated that, by 1893, Billy Bonney's own rising fame stimulated Wallace's competitive spirit, since he waved the banner of his best-selling *Ben-Hur*, and stated outright: "The Governor's enemy was no less a personage than the illustrious "Billy the Kid," than whom no man had ever excited more terror on the frontier or given better ground for the dread in which he was held."

But the article's simple focus was to make Billy all bad. The pardon was irrelevant to that literary mission, and was omitted. In its place was a dramatic Wallace-ordered capture of outlaw Billy who was "surrounded by overwhelming numbers" of men - likely Wallace's cribbing of Secret Service Agent Azariah Wild's 1880 reports' versions of posses chasing Billy's mythical outlaw gang. Revealing Wallace's guilty conscience, was his continued lie that it was Billy who planned to come to Santa Fe to kill him. It is Wallace's reversal of his own guilt deserving of punishment; and, at an even deeper level, is a projection of his own murderous hatred of the undefeatable and brilliant boy. The article stated:

LEW WALLACE'S FOE.
Threatened by
"Billy the Kid"
The Writing of "Ben-Hur"
Interrupted.
An Incident of the Soldier-
Author's Career in New Mexico.

General Lew Wallace, best known to the general public by his two great books, "Ben-Hur" and the "Prince of India," is a man of many roles. He has been successful as a soldier, politician, diplomat and author, and some startling experiences have fallen to his lot.

His career on the battlefield, his life in Turkey, When he was Minister to Constantinople, and his later triumphs in the world of literature have all gone to make an eventful record, and they have all been so often recounted in the public prints that it would seem that every incident of his life would be familiar to those who keep themselves posted on the careers of public men. Yet there is one ordeal through which General Wallace has passed, and which he probably will never forget, that has escaped the vigilance of the scribes. It is, probably, not generally remembered that General Wallace was once Governor of the Territory of New Mexico, but it is a fact that in 1880, and for a year or so after that, he occupied the former palace of the Captains-General of Spain, in the historic old town of Santa Fe, N.M. He was the chief executive of the Territory, by appointment of President Garfield [Hayes], and it was during his administration that he fell under the ban of an assassin, and was given very good reason to believe that he would have to look down the ugly barrel of a 45-caliber revolver, and to defend his life as best he might.

The Governor's enemy was no less a personage than the illustrious "Billy the Kid," than whom no man had ever excited more terror on the frontier or given better ground for the dread in which he was held. He had perpetrated murder after murder and there were few crimes of which he was not believed to be capable. He boasted that he had killed more men than he was years of age and would shoot a man if he felt so disposed, "just to see him kick."

After "Billy the Kid" had been carrying things with a high hand for a long time Governor Wallace offered a reward for his capture. It proved a tempting bait to the "gun fighters" and officers of the law in the Territory. There were plenty of men among them who would not shirk from a hunt through the mountain fastnesses, even after such formidable game as this border bully, and the result of the Governor's offer was that after a most exciting pursuit **"Billy the Kid" was surrounded by overwhelming numbers and forced to surrender**. He was taken to Santa Fe and thence to Lincoln County to answer a charge of murder.

Enraged at having been trapped, the outlaw swore that if he ever regained his liberty he would kill three men. One was a judge who had passed sentence upon him, one was Pat Garrett of Lincoln county, who had been conspicuously active in effecting his capture, and the third was Governor Lew Wallace.

"After I have settled accounts with these three men," said the desperado, "I will be willing to surrender and be hanged. **When I get out I will ride into Santa Fe, hitch my horse in front of the Palace, and walk in and put a bullet through Lew Wallace**.

This seemed idle boasting at the time, because there appeared to be not the remotest possibility of the prisoner's escape. He was in the custody of Sheriff Garrett in the County Jail of Lincoln, and the Sheriff, besides being a cool, courageous and reliable man, had every incentive to be watchful of his charge. It was thought a pretty sure thing that Garrett would never let the "Kid" go, and Governor Wallace felt fairly secure in his office away off in Santa Fe.

Garrett appointed as guards over the "Kid" Bob Ollinger [Olinger] and John [James] Bell. They were his personal friends, both big, burley **six-footers, who towered over their diminutive prisoner**. In addition to this physical superiority over him, they counted themselves as his equals when it came to a fair and square gun-fight. If anyone had told them that the "Kid" would outwit them and escape they would have laughed at the very thought of it.

For months the "Kid" was a docile as a kitten. The guards became used to him, then familiar, and then friendly. He seemed to have forgotten that they had helped to cage him and were his custodians, and as time passed the trio became boon companions. The guards laughed at the "Kid's" stories of his exploits, played cards with him during their long watches and would often remove one of the "cuffs" from his wrist, so that he could manipulate his cards or ply knife and fork at meal times. Whenever this was done both handcuffs were fastened to the right wrist, and thus locked in a cell with one of his stalwart guards the little cutthroat was safe enough.

Ollinger and Bell took turns watching in the jail and relieved each other to go to dinner. One day when Ollinger had gone across the street to a restaurant Bell took the "Kid" from his cell to an up-stairs room in the little two-story adobe jail. He put some food on a table for him and then unfastened the left cuff and locked it on the prisoner's right wrist.

The "Kid" sat down and began to eat without the slightest apparent concern. While he was munching the coarse prison fare Bell strode restlessly up and down the room. He wore no coat and his heavy revolver protruded from the holster attached to his cartridge belt. Each time he walked the room he passed within two feet of where the "Kid" sat, and once when he came within reach the "Kid," with the quickness of a cat, leaped upon his chair and dealt him a rap on the head with the handcuffs. Bell staggered under the blow, and before he could recover the "Kid" has snatched the revolver from the holster and sent a bullet through Bell's body. The guard tottered and fell and in a few moments was dead.

Ollinger was across the street and had, no doubt, heard the shot. The outlaw seized a double-barreled shotgun and ran out on the front balcony. Already Ollinger had crossed the street. He had come on the run, but before his foot struck the steps he fell with a load of buckshot in his heart.

The murderer walked carelessly down the stairs, stepped over Allinger's [Olinger's] prostrate form and strutted down the street with the revolver and shotgun in his hands. A blacksmith was shoeing a horse in a neighboring shop, and "Billy the Kid" easily persuaded him to desist, **then mounted and rode out of town at a walk, saying just before he** started: "Now for the Governor."

The news of the escape quickly reached Santa Fe, and Governor Wallace's friends became very uneasy lest the "Kid" should carry out his threat. The Governor himself was not entirely tranquil in the circumstances. It is one thing to face an enemy in the open field and quite another to have a treacherous one dogging one's footsteps.

Brave as Governor Wallace had shown himself to be, he recognized his danger and prepared to meet it. At that time he had already begun "Ben-Hur," and used to sit for hours in his office each day engaged upon the absorbing work. From the day upon which "Billy the Kid" escaped from the Lincoln County Jail a close observer entering the office might have detected lying on the table, partially hidden among papers and scraps of manuscript, the glint of a pistol, for the Governor was never without one while he knew that his arch-enemy was at large.

The people of Santa Fe were well aware that the head of the Territorial Government was preparing for war for every morning about 7 o'clock the sharp crack of a revolver being fired rapidly resounded from the corral in the rear of the gubernatorial residence. It soon became known that it was Governor Wallace improving himself as a pistol shot preparatory to an impromptu duel with "Billy the Kid." A figure had been marked on the adobe wall of the corral, and the Governor filled it full of holes. He became so expert that he could knock an imaginary eye out of the figure at twenty paces. He made no bones of the matter and, in fact, could be easily seen from the adjoining houses.

During the weeks which elapsed before the termination of this period of suspense Pat Garrett was in hot pursuit of "Billy the Kid." It was a most remarkable and exciting chase. The whole Territory was deeply intent upon it, and news of the whereabouts of the two men was eagerly looked for. Governor Wallace repeatedly said to the writer: "When these two men meet one or both of them will bite the dust."

He was right. The announcement finally came from Fort Sumner that Garrett had forever rid the country of the "Kid." He had tracked him to the house of Peter Maxwell, near Fort Sumner, and, concealing himself in one of the rooms, had fired one shot at his man. That shot passed through the desperado's heart and he fell dead in his tracks.

Governor Wallace breathed easier, and the next night a reporter found tall, muscular Pat Garrett waltzing with a four-foot Mexican girl in a dance hall of Santa Fe.

ARTICLE OF JUNE 23, 1900

For *The Indianapolis Press* on June 23, 1900, Lew Wallace repeated his outlaw myth with "Gen. Wallace's Feud with Billy the Kid, When the General Was Governor of New Mexico and Billy Bonne Was the Most Dangerous Western Outlaw, He Was a Waif and was Reared in Indiana." In this article, Wallace created the mythical tally: "[H]e killed a man for every one of the twenty-two [later changed to twenty-one] years he lived." Noteworthy is that in all his outlaw fabricating, Lew Wallace never mentioned counterfeiting as a Billy the Kid crime; and Wallace had met with Secret Service Operative Azariah Wild during Wild's late 1880 assistance in Billy's pursuit of the "Wilson & Kid gang."

The article stated:

GEN. WALLACE'S FEUD WITH BILLY THE KID
When the General Was Governor of New Mexico and Billy Bonne Was the Most Dangerous Western Outlaw
HE WAS A WAIF AND WAS REARED IN INDIANA

(By a Staff Correspondent)
CRAWFORDSVILLE, Ind., June 23. –

"Yes, **he killed a man for every one of the twenty-two years he lived**, and died in his stocking feet – a marvelous, far more than marvelous, career his was – a nightmare of existence."

Gen. Lew Wallace's shaggy brows contracted with a frown as he closed his eyes as though to shut out from his memory unpleasant things. There was a pause. He arose from his chair, and after walking up and down his study in silence, finally said:

"So long as I live, I will never lose the image of Billy the Kid, as I saw him that midnight in old Santa Fe, back in 1879. There he stands in the doorway of the little adobe house, form outlined by moonlight at his back, face illuminated by glow of the little lamp. The clock had made its first stroke of the midnight hour, when by appointment to the second there was a knock at the door that I can hear yet. 'Come in,' I said. The door flew open and there stood the most feared, the most adored, the most reverenced man in New Mexico, hunted by every limb of the law as a criminal, and sought by every Spanish senorita as her lover. The room was covered by a Winchester rifle held in one hand. In the other was a Colt's revolver. It was a musical growl that said, "I was to meet the Governor here at midnight. It is midnight: is he here?"

"I asked him to come in for a conference, and told him that I was the Governor of New Mexico.

"Your note gave me the promise of protection," he said.

"There is no one here but us three," replied I, pointing to the owner of the cottage.

"Billy threw his gun over his arm and came straight to the table near which I sat. I looked at him in wonder. This was the man that had killed his scores: the man whom every officer hunted. I was not expecting to see a stripling, with rounded shoulders, slightly stooping stature, slender, effeminate physique. His face was smooth and soft, and yet character and firmness were shown in every line. His voice was as musical as that of a society belle. **Over him, with a majesty, hung the cloak of fearlessness and alertness penetrated only by two eyes that looked deep into every man's intentions.**"

Reared in Indiana.

The General passed from the thoughtful to the narrative and said: "Billy the Kid, the New Mexican outlaw that attracted the attention of a nation, and under whose fearful vendetta I was placed while Governor of New Mexico, was a New York waif whose name was William Bonne. He was brought to Indiana when he was a small boy and was reared in Indianapolis and Terre Haute. He was about 17 years old in 1876, when he went West. During his early years he had been a close reader of blood-and-thunder literature. He outdid in reality the lurid pictures of the literature in which he was schooled.

"It was not long until 'Billy the Kid' became the most daring and notorious of desperadoes. Stories of his crimes, his escapes, his fascinating faculties were the nursery tales of the Territory. He started to grow up with the country by taking employment of John Chisum, who was known as the 'Cattle King,' was a hard taskmaster and disputed Billy's account. The latter swore that he would square matters by killing Chisum's herdsmen: that for each man he killed he would credit the cattleman with $5, but if he killed Chisum himself then the whole account would be wiped out.

[AUTHOR'S NOTE: Wallace makes Chisum Billy's killing motive to hide Lincoln County War issues.]

Midnight Meeting Arranged.

"A young lawyer named Chapman was murdered at Lincoln. Four men were arrested, among them the notorious Jesse James.

[AUTHOR'S NOTE: New Mexico Territory outlaw, Jessie Evans, here becomes famous Jesse James!]

The witnesses to the killing were filled with terror and fled the country. Because of the lack of evidence the prisoners were about to be released on a writ of habeas corpus. I had been sent to pacify the country and had realized this was an opportunity I could not let slip. At last I heard that Billy the Kid had witnessed the murder.

[AUTHOR'S NOTE: Wallace hides Billy's pardon bargain to make himself the hero.]

In the outskirts of Santa Fe lived an old 'squire,' who was one of Billy's friends.

[AUTHOR'S NOTE: Wallace changes the actual Lincoln meeting to Santa Fe to dispense with Lincoln County War issues.]

I went to him one evening and told him I wanted the young outlaw to meet me promptly at midnight. He professed that he had no connection with the sought-for youth. I ordered pen and ink and wrote a note, and, leaving it, told him that I would expect it to be delivered to Billy. In the note I said I understood he was the only remaining man that had witnessed the murder, and that if he would appear before the Grand Jury and court and convict them I would pardon him for all his crimes.

[AUTHOR'S NOTE: Though reversing roles with Billy as to proposing the pardon, Wallace now admits to it. That will require his later concealing of his betrayal.]

"The midnight meeting was as I have described. When he heard from my lips my proposition he said: 'My God, Governor, they would kill me.' 'But that can be arranged,' I replied.

[AUTHOR'S NOTE: Wallace lies that he devised the sham imprisonment.]

It was decided that Billy was to be taken the next morning while asleep in a cabin back in the mountain. He picked the men that were to capture him. He required me to keep him in irons during confinement, that his reputation not be marred" ...

[AUTHOR'S NOTE: Wallace hides the Lincoln location of the jail for this lie.]

Was Something of a Hypnotist.

"It was a week before the trial. Billy had been taken to dinner in his chains. After the meal he said: "Well, I wish you would tell the Governor that I am tired. Much obliged boys,' and leaving them as though in a trance, he quietly walked across the street, and, unhitching a horse, dashed out of town. There could be no suspicion that the guards had conspired for his release. They were victims of that mysterious something that Billy exerted over men.

[AUTHOR'S NOTE: Here is Wallace's perfidy: hiding Billy's testimony that fulfilled the pardon bargain, substituting a dream-like escape, as if Billy could not stick to his pardon deal.]

"Later Billy was arrested for a series of murders.

[AUTHOR'S NOTE: Billy arrest by Pat Garrett was only for Brady-Hindman-Roberts indictments.]

He had kept my note offering pardon in the affair. He had been in jail a week when he addressed me: 'Governor, why haven't you come to see me?' I paid no attention to it. A few days later there was a second note: 'Governor, I have some papers you would not want to see displayed. Come to the jail.' I knew what he meant.

[AUTHOR'S NOTE: Wallace here reworked Billy's jail letters as blackmailing.]

I sent a copy of the old note and the story over to the paper and it was published. I sent him a copy of the paper and drew his fire. It was then that he swore his vendetta on my life and on that of Pat Garrett, the sheriff of Lincoln County.

[AUTHOR'S NOTE: This fake "Billy vendetta" against himself is a projection of his hostility and an unconscious expression of guilt and his own deserved punishment. Wallace's adding of Garrett, reflects his request to Garrett to report back to him after Billy's hanging death, like a compatriot in his murderous plan.]

He was convicted for murder and sentenced to be hanged. When the sentence was read, he arose in court and said:

" 'Judge, that doesn't frighten me the least bit. Billy the Kid was not born to be hung.'

"This young desperado was a thorough fatalist. He believed that for the time he had a charmed life: that he had nothing to fear from the weapons of enemies, and that he would not go 'until his time came,' and the time was not at hand.

"He had gone through many a danger. At one time, surrounded in a Mexican house, 'the Kid' fought nine men. The house was set on fire, and he made a dash for liberty and escaped through all the musketry of the guards. There were a dozen bullet holes in his clothing and his necktie had been cut away at the throat by a bullet, but Billy received not a mark on his skin.

[AUTHOR'S NOTE: This is Wallace's faking of the Lincoln County War as a "surrounded Mexican house," to hide it as an anti-Ring fight.]

"From his trial," continued General Wallace, "Billy was taken back to jail. He was in no wise disturbed. A day before the execution nine guards were watching him. At dinner time all but one left. Billy was in chains. The guard on duty received a tray that bore Billy's dinner. As the guard stood to place the tray on the floor, Billy the Kid struck him on the head with the handcuffs, crushing the skull. Then he took the guard's revolver, routed all the other guards that appeared, forced a blacksmith near by to break the handcuffs, mounted a good horse near at hand and rode away. He said as he started: 'Tell the Judge that I said that Billy the Kid was not born to be hung.'"

[AUTHOR'S NOTE: This fictional escape, multiplies the number of Billy's guards.]

End of Billy the Kid.

"It is needless to touch upon my danger under the vendetta," returned Gen. Wallace. Sufficient it is to say that he started for Santa Fe at once, and, determined to have a shot in return, I started out to meet him, but for some reason he never reached the point.

[AUTHOR'S NOTE: Wallace continues his coat-tailing on Billy's great escape, though, by then, he was likely the last thing on Billy's mind.]

Sheriff Pat Garrett was the only man in New Mexico not afraid of Billy and his charmed life. Garrett started out to make his capture, and it was a scout lasting for weeks, each man waiting to get the drop. All New Mexicans had their eyes on the two, and every morning the general question was, 'Has Pat and the Kid met yet?' It was a long siege, but Billy fell through love.

"Pat received information that Billy had gone back to an old fort in the mountains to see his sweetheart. Garrett journeyed there. He lay in wait in the dooryard of Billy's love, and finally saw the door open one night and a man come out in stocking feet. His hat was off; he wore only shirt and trousers. He passed out into the night. Garrett walked in and covered the girl's father with a gun. 'Not a word,' he whispered, as he passed behind the headboard of the bed with gun in hand. The door opened again. Billy seemed to smell danger, as a camel smells rain. He knew by instinct that something was wrong. He cried to the old man in Spanish, 'Who's there? Who's there?' Garrett raised his revolver. There were two reports. Billy the Kid jumped into the air and fell in his tracks. There were two bullet holes through his heart."

As he concluded the story there was a tremble in Gen. Wallace's voice that indicated that with the horrible picture there was a feeling of admiration for Billy. There was a pause and he said: "And he was only twenty-two."

E.I. LEWIS

ARTICLE OF JUNE 8 1902

Twenty-one years after Billy's killing, two years after *The Indianapolis Press's* "Gen. Wallace's Feud with Billy the Kid," Lew Wallace made his final Billy the Kid fiction. For *New York World Magazine* on June 8, 1902, he presented a novella as "General Lew Wallace Writes a Romance of 'Billy the Kid' Most Famous Bandit of the Plains, Thrilling Story of the Midnight Meeting Between Gen. Wallace, Then Governor of New Mexico, and the Notorious Outlaw, in a Lonesome Hut at Santa Fe."

In it, Wallace confirmed the pardon bargain as: " 'Testify,' I said ... 'and convict the murderer of Chapman and I will let you go scot-free with a pardon in your pocket.' " But this reworking reveals Wallace's unremitting rage at Billy's egalitarian self-confidence, with particular offense at Billy's threat to expose his pardon promise letter and his hypocrisy. In fact, Wallace's pique was still so hot, that he abandoned his 1900, "Gen. Wallace's Feud" article's having Billy's "most phenomenal exhibition of shooting," replacing it with a catty remark that Billy "missed his aim." This version was incorporated into his *Autobiography*. The 1902 article stated:

GENERAL LEW WALLACE WRITES A ROMANCE OF 'BILLY THE KID' MOST FAMOUS BANDIT OF THE PLAINS

Thrilling Story of the Midnight Meeting Between Gen. Wallace, Then Governor of New Mexico, and the Notorious Outlaw, in a Lonesome Hut at Santa Fe.

Gen. LEW WALLACE, author of "Ben Hur," is completing his autobiography, which will be issued in a few weeks.

The most thrilling chapter in this remarkable personal narrative tells of the midnight meeting in a lonely hut between Gen. Wallace, at the time Governor of the Territory of New Mexico, and "Billy the Kid," the most notorious outlaw the far West has ever produced.

From advance sheets of Gen. Wallace's book the following account of this strange rendezvous has been copied and compiled for the Sunday World Magazine. The story has never been printed in any newspaper or magazine before.

The episode occurred in 1879. The outlaw was at the zenith of his wild career. Gen. Wallace conceived the idea that he might gain certain important information by a face-to-face talk with the outlaw. With much difficulty the meeting was finally arranged. It was not without a strong element of danger to both participants, but they trusted each other and the trust was not betrayed.

The Midnight Rendezvous.

On the night of the meeting two men sat, shortly before midnight, silent and expectant, in the hut which had been chosen for the rendezvous, which was on the outskirts of Santa F, N.M.

Their gaze was fastened on the door, and, as the minutes slipped away the tension grew more severe, the silence more oppressive.

One man was the owner of the rude home that stood desolate in the shifting sands of the great mesa.

The other was Gen. Lew Wallace, Governor of New Mexico.

The hands of the clock pointed to 12.

The hush deepened. Suddenly it was broken by the sound of a resolute knock on the door of the cabin.

"Come in," said the Governor of New Mexico.

The door flew open and, standing with his form outlined by the moonlight behind him, was "Billy the Kid." In his left hand he carried a Winchester rifle. In his right was a revolver. The weapons, quick as a flash, covered the two occupants in the room.

"I was to meet the Governor here at midnight. It is midnight: Is the Governor here?"

The light of the candles flickered against a boyish face, yet the man who stood in the doorway was the most notorious desperado in all the West. He had killed scores of men: he was the quarry of every sheriff from the Rio Grande to the bordering foothills that shut in Death Valley.

The Boy Outlaw.

In facial features "Billy the Kid" was a mere stripling. His narrow shoulders were rounded, his posture slightly stooping, his voice low and effeminate. But his eyes were cold and piercing, steady, alert, gray like steel.

Gen. Wallace rose to his feet and held out his hand, inviting the visitor forward for a conference.

"Your note gave the promise of absolute protection," said the outlaw, warily.

"I have been true to my promise," replied the Governor. "This man," pointing to the owner of the cabin, "and myself are the only persons present."

The rifle was slowly lowered, the revolver returned to its leather holster. "Billy" advanced and the two seated themselves at opposite sides of the narrow table.

Gen. Wallace was able to effect an important arrangement with the outlaw, of which he gives the details. In fact, a very friendly understanding was established between the two.

Explaining the purpose of the interview and its result with "Billy," Gen. Wallace says:

"Shortly before I had become Governor of New Mexico, Chapman, a young attorney in Lincoln, had been murdered.

[AUTHOR'S NOTE: This faked date of Chapman's murder is to hide Wallace's blame. It was on February 18, 1879, 4½ months into his term; and Wallace was blamed for having never come to Lincoln County.]

Half a dozen men were arrested, accused of the crime. Among them was Jesse James.

[AUTHOR'S NOTE: Lying Wallace makes Jessie Evans Jessie James.]

While it was more than probable that one or more of the men charged with the murder were guilty, it was impossible to prove the allegation, for the witnesses, filled with terror, fled the country. When I reached New Mexico it was declared on every hand that "Billy the Kid" had been a witness to the murder. Could he be made to testify?

"That was a question on the tip of every tongue.

"I had been sent to the Southwest to pacify the territory; here was an opportunity I could not afford to pass by. Therefore I arranged the meeting by note deposited with one of the outlaw's friends, and at midnight was ready to receive the desperado should he appear. He was there on time – punctual to the second.

[AUTHOR'S NOTE: This summarizes lying Wallace's reversals.]

"When 'Billy the Kid' stepped to the chair opposite mine, I lost no time in announcing me proposition.

Agrees to the Plan.

" 'Testify,' I said, 'before the Grand Jury and the trial court and convict the murderer of Chapman and I will let you go scot-free with a pardon in your pocket for all your misdeeds.'

[AUTHOR'S NOTE: Wallace confirms the bargain.]

" 'Billy' heard me in silence; he thought several minutes without reply.

" 'Governor,' said he, "if I were to do what you ask they would kill me."

" 'We can prevent that," said I.

[AUTHOR'S NOTE: Wallace inverts the sham jailing.]

"Then I unfolded my plan. 'Billy' was to be seized while he was asleep. To all appearances, his capture was to be genuine. To this he agreed, picking the men who were to effect his capture. He was afraid of hostile bullets and would run no risk. Another stipulation was to the effect that during his confinement he should be kept in irons. 'Billy the Kid' was afraid also of the loss of his reputation as a desperate man."

[AUTHOR'S NOTE: Wallace snidely makes Billy worried only about "reputation."]

The plan agreed upon in the cabin on the lonely mesa at midnight was carried out to the letter. "Billy the Kid" was seized the following morning and confined in the Lincoln County jail. It was here that Gen. Wallace, in spite of the fears of the guards, permitted the outlaw to give an exhibition of his skill with the revolver and the rifle. "Billy," standing or riding, using either the one weapon or the other, sent every bullet true to its mark.

"Billy," said the General, "there's some trick to that shooting. How do you do it?"

"Well, General," replied the desperado, "there is a trick to it. When I was a boy I noticed that a man in pointing to anything he wished observed, used his index finger. With long use, unconsciously, the man had learned to point it with unerring aim. When I lift my revolver, I say to myself, 'Point with your finger.' I stretch the finger along the barrel and, unconsciously, it makes the aim certain. There is no failure; I pull the trigger and the bullet goes true to its mark."

"Billy," though at his own request kept in irons, did not remain long confined. One morning the guards led him to breakfast. Returning, the desperado drawled in the feminine voice that was a part and parcel of his character:

"Boys, I'm tired. Tell the Governor I'm tired."

[AUTHOR'S NOTE: Wallace denigrates Billy as "effeminate" and too "tired" for the bargain.]

The manacles slipped like magic from his wrists. The guards stood stupefied, and "Billy the Kid," laughing mockingly, walked leisurely from the jail yard, through the gate and across the street. Easily, gracefully, he threw himself into the saddle on the back of a horse standing near at hand and, putting spurs to the animal, dashed away. "Billy" was gone. He had not escaped in the night; he had walked away in the broad light of day, with his guards, heavily armed, standing about him.

[AUTHOR'S NOTE: This hides Billy's testifying, and that he left only after the lack of pardon risked his life by potential transport to a Mesilla trial.]

"Boys," I'm tired," he said, and looked them straight in the eyes.

They were not in collusion with the desperado; Gen. Wallace satisfied himself of the fact.

But how account for "Billy's" escape?

Hypnotism, some say – hypnotism or that strange something that lurked in the depths of the steel-gray eyes.

The desperado's freedom, however, was not long-lived. He was arrested soon afterward for a series of murders, and was brought again to the Lincoln County Jail. Patrick Garrett was Sheriff. He was probably the one man in New Mexico who did not fear "Billy the Kid." He was his match in every respect – as calm, as desperate, as certain.

[AUTHOR'S NOTE: Wallace's outlaw myth of Billy continues by fabricating murders.]

Perhaps "Billy" knew this. At any rate he must have considered himself in desperate straits. He sent for Gen. Wallace. The General refused to respond. Then the outlaw sent him a note. The note said:

"Come to the jail. I have some papers you would not want to see displayed."

"I knew what he meant," said Gen. Wallace, reminiscently. "He referred to the note he received from me in response to which he appeared in the hut on the mesa. He was threatening to publish it if I refused to see him. I thwarted his purpose by giving a copy of the latter and a narrative of the circumstances connected with it to the paper published in the town. It was duly printed and upon its appearance a copy was sent to "Billy" in his cell. He had nothing further to say."

[AUTHOR'S NOTE: A source of Wallace's guilty obsession was existence of his pardon promise letters.]

Not Daunted by His Sentence.

In the end the desperado was convicted and sentenced to be hanged. When the sentence was read he stood before the trial judge and said:

"Judge, that doesn't frighten me a bit. 'Billy the Kid' was not born to be hung."

He was a thorough fatalist. He believed he bore a charmed life. He believed he would not die until his "time came," and then death was inevitable.

From the court-room "Billy" was led back to the jail. Nine men were put on guard, and he was never allowed a moment from the sight of one of them.

On the day before that set for his execution one man sat in front of Billy while he ate his dinner. During the meal the guard forgot himself and suddenly stooped. "Billy's" quick eye took in the situation in a glance.

With a leap he sprang upon the bending man and dashed his brains out with his handcuffs. He seized the dead guard's revolver and, his steel-gray eyes gleaming, he walked forward deliberately and routed all the other guards, who ran to the assistance of their comrade.

Once more "Billy the Kid" escaped in the full light of day through the doors of the jail. He forced a blacksmith to break the manacle chains, seized a good horse that stood nearby and rode away.

He called back as he spurred the animal into a gallop:

"Tell the judge that I said 'Billy the Kid' was not born to be hung."

But "Billy" had forgotten one thing; he had not reckoned on the character of the man who was Sheriff of the county. He had forgotten Patrick Garrett. Garrett shut his teeth hard, like a man who is determined to accomplish his purpose, no matter the obstacles presenting themselves. He set out to take "Billy the Kid," dead or alive.

Garrett received information that "Billy" had gone back to an old fort in the mountains to see his sweetheart. Garrett followed. He lay in wait in the dooryard of the home of "Billy's" love, and finally his vigil was rewarded when he saw the door open one night and a man step out into the white light of the moon.

His hat was off, he was in his stocking feet and he wore only shirt and trousers. He passed out into the night.

Garrett crept to the door and passed in.

He covered the girl's father with his gun.

"Not a word," he said, and slid behind the headboard of the bed.

The Death of "Billy the Kid."

The door opened again and "Billy the Kid" entered. He seemed to scent danger as a camel scents rain; instinct taught him that something was wrong. He cried to the cowering old man in Spanish:

"Who's here?" he asked. "Who's here?"

Garrett raised his revolver; two shots rang out on the quiet air and the room filled with smoke. A form tottered, then crashed to the floor. In the nerveless hand was a smoking revolver; for the first and last time the notorious New Mexican outlaw had missed his aim. Garrett escaped unwounded. But there were two bullet wounds in the body of "Billy the Kid" and both pierced the heart. Garrett's aim was unerring.

To-day there is a little lowly heap of earth located in Las Cruces, N.M. [sic – Fort Sumner] To the curious stranger some idle native may, now and again, point out this little grave and explain, with a certain pride, that Las Cruces possesses the final resting place of the worst bad man that ever infested the Southwestern border. An ancient Mexican, who sometimes shows this grave to visitors, once made the cautious remark regarding its occupant that, had he lived, he would probably have turned out to be a bad man.

"And how old was 'Billy' when he died?" asked one curious stranger.

"Twenty-one, senor," replied the ancient. "He died, almost one might say, before he fully began to live."

"You say he was bad?" remarked another stranger.

"He is said to have killed many men."

"How many? How many, amigo, had this man killed at the time he himself died?"

"He had killed," replied the ancient Mexican, "twenty-one men, one for each year of his age, may the saints defend us," said the Mexican.

[AUTHOR'S NOTE: Wallace settled for his final version of the outlaw myth on 21 men for his 21 years. It made it to one of Billy's gravestones.]

"He was a good man, and very kind to poor people. Yet, had he lived, he might, according to the opinion of some, have turned into a bad man."

Gen. Wallace also tells in his autobiography how and why "Billy the Kid" started on his career of crime:

A Waif of New York City.

"The man whose deeds of blood had drawn upon him the eyes of an entire nation, was born a New York waif. Before he was more than ten years of age he was brought to Indiana, and in Terre Haute and Indianapolis, where he was reared, he was known as William Bonne. In 1876, when he was about seventeen years old, he suddenly left his home, crossed the Mississippi and went to the country of the men of his kind – the frontier of the far West.

"Billy began his career with an oath to kill John Chisum, his first employer when the lad reached the plains. Chisum and the "Kid' had been unable to agree on terms of settlement for a season's work. The result was the lad's fearful vendetta, sworn not only against Chisum, but against all of Chisum's other employees as well.

" 'For each herdsman employed by you whom I kill," Billy sent him word, "I will deduct $5 from our unsquared account. If I kill you,' he added grimly, 'my bill will be receipted in full.'

"Then his bloody career began.

[AUTHOR'S NOTE: Wallace fabricates Chisum conflict as Billy's killing motive to omit the anti-Ring Lincoln County War.]

It was not long until William Bonne, the waif, reared in the peaceful surroundings of Indiana, became the most feared man in the Southwest. At the same time, he was the most revered, the most adored and the most respected man in the Territory.

"It was the kind of good reward that sometimes comes to bad men."

[AUTHOR'S NOTE: Wallace's admission of Billy's being "revered," "adored," and "respected" admitted Billy's inescapable real fame.]

PAT GARRETT'S OUTLAW MYTH OF BILLY THE KID

The 1881 killing of Billy the Kid had viral fame, inspiring Pat Garrett to ally with his journalist boarder, Ashmun "Ash" Upson, to create his ghostwritten book, issued the following year: *The Authentic Life of Billy the Kid The Noted Desperado of the Southwest, Whose Deeds of Daring and Blood Made His Name a Terror in New Mexico, Arizona, and Northern Mexico.*

Though it used that period's lurid dime novel style, and though the history of Billy Bonney had not yet been researched, so was fictionalized, both men knew Billy. Upson had been a border with his family in Silver City; and Garrett, having met him in 1878, when both spent time in Fort Sumner, certainly knew the specifics of his own tracking, capturing, jailing, and killing of him.

Garrett's lethality was undisputable, with his first killing of two of Billy's companions in his attempt to kill him. On December 19, 1880, he and his Texan posse ambushed Billy's group returning to Fort Sumner. Tom O'Folliard was fatally shot. Garrett then tracked Billy and his companions, attempting to escape the Territory, to the windowless, stacked rock, line cabin in Stinking Springs. In the morning of December 22, 1881, with Billy and his group having spent the night in the cabin, Charlie Bowdre emerged first wearing either Billy's hat, or one that looked like it, and was immediately killed in ambush by Garrett as mistaken for Billy. Only then did Garrett relent to capturing Billy for certain hanging trials.

As to his finally killing Billy, his book described his coming to Fort Sumner with his Deputies John William Poe and Thomas "Kip" McKinney; and, late that moonlit night of July 14, 1881, stationing them on the porch of the Maxwell family mansion, while he went inside to check with the town's owner, Peter Maxwell, in his dark bedroom. His book stated:

> I left Poe and McKinney at the end of the porch, and about twenty feet from the door of Pete's bedroom, while I myself entered it. I walked to the head of the bed and sat down near the pillow and beside Maxwell's head. I asked him as to the whereabouts of the Kid. He replied that the Kid had certainly been about, but he did not know whether he had left or not. At that moment, a man sprang quickly

in the door, and looking back, called twice in Spanish, "Quien es? Quien es? (Who comes there?)" No one replied, and he came into the room. I could see he was bareheaded, and from his tred I could perceive he was either barefooted or in his stocking feet. He held a revolver in his right hand and a butcher knife in his left.

He came directly towards me while I was sitting at the head of Maxwell's bed. Before he reached the bed, I whispered, "Who is it, Pete?" but received no reply for a moment. It struck me that it might be Pete's brother-in-law, Manuel Abreu, who had seen Poe and McKinney on the outside and wanted to know their business. The intruder came close to me, leaned both hands on the bed, his right almost touching my knee, and asked in a low tone "Who are they, Pete?" At the same instant Maxwell whispered to me, "That's him!"

Simultaneously the Kid must have seen or felt the presence of a third person at the head of the bed. He raised quickly his pistol – a self-cocker – within a foot of my breast. Retreating rapidly across the room, he cried, "Quien es? Quien es? (Who is that? Who is that?)" All this happened more rapidly than it takes to tell it. As quick as possible I drew my revolver and fired, threw my body to one side, and fired again. The second shot was useless. The Kid fell dead at the first one. He never spoke. A struggle or two, a little strangling sound as he gasped for breath, and the Kid was with his many victims. (Garrett, Pages 215-216)

Garrett's description matched Peter Maxwell's witness statement to the Coroner's Jury the next day: "I being in my bed in my room, at about midnight on the 14th day of July, Pat F. Garrett came into my room and sat down. William Bonney came in and got close to my bed with a gun in his hand and asked me "who is it" and then Pat F. Garrett fired two shots at the said William Bonney and the said William Bonney fell near my fire place and I went out of the room and when I came in again about three or four minutes after the shots the said William Bonney was dead."

As to the outlaw myth, Garrett and Upson portrayed Billy as evil in *The Authentic Life of Billy the Kid*; stating:

> The Kid had **a devil lurking in him**. It was a good-humored jovial imp, or a cruel and bloodthirsty fiend, as circumstances prompted. Circumstances favored the worser angel, and the Kid fell.

To be noted is the influence of the Garrett book, on the early pseudo-histories that followed. Journalist Walter Noble Burns, for his 1926 book, *The Saga of Billy the Kid*, merely added his own florid elaborations making Billy the incarnation of evil; writing:

> **[Billy] placed no value on human life ... He killed a man as nonchalantly as he smoked a cigarette. Murder did not appeal to Billy the Kid as tragedy; it was merely a physical process of pulling a trigger** ... In his murders, he observed no rules of etiquette ... As long as he killed a man he wanted to kill, it made no difference to him how he killed him ...
>
> It is impossible now to name twenty-one men that he killed, though, if Indians be included, it is not difficult to cast up the ghastly total ...
>
> The Lincoln County war and the subsequent reign of terror Billy the Kid had set up had given the territory [of New Mexico] an evil reputation.

THE ANTIQUE FOUNDATION

So one can say that the history of Billy the Kid was born in outlawry; but the outlawry was not his. The creators of his mythology had ulterior motives which necessitated leaving out the reality of Billy Bonney's freedom fighter role, and the grandeur of the Lincoln County War's life-and-death resistance to the Santa Fe Ring.

The creators of outlaw mythology also dated themselves. As scholarly research grew in the second half of the 20th century, their old-fashioned fables became increasingly obvious.

The outlaw myth of Billy the Kid lived on instead with windbag old-timers of the first half of the 20th century, as they strove for attention by fables of being or knowing Billy the Kid; with made-up memories using the Pat Garrett and Walter Noble Burns books, and the outlaw myth press of the Santa Fe Ring and Lew Wallace.

And this throw-back garbage, from history's junkyard, would become the fodder for modern Billy the Kid hoaxers, who tried to dress-up the old fakery for profiteering reruns, or created new hoaxes about the outlaw Billy the Kid; with the recent one portraying him as a counterfeiter-rustler being the subject of this book.

CHAPTER 2
REAL HISTORY

REALITY VERSUS FICTION

The actual history of Billy Bonney took a long time to untangle from its original fictionalizing. Even the scholarly books of the late 20th century avoided the Santa Fe Ring as a causal agent in unfolding events, preferring to plaster newly discovered documents on the antique, outlaw myth armature. But leaving out the Santa Fe Ring, is like writing about the Civil War and omitting slavery. The rendition of the history makes no sense, because the causality of events is missing.

Billy the Kid imposters were dead by the renaissance in Billy the Kid scholarship in the second half of the 20th century. In 1957, William Keleher's *Violence in Lincoln County 1869-1881* published both the original Spanish and translated Coroner's Jury Report. The unsurpassed scholarly researcher of the period, Frederick Nolan, published his *The Life and Death of John Henry Tunstall* in 1965; *The Lincoln County War: A Documentary History* in 1992; and *The West of Billy the Kid* in 1998. Billy's early adolescence in Silver City, New Mexico Territory, and Bonita, Arizona Territory, were unavailable until 1993 with Jerry Weddle's book, *Antrim is My Stepfather's Name: The Boyhood of Billy the Kid*. Other modern historians were Joel Jacobsen in 1994 with *Such Men as Billy the Kid. The Lincoln County War Reconsidered*; Philip Rasch with his 1995 compendium, *Trailing Billy the Kid*; and Robert Utley, with his 1989 *Billy the Kid: A Short and Violent Life*.

My own 21st century books, using major historical collections and new interpretations, added understanding of the role of the Santa Fe Ring from its 1866 origin, to its bloody Territorial take-overs of the 1870's, and its continuation to the present. There are 2012's *Billy the Kid's Writings, Words, and Wit;* 2017's *The Lost Pardon of Billy the Kid: An Analysis Factoring in The Santa Fe Ring, Governor Lew Wallace's Dilemma, and a Territory in Rebellion;* 2018's *The Santa Fe Ring: The Making of an American Monster;* and 2019's *The Coroner's Jury Report of Billy the Kid: The Inquest that Sealed the Fame of Billy Bonney and Pat Garrett*. And, in multiple books, I have made it my mission to expose the profiteering hoaxes, from early 20th century origins to the present, that ride on Billy the Kid's coattails.

Pat Garrett himself got a major biographer, Leon Metz; whose *Pat Garrett: The Story of a Western Lawman* came out in 1974, and countered the defamation intrinsic in the pretender hoaxes based on Billy the Kid's not being killed by him on July 14, 1881.

And some of these later sources would reveal subsequent fakery, since the next generation of hoaxing authors surreptitiously used their new facts to fix-up the old imposter scams, which they backed. The "Billy the Kid's Bad Bucks" hoax is an example of this development, by faking sources discovered by the later scholars for an audience relatively naïve about the facts.

SALVATION BY PUBLIC IGNORANCE

The old imposters, their scamming authors, and modern-day hoaxers got a hearing because of public ignorance of Billy the Kid's complex history. That enabled those fraudsters to spin tales using the original outlaw mythology of Billy the Kid, which had proliferated as books and movies.

Unknown, to this day, is that the Lincoln County War was a freedom fight of Anglo homestead farmers and disenfranchised Hispanic people against the land grabbing Santa Fe Ring seeking ranching and mercantile monopolies, while using outlaw gangs to rustle from cattle king, John Chisum's 80,000 head to fulfill beef contracts and terrorize opponents. Unknown is Billy Bonney's bi-cultural role in bridging those two victimized sub-cultures, and bringing Mexican fighters from Patricio and Picacho into that War's final battle. Unknown was Billy's risk to the Ring as leading another uprising (along with Hispanics, like his friend, Yginio Salazar). Unknown was Billy's more immediate risk to the Ring by testifying against its assassins - unless he was eliminated first. Certainly unknown, except by an occasional dropped name, were almost all the other historical participants in that unsung period when New Mexicans were willing to risk their lives to fight for their democratic rights.

So Billy the Kid's massive fame and popularity, plus massive ignorance about him, added up to an ideally non-critical but receptive audience for old imposters and modern hoaxers.

REAL HISTORY

Central to debunking the misinformation in the Billy the Kid hoaxes, is Billy Bonney's real history. It is a complex, colorful, traumatic life of a brilliant, charismatic, teenaged, literate, bi-cultural resistance fighter against the Santa Fe Ring; fit amazingly into just 21 years. Most of it was unknown to his old-timer impersonators and modern hoaxers.

****

In a hot, full-mooned, New Mexico Territory night as bright as day, the 21 year old, homeless youth, Billy Bonney, with trusting stockinged feet, approached the porticoed, two story, Fort Sumner mansion of the Maxwell family, at about a quarter to mid-night.

That day, July 14, 1881, was the third anniversary of the Lincoln County War's start, which had left him branded as the outlaw, "Billy the Kid;" though, to himself, he was a freedom fighter: the last Regulator and that War's only participant to be convicted and sentenced to hanging.

That July night, he intended to cut a dinner steak from the side of beef hanging, at the patrón's generosity, on the mansion's north porch. But first he would check in with that patrón and town owner, well, at his south porch's corner bedroom.

Asleep in that mansion was Billy's secret lover, Maxwell's sister, Paulita, seventeen, and just pregnant with Billy's child. Also there, lived a never-emancipated Navajo slave, Deluvina; purchased, as a child, by Peter's and Paulita's fabulously wealthy, deceased father, Lucien Bonaparte Maxwell. Then, the family lived in Cimarron, a New Mexico Territory town in Colfax County, which Lucien had created on his and his wife's almost two million acre land grant; later named after himself.

That was before Lucien was cheated in the sale of that Maxwell Land Grant by unscrupulous lawyers, Thomas Benton Catron and Stephen Benton Elkins, who used their profits to propel their Santa Fe Ring. As Billy knew, that corrupt collusion of public officials still held New Mexico Territory in a stranglehold. As a hero in the failed Lincoln County War of 1878, Billy had fought that Ring. If Billy was thinking about his mortal danger, he knew its source was the Ring. If he thought about injustice, its focus would have been his promised pardon withheld by departed Territorial Governor Lew Wallace.

That July of 1881 day was 2½ months since Billy's jailbreak escape from his scheduled hanging on May 13th. He knew that Lincoln County Sheriff Pat Garrett would be in pursuit. Garrett had captured him on December 22, 1880 at Stinking Springs for his hanging trial. And in Billy's April 28, 1881 escape from Garrett's Lincoln jail, he had shot dead his deputy guards: James Bell and Robert Olinger. Garrett would kill him on sight.

When first tracking Billy in late 1880, Garrett had killed Billy's friends, Tom O'Folliard and Charlie Bowdre - missing Billy only by accident in two consecutive ambushes: at Fort Sumner and Stinking Springs. In fact, at the Stinking Springs capture of Billy and his companions, Garrett killed Bowdre by mistaking him for Billy: the prize for which the Ring had made Garrett a Sheriff.

To be near Paulita, Billy had recklessly chosen return to Fort Sumner, instead of fleeing to Old Mexico, the natural choice given his bi-culturalism. But he relied on the Maxwell family's protection, as well affection of the townspeople he had known since late 1877. It would take betrayal to bring his death.

Billy's life had been traumatic. Likely illegitimate, he was a second son, born on November 23, 1859, in New York City, as William Henry McCarty. Raised in Kansas and Indiana with his brother, Josie, by his mother, Catherine, he became "Henry Antrim" after she married a William Henry Harrison Antrim, in 1873, after they moved to New Mexico Territory. Antrim became a miner; and the family lived in Silver City. He was a rejecting father, evicting Billy at 14½ to homelessness when Catherine died of tuberculosis in 1874. But Billy's longing for a father remained, and he sometimes used the name "Antrim" for himself.

In Silver City's school, he learned Spencerian script. He also became fluent in Spanish; and, atypically, was equally comfortable in Anglo and Hispanic sub-cultures in those racist times. By 1975, 15½ year old Billy spent his last year in Silver City doing petty thievery, and butcher shop and hotel work; while altercations with local boys revealed his violent temperament.

By September, Silver City Sheriff, Harvey Whitehill arrested him for burglary, and laundry and revolver robbery; his adult accomplice having escaped. Facing ten years hard labor - the statutes making no provision for juveniles - he achieved his first dramatic escape: through the jail's chimney. He fled across the border to Arizona Territory's little town of Bonita.

In Arizona, as Henry Antrim, Billy again combined work – as a cook at a small hotel - with crime: stealing military blankets, saddles, and horses; while fatefully developing shootist skills. In 1876, incarcerated at local Fort Grant's guardhouse with his older, thieving accomplice, John Mackie, he escaped through a roof ventilation space. But he defiantly stayed in Bonita, relying on his rustling charges being dropped on a technicality, his first demonstration of risky behavior for his wish to have a "home."

On August 17, 1877, Billy's life again changed horrifically. His argument at Bonita's Atkins Cantina with a bullying blacksmith, Frank "Windy" Cahill, escalated to his fatally shooting that unknowably unarmed man. Billy escaped on a stolen horse. The Coroner's Jury declared him - as Henry Antrim - guilty of homicide, though in absentia; ignoring self-defense. So at 17½, Billy was almost hanged for murder. He escaped back to New Mexico Territory with an alias: William Henry Bonney - Billy Bonney. "Bonney" was likely his mother's maiden name.

In New Mexico Territory, by the next month of September, 1877, Billy attached himself to familiar sociopaths in Jessie Evans's murderous and rustling Santa Fe Ring-affiliated gang. And since all Ringites ended up immune to prosecution and profited financially, intelligent and energetic Billy, unknown to history, would have likely had a wealthy and long life.

But Billy had a conversion. He met kind, wealthy Englishman, John Henry Tunstall, a Ring competitor. By the next month, October of 1877, he left Jessie Evans's gang to be Tunstall's youngest ranch hand. Tunstall's men affectionately nick-named him "Kid." Tunstall became the lost father found; even gifting him, under the Homestead Act, with a ranch on the Peñasco River in partnership with another employee, half-Chickasaw, Fred Waite. That was likely Billy's proudest and most optimistic moment.

Billy had stumbled into a noble cause: ending Ring oppression. His gunman skill now elevated him as a protector of the good. His hair-trigger temper became vehemence for justice. And the town of Lincoln, as well as Tunstall's ranch on the Feliz River, became home. But Billy's tragic destiny was unrelenting. After only 4½ months, this idyllic time ended with Tunstall's Ring murder.

Lincoln, site of the future Lincoln County War, had already sustained Ring abuses through mercantile monopoly of "The House": a huge, two-story adobe, general store run by its local Ring bosses, Emil Fritz, Lawrence Murphy, James Dolan, and John Riley for secret partner, Ring boss, Thomas Benton Catron. They bled cash-poor Mexicans and Anglo homesteaders with usurious credit. Redress was impossible, since law enforcement and courts were Ring-controlled. Terror reigned. In 1875, when rancher, Robert Casey, defeated Murphy in a Lincoln election, he was assassinated the same day. Three weeks later, Lincoln's anti-Ring, Mexican community leader, Juan Patrón, was shot by Riley; though accidentally surviving as a limping cripple.

Hope began in late 1876 with arrival of English merchant, John Tunstall; persuaded to settle in Lincoln by resident attorney, Alexander McSween, a Ring opponent; but once legal counsel to "The House," and aware of its abuses. Tunstall planned to defeat the Ring by fair mercantile and ranching competition. But that inadvertently put him in direct competition with Catron's own monopolistic plans for Lincoln County: his secret control of "The House" for beef and flour contracts to Fort Stanton and the Mescalero Indian Reservation; his Pecos River cow camp fronted by "The House;" and his take-over of dying Lawrence Murphy's huge ranch, which he made his Carrizozo Land and Cattle Company, under management of his brother-in-law, Edgar Walz.

By 1877, Tunstall defiantly built, just a quarter mile northeast of "The House," a general store and the Lincoln Bank. He made Catron's major cattle competitor, cattle king John Chisum, the bank's president. And he began two cattle ranches to wrest from "The House" its beef and flour contracts. He even exposed Ringite Lincoln County Sheriff William Brady's embezzlement of tax money to buy rustled cattle for Catron's cow camp and Carrizozo Ranch. So Tunstall and McSween qualified for the Ring's hit list.

Ringmen preferred to kill with guise of legality. So they entangled Tunstall in fabricated criminality, starting with false prosecution of McSween, who was then attorney for the estate of "The House's" partner, Emil Fritz, who died intestate in 1874, but had two local siblings and a life insurance policy. The Ring seized on that policy. In 1877, McSween had gotten its $10,000 proceeds from its withholding New York City insurance company, minus $3,000 to the collections firm - leaving $7,000 minus his fees. Knowing that the House faced bankruptcy from Tunstall's competition, and would extort that sum from Fritz's local heirs, he retained it while seeking heirs in Germany.

In December of 1877, McSween left on business to St. Louis with his wife and with Tunstall's business associate, the cattle king, John Chisum, then also president of the bank in Tunstall's store. The Ring pounced, declaring McSween an absconding embezzler of the Fritz insurance money. Ring boss Catron, then

U.S. Attorney, issued his arrest warrant for capture. Chisum was also jailed in retaliation for backing Tunstall. On February 4, 1878, McSween had his hearing in Mesilla under Ringite District Judge Warren Bristol (later Billy's hanging judge), who indicted him for embezzling; intending his incarceration and killing in Lincoln by its Ringite Sheriff, William Brady. McSween was saved by the honorable Deputy Sheriff, Adolph Barrier, from his Las Vegas, New Mexico, arrest site, who kept him in personal custody.

But Judge Bristol had set the Ring's traps for assassination of McSween and Tunstall. His indictment did two things. First, he set the bail at $8,000, with approval only by Ringite District Attorney William Rynerson; who refused all bondsmen to leave McSween open to Sheriff Brady's fatal custody at any time.

The second was Tunstall's trap. Bristol attached McSween's property to the sum of $10,000 - falsely deemed the embezzled total - to ensure the money if he was convicted at that April's Grand Jury. Then Bristol lied that Tunstall was in partnership with McSween, to attach Tunstall's property also. And Bristol empowered Sheriff Brady to do attachment inventories at their properties. The intent was harassment to provoke Tunstall and his men to violence to justify his killing in "self-defense."

But Tunstall merely said that any man's life was worth more than all he owned. Billy, with Tunstall three months, must have been overwhelmed by this novel idealism.

Tunstall's businesses had bankrupted "The House," making boss Catron emerge its mortgage owner. And the April Grand Jury would likely exonerate McSween. So the Ring acted urgently, using the embezzlement case's property attachment.

On February 18, 1878, when Tunstall sought to transfer his fine horses, which were immune to the attachment, from his Feliz River Ranch to Lincoln, Brady called it theft of attached property and sent his big posse of Deputies, Ring rustlers, and Jessie Evans's outlaw gang after him and his men, including Billy. Tunstall, becoming isolated, was murdered, his horse slain; with both corpses mutilated. This martyrdom, coupled with more Ring outrages, intended to terrorize the citizens into submission, triggered the Lincoln County War.

Sheriff Brady refused to arrest the murderers. So anti-Ring Justice of the Peace John "Squire" Wilson issued warrants for James Dolan, Jessie Evans, and his other possemen. For service, he appointed Billy and Fred Waite as Deputy Constables under Town Constable Atanacio Martinez. Billy had already given

Wilson an affidavit as to first-hand knowledge of the murderers. But Brady shielded them by putting Billy, Waite, and Martinez in Lincoln's pit jail. And he confiscated Billy's Winchester '73 carbine - likely a gift from Tunstall.

Next, "Squire" Wilson defied the Ring by deputizing Tunstall's foreman, Dick Brewer; who, in turn, made Tunstall's men, including now-released Billy, his possemen to serve those murder warrants. Billy, then 18, was still a lawman.

Meanwhile, Attorney Alexander McSween, in mortal danger from Brady and the Ring, went into hiding with Deputy Sheriff Barrier; mostly in the nearby Hispanic town of San Patricio.

By March of 1878, Dick Brewer's posse had captured Tunstall murder possemen, William "Buck" Morton and Frank Baker, who were shot attempting escape. Billy was in the firing group.

At that point, including "Windy" Cahill, Billy Bonney was now involved in three killings.

The Ring hit back. Ringite Governor Samuel Beach Axtell, by illegal proclamation, removed Wilson's Justice of the Peace powers to retroactively outlaw Dick Brewer's posse; then declared Sheriff William Brady to be Lincoln County's only law enforcer.

Enraged, Tunstall's men named themselves "Regulators" after pre-Revolutionary War freedom fighters. Included were Tunstall men - Billy; Fred Waite; John Middleton; Jim "Frenchie" French; farmer cousins, George and Frank Coe; and homesteader, Charlie Bowdre - and a John Chisum cattle detective, Frank MacNab. Dick Brewer was chosen as leader. Only one month after Tunstall died, Billy was being schooled in politics of revolution.

The Ring's next chance to assassinate McSween was April 1, 1878, when he returned to Lincoln for his Grand Jury embezzlement trial. That morning, to save him, Regulators with carbines, and Billy with only a revolver, ambushed Brady and his three deputies from behind an adobe corral wall at Tunstall's store. Brady and his Deputy George Hindman died. Recklessly, Billy, with Jim French, ran out to retrieve his confiscated Winchester '73 carbine from Brady's body. Both got leg wounds from firing surviving deputy, Jacob Basil "Billy" Matthews. But Billy regained his symbol of father-figure Tunstall. (It is likely the carbine held in Billy's famous tintype two years hence.)

Three days later, on April 4, 1878, Deputy Dick Brewer, seeking stolen Tunstall horses, led Billy, John Middleton, Fred Waite, Frank Coe, George Coe, and Charlie Bowdre to Blazer's

Mill - a privately owned, way station and grist mill within the Mescalero Indian Reservation. Accidently encountered was Tunstall murder posseman, Andrew "Buckshot" Roberts, for whom they had a warrant. Roberts fired his Winchester carbine at Bowdre, who shot him in the belly. Roberts's bullet had hit Bowdre's belt buckle, ricocheted, and wrenched George Coe's revolver, mutilating his trigger finger. Another Roberts shot hit Middleton's chest, though Middleton survived. Then Roberts killed Brewer, later dying himself from Bowdre's wound. Billy had not fired a shot. Roberts had demonstrably resisted arrest murderously, necessitating self- defense response. But Ring boss Catron, as U.S. Attorney, seized on this killing to file his federal indictment against the Regulators, including Billy, claiming the murder site was the Mescalero Reservation, under federal control.

Billy's murder involvement now totaled six men; though only "Windy" Cahill was demonstrably by his hand.

At the April, 1878, Lincoln County Grand Jury, McSween was exonerated for embezzling. He continued his anti-Ring fight backed by the Regulators, though they had never been paid; John Chisum having dishonestly reneged. Revolutionary fervor sufficed. And Billy, their hot-headed fearless zealot, was becoming an inspiration - with McSween as his new father substitute.

McSween's lawful tactic was seeking high-level intervention to expose Tunstall's Ring assassination, because murder of a foreign citizen could elicit a Washington, D.C. investigation. He filed a complaint with the British ambassador and to President Rutherford B. Hayes, accusing U.S. officials of murdering Tunstall. In response, investigating attorney, Frank Warner Angel, was sent by the Departments of the Interior and Justice. Arriving May 4, 1878, Angel took 39 depositions. Billy, volunteering for one, entered the national stage.

Public optimism of Ring defeat further grew when the Lincoln County Commissioners appointed neutral John Copeland, as Sheriff replacing Brady. He even deputized Regulator, Josiah "Doc" Scurlock, to recover Tunstall's horses, stolen by the Ring. Still a lawman, Billy was on Scurlock's posse. And Wilson, ignoring Axtell's proclamation, continued as Justice of the Peace.

Optimism was short-lived. New Regulator leader, Frank MacNab, was killed in ambush on April 28, 1878 by Ringite Seven Rivers rustlers. By May 28th, because John Copeland forgot to post his tax collecting bond, Governor Axtell, by another proclamation, removed him and appointed as Sheriff, Ringite George Peppin, Brady's deputy, present at Brady's killing.

War fervor built, with furious Regulators and Mexicans calling themselves "McSweens." Billy's affiliation with local, firebrand youth, Yginio Salazar, and Billy's closeness to Hispanic residents of nearby San Patricio and Picacho, had arguably brought them all into the McSween alliance. By April 30, 1878, McSweens were skirmishing with Ring partisans, known as "Murphy-Dolans."

McSween again hid, often in San Patricio. In revenge, Sheriff George Peppin, with John Kinney's Ring-rustler gang from Mesilla, on July 3, 1878 massacred residents and destroyed farm animals and property there. On July 13th, the "Regulator Manifesto" was sent to Catron's brother-in-law, then managing his Carrizozo cattle ranch, threatening retaliation against Catron himself. Signed only "Regulator," it was likely created by Billy.

The Lincoln County War's culminating Battle began the next day: July 14, 1878. McSween, with 60 men - Regulators and Hispanic residents of San Patricio and Picacho - occupied Lincoln. Reflecting McSween's intended peaceful victory was that his wife, Susan, and her sister with five children, remained in his double-winged house; along with the sister's attorney husband's law intern, Harvey Morris.

McSween's men took strategic positions in houses throughout the mile-long town, most of whose inhabitants had fled. When Seven Rivers and John Kinney outlaws joined James Dolan and Sheriff George Peppin, Billy; his friends, Yginio Salazar and Tom O'Folliard; and San Patricio men - José Chávez y Chávez, Ignacio Gonzales, Florencio Chávez, Francisco Zamora, and Vincente Romero - rushed to McSween's house, joining guard, Jim French.

Though Ring men occupied foothills south of Lincoln, they were held at bay for five days by shooting McSweens. Regulators were about to win. But McSween did not realize that Fort Stanton's new Commander, Lieutenant Colonel N.A.M. Dudley, was beholden to the Ring. McSween was also reassured by the Posse Comitatus Act, passed the month before in Washington, baring military intervention in civilian disputes.

On July 16th, Commander Dudley began his illegal invention by sending to Lincoln, for "fact-finding," 9th Cavalry Private Berry Robinson, who was almost hit in the mutual gunfire. Next, on July 18th, James Dolan used Ringite Lincolnite, Saturnino Baca, McSween's tenant, to lie that his wife and children were at risk from the McSweens.

The next day, July 19th, violating the Posse Comitatus Act, Dudley marched on Lincoln with 39 troops - white infantry, black 9th Cavalry, and white officers - two ambulances; a mountain howitzer cannon; and a Gatling machine-gun, that period's most awesome weapon. Panicked McSweens - except for those in his besieged house - fled north across the nearby Bonito River. Dudley himself threatened McSween with razing his house if any soldier was shot. He then left three soldiers there to inhibit its defenders' shooting from it, and ordered three more to accompany Sheriff Peppin as a shield. Next, by death threats, he forced Justice of the Peace Wilson to write arrest warrants for McSween and his men as attempting murder of Private Robinson to feign reason for his intervention. Then he encamped at the east side of Lincoln.

Backed by the participating troops, Sheriff Peppin's outlaw posseman set fire to McSween's house's west wing. His family was evacuated after Dudley refused McSween's wife's plea to save him.

By nightfall, the McSween house conflagration - worsened by an exploding keg of gunpowder for bullet-making - left all trapped in the east wing. At about 9 p.m., escape was attempted into fire-lit shooting Ringites. With Billy was law intern, Harvey Morris, whom he saw fatally shot. And before Billy escaped across the Bonito River, at the property's rear - to rescue by fellow Regulators - he witnessed Dudley's treasonous crime: three of his white soldiers, imbedded with the assailants, under orders, fired a volley at those escaping. Arguably, they had even killed Morris.

Shot dead were Alexander McSween, Francisco Zamora, and Vincente Romero. Yginio Salazar survived with two bullets in his back. Symbolizing horror, McSween's starving, yard chickens ate the eyeballs of his corpse. Again was Ring murder and mutilation in Lincoln County to gain treacherous victory.

But people were unaware of Ring influence in Washington, D.C. Investigator Frank Warner Angel, after documenting crimes of Governor S.B. Axtell, U.S. Attorney Catron, and Sheriff Brady's posse, was possibly forced to deny that U.S. officials were involved in Tunstall's murder. And Catron resigned as U.S. Attorney. President Hayes scapegoated Governor Axtell, replacing him with Civil War General Lew Wallace. But Angel secretly tried to get justice by writing for Wallace a notebook listing Ringites, and sending him an exposé on the Santa Fe Ring printed in 1877.

Though most Regulators fled the Territory, Billy stayed and carried out the Regulator Manifesto's guerrilla stock rustling with Tom O'Folliard and Charlie Bowdre - who had relocated to Fort

Sumner with his wife Manuela. For his stolen stock, Billy used non-Ring outlets: Pat Coghlan in the western part of the Territory; and Dan Dedrick. Dedrick was a counterfeiter and rustler owner of Bosque Grande, a ranch 12 miles south of Fort Sumner. With his two brothers, he also owned a livery stable in White Oaks, a town about 45 miles northwest of Lincoln. Those brothers were another stock outlet for Billy. Billy also sold rustled horses in Tascosa, Texas; where he wrote a subsequently famous, bill of sale to friendly a doctor, Henry Hoyt, for an expensive sorrel horse - likely dead Sheriff Brady's. He also got money by gambling. He was again a homeless drifter. That would now be permanent.

Amidst public hope, on October 1, 1878, new Governor, Lew Wallace took office. A high-achieving elitist, he was the son of an Indiana governor; a Civil War Major General; an Abraham Lincoln murder trial prosecutor; author of best-selling novel, *The Fair God*; and was writing *Ben-Hur A Tale of the Christ*. He had sought an exotic ambassadorship, like to Turkey, not governorship of backwater New Mexico Territory. So, to dispatch quickly with Lincoln County "troubles" without confronting the Santa Fe Ring, he issued, a month after arriving, an Amnesty Proclamation; though excluding those already indicted. Billy had been indicted for the Brady, Hindman, and Roberts murders.

There were more sources of hope. The new Sheriff, George Kimbrell - having been appointed to replace Sheriff George Peppin who resigned - was anti-Ring. And McSween's intrepid widow, Susan, had brought to Lincoln Attorney Huston Chapman to charge Commander N.A.M. Dudley with the Lincoln County War Battle's murder of her husband and arson of her home.

In that atmosphere of legal scrutiny, James Dolan made peace overtures, first to Susan McSween, then to Billy - a proof of that teenager's acknowledged Ring threat. Billy and his Hispanic compatriots could instigate another uprising - as T.B. Catron feared.

The Billy-Dolan peace meeting was fatefully scheduled on the February 18, 1879 anniversary of Tunstall's murder. It ended in calamity. As James Dolan; Billy; Jessie Evans and Jessie's new gang member, Billy Campbell; and Billy's Regulator friends, Tom O'Folliard and Josiah "Doc" Scurlock, walked Lincoln's dark street after the meeting, they encountered Chapman. Dolan and Campbell fired at point-blank range, killing him, then igniting his clothing. Billy was again an eye-witness. And again there was murder and mutilation in Lincoln County.

Chapman's murder forced Governor Wallace to go to Lincoln - after procrastinating for five months after arriving. Once there, he avoided Ring confrontation, using the Ring's own concoction of vague "outlaws and rustlers" causing trouble. The Ring had given him a list of Regulators as "outlaws;" with Billy on it as "the Kid."

Focus on Billy - likely through Dolan - made Wallace put the astronomical reward of $1,000 on his head. Billy responded with his pardon plea, writing on March 13, 1879, to offer Wallace his eye-witness testimony against Chapman's murderers in exchange for annulling his Lincoln County War indictments. It was Billy's bold and calculated risk to negate Ring power over himself.

His articulate pardon plea letter, in his personalized Spencerian script, led to his March 17, 1879, nighttime meeting with Wallace in Justice of the Peace Wilson's Lincoln house. Evidence indicates that Wilson was covertly backing Billy's plea. And Billy believed Wallace agreed to his pardon bargain.

To avoid assassination before testifying, Billy requested from Wallace a sham arrest (He had already seen Ring assassinations of John Tunstall, Alexander McSween, Harvey Morris, Francisco Zamora, Vincente Romero, and Huston Chapman.) He was kept in the home of his Lincoln friend, Juan Patrón, the town Jailer. Wallace, housed next door, interviewed him and got his additional letter about Lincoln County War issues.

Billy fulfilled his pardon bargain the next month by testifying in the Grand jury. He got indictments of Chapman's killers, with James Dolan and Billy Campbell for first degree murder, and Jessie Evans as accessory. But Ringite District Attorney William Rynerson, colluding with Judge Bristol, had Billy's trial venue for his indictments switched from Lincoln to Doña Ana County to guarantee a hanging verdict. Still Wallace issued no pardon.

By that April of 1879, Alexander McSween's widow, Susan, retained Attorney Ira Leonard, Chapman's office-mate from Las Vegas, to prosecute Dudley. So Dudley, likely advised by Catron, his attorney for past court martials, got defamatory affidavits to ruin her credibility. And he requested a military Court of Inquiry, where he would be defended by Catron's law firm member, Henry Waldo. And on April 25th, the Ring tried unsuccessfully to assassinate Ira Leonard to stop the case.

Wallace, having removed Dudley as Commander, testified against him in the 1879 Court of Inquiry, though without confronting the Ring. Billy testified also, for his own anti-Ring agenda. He devastatingly reported the three white soldiers firing a volley at him and escaping others: meaning officers; meaning under Dudley's orders; meaning violating the Posse Comitatus Act and justifying court martial, and even hanging. His courage made Ira Leonard take him as client.

By July of 1879, the biased Court of Inquiry exonerated Dudley. And Billy, with no pardon and imminent transport to Mesilla for a hanging trial, exited his bogus jailing.

The Ring recouped. By October of 1879, Susan McSween lost her civil trial against Dudley in Mesilla, to which her venue had been changed by Judge Bristol. That month, Bristol also voided James Dolan's Chapman murder indictment based on no witnesses daring to appear for a trial. Dolan, certain of immunity, had even taken over Tunstall's store. Tunstall's ranch property was given by the Ring to Dolan, Riley, and Rynerson; and Billy's Peñasco River ranch went to Jacob Basil "Billy" Matthews, head posseman for Tunstall's murder. And there was a more subtle Ring victory: Lew Wallace's humiliation in the Court of Inquiry made him shun Lincoln County "troubles" and Billy's pardon.

Billy's future killer, Patrick "Pat" Floyd Garrett, had arrived in New Mexico Territory's Fort Sumner in 1878. Born to an Alabama plantation family, relocated to Claiborne Parrish, Louisiana, when 9½ - and Billy was just born - he had even been willed a slave. After the Civil War, he had drifted to Texas, where he possibly murdered a black man, before becoming a buffalo hunter from 1876 to 1878 with two partners and a kid named Joe Briscoe. Garrett murdered Briscoe, but claimed self-defense to avoid prosecution. On the range, he never met fellow buffalo hunter, John William Poe; but later, his, Poe's, and Billy's histories would merge on the night of July 14, 1881.

In Fort Sumner, tall Garrett met transient kid, Billy Bonney, gambling at Hargrove's or Beaver Smith's Saloons. They were given townspeople's nicknames, "Big Casino" and "Little Casino," for their poker playing and height discrepancies.

The original Fort Sumner was built in 1865 by the U.S. government on desert flatlands east of the Pecos River for soldiers guarding Bosque Redondo: a concentration camp for 3,500 Navajos and 400 Apaches, until their scandalous starvation caused release of the Navajos to their homeland in 1868; the Apaches having already escaped. In 1870, Fort Sumner was purchased by Lucien Bonaparte Maxwell, one of the Territory's richest men. Converting it into a town around its parade ground, and using its thousands of acres for sheep raising, he settled there with his wife, Luz Beaubien; daughters, including Paulita; and son, Peter. Retained was the military cemetery for his family. It would receive Billy's body, to lie beside Pat Garrett's earlier shooting victims: Billy's Regulator pals, Tom O'Folliard and Charlie Bowdre. Maxwell died in 1875, leaving the town to his wife and son, Peter; who became the family's ruin through mismanagement. But when Pat Garrett and Billy Bonney gambled there, Fort Sumner was still thriving.

Lucien Maxwell's wealth came from marrying Luz Beaubien, an heiress of the almost two million acre Beaubien-Miranda Land Grant, buying its shares from her siblings. In 1870, he sold it as the Maxwell Land Grant; but was cheated by his attorneys, Thomas Benton Catron and Steven Benton Elkins, who resold it for double the money. That profit fortified their Santa Fe Ring, as they enriched themselves with railroads, banks, and mines. Catron eventually owned six million acres - more than anyone in U.S. history. In the Lincoln County War period, he was Billy's lethal enemy, with the Ring branding him as the murderous outlaw "Billy the Kid" to justify killing him. By 1912's New Mexico statehood, Catron became one of the two first senators.

By 1878, before the Lincoln County War, Pat Garrett and Billy Bonney led separate lives, though connected by Fort Sumner's Gutierrez sisters: Juanita, Apolinaria, and Celsa. Billy befriended Celsa, married to her cousin, Saval Gutierrez, a Maxwell sheep herder. Billy's July 14, 1881 death walk would start at their house. Garrett married Juanita, who soon died of a possible miscarriage. In 1880, he married Apolinaria, with whom he had eight children. It was a double marriage with his Fort Sumner, friend, Maxwell's foreman, Barney Mason, later a spy assisting Garrett's capture of Billy.

In 1878, Garrett had struggled with unemployment. At Fort Sumner, he drove a wagon for Peter Maxwell; helped a local hog raiser, Thomas "Kip" McKinney; and bartended at Hargrove's Saloon. Then came 1880 and the opportunity of his life. For Lincoln County's November election, the Ring needed a compatible Sheriff. To qualify, Garrett moved with his wife, Apolinaria, to that county's town of Roswell; adding, as a boarder, an unemployed journalist named Ashmun "Ash" Upson. In 1882, Upson would ghostwrite Garrett's book about killing Billy the Kid.

By 1880, the Ring's outlaw myth propaganda had advertised Billy's gunman reputation. That almost achieved his killing on January 3, 1880 at Fort Sumner's Hargrove's Saloon. A Texan bounty hunter named Joe Grant tried to shoot him in the back. Saved by Grant's gun's misfiring, Billy retaliated fatally. Obvious self-defense, that killing was not legally pursued.

Billy was now linked to murders of seven men: Frank "Windy" Cahill, William Brady, George Hindman, Andrew "Buckshot" Roberts, William "Buck" Morton, Frank Baker, and Joe Grant.

That 1880, when his now-famous tintype photograph was taken in Fort Sumner, Billy may have heard first whispers of his outlaw myth as a rustler and murderer. The Ring was setting its legal trap for eliminating him, since he refused to flee, and was impossible to kill or capture with his partisan backing.

Apparently using "co-boss" Stephen Benton Elkins's Washington, D.C., connections, the Chief of the Secret Service, James Brooks, was contacted for what would arguably be one of that agency's first political murders. Formed in the Civil War as a branch of the Treasury Department to combat counterfeiting, the Secret Service could pursue other crimes at its discretion, and could provide funding for informers and posses.

The scheme involved co-ordination of Carton's Lincoln County Ringites, with James Dolan initiating the investigation by reporting receipt of four counterfeit $100 bills from local counterfeiters at his Lincoln store (Tunstall's prior store which he had taken over). The Operative would then be fed information by Dolan himself, Catron's brother-in-law, Edgar Walz, at his Carrizozo ranch, and by Ringite U.S. Attorney Sidney Barnes. And by 1880, the Ring was confident that Governor Lew Wallace's only mission was protecting himself, and would not pardon Billy or interfere with killing him. So Billy, and the remaining Regulators, Charlie Bowdre and Tom O'Folliard, would be presented as murderous rustlers linked to the counterfeiting gang. The only missing piece was an Operative who was adequately gullible.

By September 11, 1880, Secret Service Special Operative Azariah Wild was sent to Lincoln, and proved an ideal dupe by lazy reliance on his Ringite informers. Though he initially recognized that the counterfeit bills Dolan got were from a youth, Billy Wilson, who was linked to the main counterfeiter, Dan Dedrick, who was reputed to also have a press, he was persuaded of a link to Billy. In fact, Billy occasionally used Billy Wilson for his guerilla rustling, along a "Dirty Dave" Rudabaugh, and past Regulators, Tom O'Folliard, Josiah "Doc" Scurlock, Charlie

Bowdre, and Jim "Frenchie" French. And Billy used Dedrick as an outlet for rustled stock, as well as Dedrick's brothers, Mose and Sam, at their White Oaks livery stable.

Wild was led to believe by Dolan and Walz that Billy was in the country's largest counterfeiting and rustling gang. By that December, came the Ring's *New York Sun* article, using Wild's leaked reports for "Outlaws of New Mexico. The Exploits of a band headed by a New York Youth, War Against a Gang of Cattle Thieves, Murderers, and Counterfeiters." Now Billy was alias "the Kid." The Ring had launched his national outlaw myth.

But Ring's plot almost backfired when Wild was told by Attorney Ira Leonard that his client, Billy Bonney, would testify *against the counterfeiters* in exchange for the pardon not granted by Lew Wallace. It was obvious that in Billy's dealings with Dan Dedrick - he had even gifted him his tintype, which became famous - he had become aware of the activities. And, as with his prior pardon bargain for testifying against Ringites, he was willing to convict people doing reprehensible crimes.

On October 8, 1880, Wild wrote in his daily report to Chief James Brooks that he himself would arrange a pardon for Billy in exchange for that testimony. But Wild confided that pardon plan to his Ringite informers, who convinced this dupe that Billy, staying in Fort Sumner, was actually the leader of an immense rustling-counterfeiting gang! So, in his report for October 14, 1880, Wild wrote that he intended to arrest Billy at the meeting to discuss the pardon bargain. But Billy was cautious. He held up the stagecoach carrying Wild's mail, read that report, and avoided apprehension by avoiding the meeting with Leonard and Wild. But another pardon was lost.

The Ring, determined to eliminate Billy, expanded the scheme to getting a Lincoln County Sheriff willing do it. The current Sheriff, George Kimbrell, who had assisted in Billy's sham arrest for the pardon bargain, was a McSween-side sympathizer. The Ring chose Pat Garrett. Secretly, Wild worked with him to form a dragnet to capture Billy and his "rustler-counterfeiter gang;" while, for the upcoming sheriff's election, Garrett was advertised as a law-and-order man to new gold-rush settlers in White Oaks, unaware of Lincoln County War issues, but a third of Lincoln County's voters.

In the November 2, 1880 election, Pat Garrett got 358 votes to Kimbrell's 141. Wild, convinced by his Ring contacts that Kimbrell protected the "Kid gang," also gave Garrett Territory-wide power for the capture by appointing him Deputy U.S. Marshall. Unaware, Billy would have wrongly thought that Garret's lawman authority was limited to Lincoln County, not Fort Sumner's San Miguel County, where he stayed.

And unaware of his locally publicized "outlawry," Billy still brought stolen horses to the Dedrick's White Oaks livery.

On November 22, 1880, a White Oaks posse ambushed him, Tom O'Folliard, Billy Wilson, Tom Pickett, and "Dirty" Dave Rudabaugh at nearby Coyote Spring, shooting dead two of their horses before Billy's group escaped. Five days later, that posse attacked them again at the way station ranch of "Whiskey" Jim Greathouse, 45 miles northeast of White Oaks; accidentally killing one of their own men, Jim Carlyle, but blaming Billy.

That accusation prompted Billy's only letter of 1880 to Governor Lew Wallace. On December 12th, he wrote, denying his outlawry and murdering of Jim Carlyle. He even described his Robin Hood role of seeking justice for the downtrodden. Wallace never answered. Instead, on December 22nd, he placed a Las Vegas *Daily Gazette* notice: "Billy the Kid: $500 Reward." He would repeat it in the *Daily New Mexican* on May 3, 1881, after Billy's jailbreak. His betrayal of the pardon bargain was complete.

By December of 1880, dreadful days began for Billy. U.S. Marshall Pat Garrett, backed by Azariah Wild, had assembled Texan posses to ride after Billy, since New Mexicans, to whom he was an anti-Ring hero, refused. Garrett's first ambush was on December 19, 1880, when Billy, Tom O'Folliard, Charlie Bowdre, Billy Wilson, Tom Pickett, and Dave Rudabaugh rode into Fort Sumner. O'Folliard was shot dead. The rest escaped.

Billy's group tried to flee the Territory in a snowstorm; but stopped, about 16 miles from Fort Sumner, on December 21, 1880, at a rock-walled, windowless, shepherds' line cabin at Stinking Springs. There Garrett ambushed them the next morning, killing Charlie Bowdre, whom he mistook for Billy, his intended victim. The rest surrendered. It would be seven months before Garrett succeeded in his mission to kill Billy.

And Azariah Wild, his own mission completed, left the Territory, unperturbed that he had found no mass of counterfeit bills, no counterfeiting gang, and had not even sought Dan Dedrick's alleged printing press. His own mission was complete.

Garrett transported his prisoners by train, via Las Vegas, New Mexico, to the Santa Fe jail. Billy remained there from December 27, 1880 to March 28, 1881, because the Ring awaited completion of the railroad to Mesilla to impede any rescue. But he almost escaped by tunneling out with fellow prisoners.

From his cell, Billy wrote four unanswered letters to Wallace, in 1881, pleading for his pardon: writing on March 4th: *"I have done everything that I promised you I would, and you have done nothing that you promised me."* On March 2nd, he had threatened: *"I have some letters which date back two years and there are Parties who are very anxious to get them but I will not dispose of them until I see you."* Wallace never got over that audacity or his own guilt, reworking the pardon obsessively till the end of his life in vindictive fictionalized articles on the outlaw "Billy the Kid."

Billy's first Mesilla murder trial, under Ringite Judge Warren Bristol, began on March 30, 1881, with jurors unaware of Lincoln County War's issues, and without any Lincolnites daring to be witnesses for his defense. Attorney Ira Leonard represented him for past U.S. Attorney Catron's June 21, 1878 federal indictment, Case Number 411, the United States versus Charles Bowdre, Josiah Scurlock, Henry Brown, William Bonney alias Henry Antrim alias the Kid, John Middleton, Steven Stevens, John Scroggins, Frederick Waite, and George Coe for the murder of Andrew "Buckshot" Roberts. It was first because the Ringites likely considered it air-tight.

But, surprising everyone, Ira Leonard got it quashed as invalid, since the federal government had no jurisdiction over Blazer's Mill, the murder site; because private property, like it, was under Territorial jurisdiction. Its being surrounded by the federally-controlled Mescalero Reservation was irrelevant.

Remaining were only the Brady and Hindman Territorial indictments; and, though Billy been firing in the group of Regulators, he had only a revolver lacking accurate range.

But, suddenly, Ira Leonard withdrew, likely after a Ring threat. That was disastrous for Billy. He got Ring-biased, court appointed attorney, Albert Jennings Fountain, who considered him an outlaw, along with co-counsel John D. Bail, a Ringite Catron friend.

On April 8th and 9th of 1881, was Billy's Brady murder trial. His Spanish-speaking jury, given no translator, heard only prosecution witnesses - including James Dolan. After Judge Bristol's biased instructions (with translator) made Billy's mere presence equal to firing the fatal shot, the jury found him guilty of first degree murder; its sole punishment being hanging. On April 13th, Judge Bristol set Billy's hanging date for May 13th, to limit time for appeal. Billy was to be hanged in Lincoln by its Sheriff, Pat Garrett.

From the Mesilla jail, Billy wrote to Attorney Edgar Caypless - conducting his replevin case against Stinking Springs posseman, Frank Stewart, for stealing his racing mare at Stinking Springs - hoping to get money from her sale to pay for an appeal.

Ironically, the new Lincoln jail, where Billy was incarcerated to await hanging, was in the past "House," which Catron had sold to Lincoln County for its courthouse, with second floor as jail.

On April 21, 1881, Billy arrived to Sheriff Garrett's custody. For his 24 hour guard, Garrett deputized a White Oaks man, James Bell, and a Seven Rivers man, Bob Olinger. Garrett's further precaution was shackling Billy at wrists and ankles, with securing to a floor ring - all to guarantee his hanging death.

But on April 28th, with Garrett away collecting White Oaks's taxes, Billy escaped. He used a revolver from an accomplice's putting it in the outhouse, or by seizing Bell's. A likely accessory was caretaker, Gottfried Gauss: Tunstall's past cook, and witness to Ring's Lincoln County War atrocities. Billy shot Bell dead as the man fled down the jail's stairway to sound alarm.

Deputy Bob Olinger, across the street at the Wortley Hotel with jail prisoners, either heard the shot or was directed to the ambush. Billy was at the second-floor window, and killed him with his own Whitney double-barrel shotgun.

Billy then spent hours using a miner's pick, supplied by Gauss, to break his leg chain to enable riding; while gathered loyalist Lincoln townspeople, in passive resistance, did nothing to stop him. He finally rode away on a pony supplied by Gauss.

As of that April 28, 1881 escape, Billy was involved in the murder of nine men; James Bell and Robert Olinger adding to Frank "Windy" Cahill and Joe Grant as Billy's only provable killings.

Of the dead, Billy would have said that that Cahill's and Grant's killings were in self-defense; that he was a legal posseman at the group shooting of escaping arrested Tunstall murderers, William "Buck" Morton and Frank Baker; that his gun lacked range to hit Sheriff William Brady or Deputy George Hindman, and their killings by the Regulators were to save Alexander McSween from murder by them; that he had not shot Andrew "Buckshot" Roberts, a Tunstall murderer and murderer of Dick

Brewer firing at his group, and killed solely by Charlie Bowdre in self defense; and that Deputy James Bell, after refusing to be tied, had tried to run for help, so was killed to save himself from unjust hanging (and Bell had been on the White Oaks posse, and possibly killed Jim Carlyle, then falsely accused him).

Only Seven Rivers rustler, Bob Olinger, would have been admittedly hated as being in each Lincoln County War period crime - Tunstall's murder, Frank MacNab's ambush murder, and the War's skirmishes and battle. Billy's rage was so great, that he smashed apart Olinger's shotgun to throw it on his corpse, delaying his own escape.

That count of nine killed men - with only four certain - remained as Billy's final true tally.

Billy's escape route was across the Capitan Mountains to the Las Tablas home of his friend, Yginio Salazar. He next went south, possibly intending to go to Old Mexico, and visited friendly rancher, John Meadows. But he reversed, going northeast to Fort Sumner and Paulita, where he hid in the Maxwell's sheep camps, confident of protection by the Maxwells and townspeople. He was unaware that Pat Garrett was paying Maxwell foreman, Barney Mason, as a spy, through Secret Service Agent Azariah Wild.

Garrett's two deputies for the pursuit of Billy to Fort Sumner - John William Poe and Thomas "Kip" McKinney - did not know Billy. Poe, a buffalo hunter, past Deputy U.S. Marshall in Texas, cattle detective, and recent White Oaks settler, had met Garrett during the Wild-assisted tracking of the "Kid gang." McKinney knew Garrett from their 1878, hog farming days. And they were unaware of the Santa Fe Ring, the Lincoln County War freedom fight, or Billy's role; knowing only outlaw myth propaganda.

Once in Fort Sumner, Garrett, doubting Billy's presence as too foolhardy, was urged by Poe to stay. On July 14, 1881, Poe, a stranger to the townspeople, did recognizance of the town; and also checked with Sunnyside postmaster, Milnor Rudulph, seven miles to its north. Poe became convinced Billy was nearby. That night, he, Garrett, and McKinney planned an ambush in Peter Maxwell's bedroom, with Maxwell as traitor. Unknown accomplices likely directed Billy to Maxwell's bedroom, where Garrett waited, with Poe and McKinney outside to kill Billy if he managed to escape through the door to the porch.

Near midnight, Billy proceeded from the converted barracks house of Celsa and Saval Gutierrez, carrying their butcher knife across the parade ground to cut a dinner steak in light of the almost-full huge moon, hovering at the horizon. He first went toward Maxwell's bedroom; but seeing Poe, asked in Spanish who he was, then entered.

Inside, to Maxwell, in bed as decoy, Billy asked again in Spanish who was there, possibly sensing Garrett in the darkness. Garrett then fired. Then Garrett fired wild. But the first shot was fatal. In terror, Maxwell ran out to the porch, almost getting shot by Poe, primed for back-up killing. Then Garrett returned to the room, with Poe and McKinney, and made sure Billy was dead.

The townspeople held a night vigil for Billy in their carpenter's shop. The Coroner's Jury, the next day on July 15, 1881, had as President, Postmaster Milnor Rudulph, a loyal Ringite who had helped take over the Legislature in 1872 to block anti-Ring bills. Bi-lingual, Rudulph wrote the Coroner's Jury Report in Spanish. The frightened juryman had no alternative but to sign his conclusion: *"[O]ur verdict is that the deed of said Garrett was justifiable homicide and we are unanimous in the opinion that the gratitude of all the community is due to the said Garrett for his deed and he is worthy of being rewarded."*

Ring terrorism was now complete. Silence fell for a generation before any dared contradict the Santa Fe Ring's outlaw mythology of Billy the Kid.

CHAPTER 3
BILLY BONNEY IN HIS OWN WORDS

SPEAKING THROUGH TIME

The real Billy Bonney was spectacularly brave, brilliant, and literate; and he left a big paper trail proving all that. What comes through is his zealot's mission to fight the Santa Fe Ring by repeatedly risking his life in legal confrontations with a deposition and court testimonies, and in pardon bargains offered to Lew Wallace and Secret Service Operative Azariah Wild. One can also see his Robin Hood self image, as in his December 12, 1880 letter to Lew Wallace; stating: *"There is no Doubt but what there is a great deal of Stealing going on in the Territory. and a great deal of the Property is taken across the [Staked] Plains as it is a good outlet but so far as my being at the head of a Band there is nothing of it in Several Instances I have recovered Stolen Property when there was no chance to get an Officer to do it.* **one instance for Hugo Zuber Post office Puerto de Luna. another for Pablo Analla Same Place**.*"* This real Billy is incompatible with his outlaw myths, and the "Billy the Kid's Bad Bucks" hoax of an evil counterfeiter, tricking fellow citizens.

Surviving are Billy's 1878 affidavit and deposition on the murder of John Henry Tunstall, and his testimony in the 1879 military Court of Inquiry for possible court martial for Commander N.A.M. Dudley. His pardon bargain letters and interview with Governor Lew Wallace were retained by Wallace when he left the Territory, and were almost the only civilian documents Wallace kept. They ended up in his collected papers, donated to the Indiana Historical Society. And Billy's 1879 Grand Jury testimony against Huston Chapman's murderers was referenced by contemporaries. Also, Dr. Henry Hoyt kept the Bill of Sale that Billy wrote out for him for a horse. And as big news in his day, Billy gave many articulate and ironic press interviews.

AFFIDAVIT AND DEPUTIZING

A key factor Billy Bonney's history was his lawman status in pursuing John Tunstall's killers. On February 19, 1878, the day after Tunstall's murder, Billy and Tunstall's foreman, Dick Brewer, gave eye-witness affidavits to Lincoln Justice of the Peace John "Squire" Wilson, to enable his writing arrest warrants. It is the first time Billy's voice is publicly heard. He named Tunstall's killers as Sheriff Brady's possemen: *"James J. Dolan, Frank Baker, Jessie Evans, George Davis, A.H. Mills, W.S. Morton, [William] Moore, George Hindman, [Frank] Rivers, Pantaleon Gallegos, divers other persons unknown."* It yielded Wilson's February 19th legal arrest warrants, stating:

Territory of New Mexico)
County of Lincoln   )

Be it remembered that before the undersigned Justice of the Peace in and for the County and Territory aforesaid, personally came R.M. Brewer & **W. Bonney** *who being duly sworn according to law deposeth & saith that at the County and Territory aforesaid on the 18th day of February 1878 in and upon the [presence] of J.H. Tunstall, Robt A. Widenman[n], R.M. Brewer,* **William Boney** *[sic] & John Middleton, then and there in the Peace of the Territory an assault was made with divers deadly weapons to wit with Winchester Guns and Colts Revolvers, and divers other deadly weapons by James J. Dolan, Frank Baker, Jessie Evans, George Davis, A.H. Mills, W.S. Morton, [omitted first name] Moore, George Hindman, [Frank] Rivers, Pantaleon Gallegos, divers other persons unknown and did then and there as affiant believes wounded & killed J.H. Tunstall contrary to the statute in such case made and provided against the Peace & dignity of the Territory.*

R.M. Brewer
William Bonney.

After Sheriff Brady refused to serve them, Wilson concluded that *"there being then and there no officers to serve such warrant the undersigned as directed by law, in such cases specially empowered Richard H. Brewer to serve the same endorsing such deputation on said last mentioned warrant."* Wilson wrote:

The Territory of New Mexico)
County of Lincoln   )

    I, John B. Wilson justice of the Peace in and for precinct N⁰ 1 Lincoln County, New Mexico, do hereby certify that on or about the 19th day of February 1878 **W. Boney** [sic] and R.M. Brewer filed in my office affidavits charging John [James] J. Dolan, J. Conovair, Frank Baker, Jessie Evans, Tom Hill, George Davis, A. [Andrew] L. ["Buckshot"] Roberts, P. [Panteleon] Gallegos, T. Green, J. Awly, A.H. Mills, "Dutch Charley" proper name unknown, R.W. Beckwith, William Morton, [Deputy] George Hindman, J.B. Matthews and others with having murdered and killed one John H. Tunstall at the said County of Lincoln on or about the 18th day of February 1878, that on or about the 20th day of Feby 1878, I secured warrants on said affidavits for the arrest of the parties above named and directed the same to the Constable of for precinct N⁰ one in said County to wit: Atanacio Martines [Martinez].

    That on or about the 20th day of Feby 1878 said warrant was returned "not served" that on or about the said last mentioned day the undersigned issued an alias warrant for the apprehension of the above named persons, and there being then and there no officers to serve such warrant the undersigned as directed by law, in such cases specially empowered Richard H. Brewer to serve the same endorsing such deputation on said last mentioned warrant.

    In testimony whereof I have hereinto set my hand at Lincoln Precinct N⁰ 1 Lincoln County, N. Mexico this 31st day of August 1878.

                                  John Wilson, Justice of the Peace

    This enabled Special Constable Dick Brewer to deputize Billy and Fred Waite as Deputy Constables under Lincoln Town Constable Atanacio Martinez to serve the warrants. To block the arresting, Sheriff William Brady then illegally locked them in Lincoln's pit jail, and confiscated Billy's Winchester '73 carbine.

DEPOSITION TO FRANK WARNER ANGEL

    On June 8, 1878, Billy gave his eloquent eye-witness deposition, with characteristic meticulous attention to detail, on John Tunstall's murder, to Investigator for the Departments of Justice and the Interior, Frank Warner Angel, with Lincoln

Justice of the Peace John "Squire" Wilson, as witness. In it, Billy stated information unknown to the imposters: that he had a ranch on the Peñasco River along with another Tunstall employee, Fred Waite; that he knew about the injustice of the case against Tunstall; and that the horses being herded back to Lincoln were exempted from the case's attachments.

Lacking that still-undiscovered deposition, imposters had to fabricate Tunstall's murder scene and its motive.

And proving his Regulator zeal to attain justice, Billy was risking his life by coming to Lincoln after Ringite Governor Samuel Beach Axtell's illegal proclamation outlawing the Regulators, and after receiving his own April Grand Jury indictments for Regulator killings in the Lincoln County War. He then signed the document, as witnessed by Angel and Wilson; which Angel's transcriptionist recorded as follows:

Territory of New Mexico)
County of Lincoln   )
*   )*

William H. Bonney was duly sworn, deposand says that he is a resident of said county, that on the 11th day of February A.D. 1878 he in company with Robt. A. Widenmann and Fred T. Waite went to the ranch of J. H. Tunstall on the Rio Feliz, that **he and said Fred T. Waite at the time intended to go to the Rio Peñasco to take up a ranch** *for the purpose of farming. That the cattle on the ranch of said J. H. Tunstall were throughout the County of Lincoln, known to be the property of said Tunstall; that on the 13th of February A.D. 1878 one J.B. Matthews claiming to be a Deputy Sheriff came to the ranch of said J.H. Tunstall in company with Jesse Evans, Frank Baker, Tom Hill and [Frank] Rivers, known outlaws who had been confined to the Lincoln County jail and had succeeded in making their escape, John Hurley, George Hindman, [Andrew] Roberts and an Indian aka Ponceāro the latter said to be the murderer of Benaito Cruz, for the arrest of murderers of whom (Benaito Cruz) the Governor of this Territory offers a reward of $500. Before the arrival of said J.B. Matthews, deputy Sheriff, and his posse, having been informed that said deputy sheriff and posse were going to round up all the cattle and drive them off and kill the persons at the ranch, the persons at the ranch cut portholes into the walls of the house and filled sacks with earth, so that they, the persons at the ranch,* should they be attacked or murder attempted, could defend themselves, this course being thought necessary **as the sheriffs posse was composed of murderers, outlaws, and desperate characters none of whom has any interest at stake in the County, nor being residents of said County**. That said Matthews when within about 50 yards of the house was called to stop and advance alone and state his business, that said Matthews after arriving at the ranch said that he had come to attach the cattle and property of A.A McSween, that **said Matthews was informed that A.A. McSween had no cattle or property there**, but that if he had he, said Matthews could take it. That said Matthews said that he thought some of the cattle belonging to R. M. Brewer whose cattle were also at the ranch of J.H. Tunstall, belonged to A.A. McSween, that said Matthews was told by said Brewer that he Matthews could round up the cattle and that he, Brewer, would help him. That said Matthews said that he would go back to Lincoln to get new instructions and if he came back to the ranch he would come back with one man. That said Matthews and his posse were then invited by R.M. Brewer to come to the house to get something to eat.

Deponent further states that Robert A. Widenmann told R.M. Brewer and the others at the ranch, that he was going to arrest Frank Baker, Jesse Evans and Tom Hill said Widenmann having warrants for them. That said Widenmann was told by Brewer and the others at the ranch that the arrest could not be made because if it was made they, all the persons at the ranch would be killed and murdered by J.J. Dolan and their party. That said Evans advanced upon said Widenmann, said Evans swinging his gun and catching it cocked and pointed directly at said Widenmann. That said Jesse Evans asked said Widenmann whether he Widenmann, was hunting for him, Evans, to which Widenmann answered that if he was looking for him, he, Evans, would find it out. Evans also asked Widenmann whether he had a warrant for him; Widenmann answered that it was his (Widenmann's) business. Evans told Widenmann, that if he ever came to arrest him (Evans) he, Evans would pick Widenmann as the first man to shoot at, to which Widenmann answered that that was all right, that two could play at that game. That during the talking Frank Baker stood near said Widenmann, swinging his pistol on his finger, catching it full cocked pointed at said Widenmann.

The persons at the ranch were R. M. Brewer, John Middleton, G. Gayss [Gauss], M. Martz, R.A. Widenmann, Henry Brown, F.T.

Waite, Wm McClosky and this deponent. J.B. Matthews after eating started for Lincoln with John Hurley and Ponceano the rest of the party or posse saying they were going to the Rio Peñasco. Deponent started to Lincoln with Robert A. Widenmann and F.T. Waite and arrived at Lincoln the same evening and again left Lincoln on the next day, February the 14th in company with the above named persons, having heard that said Matthews was going back to the ranch of said J.H. Tunstall with a large party of men to take the cattle and deponent and Widenmann and Waite arrived at said ranch the same day.

Deponent states that on the road to Lincoln he heard said Matthews ask said Widenmann whether any resistance would be offered if he Matthews returned to take the cattle, to which said Widenmann answered that no resistance would be offered if the cattle were left at the ranch but if an attempt was made to drive the cattle to the Indian Agency and kill them for beef as he, said Matthews had been heard to say would be done, he, said Widenmann, would do all in his power to prevent this.

Deponent further says that on the night of the 17th of February A.D. 1878 J.H. Tunstall arrived at the ranch and informed all persons there that reliable information had reached him that J.B. Matthews was gathering a large party of outlaws and desperados as a posse and the said posse was coming to the ranch, the Mexicans in the party to gather up the cattle and the balance of the party to kill the persons at the ranch. It was thereupon decided that all persons at the ranch excepting G. Gauss, were to leave and Wm McClosky was that night sent to the Rio Peñasco to inform the posse who were camped there, that they could come over and round up the cattle, count them and leave a man there to take care of them and that Mr. Tunstall would also leave a man there to help round up and count the cattle and help take care of them, and said McClosky was also ordered to go to Martin Martz, who had left Tunstalls ranch when deponent, Widenmann and Waite returned to the town of Lincoln on the 13th of February and asked him said Martz to come to the ranch of said Tunstall and aid the sheriffs posse in rounding up and counting the cattle and to stay at the ranch and take care of the cattle.

Deponent left the ranch of said Tunstall in company with J.H. Tunstall, R.A. Widenmann, R.M. Brewer, John Middleton, F.T. Waite, said Tunstall, Widenmann, Brewer, Middleton and deponent driving the loose horses, Waite driving the wagon. Said Waite took the road for Lincoln with the wagon, the rest of the party taking the trail with the horses. **Deponent says that all the horses which he and the party were driving, excepting 3 had been released by sheriff Brady at Lincoln that one of these 3 horses belonged to R.M. Brewer, and the other was traded by Brewer to Tunstall for one of the released horses.**

Deponent further says, that when he and the party has traveled to within about 3 miles from the Rio Ruidoso he and John Middleton were in drag in the rear of the balance of the party as just upon reaching the brow of a hill they saw a large party of men coming towards them from the rear at full speed and that he and Middleton at once rode forward to inform the balance of the party of the fact. Deponent had not more than barely reached Brewer and Widenmann who were some 200 or 300 yards to the left of the trail when the attacking party cleared the brow of the hill and commenced firing at him, Widenmann and Brewer. Deponent, Widenmann and Brewer rode over a hill towards another which was covered with large rocks and trees in order to defend themselves and make a stand. But the attacking party, undoubtedly seeing Tunstall, left off pursuing deponent and the two with him and turned back at the caño in which the trail was. Shortly afterwards we heard two or three separate and distinct shots and the remark was then made by Middleton that they, the attacking party must have killed Tunstall. Middleton had in the meantime joined deponent and Widenmann and Brewer. Deponent then made the rest of his way to Lincoln in company with Robt. A. Widenmann, Brewer, Waite and Middleton stopping on the Rio Ruidoso in order to get men to look for the body of J.H. Tunstall.

Deponent further says that neither he nor any of the party fired off either rifle or pistol and that neither he nor the parties with him fired a shot.

William H. Bonney

Sworn and subscribed before me this eighth day of June A.D. 1878.

John B. Wilson
Justice of the Peace

"REGULATOR MANIFESTO"

On July 3, 1878, during the multiple skirmishes in the Lincoln County War, and leading to the final Battle, there occurred a retaliatory Santa Fe Ring massacre at anti-Ring San Patricio: the Hispanic community which was like bi-cultural Billy's second home. On July 13, 1878, ten days after it, Billy took action: challenging the Ring, in what I named the "Regulator Manifesto." It is the anti-Ring declaration of the Lincoln County War Battle, starting the next day. It is signed only *"Regulator."*

Existing as a copy, it was first attributed to Charles Bowdre by early historian, Maurice Garland Fulton, who claimed implausibly that its recipient, Ring head, T.B. Catron's, brother-in-law, Edgar Walz, recognized Bowdre's handwriting. But I believe it was Billy's production, either dictated to Bowdre, or wrongly attributed to him by Walz. And it heralds Billy's future retaliative guerrilla rustling from Ringites, like Catron and Walz. It stated:

In Camp, July 13, 1878.
Mr. Walz. Sir: - We are all aware that your brother-in-law, T.B. Catron sustains the Murphy-Kinney party, and take this method of informing you that if any property belonging to the residents of this county is stolen or destroyed, Mr. Catron's property will be dealt with as nearly as can be in the way in which the party he sustains deals with the property stolen or destroyed by them.

We returned Mr. Thornton the horses we took for the purpose of keeping the Murphy crowd from pursuing us with the promise that these horses should not again be used for that purpose. Now we know that the Tunstall estate cattle are pledged to Kinney and party. If they are taken, a similar number will be taken from your brother [in-law, Catron]. It is our object and efforts to protect property, but the man who plans destruction shall have destruction measured on him. Steal from the poorest or richest American or Mexican, and the full measure of the injury you do, shall be visited upon the property of Mr. Catron. This murderous band is harbored by you as your guest, and with the consent of Catron occupies your property.
Regulator

HOYT BILL OF SALE

After the lost Lincoln County War, refusing to leave the Territory, like most Regulators, Billy earned money by gambling and retaliatory rustling from Ringites, as threatened in his July 13, 1878 "Regulator Manifesto." He would have denied being a common rustler - as he later labeled Seven Rivers rustlers to Governor Lew Wallace in a March 23, 1879 interview.

Billy used non-Ring outlets for stock, and sold horses himself in Tascosa, Texas. There, on October 24, 1878, he "sold" to Dr. Henry Hoyt a sorrel horse - likely Sheriff William Brady's Dandy Dick stolen from Catron's Carrizozo ranch. He priced it high for its bill of sale, which also demonstrated legalese he had possibly learned from Alexander McSween; and with proper witnessing by saloon owners, James E. McMasters and George J. Howard. That skill would be used in 132 days to write his first pardon plea letter to Governor Lew Wallace.

Billy's abilities impressed Hoyt enough for him to keep the document. On April 27, 1929, Hoyt sent its copy to Lew Wallace Jr.; writing: "I am one of the very few men living who was well acquainted with that famous outlaw 'Billy the Kid' and for many years supposed I had the only specimen of his handwriting in existence [until learning about the Lew Wallace letters], **a Bill of Sale for a horse he presented me with, and wrote out himself,** to protect me should my ownership ever be questioned, a very important matter in that part of the world at that period. This paper I have preserved all these years."

The Hoyt Bill of Sale stated:

Tascoso Texas
Thursday Oct 24th 1878

Know all persons by these presents that I do hereby Sell and deliver to Henry F. Hoyt one Sorrel Horse Branded BB on left hip and other indistinct Branded on Shoulders for the sum of Seventyfive $ dollars in hand received
W HBonney

Witness
Jas. E. McMasters
Geo. J. Howard

LETTER OF MARCH 13, 1879
TO LEW WALLACE

On approximately March 13, 1879, Billy began his pardon plea to Governor Lew Wallace, offering eye-witness testimony against Ringite murderers of Attorney Huston Chapman on February 18, 1879 for an exchange, since Wallace's November 13, 1878 Amnesty Proclamation had excluded those indicted, like him. Noteworthy is that Billy asked to *"annuly"* - meaning annul - his indictments for the murders of William Brady, George Hindman, and Andrew "Buckshot" Roberts. That was correct: a pardon is post-sentencing; annulment is before. And Billy's ability to spell even "indicted," contrasts the pretenders' low literacy. He wrote:

To his Excellency the Governor.
General Lew. Wallace
Dear Sir I have heard that You will give one thousand $ dollars for my body which as I can understand it means alive as a witness. I know it is as a witness against those that murdered Mr. Chapman. if it was so as that I could appear at Court, I could give the desired information. but I have indictments against me for things that happened in the late Lincoln County War and am afraid to give up because my Enimies would Kill me. the day Mr. Chapman was murdered I was in Lincoln, at the request of good citizens to meet Mr. J.J. Dolan to meet as Friends. So as to be able to lay aside our arms and go to Work. I was present when Mr. Chapman was murdered and know who did it and if it were not for these indictments I would have made it clear before now. if it is in your power to Annully those indictments I hope you will do so so as to give me a chance to explain. please send me an annser telling me what you can do. You can send annser by bearer.

I have no wish to fight any more indeed I have not raised an arm since Your proclamation. as to my Character I refer to any of the Citizens, for the majority of them are my Friends and have been helping me all they could. I am called Kid Antrim but Antrim is my stepfathers name.
Waiting for an annser I remain
Your Obedient Servant
W.H. Bonney

LETTER OF MARCH 20, 1879
TO "SQUIRE" WILSON

Billy began a flurry of March 20, 1879 letters by writing to Justice of the Peace John "Squire" Wilson to check with Lew Wallace about his planned feigned arrest for his pardon bargain, since many of the men he was supposed to testify against for the Huston Chapman murder had escaped from their Fort Stanton imprisonment. He wrote from his safe-haven:

> S<u>an</u> Pa<u>tricio</u>
> Thursday 20th 1879
> Friend Wilson.
> Please tell You know who that I do not know what to do, now as those Prisoners have escaped. So send word by bearer. a note through You it may be he has made different arrangements if not and he still wants it the same to Send :William Hudgins [Hudgens]: as Deputy, to the Junction tomorrow at three Oclock with some men you know to be all right. Send a note telling me what to do
> WHBonney
> P.S. do not send Soldiers

LETTER OF MARCH 20, 1879
TO LEW WALLACE

Wallace responded to Wilson with arrangements, and enclosed a vague *"note"* for Billy about their *"understanding."* Billy responded with a precautionary scenario for his sham arrest:

> San Pa<u>tricio</u>
> Lincoln <u>County</u>
> Thur<u>sday</u> 20th <u>1879</u>
> General. Lew. Wallace:
> Sir. I will keep the appointment I made. but be Sure and have men come that You can depend on I am not afraid to die like a man fighting but

I would not like to be killed like a dog unarmed. tell Kimbal [Kimbrell] to let his men be placed around the house and for him to come in alone: and he can arrest us. all I am afraid of is that in the Fort we might be poisoned or killed through a window at night. but You can arrange that all right. tell the Commanding Officer to watch)Let Goodwin(he would not hesitate to do anything there Will be danger on the road of Somebody Waylaying us to kill us on the road to the Fort. You will never catch those fellows on the road Watch Fritzes. Captain Bacas ranch and the Brewery they Will either go to Seven Rivers or to Jicarillo Mountains they will stay around close untill the scouting parties come in. give a spy a pair of glasses and let him get on the mountain back of Fritzes and watch and if they are there there will be provisions carried to them. it is not my place to advise you, but I am anxious to have them caught, and perhaps know how men hide from Soldiers, better than you. please excuse me for having so much to say

and I still remain Yours Truly
W H. Bonney

P.S.
I have changed my mind Send Kimbal [Kimbrell] to Gutieres just below San Patricio one mile, because Sanger and Ballard are or were great friends of Camels [Billy Campbell's] Ballard told me ~~today~~ yesterday to leave for you were doing everything to catch me. it was a blind to get me to leave tell Kimbal [Kimbrell] not to come before 3 oclock for I may not be there before

THE LEW WALLACE INTERVIEW

For his sham arrest in Lincoln, Lew Wallace and Billy were housed next door to each other; with Billy in his friend, jailor Juan Patrón's, house, and Wallace at José Montaño's. On March 23, 1879, Wallace interviewed Billy, asking nothing about the Lincoln County War. At this period, Wallace was also collecting information about Territorial outlawry, and Billy seems to have responded to that quest by telling him about the Santa Fe Ring's network of cattle rustlers, who fulfilled the beef contracts for Fort Stanton and the Mescalero Indian Reservation; which were held by the local Ring front, "The House," then controlled by James J. Dolan and John Riley. Noteworthy is Billy's vast fund of local information and geography. The notes stated:

William Bonney ("Kid")
relative to arrangement
with him.
Notes:

3-23-1879

Statements by Kid, made Sunday night March 23, 1879

1. There is a cattle trail beginning about 5 miles above Yellow Lake in a cañon, running a little west of north to Cisneza del Matcho (Mule Spring) and continuing around the point of the Capitan Mountains down toward Carrizozo in the direction of the Rio Grande. Frank Wheeler, Jake Owens and Dutch Chris are supposed to have used this trail taking a bunch of cattle over. Vansickle told K. so. They stopped and killed two beavers for Sam Corbett – hush money to Vansickle to whom they gave the beavers. Vansickle also said the Owens-Wheeler outfit mentioning "Chris" Ladbessor using this trail for about a year, but that lately their horses had given out, and of 140 head which they started to work they had only got through with 40. That now they were going to the Reservation to make a raid on the Indian horses to work on.

The Rustlers.

The "Rustlers," Kid says: were organized in Fort Stanton. Before they organized as "Rustlers" they had been with Peppin's posse. They came from Texas. Owens was conspicuous amongst them. **They were organized before the burning of McSween's house**, and after that they went on their first trip down the county as far as the Coe's ranch and **thence to the Feliz where they took the Tunstall cattle.** From the Feliz they went to the Pecos, where some of them deserted, Owens amongst them. (Martin, known to Sam Corbett) was in charge of the Tunstall cattle, and was taken prisoner, and saw them kill one of their own party. On the same trip they burnt Lola Wise's house, and took some horses. Coe at the time was ranching at the house. On this trip they moved behind a body of soldiers, one company, and a company of Navajo Scouts. They moved in sight of the soldiers, taking horses, insulting women. Lorenzo Trujillo (Jus. Peder) Juan Trujillo, Jose M. Gutierres, Pancho Sanchez, Santos Tafoya, are witnesses against them. They stopped on Pecos at Seven Rivers. Collins, now at Silver City, was one of the outfit – nick-named the Prowler by the cowboys. At Seven Rivers. There joined them Gus Gildey (wanted at San Antonio for killing Mexicans) Gildey is carrying the mail now from Stockto n to Seven Rivers – James Irvin and

Reese Gobles, (rumored that their bodies were found in a drift down the Pecos) – Rustling Bob (found dead in the Pecos, killed by his own party) – John Selman (whereabouts unknown) came to Roswell while [Captain] Carroll was there –

The R's [Rustlers] stayed at Seven Rivers; which they left on their second trip via the Berenda for Fort Stanton. On their return back they killed Chavez boys and the crazy boy, Lorenzo – and the Sanchez boy, 14 years old. They also committed many robberies. They broke up after reaching the Pecos, promising to return when some more horses got fat.

Shedd's Ranch

The trail used going from Seven Rivers to Shedd's was round the S.W. part of the Guadalupe Mts. by a tank on the right hand of trail: from Shedd's the drives would be over to Las Cruces Jesse Evans, Frank Baker (killed) Jim [James] McDaniels (at Cruces, ranging between Cruces and El Paso) Reed at Shedd's bought cattle from them – also sold cattle to E.C. Priest, butcher in Cruces. "Big Mose" (at Cruces last heard from) and [blank], deserter from cavalry – (went to Arizona)

Mimbres

Used to be called Mormon City – situated 30 miles on the road to Cruces from Silver City south. A great many of what are known as "West Harden gang" are there. Among them Joe Olney, known in Mimbres as Joe Hill; he has a ranch in old Mexico somewheres near Coralitos. He makes trips up in this country: was at Penasco not long ago.

San Nicholas Spring

Is about 18 miles from Shedd's Ranch on the road to Tularosa, left hand road. There's a house at the spring and about 4 or 5 miles from it N.W. is another corral of brush and a spring, situated in a cañon. There Jim [James] McDaniels used to keep stolen Indian horses. McD. one of the Rio Grande posse. Kid says the latter is still used.

The Jones Family

Came from Texas. Used to keep saloon at Fort Griffin. The family consists of the father, Jim Jones, John Jones, boy about 10 years old, a girl about 13, and the mother. Marion Turner lives with the family, and he killed a Mexican man at Blazers Mill "just to see him kick." He had no cattle **when the War started**. The Jones, John and Jim, killed a man named Riley, a partner of theirs, on the Penasco 3 or 4 years ago.

THE "BILLIE" LETTER TO LEW WALLACE

On a likely March 24, 1879, Billy wrote a letter to Wallace about Lincoln County War events. It exists now as a one-page fragment, signed "Billie." I dated and authenticated it in my 2012 book, *Billy the Kid's Writings, Words, and Wit.* It stated:

... on the Pecos. All that I can remember are the So Called Dolan Outfit but they are all up here now. and on the Rio <u>Grande</u> this man Cris Moten I believe his name is he drove a herd of 80 head one Year ago last December in Company with Frank Wheeler Frank <u>Baker</u> deceased Jesse Evans George Davis alias Tom Jones. Tom Hill, his name in Texas being Tom Chelson also deceased, they drove the cattle to the Indian Reservation and sold them to John Riley and JJ Dolan. and the cattle were turned in for Beef for the Indians the Beckwith family made their boasts that they came to Seven Rivers a little over four years ago with one Milch Cow borrowed from John Chisum they had when I was there Year ago one thousand six hundred head of cattle. the male members of the family are Henry Beckwith and John Beckwith Robert <u>Beckwith</u> was killed the time McSween's house was burned. Charles [blank] Robert Olinger and Wallace Olinger are of the same gang. their cattle ranch is Situated at Rock Corral twelve miles below Seven Rivers on the Pecos. Paxton and Pierce are Still below them forty miles from Seven Rivers there are four of them Paxton: Pierce: Jim Raymers, and Buck Powel. they had when I seen them last about one thousand head of cattle: at Rocky Arroyo there is another Ranch belonging to [blank] Smith who Operated on the Penasco last year with the Jesse Evans gang those and the places I mentioned are all I know of this man Chris Moten at the time they stole those Cattle was in the employ of <u>Dolan</u> and <u>Co</u>. I afterwards Seen Some of the cattle at the Rinconada Bonita on the reservation those were the men we were in search of when we went to the Agency. the Beckwith family were attending to their own Business when this War started but G.W. Peppin told them that this was John Chisums War. and so they took a hand thinking they would lose their Cattle in case that he Chisum won the fight. this is all the information I can give you on this point

Yours Respectfully Billie

LOST GRAND JURY TESTIMONY

Billy fulfilled his side of the Lew Wallace pardon bargain by testifying against the murderers of Attorney Huston Chapman - James Dolan, Billy Campbell, and Jessie Evans - in the April 1879 Lincoln County Grand Jury. By doing that, he was also implicating the Santa Fe Ring and risking his life. His testimony achieved those men's murder indictments (James Dolan and Billy Campbell for murder; Jessie Evans for accessory to murder).

That testimony was confirmed in *The Grant County Herald* of May 10, 1879, as reprinted from the Mesilla *Thirty Four*: "At the recent term of court in Lincoln, about 200 indictments were found. Among them, Col. Dudley and George W. Peppin for burning McSween's house, **Dolan and Campbell for the Chapman murder, in which the Kid is the principal witness**."

TESTIMONY AGAINST N.A.M. DUDLEY

Proof of Billy Bonney's anti-Ring commitment was his testifying against past Fort Stanton Commander N.A.M. Dudley on May 28th and 29th, 1879, since it was not part of his pardon bargain, and it risked his life. But he was seeking justice for Dudley's illegal military intervention in the Lincoln County War Battle, enabling the murders of Billy's compatriots: Alexander McSween, Harvey Morris, Francisco Zamora, and Vincente Romero. Billy twice made the unprotected, nine mile trip from his Lincoln sham custody to the courtroom in the Fort Stanton Adjutant's office for his court appearances.

His Regulator zeal, plus his courage and intellectual brilliance, made him unshakable under Dudley's lawyer's abusive cross-examination. Billy's precise and devastating testimony alone should have yielded a court martial after this interchange: "*How many soldiers fired at you? ... Three ... How many shots did those soldiers fire, that you say shot from the Tunstall building? ... I could not swear to that on account of firing on all sides, I could not hear. I seen them fire one volley ... Were the soldiers which you say fired at you as you escaped from the McSween house on the evening of July 19th last, colored or white? ... White troops.*"

A volley meant the three soldiers fired in unison. That required Dudley's order. "White" meant they were officers. That directly linked Dudley to ordering his soldiers to murder civilians. That was Dudley's treasonous Posse Comitatus Act violation. So dangerous was this evidence, that Dudley's lawyer's closing argument devoted a large part to a false attack on Billy.

Noteworthy, is that the Ring had already bestowed his outlaw moniker, "Billy the Kid;" and Billy was still uncertain about it under questioning. His transcript stated:

WILLIAM BONNEY, *a witness being duly sworn, testified as follows.*

Q. by Recorder. What is your name and place of residence?
Answer. My name is William Bonney. I reside in Lincoln.
Q. by Recorder. Are you known or called Billy Kidd, also Antrim?
Answer. Yes Sir.
Q. by Recorder. Where were you on the 19th day of July last and what, if anything, did you see of the movements and actions of the troops in that city, state fully?
Answer. I was in the McSween house in Lincoln, and I saw soldiers come from the post with the sheriff's party, that is the sheriff's posse joined them a short distance below there, the McSween house. Soldiers passed on by and the men dropped off and surrounded the house, the sheriff's party. Shortly after, the soldiers came back with Peppin, passed the house twice afterwards. Three soldiers came and stood in front of the house, in front of the windows. Mr. McSween wrote a note to the officer in charge asking what the soldiers were placed there for. He replied saying that they had business there, that if a shot was fired over his camp, or at Peppin, or at any of his men, that he had no objection to blowing up, if he wanted, his own house. I read the note myself, he handed it to me to read. I saw nothing further of the soldiers until night. I was in the back part of the house. **When I escaped from the house three soldiers fired at me from the Tunstall store, outside corner of the store.** That's all I know in regards to it.
Q. by Recorder. Did the soldiers that stood in front of the windows have guns with them while there?
Answer. Yes Sir.
Q. by Recorder. Who escaped from the house with you and who was killed at the time, if you know, while attempting to make their escape?
Answer. Jose Chavez [Chávez y Chávez] escaped with me, Vincente Romero, Francisco Zamora and McSween.
Q. by Recorder. How many persons were killed in that fight that day, if you know, and who killed them, if you know?

Answer. I seen five killed, I could not swear to who killed them, I seen some of them that fired.

Q. by Recorder. Who did you see that fired?

Answer. Robt. Beckwith, John Hurley, John Jones, **those three soldiers, I don't know their names.**

Q. by Recorder. Did you see any persons setting fire to the McSween house that day, if so, state who it was, if you know?

Answer. I did, Jack Long, and there was another man I did not recognize.

Recorder stated he had finished with the witness.
Cross examination.

Q. By Col. Dudley. What were you, and the others there with you, doing in McSween's house that day?

Answer. We came here with McSween.

Q. By Col. Dudley. Did you know, or had you not heard, that the sheriff was endeavoring to arrest yourself and others there with you at the time?

Answer. Yes Sir. I had heard so, I did not know.

Q. By Col. Dudley. Then were you not engaged in resisting the sheriff at the time you were in the house?

Objected to by Recorder. The Court has already ruled that nothing extraneous from the actual occurrence that took place, and Col. Dudley's actions in connection therewith, should be further inquired into ... it cannot be a matter of defense of Col. Dudley or justify his actions however much the parties may have been resisting the sheriff or civil authorities.

Lt. Col. Dudley, by his Counsel, states he does not deem it necessary to make reply to the objection.

Objection sustained.

Q. By Col. Dudley. In addition to the names you have given, are you also known as the "Kid?"

Answer. I have already answered that question, Yes Sir, I am, but not "Billy Kid" that I know of.

Q. By Col. Dudley. Were you not and were not the parties with you in the McSween house on the 19th day of July last and the days immediately preceding, engaged in firing at the sheriff's posse?

Court objects to the question.

Lt. Col. Dudley, by his Counsel, asks, does the Court intend to rule her McSween house by the testimony of this witness, it is not permissible to show all the circumstances under which this firing took place ...

Court cleared and closed.

Court opened and its decision announced ...

The Court directs the case to proceed calling attention to its previous rulings which were deemed sufficient by explicit.

Q. By Col. Dudley. Whose name was signed to the note received by McSween in reply to the one previously sent by him to Col. Dudley?

Answer. Signed N.A.M. Dudley, did not say what rank, he received two notes, one had no name signed to it.

Q. By Col. Dudley. Are you as certain of everything else you have sworn to as you are to what you have sworn to in answer to the last proceeding question?

Answer. Yes Sir.

Q. By Col. Dudley. From which direction did Peppin come the first time the soldiers passed with him?

Answer. Passed up from the direction of where the soldiers camped, the first time I saw him.

Q. By Col. Dudley. What direction did he come from the second time?

Answer. From the direction of the [Wortley] hotel from the McSween house.

Q. By Col. Dudley. In what direction did you go upon your escape from the McSween house?

Answer. Ran towards the Tunstall store, was fired at, and there turned towards the river.

Q. By Col. Dudley. From what part of the McSween house did you make your escape?

Answer. The northeast corner of the house.

Q. By Col. Dudley. How many soldiers fired at you?
Answer. Three.

Q. By Col. Dudley. How many soldiers were with Peppin when he passed the McSween house each time, as you say?

Answer. Three.

Q. By Col. Dudley. The soldiers appeared to go in company of threes that day, did they not?

Answer. All that I ever saw appeared to be three in a crowd at a time after they passed the first time.

Q. By Col. Dudley. Who was killed first that day, Bob Beckwith or McSween men?

Answer. Harvey Morris, McSween man, was killed first.

Q. By Col. Dudley. How far is the Tunstall building from the McSween house?

Answer. I could not say how far, I never measured the distance. I should judge it to be 40 yards, between 30 and 40 yards.

Q. By Col. Dudley. How many shots did those soldiers fire, that you say shot from the Tunstall building?

Answer. I could not swear to that on account of firing on all sides, I could not hear. I seen them fire one volley.

Q. By Col. Dudley. What did they fire at?

Answer. Myself and Jose Chávez [Chávez y Chávez].

*Q. By Col. Dudley. Did you not just now state in answer to the question who killed Zamora, Romero, Morris, and McSween that you did not know who killed them, but you saw Beckwith, John Jones, **and three soldiers fire at them**?*

Answer. Yes Sir. I did.

*Q. By Col. Dudley. Were these men, the McSween men, there with you **when the volley was fired at you and Chavez by the soldiers**?*

Answer. Just a short ways behind us.

Q. By Col. Dudley. Were you looking back at them?

Answer. No Sir.

Q. By Col. Dudley. How then do you know they were just behind you then, or that they were in range of the volley?

Answer. Because there was a high fence behind, and a good many guns to keep them there. I could hear them speak.

Q. By Col. Dudley. How far were you from the soldiers when you saw them?

Answer. I could not swear exactly, between 30 and 40 yards.

Q. By Col. Dudley. Did you know either of the soldiers that were in front of the window of McSween's house that day? If so, give it.

Answer. No Sir, I am not acquainted with them.

Redirect.

Q. by Recorder. Explain whether all the men that were in the McSween house came out at the same time when McSween and the others were killed and the firing came from the soldiers and others?

*Answer. Yes Sir, all came out at the same time. **The firing was done by the soldiers until some had escaped.***

Recorder stated that he had finished with the witness.

Q. by Col. Dudley. How do you know if you were making your escape at the time and the men Zamora, Morris and McSween were behind you that they were killed at that time, is it not true that you did not know of their death or the death of either of them until afterwards?

Answer. I knew of the death of some of them, I did know of the death of one of them. I saw him lying down there.

Q. by Col. Dudley. Did you see any of the men last mentioned killed?

Answer. Yes Sir, I did, I seen Harvey Morris killed first, he was out in front of me.

Q. by Col. Dudley. Did you not then a moment ago swear that he was among those who were behind you and Jose Chavez [Chávez y Chávez] when you saw the soldiers deliver the volley?

Answer. No Sir, I didn't think I did. I misunderstood the question if I did. I said he was among them that was killed not behind me.

Witness then withdrew ...

In Billy's second day of testimony on May 29th, he confirmed that Dudley's white officers fired at escaping McSweens, including himself; and that visibility came from the burning McSween house that made the area *"almost light as day."* The transcript stated:

Q. by Court. Were the soldiers which you say fired at you as you escaped from the McSween house on the evening of July 19th last, colored or white?

Answer. White troops.

Q. by Court. Was it light enough so you could distinctly see the soldiers when they fired?

Answer. The house was burning. Made it almost light as day for a short distance all around.

LETTER OF DECEMBER 12, 1880 TO LEW WALLACE

After Governor Lew Wallace betrayed the pardon bargain, Billy was publicly outlawed in lurid press. On December 12, 1880, he wrote to Wallace to deny a December 3, 1880 *Las Vegas Gazette* article by J.H. Koogler, titled "Desperadoe's Stronghold."

Billy's letter made clear that he did not consider himself an outlaw. He wrote: "*I noticed in the Las Vegas Gazette a piece which stated that, Billy "the" Kid, the name by which I am known in the Country was the captain of a Band of Outlaws who hold Forth at the Portales.* **There is no such Organization in Existence. So the Gentleman must have drawn very heavily on his Imagination.**" In addition, the letter shows his self-assured legal knowledge, describing to Wallace that he considered the posse illegal, for lack of proper arrest warrants: "*I asked for their Papers [warrants] and they had none. So I concluded that it amounted to nothing more than a mob.*"

By that December 12th, he had endured Secret Service pursuit, another lost pardon through a possible Secret Service bargain, two White Oaks posse ambushes, and a false murder accusation for Jim Carlyle. Seven days later, Garrett's posse would ambush Billy's group near Fort Sumner, killing Tom O'Folliard, intending to kill him. Ten days away was Billy's Stinking Springs capture, where Garrett would shoot dead Charlie Bowdre when mistaking him for Billy. Billy wrote:

Fort Sumner
Dec. 12th 1880
Gov. Lew Wallace
Dear Sir

I noticed in the Las Vegas Gazette a piece which stated that, Billy "the" Kid, the name by which I am known in the Country was the captain of a Band of Outlaws who hold Forth at the Portales. There is no such Organization in Existence. So the Gentleman must have drawn very heavily on his Imagination. *My business at the White Oaks at the time I was waylaid and my horse killed was to See Judge Leonard who has my case in hand. he had written me to come up, that he thought he could get Everything Straightened up I did not find him at the Oaks & Should have gone to Lincoln if I had met with no accident. After mine and Billie Wilsons horses were killed we both made our way to a Station, forty miles from the Oaks kept by Mr Greathouse. When I got up the next morning The house was Surrounded by an outfit led by one Carlyle, Who had come into the house and Demanded a Surrender. I asked for their Papers [warrants] and they had none. So I concluded that it amounted to nothing more than a mob and told Carlyle that he would have to Stay in the house and lead the way out that night. Soon after a* note was brought in Stating that if Carlyle did not come out inside of five minutes they would Kill the Station Keeper)Greathouse) who had left the house and was with them. in a Short time a Shot was fired on the outside and Carlyle thinking Greathouse was Killed jumped through the window. breaking the Sash as he went and was killed by his own Party they think it was me trying to make my Escape. the Party then withdrew.

    they returned the next day and burned an old man named Spencer's house and Greathouses also

    I made my way to this Place afoot and During my absence Deputy Sheriff Garrett Acting under Chisum's orders went to the Portales and found Nothing. on his way back he went by Mr Yerby's ranch and took a pair of mules of mine which I had left with Mr Bowdre who is in Charge of mr Yerby's cattle. he (Garrett) claimed that they were stolen and even if they were not he had no right to Confiscate any Outlaws property.

    I had been at Sumner Since I left Lincoln making my living Gambling the mules were bought by me the truth of which I can prove by the best citizens around Sumner. J.S. Chisum is the man who got me into Trouble and was benefited Thousands by it and is now doing all he can against me There is no Doubt but what there is a great deal of Stealing going on in the Territory. and a great deal of the Property is taken across the [Staked] Plains as it is a good outlet but so far as my being at the head of a Band there is nothing of it in Several Instances I have recovered Stolen Property when there was no chance to get an Officer to do it.

        one instance for Hugo Zuber Post office Puerto de Luna. another for Pablo Analla Same Place.

    if Some impartial Party were to investigate this matter they would find it far Different from the impression put out by Chisum and his Tools.

                Yours Respect
                      William Bonney

SANTA FE JAIL LETTER: JANUARY 1, 1881

After capture, Billy was kept in the Santa Fe jail, awaiting transport to Mesilla for his hanging trial. On January 1, 1881, four days after arriving, he wrote to Lew Wallace:

Santa Fe
Jan 1st 1881

Gov. Lew Wallace
Dear Sir
I would like to see you for a few moments if You can spare the time.
Yours Respect.
W.HBonney

SANTA FE JAIL LETTER: MARCH 2, 1881

On March 2, 1881, Billy sent his second jail letter, which Wallace considered "blackmail." Billy wrote:

Santa Fe Jail New Mex
March 2nd 1881
Gov. Lew Wallace
Dear Sir
I wish you would come down to the jail to see me. it will be to your interest to come and see me. **I have some letters which date back two years, and there are Parties who are very anxious to get them but I shall not dispose of them until I see you. that is if you will come immediately**
Yours Respect
W<u>m</u> H Bonney

SANTA FE JAIL LETTER: MARCH 4, 1881

On March 4, 1881, Billy wrote his third jail letter in tragic confirmation of the pardon's betrayal: "*I have done everything that I promised you I would, and You have done nothing that You promised me.*" Billy wrote:

> Santa Fe. In jail.
> *March 4th 1881*
> *Gov. Lew Wallace*
> *Dear Sir*
> *I wrote You a little note the day before yesterday but have received no annser. I Expect you have forgotten what you promised me, this Month two Years ago. but I have not, and I think You had ought to have come and seen me as I requested you to.* **I have done everything that I promised you I would, and You have done nothing that You promised me.**
>
> *I think when You think the matter over, You will come down and See me, and I can then Explain Everything to You.*
>
> *Judge Leonard, Passed through here on his way East, in january and promised to come and See me on his way back. but he did not fulfill his Promise. it looks to me like I am getting left in the Cold. I am not treated right by [U.S. Marshal John] Sherman. he lets Every Stranger that comes to See me through Curiosity in to See me, but will not let a Single one of my friends in, not Even an Attorney.*
>
> *I guess they mean to Send me up without giving me any Show. but they will have a nice time doing it. I am not entirely without friends.*
> *I shall Expect to See you Sometime today*
> *Patiently Waiting*
> *I am Very truly Yours, Respect.*
> *Wm H. Bonney.*

SANTA FE JAIL LETTER: MARCH 27, 1881

On March 27, 1881, Billy wrote to Wallace for the last time, emphasizing the pardon bargain, possibly hoping that it would be issued after sentencing in the Mesilla trial. He wrote:

> *Santa Fe New Mexico*
> *March 27th/81*
> *Gov Lew Wallace*
> *Dear Sir*
> *for the last time I ask: Will you keep Your promise. I start below tomorrow. Send Annser by bearer.*
> *Yours Respt*
> *WBonney*

LETTER TO ATTORNEY EDGAR CAYPLESS

After Billy's unjust hanging sentence for the Regulators' killing of Sheriff William Brady, handed down by Ringite Judge Warren Bristol on April 13, 1881, Billy wanted to appeal. Two days later, on April 15th, he wrote to Las Vegas attorney, Edgar Caypless, whom he had earlier hired on contingency to file his audacious replevin (rustling) suit for recovery of his bay mare from Pat Garrett's posseman, Frank Stewart, who had stolen her at Billy's Stinking Springs capture. Billy hoped to sell her to pay an appeal lawyer, with grounds that his Spanish-speaking jurymen had been deprived of a translator.

Caypless prevailed in the replevin case, but only after Billy's death; and he kept the mare's sales price as fee.

For his last known letter, Billy wrote:

Dear Sir. I would have written before this but could get no paper. My United States case was thrown out of court and I was rushed to trial on my Territorial charge. was convicted of murder in the first degree and am to be hanged on the 13th day of May. Mr. A.J. Fountain was appointed to defend me and has done the best he could for me. He is willing to carry the case further if I can raise the money to bear his expense. The mare is about all I can depend on at present so hope you will settle the case right away and give him the money you get for her. If you do not settle the matter with Scott Moore [to whom Frank Stewart sold the mare] and have to go to court about it either give him [Fountain] the mare or sell her at auction and give him the money. please do as he wishes in the matter. I know you will do the best you can for me in this. I shall be taken to Lincoln tomorrow. Please write and direct care of Garrett, sheriff. excuse bad writing. I have my handcuffs on. I remain as ever

Yours respectfully,
W.H. Bonney

NEWSPAPER INTERVIEWS

Billy Bonney's press interviews occurred after his Stinking Springs capture, and after his Mesilla hanging verdict. He was already nationally famous, and making ironic commentary like in his April 3, 1881's Santa Fe *Daily New Mexican's* "Something About the Kid": "At least two hundred men have been killed in Lincoln County during the past three years, but I did not kill all of them."

On December 27, 1880, the *Las Vegas Daily Gazette* published editor, Lucius "Lute" Wilcox's, article about the Stinking Springs capture and prisoner transport to Las Vegas, titled: 'The Kid. Interview with Billy Bonney The Best Known Man in New Mexico." Billy teased his outlaw myth; stating about onlookers: "Well, perhaps some of them will think me half man now; everyone seems to think I was some sort of animal." Wilcox wrote:

With its customary enterprise, the *Gazette* was the first paper to give the story of the capture of Billy Bonney, who has risen to notoriety under the sobriquet of "the Kid," Billy Wilson, Dave Rudabaugh and Tom Pickett. Just at this time everything of interest about the men is especially interesting, and after damning the men in general and "the Kid" in particular through the columns of this paper we considered it the correct thing to give them a show.

Through the kindness of [San Miguel County] Sheriff Romero, a representative of the *Gazette* was admitted to the jail yesterday morning.

Mike Cosgrove, the obliging mail contractor, who has met the boys frequently while on business down the Pecos, had just gone in with four large bundles. The doors at the entrance stood open, and the large crowd strained their necks to get a glimpse of the prisoners, who stood in the passageway like children waiting for a Christmas tree distribution. One by one the bundles were unpacked disclosing a good suit of clothes for each man. Mr. Cosgrove remarked that he wanted "to see the boys go away in style."

"Billy the Kid," and Billy Wilson who were shackled together stood patiently while a blacksmith took off their shackles and bracelets to allow them an opportunity to make a change of clothing. Both prisoners watched the operation which was to set them free for a short while, but Wilson scarcely raised his eyes, and spoke but once or twice to his compadres. **Bonney on the other hand, was light and chipper, and was very communicative, laughing, joking and chatting with the bystanders.**

"You appear to take it easy," the reporter said.

"Yes! What's the use of looking at the gloomy side of everything. The laugh's on me this time," he said. Then looking about the placita, he asked: "Is the jail at Santa Fe any better than this?"

This seemed to trouble him considerably, for as he explained, "this is a terrible place to put a fellow in." He put the same question to every one who came near him and when he learned that there was nothing better in store for him, he shrugged his shoulders and said something about putting up with what he had to.

He was the attraction of the show, and as he stood there, lightly kicking the toes of his boots on the stone pavement to keep his feet warm, one would scarcely mistrust that he was the hero of "Forty Thieves," romance which this paper has been running in serial form for six weeks or more.

"There was a big crowd gazing at me wasn't there?" he exclaimed, and then smiling continued: **"Well perhaps some of them will think me half a man now; everyone seems to think I was some kind of an animal."**

He did look human, indeed, but there was nothing very mannish about him in appearance, for he looked and acted like a mere boy. He is about five feet, eight or nine inches tall, slightly built and lithe, weighing about 140; a frank and open countenance, looking like a school boy, with the traditional silky fuzz on his upper lip, clear blue eyes, with a roguish snap about them, light hair and complexion. He is, in all, quite a handsome looking fellow, the only imperfection being two prominent front teeth, slightly protruding like a squirrels' teeth, and he has agreeable and winning ways.

On December 28, 1880, for the *Las Vegas Gazette*, from inside the train to Santa Fe, for "Interview with the Kid," Billy's steely self-control is evident when one realizes it was detained by a mob, either to lynch or to rescue him. The article stated:

We saw him again at the depot when the crowd presented a really war like appearance. Standing by the car, out of one of the windows from which he was leaning, he talked freely with us of the whole affair:

"I don't blame you for writing of me as you have. You have had to believe others' stories, but then **I don't know as anyone would believe anything good of me, anyway,**" he said. "**I really wasn't the leader of any gang.** I was for Billy all the time. About that Portales business, I owned the ranch with Charlie Bowdre. I took it up and was holding it because I knew that at some time a stage line would run there, and I wanted to keep it for a station. **But I found that there were certain men who wouldn't let me live in the country and so I was going to leave.**

We had all our grub in the house when they took us in, and we were going to a place six miles away in the morning to cook it and then light out. I haven't stolen any stock. I made my living by gambling, but that was the only way I could live. **They wouldn't let me settle down; if they had I wouldn't be here today,"** and he held up his right arm on which was the bracelet.

"Chisum got me into all this trouble and then wouldn't help me out. I went up to Lincoln to stand my trial on the warrant that was out for me, but the Territory took a change of venue to Dona Ana, and I knew I had no show, and so I skinned out ...

If it had not been for the dead horse in the doorway I wouldn't be here in Las Vegas. I would have ridden out on my bay mare and taken my chances of escaping. But I couldn't ride over that for she would have jumped back **and I would have got it in the head**. We could have stayed in the house but there wouldn't have been anything gained by that for they would have starved us out. I thought it was better to come out and get a square meal - don't you?"

The prospects of a fight exhilarated him, and he bitterly bemoaned being chained. "If I only had my Winchester, I'd lick the whole crowd" was his confident comment on the strength of the attacking party. He sighed and sighed again for the chance to take a hand in the fight and the burden of his desire was to be set free to fight on the side of his captors as soon as he should smell powder.

As the train rolled out, he lifted his hat and invited us to call and see him in Santa Fe, calling out *"adios."*

Billy's loyal attorney, Ira Leonard, protectively accompanied him on the train ride to Mesilla, via the Rincón depot. From there, they took the stagecoach to Las Cruces. With them were guards and prisoner, Billy Wilson, also transported to Mesilla. At Las Cruces, a crowd had gathered to see the famous outlaw, Billy the Kid. The arrival was covered in the April 3, 1881 Santa Fe *Daily New Mexican* in: "Something About the Kid." It stated:

An extract of a letter written by W.S. Fletcher from Mesilla to a gentleman in the city reads about as follows: Tony Neis and Francisco Chaves, deputy U.S. Marshals, arrived Thursday night with **Billy, the Kid,** and Billy Wilson. They met an ugly crowd at Rincon, where some threats were made, but Tony's crowd were too much for them. **At Las Cruces an impulsive mob gathered around the coach and someone asked which is "Billy the Kid." The Kid himself answered by placing his hand on Judge Leonard's shoulder and saying "this is the man."** The Kid weakened somewhat at Las Cruces, where he found quite a number of Lincoln County men, who were to appear against him as witnesses.

[AUTHOR'S NOTE: Billy had no defense witnesses. The prosecution had Ringites James Dolan, Saturnino Baca, and Sheriff William Brady's deputy, Billy Matthews; and subpoenaed Lincolnite, Isaac Ellis.]

He says at least two hundred men have been killed in Lincoln County during the past three years, but that he did not kill all of them. I think twenty murders can be charged against him. He was arraigned yesterday (Wednesday) before the United States court for the murder of Roberts, on the Mescalero Apache reservation, in 1878. Judge Leonard was assigned to his defense. Judge Newcomb gave notice that he had three other indictments for murder against him, and it looks as if he had no show to get off. His counsel asked today for time to send to Lincoln, which was granted, so that his trial will not commence for at least ten days. Billy Wilson's case is before the grand jury. He is charged with passing counterfeit money. He has retained Judge Thornton as his counsel. He seems to have friends here while the Kid has none.

No mails between Rincon and Doña Ana for the past week. Mosquitoes and flies abound and weather hot as blazes.

Billy's articulate response to the hanging verdict was in an April 16, 1881 article in the *Mesilla News*. He summarized Santa Fe Ring injustice: "I think it hard that I should be the only one to suffer the extreme penalty of the law." He called his court "mob law;" ending with facetious "personal advice": "If mob law is going to rule, better dismiss judge and sheriff and let all take chances alike." And he said sarcastically: "Advise persons never to engage in killing." About Lew Wallace's pardon, he said curtly: "Don't know that he will do it." The article stated:

Well I had intended at one time not to say a word on my own behalf because persons would say, "Oh he lied." Newman, editor of the *Semi-Weekly*, gave me a rough deal; he created prejudice against me, and is trying to incite a mob to lynch me. He sent me a paper which showed it; I think it a dirty mean advantage to take of me, **considering my situation and knowing that I could not defend myself by word or act. But I suppose he thought he would give me a kick down hill.** Newman came to see me the other day. I refused to talk to him or tell him anything. But I believe the *News* is always willing to give its readers both sides of a question. **If mob law is going to rule, better dismiss judge and sheriff and let all take chances alike.** I expect to be lynched going to Lincoln. **Advise persons never to engage in killing.**
 Considering the active part Governor Wallace took on our side and the friendly relations that existed between him and me, and the promise he made me, I think he ought to pardon me. Don't know that he will do it. When I was arrested for that murder he let me out and gave me freedom of the town, and let me go about with my arms. When I got ready to leave Lincoln in June, 1879, I left. **I think it hard that I should be the only one to suffer the extreme penalty of the law.**

For his secret transport to Lincoln for hanging, to prevent his partisans' rescue, in darkness, on April 17, 1881, Billy was taken by wagon from the Mesilla jail. April 20, 1881's *Newman's Semi-Weekly* reported his departure, with Billy, as usual, joking:

On Saturday night about 10 o'clock Deputy U.S. marshal Robt. Ollinger [sic] with deputy sheriff David Wood and a posse of five men (Tom Williams, Billy Mathews [sic], John Kinney, D.M. Reade and W.A. Lockhart) started for Lincoln with Henry Antrim *alias* the Kid. The fact that they intended to leave at that time had been purposely concealed and the report circulated that they would not leave before the middle of the week in order to avoid any possibility of trouble, it having been rumored that the Kid's band would attempt a rescue. They stopped in front of our office while we talked to them, and we handed the Kid an addressed envelope with some paper and he said he would write some things he wanted to make public. **He appeared quite cheerful and remarked that he wanted to stay until their whiskey gave out, anyway.** Said he was sure that his guard would not hurt him unless a rescue should be attempted and he was certain that it would not be done, unless, perhaps, "those fellows at White Oaks come out to take me," meaning to kill him. **It was, he said, about a stand-off whether he was hanged or killed in the wagon ...** He was hand-cuffed to the back seat of the ambulance. Kinney sat beside him, Olinger on the seat facing him, Mathews on the seat facing Kinney, Lockhart driving, and Reade, Wood and Williams riding along on horseback on each side and behind. The whole party was armed to the teeth and anyone who knows the men of whom it was composed will admit that a rescues would be a hazardous undertaking. Kid was informed that if trouble should occur he would be shot first and the attacking party attended to afterwards.

CONCLUSION

Real Billy Bonney's high intelligence, literacy, fund of knowledge, and freedom fighting idealism - proved by his own writings and recorded words - disprove his incompatible outlaw myths.

CHAPTER 4
BILLY BONNEY'S CHAMPIONS

RESPECT FOR A FREEDOM FIGHTER

In the 20th century, Billy Bonney's aging Lincoln County War period contemporaries finally contradicted the Santa Fe Ring's outlaw myth propaganda in print. They confirmed his brilliance, bi-culturalism, and militant zeal as a freedom fighting soldier.

FRANK AND GEORGE COE

John Tunstall's employees, Homestead Act farmers, cousins Frank and George Coe, 26 and 21 respectively, nick-named new, 17 year old ranch hand, Billy Bonney, as "Kid." By 1878, after Tunstall's murder, they became his fellow Regulators. After the lost Lincoln County War Battle, they fled to the Territory's northwest, near Farmington.

FRANK COE

On August 3, 1926, Frank Coe wrote about Billy in an unpublished letter to a William Steele Dean. He emphasized Billy's multiculturalism: "[He was] 5ft 8in, weight 138 lb stood straight as an Indian, fine looking a lad as I ever met. He was a lady's man, the Mex girls were all crazy about him. He spoke their language well. He was a fine dancer, could go all their gaits and was one of them. He was a wonder, you would have been proud to know him."

On September 16, 1923, Frank - like Billy, considering himself a Regulator soldier - gave a quote to the *El Paso Times*: "[Billy] was brave and reliable, one of the best soldiers we had. He never pushed his advice or opinions, but he had a wonderful presence of mind; the tighter the place the more he showed his cool nerve and quick brain."

GEORGE COE

In 1934, George Coe published *Frontier Fighter: The Autobiography of George Coe Who Fought and Rode With Billy the Kid*. The title demonstrated Coe's Regulator pride, since he and Billy fought side-by-side against the Santa Fe Ring.

He described employer, John Tunstall's, paternal affection for Billy: "Tunstall seemed really devoted to the Kid. One day I was in Lincoln and I asked him about Billy. 'George, that's the finest lad I ever met," he said. "He's a revelation to me every day and would do anything to please me. I'm going to make a man out of that boy yet. He has it in him.' "

About the Lincoln County War, George quoted Billy's militant fervor: "As for ... giving up to that outfit, we'll die first." Billy repeated that bravery in his March 20, 1879 pardon bargain letter to Governor Lew Wallace; writing: *I am not afraid to die like a man fighting but I would not like to be killed like a dog unarmed.*"

George gave a telling anecdote about Billy's teasing bravado on April 3, 1878 in the lead-up to the Lincoln County War Battle. It showed how this teenager inspired grown men:

"We made a big bonfire, and sat around swapping lies and bragging ... Then we talked about riding into Lincoln and setting in short order all the difficulties that were troubling the people there. We were a brave band as we told it. Our guns, which formed the most important part of our possessions, had been placed carelessly around against nearby trees. Billy sized up the situation and, looking for a little fun and excitement with an inexperienced bunch of greenhorns, he slipped about five or six cartridges out of his belt and tossed them into the fire. In less than a minute they began to go off, and such a mad dash for tall timber you have never seen ... I looked back as I ran, and there stood the Kid with his arms folded, perfectly unconcerned ... "Well, you're a damn fine bunch of soldiers. Run like a bunch of coyotes and forget to take your guns. I just wanted to break you in a little before we met the enemy, and, boys, I'm sure proud of your nerve."

YGENIO SALAZAR

Quoted in Maurice Garland Fulton's 1926 *The Saga of Billy the Kid*, Billy's good friend, Ygenio Salazar stated: " 'Billy the Kid' ... was the bravest fellow I ever knew. All through the three-days' battle [sic – six day Lincoln County War Battle] he was as cool and cheerful as if he were playing a game instead of fighting for his life." (Fulton, Page 144)

GOTTFRIED GAUSS

German-born Gottfried Gauss, 56 at Billy's great escape from Lincoln's courthouse-jail, was part of Billy's Lincoln County history from that teenager's October of 1877 arrival as a John Tunstall ranch hand - when Gauss was Tunstall's cook - through the Lincoln County War period, and to Billy's 1881 jailbreak, when Gauss was the Lincoln courthouse-jail's caretaker and likely supplier of Billy's escape revolver.

Gauss's anti-Ring stance went back to 1876 when he was employed in "The House," and was cheated out of his wages and profits from its brewery, which he ran.

Billy himself mentioned Gauss in his June 8, 1878 deposition to Investigator Frank Warner Angel as being at Tunstall's Feliz River ranch before Tunstall's ambush-murder, as well as during an earlier intimidation of its ranch hands by Sheriff William Brady's possemen. Billy's transcriptionist wrote: *"The persons at the ranch were R. M. Brewer, John Middleton, G. Gauss, M. Martz, R.A. Widenmann, Henry Brown, F.T. Waite, W$\underline{m}$ McClosky and this deponent."*

And the night before Tunstall made his fatal return ride with his men and horses to Lincoln from that ranch, he assigned Gauss to stay. Thus, Gauss witnessed the arrival of Sheriff William Brady's posse, on its way to murder John Tunstall. By shared traumas, he was Billy's steadfast friend.

On March 1, 1890, in an interview with the *Lincoln County Leader* about Billy's 1881 jailbreak, Gauss implied enabling by non-intervening Lincolnites, as well as his own sympathy for Billy. Gauss may even have directed Deputy Bob Olinger to the courthouse's east side, where Billy shot him. Gauss stated:

I was crossing the yard behind the courthouse, when I heard a shot fired then a tussle upstairs in the courthouse, somebody hurrying downstairs, and deputy sheriff Bell emerging from the door running toward me. He ran right into my arms, expired the same moment, and I laid him down, dead ...

When I arrived at the garden gate leading to the street, in front of the courthouse, I saw the other deputy sheriff Olinger, coming out of the hotel opposite, with the four or five other county prisoners, where they had taken their dinner. I called to him to come quick. He did so, leaving his prisoners in front of the hotel. When he had come up close to me, and while I was standing not a yard apart, I told him that I was just after laying Bell dead on the ground in the yard behind. Before he could reply, he was struck by a well-directed shot fired from a window above us, and fell dead at my feet. I ran for my life to reach my room and safety, when Billy the Kid called to me: "Don't run, I wouldn't hurt you – I am alone, and master not only of the courthouse, but also of the town, for I will allow nobody to come near us." "You go," he said, "and saddle one of Judge (Ira) Leonard's horses, and I will clear out as soon as I have the shackles loosened from my legs." With a little prospecting pick I had thrown to him through the window he was working for at least an hour, and could not accomplish more than to free one leg. He came to the conclusion to wait a better chance, tie one shackle to his waistbelt, and start out. Meanwhile I had saddled a small skittish pony belonging to Billy Burt (the county clerk), as there was no other horse available, and had also, by Billy's command, tied a pair of red blankets behind the saddle ...

When Billy went down the stairs at last, on passing the body of Bell he said, "I'm sorry I had to kill him but I couldn't help it."
On passing the body of Olinger he gave him a tip with his boot, saying, "You are not going to round me up again." And so Billy the Kid started out that evening, after he had shaken hands with everybody around and after having a little difficulty in mounting on account of the shackle on his leg, he went on his way rejoicing.

IRA LEONARD

Billy Bonney's best friend in a high place was his attorney, Ira Leonard, met during his 1879 pardon bargain's sham arrest with Governor Lew Wallace. And Billy helped Leonard as his prosecution witness for Commander N.A.M. Dudley's Court of Inquiry for possible court martial.

Leonard backed the pardon bargain, informing Wallace on his fulfillment by testifying in the April of 1879 Grand Jury against the Ringite murderers of Attorney Huston Chapman. To Wallace, on April 20, 187, Leonard described Billy's pressured testimony: "*I will tell you Gov. that the prosecuting officer of this Dist. [Ringite William Rynerson] is no friend to the enforcement of the law. He is bent on going for the Kid & ... is proposed to destroy his testimony & influence. He is bent on pushing him to the wall. He is a Dolan man and is defending him by his conduct all he can.*"

By April 25, 1879, the Ring tried to assassinate Leonard in Lincoln, just 66 days after James Dolan, Billy Campbell, and Jessie Evans had murdered his office mate, Huston Chapman, there, on February 18, 1879. But idealistic Leonard refused to stop prosecuting Dudley, or representing Ring enemy, Billy Bonney. Importantly, Leonard had no doubt about the Ring's existence. To Lew Wallace he wrote on May 20, 1879 that "*[Murphy and Dolan] were a part and parcel of the Santa Fe Ring that has been so long an incubus on the government of this Territory.*"

And when the Secret Service was trying to frame Billy Bonney as a counterfeiter, Leonard negotiated a second pardon option of Billy's testifying against real counterfeiters; but was thwarted by Ringites' manipulation of the gullible Operative.

HENRY HOYT

Henry Hoyt was a 24 year old medical doctor, working as a mail rider, when he met Billy Bonney in Tascosa, Texas, three months after the lost Lincoln County War Battle. Billy and fellow Regulators, Charlie Bowdre and Tom O'Folliard, were selling horses, rustled in retaliation from Ringmen, as forewarned in Billy's "Regulator Manifesto" letter of July 13, 1878 to Catron's Carrizozo cattle ranch manager and brother-in-law, Edgar Walz.

Billy gifted Hoyt a horse, likely dead Sheriff William Brady's, writing a legally protective bill of sale, dated October 24, 1878.

Hoyt admired Billy's intelligence and bi-culturalism. In his autobiographical, 1929 book, *A Frontier Doctor*, he wrote: "After learning his history directly from himself and recognizing his many superior natural qualifications, I often urged him, while he was free and the going was good, to leave the country, settle in Mexico or South America, and begin all over again. He spoke Spanish like a native and although only a beardless boy was nevertheless a natural leader of men. With his poise, iron nerve, and all-around efficiency properly applied, he could have made a success anywhere."

And, as Hoyt recorded in *A Frontier Doctor*, he also witnessed Billy the following year in Las Vegas, New Mexico, in company with Jesse James; though Billy denied to him any outlaw alliance.

JOHN P. MEADOWS

A cattle rancher living in New Mexico Territory from early 1880, John P. Meadows, gave interviews about having known Billy; and performed "Days of Billy the Kid in Story, Song and Dance" on February 26, 1931 in Roswell, New Mexico. He later used the act for newspaper accounts in the *Roswell Daily Record* on March 2nd, 3rd, and 4th of 1931, when he also wrote a manuscript on Billy. And from August 8, 1935 to June 25, 1936, the *Alamogordo News* printed almost 40 articles by him, now collected in a 2004 book titled *Pat Garrett and Billy the Kid as I Knew Them: Reminiscences of John P. Meadows*. It shows how Billy inspired others: "When he was rough, he was as rough as men ever get to be, yet he had a good streak in him."

E.C. "TEDDY BLUE" ABBOTT

E.C. "Teddy Blue" Abbott, a cowboy about Billy's age, in New Mexico Territory in 1878, and having merely heard of him, recorded his atypical multi-culturalism in his 1955 book, *We Pointed Them North: Recollections of a Cowpuncher*. Abbott reported: "The Lincoln County troubles was still going on, and you had to be either for Billy the Kid or against him. It wasn't my fight ... it was the Mexicans that made a hero of him."

CHAPTER 5
THE CORONER'S JURY REPORT OF JULY 15, 1881

PROVING BILLY BONNEY'S DEATH

The July 15, 1881 Coroner's Jury Report, in Spanish, contradicted the imposter hoaxes by proving Billy Bonney's death. **[APPENDIX: 1]**

1) **It confirmed the Report's proper filing with the District Attorney of the First Judicial District, William Breeden:** "To the District Attorney of the First Judicial District of the Territory of New Mexico, Greetings."

2) **It presented the proper action of San Miguel County Justice of the Peace Alejandro Segura, as** *ex officio* **coroner:** "[I]mmediately upon receiving said information [of a murder in Fort Sumner] I proceeded to the said place and named Milnor Rudulph, Jose Silva, Antonio Saavedra, Pedro Antonio Lucero, Lorenzo Jaramillo and Sabal Gutierres a jury to investigate the case."

3) **The body was identified:** "[The jury] found the body of William Bonney alias "Kid" with a shot in the left breast."

4) **The eye-witness was interviewed and corroborated the victim's identity:** "[The Jurymen]examined the evidence of Pedro Maxwell [Peter Maxwell, owner of Fort Sumner], which evidence is as follows: "I being in my bed in my room, at about midnight on the 14th day of July, Pat F. Garrett came into my room and sat down. William Bonney came in and got close to my bed with a gun in his hand and asked me "who is it" and then Pat F. Garrett fired two shots at the said William Bonney and the said William Bonney fell near my fire place and I went out of the room and when I came in again about three or four minutes after the shots the said William Bonney was dead."

5) **The jurymen's verdict denied murder, stating:** "[T]he deed of said Garrett was justifiable homicide."

6) **Garrett was praised:** "[H]is deed and is worthy of being rewarded."

THE TRANSLATED CORONER'S JURY REPORT

Territory of New Mexico) Precinct No. 27
County of San Miguel)

To the District Attorney of the First Judicial District of the Territory of New Mexico,

Greetings:

On this 15th day of July, A.D. 1881, I, the undersigned, Justice of the Peace of the above named precinct, received information that a murder had taken place in Fort Sumner, in said precinct, and immediately upon receiving said information I proceeded to the said place and named Milnor Rudulph, Jose Silva, Antonio Saavedra, Pedro Antonio Lucero, Lorenzo Jaramillo and Sabal Gutierres a jury to investigate the case and the above jury convened in the home of Luz B. Maxwell and proceeded to a room in the said house where they found the body of William Bonney alias "Kid" with a shot in the left breast and having examined the body they examined the evidence of Pedro Maxwell, which evidence is as follows:

"I being in my bed in my room, at about midnight on the 14th day of July, Pat F. Garrett came into my room and sat at the end on my bed to talk with me. A little while after Garrett sat down, William Bonney came in and got close to my bed with a gun in his hand and asked me "Who is it Who is it?" and then Pat F. Garrett fired two shots at the said William Bonney and the said Bonney fell near my fire place and I went out of the room and when I came in again about three or four minutes after the shots the said Bonney was dead."

The jury has found the following verdict:

We the jury unanimously find that William Bonney has been killed by a bullet in the left breast in the region of the heart, the same having been fired from a pistol in the hand of Pat F. Garrett, and our verdict is that the act of said Garrett was justifiable homicide and we are unanimous in the opinion that the gratitude of all the community is due to the said Garrett for his deed and is worthy of being rewarded.

>M. Rudulph, President
>Anto Sabedra
>Pedro Anto Lucero
>Jose x Silba
>Sabal x Gutierrez
>Lorenzo x Jaramillo

All which information I put at your disposal.

>Alejandro Segura Justice of the Peace

PAT GARRETT'S LETTER TO THE ACTING-GOVERNOR

On July 15, 1881, the day after killing Billy Bonney, Pat Garrett sent a letter, enclosing a copy of that day's Coroner's Jury Report, to Territorial Acting-Governor, William Ritch, confirming the killing and its circumstances.

The letter was quoted in July 23, 1881's Las Cruces *Rio Grande Republican* as "Kid the Killer Killed, Wm. Bonney alias Antrim, alias Billy the Kid, Fatally Meets Pat Garrett, the Lincoln County Sheriff." It stated: "Below is given Sheriff Garrett's report as made to Acting Governor Ritch which contains also the verdict of the coroner's jury [with English translation, but explaining: 'The verdict is given in Spanish in Garrett's report']." The article stated:

William Bonney, alias 'the Kid,' is dead. No report could have caused more general feeling of gratification than this, and when it was further announced that the faithful and brave Pat Garrett, he who had been the mainstay of law and order in Lincoln county, the chief reliance of the people in the dark days, when danger lurked at every hand, has accomplished the crowning feat of his life by bringing down the fierce and implacable foe single-handed, the sense of satisfaction was heightened to one of delight. The following is Sheriff Garrett's official report to the chief executive of the territory.

It is as follows. – Fort Sumner, N.M., July 15. - Fort Sumner, N.M., July 15, '81 - To his Excellency the Governor of New Mexico:

"I have the honor to inform your Excellency that I had received several communications from persons in and about Fort Sumner, what William Bonney, alias the Kid, had been there, or in that vicinity for some time.

"In view of these reports I deemed it my duty to go there, and ascertain if there was any truth in them or not, all the time doubting their accuracy; but on Monday, July 11, I left home, taking with me John W. Poe and T.L. McKinney, men in whose courage and sagacity I relied implicitly, and arrived just below Fort Sumner, on Wednesday, 13th [sic]. I remained concealed near the houses, until night, and then entered the fort about midnight, and went to Mr. P. Maxwell's room. I found him in bed, and had just commenced talking to him about the object of my visit at such an unusual hour, when a man entered the room in stockinged feet, with a pistol in one hand and a knife in the other. He came and placed his hand on the bed just beside me, and in a low whisper, "who is it?" (and repeated the question) he asked Mr. Maxwell.

I at once recognized the man, and knew he was the Kid, and reached behind me for my pistol, feeling almost certain of receiving a ball from his at the moment of my doing so, as I felt sure he had now recognized me, but fortunately he drew back from the bed at noticing my movement, and, although he had his pistol pointed at my breast, he delayed to fire, and asked me in Spanish, "Quien es? Quien es?" This gave me time to bring mine to bear on him, and the moment I did so I pulled the trigger and he received his death wound, for the ball struck him in the left breast and pierced his heart. He never spoke, but died in a minute. It was my desire to have been able to take him alive, but his coming upon me so suddenly and unexpectedly leads me to believe that he had seen me enter the room, or had been informed by someone of the fact; and that he came there armed with pistol and knife expressly to kill me if he could. Under that impression I had no alternative but to kill him or to suffer death at his hands.

I herewith annex a copy of the verdict rendered by the jury called in by the justice of the peace (ex officio coroner), the original of which is in the hands of the prosecuting attorney of the first judicial district."

(The verdict is given in Spanish in Garrett's report, and upon being translated is as follows:

"We the jury unanimously say that William Bonney came to his death by a wound in the breast in the region of the heart, fired from a pistol in the hand of Pat F. Garrett, and our decision is that the action of said Garrett, was justifiable homicide; and we are united in opinion that the gratitude of all the community is due to said Garrett for his action, and he deserves to be compensated."

(Signed) M. Rudulph, Foreman,
Antonio Saavedra,
Pedro Antonio Lucero,
Sabal Gutierres,
Lorenzo Jaramillo

I am Governor, very respectfully your Excellency's obedient servant,
Pat F. Garrett

THE ISSUE OF NO CULPABILITY

Pat Garrett's letter of July 15, 1881 to Acting-Governor William Ritch confirmed that he had followed proper legal procedure and sent the original Coroner's Jury Report to the District Attorney for the First Judicial District, William Breeden, responsible for San Miguel County, in which was the homicide site of Fort Sumner. Garrett's letter to Ritch had stated: "I herewith annex a copy of the verdict rendered by the jury called in by the justice of the peace (*ex officio* coroner, meaning by virtue of his position or status), **the original of which is in the hands of the prosecuting attorney of the first judicial district."**

Breeden, also Territorial Attorney General, would have checked the verdict: "[O]ur verdict is that the action of said Garrett was justifiable homicide." That meant the killing as self-defense, as was subsequently confirmed by prosecutor Breeden's filing no murder charge against Garrett, and later by his assisting Acting-Governor Ritch in processing Garrett's reward payment. There were no grounds for a cold case murder accusation against Garrett.

ISSUES COMPLICATING REWARD COLLECTION

Garrett's letter to Acting-Governor Ritch also initiated the process of collecting his reward. The Coroner's Jury Report had presented no problem with its conclusion stating: "[H]e deserves to be rewarded." But issuing the reward to him was complicated by two variables: its being a **private offer** by past-Governor Lew Wallace, and its **not being a dead-or-alive offer**.

The reward offer, published by Lew Wallace, in his own name, in December 22, 1880's *Las Vegas Daily Gazette*, and May 3, 1881's *Santa Fe Daily New Mexican*, had stated:

> **BILLY THE KID**
> **$500 REWARD**
> I will pay $500 reward to any person or persons who will capture William Bonney, alias The Kid, and deliver him to any sheriff of New Mexico. Satisfactory proofs of identity will be required.
>   LEW. WALLACE,
>   Governor of New Mexico

Its stipulating capture and delivery "to any sheriff" meant alive. To cover that Bonney was now dead (i.e., not deliverable alive), Garrett's letter to Ritch had explained that killing had been the only option: "I had no alternative but to kill him or to suffer death at his hands." So death instead of capture presented no problem to all concerned in justifying the reward.

REWARD NEEDING LEGISLATIVE INTERVENTION

Acting-Governor William Ritch could not simply issue payment of Garrett's reward. He hesitated to use Territorial funds to cover Lew Wallace's private offer. And Wallace had left the Territory and his governorship in May of 1881.

So Ritch sought legal advice from the ideal person: William Breeden. Not only was he the proper prosecutor as District Attorney of the First Judicial District, who himself possessed the original of the Coroner's Jury Report, and who knew Garrett's killing had been in self-defense; but he was also the Territorial Attorney General, who could advise on the proper legal solution of conversion of a private reward to a Territorial one.

Garrett himself met with Ritch on July 20, 1881, as reported by the July 21, 1881 *Santa Fe Daily New Mexican*. Ritch was quoted as "willing to pay the amount, and was willing to do so," but made clear that the delaying issue was that proper procedure had to be followed first. The article stated:

> Yesterday afternoon Pat. Garrett; accompanied by Hon. T.B. Catron and Col. M. Brunswick, called upon acting-Governor Ritch in regard to the reward offered by ex-Governor Lew Wallace for the Kid. The reward was fixed at five hundred dollars, and the offer was published in the papers. <u>Governor Ritch announced that he was willing to pay the amount, and would be glad to do so, but that he would have to look at the records first</u>. He was not in the city when the offer was made, and had never received any notification of it, consequently did not know whether or not it was on record. In consequence of the state of affairs, the question of the reward was not settled.

Ritch recorded his consultation with Breeden in his July 21, 1881 *Executive Record Book 2* entry as: "In the matter of the application by Patrick F. Garrett for a reward claimed to have been offered May-1881 for the capture of Wm Bonney alias 'the Kid.' " It confirmed that Breeden agreed that the reward was a private offer, since Wallace had not filed it with his office or that of the Territorial Secretary [then Ritch himself], converting it to a Territorial offer. Breeden stated: "*In addition, we will add as fact that there was no record whatever in this [Attorney General's] office or at the Secretary's office of there having been a reward offered as* set forth by Attorney General, nor was there any reward or file in said offices of a corresponding reward in any form." So the issue was converting Wallace's private reward to a Territorial reward.

Ritch's July 21, 1881 *Executive Record Book 2* entry transcribed Breeden's opinion; stating:

Executive Department
Territory of New Mexico
July 21st 1881

July 20th 1881 Pat F. Garret [sic- throughout] Sheriff of Lincoln County appeared and presented a bill for $500. claiming it as a reward offered on or about the 7th of May 1881 by the late Governor Lew Wallace, for the capture of said Bonny [sic, throughout].

As evidence of said offer having been made the affidavit of publication thereof made by Chas. H. Green [sic – Greene] the editor and manager of the Daily <u>New Mexican</u> was presented with said bill, as also was presented a statement of the proceedings and verdict of a coroner's jury at Fort Sumner in San Miguel County upon the body of the said Bonny, captured as aforesaid, and a statement of Garret directed to this office of his doings in the premises.

Upon examination of said papers it was deemed important that the opinion of the Attorney General be taken thereon and they were at once transmitted to that office. On the following day the papers with the opinion of Hon. Wm Breeden Attorney General were filed.

Said opinion is quite full. We quote the closing paragraphs as sufficient in this connection, to with

"The offer by the Governor, or the notice thereof, which is all there is to show such an offer, is as follows –

Billy the Kid
$500 Reward

"I will pay five hundred dollars reward to any person or persons, who will capture William Bonny, alias the Kid, and deliver him to any Sheriff of New Mexico. Satisfactory proof of identity will be required.

Lew Wallace
Governor of New Mexico

"This certainly appears to be the personal offer of Governor Wallace, and it seems he did nothing to indicate that it was intended as an executive act on behalf of, and to bind the Territory.

"If the reward should be paid, it is very probable that the Legislature would approve the payment if so desired, and that no objection would be raised, or that it will provide for its payment if it remained unpaid, at the next session thereof;

[AUTHOR'S NOTE: Breeden saw no problem with the Legislature's eventual approving of reward payment.]

but if the Governor [Ritch] should now direct the payment of the claim, he would doubtless expose himself to the charge of misappropriation of the Territorial funds, in case the Legislature should refuse to ratify or approve the payment."

[AUTHOR'S NOTE: So Breeden said if Ritch paid the reward himself *before proper procedure of legislative approval*, it could be criticized as misappropriating funds. Ritch next returned to presenting his own words.]

In addition we will add as a fact that there was no record whatsoever; either in this office or at the [Territorial] Secretary's office of there having been a reward offered as set forth by Attorney General, nor was there any record or file in said offices of a corresponding reward in any form.

[AUTHOR'S NOTE: Ritch confirmed that Wallace had not converted his reward offer into a Territorial offer.]

The opinion of the Attorney General appearing to be consistent with the law and the facts. Decision is rendered accordingly and the Governor [Ritch] declines to allow the reward at this time. <u>Believing however, that Mr Garret has an equitable claim against the Territory for said reward, the action at this office will simply be suspended until the case can properly be represented to the next Legislative Assembly.</u>

      Ritch
      Act Governor NM

[AUTHOR'S NOTE: Ritch confirmed that the reward was justified, but had to be converted to a Territorial reward, though that made a delay till the legislative meeting.]

REWARD GRANTED TO GARRETT BY THE LEGISLATURE

The Act granting Pat Garrett his reward made clear that only the conversion "technicality" had caused the delay. It stated:

AN ACT FOR THE RELIEF OF PAT. GARRETT
CONTENTS

SECTION 1. Authorizes payment of $500 reward for the arrest of "the Kid."

WHEREAS, The Governor of New Mexico did, on or about the 7th day of May, A.D., 1881, issue certain proclamation in words and figures as follows, to-wit:

"I will pay five hundred dollars reward to any person or persons who will capture William Bonney, alias 'The Kid,' and deliver him to any sheriff of New Mexico. Satisfactory proof of identity will be required."

(Signed)   Lew. Wallace
                 Governor of New Mexico.

AND, WHEREAS, Pat. Garrett was at that time sheriff of Lincoln county, and did, on or about the month of August, 1881, in pursuance of the above reward, and by virtue of a warrant placed in his hands for the purpose, attempted to arrest said William Bonney, and in said attempt did kill said William Bonney at Fort Sumner, in the county of San Miguel, in the Territory of New Mexico, and wherefore, said <u>Garrett is justly entitled to the above reward, and payment thereof has been refused upon a technicality</u>. Therefore

Be it enacted by the Legislative Assembly of the Territory of New Mexico:

SECTION 1. The Territorial Auditor is hereby authorized to draw a warrant upon the Territorial Treasurer of the Territory of New Mexico, in favor of Pat. Garrett for the sum of five hundred dollars, payable out of any funds in the Territorial treasury not otherwise appropriated, in payment of the reward of five hundred dollars heretofore offered by his Excellency, Governor

Lew. Wallace, for the arrest of William Bonney, alias "The Kid."

SEC. 2. This act shall take effect and be in force from and after its passage.

Approved February 18, 1882.

LATER FINDING OF THE REPORT

After the Coroner's Jury Report fulfilled its uses, it was filed away by William Breeden. It was indirectly referenced in a 1935 book by a Frank M. King titled *Wranglin' the Past: Reminiscences of Frank M. King*, in the chapter titled "The Kid's Exit." King wrote that Garrett's letter to Acting-Governor William Ritch, which cited the Report's its copy, had recently been located in old files of the Secretary of State of New Mexico.

And the original William Bonney Coroner's Jury Report of July 15, 1881 - sent to William Breeden, as District Attorney of the First Judicial District, and also legally analyzed by him as Attorney General - was found in 1932 by a Harold Abbott, employed from 1931 to 1933 in Santa Fe in the State Land Office, when he discovered it in the basement of the state capitol. He made copies of it for himself and others, including his brother George. Harold died in 1937; George in 2006.

So George Abbott lived to see his brother's finding of the Coroner's Jury Report making the front page of November 30, 1950's *Alamogordo News* as "Sumner Jury Thought The Kid Had Been Killed." It stated:

Although the perennial controversy over whether the infamous Billy the Kid still lives, has again arisen, at least one Alamogordo man, Frank Phillips, 84, claims personal knowledge of his death in 1881 at the hands of the late Sheriff Pat Garrett, and George Abbott, also of Alamogordo has in his office at the Pioneer Abstract Co., a photostatic copy of the verdict of the coroner's jury which viewed the remains of the late Wm. Bonney

Some twenty years ago, when the late Harold Abbott, brother of George, was an employee of the state land office in Santa Fe, he, with other employees, were going over some old records in the basement of the state capitol. There they ran across, in the San Miguel court records, the original

copy of the coroner's jury, dated July 15, 1881, and written in Spanish. The document covered three pages of which they made photostatic copies.

As the reader will see from the document, translated below, the six men serving on the jury and the Justice of the Peace who empanneled them, seemed convinced that Wm. Bonney, known as "Kid," was quite dead, and that he had been killed by Pat Garrett.

The most recent controversy arose when a firm of El Paso lawyers appealed to Governor Mabry for a full pardon for Wm. Bonney, who claims that the man killed at Fort Sumner by Pat Garrett was another outlaw, and not the Kid at all; that the Kid left the country, assumed the name of ["Brushy Bill"] Roberts, and has lived in Old and New Mexico all this time.

The documentary evidence of the Kid's death is translated as follows:
Territory of New Mexico
San Miguel County
Precinct No. 27
To the attorney of the 1st Judicial district of the Territory of New Mexico:
Greetings: [The English Translation followed]

FROM BREEDEN TO HAROLD ABBOTT

One can trace the Coroner's Jury Report's storage in the state Capitol Buildings. First was William Breeden's Palace of the Governors office. Breeden apparently filed the Report in his capacity as District Attorney for the First Judicial District under San Miguel County court records, as he categorized this Fort Sumner killing in that county. As Attorney General also, his office was in rooms 5, 6, and 8, according to Clinton P. Anderson in his 1944 *New Mexico Historical Review* article titled "The Adobe Palace." (Anderson, Page 110) **[FIGURE: 1]** Anderson noted that Breeden kept that office till 1889. (Anderson, Page 112)

Next occupying Breeden's office area in that Palace of the Governors Capitol Building was the State Land Office's Commissioner.

A Jesse Nusbaum's 1909 journal recorded Palace of the Governor's rooms; being published in 1978 by Rosemary Nusbaum, as: *The City Different and the Palace, The Palace of the Governors: It's Role in Santa Fe History*. It stated that "the block of five rooms west of the Historical Society's quarters were occupied by Robert P. Ervin, Commissioner of Lands." (Nusbaum, 86)

Robert P. Ervin served as State Land Commissioner from 1907 to 1918. And though the Palace of the Governors was renovated from Breeden's period to the Ervin one, the general office location stayed the same. And apparently Breeden's old records were stored along with those of the State Land Office.

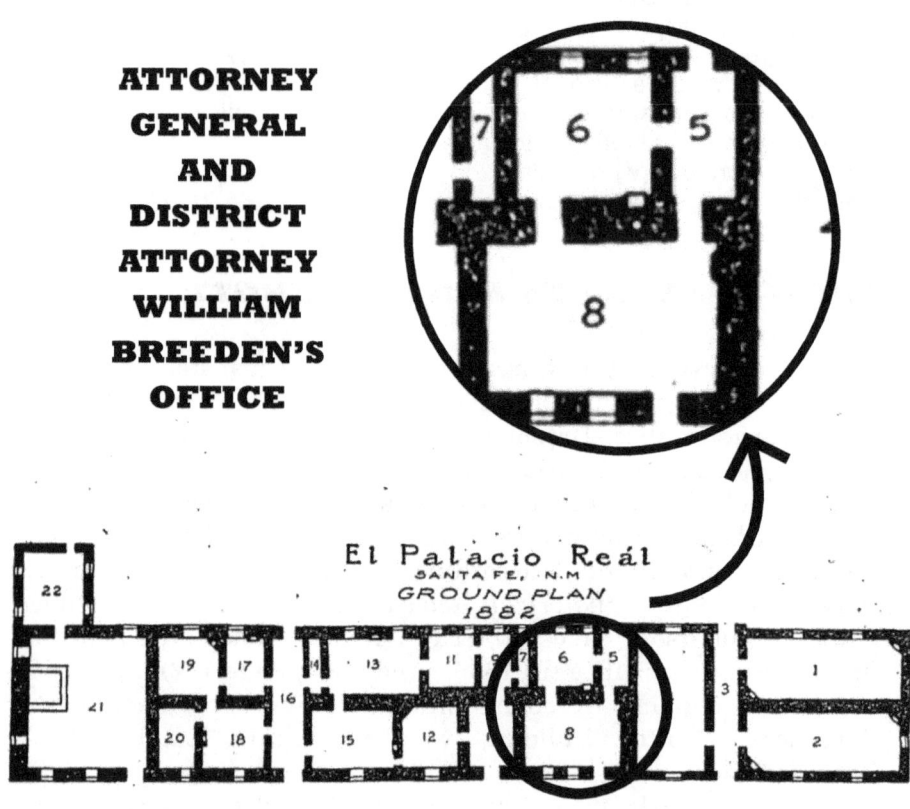

FIGURE: 1 Palace of the Governors in 1882, showing Attorney General William Breeden's office as rooms 5, 6, and 8. From Clinton P. Anderson's 1944 *New Mexico Historical Review*

The office's combined records joined the history of the Capitol Building's relocations. Harold Abbott had stated that in 1932 "he, with other employees, were going over some old records **in the basement of the state capitol**;" so those records presumably related to his Land Office job. But his finding of Breeden's **"San Miguel court records"** with them indicates that they had stayed together since their first Palace of the Governors storage.

But the Capitol Building in Harold Abbott's day was not the one after the Palace of the Governors. From 1850 to 1886 one was under construction, but ended up as the Territorial Courthouse.

In 1886, another building became the Capitol, replacing the Palace of the Governors, but burned down in six years, on May 12, 1892; though its archives were saved.

Then the Territorial Courthouse became the temporary Capitol Building until another was completed in 1900. That one was used for 66 years, until today's Capitol Building, "the Roundhouse," was dedicated in 1966. And the previous Capitol Building was renamed as the Bataan Memorial Building.

So by Harold Abbott's 1932 finding of the Coroner's Jury Report in the Capitol Building's basement (of the future Bataan Memorial Building), the old Palace of the Governors' records might have been moved multiple times. Additionally, Frank M. King had reported in his 1935 book, *Wranglin' the Past*, that Garrett's July 15, 1881 letter to Ritch, with the Coroner's Jury Report copy, was found in old files of New Mexico's Secretary of State. And the Secretary of State's offices were also in that Capitol Building, according to a 1932 article in the *Santa Fe New Mexican* titled "Call for Bids."

Demonstrated is that governmental personnel had done a good job in keeping San Miguel County legal records together. And the found Coroner's Jury Report proves their achievement! The only way around it for Billy the Kid hoaxers way lying.

PART II

A HISTORY OF HOAXING HISTORY

CHAPTER 1
OLD HOAXERS DOING NEW TRICKS

OVERVIEW

The people participating in the "Billy the Kid's Bad Bucks" hoax, were all old hands at faking Billy Bonney's history. W.C. Jameson, who featured it in his 2018 book, *Cold Case Billy the Kid: Investigating History's Mysteries*, played approving narrator for its creators: past Lincoln County Deputy Sheriff Steve Sederwall, and U.S. Marshals Service Historian David Turk. Both these men were active in the gigantic 21st century "Billy the Kid Case" forensic DNA hoax, in which Jameson had also participated. And an early promoter of the "Bad Bucks" hoax, had been glossy *True West* magazine's Editor-in-Chief, Bob Boze Bell, who had also backed the "Billy the Kid Case" hoax in his publication.

But the blame for encouraging this latest round of hijacking Billy the Kid's history goes to the originators of the "Billy the Kid Case" hoax: past New Mexico Governor Bill Richardson; his major political donor, Attorney Bill Robins III; and his appointed historian, University of New Mexico professor, Paul Hutton, who also wrote, co-produced, and narrated a Discovery Channel pseudo-documentary for it. Furthermore, Richardson corruptly shielded the Lincoln County Sheriff's Department's Sheriff and Deputies, including Steve Sederwall, after they illegally exhumed an Arizona Billy the Kid imposter named John Miller in 2005 for that hoax, inspiring their certainty of immunity to the law.

That, coupled with international publicity sparked by the "Billy the Kid Case" hoax, appears to have inspired the lesser players subsequently to devise their own hoaxes, following the formula of the original publicity-grabbing fabrications.

One can get perspective on the "Billy the Kid's Bad Bucks" chicanery from examples of past hoaxing by W.C. Jameson, Steve Sederwall, David Turk, and Bob Boze Bell.

THE "BRUSHY BILL" ROBERTS IMPOSTER HOAX

IMPERSONATING BILLY THE KID

There was a peculiar side-effect of Billy Bonney's posthumous fame: the emergence of addled, attention-seeking old men, in the second quarter of the 20th century, who claimed to be him. Since Billy was fatally shot in Fort Sumner on July 14, 1881 by Pat Garrett, that necessitated a second fabrication: accusing Garrett of covering up killing the wrong man.

The most successful Billy the Kid imposter hoax was invented by a mentally and vocationally disabled man named Oliver Pleasant Roberts, self-named "Brushy Bill" and "William Henry," who was born 20 years after Billy Bonney. Also a Social Security benefits fraudster, he had first aged himself by 10 years to qualify for benefits. His multiple delusions of being famous Old West people included Frank James, as well as Billy the Kid. In 1987, he was exposed by his full brother's daughter, Geneva Pittmon, who had his birth date in the family Bible, and whose family had helped to house this impaired man as an adult. "Brushy's" fabricated genealogy was further exposed by his relative, Roy L. Haws, a descendant of "Brushy's" father's first wife, in his 2015 book: *Brushy Bill: Proof His Claim to Be Billy the Kid Was a Hoax*.

"BRUSHY'S" FIRST AUTHORS

"Brushy's" success was owed to his promoting, and hoaxing authors: William V. Morrison and Charles Leland "C.L." Sonnichsen. Morrison, was an imposter himself, who claimed to be an attorney when being just a traveling salesman who did some probate research. Before "Brushy," he had also promoted another pretender named J. Frank Dalton, as being Jesse James. Sonnichsen was an English teacher with pretentions of being an historian, who got perverse satisfaction by faking that legitimate Billy the Kid historians were wrong, and he was right.

Step one of the hoax, was Morrison's publicity-grabbing attempt to get "Brushy" the gubernatorial pardon promised to Billy Bonney by Governor Lew Wallace. "Brushy" failed his interview with modern Governor Thomas Jewett Mabry, who correctly declared him a fraud on November 30, 1950.

In 1955, after "Brushy's" death five years earlier, Morrison and Sonnichsen published a book titled *Alias Billy the Kid*, in which they repeated the fakery, lied that no Coroner's Jury Report existed to prove the corpse was Billy Bonney's, and added conspiracy theories about historians and monied interests not wanting to admit that "Brushy" was Billy the Kid.

I exposed that hoax, with its error-filled sources for coaching "Brushy," who then parroted the errors; and its fakery that he was illiterate and could not study-up in my books: 2010's *Billy the Kid's Pretenders: Brushy Bill and John Miller*; and in my 2019's *Cracking the Imposter Hoax of Brushy Bill Roberts*; *The Cold Case Billy the Kid Megahoax: The Plot to Steal Billy the Kid's Identity and Defame Sheriff Pat Garrett as a Murderer*; and *The Coroner's Jury Report: The Inquest That Sealed the Fame of Billy Bonney and Pat Garrett*.

The "Brushy" hoax, of necessity, invented an alternative death scene, with Pat Garrett accidentally killing "Brushy's" (fictional) friend, Billy Barlow, because they looked the same; **and it was a dark and moonless night making the accident possible**. Importantly, that fiction by "Brushy," undid the rest of his hoax, since the night of July 14, 1881 had bright moonlight, making it almost as light as day, and proving he was not there.

Dishonest Sonnichsen, who used Morrison's tape recorded "Brushy" coaching interviews, caught this moon error, because they were also using, as sources, Pat Garrett's 1927 edition of *The Authentic Life of Billy the Kid* and Deputy John William Poe's 1933, which described the reality. So he secretly forged "Brushy's" words to put moonlight into the death scene.

"BRUSHY'S" NEXT AUTHORS

That dark-night-to-bright-moonlight tomfoolery would have gone unnoticed, except for "Brushy's" next authors, who were true-believers duped by Morrison and Sonnichsen: W.C. Jameson, a country music singer; and Frederick Bean, a novelist. They wrote 1998's "Brushy"-backing book, *The Return of the Outlaw Billy the Kid*.

Since Jameson and Bean knew no real history, having avoided the scholarly books written since "Brushy's day, they had the naïve and misguided strategy of convincing readers that "Brushy" was Billy the Kid by letting them see *his own words transcribed from his tapes* - which to them seemed so detailed that they proved he was Billy. So, not realizing that some delusional people, like "Brushy," confabulate by elaborate over-descriptions, and without realizing its damning significance, they repeated "Brushy's" real words about the dark night of July 14, 1881 being the reason for Garrett's accidental killing of Billy Barlow.

Then something new happened besides Frederick Bean's dying. In 2004, W.C. Jameson became part of the "Billy the Kid Case" hoax by being cast as a talking-head voucher for "Brushy Bill" in Professor Paul Hutton's, hoaxing TV program: "Investigating History: Billy the Kid." The hoaxers were apparently a bad influence, because Jameson became one himself in his determination to convince people that "Brushy" was Billy.

So he published 21st century books fixing-up "Brushy" by forging his transcript words, just as had Sonnichsen and Morrison, to better match Billy Bonney's history. Though Jameson did multiple dishonest alterations to trick readers, as will be seen below, one can track "Brushy's" fatal moon error to reveal Jameson as a hoaxer; since, by his 2012 *Billy the Kid: The Lost Interviews*, and his 2018 *Cold Case Billy the Kid: Investigating History's Mysteries*, his pseudo-"Brushy" was mouthing the bright moonlight in his alleged (but forged) transcripts.

Jameson was, thus, no innocent to hoaxing when he became the promoter of his fellow past "Billy the Kid Case" hoaxers' fakery of Billy Bonney as a counterfeiter in his *Cold Case Billy the Kid* book, which also promoted his "Brushy" hoaxing and "Billy the Kid Case" hoaxing.

THE "BILLY THE KID CASE" IMPOSTER HOAX ADDING FAKED DNA

THE HOAX AND ITS BLOCKADES

Named the "Billy the Kid Case" by its hoaxers, it began in 2003 as a self-serving publicity stunt by corrupt New Mexico Governor Bill Richardson, then contemplating a 2008 run for President; and as a likely pay-to-play for his major political donor, Attorney Bill Robins III, who was a "Brushy Bill" believer. Besides newspapers publishing his fake news, Richardson's hoax was disseminated by University of New Mexico Professor Paul Hutton, whom he made its official historian; and who created a History Channel pseudo-documentary on it as "Investigating History, Billy the Kid." Hutton also co-produced it with the Bill Kurtis Production Company, with intended future fake exhumation "documentaries" on Billy. And Hutton and Bill Kurtis added notorious Dr. Henry Lee for the fake forensics. Also hoax-backing was *True West* magazine's Editor-in-Chief, Bob Boze Bell.

The "Billy the Kid Case" was a forensic fraud with covert goal of crowning "Brushy" as Billy the Kid by faking DNA matchings, with the claim that Pat Garrett murdered an innocent victim on July 14, 1881. Garrett's "murder" was to be proved by matching DNA from Fort Sumner's Billy the Kid grave to his mother, buried in Silver City; with no match meaning a stranger was in Billy's grave; ergo, Garrett killed Billy Barlow. Then "Brushy's" DNA would be matched to the mother's DNA; with a match proving she was his mother; ergo, he was surviving Billy the Kid.

But reality was the blockade. So the hoaxers kept the truths secret, and lied. Here are the impassable hurdles:

1) **VICTIM IDENTIFIED AS BILLY THE KID**: The July 15, 1881 Coroner's Jury Report of William Bonney identified him as the corpse, and also quoted eye-witness, Peter Maxwell:

> "I being in my bed in my room, at about midnight on the 14th day of July, Pat F. Garrett came into my room and sat down. William Bonney came in and got close to my bed with a gun in his hand and asked me "who is it" and then Pat F. Garrett fired two shots at the said William Bonney and the said William Bonney fell near my fire place and I went out of the room and when I came in again about three or four minutes after the shots the said William Bonney was dead."

Furthermore, about 200 townspeople, who knew Billy, viewed his body at a night vigil in the carpenter's shop before he was buried on July 15, 1881.

2) **NO MURDER BY GARRETT OCCURRED:** The Coroner's Jury of July 15, 1881 cleared Garrett of murder because of his self-defense act; stating: "[T]he deed of said Garrett was justifiable homicide." And the innocent victim claim was merely part of Billy the Kid imposter hoaxing.

3) **IMMUNITY TO FUTURE MURDER PROSECUTION**: Garrett was also immune to murder prosecution by New Mexico Territory's Statute of Limitations on murder in the 1876 *Acts of*

the Legislative Assembly of the Territory of New Mexico, which appeared in 1882's *The General Laws of New Mexico* under "Limitation of Criminal Actions, Acts of the Legislative Assembly of the Territory of New Mexico, Twenty-Second Session, Chapter 13. Section 1." Permitted was only a 10 year window for prosecution after the act, making Garrett's prosecution impossible after 1891.

4) **USELESS DNA:** There was no valid DNA available for matching with anyone from the graves of Billy the Kid and his mother, Catherine Antrim, since they were just tourist markers. The mother's site was just overlapping plots, without verifiable remains. And Billy's grave's location in the Fort Sumner cemetery was uncertain. On this basis, the New Mexico Office of the Medical Investigator (OMI) refused the hoaxers' permits for their exhumations as forensically invalid. (Forensically valid DNA is called "reference DNA" and has 100% certainty of being from an individual in question. It is the only kind valid for identity matchings.) And the hoaxers' plan to match the mother's "DNA" to "Brushy Bill" was also meaningless, because mitochondrial DNA was to be used; and it was for proving a *mother's* offspring, and "Brushy" denied being her son.

5) **PRECEDENT CASE BLOCKING BILLY THE KID'S EXHUMATION:** The 1961-1962 Billy the Kid exhumation petition by a Lois Telfer was denied based on uncertain grave location, and the possibility of illegally disturbing other remains.

6) **FAKING DNA:** The hoaxers also claimed to have gotten the blood DNA of Billy the Kid from the carpenter's bench on which he had been laid out. This was pure fakery. In fact, they never established that blood was present. And the bench samples taken by complicit Dr. Henry Lee yielded no DNA anyway. [APPENDIX: 2] So they lied that they had gotten Billy the Kid's "bench-blood-DNA" to justify exhumations for "matchings" with it.

GOVERNOR RICHARDSON'S ANNOUNCEMENTS

The "Billy the Kid Case" hoax entered public awareness at a stratospheric level; though decades of "Brushy Bill's" ridicule necessitated covert action. On June 5, 2003, Governor Bill Richardson announced his scam to the world in a front page, fake news, *New York Times* article titled "122 Years Later, The Lawmen Are Still Chasing Billy the Kid."

Its reporter, Michael Janofsky, apparently doing zero research, mouthed that Richardson was just investigating about pardoning Billy the Kid. But Richardson's "experts" were just "Brushy"-believers and complicit lawmen. And faked DNA matchings were intended to make "Brushy" Billy the Kid so Richardson could pardon *him for his long and law-abiding life*!

But incompetent or complicit reporter, Janofsky wrote that Richardson was seeking **"evidence to a long-held alternative theory that Garrett shot someone other than the Kid and led a conspiracy to cover up his crime;"** and that a Jannay Valdez, owner of a "Billy the Kid ["Brushy Bill"] Museum" in Canton, Texas, said: **"I'm absolutely convinced that Garrett killed someone else and that Brushy Bill was the Kid."** Listed lawmen were Lincoln County Sheriff Tom Sullivan, and his Deputy, Steve Sederwall, filing the murder case against Pat Garrett; as well as a Texas law firm for the case [**Attorney Bill Robins III**]. Richardson's spokesman [Billy Sparks] stated "the state would assist by clearing any legal hurdles to gain access to the mother's body." As to the pardon, Janofsky wrote that Governor Lew Wallace had promised it. The article stated:

LINCOLN, NEW MEXICO – For more than 120 years, Pat Garrett has enjoyed legendary status in the American West, a lawman on a par with Wyatt Earp, Bat Masterson, even Matt Dillon. As sheriff here in Lincoln County in 1881, Garrett is credited with shooting to death the notorious outlaw known as Billy the Kid, a killing that made Garrett a hero. For years, a patch bearing his likeness has adorned uniforms worn by sheriff's deputies here.

But now, modern science is about to interrupt Garrett's fame in a way that some say could expose him as a liar who covered up a murder to save his own skin and reputation.

Officials in New Mexico and Texas are working out plans to exhume and conduct genetic tests on the bodies of a woman buried in New Mexico who was believed to be the Kid's mother and a Texas man known as Brushy Bill Roberts, who claimed to be the Kid and died in 1950 at the age of 90. If test results suggest that the two were related, it would add new evidence to a long-held alternative theory that Garrett shot someone other than the Kid and led a conspiracy to cover up his crime.

Such skepticism is hardly uncommon. Disputes over

major events in the Old West have engaged historians almost since they happened. The debate over Billy the Kid is one of the longest-running.

Beyond renewing interest in the Kid saga, the possibility that testing could enlarge Garrett's reputation or destroy it has even caught the fancy of Gov. Bill Richardson of New Mexico, who has offered state aid for the investigation and a possible pardon that an earlier New Mexico governor had once promised the Kid for a murder he committed.

"The problem is, there's so much fairy tale with this story that it's hard to nail down the facts," said Steve Sederwall, the mayor of Capitan, N.M., who is working with Lincoln County's current sheriff, Tom Sullivan, to resolve the matter. "All we want is the truth, whatever it is. If the guy Garrett killed was Billy the Kid, that makes him a hero. If it wasn't, Garrett was a murderer, and we have egg on our face, big time."

No matter what the genetic testing may show - and it might not show much of anything – it is hard to overstate the prominence of Garrett and the Kid in Western lore, especially here in southeastern New Mexico where their lives converged during and after the gun battles for financial control of the region that were known as the Lincoln County War. The Kid's notoriety grew after he and friends on one side of the conflict killed several men in an ambush, including Garrett's predecessor, Sheriff William Brady. For that, the Kid was hunted down, captured by Garrett, found guilty of murder and taken to the Lincoln jail, where he was placed in shackles to await hanging. He was only 21.

Today the tiny town of Lincoln, population 38, is a memorial to what happened next. More than a dozen buildings, including one that housed the jail, have been preserved as a state monument that attracts as many as 35,000 visitors a year.

Historians generally agree that the Kid, born Henry McCarty and known at times as William H. Bonney, escaped after it became apparent that Gov. Lew Wallace had reneged on a promise to pardon him in exchange for information about another killing in the county war. On April 28, 1881, the Kid managed to get his hands on a gun, kill the two deputies assigned to watch him and leave the area on horseback.

But then the stories diverge, providing fuel for two major theories of where, when, and how the Kid's life ended.

The version embraced here and supported by numerous books and Garrett relatives is that the Kid made his way to a friend's ranch in Fort Sumner, about 100 miles northeast of Lincoln. The ranch owner, Pete Maxwell, was also a friend of Garrett and somehow got word to Garrett that the Kid was in the area. After arriving, Garrett posted two deputies at the door.

As the Kid approached on the night of July 13 [sic], he spoke a few words in Spanish to the deputies, who did not recognize him. But Garrett, waiting inside, knew the voice. When the Kid walked in, Garrett turned and shot him in the heart.

William F. Garrett of Alamogordo, N.M., who is Garrett's grand-nephew, said years of research, including conversations with his cousin Jarvis, the last of Garrett's eight children, convinced him there is "no question about it" that his great-uncle killed Billy the Kid at Maxwell's. Jarvis died in 1991 at the age of 86.

"He was hired to get the Kid, and he got the Kid," Mr. Garrett said in an interview. "uncle Pat was a person of integrity who did his job. He was a law abider, not a law breaker."

But just as the story of Garrett as hero has flourished over the years, so have others, including the tale of Brushy Bill of Hico, Tex. His trip to New Mexico in 1950 to seek the pardon he said he was denied nearly 70 years before gave new life to an alternative possibility, that Garrett had not killed the Kid at all, but a drifter friend of the Kid's named Billy Barlow.

This story holds that Garrett and the Kid may have been in cahoots for some reason and that Garrett had stashed a gun at the outhouse at the jail that the Kid used to kill the deputies and escape.

Even if only part of that is true, it would strongly suggest that Garrett killed the wrong man.

Speaking with the same person as Garrett's great-nephew, Jannay P. Valdez, curator of the Billy the Kid Museum in Canton, Tex., said he had no doubt that Garrett killed someone else and that Brushy Bill was the Kid. "I'm absolutely convinced," he said here on Monday after meeting with Mr. Sederwall to discuss theories and how to begin the kind of genetic testing that has been used to ascertain lineage of other historical figures like Thomas Jefferson and Jessie James. "I'd bank everything I have on it."

As longtime friends, Mr. Sederwall and Sheriff Sullivan decided they wanted to settle the matter once and for all but could do so only through scientific analysis. To justify the effort that would require much of their time and, perhaps at some point, taxpayer money, they needed an official reason. So in April, they opened the first-ever investigation into the murders of the two deputies shot in the Kid's escape, James W. Bell and Robert Olinger, to examine what happened at the jail and Maxwell's ranch.

[AUTHOR'S NOTE: Janofsky is parroting the hoax, which claimed that Garrett helped the Kid escape.]

As Mr. Sederwall said, "There's no statute of limitations on murder."

[AUTHOR'S NOTE: This announces the real murder case; and hides New Mexico's statute of limitations.]

The goal now, he said, is to compare genetic evidence of Catherine Antrim, believed to be the Kid's mother, who died of tuberculosis in 1874 and is buried in Silver City, N.M., and of Brushy Bill, who lived out his life in Texas. A Dallas firm [sic Houston] has agreed to help, and a spokesman for governor Richardson said the state would assist by clearing legal hurdles to gain access to the mother's body.

The Kid was buried at Fort Sumner, N.M., although the whereabouts of the grave are uncertain; he has no known living relatives. Mr. Valdez said he had already secured permission to exhume the body of Brushy Bill, who is buried 20 miles from Hico in Hamilton, Texas.

But solving the mystery might not be so simple. For one thing, Mr. Valdez said he was certain that the woman buried in Silver City was but "a half aunt." And even if tests disqualify Brushy Bill as Billy the Kid, other "Kids" have emerged over the years, including a man named John Miller, who died in 1937 and is buried in Prescott, Ariz. Mr. Sederwall said that efforts would be made to exhume his body as well.

The investigators conceded that much is riding on their quest. Sheriff Sullivan, a tall, strapping man who carries a turquoise-handled .357 magnum on his right hip, said he, like so many others in the West, revered Garrett for gunning down the Kid. The uniform patch with Garrett's likeness was his design. Now, the legend is threatened.

"**I just want to get to the bottom of it," said Sheriff Sullivan**, who is retiring next year. "My integrity's at stake. So's my department's. So's what we believe in and even New Mexico history. If Garrett shot someone other than the Kid, that makes him a murderer and he covered it up. He wouldn't be such a role model, then, and we'd have to take the patches off the uniforms."

On June 10, 2003, Richardson held a press conference, with a press release repeating his Janofsky article's fakery. Present were his key hoaxers: Lincoln County's Sheriff Tom Sullivan and Deputy Steve Sederwall; De Baca County's Sheriff Gary Graves; and University of New Mexico professor Paul Hutton, appointed by Richardson as the hoax's "historical advisor." Richardson revealed that Lincoln County Sheriff's Department murder case against Pat Garrett had been flied as No. 2003-274. The press release promised use of forensic DNA to prove that the Kid deserved a pardon. It stated:

State of New Mexico
Office of the Governor

Bill Richardson
Governor
For immediate release
6/10/03

Contact: Billy Sparks
telephone number

GOVERNOR BILL RICHARDSON ANNOUNCES STATE SUPPORT OF BILLY THE KID INVESTIGATION

SANTA FE – Governor Bill Richardson today outlined how the state of New Mexico will support the investigation efforts to investigate the life and death of Billy the Kid.

Governor Richardson delivered the following remarks during a news conference today in the State Capitol:

This is an important day in the history of New Mexico and the American West. I am announcing my support and the support of the state of New Mexico for the investigation into the life and death of Henry McCarty, also known as William Bonney. To millions around the world, he was called Billy the Kid. How he captured the world's imagination is well worth exploring. His life, though ended at the age of 21, is part of what makes New Mexico and an American West, unique.

My goal is to shed new light on old history.

I am pleased to be joined here by Lincoln County Sheriff Tom Sullivan, Capitan Mayor Steve Sederwall, De Baca County Sheriff Gary Grays [sic - Graves]. Grant County Attorney Sherry Tippett, University of New Mexico History Professor, Doctor Paul Hutton and State Police Major Tom Branch.

Let me tell you how this all came about.

Last month I was contacted by Lincoln County Sheriff, Tom Sullivan and Capitan Mayor, Steve Sederwall, to support reopening the case. Case number 2003-274 seeks to answer key questions that have lingered for over 120 years surrounding the life and the death of Billy the Kid.

This episode in the history of New Mexico and the history of the old west is both fact and legend and continues to stir the imagination and interest of people all over the world.

By utilizing modern forensic, DNA and crime scene techniques, the goal of the investigation is to get to the truth. In the process, the reputation of Pat Garrett, still a hero in Lincoln County law enforcement, hangs in the balance. **The question is did Sheriff Garrett kill Billy the Kid at Fort Sumner, New Mexico on July 14. 1881?**

This investigation will also seek to shed new light on the events surrounding the escape of Billy the Kid from the Lincoln County Jail on April 28, 1881. The shooting of Deputies J.W. Bell and Bob Olinger by Billy the Kid has never been officially investigated. Where did Billy get his gun and what really happened?

I have contacted the national Labs, Los Alamos and Sandia and have been assured that they will volunteer their support in this effort. Los Alamos Lab can assist us by providing ground penetrating radar, DNA expertise and technical forensic assistance. Sandia Labs will allow their experts to volunteer their time to help us uncover the facts.

The State Police will help supervise the investigation and crime scene analysis of the evidence uncovered in the investigation.

I have also asked University of New Mexico Professor of History and Executive Director of the Western History Association, Doctor Paul Hutton, to serve as our historical advisor. Dr. Hutton has served as President of the Western Writers of America and has won several national honors for his works on western history.

I intend to hold hearings at Fort Sumner, Lincoln, Silver City and Mesilla. I will appoint a defense counsel and a prosecutor to present the evidence. **[Never done.]**

As Governor, I will examine the events surrounding the alleged offer of a pardon to Billy the Kid by former New Mexico Governor Lew Wallace. I will evaluate the evidence uncovered and make a decision.

There is no question that this story deserves our attention and that the history of New Mexico and the American West is important to all of us. If we can get to the truth we will. I have total confidence in the team you see here today to conduct a professional, honest and exhaustive investigation of the facts and report back to me and to the rest of the world what really happened here in New Mexico.

The benefits to our state and to the history of the West far outweigh any cost we may incur. I expect the actual cost to be nominal. Just since this investigation was announced, it has sparked news articles about New Mexico and Lincoln County from New York to London to India. Getting to the truth is our goal. But, if this increases interest and tourism in our state, I couldn't be happier.

I understand that Movie Producer Ron Howard has donated the cabin used in shooting his movie "The Missing", being shot in Santa Fe, to Silver City. The cabin is a replica of a Billy the Kid era home. The cabin will be delivered to Silver City this week.

The potential benefit from this investigation to all of New Mexico is already being felt and is well worth the effort.   #30#

Proved was only Richardson's list of his morally vulnerable bottomfeeders, poised for profit beyond their wildest dreams. Not listed were his pocket judges, Henry Quintero and Ted Hartley, just appointed by him for the Grant County and De Baca County District Courts respectively, to rubber-stamp the fake exhumation petitions of lawmen Sullivan, Sederwall, and Graves.

THE "BILLY THE KID CASE" PROGRESSION

The genius of the "Billy the Kid Case" hoax was to legitimize exhumations by claiming they were for *a real, filed, "cold case" murder investigation against Garrett* for murdering his non-Billy victim. It was filed by the hoaxer lawmen as Sheriffs Department murder Case 2003-274 in Lincoln County, and as Case No. 03-06-136-01 in De Baca County. But I blocked them in District Courts.

So the hoaxers rewrote their hoax. They made-up that Billy *was shot* in Fort Sumner in an escape plot with Garrett, and played dead on a carpenter's bench for the vigil that night. They claimed to have that bench with "blood-DNA-of-Billy-the-Kid" for matchings. Deputy Steve Sederwall said, on October 6, 2005, reporter, Julie Carter, in her *RuidosoNews.com's* "Follow the Blood: In the Billy the Kid Case, Miller Exhumed," that bench "blood" proved Billy was alive, because "dead men don't bleed."

But that was not true. Dead men do bleed through exit wounds by gravity and residual blood pressure. And someone shot in the chest cannot "play dead," because they hyperventilate. Key, however, was they had no "blood." Complicit Dr. Henry Lee's "blood" testing was also for rust - obvious on a carpenter's bench. And his lab results later showed no testing for blood and no DNA. **[APPENDIX: 2]** Even if there had been blood, they had no "reference DNA" to prove it as Billy's - like a random fingerprint, with none available of the actual person for establishing identity.

So the hoaxers lied about having Billy's bench DNA to dig up illegally an Arizona pretender named John Miller and a random man buried beside him. Only corrupt intervention by Governors Richardson and Janet Napolitano saved them from felonies.

I subsequently did open records litigation against the hoaxing lawmen, with them stonewalling for seven years to hide the proofs of their forensic hoax and illegal exhumations; while the records were available on the day I first requested them.

Adding more fakery, during the litigation, Steve Sederwall forged Dr. Henry Lee reports to trick the judge in an attempt to hide his own role as a Deputy Sheriff in the case, as well as to hide Dr. Lee's more equivocal conclusions about the findings. Though I won the case, the corrupt higher courts then removed all the lawmen's penalties (with the Chief Justice of the state Supreme Court being a major Richardson political donor and married to Richardson's own attorney and used for the hoax).

I exposed this hoax in my 2014 book, *Cracking the Billy the Kid Case Hoax: The Plot to Exhume Billy the Kid, Convict Sheriff Pat Garrett of Murder, and Become President of the United States*; and my 2019 book, *The Cold Case Billy the Kid Megahoax: The Plot to Steal Billy the Kid's Identity and Defame Sheriff Pat Garrett as a Murderer*. The fact is, without my efforts, the history would have been destroyed beyond retrieval by these hoaxers.

Importantly, the result was that the untouched, bottom level hoaxers were inspired by their brush with fame; and their immunity to consequences of lying, forging, and grave-robbing. So they tried to return to the limelight with repeats of the "Billy the Kid Case" hoax claims and by fabricating new hoaxes to ride on Billy the Kid's coattails. That was how profiteering Steve Sederwall, David Turk, Gary Graves, and Dr. Henry Lee, joined forces with W.C. Jameson to try again to hijack Billy the Kid history in his 2018 book: *Cold Case Billy the Kid*.

THE "COLD CASE BILLY THE KID" MEGAHOAX

In 2018, "Brushy"-believer and author, W.C. Jameson, partnered with past "Billy the Kid Case" hoaxers, to combine the "Brushy Bill" and "Billy the Kid Case" hoaxes in his book: *Cold Case Billy the Kid: Investigating History's Mysteries*. Hoping to show that history was not as written, he indiscriminately narrated fakery, including the "Billy the Kid's Bad Bucks" hoax.

THE FOUNDATION OF FAKERY

The important perspective is that the "Billy the Kid's Bad Bucks" hoax was built on a foundation of multiple profiteering hoaxes for "Brushy Bill," the "Billy the Kid Case," and the "Cold Case Billy the Kid." The common denominator was cheats pretending to be historians by feeding the public non-historical claims as attention-grabbing discoveries.

CHAPTER 2
W.C. JAMESON'S HOAXING OF "BRUSHY BILL'S" MOON ERROR

A TRUE-BELIEVER TURNED HOAXER

William Carl "W.C." Jameson, a country music singer, was taken-in by C.L. Sonnichsen's and William V. Morrison's the "Brushy Bill" hoax in their 1955 *Alias Billy the Kid*. He partnered with novelist, Frederick Bean, to publish an updated version of the claims in a 1998 book titled *The Return of the Outlaw Billy the Kid*. It is a milestone in Jameson's evolution from dupe to hoaxer, since, at that early date, he and Bean were so convinced of "Brushy's" words as gospel, that they chose to reproduce them, so he could convince readers of his special knowledge, as proof that he was Billy the Kid. Ignorant of actual history, Jameson and Bean, thus, presented "Brushy's" gaffes, which had been edited out by actively hoaxing author, C.L. Sonnichsen, for his *Alias Billy the Kid* book with co-author William Morrison. So *The Return of the Outlaw Billy the Kid* is great for hoaxbusting.

But, apparently, after his 2004 participation in the "Brushy"-backing "Billy the Kid Case" hoax as a talking head in hoaxing Professor Paul Hutton's History Channel Documentary "Investigating History: Billy the Kid," with its taste of media fame, and his 2006 chance meeting with Deputy Steve Sederwall, Jameson changed. He made an alliance with the now "out-of-work" "Billy the Kid Case" hoaxers, and became one himself, with particular reliance on glib opportunist Sederwall; whom he added to his pantheon of "Brushy," Morrison, and Sonnichsen. And Jameson proceeded to create a fixed-up pseudo-"Brushy," to sell to readers in an of outpouring books. The "Billy the Kid's Bad Bucks" counterfeiting hoax would be a culmination.

ALIAS BILLY THE KID'S DEATH SCENE'S BRIGHT MOON

One can track W.C. Jameson's descent into hoaxing by using "Brushy's" fatal dark night moon error.

Billy Bonney's real Fort Sumner death scene of July 14, 1881 had three well known elements: *bright moonlight*; Billy walking to the Maxwell house to cut himself a steak from the side of beef hanging on the north porch; and his entering Peter Maxwell's bedroom where hiding Pat Garrett fatally shot him in ambush.

For the original "Brushy Bill" hoax in C.L. Sonnichsen's and William V. Morrison's 1955 *Alias Billy the* Kid, the death scene chapter title is "Death **by Moonlight**."

For his survival, "Brushy" made-up an "innocent victim" mistaken for himself (as Billy the Kid) by Pat Garrett. That victim was his claimed partner, Billy Barlow. The key, as "Brushy" conceptualized his fakery, was Barlow "mistaken for himself." He had told Governor Mabry that they were like two peas in a pod.

"Brushy's" killing scene occurs after a Jesus Silva (the dropped name of Peter Maxwell's foreman) was cooking a meal for him and Billy Barlow; and Barlow wanted "fresh beef." Sensing a "trap," "Brushy" lets Barlow go to the Maxwell house, where Barlow is shot on the back porch - not inside the bedroom! (Page 49)

But the litmus test for active hoaxing was the moon. "Brushy" is quoted by Sonnichsen, allegedly from his taped interview with Morrison, about the shooting scene: "I ran through the gate into Maxwell's back yard **in the bright moonlight**." (Page 49) The moonlight was correct, and came from the book's source footnote: Garrett's Deputy, John W. Poe's, 1933 *The Death of Billy the Kid*, which stated: **"[T]he moon was shining very brightly**." (Poe, Page 28) That was also in their source book, Walter Noble Burns's 1926 *The Saga of Billy the Kid*: **"The Kid's figure stood out clearly in the moonlight."** (Burns, Page 281) It would take 43 years until Jameson's and Bean's *The Return of the Outlaw Billy the Kid* to recognize how fatal to "Brushy's" hoax, and to his hoaxing accomplices, that night's moonlight had been.

And Jameson's adulation of Sonnichsen added another clue to the hoaxing. He had stayed in contact with that man from 1962, when he had been in his University of Texas in El Paso English class, till the man's 1991 death. Jameson recounted in his 2012 "Brushy"-backing book, *Billy the Kid: The Lost Interviews*, that

Sonnichsen told him that he had authored *Alias Billy the Kid* using Morrison's notes and taped interviews of "Brushy." (*Billy the Kid: The Lost Interviews*, Pages 28-29) **And, without disclosure, he had altered them!** As Jameson wrote: "It became clear that Sonnichsen used a relatively small amount of the information ... [and he] heavily edited Roberts' grammar, even adding and deleting words ... In other places, Sonnichsen merely summarized." (*Billy the Kid: The Lost Interviews*, Pages 42) Jameson, thus, guilelessly revealed willful fixing-up of "Brushy" to match Billy Bonney. And, as will be seen, "Brushy's" moon error was one of Sonnichsen's fix-ups.

THE RETURN OF THE OUTLAW BILLY THE KID'S DEATH SCENE'S DARK MOON

In 1998, 43 years after C.L. Sonnichsen's and William V. Morrison's *Alias Billy the Kid*, W.C. Jameson and, now deceased Frederic Bean published their *The Return of the Outlaw Billy the Kid*, dedicated to Sonnichsen and Morrison. As Jameson, then just a dupe, said in their book: "This amazing story captivated me such that for the next twenty-eight years I investigated it at every opportunity." (Page vii) Both stated: "We believe the case for William Henry Roberts ["Brushy's" made-up name] as Billy the Kid is stronger than the case against it." (Page 207) Both wrote: "Roberts' recollections of people, places, and events were too 'detailed and precise' for a semiliterate man to have come from sources other than from personal experience." (Page 165) This revealed their quirk. Since the hoax's 1950's origin, scholarly books making clear "Brushy's" fakery had been published; but their faith was immune to facts. "Brushy" was gospel.

To them, missing was just more "proof." Part of that starry-eyed strategy was letting "Brushy" speak for himself through Morrison's interview tapes. (Page vii) Not till Jameson's 2012 book, *Billy the Kid: The Lost Interviews,* was it explained that Frederick Bean had gotten them in 1989 from "Brushy's" last wife's family, made a transcript, then returned them.

The goal was to let "Brushy" present himself. Nevertheless, Sonnichsen's admitted editing was corrupting, inspiring Jameson's and Bean's fix-ups. They added historical names - like "Regulators" - unknown to "Brushy."

Nevertheless, *The Return of the Outlaw Billy the Kid* froze "Brushy" in amber of their adoration for all to see. And what was revealed, by comparing their text to *Alias Billy the Kid's*, were the sly changes in that book and theirs. And, as Jameson descended to forgery of "Brushy's" words in later books, he hid this naive book.

ACCIDENTALLY LETTING "BRUSHY" REVEAL HIS DEATH SCENE MOON ERROR

To Jameson and Bean, the death scene was the holy grail. So their faith in "Brushy's" words, combined with their historical ignorance, give a view of "Brushy" in the raw. So Jameson and Bean opened a can of worms for "Brushy!"

The chapter "William Henry Roberts' Story Part I: 1859-1881," merely lifted *Alias Billy the Kid's* death scene summary, and mindlessly repeated: "Billy, **easily seen in the moonlit yard**, immediately drew return fire from the lawmen." (Page 73)

Hoaxbusting treasure is in the chapter "Quien es? A Reexamination of the Shooting in Fort Sumner" (Pages 101-133) where "Brushy" finally speaks. **And he says July 14, 1881's night was dark!** In truth, the near-full moon, had hovered at the horizon, making night as light as day!

But "Brushy's" dark night was **not in *Alias Billy the Kid***. Hoaxing Sonnichsen, as supposedly quoting him for the death scene," in the chapter he slyly titled "Death **By Moonlight**," wrote: "I ran through the gate into Maxwell's back yard **in the bright moonlight**." (*Alias Billy the Kid,* Page 49) This explains Jameson's and Bean's naive copying of *Alias Billy the Kid's* "Brushy" being "**easily seen in the moonlit yard**." (Page 73)

But ignorant of the moon's significance, they left it untampered when quoting "Brushy's" own words from the tapes' transcript: "[After hearing the shot from Pete Maxwell's place] I pulled one of my .44's and ran through the door, **trying to see in the dark**. Two more shots came from the shadow beside the Maxwell house. **I couldn't find a target. It was too dark to see**." (Page 112) "Brushy stuck to darkness for his faked scene: "emptying my six-shooter at the shadow where I saw the muzzleflash." (Page 113)

Key is that "Brushy" used the darkness for his fabrication *to explain the accidental killing of Barlow:* "Garrett knew by now that he'd **killed the wrong man in the dark**." (Page 117)

Also, "Brushy" had Celsa Gutierrez say: "They took the body of your friend inside the house and they say it is yours ...**Your partner looks very much like** *you in the dark.*" (Page-117)

CRACKING THE "BRUSHY BILL" IMPOSTER HOAX: Thus, "Brushy's" dark night moon error, in one fell swoop, proved not only that he was not present in Fort Sumner on the night of July 14, 1881; but that Sonnichsen and Morrison had willfully, dishonestly, and despicably fixed-up and concealed his fatal error to perpetrate their hoax of him as being Billy the Kid. And by Jameson's later books, his newly fixed-up bright moonlight would prove his fall into active hoaxing himself.

RETURN OF THE DARK MOON IN *BILLY THE KID: BEYOND THE GRAVE*

MAKING A BETTER "BRUSHY"

In his 2018 book, *Cold Case Billy the Kid*, W.C. Jameson stated that he first met Steve Sederwall in 2006 at a book signing for his 2005 *Billy the Kid: Beyond the Grave*. Strangely, though Jameson had participated in the "Billy the Kid Case" hoax, he omitted that entire case, stating only that he knew Sederwall "by reputation," from newspapers and TV, where "his aggressive investigations into a variety of Billy the Kid-related events ... were based on solid police work, and they differed, sometimes dramatically, from established history." Jameson added that Sederwall "irritated" "self-anointed experts," but ignored them. (*Cold Case*, Page v) So he was ripe for duping by Sederwall.

But *Billy the Kid: Beyond the Grave* was published before his Sederwall meeting. Nevertheless, the hoaxers' chicanery had influenced him. By this book, he was less the innocent who had co-authored 1998's *The Return of the Outlaw Billy the Kid*. Hoaxing, plus the "Billy the Kid Case's" "Brushy" push, had emboldened him to do clandestine fix-ups of "Brushy" for a new millennium of dupes. The means became justified by that end. So he hid his *The Return of the Outlaw Billy the Kid*, with its accidental exposures, and now proceeded to contradict his old self.

But in 2005, Jameson, as lone author, and acknowledging none of the "Billy the Kid Case" hoaxers, was relatively naïve, just before plunging into heavy hoaxing in his future *Billy the Kid: The Lost Interviews, Pat Garrett: The Man Behind the Badge,* and *Cold Case Billy the Kid.* That made his *Billy the Kid: Beyond the Grave* great for hoaxbusting, because it has his last accidental exposure of "Brushy's" fatal dark night moon error. Nevertheless, Jameson's secret fix-ups of "Brushy's" other glaring errors, and his additions of historical information unknown to "Brushy," but presented as his words, show his increasing dishonesty.

THE HOAXBUSTING MOON OF JULY 14, 1881

In *Billy the Kid: Beyond the Grave,* for Jameson, as for "Brushy" himself, the dark night explained Pat Garrett's mistaking Billy Barlow for "Brushy" **because it was so dark**.

Thus, for this book, still relying on "Brushy's" original transcript, Jameson wrote: "**William Henry Roberts recalled that the night was dark but there was enough moonlight to make shadows**." (Page 57) And after "Brushy was shot, Jameson quoted from "Brushy's" transcript: "**I lost my footing and fell on my face in the darkness**." (Page 61) And from the transcript came "Brushy" stating: "**Garrett knew by now that he killed the wrong man in the dark.**" (Page 64)

This dark night matched Jameson's *The Return of the Outlaw Billy the Kid,* which had "Brushy" say: "**[After hearing the shot from Pete Maxwell's place] I pulled one of my .44's and ran through the door, trying to see in the dark. Two more shots came from the shadow beside the Maxwell house. I couldn't find a target. It was too dark to see.**" (*The Return of the Outlaw Billy the Kid,* Page 112) That dark night was repeated in that book in "Brushy's" quote explaining Billy Barlow's killing: "**Garrett knew by now that he'd killed the wrong man in the dark.**" (*The Return of the Outlaw Billy the Kid,* Page 117)

But Jameson, in his upcoming alliance with "Billy the Kid Case" hoaxers for his next "Brushy"-backing books, would never again reveal that dark night moon error.

But it was too late. **Every time Jameson lied that "Brushy" claimed that night's bright moonlight," it would brand him as a hoaxer and a forger of "Brushy's" transcribed words.**

RETURN OF THE BRIGHT MOON IN *BILLY THE KID: THE LOST INTERVIEWS*

FAKING "BRUSHY'S" WORDS

In 2012's *Billy the Kid: The Lost Interviews*, W.C. Jameson created a fictionalized, grammatically-sophisticated, politically correct, pseudo-"Brushy," glossed with newly accurate historical spellings; all intended to fake a match with real Billy. And, since hoaxer, Steve Sederwall's, input was implied by Jameson, it is possible that this hoaxing is also attributable to him.

Billy the Kid: The Lost Interviews is intentionally misleading, as if based on newly found, convincing, "lost interviews" of Brushy Bill." In fact, they were the same taped 1949-1950 William V. Morrison interviews that C.L. Sonnichsen had used to write *Alias Billy the Kid*; and that Frederick Bean had located in 1989, and were quoted from his transcript of them in his and Jameson's 1998 book, *The Return of the Outlaw Billy the Kid*. The change was in Jameson. He was now in league with hoaxers. And I exposed his hoaxing in this book in my 2019 books: *Cracking the Billy the Kid Imposter Hoax of Brushy Bill* Roberts; and *The Cold Case Billy the Kid Megahoax: The Plot to Steal Billy the Kid's Identity and Defame Sheriff Pat Garrett as a Murderer*.

Tellingly, Jameson now enthused in his "Preface" about Steve Sederwall as a "retired federal investigator ... [who] got "information and facts heretofore unknown." But the "Billy the Kid Case" is concealed, and Sederwall's input is not described.

On the surface, the book appears to repeat *The Return of the Outlaw Billy the Kid's* formula of letting "Brushy" speak for himself. Except, that book is now hidden, and the quotes are by a pseudo-"Brushy," mouthing new facts and conspiracy theories in a forged transcript of his alleged words! And the little bibliography reveals modern sources likely used for the upgrades.

Fortunately, however, Jameson's true-believer bedazzlement and historical ignorance leave most of "Brushy's" error-filled fables untouched; while his fix-ups stand out as wrong or obviously discovered after "Brushy's" day.

Key is that **"Brushy's" death scene has a bright moon**. As reprehensible, Jameson's pseudo-"Brushy" even uses "Billy the Kid Case" hoax's claims, made over fifty years after his death!

THE DEATH SCENE GETS A BRIGHT MOON

Active hoaxing and Jameson's forging of "Brushy's" transcript yield a pseudo-"Brushy" mouthing the "bright moonlight," about which real "Brushy" had been fatally ignorant.

These are examples:

1) "Brushy" says about the shooting: "I pulled one of my .44's and ran through the door, trying to see in the dark. I ran through the gate into Maxwell's back yard **into the bright moonlight**. Two more shots came from a shadow beside the Maxwell house. I started shooting at the shadows along the house." (Page 124)

JAMESON EXPOSED AS A HOAXER BY HIS FAKED TRANSCRIPT: In *Alias Billy the Kid*, Morrison and Sonnichsen had fixed-up "Brushy's" dark night with chapter title "Death <u>by Moonlight</u>" (*Alias Billy the Kid*, Page 48), and a faked quote: "I ran through the gate into Maxwell's back yard **in the bright moonlight**." (*Alias Billy the Kid*, Page 49)

In Jameson's and Bean's 1998, *Return of the Outlaw Billy the Kid*, as naïve true-believers, they honestly quoted "Brushy" from his transcript: "[After hearing the shot from Pete Maxwell's place] I pulled one of my .44's and ran through the door, <u>trying to see in the dark</u>. Two more shots came from the shadow beside the Maxwell house. I couldn't find a target. <u>It was too dark to see</u>." (*Return of the Outlaw*, Page 112) And they accepted his dark night quote as his explanation for the Barlow's killing: "Garrett knew by now that he'd <u>killed the wrong man in the dark</u>." (*Return of the Outlaw*, Page 117) Thus, they accidentally proved the dishonest Morrison-Sonnichsen fix-up.

But debased Jameson now hid "Brushy's" error. To trick readers, as Morrison-Sonnichsen had intended, he deleted "Brushy's" disastrous quote from his *The Return of the Outlaw Billy the Kid*: "I pulled one of my .44's and ran through the door, <u>trying to see in the dark</u>. Two more shots came from the shadow beside the Maxwell house. I couldn't find a target. <u>It was too dark to see</u>." (*Return of the Outlaw*, Page 112) For *Billy the Kid: The Lost Interviews*, Jameson wrote: "I pulled one of my .44's and ran through the door, trying to see in the dark. I ran through the gate into Maxwell's back yard into the bright moonlight" – adding "bright moonlight," which "Brushy" never said. This is despicable and willful forgery to hide that "Brushy" could not have been in Fort Sumner on the night of July 14, 1881.

Nevertheless, hoaxing Jameson still seemed unaware of just how dangerous to the hoax the error was, since he was careless in "cleaning up" all "Brushy's quotes. Later in the text, he fabricated "Brushy" ruminating to Morrison about the Billy Barlow killing, and has "Brushy" repeat the darkness: "Barlow looked a little like me but he was half-Mex. I could imagine Garrett couldn't tell us apart in the real dark, except Barlow had a beard." (Page 133)

THE "BILLY THE KID CASE" HOAX GETS PLUGGED

1) "Brushy" has a long passage before the Fort Sumner shooting saying he wanted to "have a talk with Mr. Pat Garrett" to set things "straight between us" because "[w]e used to be friends before the Lincoln County War." (Page 121)

HOAXING THE TRANSCRIPT: This was not in *Alias Billy the Kid.* But it fabricates a friendship between "Brushy" and Pat Garrett like in the "Billy the Kid Case" hoax. "Brushy's" version merely had an accidental killing of his look-alike, Billy Barlow, in the dark, when Garrett was trying to kill *him.*

2) "Brushy" says: "**It crossed my mind that Garrett might be trying to help me. We'd been friends once**, back when he first came to this country." (Page 132) "Brushy's" earlier confabulation (lifted from a prompt source) for showing special knowledge that Garrett had been a buffalo hunter who killed a partner over hides is then inserted here as proof of "friendship." "Brushy" continues that, as Lincoln County Sheriff, Garrett had to pursue him, but wonders if "he saw his chance to let me get away clean and make a fresh start for myself" by pretending Barlow was Billy the Kid. (Pages 132-133)

EXPOSING JAMESON AS A COMPLICIT "BILLY THE KID CASE" HOAXER BY HIS FAKED TRANSCRIPT: This is not in *Alias Billy the Kid*, except for the erroneous description of buffalo hunter Garrett's killing, which was copied from "Brushy's" earlier confabulation based on a prompt source and in a different context. (*Alias Billy the Kid*, Page 36)

This shockingly appears to be Jameson's making-up quotes to make "Brushy" fit the "Billy the Kid Case" hoax - which relied on a fake Garrett friendship motive for the innocent victim killing to let Billy go free. It should be noted that this book first came out in 2012, and Jameson was a participant in the latter hoax since 2004; and hoaxer, Steve Sederwall, was also participating with Jameson for this book. And Jameson's unwieldy fusing of that hoax, and its hoaxers, to his "Brushy" hoaxing culminated six years later in his *Cold Case Billy the Kid*.

Used here, however, it contradicts real "Brushy's" own description of Garrett's effort to kill him as Billy the Kid. As Jameson's own "Brushy" text quoted: "**My partner walked right into the trap, and the trap had likely been set for me ... I knew I had to get away from Maxwell's before they killed me.**" (Pages 124-125) And Jameson himself had first stuck to the theme of Garrett's intent to kill "Brushy" as Billy, by the quote: "**Barlow looked a little like me but he was half-Mex. I could imagine Garrett couldn't tell us apart in the real dark.**" (Page 133) That meant Garrett intended to kill the Kid in the world according to "Brushy." Jameson could not keep his hoaxing straight.

3) "Brushy" is quoted that Garrett could keep the corpse identity secret because the only people who knew it was not him were Celsa, Jesus Silva, the Mexican woman who took him in, and a Frank Loboto; and they would keep a secret.

FAKING THE TRANSCRIPT: This is not in *Alias Billy the Kid*. It appears to be Jameson's fiction to have pseudo-"Brushy" mouth conspiracy theories of Sonnichsen and himself. Of course, this maintains the "Brushy" hoax's key lies of hiding the night vigil over Billy's body and Billy's Coroner's Jury Report.

4) "Brushy" states a flashback of a **Frank "Lovoto"** having checked Fort Sumner and reporting to him that Barlow's body had been taken to the carpenter's shop wrapped in a sheet to hide its identity; Poe could not recognize him, so could not identify the body; Garrett sealed the house to prevent viewing of the body; and a "coroner's jury was appointed to sign the death certificate so Garrett could file for the reward." "Brushy" adds that there were two coroner's jury reports, with the first lost and Garrett making people sign a second with different signers; that Milnor Rudulph was not the real president, and never viewed the body. And he says Garrett succeeded by burying Barlow in the Billy the Kid grave, and by taking the fake coroner's jury report to Santa Fe to get his reward. (Pages 134-135)

EXPOSING JAMESON AS AN ACTIVE HOAXER AND COMPLICIT WITH THE "BILLY THE KID CASE" HOAX BY HIS FAKED TRANSCRIPT: This fabricated flashback quote, is not in *Alias Billy the Kid*. It is an awkward fix-up to match the "Brushy" hoax to the "Billy the Kid Case" hoax's faking DNA from the carpenter's bench by putting Barlow's body on it, hiding the body with a sheet to counter the actual townspeople's viewing, and announcing a fake coroner's jury shielding Garrett. For the "Brushy" hoax, it puts into pseudo-"Brushy's" mouth Sonnichsen's fake conspiracy theory of two coroner's jury reports.

This is now brazenly out-of-control hoaxing and forging. And it ridiculously requires sheepherder, Frank Lobato, to know insiders' information about a cover-up of the innocent victim. And, if real Loboto had found it out, it would prove general gossip among townspeople, and no postulated conspiracy of them to keep the secret!

PARTNERSHIP IN HOAXER HEAVEN

Jameson had crossed-over to no-holds-barred flimflam. He ended *Billy the Kid: The Lost Interviews* by stating: "Steve Sederwall's ongoing research and investigative work applied to Billy the Kid and the Lincoln County war continues to yield new and exciting results." ("Acknowledgments") Sederwall would now be in the driver's seat for this newly ambitious dupe.

PAT GARRETT: THE MAN BEHIND THE BADGE AND THE MOON

DEFAMING PAT GARRETT AND HOAXING BRIGHT MOONLIGHT

W.C. Jameson's 2016 *Pat Garrett: The Man Behind the Badge*, represented a new direction in his pursuit of "Brushy" as Billy: simply claiming that "history is not as written": the mantra of the "Brushy" and "Billy the Kid Case" hoaxes. And, though not a co-author, Steve Sederwall was his acknowledged source. As Jameson wrote: "Intrepid investigator Steve Sederwall turned over more stones and found more pertinent information and evidence regarding Pat Garrett ... Billy the Kid, and others than all the so-called experts put together." (Page 223) The illogic was to defame Garrett, then leap to claiming he was so bad that he could kill someone instead of Billy the Kid and hide it; so he did!

And wised-up Jameson immediately took no chance with "Brushy's" fatal "dark night" moon error, which he had naively left in his 1998 *The Return of the Outlaw Billy the Kid*. He now announced in his "Prologue" that July 14, 1881's moon was full three nights earlier, in waning phase, with 87 percent brightness! (Page x) And for his killing scene chapter, "The Shooting," there is no mention of the moon at all! (Pages 66-70)

HEADING TO A MEGAHOAX

In Jameson's 21st century books, the original "Brushy" hoax was bloating into the monstrosity that would emerge in two more years, as Jameson's 2018 megahoax collusion with "Billy the Kid Case" hoaxers for his book: *Cold Case Billy the Kid: Investigating History's Mysteries*. There, the "Billy the Kid's Bad Bucks" hoax would have pride of place for the history-is-not-as-written scam - forcing Jameson to ignore that it demolished "Brushy" as Billy, since he knew nothing of its claims, and he was supposed to be the Billy the Kid being portrayed!

Jameson apparently now had a new and simpler goal: profiteering from tabloid-level "history's mysteries" of fake TV "documentaries," books, and press. That was the realm of the cynically opportunistic hoaxers he now joined and promoted.

CHAPTER 3
STEVE SEDERWALL'S "BILLY THE KID CASE" HOAXES

A PROLIFIC HOAXER

Steven M. "Steve" Sederwall's Billy the Kid hoaxing began with the "Billy the Kid Case." Though just a Lincoln County Deputy Sheriff for it, he wrote its key documents; participated in its forensic fakery with Dr. Henry Lee; was in its 2004 TV pseudo-documentary: "Investigating History: Billy the Kid;" and participated in the illegal exhumation of pretender, John Miller, making false claims that Miller matched Billy the Kid.

After I stopped that hoax, Sederwall allied with hoax-backing *True West* magazine Editor-in-Chief Bob Boze Bell and "Brushy"-backing W.C. Jameson, to recycle, in print, "Billy the Kid Case" fakery, while adding new hoaxes hijacking Billy the Kid history.

Sederwall's hoaxes all relied on historical ignorance of his audience, misstating historical documents, illogical "what-if" reasoning, old-timers' discredited hearsay accounts, fake conspiracy theories, and pure fabrications. His productions for the "Billy the Kid Case," and later for Jameson's books - 2016's *Pat Garrett: The Man Behind the Badge* and his 2018 *Cold Case Billy the Kid: Investigating History's Mysteries* - were characterized by defamation of Sheriff Pat Garrett, and accusing him of murdering an innocent victim, not Billy the Kid.

In keeping with imposter hoaxes, and lacking knowledge of history and documents, Sederwall promoted the antiquated myth of the outlaw Billy the Kid in his hoaxing.

And though the low man on the "Billy the Kid Case" hoax totem pole as a Deputy Sheriff, in his recycling of that hoax for Jameson's books, he *hoaxed himself* as its lone and private "investigator" "cop," using the other participants for *his* case!

HOAXING "BRUSHY" AS BILLY

Steve Sederwall created the first "Billy the Kid Case" document in May of 2003, as Mayor of Capitan, New Mexico, and a Lincoln County Deputy Sheriff for the case. It was his "Mayor's Report" to his constituents in his "Capitan Village Hall News." He opportunistically backed "Brushy Bill," the thrust of Governor Richardson's soon to be announced scam. Sederwall wrote:

> On April 28, 2003, at five minutes after noon, one of our citizens, Sheriff Tom Sullivan fired two shots in Lincoln, New Mexico. The floor under my feet shook at each report of his pistol. The gun smoke hung in the air just as in a western novel would describe it. As I heard the shots a cold chill ran down my back knowing that J.W. Bell heard the shots that killed him.
>
> A 122 years before, just minutes after twelve, noon, on April 28, 1881, two lawmen lay dead, in the yard of the courthouse in Lincoln , New Mexico, from gunshot wounds. Quicker than it took New Mexico breeze to clear the gunsmoke, history was clouded with the myth of the shooting and escape of William H. Bonney a.k.a. Billy the Kid from the make-shift jail where he awaited the date with the hangman.
>
> Sheriff Sullivan and I have opened a case into that shooting in 1881. As part of the investigation Sheriff Sullivan fired off two rounds from a .45 Long Colt to see if the shots could be heard from the Wortley Hotel. To our surprise the black powder rounds loaded for us by Virgil Hall could be heard in nearly every part of town.
>
> **This investigation came about after Sheriff Sullivan and I talked about a man by the name of Brushy Bill Roberts. In 1950 Roberts ["Brushy Bill"] came to the Governor of New Mexico with his attorney [sic - William Morrison, not an attorney]; saying he was Billy the Kid. He said that Pat Garrett shot a man by the name of Billy Barlow and buried his body claiming to be that of Billy the Kid. Roberts said he lived out a life within the bounds of the law under an assumed name and wanted a pardon that was promised to him by Governor Wallace.**

[AUTHOR'S NOTE: This is the hoax's first known reference connecting the "Billy the Kid" hoax's claim that Garrett did not kill the Kid, to the "Brushy Bill" Roberts hoax.]

On the surface of this story [Brushy Bill Roberts's] you would say "so what?" But if you look at this man's claim he is saying our Sheriff Pat Garrett is a murderer. Garrett knew the Kid and killed someone else. What this says also is that Pete Maxwell who said the body is of The Kid is a co-conspirator in a murder. There is no statute of limitations on Murder [sic], so the Lincoln County Sheriff''s Office has opened a case to pursue the investigation. If Brushy Bill Roberts is Billy the Kid then history changes. But if he is lying, we need to clear Garrett's name.

[AUTHOR'S NOTE: Confirmed is a Sherriffs Department murder filing with a "Brushy" emphasis. Against Garrett, it is absurdly claimed for clearing his name - though he and Sullivan were the accusers! Also, New Mexico *did* have a statute of limitations which expired in 1891 for prosecuting Garrett.]

I feel this investigation will put a positive light on the county, our town and the state in whole. Tom Sullivan and I have been in touch with the Governor's office and he is behind us. People who are conducting DNA on victims of the World Trade Center have agreed to complete DNA tests for us on remains of persons believed to be Billy the Kid. We have a filmmaker creating a made-for-TV story about this investigation. We have recruited some of the best investigators in the country from other states to assist in this investigation. The Sheriff and I feel this should not only clear up a 122-year-old mystery but also bring money into our village ...

Tom Sullivan and I know it is a crazy idea but won't it be fun.

Sederwall was also a participant the next year, in August of 2004, in Governor Bill Richardson's "Billy the Kid Case" hoax pseudo-documentary on the History Channel, written, co-produced, and narrated by the case's official historian, University of New Mexico Professor Paul Hutton, as "Investigating History Billy the Kid." For it, Sederwall again posed as a "Brushy"-believer, along with the rest of the hoaxers. Hutton narrated, as *Alias Billy the Kid's* cover loomed: "Over the years that story has gained some credence." W.C. Jameson states that the "Coroner's Jury Report was never found," and there was "no evidence jurymen saw the body." **Sederwall adds, "If "Brushy Bill" is Billy the Kid, it comes down to this ... Garrett had to have let him escape in Fort Sumner."**

HOAXING PAT GARRETT AS MURDERING AN INNOCENT VICTIM

Steve Sederwall claimed to have written the key document in the "Billy the Kid Case" hoax: its 2003 "Probable Cause Statement" for Lincoln County Sheriff's Department's Case No. 2003-274 to establish Pat Garrett as the murderer of an innocent victim, not Billy the Kid. To fake Garrett's murder motive, he also made-up a sub-investigation fabricating Garrett as Billy's super-friend, who helped Billy escape jail by supplying him with the revolver to murder his guard, Deputy James Bell. Professor Paul Hutton later made this a re-enactment in his 2004 "Investigating History: Billy the Kid," by having Garrett put a revolver in the outhouse;" and by fellow hoaxer, Dr. Henry Lee, in 2004, doing fake forensics for "Bell's blood" in the old Lincoln Courthouse.

THE "PROBABLE CAUSE STATEMENT"

The key to the "Billy the Kid Case" hoax was gaining legal access to graves to fake self-serving DNA matches. That meant filing real murder investigations. And a Probable Cause Statement establishes, with probability, the guilt of a suspect.

Sederwall's December 31, 2003 "Probable Cause Statement for Case No. 2003-274" is 11 pages of single-spaced footnoted text, combining double-talk, lies, and mock erudition. A contributor was fellow hoaxer, U.S. Marshals Service Historian David Turk.

It had two thrusts: First, calling Garrett a murderer by made-up "suspicions," misinformation, and fake DNA claims. Second, was fabricating his murder motive as friendship to Billy. Billy's survival used old-timers' malarkey of post-death sightings.

Sederwall claimed Garrett's guilt would be proven by DNA comparisons of remains of Billy the Kid' and his mother (to show Garrett's unknown victim lay in Billy the Kid's grave when no DNA match resulted).

The "Probable Cause Statement," as mere hoaxing, failed to establish any reason to assume that Pat Garrett did not kill Billy the Kid. But its labor in production reveal Sederwall's dogged determination to hijack history by devious means. And one can guess that, expecting no opposition, he and his Sheriff, Tom Sullivan, intended it for Richardson's complicit District Court judges, who were expected to rubber-stamp their exhumations, but might have wanted backing to bear scrutiny. It stated:

LINCOLN COUNTY SHERIFF'S DEPARTMENT
CASE # 2003-274
Probable Cause Statement

In the struggle dubbed the "Lincoln County War" investigators [Sullivan and Sederwall] soon learned that nothing was as seemed.

[AUTHOR'S NOTE: For lack of any evidence, this is the familiar "suspicion" used by Billy the Kid imposters' authors.]

As they poured through the volumes of information, documents, paperwork, reports, county records, books and examined newly discovered evidence, it became apparent no clear lines could be drawn as to who was working with or for whom. What first appeared to be clear quickly became clouded as new information was uncovered,

[AUTHOR'S NOTE: No new evidence is ever presented.]

it's difficult to judge who the "good guys" and the "bad guys" were. One would think that the Lincoln County Sheriff''s Department would be on the side of the law. However, it was a duly sworn posse of Lincoln County Deputies that shot and killed John Tunstall, in what investigators in clean conscience can only cauterize [sic] as an unprovoked murder.

[AUTHOR'S NOTE: Tunstall's murder is irrelevant. It occurred when William Brady was Sheriff of Lincoln County; and was 3½ years before Garrett killed the Kid. Of course, Brady's dishonesty is irrelevant to Garrett as a murderer.]

Evidence shows that posse-men, Hill and Morton

[AUTHOR'S NOTE: Error: Tom Hill was not Brady's official posseman; he was in Jessie Evans's outlaw gang. Brady, in writing, swore he used no known outlaws on that posse.]

committed murder when "*Hill called to him* (Tunstall) *to come up and that he would not be hurt; at the same time both Hill and Morton threw up their guns, resting their stocks on their knees; that after Tunstall came nearer, Morton fired and shot Tunstall through the breast, and then Hill fired and shot Tunstall through the head ...*" [1]([1]Deposition of Albert Howe, Angel Report) Although these deputies were acting under the color off the law they were not acting within the law. This behavior permeates the Lincoln County War and investigators will not make judgments on that behavior but rather uncover the facts and present the facts without varnish.

[AUTHOR'S NOTE: Repeating that lawman can be dishonest, is irrelevant to proving Garrett a murderer.]

No one from the Governor to the District Attorney to the Sheriff of Lincoln County is beyond suspicion of deception and covering up the true facts in this case.

[AUTHOR'S NOTE: Vague "suspicion" is irrelevant to Garrett.]

This can be seen in a number of examples. In a letter to Riley and Dolan of the Murphy-Dolan faction from District Attorney W. L. Rynerson of the 3rd Judicial District, the attorney clearly demonstrates he himself plays a part in the hostile actions when he writes, "*Shake that McSween outfit up until it shells out and squares up and then shake it out of Lincoln. I will aid to punish the scoundrels all I can.*"[2] (^{2}Rynerson letter to Riley and Dolan, Feb. 7 [sic], 1878, University of Arizona Special Collection)

[AUTHOR'S NOTE: Error: The letter is dated February 14, 1878; is about murdering Tunstall; and is irrelevant to Garrett.]

When investigators began to look at the murder of Deputy Sheriff J.W. Bell and Deputy Robert Olinger on April 28, 1881, it was found that much of the information we now know as "history" came from Pat F. Garrett's book, "The Authentic Life of Billy the Kid" published in 1882.

[AUTHOR'S NOTE: Error: Bell/Olinger eye-witness murder information was not claimed by Garrett, who was away at White Oaks; but was from, Gottfried Gauss, the caretaker.]

Investigators learned that much of this history is flawed for the reason historian Robert Utley writes: "*Although not many copies of the Authentic Life were sold, it nevertheless had a decisive impact on the Kid's image. More than any other single influence, the Garrett-Upson book fed the legend of Billy the Kid. As the legend blossomed, writers turned to the Authentic Life for details. Ash Upson's fictions became implanted in hundreds of " histories" that followed. For more than a century, only a few students thought to question the wild fantasies that flowed from Ash's imagination. In the evolution of the Kid's image, the Authentic Life is a book of enormous consequence.*"[3] (^{3}Robert M. Utley. Billy the Kid a short and violent life. University of Nebraska Press, 1989.)

[AUTHOR'S NOTE: Utley is merely describing evolution of the legend, not history. And Garrett's book confirms his shooting of Billy. All subsequent scholarly historians, including Utley, confirmed that Garrett fatally shot Billy the Kid.]

On March 23 [sic – 17], 1879, Governor Lew Wallace met with William Bonney (Kid) in Lincoln. In this meeting it is demonstrated that Wallace convinced the Kid that it would be to his advantage to work for the government.

[AUTHOR'S NOTE: Wrong. Billy proposed to Wallace, by a letter of about March 13, 1879, to give eye-witness Grand Jury testimony against the murderers of Huston Chapman in exchange for Wallace's annulling his Lincoln County War indictments. But a straw man argument is being set up.]

The Kid becomes, what would be referred to in today's terminology as a "Confidential Informant." In Governor Wallace's hand we read "Statements made by Kid, Made Sunday night March 23, 1879."[4] ([4]Statements by Kid, Lew Wallace Collection, Indiana Historical Society Library) It was through this meeting Wallace devised a plan and attempted to deceive when he and the Kid entered into an agreement where by the Kid would appear to have been arrested.

[AUTHOR'S NOTE: Saying there was an attempt "to deceive" is a misleading switcheroo. The hoaxers have admitted to Billy's confidential informant status. The arrest plan was devised by both Wallace and Billy to prevent Billy's being killed before his Grand Jury testimony against Chapman's murderers. The hoaxers, however, are still pumping the irrelevant claim that everyone was deceptive. Of course, that claim is irrelevant to their Garrett as murderer fakery.]

The Kid later talks of this and says he was allowed to wear his guns and he left when he wanted to leave.

David S. Turk, Historian for the United States Marshals Service has discovered other such deceptions in his study of official records.

[AUTHOR'S NOTE: Referring to "other such deceptions" is fake. Turk's "other deceptions" are never given. And Turk, an active "Billy the Kid Case" hoaxer, contributed his own fake Probable Cause addendum to the hoax. (See pages 322-325 below)]

It is commonly believed

[AUTHOR'S NOTE: Misstatement: It is a *known*.]

that Lincoln County Sheriff Pat F. Garrett arrested the Kid in December of 1880 in Stinking Springs near Fort Sumner. But the records show that Garrett was elected in November of 1880 and did not take office until January of 1881.[5] ([5]Lincoln County Commissioners Records, November 8, 1880).

[AUTHOR'S NOTE: This leads to a fake claim that he did not have proper authority to capture Billy.]

He went to Fort Sumner as a Deputy United States Marshall, but even that Commission and authority are now questioned. Secret Service Special Operative Azariah F. Wild of New Orleans writes in his daily logs *"I this day went to Lincoln to meet Capt. Lea & Garrett who are to organize the Posse Comatatus (sic) to make a raid on Fort Sumner to arrest counterfeiters."*[6] ([6]Report of Azariah F. Wild, November 11, 1880, Record Group 87, National Archives) Garrett shot and killed Charles Bowdre and Tom O'Folliard during the chase and arrested the Kid. Later, Secret Service Special Operative Azariah F. Wild writes to his superior and admits he was deceptive in his commission of Garrett. *"I will respectfully state that I applied to Marshall Sherman to appoint P.F. Garrett as a Deputy Marshall to which he paid no attention. I was in great need of Mr. Garrett [sic – Mr. Garrett's <u>aid</u>] at that time and took one of the Commissions Sherman sent to John Hurley (he having sent two) and substituted P.F. Garrett the very man who has rendered the Government such a valuable service in killing and arresting these men who I was in pursuit."*[7] ([7]Report of Azariah F. Wild, January 4 [sic -3], 1881, Record Group 87, National Archives)

[AUTHOR'S NOTE: This is a fake attempt to cast doubt on Garrett's commission and Wild's veracity. In fact, Wild, needing Garrett's aid, requested paperwork from U.S. Marshal John Sherman, and erroneously received two for John Hurley. So he crossed out Hurley's name on one, and added Garrett's. It was not done secretly, since Wild put it in his daily report to Secret Service Chief James Brooks. And it was accepted. To be noted, is that Sederwall recycled this fabrication in W.C. Jameson's 2018 book titled *Cold Case Billy the Kid*.]

No one in 122 years has been able to speak with clear certainty where the gun came from that William Bonney used to kill Deputy J.W. Bell.

[AUTHOR'S NOTE: A switch to a sub-investigation begins to fake Garrett as Billy's escape accomplice.]

With the information investigators have seen they question Garrett's involvement in the Kid obtaining a weapon.

[AUTHOR'S NOTE: No such information is ever given. There are just fake "what-ifs": *If* **Garrett was Billy's friend, he would give him an escape gun.** *If* **he gave an escape gun, he would later kill the innocent victim so Billy could escape again.]**

It would go to reason that if the body in Fort Sumner is anyone other than William Bonney then Garrett no doubt had a hand in allowing the Kid to escape on July 14, 1881.

[AUTHOR'S NOTE: This is fakery. No one says anyone but Billy was buried. It is just hoaxing.]

If the body at Fort Sumner is anyone other than William Bonney, then Garrett, whether by accident or design, is responsible for homicide of the person resting in that grave.

[AUTHOR'S NOTE: Here are more meaningless "what ifs."]

If it is not Bonney in the grave at Fort Sumner it would also go to reason that Garrett would be looked at as a suspect in furthering the escape of the Kid on April 28, 1881 when the two Lincoln County Sheriffs were murdered.

[AUTHOR'S NOTE: Here is the switcheroo. Now the fake "what-ifs" are used as fact: that Garrett helped Billy escape. **THIS FAKERY IS THE HOAXERS' SOLE PROBABLE CAUSE FOR GARRETT AS A MURDERER.** In fact, no evidence has been given; and none exists. And Pat and Billy were not friends.]

[AUTHOR'S NOTE: What follows next is built on the hoaxers' lying that (1) they established Garrett's murder motive, and that (2) they established need to check Billy's grave for Garrett's "innocent victim."]

Although the investigation will deal with what happened in the Lincoln County court house on April 28, 1881, this writing will deal with the alleged shooting of William Bonney at Fort Sumner on the night of July 14, 1881.

[AUTHOR'S NOTE: Do not let this fast-one slip by. The deputy murders "sub-investigation" at the courthouse consisted merely of: (1) firing a gun inside to test if it could be heard across the street; and (2) bringing in a forensic consultant, Dr. Henry Lee, whose finding of "blood" on the upstairs hallway floorboards was a hoaxer lie. Lying more, the hoaxers said the "blood" was Bell's. Olinger was left out. Also left out is that this "investigation" has nothing to do with the gun used to shoot Bell. And, even if it did, that would have nothing to do with whether Garrett gave it to Billy, or whether Garrett murdered an innocent victim 2 ½ months later. The "upstairs blood," though irrelevant, will be debunked later with the rest of the fake forensic claims.]

[AUTHOR'S NOTE: At this point, the hoaxers abandon the deputy murders and the Garrett murder motive. But they pretend that they: (1) established Garrett's Billy friendship; (2) Garrett's escape weapon involvement; (3) Garrett's murder motive; and (4) Garrett's murder of the innocent victim.]

This writing will set forth probable cause as to why investigators question who is in the grave in Fort Sumner and seek DNA from Catherine Antrim.

[AUTHOR'S NOTE: Probable cause of Garrett as a murderer has not been established. But this double exhumation is the hoaxers' goal.]

[AUTHOR'S NOTE: What follows is the hoaxers' attempt to fake that someone other than William Bonney was shot by Garrett. It is back to "what-ifs": *If* **there was any inconsistency in reporting of events around the murder, something is "suspicious;" ergo, Garrett killed someone else. But the hoaxers only fabricate some "inconsistencies."]**

The detractors of this investigation hold up the statements of Lincoln County Sheriff Pat F. Garrett, Deputy Sheriff John W. Poe, and the Coroner's Jury report as proof it is William H. Bonney that Sheriff Garrett shot and killed on July 14, 1881 and that the Kid is buried in Ft. Sumner.

[AUTHOR'S NOTE: Hidden are the multiple corpse identifications. Later, in this document, in slip-ups, the hoaxers accidentally present more of them!]

Historian Philip J. Rash [sic - Rasch] tells the story history puts forth about the shooting of the Kid in the following manner:

Garrett led them to the mouth of Taiban Arroyo, arriving after dark on 13 July. When Brazil failed to appear, Poe, who was unknown in the area, agreed to ride into fort Sumner the next morning to see what he could learn. Finding the inhabitants suspicious and uncommunicative, he proceeded to Sunnyside, about seven miles north, to visit Milnor Rudolph [sic], the postmaster and an old friend of Garrett's. Rudolph was nervous and evasive. He denied all knowledge of the Kid's whereabouts, but Poe was sure he was concealing something.[8] ([8] Poe, John W. *The Death of Billy the Kid*. New York: Houghton Mifflin Company, 1933) *There is a curious story that while the officer was on the way to Sunnyside, John Collins (Abraham Gordon Graham), a former member of Billy's gang, headed to Lobato's camp to warn the outlaw that officers were in the vicinity. On the way he met the Kid, bound for Fort Sumner. "Billy," he warned, "don't go down there. I just saw Poe, and no doubt Pat Garrett and a posse are around town looking for you."*

[AUTHOR'S NOTE: Recall that Poe was unknown to the locals; so this irrelevant hearsay further lacks credibility.]

The Kid merely laughed and answered, "Oh, that's O.K. I'll be alright," and rode on, leaving Collins badly puzzled."[9] (*[9]Ben Kemp. Dead Men, Who Rode Across the Border.* Unpublished. No date.)

That night Poe rendezvoused with Garrett and McKinney at La Punta de la Glorietta [sic], four miles north of Fort Sumner. Poe's report of both his failure to learn anything definite and his suspicions that there was so much smoke there must be some fire only increased the sheriff's skepticism. After some discussion he commented that the Kid was a frequent visitor to the house of Celsa Gutierrez (sister of Pat's wife Polineria [sic] Gutierrez) and suggested that they watch her home. Their vigil proved fruitless. As midnight approached Garrett and Poe decided that there was only one other possible source of information - Peter Maxwell, the town's most prominent citizen.

The officers arrived at his home about 12:30 AM on Friday, the 15th [sic]. Pat instructed Poe and McKinney to wait outside while he went in to talk to Maxwell. Sitting down on the edge of the bed, he asked in a low voice whether the Kid was on the premises. Maxwell became very agitated, but answered that he was not. At that point a bare headed, bare footed man in his shirt sleeves, carrying a butcher's knife in his left hand and a revolver in his right sprang through the door and asked Maxwell who the two men outside were.

Maxwell whispered, "That's him."

[AUTHOR'S NOTE: Note the hoaxer slip-ups in presenting this source: (1) *This* **Garrett cannot recognize Billy, though they claimed he and Billy were such good friends that Garrett killed for him; and (2) Maxwell identifies the victim as Billy!]**

Sensing a third person in the room, the intruder backed toward the door, at the same time demanding, "Quien es? Quien es?"

Pat jerked his gun and fired twice.[10] [11] (*[10]Las Vegas Daily Optic, July 18, 1881.* [11]*Santa Fe Daily New Mexican, July 21, 1881) As the man fell Maxwell plunged over the foot of the bed and out the door, closely followed by the sheriff. Maxwell would surely have been shot by Poe if Garrett had not struck the latter's gun down saying, "Don't shoot Maxwell." He added, "That was the Kid that came in there onto me, and I think I have got him."*

[AUTHOR'S NOTE: This is Peter Maxwell's second dead Billy identification; and is not contradicting Garrett's statement.]

Poe was not so sanguine. "Pat," he answered, "the Kid would not come to this place, you shot the wrong man." All was quiet inside. After some persuasion Maxwell brought a tallow candle and placed it on the outside of the window sill. By its light the body of a man could b e seen.

Deluvina Maxwell, a Navajo servant, entered the room, examined the body, and found that it was indeed the Kid's.

[AUTHOR'S NOTE: This is a third identification of Billy! And Deluvina knew him, as he hoaxers later confirm themselves. She also reported his killing in a June 24, 1927 interview by J. Evetts Haley. And Poe's quote, in his 1933 book, *The Death of Billy the Kid*, expressed initial disbelief of Billy's coming there – and he did not know him. It does not disprove the victim.]

Garrett's first shot had struck him in the left breast just above the heart; the second had gone wild. Later it was learned that Billy had been staying at the house of Juan Chavez.

[AUTHOR'S NOTE: A fourth Billy identification!]

Becoming hungry, he had gone to Maxwell's to slice a steak from a yearling Pete had killed that morning.

The corpse was taken to a carpenter's shop and laid on the work bench.

[AUTHOR'S NOTE: The carpenter's bench would later became the hoaxers' focus for faking DNA claims.]

Fearing an assault from Billy's friends, the officers remained awake and on guard the rest of the night. However, it passed without incident.

[AUTHOR'S NOTE: The townspeople join the list confirming the body as Billy's, and are called "Billy's friends." Note also that Garrett does not try to conceal the body of the supposed innocent victim of his "murder."]

When morning came, Justice of the Peace Alejandro Segura convened a jury, with Rudolph as president.

[AUTHOR'S NOTE: The Justice of the Peace convened the Coroners Jury. Later the hoaxers will switch this fact.]

They rendered a verdict that William Bonney, Alias "Kid," had been killed by Garrett and were "unanimous in the opinion that the gratitude of the whole community is due the said Garrett for his act and that he deserves to be rewarded".

[AUTHOR'S NOTE: Note that the job of a Coroners' Jury was to identify the body. They did. Billy was known to them. The hoaxers already quoted historian Philip Rasch saying Rudulph was nervous when interviewed by Poe - indicating he knew Billy, and knew he was in the area. Crucial also is that the Coroner's Jury declared the killing justifiable homicide. That closed the case legally. Re-opening it is double jeopardy.]

That afternoon Jesus Silva and Vincente Otero dug a grave for the outlaw in the old military cemetery.[12] ([12]Philip Rasch. *Trailing Billy the Kid* by Philip J. [sic - Rasch] Outlaw-lawman research series Volume 1, University of Wyoming, Laramie, Wyoming, 1993.)

On face value this looks to be the truth. However, if you study the statements of the eye witness [sic] and the documents they do not match up and both can not be true.

[AUTHOR'S NOTE: This is to fake "inconsistencies."]

Deputy John Poe says the following:

It was understood when I left my companions in the morning that in case of my being unable to learn any definite information in Fort Sumner, I was to go to the ranch of Mr. Rudolph (an acquaintance and supposed friend of Garrett's) whose ranch was located some seven miles north of Fort Sumner at a place called "Sunnyside," with the purpose of securing from him, if possible, some information as to the whereabouts of the man we were after. Accordingly I started from Fort Sumner about the middle of the afternoon for Rudolph's ranch,

[AUTHOR'S NOTE: Remember "in the middle of the afternoon." It will later be switched to Poe leaving for Rudulph's at night.]

arriving there sometime before night. I found Mr. Rudolph at home, presented the letter of Introduction which Garrett had given me, and told him that I wished to stop overnight with him.[13] ([13]Poe, John W. Billy the Kid. Privately published by E.A. Brininstool. Los Angeles, CA.)

[AUTHOR'S NOTE: With this unpublished, Brininstool source - and reasonable assumption of its unavailability to readers – the hoaxers are about to construct a fake argument.]

In this part of Deputy Poe's statement he tells us he was sent to Rudolph's ranch by Garrett because Rudolph was *"an acquaintance and supposed friend of Garrett's,"* that the ranch was located seven miles north of Ft. Sumner, at Sunnyside. Poe also tells Rudolph he is going to spend the night at the ranch.

[AUTHOR'S NOTE: The fakery here is leaving out part of the quote. Brininstool information is as follows: There was no "Brininstool book." Poe wrote his account, including the Rudulph episode, for Charles Goodnight in 1917. In 1919; and an Edward Seymour in New York contacted Goodnight for information on the Kid. Goodnight referred him to Poe. Poe sent his account of Billy's death to Seymour, who sent it to Brininstool, who published it in British *Wild World Magazine*, in December of 1919, later making it a brochure. It was also used in in Poe's book, *The Death of Billy the Kid*, which the hoaxers

earlier cited. On its page 22, Poe states he <u>declined</u> the invitation to spend the night. But the hoaxers omitted its pages 25-26. There, Poe states: "Darkness was now approaching, and I said to Mr. Rudulph that inasmuch as myself and my horse were by this time pretty well rested, having had a good meal, I had changed my mind, and instead of stopping with him, would saddle up and ride during the cool of the evening to meet my companions. This I accordingly did, much, I thought, to the relief of Rudulph." So there was no inconsistency]

In Sheriff Garrett's statement he gives about the same facts of where he was headed and how far it was from Ft. Sumner. Garrett differs with Poe in one area when he says he "arranged with Poe to meet us that night at moonrise" rather then spend the night with Rudolph, as can be seen below:

[AUTHOR'S NOTE: This is to fake Garrett as making contradictions. But Poe *did not* spend the night. The hoaxers merely hid Poe's quote saying that he did not spend the night.]

I advised him (Poe) *also, to go to Sunnyside, seven miles above Sumner, and interview M. Rudolph Esq. In whose judgment and discretion I had great confidence. I arranged with Poe to meet us that night at moonrise, at La Puenta de la Glorietta, four miles north of Fort Sumner.*[14] ([14]Garrett, Pat F. The Authentic Life of Billy the Kid. University of Oklahoma Press, Norman. Oklahoma. 2000)

[AUTHOR'S NOTE: That was it: the hoaxers' alleged inconsistency: whether Poe did or did not spend the night at Milnor Rudulph's! But both Poe and Garrett agree that Poe did not. There was no inconsistency. Nevertheless, this hoaxer flimflam is later repeated on the same subject.]

Deputy Poe then gives his account of when he says he first saw the Kid when he writes:

I observed that he was only partly dressed, and was both bareheaded and bare-footed - or rather, had only socks on his feet, and it seemed to me that he was fastening his trousers as he came toward me art a very brisk walk.

As Maxwell's was the one place in Fort Sumner that I considered above suspicion of harboring "The Kid," I was entirely off my guard, that thought coming into my mind that the man approaching was either Maxwell

[AUTHOR'S NOTE: This quote dovetails with Poe's question about the correct man, since he could not identify Billy. Also note Poe's lack of alarm. It will be misstated by the hoaxers.]

or some guest of his who might have been staying there. He came on until he was almost within arm's length of where I sat before he saw me, as I was partly concealed from his view by the post of the gate. Upon his seeing me he covered me with his six-shooter as quick as lightening, sprang onto the porch, calling out in Spanish, "Quien es?" (Who is it?), *at the same time backing away from me toward the door through which Garrett only a few seconds before had passed, repeating his query, "Quien es?" in Spanish several times. At this I stood up and advanced toward him, telling him not to be alarmed: that he should not be hurt, and still without the least suspicion that this was the very man we were looking for.*

This statement raises many questions with investigators. Poe says he sees a man *"partially dressed, and was bare-headed and bare-footed - or rather, had only socks on his feet, and it seemed to me that he was fastening his trousers as he came toward me art a very brisk walk."* Then the man covers him with his six shooter. Where did the man put the *"six-shooter"* when he was *"fastening his trousers"*?

[AUTHOR'S NOTE: This is an accidentally hilarious hoaxer contrivance of the impossibility of doing two things at once! Actually, one can hold a revolver and button one's pants. And Billy was a gunman and ambidextrous, so even more able! Amazingly, this silliness would be repeated by Sederwall for W.C. Jameson's 2018 book, *Cold Case Billy the Kid*.]

He did not stop and lay it down because Poe says he *"he came toward me art a very brisk walk."*

[AUTHOR'S NOTE: Triple tasking!]

Another question that investigators struggle with is would it not go without saying Poe would have had a description of the Kid as he ventured into Ft. Sumner to scout around and gather information. It is beyond reason that he would go searching for a man without at least having a description of the man for whom he was searching?

[AUTHOR'S NOTE: It is not beyond reason. Garrett was not an experienced lawman. And Poe's task was not to search for Billy, but to find out from locals about Billy's whereabouts.]

In a town of about 200 people, many of which were Hispanic would Poe be unable to recognize the Kid from this description as he claims?

[AUTHOR'S NOTE: What description? It seems Poe had none. Also, this is racist. Many people of Hispanic background could be as fair as Billy.]

Deputy Poe continues his statement with these words:

As I moved toward him trying to reassure him, he backed up into the doorway of Maxwell's room, where he halted for a moment, his body concealed by the thick adobe wall at the side of the doorway, from whence he put his head out and asking in Spanish for the fourth or fifth time who I was. I was within a few feet of him when he disappeared into the room.

When the Kid asks Poe who he is in Spanish and has his pistol pointed at the deputy, what is Deputy McKinney doing at this time? Why is he not shouldering his rifle, and at least deploying to the side to cover his partner Deputy Poe from this very real threat? Today the shooting policy for police officers is tight and narrow: in 1881 a shooting policy was non-existent. Investigators believe the deputies had to have a description for whom they were searching. With a threat such as Poe describes, a man with a gun, added to the description of the most wanted man in New Mexico, there would have been cause for both deputies to have fired on the suspect.

[AUTHOR'S NOTE: Here comes fakery. Who says Poe had the description, or thought the gun was a threat? Back then, most men were armed. Poe even shows lack of alarm by reassuring the stranger. This fakery was repeated by Sederwall for W.C. Jameson's 2018 book, *Cold Case Billy the Kid*.]

Even if the deputies chose not to fire, would they have allowed the man who was threatening their lives with a gun

[AUTHOR'S NOTE: Note this switcheroo from a fake claim of alarm at "threatening their lives," to making it a fact.]

to walk in on the unaware Sheriff in the dark? If they chose to allow the man with a gun to walk in on the Sheriff would these seasoned lawmen

[AUTHOR'S NOTE: Kip McKinney was just a hog farmer.]

not at least have warned the Sheriff of the danger?

[AUTHOR'S NOTE: No danger is established.]

In Garrett's statement he relates the following:

From his step I could perceive he was either barefooted or in his stocking feet and held a revolver in his right hand and butcher knife in his left.

He came directly towards me. Before he reached the bed, I whispered, "Who is it Pete?"

[AUTHOR'S NOTE: If Garrett cannot recognize Billy, there goes the hoaxers' best-buddies-murder-plot case centerpiece! Note also that Maxwell provides another Billy identification!]

But I received no response for a moment. It struck me that it might be Pete's brother-in-law, Manuel Abreu, who had seen Poe and McKinney and wanted to know their business. The intruder came close to me, leaned both hands on the bed, his right and almost touching my knee, and asked in a low tone: "Who are they, Pete?" At the same moment Maxwell whispered to me, "That's him!" Simultaneously the Kid must have seen, or felt, the presence of a third person at the head of the bed. He raised quickly his pistol, a self cocker, within a foot of my breast. Retreating rapidly across the room he cried: "Quien es? Quien es? (Who's that? Who's that?) All this occurred in a moment. Quickly as possible I drew my revolver and fired, threw my body aside, and fired again. The second shot was useless: The Kid fell dead ..."

Investigators find it hard to believe that Garrett could see a 6 inch knife in the Kid's hand.

[AUTHOR'S NOTE: That night had a bright moon. When Billy opened the door, a held weapon would have been visible.]

Yet the Kid could not see a six foot, five inch man.

[AUTHOR'S NOTE: It was dark in the room. Note that at this half-way point in the Probable Cause Statement, with killing done, nothing indicates the victim was not Billy.]

Deputy Poe talks about what happened after the shooting of the Kid. He writes:

Within a very short time after the shooting, quite a number of the native people had gathered around, some of them bewailing the death of their friend,

[AUTHOR'S NOTE: From Poe's *The Death of Billy the Kid*, comes this slip-up: These people, who can recognize Billy, will later be given his body to lay out.]

while several women pleaded for permission to take charge of the body, which we allowed them to do. They carried it to the yard to a carpenter's shop, where it was laid on a workbench, the women placing candles lightened around it, according to their ideas of properly conducting a "wake" for the dead.

[AUTHOR'S NOTE: By this point, there are profuse eye-witness identifications of Billy!]

Investigators keep Deputy Poe's statement in mind as they studied the Coroner's Jury Report:

Greetings:

On this 15th day of July, A.D. 1881, I, the undersigned, Justice of the Peace of the above named precinct, received information that a murder had taken place in Fort Sumner, in said precinct, and immediately upon receiving said information I proceeded to the said place and named Milnor Rudolph, Jose Silva, Antonio Sevedra, Pedro Antonio Lucero, Lorenzo Jaramillo and Sabal Gutierres a jury to investigate the case and the above jury convened in the home of Luz B. Maxwell and proceeded to a room in the said house where they found the body of William Bonney alias "Kid" with a shot in the left breast and having examined the body they examined the evidence of Pedro Maxwell, which evidence is as follows: "I being in my bed in my room, at about midnight on the 14th day of July, Pat F. Garrett came into my room and sat down. William Bonney came in and got close to my bed with a gun in his hand and asked me "who is it" and then Pat F. Garrett fired two shots at the said William Bonney and the said William Bonney fell near my fire place and I went out of the room and when I came in again about three or four minutes after the shots the said William Bonney was dead."

[AUTHOR'S NOTE: This is a definitive Jury, plus Maxwell, identifying the victim as William Bonney.]

The jury has found the following verdict: We the jury unanimously find that William Bonney has been killed by a shot on the left breast near the region of the heart, the same having been fired with a gun in the hand of pat F. Garrett and our verdict is that the deed of said Garrett was justifiable homicide and we are unanimous in the opinion that the gratitude of all the community is due to the said Garrett for his deed and is worthy of being rewarded.

M. Rudolph, President   Anto, Sevedra(signature)
Pedro Anto. m. Lucero (signature)
Jose Silba (x)   Sabal Gutierez (x)   Lorenzo Jaramillo (x)

All said information I place to your knowledge.
   Alejandro Segura Justice of the Peace (signature)

[AUTHOR'S NOTE: This is a legally binding document confirming victim identification. To reopen the case is double jeopardy. Further confirmation of jurymen's certainty, is that no murder indictment was later made with the District Attorney of the First Judicial District Attorney against Garrett.]

Investigators remembered Deputy Poe's statement and Sheriff Garrett's statement as to where Poe had been that night.

[AUTHOR'S NOTE: The hoaxers hope the reader believed their faked contention that Poe spent the night at Rudulph's. What follows is more fakery to manufacture "inconsistencies."]

Earlier that evening

[AUTHOR'S NOTE: The time was afternoon, as quoted by the hoaxers earlier, and tagged by me to prepare for this switcheroo where they need night for their fake argument.]

Garrett had dispatched Deputy Poe to interview M. Rudolph in Sunnyside, seven miles north of Fort Sumner. Poe says he left Rudolph and rode to meet Garrett and McKinney. All records show that the shooting took place about midnight and Historian Philip I. Rash [sic] sets the time at 12:30 AM on July 15th. If this were true then the time does not allow for the statement of Poe and the coroner's jury report to both be true.

[AUTHOR'S NOTE: Their hoaxers' time switcheroo is done to discredit the Coroner's Jury Report: their bugbear. But, even if granted them, it does not work because of the length of the ride. Poe could cover the 7 miles to Sunnyside in 1½ hours. Puenta de la Glorietta was 4 miles north of Fort Sumner on the way. So Poe's return journey to meet his companions was only 3 miles, or about 45 minutes: easy to meet them by evening: a fact he and Garrett confirmed. No time inconsistency exists.]

If, after the shooting, Garrett had to get some order to the scene, locate a rider to ride to Sunnyside to get Rudolph,

[AUTHOR'S NOTE: The above Coroner's Jury Report clearly states that the appointment - and contacting - of Rudolph was a legal duty performed by the appropriate official: Justice of the Peace, Alejandro Segura; certainly not Garrett, then a suspect as to his legality in Billy Bonney's killing.]

and the rider then had to get his horses [sic] caught, saddled and ready to go all of which would take the better part of an hour,

[AUTHOR'S NOTE: Timing here is faked. Maxwell had a stable and workers. A horse could be readied quickly.]

the time would be 1:30 am.

[AUTHOR'S NOTE: The hoaxers are faking time "inconsistency. Yet they know that the Coroner's Jury met sometime during daytime of the 15th. There was no need for extreme urgency; and no evidence that it occurred.]

It would take a rider who was in shape, on a good horse, and riding fast, an hour and a half to cover the seven miles to Rudolph's ranch, putting the time at 2:30 am. Adding an hour for the rider to wake Rudolph up and for Rudolph to catch his horse and saddle the horse the time would be 3:30 am. If Rudolph was in good shape, on a good horse it would be another hour and a half on the return trip to Fort Sumner putting the time at 4:30 am. Add another hour to put together a jury, and the time is now 5:30 am. This is if everyone worked smoothly.

In the jury's report we find the words:

... a jury to investigate the case and the above jury convened in the home of Luz B. Maxwell and proceeded to a room in the said in said house where they found the body of William Bonney alias "Kid"...

Either the jury found the Kid in the Maxwell's home, or he was not given to the women to put on the carpenters workbench as Poe says, or the jury report is deceptive.

[AUTHOR'S NOTE: The hoaxers hope they convinced readers of that conclusion to fake an inconsistency. But there was enough time to carry the corpse from the Maxwell house, across about 300 yards of parade ground, to the carpenter's shop. In the morning, it could be returned to the Maxwell's house for the jurymen. This fakery was recycled by Sederwall for W.C. Jameson's 2018 book, *Cold Case Billy the Kid*.]

Deputy Poe also says:

The next morning we sent for the justice of the peace,

[AUTHOR'S NOTE: Here is undone the fakery of the night riding by giving this quote about the next morning.]

who held an inquest over the body, the verdict of the jury being such as to justify the killing, and later, on the same day, the body was buried in the old military burying ground at Fort Sumner.

If the Kid's body was taken to the carpenter shop then the jury did not find the body at Maxwell's house as stated and makes investigators wonder why they would lie in the report.

[AUTHOR'S NOTE: This fabrication leads to a "lie" accusation. But nothing indicates that the body was not brought to the house from the carpenter's shop. But the hoaxers are still trying to discredit the Coroner's Jury Report by fake "contradictions;" though, of course, that is irrelevant to establishing the victim's identity.]

Deputy Poe says something else that raised investigators suspicions when he writes about the shooting itself:

[AUTHOR'S NOTE: This switcheroo distracts from the sly misstatements slipped past. And though the hoaxers never say what is "suspicious" in Poe's quote – which is merely repeating Garrett's description - they are setting the stage for their fake "investigation" to be described next.]

An instant later a shot was fired in the room, followed immediately by what everyone within hearing distance thought was two shots fired, the third report, as we learned afterward, being caused by the rebound of the second bullet which had struck the adobe wall and rebounded against the headboard of the wooden bedstead.

[AUTHOR'S NOTE: Let us take stock now. Nothing so far indicates a victim other than profusely identified Billy Bonney. Nor are there any "contradictions." Later, when exhumations were blocked, the hoaxers contradicted this document: stating Billy *was* shot, laid out on the bench, but played dead to bleed as a source of DNA, before evil Garrett switched him with the murdered innocent victim!]

[AUTHOR'S NOTE: Note that the second bullet hit the headboard. But the hoaxers will do fake forensics on a washstand instead! So next is a faked CSI-style investigation.]

On August 29, 2003, Deputy Sederwall of the Lincoln County Sheriff''s Department

[AUTHOR'S NOTE: Sederwall calls himself a deputy; years later, when hiding the case's DNA documents from my open records case, he would lie that he did the case as his "hobby!"]

located the carpenter bench where the Kid's body was placed on July 14, 1881.

[AUTHOR'S NOTE: Error: earliest morning of July 15th]

On September 13, 2003, investigators located all the furniture that was in Pete Maxwell's bedroom the night of the shooting, July 1881.

[AUTHOR'S NOTE: This Maxwell furniture - including the carpenter's bench - became necessary for hoax survival after exhumations were blocked in 2004. But the furniture is of doubtful provenance, and is forensically useless. The Maxwell family sold Fort Sumner on January 15, <u>1884</u> to Lonny Horn, Sam Doss, Daniel Taylor and John Lord in partnership with the New England Cattle Company, which transferred its operations there. The Maxwell house was torn down in 1887; and its lumber was used to build the Pigpen Ranch south of Melrose, New Mexico.

After the 1884 sale, Peter Maxwell moved outside town (see page 306 below), dying there in 1898. His furniture would have been from that house. One of Peter's sisters, Odile, married a Manuel Abreu, settling near the town. She had family furniture, but Peter's would have come after his death. In about 1926, her 15 year old daughter, Stella, made a little "Billy the Kid Museum" in a shack for tourists. Stella labeled Odile's furniture as from Maxwell's bedroom and the vigil's carpenter's bench. But, as she told historian, Richard Weddle, in old age, she merely got the bench from a local. Her Museum closed in 1936. In 1940 she put the furniture in her Santa Rosa gas station run with her husband, Kenneth Miller. It was again stored before being moved, in 1959, to their converted chicken coop in Albuquerque. Her son, Mannie Miller, showed it to the hoaxers. He died on March 20, 2011; and it was sold to a collector. In fact, all one can say is that 45 years after Billy's killing, Stella made unprovable claims about furniture for profit, with the cheap-looking items more likely from Peter's new bedroom. And the random bench was never in the family.]

Among these items is the headboard of the bed that was in Maxwell's room that night. There is no bullet hole in the headboard.

[AUTHOR'S NOTE: That finding is part of the hoaxers' fake forensics to contradict Poe's eye-witness statement that the headboard was hit. The fakery omitted mention that Stella Abreu's museum's headboard was just a frame around the huge hole of the missing headboard. There is no place for a bullet hole! This fakery would be recycled by Sederwall in W.C. Jameson's 2018 book, *Cold Case Billy the Kid*.]

In a statement made by Deluvina Maxwell she says the following:

… There was a washstand with a marble top in Pete Maxwell's bedroom, which Garrett had seen in the moonlight and shot at, thinking it was Bonney trying to get up.

[AUTHOR'S NOTE: This is a faked Deluvina quote. Its footnote states: "^{15}**Deluvina Maxwell's story <u>as related to Lucien B. Maxwell grandchildren</u>, unpublished." This is just hearsay, without even a source. It is being used to fake legitimacy of the hoaxers' claim that the washstand was shot by Garrett.]**

It was an old Spanish custom that the night before the burial of a person, people would take turns staying with the body and reciting prayers. William Bonney had a proper funeral. The people took turns and stayed through the night.

[AUTHOR'S NOTE: Another body identification as Billy!]

He was buried in the old government cemetery in Fort Sumner. For many years Deluvina left flowers on his grave in the summer time.[15]

[AUTHOR'S NOTE: This third person statement again shows the quote was not Deluvina. But she did lay flowers for decades, proving the body was Billy's!]

Deluvina lends credibility to the story of the Kid's body being laid on the carpenter bench.

[AUTHOR'S NOTE: Here is a hoaxer slip that ends their case: Billy's corpse on bench! And it ends "Brushy's" hoax too! To get out of that problem, the hoaxers later fabricated that Billy was just "playing dead!"]

In the items investigators located on September 13, 2003 was that wash stand.

[AUTHOR'S NOTE: This washstand is unsubstantiated as from Pete Maxwell's bedroom - as is the rest of the furniture from Stella Abreu's Billy the Kid Museum. And this washstand is implausibly toy-sized. Furthermore, eye-witness Poe said the headboard was hit. But what follows is a fake "crime scene investigation" using the unsubstantiated washstand.]

The was stand was dark in color and 29 1/2 inches wide, with a splash board on the back that measured 5 inch at the middle and tapered down to the ends in a decorative curve. From front to back the wash stand measured 16 inches. It stood 29 inches with three drawers with rusted locks on each drawer. There was what appeared to be a bullet hole through the stand.

Deputy Sederwall removed a .45 caliber pistol round from his deputy weapon and noticed the round was just a little bit bigger than the hole. The night of the shooting Sheriff Garrett was shooting a Colt Single Action Army Revolver, Serial Number 55093, caliber .44/40.[16] ([16]Typed letter from P.F. Garrett dated April 16, 1906. James H. Earl Collection, from County Clerk's office, El Paso, Texas.)

[AUTHOR'S NOTE: Note that there is no bullet, just holes. Claiming .44/40 ammunition is fakery to match Garrett's known weapon's caliber. Actually, there is no link to Garrett or to Maxwell's bedroom. There is even no link to anyone being shot, since accidental discharges happened in New Mexico where owning guns was common from the 19th century to the present – the time frame for "shooting" the tiny washstand!]

The bullet pierced the left side of the washstand, both sides of the drawer and exited out the right side of the stand.

The bullet struck the left side of the stand 22 1/4 inches on the center up from the bottom and 6 1/2 inches on the center of the back of the stand. The bullet exited to the right side 20 1/2 inches on the center up from the bottom and 6 1/2 inches on center from the back of the washstand. On the inside of the left side panel the wood was somewhat splintered indicating that was where the bullet entered the stand. On the right side panel the outside of the panel was splintered indicating the exit of the bullet.

The owner of the washstand, whose name investigators do not wish to release at this time

[AUTHOR'S NOTE: The hoaxers later named Mannie Miller.]

says it was inherited along with the bed from Maxwell's bedroom. The discovery of this evidence makes Deluvina's statement believable.

[AUTHOR'S NOTE: Historically real or not, the furniture examination is irrelevant to Garrett's victim's identity.]

Many questions remain. Why would the coroner's jury report and the eye witness reports be so at odds?

[AUTHOR'S NOTE: They are not at odds. The hoaxers simply made up some "discrepancies." But the hoaxers were heading to additional fakery, once again to attach the hated Coroner's Jury Report that undid their hoaxing.]

A hint can be found in a document discovered in July of 1989 by Joe O. Bowlin.

[AUTHOR'S NOTE: This is a low blow to a dead man. Joe Bowlin, with his wife Marlyn, founded the Billy the Kid Outlaw Gang to "preserve, protect, and promote the history of Billy Bonney and Pat Garrett." This hoax would have been anathema to Joe Bowlin. What follows misstates a book Bolin published posthumously for its old-timer author, A.P. "Paco" Anaya.]

The document is a story, according to Louis Anaya of Clovis, New Mexico as told to his father, Paco Anaya, a friend of Billy the Kid.

[AUTHOR'S NOTE: Note the admitted friendship of Paco Anaya and Billy. It will catch the hoaxers in another slip-up about the victim being Billy.]

This story was translated from Spanish and then printed in book form. In this transcript you will find the following:

Also, I will have to tell you a lot in reference to the reports that Pat Garrett made about the sworn declaration that appears in the records of the Secretary of State and more, concerning what he said about the

Coroners Jury that investigated the death of Billy the Kid when Pat killed Billy.

In this report, I find that the Coroners Jury that investigated the death of Billy the Kid when he was dead is not part of the same report that acted as a Coroners Jury, neither the form or the verdict of the Coroners Jury. The verdict is recorded in the office of the Secretary of State in Spanish, and they (the jury) are not the same men. There are two that did not even live in Fort Sumner.[17] ([17]Anaya, A. P. *I Buried Billy*. Creative Publishing Company. 1991.)

Paco Anaya goes on to list the members of the Jury that he remembered holding the inquest over the body. They are not the same as the jury report as is held up as proof that Garrett killed the Kid.

[AUTHOR'S NOTE: This is the two coroner's jury report claim made up by windbag "Paco" Anaya, spewing malarkey for his manuscript devoid of historical knowledge. He was used first as an "expert" in the "Brushy Bill" hoax; and subsequently recycled as a staple in all Billy the Kid imposter hoax books to follow – including W.C. Jameson's *Cold Case Billy the Kid*]

One of the differences is Illeginio Garcia [sic - poor legibility - unclear spelling] as the Jury President and not M. Rudolph.

Paco Anaya says that Garrett wrote the first version in English himself. Anaya says that Garrett later came back and wrote another report in Spanish with the help of "Don Pedro Maxwell and Don Manuel Abrea," [sic - Abreu] Maxwell's brother-in-law.

This makes the investigators ask, if Garrett wrote the verdict is that why the words are found, "...*we are unanimous in the opinion that the gratitude of all the community is due to the said Garrett for his deed and is worthy of being rewarded*"?

It should be noted that in the Coroners Jury Report that Garrett puts forth

[AUTHOR'S NOTE: Note the switcheroo. Garrett did not "put forth" the Coroner's Jury Report. It was a legal document done by authority of Justice of the Peace, Alejandro Segura. Garrett was the *subject* of their investigation. The document was available to him after he was cleared of wrongdoing, to send to District Attorney William Breeden. And it surely was not available to humble citizen Anaya. But the hidden punch line is that Anaya's posthumously published manuscript was titled *I Buried Billy*, confirming the body as Billy Bonney's.]

it is interesting to note that two of those listed were in Garrett's wedding, Sabal Gutierrez is his brother-in-law, and Garrett admits in his statement that Rudolph [sic] is a close friend.

[AUTHOR'S NOTE: Note the lie. Garrett did not pick the jurymen; the Justice of the Peace did. All the fakery has done nothing to show that Garrett murdered anyone but Billy.]

[AUTHOR'S NOTE: Next is the hoaxer' last try: using fellow hoaxer, David Turk, for useless hearsay and his fancy title.]

David Turk, Historian for the United States Marshal's Service has pointed out other documents

[AUTHOR'S NOTE: Only one document is presented; though Turk came to New Mexico in December of 2003, possibly to assist in writing this Probable Cause Statement.]

bringing into question Garrett's involvement in the Kid's escape.

[AUTHOR'S NOTE: Note that Turk was, thus, involved in faking Garrett as assisting jailbreak and by the victim murder.]

Mr. Turk has produced a Works Progress Administration, Federal Writer's Project interview where the following statement was taken:

The people around Lincoln

[AUTHOR'S NOTE: The killing was 150 miles from Lincoln; and Turk's old-timer reports are useless hearsay. He also supplied the hoax with his own slip-shod and pretender-oriented booklet titled "U.S. Marshals Service and Billy the Kid."]

say Garrett didn't kill Billie (sic) the Kid. John Poe was with Garrett the night he was supposed to ... said that he didn't see the man that Garrett killed.

[AUTHOR'S NOTE: Besides the fact that Poe's statements all refer to seeing the victim, Poe did not know Billy.]

I can take you to the grave in Hell's High Acre, an old government cemetery, where Billie (sic) was supposed to be buried and show you the grave.

The cook at Pete Maxwell's was always putting flowers on the grave and praying at it. This woman thought a lot of Billie (sic), but after Garrett killed the man at Maxwell's home her grandson was never seen again

[AUTHOR'S NOTE: No "grandson" was part of this history.]

and Billie (sic) was seen by Bill Nicholi an Indian scout. Bill saw him in Mexico.[18] ([18]Frances E. Tolly [Totty], comp. "Early Days in Lincoln County," Charles Remark Interview. February 14, 1938, Works Progress Administration, Federal Writer's Project, Folklore-Life Histories, Manuscript Division. Library of Congress.)

[AUTHOR'S NOTE: So this sole "evidence" that Garrett did not kill Billy is old-timer malarkey 57 years later, by someone unconnected to the event, and titled as "folklore."]

[AUTHOR'S NOTE: Next comes the conclusion pretending they proved their contentions.]

Discovering the headboard of Maxwell's bed that does not have a bullet hole in it, as Deputy Poe says it did, leads investigators to question if Poe was in fact in the room after the shooting of William Bonney as he said.

[AUTHOR'S NOTE: Omitted is that the headboard is just an empty frame. And claiming if it was not shot, Poe was not in the room" is absurd; and also irrelevant to victim identity.]

However, the discovery of the Maxwell wash stand with the bullet hole through it indicates someone was shot in Maxwell's room on the night of July 14, 1882].

[AUTHOR'S NOTE: Why? A shot washstand does not mean a shot person - or anything at all about who Garrett shot.]

The question remains as to who is in William H. Bonney's grave at Fort Sumner.

[AUTHOR'S NOTE: No question remains. This is all fakery.]

Investigators believe with the conflicts of Sheriff Pat F. Garrett and Deputy John Poe and the fact that these statements are at odds with the Jury Report as shown above,

[AUTHOR'S NOTE: This is fakery. The "conflicts" do not exist; and had nothing to do with whom Garrett shot.]

coupled with the evidence discovered by deputies,

[AUTHOR'S NOTE: There has been no legitimate evidence.]

probable cause exist [sic] to warrant the court to grant investigators the right to search for the truth in criminal investigation 2003-274 through DNA samples obtained from Catherine Antrim.

[AUTHOR'S NOTE: Without any probable cause of a murder, the hoaxers, contrived their objective: exhumation of Billy and his mother.]

[AUTHOR'S NOTE: Signatures follow; typed and written.]

Steven M. Sederwall: Deputy Sheriff, Lincoln County (12/31/03)

Tom Sullivan: Sheriff Lincoln County (12/31/03)

HOAXING THE JAILBREAK SUB-INVESTIGATION WITH DR. HENRY LEE

ADDING A HOAXING FORENSIC EXPERT

Deputy Steve Sederwall had contacted Dr. Henry Lee through fellow hoaxer, "Billy the Kid Case" official historian, Paul Hutton; as Sederwall testified in his June 26, 2012 deposition for my open records litigation against the lawmen: "Paul Hutton wanted me to be on some investigative history ... I said, "You know, I'm looking at bringing Henry Lee out here ... Tell Kurtis I'll let him film it if he wants to, or whatever, if he can get Henry out here." So [Hutton] jumped on it."

Henry Lee jumped on it too, getting the flood of publicity that accompanied media magnet, Billy the Kid; and that Lee craved for what his scornful colleagues call his "show-biz forensics. And he had national name recognition by helping O.J. Simpson walk free in his 1996 murder trial. As to reputation for veracity, that was another story.

Prosecutor, Vincent Bugliosi, in his book, *Outrage: The Five Reasons Why O.J. Simpson Got Away With Murder*, called Henry Lee "nothing short of incompetent." Bugliosi was avoiding "liar." An example from *Outrage* was Lee's testifying that "crime-scene" shoe "imprints" on murder victim Nicole Simpson's walkway did not match O.J. Simpson's incriminatory, "size-12 Bruno Magli bloody shoe prints" - also at the scene. But the smaller "prints" Lee used, according to Bugliosi, had been hardened into the concrete during its laying "ten years earlier!"

Helpful Dr. Lee resurfaced for the 2007 murder trial defense for music impresario, Phil Spector; accused, and ultimately convicted, of fatally shooting actress, Lana Clarkson. But Attorney Sara Caplan - in Spector's first defense team - testified to the judge, Larry Paul Fidler, that, at the crime scene, Lee bottled dead Clarkson's torn-off fingernail, which indicated possible struggle - not Spector's defense's claim of her committing suicide. Then that fingernail disappeared. Judge Fidler declared destruction of evidence. The CNN.com AP headline of May 25, 2007 was: "Famed expert's credibility takes a hit at Spector trial."

Lee's involvement in a 2016 documentary, "The Case of JonBenet Ramsey," accusing her nine year old brother, Burke

Ramsey of murdering her, resulted in Burke's $750 million defamation suit, which included Lee. On January 5, 2019, Dailymail.com reporter Maxine Shen wrote: "CBS and the brother of JonBenet Ramsey settle their $750m defamation lawsuit to the 'satisfaction of both parties.' " It stated: "Beyond CBS and the documentary production company Critical Content, LLS, Burke's lawsuit named **forensic scientist Henry Lee** and forensic pathologist Werner Spitz among several others who appeared in the broadcast."

So Henry Lee was the perfect "expert" to keep secret that no verifiable DNA of Billy the Kid existed on the planet - and fake some. He sham-tested for "blood" wherever he was pointed; and made up crime scene scenarios however he was directed - as long as Bill Kurtis Productions kept filming.

Lee was part of the "Billy the Kid Case" hoaxers' team from 2004 onward; and was acknowledged in 2018's *Cold Case Billy the Kid*. Wearing a cowboy hat in a 2010 photo, he was even a "posse" member in Sederwall's then website, BillytheKidCase.com, selling Case 2003-274's free public documents.

Lee was funded by Bill Kurtis, who wrote Sederwall a letter (eventually an exhibit in my open records litigation) stating: "This letter is provided as official verification that Kurtis Productions, LTD located in Chicago, Illinois paid all expenses for Dr. Henry Lee and his participation in the making of the documentary *Investigating History: Billy the Kid*. Dr. Lee was flown to New Mexico on July 30, 2004 and departed on August 1, 2004 at the expense of Kurtis Productions, LTD."

Lee's joining the "Billy the Kid Case" was announced by hoax-backing *Albuquerque Journal* reporter, Rene Romo. On August 2, 2004, Romo splashed, "Forensic Expert on Billy's Case: Questions Remain on Outlaw's Fate" Romo declared: "Dr. Henry Lee, one of the nation's leading forensic scientists ... has added the Billy the Kid slaying to his case files ... "This is an extremely interesting case of some historical importance,' Lee said in an interview ... 'That's why I agreed to spend some of my own time to work with them ... **It's basically a worthwhile project and legitimate**."

So famous Dr. Lee called the "Billy the Kid Case" "a worthwhile project and legitimate." What else was the public to think? And Romo confirmed: "Lee's expenses were paid by Illinois-based Kurtis Productions, headed by Bill Kurtis, host of the History Channel series 'Investigating History.' "

Lee's profit motive was further elucidated in the August 12, 2004 *Lincoln County News* article by Doris Cherry: "Forensics 101 for 'Billy." She quoted Sheriff Tom Sullivan: "Along with Sullivan and Lee were a crew from Curtis [sic] Production Company filming for the History Channel and Court T.V. **Dr. Lee also has a show produced by Curtis [sic] Production.**"

So "Billy the Kid DNA" exhumations and "matchings" were to be churned out by Lee and Kurtis for their enterprise. No wonder Lee called the project "worthwhile." He was intending an exhumation franchise for himself.

But the public was fed a different bill of goods via the hoaxers. By April 13, 2006, deceived reporter, Leo W. Banks of the *Tucson Weekly*, in "The New Billy the Kid?" had Lee pleading; as in: "Everybody wants a piece of the Kid, even a celebrity like Henry Lee ... when he heard about the Kid dig-up efforts, **he called Sederwall to volunteer his services.**"

The "Billy the Kid Case" hoaxers plugged Lee extravagantly. Rene Romo's August 2, 2004 *Albuquerque Journal* article even used their "Probable Cause Statement's" complicit historian: "You're getting the top guy ... I think that will go a long way to finding out what happened in Lincoln," said **David S. Turk**, historian with the U.S. Marshals Service ... who is cooperating on the case."

Added was that a Calvin Ostler, a Utah Medical Examiner - would participate. Unmentioned, was that Ostler was Lee's business partner. So Lee-Turk-Ostler did ricochet validation, without public awareness that they were all in cahoots for the trash "documentary" by Bill Kurtis and Professor Paul Hutton - all doing their job for Governor Bill Richardson.

LEE HOAXES BELL'S "BLOOD"

Sederwall's Deputy Bell killing sub-investigation for the Case 2003-274 "Probable Cause Statement" became a fake forensic investigation by Dr. Henry Lee. In the "Probable Cause Statement," Sederwall had fabricated Pat Garrett as being Billy's accomplice to Bell's killing, to fabricate that Garrett's murder motive for later killing the innocent victim was that same friendship. It used fake "what-if" reasoning: *if* Garrett gave Billy the escape gun, then he was Billy's friend, and would later kill to save him in Fort Sumner. In fact, there existed no Garrett friendship, no giving of the gun, and no known weapon.

So hoaxing Lee's task was to create a fake Deputy Bell killing scene to call Pat Garrett a liar. And with the hoax's usual "what-if" illogic, it was to claim that *if* Garrett lied about that scene, *then* he lied about the Fort Sumner victim's identity.

The actual scene was not witnessed by Garrett. It was told to him by courthouse care-taker, Gottfried Gauss, who stated that

Billy shot Bell as the man ran down the stairway; and that he found Bell dying *at its bottom*, and dragged him out the back door.

So, Lee would fake that the dying scene was at the top, not the bottom of the stairs to make Garrett a liar! For that hoaxing, Sheriff Sullivan and Deputy Sederwall took Lee to the old Lincoln courthouse on August 1, 2004. Lee tested for "blood" on upstairs floorboards and a wall. Of course, he found "blood."

Lee's original report of February 25, 2005, titled "Forensic Research & Training Center Forensic Examination Report" had this floorboard "investigation" under "Examination of Lincoln County Court House." Listed as present were "Calvin Ostler, Forensic Consultant, Riverton, Utah;" [Lee's partner] "Tom Sullivan, Sheriff, Lincoln County, New Mexico;" "Steve Sederwall, Deputy Sheriff, Lincoln County;" and "David Turk, US Marshall [sic], United States Marshall [sic] Service;" and Bill Kurtis of Bill Kurtis Productions - presumably getting his TV footage.

Lee called the staircase "repainted," when it was actually *replaced* in the 1980's. Lee gave a photo of the "target area" showing brown drips down on the wall under the stairway. Not only do they look like rusted water from a broken pipe or leaking roof, but the upstairs hall was not part of the historical shooting.

To test those stains, Lee used O-tolidine, a non-specific chemical for iron-containing compounds - like rust or blood. So cagy Lee called the drips *"blood-like* stains;" and stated they merited "presumptive blood tests." So, in his report's "Conclusions," he stated: "[T]hose stains could be bloodstains." Omitted is that for the amount of dripping, a massacre was needed on the second floor, not one man bleeding; and that from 1881 to 2004, the bloody mess would have been cleaned up.

And, as an expert, Lee should obviously have asked if there were Bell remains or Bell kin for "reference DNA" to establish if the "blood" was Bell's. The answer is: no remains and no kin. Nevertheless, hoaxing Lee, indifferent to real forensics, concluded: "Various stains were observed on the surface and underside of the floorboards. **Chemical tests for the presence of blood were positive with some of these stains. These results indicate presence of Heme or Peroxidase like activity with those stains tested positive, which suggests that those stains could be bloodstains. Further DNA testing could reveal the nature and identity of those blood-like stains.**"

The day after Lee's fake "investigation," on August 2, 2004, in the *Albuquerque Journal's* "Forensic Expert on Billy's Case," the hoaxers' mouthpiece, Rene Romo, reported the find of Deputy

Bell's "blood!" And Lee had reconstructed a "crime scene" of Bell's killing - though neither blood nor a link to Bell existed! Romo wrote: "Lee and the investigators Sunday afternoon also found several positive indications of blood residue below floor-boards at the top of a stairwell in the old Lincoln County courthouse. Such evidence could support Sederwall's theory that **the Kid fatally shot deputy J.W. Bell there, at the top of the stairs,** in his infamous escape from the Lincoln County jail. **That version would also contradict Garrett's account that the Kid, at the top of the stairs, shot Bell who was at the bottom of the stairwell.**"

Lincoln County News reporter Doris Cherry followed suit with her August 12, 2004 "Forensics 101 for 'Billy' ": "**Sullivan said that after studying the courthouse and the shooting he contended Bell was really killed at the top of the stairs, not near the bottom of the stairs as legend has it.**"

So the hoaxers claimed that Bell was shot on *the top, versus bottom, of the stairway*, based on no blood, no stairway from the period, and no connection to Bell!

On March 13, 2010, erstwhile Deputy, Steve Sederwall, appeared in a National Geographic International TV program, produced by British Parthenon Entertainment for the Discovery ID channel, to give this top-of-stairs scam to call Garrett a liar, and therefore a likely murderer of an innocent victim!

HIDING LEE'S RECORDS AND LAB RESULTS

Ultimately, by my open records litigation and subpoena of Lee's Orchid Cellmark Lab, on April 20, 2012, I got the 133 pages of Lee's DNA records that the hoaxers obviously tried to hide. The records showed that Lee's Deputy Bell shooting, courthouse investigation of floorboards **yielded no valid DNA**, as reported in October 15, 2004's "Laboratory Report, Forensic Identity, Mitochondrial Analysis, Results and Conclusions." One specimen yielded no DNA, and his second specimen showed an useless "**mixture of two or more mitochondrial profiles.** Consequently no sequence data are reported." The conclusion was: "[P]rofiles are therefore inconclusive." **And even if there had been valid floorboard DNA, there was no Bell DNA with which to compare it.**

DNA expert and President of San Francisco's Lexigen, Dr. Simon Ford clarified: "Mixed DNA results are very common in forensic casework," and "two or more ... profiles," **merely means "at least two;" not that there are two**. And the only way to sort out a mixed specimen to use <u>reference DNA</u> of all possible individuals in the sample. [But there was no Bell " reference DNA."] And if the DNA had degraded, no separate individuals could be identified in the mix anyway. Dr, Ford added: "[B]ased on DNA technology alone, there is no way of knowing from which kind of cell a particular DNA profile originated **[meaning DNA results cannot prove a blood source].**

HOAXING THE BELL KILLING "SUB-INVESTIGATION" HOAX AS HIS OWN "INVESTIGATION"

PARTNERING WITH W.C. JAMESON

Steve Sederwall recycled his Deputy James Bell killing "Probable Cause Statement" sub-investigation for W.C. Jameson's 2018 *Cold Case Billy the Kid: Investigating History's Mysteries*. But Sederwall now hoaxed it as his own private "investigation," and hid the "Billy the Kid Case." Sederwall fabricated his fellow "Billy the Kid Case" hoaxers as his assistants; with Dr. Henry Lee working for *him*.

In 2010, he had also forged Dr. Lee Reports to remove Case 2003-274 and his own Lincoln County Deputy title, to try the same trick on the District Court judge in my open records litigation against him and his fellow "Billy the Kid Case' lawmen.

But oblivious Jameson merely gushed: "Steve Sederwall revealed elements of this gripping event that had long escaped the notice of earlier researchers and writers;" (Page 95); though, in fact, there are different versions of that escape, with none certain. Jameson gives a "Garrett version" from *The Authentic Life of Billy the Kid* with a gun left in the outhouse, Billy getting ahead of Bell on the steps, and Billy shooting down the stairway to kill Bell. (Page 97).

HOAXING: Since Garrett was away collecting taxes, he was not a witness; so he only quoted witnesses. The favored version is of Gottfried Gauss leaving the gun in the outhouse; Billy, on returning to the jail, getting first to the second floor hall ahead of his guard, James Bell; then wanting to tie him. But Bell bolted down the stairs, was fatally shot by Billy, stumbled to the bottom landing, and was taken outside by Gauss to be concealed.

Jameson segues to Sederwall by fabricating that Garrett never did an "investigation" into the killings of Deputy guards, James Bell and Robert Olinger. So Sederwall would now apply "modern crime-solving and investigative techniques." (Page 101)

RECYCLING FAKE FLOORBOARD FORENSICS

Duped Jameson devoted two chapters to narrating Sederwall's hoaxed "investigation": "Lincoln County Courthouse Crime Scene Investigation" (Pages 102-111), and "An Escape Plot." (Pages 112-119). Jameson wrote; "Sederwall's cop instinct kicked into gear after studying Garrett's account of the escape." (Page 102).

So Sederwall secretly recycled his Case 2003-274's "Probable Cause Statement," and his forged Dr. Henry Lee "Floorboard Reports," as cited by unaware Jameson in his "Bibliography."

Repeated was Sederwall's usual fake reasoning by "what-ifs": What if Pat Garrett killed the innocent victim? What if he helped Billy escape jail by giving him the gun? That means they were friends. That means Pat would kill for Billy. That means Pat *did kill* for Billy and is a murderer. (It should be noted that "Brushy Bill" never claimed this plot when impersonating Billy.)

Here again is Sederwall's "Probable Cause Statement's" presentation of its Deputy Bell killing sub-investigation:

> No one in 122 years has been able to speak with clear certainty where the gun came from that William Bonney used to kill Deputy J.W. Bell. With the information investigators have seen they question Garrett's involvement in the Kid obtaining a weapon.
>
> It would go to reason that if the body in Fort Sumner is anyone other than William Bonney then Garrett no doubt had a hand in allowing the Kid to escape on July 14, 1881.
>
> If the body at Fort Sumner is anyone other than William Bonney, then Garrett, whether by accident or design, is responsible for homicide of the person resting in that grave.
>
> If it is not Bonney in the grave at Fort Sumner it would also go to reason that Garrett would be looked at as a suspect in furthering the escape of the Kid on April 28, 1881 when the two Lincoln County Sheriffs were murdered.
>
> Although the [sub] investigation will deal with what happened in the Lincoln County court house on April 28, 1881, this

writing [Probable Cause Statement] will deal with the alleged shooting of William Bonney at Fort Sumner on the night of July 14, 1881 [as the murder case].

So Sederwall, faking the "investigation" as solely his, rolled out its full forensic hoaxing for fake "suspicions," while keeping secret its silly top-of-the-stairs direction; as follows:

1) It was "suspicious" that Garrett described the scene, since he was away at White Oaks collecting taxes. **[But Garrett made clear he was recounting the escape from eye-witnesses.]**

2) It was "suspicious" that Garrett said the armory door could be opened by a "firm push." **[Concealed is that in *The Authentic Life of Billy the Kid* Garrett was just saying that "Lincoln did not then have a jail that would hold a cripple." Prisoners were merely housed on the second floor of the courthouse, and chained to steel rings in the floor. That is why Garrett took extra precaution with Billy by keeping him alone, with wrist and ankle shackles, and two 24 hour deputy guards (Bell and Olinger).]**

3) It was "suspicious that Garrett blamed Bell and Olinger. **[Why not? They were the responsible guards.]**

With himself as sole investigator, Sederwall then presented himself as the hero to "remedy the situation" of Garrett's "lying." On August 4, 2002, he leads New Mexico lawmen and forensic expert Dr Henry Lee (presented in a photo wearing a cowboy hat along with Sederwall wearing a badge) to examine the area claimed for the Bell killing. (Page 104) Admitted is that the stairway was replaced. [Omitted is that the shooting of Bell had occurred on it - so there was no longer an evidence source!] Stating that the original floorboards on the second floor were then exposed for Lee, Sederwall has him perform his "presumptive blood tests" with o-Tolidine, called a test for blood (omitting it was for any iron-containing compound, like rust). Sederwall portrays Lee as swabbing the flooorboards, and **quotes him as saying: "Positive for blood."** (Page 105) Sederwall added: **"The tests showed positive reactions for blood in several areas on the landing ... Lee's conclusion was that 'chemical tests for the presence of blood were positive with some of [the floorboard] stains."** (Page 105)

LYING: Dr. Lee's quote and conclusion are made-up by Sederwall, proving why, in his forged Lee reports, he removed Lee's "Results and Conclusions."

Lee, though a hoaxer himself, had approximated truth. So in his real report of February 25, 2005, he called the stains "blood-like" and "could be bloodstains." Lee concluded: "Various stains were observed on the surface and underside of the floor boards. Chemical tests for the presence of blood were positive for some of those stains. These results indicate the presence of Heme or Peroxidase like activity with those stains tested positive, <u>which suggests that those stains could be bloodstains</u>. Further DNA testing could reveal the nature and identity of those blood-like stains."

Most important, is that Sederwall, and likely Lee, knew that there existed no DNA of Bell to compare the "blood" to, since his gravesite is unknown and there are no kin. There was no way to prove blood, if found, was Bell's. And omitted is that Lee's Lab, Orchid Cellmark, did not test for blood anyway. And, by Jameson's 2018 book, Sederwall knew and concealed that no valid DNA came from Lee's floorboard specimens at Orchid Cellmark.

JAMESON AS INADVERTENTLY COMPLICIT: Dupe Jameson cited Sederwall's forged Dr. Lee report in his Bibliography under "Reports," with yet another faked title and faked date as "Forensic Examination Report (Lincoln County Courthouse), May 22, 2004." Lee's actual and sole report was dated February 25, 2005 and titled "Forensic Research & Training Center Forensic Examination Report;" and combined all his investigations as: "Item #1 Workbench;" "Item #2 Washstand;" "Item #3 A piece of Headboard;" Item #4 "Examination of Lincoln County Court House;" and "Results and Conclusion." <u>The "May 22, 2004" was the "Date of Request" lifted from Lee's report</u>.

Out-of-control Sederwall next lied that blood had been confirmed, claimed Bell's was the only bloodshed in the courthouse's history, made-up a "significant amount," and concluded the "blood" must be Bell's. (Pages 105-106; 110) He then made-up that Garrett must have lied because he did not mention so much blood on the second floor. (Page 106)

Sederwall then quoted witness Gauss about hearing a "tussle upstairs, somebody hurrying down the stairs," and Bell coming out the door to him. This is the conventional scene in which Bell struggled with Billy, ran down the back stairs, was shot on the way down, got to the back door at the base of the landing, and was taken outside by Gauss as he died. Sederwall stated that this meant Bell was "upstairs," because he ran downstairs. (Page 106)

HOAXING: Running down the stairway, has nothing to do with proving bleeding on its top.

Sederwall then misrepresented a quote of Sophie Poe, from her 1936 book titled *Buckboard Days*, about when she lived in the courthouse. As the wife of John William Poe, who replaced Pat Garrett as Lincoln County Sheriff, she commented on blood on its stairway - while forgetting that Bell was heading down, not up, when shot. She stated: "The back stairway ... which I had to travel many times during the day, was still stained with blood, a grim reminder of the day ... when Billy the Kid had shot and killed his guard, James W. Bell. Bell had been climbing those stairs and his body had fallen to the bottom of them." (Sophie Poe, Page 205) The place she referenced is preserved for tourists, as where the bullet passed sideways through turning Bell, hitting the wall half-way down the stairway, to the right of descent.

But Sederwall lied that she referenced **blood on the second floor**. (Page 106) Then he quibbled about her saying that Bell had fallen "to the bottom of the stairs." She obviously meant that was were he collapsed. But Sederwall claimed she saw blood from the top to the bottom of the stairs. Then he claimed Garrett lied by not describing that too.

HOAXING: Sederwall is faking scenarios from made-up evidence. Bell was shot in the middle of the stairway while heading down; dying soon after he made it to the bottom.

Sederwall faked "discrepancies" in Garrett's account; questioning Billy slipping handcuffs, and ruminating about how to wipe yourself in the latrine if your hands were cuffed behind your back (which was never claimed for Billy). (Pages 107-108)

FAKE ANALYSIS: Sederwall omitted that Garrett might not have been given the true manner of escape, especially if Billy had an accomplice, like Gottfried Gauss, supplying the information, and obviously concealing a plot. So any discrepancies that Garrett got second-hand would not implicate him of willful misinformation. And none of this indicated that Billy was not killed in Fort Sumner.

Sederwall then gave the gun-left-in-the-outhouse version, and ruminated about why Billy did not shoot Bell then. And he gave the known scenario that Billy wanted to take Bell prisoner, not kill him. But he added Bob Olinger to that plan. And he made-up scenes of Billy's confronting Bell with the gun, and wounding Bell's head, usually seen as Billy's attempt to subdue him to enable tying-up. But Sederwall now faked Bell's head's blood as on the floorboards in Dr. Lee's fake forensics. (Pages 108-110)

By then, Sederwall's had blood pouring out. And he lied that Lee had said "Bell lost a great deal of blood." (Page 110)

THEN CAME THE WHOLE POINT OF JAMESON'S BOOK: THE FUSING OF THE "BRUSHY" AND "BILLY THE KID CASE" HOAXES INTO A MEGAHOAX: SEDERWALL QUOTED "BRUSHY" HIMSELF FOR AN ESCAPE SCENARIO TO GO WITH FOR HIS FAKE FORENSICS! In the quote, Sederwall had "Brushy" ask to go to the latrine. While Bell goes to get the key, he slips out of his handcuff, hits and stuns returned Bell on the head, grabs his gun and key, and wants to be taken to the armory. On the way there, Bell runs for the stairway, pauses at the hall on top of the stairs so "copious amounts of blood" can fall. Then Billy's fatal bullet ricochets on the wall. So Sederwall says this explains the "blood" he and "his investigative team" found "a century and a quarter later."(Page 111)

HOAXING "BRUSHY'S HOAX: This, at last, unites two liars: "Brushy" impersonating Billy; and Sederwall impersonating a valid investigator using "Brushy" for "evidence" that Bell-head-wound-blood was on the upstairs hallway.

But Sederwall was hoaxing "Brushy's" tale. In fact, "Brushy" was lying by combining two different escape tales. "Brushy" said: "Sam Corbett [actually Tunstall's past shopkeeper] and his wife came in to see me. Sam had hid a six-shooter in the latrine. But I didn't need Sam's six-shooter. ["Brushy" had Olinger leave, and himself alone with Bell in the east room where Billy was kept. Bell goes to Garrett's office to the west of it get the key. "Brushy" slips his shackle, and when Bell returns, he states] I hit him in the back of the head. He tumbled over on the floor ... [NOTE: "Brushy" said he hit Bell in the east room used for the incarceration, not the hallway scenario Sederwall made-up as by him.] I told him to walk through [Garrett's] office and unlock the armory door." (*Alias Billy the Kid*, Pages 43-44) Then "Brushy" has Bell's flight down the stairs, and the shot hitting the wall, as "Brushy" would have seen himself when taken on a Lincoln tour by his prompting backer, William V. Morrison.

And, a key discrepancy to note is that "Brushy" never claimed that Pat Garrett played a part in his escape as Billy the Kid. This was unique to the "Billy the Kid Case" hoax, and Sederwall's later recycling of it.

RECYCLING GARRETT AS BILLY THE KID'S ESCAPE MURDER ACCOMPLICE

By the next chapter in *Cold Case Billy the Kid*, "An Escape Plot," building on his fake courthouse forensics, and based on no real evidence at all, Sederwall accused Garrett of "perfidy;" to sneer: "[H]e may have been more involved in the Kid's escape than we have been led to believe." (Page 112)

A BAD FIT OF HOAXES: Since the "Brushy" hoax is a bad fit for the "Billy the Kid Case" hoax, contradictions like this arise: "Brushy" did not claim Garrett helped his escape, or that Garrett killed Billy Barlow to save him. But the "Billy the Kid Case" hoax, and now Sederwall, was using the Bell killing to fake Garrett's friendship for Billy, for a future murder motive for Garrett.

Adding to the basic "Billy the Kid Case" hoax, Sederwall, continued to attempt Garrett's character assassination by faking history-not-as-written. He faked "discrepancies" about Garrett's report of Billy's escape, with his usual "what ifs": What if Garrett had been away collecting taxes on purpose? (Pages 113-114)

HOAXING: Tax collecting was required. When new Sheriff John Copeland neglected filing his tax collecting bond in his first month, on May 28, 1878, Governor S.B. Axtell issued a Proclamation removing him as Sheriff.

Sederwall provided Garrett's report about the escape horse being Billy Burt's, Billy's promise to return it, and an "Andrew Nimley" [sic] retrieving it; and concluded Garrett lied because he gave too much information! (Page 116)

He then tried a history-not-as-written trick to claim the escape horse was Garrett's. He cited old-timer windbag malarkey of a Gorgonio Wilson, a self-proclaimed eye-witness, who stated in an August 7, 1955 (!) *El Paso Times* article, when 89, that Billy called him from a window to saddle *Garrett's horse* for him. And the daughter of a non-historical Robert Corn said her father said Billy used *Pat's horse*. And in 1977, an Ygenio Salazar relative claimed *Garrett's horse*. (Page 116-117) So Sederwall concluded that sharing his horse meant Garrett and Billy were friends.

FAKE EVIDENCE: First of all, the Tularosa Ditch War prisoner was Alexander Nunnelly, not "Andrew Nimley;" and he did not retrieve Billy's escape pony.

As to the escape horse, Sederwall used meaningless hearsay. And it involved hiding that Lincoln's gathered residents eye-witnessed Billy's escape. And no legitimate witness reported Garrett's horse used for it. But, if his horse had been stolen for it, Garrett would have reported it himself. Also, he would have ridden his horse to White Oaks for his tax collecting, so it would not have been there.

Furthermore, Garrett's wanting to give a detailed account about the embarrassing fact of the escape of his most important prisoner means just that. Sederwall is merely blowing smoke by calling it too much information.

And a crucial real discrepancy is to be noted: Sederwall had destroyed "Brushy" as Billy! "Brushy" had no tale of escaping on Garrett's horse.

Next, Sederwall presented known scenarios of Gauss's involvement in the escape, and of the Kid's going to the outhouse to get the gun; but rejected them as "lies." (Pages 117-118)

FAKE ANALYSIS: Since Sederwall is faking evidence to fabricate Garrett an accomplice in the escape (and ultimately a murderer of the innocent victim), he has to discount the likely and accepted truth that *Gauss* was actually Billy's accomplice. He gives no evidence that the Gauss-gun-in-outhouse scenario is "lies."

And he omits the likely motives for Gauss's willingness to risk his life by hanging as a murder accomplice of Billy's deputy killings. In fact, Gauss, was bitterly anti-Ring. He had first been employed in running the brewery for "The House" in its sutler store beginnings, and had been cheated out of his wages. As anti-Ring, John Tunstall's, cook, he would have met Billy by October of 1877, and had been present at every subsequent Ring atrocity. He was the only one left at Tunstall's Feliz River ranch when Brady's murderous posse came looking for Tunstall, then murdered him. He knew about the illegal Proclamation of Governor S.B. Axtell outlawing the Regulators, and might even have been in Tunstall's store at the Regulator's Brady ambush. And he would have known the horror of the murder of Alexander McSween, whom he knew, in the Lincoln County War Battle. He would have believed Billy's hanging sentence was unjust, especially since all the Ring murderers had been shielded from penalties. And he was now caretaker of the courthouse, in an ideal position to intervene. Furthermore, he was above suspicion, because Pat Garrett was a late entry to Lincoln County, and would have been unaware of his partisanship. And it is obvious that Gauss and Billy would have used the outhouse plan when Garrett was out of town - as Garrett would have represented their greatest risk to success.

Adding to his fakery of Garrett as Billy's accomplice, Sederwall relied on his usual meaningless "what ifs;" now so bizarre they knock your sox off: What if Garrett made up that Billy was a bad outlaw to build himself up as a hero by contrast? What if Garrett blamed his deputies for incompetence to spare himself? What if, on purpose, he did not seal off the town to further investigate the deputy killings? (Pages 118-119)

The Jameson-Sederwall duo conclude: "The evidence clearly shows that Garrett lied. The evidence is highly suggestive of [his] possible role in the escape plot."

HOAXING: All this fakery was irrelevant to Garrett not killing Billy, or "Brushy" being Billy. But one can guess that for gullible W.C. Jameson, this courthouse forensics blather and lying looked like real science and real "cop" investigations adding useful evidence. And saying bad things about Garrett was a legacy of the "Brushy" hoax in *Alias Billy the Kid*. So, to fuzzy-headed Jameson, this may all have seemed helpful to his cause. Instead, possibly unbeknownst to himself, as sole author, Jameson was now perpetrating a massive hoax by his inability to vet his own sources.

HOAXING CARPENTER'S BENCH "BLOOD DNA OF BILLY THE KID"

IN THE "BILLY THE KID CASE" HOAX

The carpenter's bench first appeared in Steve Sederwall's "Probable Cause Statement" for Case 2003-274, promoting himself as its Deputy Sheriff. He had written: "On August 29, 2003, Deputy Sederwall of the Lincoln County Sheriff''s Department located the carpenter bench where the Kid's body was placed on July 14, 1881."

And after I blocked the exhumations of Billy and his mother, Sederwall helped create Version II of the hoax, which featured the bench as the source of "blood-DNA-of-Billy-the-Kid." He also appears to have created its bizarre fabrication that Garrett shot Billy non-fatally in an escape plot, and Billy played dead on the bench for the night vigil, while leaving his blood on the bench (for future DNA). This is evidenced by Sederwall's making the false claim that "dead men don't bleed," to reporter, Julie Carter, for her October 6, 2005 *RuidosoNews.com's* "Follow the Blood: In the Billy the Kid Case, Miller Exhumed," as proof of this scenario. She quoted him: "Whoever was laid on that, whether it was Billy the Kid or not," said Sederwall, "he left his DNA." The investigators said the amount of blood found on the bench indicated that whoever was on that bench must have been still alive. **"Dead men don't bleed," explained Sederwall. "and we witnessed a large amount of blood."** The hoaxers were put back in business with a new hoax and exhumation hopes thanks to creatively faking Sederwall.

THE INVALID CARPENTER'S BENCH

The carpenter's bench was not forensically valid, since its being the real one is unprovable. The hoaxers had found it in the Albuquerque converted chicken coop of a Mannie Miller, son of Stella Abreu Miller, who had it in her 1926-1936 Fort Sumner Billy the Kid Museum, with supposed Peter Maxwell bedroom furniture. (See page 168 above) But it had no provenance from 1881 to 1926; during which was Fort Sumner's sale in 1884, and massive flooding. Furthermore, historian, Richard Weddle, informed me that he had interviewed Stella in Albuquerque in her old age, and she had stated that she had gotten the bench from a local man in 1926 just for her museum display.

Stella showed it to early historian, Robert Mullin; and another historian, Maurice Garland Fulton, photographed it. That is how it became *the* carpenter's bench of the death scene - without being a Maxwell family possession or the real bench.

But fellow "Billy the Kid Case" hoaxer Paul Hutton "authenticated" it. And, in 2007, for his Albuquerque Museum of Art and History Billy the Kid show, with curator, Deb Slaney, Hutton labeled it as having "human blood."

Hoaxer, U.S. Marshals Service Historian David Turk, also gave its fake authentication. On August 8, 2006, I made an open records request on how Turk could "authenticate" it. On August 31, 2006, a Nikki Cedric at his Public Affairs office answered: "Mr. Turk ... has seen the said workbench; *however, he did not state that any particular person was on the bench. This is for the lab to determine.* The bench does match descriptions given in other sources and he believes it to be the one described."

So on April 19, 2006, hoax-backing reporter, Julie Carter, in *RuidosoNews.com*, reported in "Digging up Bones": "UNM History professor Paul Hutton and U.S. Treasury [sic - Marshals Service] historian Dave Turk have both authenticated the bench."

HOAXING BENCH BLOOD

But claiming "blood" - not necessarily *real* blood - was the hoaxers' only bench concern. So Sederwall faked it for the press.

On August 14, 2004, for the *Lincoln County News,* reporter Doris Cherry's "Forensics 101 for 'Billy," quoted Sederwall: "The bench has been in the Maxwell family descendents since 1881 and has been stored out of weather, protecting the blood evidence ... Only once was the blood exposed to the elements, when a family member who took the bench without family approval returned it to the Maxwell family home in Fort Sumner and left it outside to get rained on once. So the odds of finding blood evidence were very good."

ADDING DR. HENRY LEE FOR MORE FAKING

As stated above, when a Lincoln County Deputy, Steve Sederwall had contacted Dr. Henry Lee, through fellow hoaxer, and the case's official historian, Paul Hutton, to do "Billy the Kid Case" forensics. (See page 174 above)

By the time Dr. Henry Lee arrived on the scene, it was indisputable that no valid DNA existed for the Billy the Kid Case."

Without "reference DNA," carpenter's bench "blood" would be like a random fingerprint, with no actual fingerprints existing of the individual in question to compare with it.

But legitimate DNA forensics were not Dr. Henry Lee's worry. His worry was *DNA film footage for Bill Kurtis Productions*. Anything that could be claimed as linked to Billy the Kid sufficed. The bench was just fine for Dr. Lee. And when Lee looked at the bench, unsurprisingly, he found "blood."

Rene Romo's August 2, 2004, *Albuquerque Journal's* "Forensic Expert on Billy's Case" gave this new hoaxed finding: "Lee, assisted by Calvin Ostler ... performed tests on the bench that Sederwall believes to be the one on which the Kid's body was laid out after Garrett gunned him down. Preliminary results indicated **trace evidence of blood**, but, without further testing, it is not certain whether the blood was human, Lee said."

In fact, it was not even certain that it was blood! Since I too had seen the bench; it just looked like a few rust-colored discolorations - like expected on a carpenter's bench.

By August 12th, reporter Doris Cherry, for her *Lincoln County News*, "Forensics 101 for 'Billy,' " wrote: "Dr. Lee proved the good odds by utilizing a laser to bore into the wood of the bench to take samples and he took scrapings from the top and underneath of the bench. '**Then he swabbed it with the chemical that changes color to indicate the presence of blood,'** Sullivan said."

The hoaxers were just hoaxing. Lee, as he stated in his report, had merely tested with Luminol, a non-specific chemical that fluoresces with iron-containing substances. Besides blood, it lights up for rust, paints, and cleaning agents - all more likely on a carpenter's bench than blood. **And no other testing would *ever* be done by that hoaxing group to verify blood - or to connect it to Billy Bonney (which was impossible).**

Next, hoaxing Sullivan and Sederwall got carried away. Romo's original **"trace,"** in his August 2, 2004, "Forensic Expert on Billy's Case," started bleeding like stigmata. In Doris Cherry's "Forensics 101 for Billy," **Sullivan stated that Lee "found a lot of blood."** For Julie Carter's "Follow the Blood," **Sederwall said: "We witnessed a large amount of blood;" and he creatively lied that it proved "an upper chest wound."** By April 13, 2006, "blood" was almost dripping off the bench. Leo Banks of the *Tucson Weekly*, in "The New Billy the Kid," reported that **Sederwall said the bench was "saturated!"**

Obviously the hoaxers hid Lee's actual report. It took me five years of open records litigation against the lawmen to get it on

January 31, 2012. At 25 pages, it was dated February 25, 2005, and titled "Forensic Research & Training Center Forensic Examination Report." Its header listed "Requested by: Lincoln County Sheriff's Office, New Mexico; Investigation History Program, Kurtis Production." "Local Case No." was "2003-274." The "Report To:" was Steve Sederwall, Lincoln County Sheriff's Office, New Mexico." Recorded for the "forensic investigation team" were: "Calvin Ostler, Forensic Consultant, Riverton, Utah;" "Tom Sullivan, Sheriff, Lincoln County, New Mexico;" "Steve Sederwall, Deputy Sheriff, Lincoln County;" and "David Turk, US Marshall [sic], United States Marshall [sic] Service." The carpenter's bench was reported under "Item # 1 Workbench." Lee concluded:

> After a detail examination of the evidence and review of all the results of field testing, the following conclusion was reached.
> 1. Brownish dark stains were observed on different areas of the workbench. These areas were subjected to chemical presumptive blood tests. Some of those samples give a positive reaction. These results indicate the presence of Heme or Peroxidase like activity with those stains testing positive, **which suggest that those stains could be bloodstains**. Further DNA testing could reveal the nature and identity of these blood-like stains.

Lee had proved himself a true "Billy the Kid Case" hoaxer by omitting more likely rust. And his lab, Orchid Cellmark, did not test for blood. And finding DNA would not even connect it to those stains, since no controls were done for DNA from non-stained areas. Nor were controls taken from all people present at his testing to check for *their* contaminating DNA (think sneeze!). Lastly, Lee was lying that "[f]urther DNA testing could reveal the nature and identity of these blood-like stains." He was hiding the lack of "reference DNA of Billy the Kid."

"BLOOD OF BILLY THE KID" GETS A DNA LAB

Next, Dr. Henry Lee had to turn his fake "blood of Billy the Kid" into fake "DNA of Billy the Kid." So he sent his bench swabbing and scraping specimens to Orchid Cellmark Lab.

Reporter, Doris Cherry, in her August 12, 2004, "Forensics 101 for 'Billy' " stated: "Each swab and all scrapings from the bench were sealed in preparation to shipping to the Orchard Selmark [sic - Orchid Cellmark] Lab in Dallas. Sullivan said Dr. Lee uses the lab for most of his work, and the lab is also famous for its forensic work to determine DNA of the 9-11 victims."

Kept secret was that Orchid Cellmark does not test for blood; that objects in a human environment pick up human DNA; that no controls were done; and no "reference DNA" existed. Soon, the nervous hoaxers called their lab's name "secret."

In fact, Orchid Cellmark had "secrets." On August 9, 2004, I had contacted its then director, Mark Stolorow, explaining the "Billy the Kid Case" hoax. He was amused. On August 18th, we spoke again. Stolorow was defensive. Orchid Cellmark, he told me, was under a "gag order" on the case. Dr. Lee was now in charge!

Three months later, Orchid Cellmark was caught faking DNA computer data on another case. That scandal appeared on November 18, 2004, in "TalkLeft.com," as "Fraud alleged at Cellmark, DNA Testing Firm." It stated: "This is shocking to the forensic community which has always believed that raw data cannot be electronically manipulated." It concluded: "Bottom line: A lot of defendants will be seeking retesting by an independent lab when the prosecution is relying on results by Cellmark." That scandal reduced Orchid Cellmark to one lab in Farmers Branch, Texas.

Mark Stolorow was replaced as Orchid Cellmark's director by Dr. Rick Staub. Unlike Stolorow, he seemed indifferent to scandal, or that his lab found no DNA at all in Henry Lee's bench specimens! **[APPENDIX: 2] But that did not stop the hoaxers from claiming they had the DNA of Billy the Kid for identity matching, and doing exhumations based on it!** And Dr. Lee, in charge of the forensics, never objected. And Dr. Rick Staub was right there in Arizona with his bone bags, along the backhoe, to take dismembered body-parts back across state lines to Texas. After all, Bill Kurtis Productions was filming another TV program; and he would be featured, along with famous Dr. Lee!

NO BENCH DNA ANYWAY

Ultimately, by my open records litigation and subpoena of Lee's Orchid Cellmark Lab, on April 20, 2012, I got the 133 pages of Lee's DNA records, which the hoaxers had desperately tried to hide. October 15, 2004's "Laboratory Report, Forensic Identity, Mitochondrial Analysis, Results and Conclusions" for Orchid Cellmark's in-house Case 4444-001B-004B (done for Case 2003-274) for the carpenter's bench **SHOWED LEE'S BENCH**

SPECIMENS HAD NO DNA! THE HOAXER'S CLAIM TO HAVE BENCH-BLOOD-DNA OF BILLY THE KID FOR DNA MATCHINGS WAS A LIE! [APPENDIX: 2] It stated that Lee's bench specimens "**failed to yield amplifiable DNA.**" The "**Conclusions**" recorded: "**no mitochondrial [DNA] sequence data were generated.**"

And the hoaxers knew that by October 15, 2004. There was no justification to dig up anyone at all in their "investigation" for "identity matching with Billy the Kid!"

Nevertheless, during my open records litigation, Steve Sederwall forged a Dr. Lee report on the carpenter's bench to hide the case as for the Lincoln County Sheriff's Department, to hide his own lawman status, and to hide Lee's devastating results.

HOAXING CARPENTER'S BENCH "BLOOD DNA" RESULTS FOR MY OPEN RECORDS ACT LITIGATION

Just how close the history of Pat Garrett and Billy the Kid came to complete annihilation by the "Billy the Kid Case" hoax was demonstrated by Steve Sederwall's hoaxing of carpenter's bench results for my open records case against him and his fellow lawmen hoaxers of Lincoln County Sheriff's Department Case 2003-274. Had my litigation not exposed their actual DNA records before they made their fake claims international news, it would have been impossible to repair the damage.

For his hoaxing in my litigation, Sederwall made-up that, as a hobbyist, he was in contact with Orchid Cellmark's Director, Dr. Rick Staub, about Lee's bench specimens, so knew the results. And in his deposition in 2008, and his courtroom testimony in 2011, he presented the lies that could have been used by hoax head, Governor Bill Richardson, to fabricate Pat Garrett as a murderer and to give "Brushy Bill" the Billy the Kid pardon.

HOAXING FINDING BENCH BLOOD

After my blocking of the exhumations of Billy Bonney and his mother, the hoaxers had been left with the desperate claim of "bench-blood-of-Billy-the-Kid" as their sole source for faking DNA. So in his deposition of August 18, 2008, Sederwall testified, under oath to my attorney, that Orchid Cellmark Director Rick Staub had confirmed to him that blood was found from Dr. Henry Lee's bench specimens. Sederwall stated:

> Q. Do you know if [Orchid Cellmark] tested for blood?
> A. They did.
> **Q. Did they find blood?**
> **A. They did.**

Left out was that Orchid Cellmark does not test for blood. And, when its records were subpoenaed in April of 2012, they obviously showed no "testing" for blood or claim of blood.

HOAXING A MIXED DNA SPECIMEN

Sticking to the script of Version II of the "Billy the Kid Case" hoax - with shot Billy "playing-dead" on the bench and replaced by Garrett's murdered innocent victim - Sederwall built a hoax around Orchid Cellmark's reporting a "mixed DNA" result as from two or more sources. Though that result had only come from Lee's courthouse floorboards' specimen and for random man, William Hudspeth's, jawbone, Sederwall pretended it was found for the carpenter's bench. And Sederwall made up the claim that the lab had found the DNA of just two individuals mixed together.

So he lied in an Evidentiary Hearing in my open records litigation: "[Staub] told me it was blended, that there was two DNA ... Before they could do anything with it, they would separate it. [Staub] said, 'We are talking about probably **$50,000 [so they could not afford the separating]**." (Transcript 1/21/11, p. 172)

In truth, when I got the subpoenaed Orchid Cellmark records on April 22, 2012, they proved that the work was for Case 2003-274, not Sederwall personally; and that there had been **no DNA at all from Lee's bench specimens. [APPENDIX: 2]**

Furthermore, as mentioned, forensic expert, San Francisco's Lexigen President, Dr. Simon Ford, stated that mixed specimens commonly occur in forensic samples, and that notation means only that DNA was mingled from *two or more* individuals - not *just* two. And "**most labs charge about $1,000 for testing ...** Some labs have a surcharge of between $300 and $500 for "difficult" samples, such as bone or tissue. The interpretation (matching and statistical calculation) is usually included in the cost of the testing."

Of course, the bench specimens had no DNA at all.

RECYCLING THE BENCH BLOOD DNA HOAX AS HIS PRIVATE INVESTIGATION

Fourteen years after he knew the bench had neither blood nor DNA, Steve Sederwall recycled Case 2003-274's bench blood hoax for W.C. Jameson's narration in his 2018 *Cold Case Billy the Kid*. Sederwall further hoaxed the case as his own "investigation," and hid his forged Dr. Henry Lee report about it. He called Fort Sumner an active crime scene (Page 154), echoing the fake title of Jameson's book as a "cold case" involving Billy the id.

HOAXING: Fort Sumner was not a crime scene after the Coroner's Jury's July 15, 1881 decision: *"[O]ur verdict is that the deed of said Garrett was justifiable homicide."*

HOAXING BENCH FORENSICS

Sederwall, as sole "investigator," of the pretend crime scene, recycled the "Billy the Kid Case's" carpenter's bench hoax, with added hoaxing. He called the bench an **important source of "bloodstains from the slain intruder"** (Page 155) - his new name for the innocent victim - **as a source of DNA**.

Research is claimed on the Maxwell family (Pages 155-159) - though the bench had not been in their possession. Other furniture from Stella Abreu's Museum is included, and traced to Peter Maxwell's sister Odelia, who married Manuel Abreu (and had Stella). Hilariously inserted is another Sederwall hoax, discussed later of an old-timer named Bundy Avant meeting "Pete Maxwell" in the San Andres mountains. (See pages 304-306 below) Avant's fabricated "Pete" was a chuck wagon cook. So Sederwall made up that Peter Maxwell gave away his furniture after being reduced to "cooking for 'wagon outfits!' " Sederwall gives his tracing of the bench to the Albuquerque home of Stella Abreu Maxwell's son, Mannie Miller. (Pages 158-160) [Oddly, a photo of the bench, labeled as in the "Steve Sederwall Collection" (Page 160) does not match the Mullin Collection photo, or the bench I saw in 2010 with Kenny Miller at deceased Mannie's chicken coop. The Sederwall one is falling apart, with one of its top boards cracked. It may have been repaired, with possible board replacement, which would then match the one later photographed by Dr. Lee - adding to its invalidity for forensics.]

As to Dr. Henry Lee, Sederwall claims that "**a number of locations**" **on the bench's top and bottom tested positive for blood** by "presumptive blood test reagents phenolphthalein and o-toloidine." **He states that this "blood" was from "two different human beings,"** and its future separation could identify the "**slain intruder.**" (Page 163) A Lee report is not cited, but one is in the Bibliography as: "Lee, Dr. Henry. Forensic Examination Report (Examination of Furniture From Pete Maxwell's of July 15, 1881) 22 May 2004." (Page 187)

HOAXING: Sederwall is lying. No blood was identified. Dr. Lee's sole report of February 25, 2005 merely hoaxed "blood-like" stains; and Orchid Cellmark Lab <u>got no blood or DNA from the bench.</u> [APPENDIX: 2] <u>The meaningless mixed sample was from the courthouse floorboards</u>.

The cited Lee report seems to be one of Sederwall's forgeries, newly dated May 22, 2004 from Lee's "Date of Request." The one he used to trick the District Court judge was "Forensic Research and Training Center Forensic Examination Report: "Examination of furniture from Pete Maxwell's of July 15, 1881," dated February 25, 2005.

Sederwall's "**bloodstains from the slain intruder**" were his fiction, repeating the "Billy the Kid Case" hoax's lie about the bench having "mixed DNA" of two people bleeding on the bench to fake playing-dead-Billy first, then switched shot innocent victim (possibly Billy Barlow).

IRRELEVANT: Not only did this fakery give no proof that Garrett did not kill Billy, it contradicted "Brushy's" death scene with shot-Billy-bleeding-on-the-bench-for-DNA.

HOAXING A CRIME SCENE FOR THE "BILLY THE KID CASE"

LEE ATTACKS GARRETT WITH FURNITURE

Dr. Henry Lee knew the "Billy the Kid Case's bad guy was Pat Garrett as a liar and murderer. So he attacked Garrett with fake "forensics." But having no crime scene to investigate - with the Maxwell house torn down in about 1887 - had left the hoaxers with just Stella Abreu's Museum furniture.

Steve Sederwall's "Probable Cause Statement" had introduced a "washstand" from Stella's collection to fabricate that Garrett had lied that his second shot hit Maxwell's headboard. In his 1933 *The Death of Billy the Kid*, Deputy John William Poe had reported that: "[A] shot was fired in the room, followed immediately by what everyone within hearing distance thought were two other shots. However, there were only two shots fired, the third report, as we learned afterward, being caused by the rebound of the second bullet, which had struck the adobe wall and **rebounded against the headboard of a wooden bedstead**."

But Sederwall made-up that it was the washstand that Garrett hit. So, by his fake "what-if" reasoning, Sederwall had claimed that *if* Garrett lied about hitting the washstand, then he had lied about the corpse's identity!

To back the washstand in the "Probable Cause Statement," Sederwall had faked a Deluvina Maxwell quote: *"There was a washstand with a marble top in Pete Maxwell's bedroom, which Garrett had seen in the moonlight and shot at, thinking it was Bonney trying to get up."* [**The quote was actually from Lucien Maxwell's "grandchildren," from an uncited source. (See page 168 above) And hidden is real Deluvina Maxwell's confirming the victim as Billy on June 24, 1927 to historian J. Evetts Haley: "I came here about [1869] and was here when Billy the Kid was killed ... I did not see Billy the night after he was killed, but I saw him the following morning."**]

But all that was important was that the washstand was all the hoaxers had to give to Lee to fake a "crime scene." So the "Probable Cause Statement" said: "On September 13, 2003, investigators located all the furniture that was in Pete Maxwell's bedroom the night of the shooting, July 1881. **In the items investigators located on September 13, 2003 was that wash stand."**

LEE AND A WASHSTAND

This "washstand" was a box, the size of a toy! [FIGURE: 2] Its measurements by Dr. Lee were: 28¾" x 16", x 30" high. It had bullet holes, but no bullet. So, with Lee on board, and willing to claim anything needed, they recycled their washstand-headboard scam as his "investigation" to incriminate Garrett as a liar.

Lee fabricated a crime scene based on the toy's tiny height. Hoax-helping reporter, Rene Romo, presented it in his August 2, 2004 *Albuquerque Journal*'s "Forensic Expert on Billy's Case":

Lee and the investigators [Sullivan, Sederwall, and Calvin Ostler] also examined a washstand that was purportedly struck by a bullet when Garrett shot the Kid in a bedroom of the outlaw's friend, Pete Maxwell, in Fort Sumner ... Lee and the investigators used laser technology Saturday to determine the trajectory of the bullet as it entered the left side of the washstand and exited the right at a downward angle. Given the washstand's likely location in the room, the investigation has already cast some doubt on Garrett's account of the fatal shooting, Sederwall and [Calvin] Ostler said.

'The evidence we are seeing does not corroborate the popular legend,' Ostler said. 'Something's askew' ...

One simple explanation that Lee offered is that Garrett may have shot defensively at the Kid as he fled and struck the washstand from the side instead of head on. Garrett's official story may have omitted that embarrassing detail. "You don't want to paint yourself as a chicken," Lee suggested.

Omitted is no bullet for dating; and no relationship of the washstand to Garrett or to Billy or to Peter Maxwell or to the shooting. And Lee made-up his groveling Garrett from the box being toy-sixed, needing one to crouch to hit it! And the hoaxers missed that their Maxwell would have had to kneel to wash!

In his February 25, 2005 report titled "Forensic Research & Training Center Forensic Examination Report" under "Item # 2 Washstand," Henry fabricated: "The angles produced in the examination tell us two things: First, the bullet was fired from no more than 41" from the floor given the reported limitations of the room. The room was reported to be 20' by 20'; the maximum distance is assumed to be 20'. If the firearm was a maximum of 41" off the floor it is unlikely that the shooter was standing. It is more likely the shooter was kneeling, squatting, or close to the floor. Second, the horizontal angle is such that if the Washstand was positioned so that the back was against the wall, the shot could not have been fired from more than approximately 40 inches from the Washstand, because the wall would have been in the way. The angle of trajectory intersects the back plane of the Washstand at approximately 45 3/16", and no more than 46". Lee's conclusion reflected his well-known caution about putting his lies in writing: "Two bullet holes were located on the side panels of the Washstand. The hole on the left side panel is consistent with a bullet entrance hole while the hole on the right side panel is consistent with a bullet exit hole. However, it is not possible to determine when those bullet holes were produced at this time."

Item # 2 Washstand

This Washstand measures approximately 28 ¼" long by 16" deep by 30" tall. Figure 6 is a sketch diagram of the washstand. This washstand is made of wood with a black color finish on it.

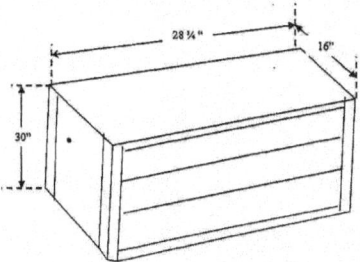

Figure 6, Washstand

Photograph # 3 shows the left side panel of the washstand and photograph # 4 depicts a view of the right side panel of the washstand. Visual examination of the external surfaces of the washstand reveals two holes, one single hole in each end of the side panels of the washstand. Examination of these holes indicates that they are consistent with bullet holes.

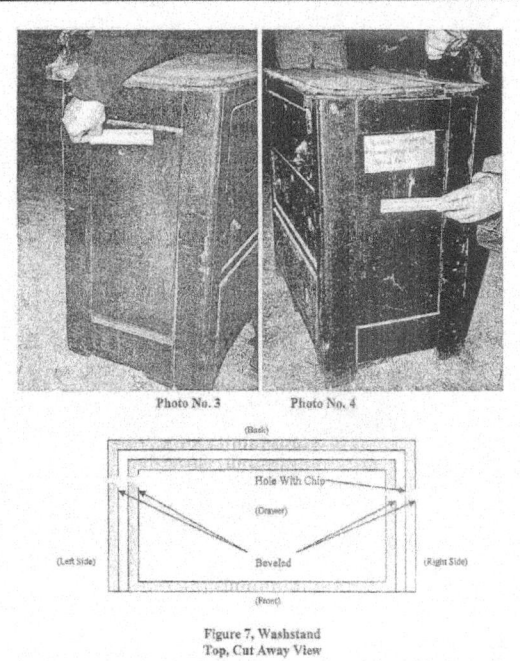

Photo No. 3   Photo No. 4

(Back)

Hole With Chip
(Drawer)
(Left Side)   Beveled   (Right Side)
(Front)

Figure 7, Washstand
Top, Cut Away View

Figure 7 is a cut away diagram of the washstand. This diagram depicts the relative locations of the two holes on the side panels of the washstand.
The hole on the left side panel is round and well defined. The hole on the right side panel is chipped and beveled. The left side panel hole is consistent with a bullet entrance hole.

FIGURE: 2. "Washstand" from Stella Abreu's Fort Sumner Billy the Kid Museum, 1926-1936

FIGURE: 3. Headboard without its center from Stella Abreu's Fort Sumner Billy the Kid Museum, 1926-1936 (Courtesy of Kenny Miller)

LEE AND A HEADBOARD

The lawmen also gave Dr. Lee Stella's museum's headboard to "investigate." Important for their fake argument of Garrett as a liar, was finding that it had no bullet hole as claimed by him and Poe. So that is what Lee gave them.

Lee's February 25, 2004 report titled "Forensic Research & Training Center Forensic Examination Report" - which I got during the open records litigation against the hoaxing lawmen - under its topic, **"Item # 2 Headboard;"** stated: **"No bullet hole and no observable damage, no sign of bullet ricocheted type of defects were found on the Headboard. No blood or biological materials were observed on the Headboard."**

What Lee left out, is that Stella's "headboard" is just a rim around a huge hole. **[Figure: 3]** There was no headboard to have the hole! So Lee and Calvin Ostler had lied to Rene Romo for his August 2, 2004 *Albuquerque Journal*'s "Forensic Expert on Billy's Case" by stating: "The evidence we are seeing does not corroborate the popular legend."

Deputy Steve Sederwall was soon spouting Dr. Lee's fable in Julie Carter's October 2005, "Follow the Blood;" stating: "Using high-tech lasers and other modern crime scene methods, investigators learned that the shooting of the Kid in Pete Maxwell's bedroom was not in the way history has portrayed it. Tests indicate that Garrett fired his second shot from the doorway while on his knees and with his left hand on the floor, firing back over his shoulder ... Being blinded by his first shot, it appears he was in a great hurry to get out of the room and fell to the floor.' He [Sederwall] added: 'To find the furniture from Maxwell's bedroom was great. But to have Dr. Lee recover usable evidence was truly a historical find.' "

RECYCLING DR. HENRY LEE'S FAKE CRIME SCENE FOR *PAT GARRETT: THE MAN BEHIND THE BADGE*

Steve Sederwall recycled Dr. Henry Lee's fake washstand versus headboard death scene forensics as his own private "investigation" in W.C. Jameson's 2016 *Pat Garrett: The Man Behind the Badge.*

As introduction, Jameson questioned where Garrett's second shot ended up, and duplicitously presented, as if fact, Lee's fake forensics that Garrett must have lied about his position in the shooting, since his bullet hit a washstand "fifteen feet" away "at an angle that indicted he was on his knees in the far corner of the room when he fired." As to the search by Garrett and his Deputies for the second bullet strike, Jameson claimed Garrett hid the washstand holes, because they proved a different positioning than his lie. (Page 76)

Steve Sederwall enters for "Crime Scene Investigation: The Washstand" in "Appendix II." (Pages 206-207) Hidden is that it was part of Lincoln County Sheriff's Department Case No. 2003-274, "Billy the Kid Case." Instead, as mere "investigators," are listed, Steve Sederwall (first, with "Deputy" hidden), Tom Sullivan (with "Sheriff" hidden), Kim [sic – Calvin] Ostler, Dr. Henry Lee, David Turk (as from the U.S. Marshals Service, but with "Historian" hidden to fake him as a Marshal), and Mike Haag (as a firearms examiner). They are to examine the washstand, claimed as from Peter Maxwell's bedroom on July 14, 1881. Its measurements and two holes are presented, with Lee's laser as showing a "bullet path." The conclusion is that Garrett "shot the holes in the washstand ... from a position that likely involved being on both knees with one hand on the floor for support while the opposite hand fired the revolver."

HOAXING: This repeated Lee's first washstand hoaxing, as debunked above. (See pages 197-199) Sederwall also forged a Lee report about the washstand and headboard for my open records litigation. Jameson unknowingly later cited that forged report in his *Cold Case Billy the Kid* book as by Henry Lee and titled "Forensic Examination Report (Examination of Furniture From Pete Maxwell's of July 15, 1881) 22 May 2004." (*Cold Case Billy the Kid*. Page 187)]

RECYCLING DR. LEE'S FAKE CRIME SCENE FOR *COLD CASE BILLY THE KID*

For W.C. Jameson's 2018 *Cold Case Billy the* Kid, Steve Sederwall again recycled Dr. Henry Lee's fake washstand-headboard death scene for the "Billy the Kid Case" hoax, and faked it as his own "investigation." The objective, like from its first invention, was to discredit Pat Garrett's veracity, with the illogic that if he lied about death scene specifics, he lied about the corpse's identity; ergo, he killed the innocent victim. And since

Deputy Poe presented the same claim of the shot headboard, he must by lying too in order to hide the corpse's identity.

It should be noted, since "Brushy"-backing W.C. Jameson was showcasing this fakery in his books, that it contradicted "Brushy Bill's" own version from C.L. Sonnichsen's and William V. Morrison's *Alias Billy the Kid* in which "Brushy's" partner, Billy Barlow, is shot on *Peter Maxwell's back porch* when mistaken for him. "Brushy" had no bedroom shooting death scene! One is left to wonder if Jameson simply let Sederwall write his books.

HOAXING THE HEADBOARD

Sederwall, as narrated by Jameson, reminds the reader that Deputy Poe had said Garrett's second shot rebounded from the wall and hit the headboard of Maxwell's bed. He then states that Lee found "nothing resembling the impact of a bullet, even a scratch." So Poe is called a liar. (Pages 160-161) No mention is made of Lee's report, but the Bibliography cites "Lee, Dr. Henry. Forensic Examination Report (Examination of Furniture From Pete Maxwell's of July 15, 1881) 22 May 2004." (Page 187)

HOAXING: Sederwall is tricking readers, since the "headboard" is just a big empty hole with a frame, having no place for the bullet hit. [FIGURE: 3] But scorning readers' intelligence, he gives its photo. Wily Dr. Lee had omitted a it in his actual February 25, 2005 report for his own fake "investigation."

The Lee report in the Bibliography appears to be one of Sederwall's forged ones, with the date now May 22, 2004 (lifting Lee's "Date of Request.") The one he first gave me was his forged "Forensic Research and Training Center Forensic Examination Report: "Examination of furniture from Pete Maxwell's of July 15, 1881," dated February 25, 2005. Its second forged version, with different font and deleted "Results and Conclusions," went to the Court in my open records litigation to trick the judge as Exhibit E.

Lee's, actual report of February 26, 2005 had stated dishonestly: "No bullet hole and no observable damage, no sign of bullet ricocheted type of defects were found on the Headboard. No blood or biological materials were observed on the Headboard."

This is pure hoaxing by both Sederwall and Lee; as well as records forgery, as found by the Court, for Sederwall.

HOAXING THE WASHSTAND

Sederwall also repeated Dr. Henry Lee's fake washstand forensics. (Pages 161-163) A photo of it (Page 162) differs from the one photographed and diagramed by Lee in his February 25, 2005 report, by having a raised back rim - with Lee's picture being only a box. [FIGURE: 2] Lee's bullet trajectory for its holes is presented, with his fictional claim of Garrett shooting from the floor. No report is mentioned, but the Bibliography cites: "Lee, Dr. Henry. Forensic Examination Report (Examination of Furniture From Pete Maxwell's of July 15, 1881) 22 May 2004." (Page 187)

HOAXING: The toy-sized washstand used, is implausible as being a real one from Maxwell's bedroom. And neither Garrett nor Poe claimed a shot washstand. So the trajectory is merely hoaxing of Garrett as shooting it, and of his position in the room.

The Lee report cited in the Bibliography is apparently a Sederwall forgery, now dated May 22, 2004. When given to me, it had been dated February 25, 2005, and Sederwall had removed its "Results and Conclusions" section.

Lee's real February 25, 2005 report was non-committal; stating: "Two bullet holes were located on the side panels of the Washstand. The hole on the left side panel is consistent with a bullet entrance hole while the hole on the right side panel is consistent with a bullet exit hole. However, it is not possible to determine when those bullet holes were produced at this time [meaning anytime from the 1880's to the 1900's]."

HOAXING JOHN MILLER AS BILLY THE KID

DIGGING UP A DEFAULT PRETENDER

After I blocked the exhumations of Billy Bonney and his mother, the "Billy the Kid Case" hoaxers were desperate for any exhumation to continue their publicity stunt. Chosen was little-known pretender, John Miller, whose backing author was Helen Airy, in her 1993 book *Whatever Happened to Billy the Kid*. She hid that Miller was almost a decade older than Billy, being no kid. Furthermore, he knew no history, and merely hinted to friends that he was Billy the Kid. Of course, the "Billy the Kid Case" hoaxers kept his total mismatch secret. They also lied that they got "bench DNA of Billy the Kid" from Dr. Henry Lee for identity matching with his remains in his Prescott, Arizona grave.

I exposed this hoax, and the "Billy the Kid Case" hoaxers' detour from their "Brushy Bill" goal, in my 2014 *Cracking the Billy the Kid Case Hoax: The Plot to Exhume Billy the Kid, Convict Pat Garrett of Murder, and Become President of the United States*; and my 2019 books: *The Cold Case Billy the Kid Megahoax: The Plot to Steal Billy the Kid's Identity and Defame Sheriff Pat Garrett as a Murderer*, and *Billy the Kid's Pretender John Miller*.

Only corruption of Governor Bill Richardson, colluding with Arizona's equally corrupt Governor, Janet Napolitano, with auspices over Miller's state-controlled Arizona Pioneers Home Cemetery, enabled the unjustified and illegal dig. Furthermore, because the hoaxers had learned from facing my attorneys and the New Mexico Office of the Medical Investigator (OMI) that they had no basis for a legal permit, they dug secretly.

But they left a paper trail. Ever-productive Lincoln County Deputy Steve Sederwall wrote the "Lincoln County Sheriff's Department Supplemental Report for Case 2003-274 for the Exhumation of John Miller." It was for Lincoln County Sheriff, Rick Virden, then in charge of carrying out the "Billy the Kid Case" hoax. It was dated on the exhumation day of May 19, 2005. It recorded that present besides Sederwall himself and Deputy Tom Sullivan, the past Lincoln County Sheriff, were Dr. Rick Staub, Director of Orchid Cellmark Lab to collect the grave-robbed bones; a moonlighting, Maricopa County, forensic anthropologist, Dr. Laura Fulginiti, nervously added to feign legitimacy; and a Bill Kurtis Productions film crew, which represented the purpose of the whole charade.

But there was an unforeseen problem with Dr. Fulginiti: she was honest, and recorded everything they did. And what they did was also exhume the random man buried beside Miller named William Hudspeth, because the cemetery had no grave-markers. And morally indifferent Dr. Rick Staub bagged Hudspeth's bones too for his meaningless DNA extractions. Of course, Hudspeth joined the many secrets kept for the "Billy the Kid Case" hoax. But the key secret of the dig was that they were lying that they had the "bench-blood-DNA-of-Billy-the-Kid" from Dr. Henry Lee's carpenter's bench specimens. **[APPENDIX: 2]**

Sederwall's exhumation report **[APPENDIX: 3]** stated:

LINCOLN COUNTY SHERIFF'S DEPARTMENT
SUPPLEMENTAL REPORT

Case # : 2003-274
Date: Thursday, May 19, 2005
Subject: Exhumation of John Miller
Location: Arizona Pioneers' Cemetery, Prescott, Arizona
Report By: Steven M. Sederwall

On Thursday, May 19, 2005, at approximately 1:00 pm the following met at the Arizona Pioneers' Cemetery at Prescott, Arizona.

Investigators:

Steven M. Sederwall, Lincoln County Deputy Sheriff

Following Sederwall, was Tom Sullivan as "Sheriff of Lincoln County, Retired," then Dale Tunnell as an "Arizona State Investigator." In line was "**Dr. Rick Staub, Orchid Cell Mark** [sic], DNA," proving the lab head himself was there for the bones.

The remaining "Investigators" were listed as "Mike Poling, Yavapai County Sheriff's Deputy [a random lawman who happened on the scene to give forensic expert, Laura Fulginiti, specimens from another case, but was slyly added to the list to fake presence of Arizona authority; and was later claimed by the lying hoaxers to be responsible for the exhumation!]; Laura Fulginiti, Forensic Scientist - Anthropologist; Kristen Hartnett, Forensic Scientist - Archeologist; Misty Rodarte, Arizona Pioneers' Administration."

Then came "Others Present." They were Pearl Tenney Romney, Anthony Rodarte, Diana Shenefield, Jesse Shenefield, Russ Hadley, Toby Deherra Jr., Pat Sullivan, Linda Fisher, Billie Martin, Dale Sams, and Clara Enest. All but Pat Sullivan, Tom Sullivan's wife, had Arizona addresses listed.

Lastly, under "Bill Kurtis Productions," were cameraman, Joel Sapatori; and the soundman, Greg Gricus.

Sederwall also posed for a trophy photo holding the skull of John Miller (or William Hudspeth) for hoax-backing reporter, Julie Carter's, October 6, 2005 *RuidosoNews.com* article, "Follow the Blood: In the Billy the Kid Case, Miller Exhumed."

Later, the lawmen would deny participation in the dig when facing criminal grave-robbing charges, and to my District Court judge when they were hiding its DNA records. The judge was not fooled, writing, when I won the case as *pro se*, for his May 15, 2014 "Findings of Fact and Conclusions of Law and Order of the Court" **[APPENDIX: 4]**:

> 8. In 2005 newly elected Lincoln County Sheriff Rick Virden (hereinafter Virden) deputized Sullivan and Sederwall to continue Case 2003-274 by exhuming Billy the Kid's identity claimants John Miller and "Brushy Bill" Roberts for DNA match with Lee's bench DNA to solve the Garrett murder.

FACING CRIMINAL CHARGES

The hoaxers had misjudged Arizona, being complacent after protection of hoax-backing corrupt New Mexico press. They got their first skeptical reporter: the *Tucson Weekly's* Leo W. Banks. In his April 13, 2006 article "The New Billy the Kid?" he made public their stealth, and that the graves were unmarked; so, unsure of Miller's location, they had hurriedly dug up his random neighbor (later named as William Hudspeth).

Even worse, Arizona amateur historian, David Snell, had kept an eye on the Arizona Pioneers' Home Cemetery for their rumored exhumation, and discovered its post-digging tire tracks of their back hoe and the Bill Kurtis Productions film crew. On March 11, 2006, Snell reported them to the Yavapai County Attorney, Shiela Polk, for grave robbing. Only their corrupt political backers, and the complicit Arizona prosecutor, spared them justified felony charges for wanton desecration of graves and grave-robbing.

CREATING A PILTDOWN MAN-STYLE HOAX

Being cornered to justify the exhumation, Steve Sederwall and Tom Sullivan faked John Miller as Billy the Kid to pretend that they had made an extraordinary find which trumped criminality. They did this by faking John Miller's bones.

Sederwall and Sullivan were inadvertently rerunning the most famous skeleton hoax of all: Piltdown Man. Between 1908 and 1912, an amateur anthropologist named Charles Dawson, claimed to have found Charles Darwin's coveted "missing link" between apes and men in and near Piltdown gravel quarry in East Sussex, England. Possible, though unproved, hoaxer, Dawson, hoped his discovery would yield a fellowship in the British Royal Society. He had "discovered" parts of a human-like skull, an ape-like jawbone, a hominid-seeming canine tooth; plus an ivory tool and Stone Age animal teeth - for a Stone Age touch. "Museum experts" assembled the skull and jawbone into a creature they named *Eanthropus dawsoni*, to honor Dawson. Popularly called "Piltdown Man," it held its spot in humans' family tree for over 40 years.

In 1953, Sir Kenneth Oakley, using a new fluorine absorption test, proved Piltdown Man was a fake composite of a medieval human skull and an antique orangutan's jawbone - all stained to match. And the ape's jawbone's teeth were filed to fit the skull.

For their own Piltdown Man hoax, desperate Sederwall and Sullivan tried to get good press from skeptical reporter, Leo Banks, by claiming that they were giving Arizona Billy the Kid!

For his April 14, 2006 *Tucson Weekly* article, "The New Billy the Kid?" Sheriff Rick Virden's Deputy, Tom Sullivan, was quoted: "Helen Airy's book triggered it for me … It made a lot of sense. I read it and thought, 'We have another Billy the Kid.' " And Deputies Sederwall and Sullivan flaunted Dr. Lee and the carpenter's bench - now "saturated with blood." Banks quoted: "When we found the bench and the other evidence, we thought, 'Let's forget about these other bodies,' " says Sullivan, referring to Catherine Antrim and the Kid. "Let's do Miller. And if that doesn't work, we'll go down to Texas and do Brushy Bill."

But Banks was the first reporter to research their "Billy the Kid Case," and called their roving extravaganza "airship Billy." He exposed that **Sullivan's and Sederwall's "Billy the Kid" skeleton claims were made by mixing-up Miller's and the random man's bones**! Banks had interviewed Dr. Laura Fulginiti. She denied their skeletal claims! Banks wrote:

> Fulginiti says the first body she studied had buck teeth and the scapula fracture that caused such a commotion with investigators.
>
> As Sederwall told the *Weekly,* "We were shocked when we got him up. He had buck teeth just like the Kid and a bullet hole in the upper left chest that exited the shoulder blade."
>
> Sullivan made a similar statement, suggesting this might be the man Garrett shot the morning of July 14, 1881.
>
> **But when contacted by the *Weekly*, Fulginiti didn't support their enthusiasm. "There was evidence of trauma on the scapula, but I couldn't tell whether it was from a gunshot wound or not," she said.**

Fulginiti also said the buck teeth were from what Banks named "Scapula Man" [Hudspeth] from his non-shot right scapula!

And Miller's skull had no teeth. Fulginiti had researched Miller as dying of a broken hip. So Banks called him "Hip Man."

Banks also contacted Orchid Cellmark Lab, discovering: **"The DNA expert present at the exhumation, Dr. Rick Staub, of Orchid Cellmark Labs in Dallas, was unable to extract useable DNA from Hip Man [Miller]. But he did get a usable sample from Scapula Man [Hudspeth]."** This was Staub's admission that John Miller's bones had yielded no DNA!

When confronted by Banks, Sullivan and Sederwall were left clumsily lying that hired forensic expert Fulginiti was wrong.

Nevertheless, it was obvious that, for their own Piltdown Man, they had assembled a "John Miller as a Billy the Kid" from random William Hudspeth's bones.

THE INCRIMINATING FULGINITI REPORT

Dutiful Dr. Laura Fulginiti had reported it all. She titled her June 2, 2005 report: "Re: Exhumation, Pioneer Home Cemetery, Prescott, Arizona." **[APPENDIX: 5]** She sent it to another "Billy the Kid Case" hoaxer, a Dale Tunnell, posing as a Ph.D. forensic expert. I got its copy from the Prescott Police Department, then starting the criminal investigation. Fulginiti had written:

On May 19, 2005 at approximately 1230 hours I am asked to assist in the exhumation of the remains of an individual known as Mr. John Miller by Dr. Dale Tunnell, President, Forensitec. The purpose of my involvement is to aid in the exhumation process as well as to assess any skeletal remains recovered. The exhumation takes place at the Arizona Pioneer [sic] Home Cemetery, Iron Springs Road in Prescott Arizona in the presence of Dr. Tunnell, several of his associates, members of the Arizona Pioneer Home staff and Kristen Harnett M.A., AMSU graduate student.

[AUTHOR'S NOTE: The unmarked grave first exhumed was later called the South Grave, and was John Miller's.

Dr. Tunnell located the alleged gravesite of Mr. Miller prior to our arrival on the scene ... At approximately 1400 hours, a backhoe began to remove the sod overlying the alleged grave, which was oriented in an East-West direction, with the head to the West. When fragments of wood began to be removed, the grave was excavated using a shovel ... The left femoral shaft, minus the head, was removed, examined, and packaged for DNA analysis [the role of Rick Staub, Director of Orchid Cellmark].

[AUTHOR'S NOTE: Tunnell then changed his mind, and they dug up the adjacent, North Grave of William Hudspeth]

Dr. Tunnell, in consultation with the cemetery staff and his other associates determined that the adjacent grave to the North was likely that of Mr. Miller and excavation shifted to that gravesite ... The backhoe removed the overlying sod until fragments of wood began to be unearthed. The excavation shifted to shovels and the top of the casket was identified. Excavation proceeded using trowels and hand tools until various aspects of the skeleton were identified and cleared ... Skeletal elements were measured for depth and location, removed from the grave and examined ... **There were extensive healed traumata on the right scapula** ... The remains were photographed, samples were harvested for DNA (tooth and femur) [Note and the skull had teeth] remains were returned to the grave and reburied.

[AUTHOR'S NOTE: Fulginiti then had doubts about the North Grave's remains being John Miller's.]

Anecdotal historical information suggested that Mr. John Miller had died from complications of a fractured hip while recuperating in the Arizona pioneer Home. The individual in the north grave, while having extensive pathological conditions, particularly in the upper body, did not have discernible pathology of the *os coxae* [pelvis].

[AUTHOR'S NOTE: The North Grave's body had no pelvic damage to go with John Miller's broken hip. So they ravished the South Grave again.]

The south grave was excavated by shovel to the point where the remnants of the casket lid were identified. Excavation resumed using trowels and hand tools until the left femoral head was identified.

The head of the femur was misshapen with bony remodeling, suggesting an **antemortem injury** ... The ischium [part of the pelvis] tapered to a point with lack of union to the pubis [another part of the pelvis], suggesting a healing fracture of the ischiopubic ramus. **This evidence led the team to believe that the individual in the south grave was, in fact, more consistent with the known facts regarding the Medical history of Mr. John Miller and additional DNA samples were recovered (femur, scalp [?], matter from inside the braincase).**

[AUTHOR'S NOTE: The South Grave was confirmed as Miller's because of its broken hip.]

The maxillae and mandible were recovered but were edentulous [had no teeth at all].

[AUTHOR'S NOTE: So Miller had NO TEETH. Random man Hudspeth had the "buck teeth" claimed as Billy the Kid's!"]

This was how Fulginiti revealed that the North Grave body with the bad scapula and alleged buck teeth was not Miller's! That was how she revealed that William Hudspeth had been dug up also; and the bad scapula and buck teeth were his! And his damaged scapula was the right one, not the left! And its damage was not from a bullet!

FAKING JOHN MILLER'S DNA

My open records litigation, with subpoena of Orchid Cellmark's records, revealed extent of the graves' ravishment. Its Case No. 4444 (for Case 2003-274) January 26, 2009's "Laboratory Report, Forensic Identity, Mitochondrial Analysis: Evidence Received," confirmed the dismemberment of John Miller in his "South Grave," and William Hudspeth in his "North Grave." Taken back to Texas by Dr. Rick Staub for meaningless DNA extractions were: Miller's "skull and mummified brains," Miller's "pelvis," Miller's "left femur," Hudspeth's "mandible and teeth," and Hudspeth's "right femur." **[APPENDIX: 6]** There was not much left in the graves. And DNA extraction destroys much of the bones.

And the hoaxers (and Dr. Staub) would have known all along that they had no DNA of Billy the Kid to compare with anything. And it was obvious that one of the two bodies represented straightforward grave-robbing of a random man (since there could not be two John Miller's).

And Bill Kurtis Productions was filming all along. But this time Bill Kurtis documented a crime scene. I was told the rumor that he subsequently destroyed or hid his footage.

THE DNA TRAVESTY

Interestingly, Dr. Rick Staub had told reporter, Leo Banks, for his April 13, 2006 *Tucson Weekly* article "The New Billy the Kid?" that **no DNA had been obtained from John Miller, and the only DNA came from random man, William Hudspeth**.

Nevertheless, when I got the Orchid Cellmark records by subpoena, a 2009 report claimed DNA extracted from both men; meaning, by then, there had been a possible fix-up - like Orchid Cellmark's other DNA faking as reported in November 18, 2004's "TalkLeft.com," as "Fraud alleged at Cellmark, DNA Testing Firm," with dishonest manipulation of data.

The Orchid Cellmark results of DNA testing from the Miller/Hudspeth exhumations were in January 26, 2009's "Laboratory Report - Forensic Identity – Mitochondrial Analysis," using the subsets of its in-house Case 4444 (for its Case No. 2003-274 specimens). **[APPENDIX: 7]** Under its Case 4444-011, John Miller's left femur from the South Grave was reported as having "a mitochondrial DNA profile obtained." For pulverized William Hudspeth, Case 4444-012 from his North Grave's mandible and teeth indicated a useless mixed sample: "Consequently no sequence data are reported ... [P]rofiles are therefore inconclusive." However, **Hudspeth's Case 4444-013 North Grave's right femur yielded the "mitochondrial DNA profile obtained,"** originally admitted by Dr. Staub to reporter Leo Banks. Of course, there was no Billy the Kid DNA anyway for identity matching. So they had nothing.

RECYCLING THE JOHN MILLER PILTDOWN MAN-STYLE HOAX

THE RETURN OF JOHN MILLER'S EXHUMATION

For W.C. Jameson's 2018 *Cold Case Billy the Kid*, Steve Sederwall recycled the John Miller exhumation as his own "ongoing investigation" (Page 165), (with dug up random man, William Hudspeth, obviously concealed).

And his dupe, Jameson, apparently did not notice that opportunistic self-promoting Sederwall was declaring that John Miller matched Billy the Kid! (To hell with "Brushy Bill!")

HOAXING JOHN MILLER AS BILLY THE KID

Reflecting Sederwall's audacity, no background is given for John Miller: like being born in 1950, almost ten years before Billy, like knowing no Billy the Kid history, like dying soon after breaking a hip, and like being toothless. His exhumation is claimed to have been done on May 9, 2005 [sic – May 19] by an unnamed "forensic anthropologist" and "authorized by the state of Arizona."(Page 165)

HOAXING: Sederwall hid his own report for that exhumation: "Lincoln County Sheriff's Department

Supplemental Report," listing "Case # 2003-274, Date: Thursday, May 19, 2005, Subject: Exhumation of John Miller, Location: Arizona Pioneers' Cemetery, Prescott, Arizona, Report By: Steven M. Sederwall, Lincoln County Deputy Sheriff."

Hidden also is that the forensic anthropologist was Dr. Laura Fulginiti, who denied his claims. [APPENDIX: 5] Hidden is having no Billy the Kid DNA to justify any exhumation for identity matching. Hidden is grave-robbing random man, William Hudspeth, buried beside Miller.

Sederwall not only recycled, but also added to his Piltdown Man-style hoax, shamelessly lying after knowing he had been exposed by Dr. Laura Fulginiti in 2005. He stated: "**The right scapula of John Miller manifested a round hole. The anthropologist observed that it appeared to be a bullet hole that had healed**" and the bullet entered the upper chest and exited his back. He added that Miller's right front incisor was placed somewhat in front of his left front incisor." So he concluded that this was Pat Garrett's bullet killing buck-toothed Billy the Kid. (Page 165)

HOAXING: Sederwall was recycling his November 6, 2006's *Albuquerque Journal's* "Billy the Kid Probe May Yield New Twist," where reporter Romo wrote: "**Sederwall ... said Miller's skeletal remains were intriguing. He said Miller had buck teeth, like the Kid, and an old bullet wound that entered his upper left chest and exited through the scapula**." Hidden, is that forensic expert, Dr. Laura Fulginiti, reported Miller having no teeth, and no damaged scapula. Hidden is that Sederwall was faking the results from random man, William Hudspeth, who had a damaged *right*, not *left* scapula, with Dr. Fulginiti denying the injury was from a bullet. (See pages 208, 210-211, 452 above and below)

Sederwall then claimed he got DNA from Miller's remains "sufficient to conduct a test." (Page 165)

HOAXING: Hidden was having no Billy the Kid DNA to compare with Miller's for any "test." Hidden was no need for DNA matching, since Miller had no historical match to Billy. Hidden was the possibility that Orchid Cellmark Lab had faked getting DNA from John Miller (after Rick Staub had denied getting Miller's DNA to reporter Leo Banks).

Jameson was apparently unaware of the "Billy the Kid Case's" press, in which the hoaxers were willing to claim any remains as Billy the Kid's to keep Bill Kurtis's cameras rolling. For Julie Carter's October 6, 2005 "Follow the Blood," Sederwall had plugged Miller; crowing: "In the light of the evidence, we see that the history of Billy the Kid will change. Those with monied interest in history remaining the same will not be happy ... As a cop I know when people fight to keep you from looking at something, they are always trying to hide something. The Lincoln County War is still going on."

For reporter Rene Romo's November 6, 2006's *Albuquerque Journal's* "Billy the Kid Probe May Yield New Twist," hoaxing Sederwall again plugged Miller, as well as faking having DNA from the carpenter's bench; stating: "If that [John Miller] DNA matches the work bench, I think the game is over."

HOAXING: This is a good example of Sederwall's incorrigible lying, even when exposed 13 years earlier for that same fakery by Dr. Laura Fulginiti.

HOAXING THE "BILLY THE KID CASE" AS ONLY ABOUT THE BELL MURDER TO HIDE ITS RECORDS

The "Billy the Kid Case" hoaxers devised new lies to hide their incriminating forensic reports from my open records requests and litigation. And since it was Case No. 2003-274's murder investigation against Pat Garrett that had the requested DNA records, the hoaxers lied that the case was actually just the investigation of the Deputy Bell's shooting - which had no DNA!

They did not realize I was behind all past anti-hoax litigation, so I had all their other records. I had their "Probable Cause Statement" for Pat Garrett as a murder suspect, with the Bell shooting as a sub-investigation as to his friendship with the Kid.

I had Bill Richardson's June 10, 2003 press release: "Last month I was contacted by Lincoln County Sheriff, Tom Sullivan and Capitan Mayor, Steve Sederwall, to support reopening the case. Case number 2003-274 ... is [to determine] did Sheriff Garrett kill Billy the Kid at Fort Sumner, New Mexico ... on July 14. 1881?"

I had all their exhumation petitions about Garrett being a murderer. As their Attorney, Sherry Tippett, stated in her October 3, 2003 Case No. MS 2003-11 "In the Matter of Catherine Antrim, Petition to Remove Remains;" stating: "This petition is made in conjunction with investigation No. 2004-274 [sic] filed in Lincoln County and case number 03-06-136-01 filed in De Baca County, for purpose of determining the guilt or innocence of Sheriff Pat Garrett in the death of William Bonney aka "Billy the Kid."

But hoaxing Lincoln County Attorney Alan Morel, responded to my records request on April 27, 2007 for Sheriff Rick Virden by lying: "The Lincoln County Sheriff's Office has extremely limited information pertaining to the case you are inquiring about, Case Number 2003-274. **Case 2003-274 involves an investigation into the escape of William H. Bonney and the murder of two Lincoln County Deputies, namely James W. Bell and Robert Olinger of April 28, 1881.**"

And four years into my litigation, Sullivan and Sederwall's attorney Kevin Brown, was still lying to the court about the Deputy killing sub-investigation for a January 21, 2011 Evidentiary Hearing, in which he claimed: "**[T]he investigation that was opened was a follow-up investigation of the escape of William Bonney and the double homicide of James and Robert Olinger. I forgot the other guy's name.**" [Transcript 1/21/11, p. 27] That segued into Brown's lying that the carpenter's bench was not in that courthouse killing; ergo, it was not part of the Case 2003-274's records I was requesting! So Brown claimed everything else - including that carpenter's bench - was a private hobby. He stated: "**Steve Sederwall – this didn't have anything to do with the courthouse investigation ... on his own, paying his own expenses, located this workbench in Albuquerque ... On July 31st, Dr. Lee examined the workbench. It wasn't part of the courthouse investigation. And DNA samples he took were given to Calvin Ostler. Cal Ostler sent the DNA to Orchid Cellmark Lab ... Steve Sederwall's position is that the workbench was personal.**" [Transcript 1/21/11, pp. 28-29, 31] In fact, that finding of the bench was in the "Probable Cause Statement," with Sederwall as deputy and as its author; stating: "**On August 29, 2003, <u>Deputy Sederwall of the Lincoln County Sheriff's Department</u> located the carpenter bench where the Kid's body was placed on July 14, 1881.**"

And Sederwall, who had claimed he wrote the "Probable Cause" statement for Garrett as a murderer, testified by lying in January 21, 2011's Evidentiary Hearing: "**The way I saw 2003-274, was Sheriff Sullivan opened up a case ... and it was a follow-up on the escape and homicide of James Bell and Robert Ollinger** [sic]." [Transcript 1/21/11, pp. 148-149]

The judge did not buy that trickery. For the January 21, 2011 Evidentiary Hearing he stated: "I'm going to find that the investigation in this case of Billy the Kid and the double homicide of James Bell and Robert Olinger and the investigation of the death of Billy the Kid are related. I'm going to find that these investigations were under the auspices of the Lincoln County Sheriff's Office. I'm going to find that any report, lab results, and anything coming out of this investigation are public documents." [Transcript 1/21/11, p. 192]

And, at the end of the District Court litigation, when I prevailed as *pro* se, the judge made clear that the Bell killing was a sub-investigation in his May 15, 2014 "Findings of Fact and Conclusions of Law and Order of the Court" **[APPENDIX: 4]**; writing:

> 5. Case 2003-274 is a murder case, filed in 2003 in the Lincoln County Sheriff's Department by Sheriff Tom Sullivan (hereinafter Sullivan) and his commissioned Deputy Steve Sederwall (hereinafter Sederwall) to be solved by forensic DNA acquisitions and matching, and accusing the suspect Pat Garrett of murdering an innocent victim instead of Billy the Kid; with a sub-investigation of Billy the Kid's double homicide of Deputies James Bell and Robert Olinger.

HOAXING THE "BILLY THE KID CASE" AS A PRIVATE HOBBY TO HIDE ITS RECORDS

Open records law applies to public officials, whose records are deemed public property that can be requested by anyone.

So Steve Sederwall and Tom Sullivan responded to my records request by a new hoax: that Case 2003-274, the "Billy the Kid Case," was actually their private hobby as amateur historians!

This was embarrassingly obvious hoaxing, since, for lack of kin to give permission, they had structured Case 2003-274 entirely as a law enforcement, Sheriffs Department, murder investigation against Pat Garrett to get the legal right to exhume graves to solve that "cold case" crime. Hobbyists do not have any legal access to graves.

Furthermore, they had made profuse exhumation petitions to the Grant County and De Baca County District Courts to exhume Billy and his mother solely in their lawman capacities in the respective Sheriffs Departments.

REALITY OF 100% LAW ENFORCEMENT CASE

Before my open records litigation, the hoaxers flaunted their lawman status. As sheriff, Tom Sullivan denied my records requests based on Lincoln County Sheriffs Department Case 2003-274's *being a law enforcement case*. For example, on October 8, 2003, he responded on his official letterhead: "**This is an ongoing investigation and until the investigation is completed and closed [the records] will not be available for release, as per Section 14-2-1(A)(4) of the inspection of Public Records Act which protects law enforcement records**."

And when the hoaxers' first attorney, Sherry Tippett, wrote her October 3, 2003 Grant County Case No. MS 2003-11 "In the Matter of Catherine Antrim, Petition to Remove Remains," she made clear their lawmen's titles and that the case was against Sheriff Pat Garrett for murder. Tippett wrote:

PETITION TO EXHUME REMAINS

Comes now **Petitioners Tom Sullivan, Sheriff of Lincoln County, Steve Sederwall, Deputy Sheriff of Lincoln County, and Gary Graves, Sheriff of De Baca County**, by and through their attorney, Sherry J. Tippett, hereby Petitions this Court to enter an Order directing the New Mexico Office of Medical Examiners [sic- Investigator] (hereinafter "OMI") to disinter the remains of Catherine Antrim for the purpose of obtaining DNA samples.

And, for the attempted exhumation of Billy the Kid, on July 26, 2004, was Attorney Mark Acuña's "County of De Baca, State of New Mexico, Tenth Judicial District, In the Matter of William H. Bonney A/K/A 'Billy the Kid' Cause No. CV-04-00005," in which his five page filing called Sullivan, Graves, and Sederwall "law enforcement officers 13 times *to deny that they were "hobbyists!"* As Acuña stated: "Sederwall, Sullivan, and Graves, all joined in on the Petition to Exhume the remains of Billy the Kid as Co-Petitioners and **in their capacity as law enforcement officers** engaged in an on-going investigation ... Petitioners assert that they maintain standing in the instant action **as law enforcement officers** engaged in the investigation of criminal violations, namely, the alleged killing of Billy the Kid by the legendary Sheriff, Pat Garrett."

And their press advertised their lawmen capacities. When Sheriff, Tom Sullivan boasted to reporter, Rene Romo, for the

December 9, 2003, *Albuquerque Journal's* "Kid's Mom May Stay Buried." Romo wrote: "**This summer, the sheriffs of Lincoln and De Baca counties opened a criminal investigation into the death of William Bonney aka Billy the Kid to resolve claims that Lincoln County Sheriff Pat Garrett killed someone other than the famous outlaw at Fort Sumner on July 14, 1881.**"

On October 21, 2005, Tom Sullivan's letter to the *RuidosoNews.com* editor stated: "Frederick Nolan dismisses the modern day law enforcement technologies we have used to recreate the crime scene in Pete Maxwell's bedroom on the night that Pat Garrett allegedly shot "the Kid" as nothing but "stunts." And now Robert Utley refers to us as "loony guys" and "two nut cases" ... Our investigation contradicts their theories written in their books. It appears that our critics all suffer from the same "kindergartenmentality." [sic] Why are they so afraid of the truth? ... **Steve and I were both sworn in as sheriff's deputies by Sheriff Rick Virden shortly after he took office**."

SEDERWALL'S HOBBYIST HOAXING

To fake that they were not public official lawmen, Deputies Steve Sederwall and Tom Sullivan presented to my open records attorney, their June 21, 2007, 18 page, "Memorandum" to Sheriff Rick Virden, **resigning their deputyships**, while claiming to be private hobbyists! But the requested records were from before 2007, when they were admittedly Virden's Deputies for conducting Case 2003-274 "Billy the Kid Case." In response, complicit Sheriff Virden claimed he had no way to recover records from them.

So in my open records litigation's September 9, 2010 Hearing for Mandatory Disclosure and Production of Records, Sederwall's attorney, Kevin Brown, stated: "[O]ur position is going to be that **Steve Sederwall is an amateur historian ... whatever he's doing on his own cannot be considered a public document**." [Transcript 9/9/10, p. 16]

This hid that, as Sheriff, Rick Virden had issued Sederwall and Sullivan full-powered **commissioned deputy cards**; with Sullivan's dated January 1, 2005, **and Sederwall's dated February 25, 2005 [FIGURE: 4]** to enable their doing exhumations. And in answer to my open records request, on November 28, 2005, Virden had responded on his official letterhead; stating: "**Tom Sullivan and Steve Sederwall are Deputies with the Lincoln County Sheriff''s Department ... Tom Sullivan and Steve Sederwall are assigned to investigate the shootings of William**

H. Bonney and Deputies Bell and Olinger." And Virden hid his 2007 letter to Hamilton, Texas, Mayor Roy Rumsey, trying to get "Brushy Bill" exhumed: "Mayor Ramsey [sic], This letter will inform you that **Tom Sullivan and Steve Sederwall are both commissioned deputies with the Lincoln County New Mexico Sheriff's Department. They have been investigating case # 2003-274**."

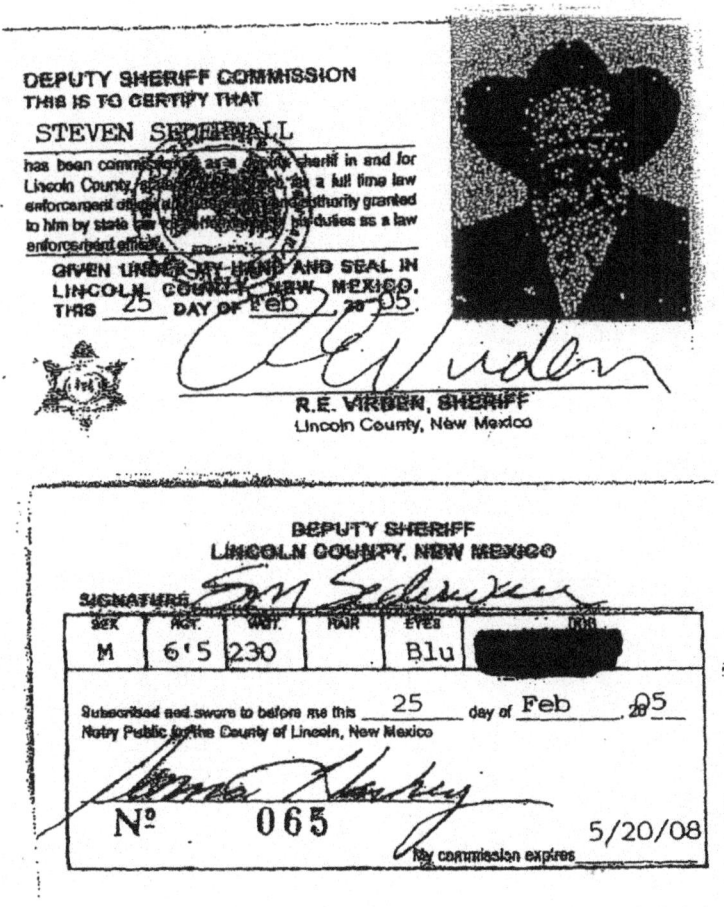

FIGURE: 4. Commissioned Deputy Card of Steve Sederwall dated February 25, 2005

SEDERWALL'S "HOBBYIST" TESTIMONIES

The most brazen "hobbyist" claims were by Steve Sederwall, claiming he had done the "Billy the Kid Case" by himself.

About Dr. Henry Lee's reporting on his carpenter's bench and courthouse floorboards specimen recoveries, Sederwall testified on January 21, 211, for an Evidentiary Hearing, that he had gotten Lee's reports at home as a private citizen hobbyist, working with a group he called the "posse." The transcript recorded him:

A. Dr. Lee called me is how it went down. He called me, and I told him ... we would try to get him involved, that would be great, because **this whole affair thing was done by – we call it a posse**. It is done on their own time and their own dime. And Dr. Lee, when we found the workbench and other items, and then we wanted to do the CSI down at the courthouse, so we called him --- I think Bill Curtis [sic] called and arranged him to come out.

Q. So did you personally ever receive a copy of Exhibit E [furniture investigation, including carpenter's bench]?

A. Yes, sir.

Q. How did you receive it?

A. Dr. Lee mailed it to me ... At my house.

Q. When you received a report at your house ... you weren't acting as a Lincoln County investigator, were you?

A. No, Sir.

Q. When you received the report, who did you think it belonged to?

A. It belonged to me. It was sent to me ...

[And the same questioning and answering was repeated for Exhibit F, the courthouse floorboard investigation.] ...

Q. Have you ever called Orchid Cellmark to talk about things?

A. Yes, sir.

Q. Tell me about those calls.

A. The first one, we asked Dr. Lee who would be some one to deal with, and he told us Orchid Cellmark. So I discussed it with them, and told them we couldn't pay them. **We were looking at a historical event, just a bunch of guys with backgrounds as criminal investigators** ... They said that would be fine. (Transcript 1/21/11, pp. 169-171)

In his June 26, 2012 Deposition (TR, p. 561), cornered about his hobbyist ploy making no sense, incorrigible con-artist

Sederwall gave a smart-alack reply: **not feeling like a deputy in his mind**! My attorney's questioning was as follows:

Q. This is a letter to [Jay] Miller [my open records proxy] from Virden. It says that you - Tom Sullivan and Steve Sederwall are assigned to investigate the shootings of William H. Bonney and Deputies Bell and Olinger? ...
A. Yes, sir ... I've never - this is the first time I've seen this letter ... Rick Virden **never gave me an assignment other than, can you go watch a horse barn, and help transport prisoners**, and work the Lincoln Days ...
Q. With the probable cause statement that I just read you and the questions and answers, we know that you were acting as a Deputy Sheriff at the time you went with Henry Lee to get the scrapings, weren't you? ...
A. **In my mind, I was, not that night, acting as a Deputy Sheriff. ... Because I'm a Deputy Sheriff, doesn't mean that I am acting on their behalf. I was not. I wasn't sent up there to do this. I was just looking. I'm a Deputy Sheriff, yes. I'm also a grandpa** ...

In fact, Lee had responded in his May 1, 2006 letter to my open records request by making clear that it was a law enforcement case: "To set the record straight, **the Lincoln County Sheriff's Department contacted me**. They requested a forensic expert to perform preliminary identification and scene reconstruction ... **We examined a wooden bench, and floorboards at the courthouse. I completed my examination of the evidence and submitted my report to the Lincoln County Sheriff's Department**." And when Lee gave his affidavit for my litigation, on August 31, 2012, he swore that his work was for the Lincoln County Sheriff's Department; stating: "In approximately late July and early August of 2004, I assisted with the collection of samples from various locations thought to be locations where there may have been residue of biological material, which could be **relevant to an investigation into the death of William Bonney, a/k/a Billy the Kid, then being performed by the Lincoln County, New Mexico, Sheriff's Department**."

And Sederwall was hiding that he had been deputized by Sheriff Tom Sullivan in 2003, had a Commissioned Deputy card from Sheriff Rick Virden dated February 25, 2005 **[FIGURE: 4]**, and had only resigned as a Deputy on June 21, 2007 after the case was done. (See page 239 below)

At the end of my District Court litigation, when I prevailed as *pro* se, the judge, in his May 15, 2014 "Findings of Fact and Conclusions of Law and Order of the Court" **[APPENDIX: 4],** ruled that Sederwall's was a public official Deputy, as well as playing hide-the-ball with the records; writing:

11. In the request phase, no records were given and their denials were improper: without valid IPRA [open records] exceptions; with Sullivan and Sederwall after having resigned their deputyship on June 21, 2007 admitting to records possession, but calling them private hobby "trade secrets;" with Virden denying having any Case 2003-274 records; and with Virden not attempting to recover records from Sullivan, Sederwall, Lee, or Orchid Cellmark ...

13. As public officials, under Section 14-2-5 NMSA 1978, Sullivan and Sederwall had to provide records as, "an integral part of the routine duties of public officers and employees."

14. As commissioned deputies, under Section 13[sic - 14]-2-11(B)(2) NMSA 1978, along with Virden, they were "responsible for the denial of records." As Virden's deputies, they were his agents. "A person may appoint an agent to do the same acts and achieve the same legal consequences by performing of an act as if he or she had acted personally." 3 Am. Jur. 2d Agency Section 18, at 422 (2002). Section 4-41-9 NMSA 1978 states, "The said deputies are hereby authorized to discharge all the duties which belong to the office of sheriff, that may be placed under their charge by their principals, with the same effect as though they were executed by the respective sheriffs."

15. Sullivan and Sederwall said they were hobbyists and the records were private property. Sullivan's and Sederwall's argument of being "unsalaried "reserve deputies" is irrelevant to the records responsibility, since "an agent is a person who, by agreement with another called the principal, represents the principal in dealings with third persons or transacts some other business ... for the principal, with or without compensation. UJI 13-401, NMRA.

16. In their June 21, 2007 "Memorandum" to Virden, Sullivan and Sederwall admitted to having Case 2003-274 records, but called them private property, while at the same time resigning their public official positions as deputies. Furthermore, from 2010 to 2012, Sederwall offered Case 2003-274 records for sale on his own billythekidcase.com website.

HOAXING THE OMI AS DENYING BILLY THE KID'S BEING BURIED IN FORT SUMNER

EXHUMATION BLOCKADE BY THE OMI

An impassable hurdle for the "Billy the Kid Case" had been the New Mexico Office of the Medical Investigator's (OMI) refusal to issue the hoaxers exhumation permits for Billy Bonney or his mother for their fake DNA quest.

But for my open records case, for convoluted rationalizing that there had been a plot to block exposing the truth of Garrett not killing Billy the Kid, Steve Sederwall made-up that the OMI's forensic anthropologist, Dr. Debra Komar, had concluded that Billy the Kid was not buried in Fort Sumner; ergo was buried in Texas as "Brushy Bill," or Arizona as John Miller.

The actual OMI opposition was as follows.

For my attorneys' litigation opposing the 2003 and 2004 exhumation attempts in Grant County (Catherine Antrim) and De Baca County (Billy Bonney), the head of the OMI, Dr. Ross Zumwalt, and its forensic anthropologist, Dr. Debra Komar, gave Affidavits. **[APPENDIX: 8]** Repeating Dr. Zumwalt, Dr. Komar's Affidavit stated: "[I]f the purpose of exhuming Catherine Antrim is to provide a "known" standard for DNA testing, **the fact that she cannot be positively identified [because her unverified remains buried in 1874 were moved from another location in 1881] renders all DNA tests suspect** ... If attempt is made to exhume the supposed body of Catherine Antrim from the burial site with her name, it is probable with a reasonable degree of scientific probability that the remains of other individuals will be disturbed. The burial site with Catherine Antrim's name is Plot D-27 at Memory Lane Cemetery. **This plot is the resting place of twelve (12) other known individuals** [who might be disturbed or confused with her remains] ... **If the purpose of the exhumation of the remains of Catherine Antrim is to compare her DNA to the remains of the believed Billy the Kid, those remains are not likely to be obtained in my opinion**. Based upon research performed by the OMI, the exact location of the Billy the Kid grave is not known, in my opinion, to a reasonable degree of scientific probability ... **If the purpose of extracting mtDNA [mitochondrial DNA] from the supposed remains of Catherine Antrim is to obtain a sample to compare against Brushy Bill Roberts in Texas, such a comparison, in** my opinion, is also scientifically flawed. **Based on research to date, I am unaware that Mr. Roberts ever claimed to be the biological child of Catherine Antrim**. Thus, a test between his mtDNA and the putative remains of Catherine Antrim would have no scientific basis to a reasonable degree of scientific probability ... Based on the fact that DNA testing of the putative remains of Catherine Antrim would have no probative value and the fact that an exhumation would likely disrupt other burial sites, **an exhumation of Catherine Antrim is scientifically unsound in my opinion.**"

In addition, Debra Komar gave a 224 page deposition on January 20, 2004 in opposition to the exhumation permits. In it, she was described as "a world-renowned forensic anthropologist who has previously worked for the United Nations in the exhumation of mass burials in Eastern Europe." (Deposition, 1/20/04, p. 11) And she repeated the forensic objections of her Affidavit.

She highlighted that "Billy the Kid is not buried in an isolated situation, but that he shares his burial with two other individuals" (Deposition, 1/20/04, pp. 17-18); and "there seems to be disagreement as to the placement of the bodies [of Tom O'Folliard, Charles Bowdre, and Billy Bonney] relative to each other; and some disagreement as to the placement of those bodies within the cemetery." (Deposition, 1/20/04, p. 22)

As to Silver City's Catherine Antrim remains, Komar described their relocation by untrained laborers from a cemetery within the city limits to one outside them at Memory Lane Cemetery; with added problem that flooding had also occurred. (Deposition, 1/20/04, pp. 24-25) She stated: "We know she's been moved. We know there's been flooding. We know when she was moved, it was in a completely uncontrolled set of circumstances. And therefore, to hold her up as some sort of standard [for DNA identification] becomes scientifically unacceptable." (Page 38) Added was that Catherine's current plot overlapped 12 other individuals! (Deposition, 1/20/04, p. 52)

As to the Fort Sumner Billy the Kid grave, where flooding "literally washed bodies out of the ground" (Deposition, 1/20/04, p. 45), there was "not a specific place where we would put a shovel in the ground ... [because the grave location is uncertain and] remains themselves may no longer still be there." (Deposition, 1/20/04, p. 69)

As to "Brushy," who denied being Catherine Antrim's son, Komar said: "[Y]ou might as well compare his [mitochondrial] DNA to mine. It would mean as much." (Deposition, 1/20/04, p. 77)

She concluded about the "Billy the Kid Case's" sought DNA of Billy and his mother: "**So if you ask the opinion of myself and the Office of the Medical Investigator why is this being done or what scientifically valid conclusions can be drawn from it, I can't find any**." (Page 81)

Key hoaxer, Attorney Bill Robins III, cross-examined her as to Catherine Antrim. He ignored the OMI's contention of invalid DNA and disturbing other remains; instead, quibbled meaninglessly about soil samples, the original grave marker, how to avoid other graves, or how long DNA lasted. Dr. Komar responded: "[W]e're arguing that we can't do that .. given that we can't then prove it's Catherine Antrim." (Deposition, 1/20/04, p. 39) She repeated the OMI's refusal: "If the purpose of using Catherine is to provide [DNA] identification for someone else that must be, for a forensic standard, based on [her] positive identification to begin with." (Deposition, 1/20/04, p. 142) "We don't exhume historical people for the sake of doing it." (Page 143) As to Billy the Kid, the same problems applied. And there was the addition of the removal of the supposed body of a soldier from the cemetery's military past, with the chance that Billy's body, not his, had been accidentally taken at that time! (Deposition, 1/20/04, pp. 70-72) So the following interchange occurred:

ROBINS QUESTION: You don't think Billy the Kid is buried at Fort Sumner, do you?
KOMAR ANSWER: I don't know. I have reason to suspect perhaps not. (Page 144)

Komar had merely repeated her Affidavit's contention that "[b]ased upon research performed by the OMI, the exact location of the Billy the Kid grave is not known." **But this interchange would subsequently be seized upon out of context and faked by Steve Sederwall in W.C. Jameson's 2018** *Cold Case Billy the Kid* **to claim she said Billy the Kid was buried elsewhere; ergo, he was "Brushy Bill" buried in Hamilton, Texas!**

In fact, Komar was also referring to her earlier statements in her deposition, in which she said about Billy: **"[T]he remains may no longer still be there. Even if they were buried there at one point.**" (Deposition, 1/20/04, p. 69) She was referring to her finding references to Billy's remains being stolen to sell soon after burial, or other digging in the area finding no remains. (Deposition, 1/20/04, p. 70) Or, in 1904, a Willie E. Griffin was hired to remove soldiers from that old military cemetery to move to Santa Fe's National Cemetery, and knew that one was supposed to be buried in association with the contiguous graves of Billy, Charles Bowdre, and Tom O'Folliard. He found only two bodies, and took one. So he is the one who may have accidentally removed Billy! (Deposition, 1/20/04, pp. 71-72)

As the OMI's Attorney, William Snead, concluded in Komar's deposition, as to the OMI's position: **"We're opposed to the principle of digging someone up where it's not going to lead to scientifically probative evidence."** (Deposition, 1/20/04, p. 203)

HOAXING DR. KOMAR'S STATEMENTS

For my open records litigation against the lawmen hoaxers, their complicit Lincoln County Attorney, Alan Morel, hiding their requested DNA records, on June 22, 2007, presented their major hoax document to my attorney titled "Memorandum, Subject: Billy the Kid Investigation," addressed to "Rick Virden, Lincoln County Sheriff," from "Steven M. Sederwall & Thomas T. Sullivan." It was signed by all three. Possibly written just by Sederwall, who later recycled it for W.C. Jameson's 2018 *Cold Case Billy the Kid*, it was seven footnoted pages, with Attachments. It was an elaborate fiction portraying him and Sullivan as martyrs for the truth, and resigning their deputyships. (See pages 228-239 below)

The "Memorandum" included a conspiracy theory hoax making up-that Dr. Komar had backed them as to Billy the Kid not being buried in Fort Sumner, but was forced by higher powers to hide that fact to protect New Mexico tourism of Billy the Kid! It stated:

> At the time investigators did not know if DNA could be obtained from a grave after 100 years, so after the Governor's news conference Sederwall met with Dr. Debra Komar an investigator with the New Mexico Office of the Medical Investigator's office. During this meeting Dr. Komar said considering the terrain, topography and climate of Silver City she judged chances of obtaining DNA from Catherine Antrim would be somewhere in the ninety percent range. Dr. Komar said she would begin investigating the graves. She and her boss were excited about working on this historical investigation ...

[AUTHOR'S NOTE: Being hidden is Dr. Komar's OMI position, in her affidavit and deposition: that the graves of Billy and his mother had no forensically valid DNA.]

As the unchecked fear spread, investigators were trying to make contact with Dr. Komar at the OMI's office but she refused to return the calls. We were advised by the girl answering the phone that she had instructions not to send our calls to Dr. Komar. The girl stated that Dr. Komar had "lawyered up" and we would have to talk to her attorney. We had never heard of a medical investigator retaining an attorney to deal with investigators.

[AUTHOR'S NOTE: This omits the OMI's blockade based on forensically useless DNA. Being fabricated is a "conspiracy against truth" by the OMI in what follows.]

We didn't understand until January 20, 2004, when Bill Robins an attorney appointed by the Governor for the Kid, deposed Dr. Komar. She was asked by Robins, on page 144 lines 7 – 10 of the record, *"You don't think Billy the Kid is buried at Fort Sumner, do you?"* Dr. Komar replied, *"I don't know. I have reason to suspect perhaps not."*

[AUTHOR'S NOTE: Taken out of context is Komar's response about Billy's body possibly being gone because of flooding, or accidental removal with soldiers' bodies

It was at this point we believed Dr. Komar had discovered information, maybe some of the same information we had, about the Kid's grave. We wondered if the fear of harming New Mexico's tourist industry had caused the state to apply pressure to Dr. Komar and told her not to talk to us, in hopes this case would die and the myth would live.

[AUTHOR'S NOTE: The "conspiracy" involves Komar and "the state;" though she merely stated that there was no valid Billy the Kid DNA in Fort Sumer. But this hoax claims she knew Billy was buried elsewhere as "Brushy!" Sederwall repeated this scam in 2018 in W.C. Jameson's book, *Cold Case Billy the Kid.* (See pages 243-245 below)]

Since doctor Komar had obtained a lawyer and refused to talk, we wrote a letter to the OMI's office under the *New Mexico Open Records Act* asking for Dr. Komar's records. Unlike our part of the investigation, it was government money that financed her studies and paid her trips to gain information, which we reasoned would make the records public.

[AUTHOR'S NOTE: The attempt was made to harass Komar into saying Billy was never buried in Fort Sumner; with added hoaxing that, unlike her, they were private hobbyists immune to open records requests!]

After nearly 5 months of letters back and forth to the OMI's office we were provided with only a list of who was buried in Silver City. We knew that Dr. Komar had more records than the state admitted because she had stated this fact when deposed by Robins. We pointed out the state had paid for her trips and we knew there was more information, we received a response saying, *"The remainder of the material requested in your public records act request is in the possession of Dr. Komar, a faculty member of the University of New Mexico, and constitutes her intellectual property under federal copyright law and the University of New Mexico's Intellectual Property Policy."* [Footnote 5: Letter from Salvatore J. Giammo, Director of Public Affairs HSC Custodian of Public Records, address to Sullivan and Sederwall, dated April 12, 2007]

It became clear the state was hiding information and was not going to share it with investigators. The nagging question remained, what was the information and why did the state feel a need to hide it?

[AUTHOR'S NOTE: Fabricated is something "hidden." The hoaxers knew the OMI's Affidavits and Komar Deposition confirmed invalid DNA in the Billy and mother graves.]

THE "MEMORANDUM" HOAXING "BILLY THE KID CASE'S" FAILURE AS A CONSPIRACY AGAINST HIMSELF AND TOM SULLIVAN

The "Memorandum" of June 21, 2007 was a major hoax document on the order of the Case 2003-274 "Probable Cause Statement." As stated above, it was likely written by Steve Sederwall, when a Deputy, with fellow Deputy (and past Sheriff) Tom Sullivan, and was addressed to Sheriff Rick Virden, in response to my open records request for the forensic records of Case 2003-274.

Like Sederwall's "Probable Cause Statement," its fabrications are labor-intensive. It was a crazy and jumbled re-write of the "Billy the Kid Case," blaming its failure on a conspiracy of Governor Richardson (biting the hand that fed him), tourist interests, and me. Its apparent intent was to create arguments for a future judge in the litigation, by stating that the case's records were immune to open records law because of being their private property. That also shielded Virden, since it intended to hide records that also incriminated him. It stated:

To: Rick Virden, Lincoln County Sheriff
From: Steven M. Sederwall & Thomas T. Sullivan
Subject: Billy the Kid Investigation
Date: Thursday, June 21, 2007

On April 28, 2003 we began a quest for the truth, looking into the *"escape of William Bonney and the double homicide of James Bell & Robert Olinger.* [Footnote 1: Lincoln County Call sheet pulled by Sheriff Sullivan April 28, 2003.] We chose this as a private venture and did not want to burden the county financially. The idea was to being modern science and police investigation methods to uncover the truth of the escape of the Kid and murder of our deputies. We had planned to file a report with the Sheriff at the end of the investigation, a report which the public could then access if they so desire.

[AUTHOR'S NOTE: Hoaxed is Case 2003-274 as the Deputy killing sub-investigation, concealing the Garrett murder case, and faking themselves as private hobbyists.]

At the beginning of the investigation, it became known that career law enforcement officers were investigating a century old cold case involving Billy the Kid and the case began to generate a great deal of press.

[AUTHOR'S NOTE: This is untrue. Publicity was from claiming Pat Garrett did not kill the Kid, and from Governor Richardson's press release to the *New York Times* calling it a real murder investigation with Case Number 2003-274.]

With the enormous amount of publicity generated by the investigation Governor Bill Richardson was prompted to call a press conference. On Tuesday, June 10, 2003 he told the world of his intentions; *"I am announcing my support and the support of the state of New Mexico for the investigation into the life and death of Henry McCarty, also known as William Bonney".*

[AUTHOR'S NOTE: This is fake time inversion; Richardson's article and press conference created the publicity.]

He told the roomful of reporters, *"By utilizing modern forensics, DNA and crime scene techniques, the goal of the investigation is to get to the truth. In the process, the reputation of Pat Garrett, still a hero to Lincoln County law enforcement hangs in the balance. The question is did Sheriff Garrett kill Billy the Kid at Fort Sumner, New Mexico on July 14, 1881"* The Governor went on to say, *"If we can get to the truth we will."*

[AUTHOR'S NOTE: This contradicts the case's being only the Deputy Bell killing investigation. Also begun is a devil-made-me-do-it accusation of Richardson as the prime mover of the Billy the Kid Case.]

On September 1, 2003, the Governor, behind the scenes, supported the investigation, by instructing Billy Sparks to hand Sheriff Sullivan three checks, from private backers, totaling $6,500.00. [Footnote 2: Three checks handed to Sheriff Sullivan in Governor's office by Billy Sparks] Standing at the threshold of the Governor's office, Sparks said, *"The governor wants to insure this investigation goes forward."*

[AUTHOR'S NOTE: This angrily exposes Richardson's "buy a sheriff scheme!" The checks, presented in Attachment 2, show the payees as the Lincoln County Sheriff's Department Case 2003-274 or the "Billy the Kid Investigation."]

The Governor also asked investigators to contact Ft. Sumner and get them *"on board."* On Friday, June 13th, Sederwall drove to Ft. Sumner and spoke with Mayor Raymond Lopez. Lopez liked the idea of worldwide attention on his village and felt it would help boost tourist dollars. He handwrote a note to the Governor, on Ft. Sumner letterhead saying, *"Mr. Steve Sederwall and I have talked and feel that we are on the same page on this Billy the Kid deal. He'll bring the information to you on the talk we had."* [Footnote 3: Handwritten note by Mayor Raymond Lopez on Ft. Sumner letterhead]

At the time investigators did not know if DNA could be obtained from a grave after 100 years, so after the Governor's news conference Sederwall met with Dr. Debra Komar an investigator with the New Mexico Office of the Medical Investigator's office. During this meeting Dr. Komar said considering the terrain, topography and climate of Silver City she judged chances of obtaining DNA from Catherine Antrim would be somewhere in the ninety percent range. Dr. Komar said she would begin investigating the graves. She and her boss were excited about working on this historical investigation.

[AUTHOR'S NOTE: This was a switch to the Garrett murder, and from the Fort Sumner grave to the mother's. Importantly, being hidden is Dr. Komar's OMI position, in her affidavit and deposition, that the graves of Billy and his mother had no forensically valid DNA.]

On June 17th, 2003, something happened that shocked the investigators. In a Ft. Sumner grocery store, Ft. Sumner's ex-mayor, David Bailey approached DeBaca County Sheriff Gary Graves and told him the Billy the Kid investigation *"had to stop."* Bailey said that if the Sheriff's [sic] were to exhume the grave of the Kid there would be a problem. Bailey said, *"You do not know what you are going to find but I do."*

On Friday, October 10, 2003, investigators were in Grant County District Court requesting a court order to exhume the body of Catherine Antrim, who is known as William H. Bonney's mother. Investigators wanted to obtain her DNA. Attorneys for Silver City and Ft. Sumner opposed the exhumation, so the judge scheduled a hearing on the matter, set for August of 2004.

[AUTHOR'S NOTE: This hides that the exhumations were all part of Case 2003-274, with themselves as its lawmen petitioners, along with Sheriff Gary Graves.]

The same day in a special meeting of the town of Silver City, Councilman Steve May objected to the exhumation by saying, *"Who cares? Who cares if it's Billy the Kid buried in Fort Sumner or if it's Brushy Bill in Texas? We might regret this if the DNA shows it's not Billy the Kid. We could shoot ourselves in the foot."*

Fear quickly spread through the "Billy the Kid" community. Anyone with an interest to protect, museum owners, authors, and entire towns became afraid of what the investigation would uncover and how it would affect their livelihood. The newspapers were full of their fears, libelous accusations and paranoia.

[AUTHOR'S NOTE: Blocked exhumations are faked as a "fearing-truth-conspiracy;" while hiding the OMI's permit refusals, and certainty that Garrett did kill the Kid.]

"What will happen if no DNA from that grave matches DNA from the Silver City site? How do we explain that? Might it be better to leave well enough alone?" – Jay Miler, syndicated columnist, *Inside the Capital* [sic], July 25, 2003.

"I think it would have a truly negative impact if that's not Billy the Kid over there (Fort Sumner) – Silver City Councilman Steve May, Silver City Sun News, October 11, 2003.

"This is an industry for us," Lopez said. *"It's no different from Intel, or Sandia Labs, or Kirkland Airforce Base. It's that big for us. We don't have much to live off other than the legend, so we have to protect it."* – Fort Sumner Mayor, Raymond Lopez, November 18, 2003, MSNBC News.

The investigation has the *"potential to destroy the existing legend and mystery and folklore surrounding Billy the Kid, badly damage the state's tourism industry, and severely impact the economy of the state, and damage the reputation of the Governor's Office."* – Letter to New Mexico Governor Bill Richardson signed by the Silver City Town Counsel [sic], June 21, 2004.

[AUTHOR'S NOTE: This was Silver City's citizens' petition, ignored by Governor Richardson, indifferent to destroying its real history - here called "legend" – while he pursued his "Brushy Bill" as Billy the Kid scheme.]

Silver City and Fort Sumner face a loss of part of their Billy the Kid legend if DNA analysis is unable to show a match between bones dug up in the two communities." ?" – Jay Miler, *Inside the Capital* [sic], July 2, 2004.

"And if bodies are exhumed and no matching DNA is found, as the Office of the Medical Investigator predicts, the effect on these communities will be considerable, especially on Fort Sumner." – Jay Miler, *Inside the Capital* [sic], September 19, 2004.

The comments were published nearly daily. Their words told us they feared the Kid was not buried in Ft. Sumner. Most of the history of the escape of the Kid as well as his alleged killing by Garrett was built on a foundation set forth in Garrett's book. Historian Robert Utley pointed out in his book, *Billy the Kid a short and violent life:* "*Although not many copies of the Authentic life were sold, it nevertheless had a decisive impact of the Kid's image. More than any other single influence, the Garrett-Upson book fed the legend of Billy the Kid. As the legend blossomed, writers turned to the Authentic life* [sic] *for the authentic details. Ash Upson's fictions became implanted in the hundreds of 'histories' that followed.*

[AUTHOR'S NOTE: This recycles the Utley misquote from the "Probable Cause Statement," where he is not talking about scholarly history, but growth of the legend.]

Investigators were searching for the truth in this story and the fact that Garrett was not truthful in his accounts was not brought to the table by investigators but historians themselves. Just as Utley voiced Garrett was not truthful, in an August 8, 2000 interview with the Associated Press, Historian Frederick Nolan made the statement that Garrett's version of the Kid's death *"may have been the biggest lie of all."*

[AUTHOR'S NOTE: This misstates Nolan, who was, like Utley, commenting on Garrett's book's dime novel style, but not denying that Garrett fatally shot Billy. Pretended is that Nolan called Garrett's report of the killing a lie.]

Yet when it became know [sic] investigators planned to use science, fear prompted the only thing that could be done to protect the books, museums, throw insults, such as, *"The three sheriffs trying to dig up Billy and his mother are a slippery bunch of varmits."* [sic] – Jay Miler, *Inside the Capital* [sic], August 9, 2004.

It was from there that the campaign to discredit the investigation and investigators was launched. Even Nolan saying that Garrett lied, feared his repeated version of the history was being questioned wrote an editor of the *Ruidoso News.* He said, *"This project is a complete and utter nonsense, and I Wouldn't be at all surprised if Sheriff Sullivan and Mayor Sederwall are already wishing they'd never got started on this benighted project."* The next day Nolan garnered more press by appearing on CCN *Live Saturday* with Frederika Whitfield, talking ill of the investigators.

As the unchecked fear spread, investigators were trying to make contact with Dr. Komar at the OMI's office but she refused to return the calls. We were advised by the girl answering the phone that she had instructions not to send our calls to Dr. Komar. The girl stated that Dr. Komar had "lawyered up" and we would have to talk to her attorney. We had never heard of a medical investigator retaining an attorney to deal with investigators.

[AUTHOR'S NOTE: This omits the OMI's blockade based on forensically useless DNA. A fabricated "OMI conspiracy against truth" follows.]

We didn't understand until January 20, 2004, when Bill Robins an attorney appointed by the Governor for the Kid, deposed Dr. Komar. She was asked by Robins, on page 144 lines 7 – 10 of the record, *"You don't think Billy the Kid is buried at Fort Sumner, do you?"* Dr. Komar replied, *"I don't know. I have reason to suspect perhaps not."*

[AUTHOR'S NOTE: As discussed above (see page 225), taken out of context is Komar's response about the Billy's body possibly not being present because of flooding, or accidental removal with soldiers' bodies

It was at this point we believed Dr. Komar had discovered information, maybe some of the same information we had, about the Kid's grave. We wondered if the fear of harming New Mexico's tourist industry had caused the state to apply pressure to Dr. Komar and told her not to talk to us, in hopes this case would die and the myth would live.

[AUTHOR'S NOTE: The faked "conspiracy" involves Komar and "the state;" though she merely explained that there was no valid Billy the Kid DNA available in Fort Sumer. But this hoax now claims that she knew Billy was buried elsewhere as "Brushy!" Sederwall repeated this scam in 2018 in W.C., Jameson's book, Cold Case Billy the Kid. (See pages 243-245 below)]

Since doctor Komar had obtained a lawyer and refused to talk, we wrote a letter to the OMI's office under the *New Mexico Open Records Act* asking for Dr. Komar's records. Unlike our part of the investigation, it was government money that financed her studies and paid her trips to gain information, which we reasoned would make the records public.

[AUTHOR'S NOTE: They were trying to force Komar to say Billy was never buried in Fort Sumner.]

After nearly 5 months of letters back and forth to the OMI's office we were provided with only a list of who was buried in Silver City. We knew that Dr. Komar had more records than the state admitted because she had stated this fact when deposed by Robins. We pointed out the state had paid for her trips and we knew there was more information, we received a response saying, *"The remainder of the material requested in your public records act request is in the possession of Dr. Komar, a faculty member of the University of New Mexico, and constitutes her intellectual property under federal copyright law and the University of New Mexico's Intellectual Property Policy."* [Footnote 5: Letter from Salvatore J. Giammo, Director of Public Affairs HSC Custodian of Public Records, address to Sullivan and Sederwall, dated April 12, 2007]

It became clear the state was hiding information and was not going to share it with investigators. The nagging question remained, what was the information and why did the state feel a need to hide it?

[AUTHOR'S NOTE: Faked is something "hidden." They knew the OMI concluded invalid DNA in the graves.]

Friday April 2, 2004, the judge in Silver City came out with a surprise ruling, not waiting for the August hearing; his ruling startled investigators would have to provide the court with DNA from Fort Sumner before he would allow the investigators to obtain DNA from Catherine Antrim.

[AUTHOR'S NOTE: This fakes that "Komar-concealed-information" was the cause of the case's 2004 transfer to Fort Sumner; not the truth that the Judge, Henry Quintero, colluded with Attorney Bill Robins III to call the case "not ripe" – meaning he wanted Billy's DNA first to justify digging up the mother for matching, as a ploy to get the case there, since they were losing in Silver City to my attorneys there. (See page 242 below)]

What no one realized was that by September 20, 2003, we had located the workbench on which Garrett claimed to have laid the Kid's body. Through our discussions with the CSI experts we felt the Kid's DNA could be obtained from that bench. We also knew historians, from as far back as the 1920's, knew the grave was not located behind the "museum and gift shop" as Ft. Sumner had led tourist [sic] to believe. [Footnote 6: Notes entitled "Bonney Grave, Ft. Sumner", by Fulton found in the Robert N. Mullin Collection, Haley Memorial Library] We also knew that digging into that empty grave would be fruitless.

[AUTHOR'S NOTE: This is a lie about Billy's grave not being in Fort Sumner's cemetery, instead of its merely having no certain location to justify exhumation. Instead, the hoax is now switched to the invalid bench as a DNA source. And still conceal is that the bench was part of Case 2003-274, not their private hobby; and that it yielded no DNA.]

Without contacting us and immediately after the judge ruled, Attorney Bill Robins filed to exhume the Kid in Ft. Sumner. The fight was on again with the village of Ft. Sumner filing motions to block Robins' attempt to look in their grave. On Wednesday July 22, 2004, Billy Sparks of the Governor's office called Sederwall at home. Sparks asked if the investigators would *'pull out of Fort Sumner"* and if so the Governor would consider it a *"personal favor."* Sparks said Silver City and Ft. Sumner were putting a great deal of pressure on the Governor to stop the dig because they feared it would destroy their tourism.

[AUTHOR'S NOTE: Besides the continued surprising biting of the hands that had fed them, this fabricates the Fort Sumner withdrawal reason. It occurred after Lincoln County Commissioner Leo Martinez threatened Sullivan with recall for doing a hoax with public money and without County Commissioners' approval. And they well knew of Robins's filing, since they were its lawmen petitioners!]

Sederwall called Mayor Lopez and attempted to talk to him about the issue and tell him it was not our desire to harm tourism in

New Mexico. When Sederwall identified himself Lopez shouted, *"fuck you!"* and hung up. This was the last time any of the investigators talk [sic] to Mayor Lopez.

[AUTHOR'S NOTE: This may be Sederwall's reworking his original thuggish threat to Lopez, as reported to me by Lopez, as: "Get your head out of your ass. We're getting this done whether you want it or not."]

That Friday we called our attorney and told him attorney Robins had filed the case on our behalf and we wanted to withdraw it. Which he did and we sat back quietly as Ft. Sumner was shorn in the press throwing a party where Frederick Nolan declared it a victory for "truth."

[AUTHOR'S NOTE: Omitted is that the Fort Sumner case had proceeded for months under their attorney, Mark Acuña; that Robins was Billy's, not their, attorney; and they withdrew days before the September 27, 2004 Hearing because of Leo Martinez's press exposure.]

During the investigation the village of Fort Sumner, the town of Silver City and the city of Hamilton, Texas, in an effort to protect tourism, fought the investigation so DNA could not be recovered.

In the case of Hamilton, Texas, Brushy Bill Roberts died under the name of Oliver L. Roberts and his date of birth, on his official death certificate sets out he was born on December 31, 1868 [Footnote 7: Death certificate of Ollie L. Roberts], which would make the man 12 years old in 1881 when the Kid shot and killed James Bell and Robert Olinger.]

[AUTHOR'S NOTE: This lie about Hamilton being a tourism conspiracy, conceals that digging up "Brushy" was refused by its County Commissioners based on the hoaxers' refusing to provide DNA records to prove they had anything for its justification (which they did not have).]

Roberts died a pauper and was buried at county expense and above his grave was placed a homemade marker of cement. [Footnote 8: Old Tombstone of Ollie L. Roberts] However, the investigators found a new tombstone on a grave located in the middle cemetery [sic] on the first row, in a very prominent place. We wondered if that grave is empty and there only for tourists. We wondered if the man was in fact buried in the back of the cemetery.

The new marker was donated and placed by the owner of the Billy the Kid Memorial Museum in Hamilton. [Footnote 9: New Tombstone for "Henry William Roberts"] Roberts name has changed from Ollie L. Roberts as listed on his death certificate and old tombstone to *Henry W. Roberts* on the new tombstone. As well, his date of birth has changed from December 31, 1868, to December 31, 1859. This would make him 21 in 1881 rather than 12 and would coincide with the history of Billy the Kid.

On May 20, 2005 [sic- May 19, 2003], the only body to be exhumed who claimed to be Billy the Kid was that of John Miller. The state of Arizona exhumed Mr. Miller and the samples were received by Dr. Rick Staub of Orchid Cellmark labs in Dallas for recovery of DNA.

[AUTHOR'S NOTE: This is the reworking of their Arizona exhumation fiasco as "the state did it." And concealed is grave-robbing of William Hudspeth. And omitted is that they did the exhumations for Case 2003-274, while lying that they had Dr. Lee's bench DNA for matching.]

Investigators agree the investigation of Billy the Kid has garnered more press and has been more troublesome than any thing we have encountered in the past. Countless letters have been written to the Village of Capitan, Orchid Cellmark, Dr. Henry Lee's office, Lincoln County, the Lincoln County Sheriff, Lincoln Counties [sic] Attorney, the New Mexico Attorney General, the United States Marshal's [sic], newspapers, magazines and to investigators in an attempt to disrupt or stop the investigation. The majority of these letters were written by Dr. Gail [sic] Cooper or Jay Miller.

[AUTHOR'S NOTE: Now the conspiracy against the truth turns to me and Jay Miller (my past proxy for my open records requests), leaving out that the "letters" were open records requests for their fake DNA records. It is also a lead-in, at this prelude to litigation, to claim that requesting is harassment.]

Miller weighed into the fight the first time on June 6, 2003 with an article accusing Governor Richardson of attempting to get publicity for the state for the investigation. Had Jay Miller read the press release, he would know that Governor Richardson admitted that fact up front.

Miller wrote letter after letter requesting files and documents concerning the financing of the investigation **but there were no records as it was privately funded by law.** Yet, Miller continued to write letter after letter. In a two month period, Jay Miller wrote the United States Marshals office, the Lincoln County Sheriff, the Lincoln County Attorney, James Jimenez, New Mexico Secretary Department Finance and Administration, the New Mexico

Governor, and countless others complaining about Sederwall and Sullivan and each rambling letter, required a response. At one point he complained to the Attorney General Sederwall was *'impersonating a police officer."*

[AUTHOR'S NOTE: Misstated are my open records requests. The issue was that they had no grounds to withhold records; and murder cases are not privately funded!]

The attacks did not center only on Sederwall and Sullivan but on anyone who dared look at the Billy the Kid Case. When Ft. Sumner heard Sheriff Gary Graves was part of the investigative team a campaign began attacking his career. On November 30, 2003 Mayor Ramon [sic] Lopez Mayor of Ft. Sumner was quoted in the paper saying Sheriff Graves was trying to start a "war" with the city over the grave of Billy the Kid. In the end, the Mayor and Ft. Sumner successfully removed Sheriff Gary Graves from office. Sheriff Graves became the first sheriff in New Mexico to be removed by a recall vote and the last sheriff taken out by Billy the Kid.

[AUTHOR'S NOTE: This lies that Sheriff Gary Graves's recall for malfeasance and misfeasance, unrelated to the Billy the Kid Case, was because of it. And Mayor Lopez did not participate. It was a citizens' group that got the necessary signatures, after Graves had stolen a prisoner's money and had repeatedly terrorized residents.]

Both the village of Ft. Sumner and the City of Hamilton, Texas own a grave marked "Billy the Kid" to draw in tourist dollars. The fact remains that a man can have but one grave. Since it is a governmental entity that owns both graves and both governments have fought to keep investigators obtaining DNA from their grave that would prove where Bonney rests, it would go to reason one or both, of these governmental agencies are guilty of perpetrating fraud against the public.

[AUTHOR'S NOTE: Omitted for this fake tourism conspiracy theory, was that they had no DNA of Billy the Kid to match with any remains. And their whole case was a hoax.]

On February 9, 2007, Sederwall and Jay Miller had lunch together in Santa Fe. Without hesitation Sederwall answered any and all questions Miller posed. Miller explained what encouraged him to fight the investigators in the Billy the Kid Case. Miller said he was born in Silver City and knew *"a lot of people up there."* He said he had received a telephone call from someone in Silver City, he chose not to identify, and the caller wanted his help to stop the investigation and the exhumation of the Kid and his mother. Miller said he began to produce the newspaper articles and the massive amount of letters knowing that we would have to answer each of them. He said that a Dr. Gail [sic] Cooper was involved and wrote most of the letters.

Miller admitted if the investigation continued it would jeopardize tourism in both Silver City and Ft. Sumner. The meeting was pleasant and as the men parted company they shook hands. Miller walked away but stopped, turned and said of Catherine Antrim, *"you know she's not in that grave don't you?"*

Even though Ft. Sumner and Hamilton know, in their hearts, Billy the Kid can have only one grave, they continue to fight the discovery of the truth and continue the fraud in the name of commerce. The Governor bending to the pressure from Ft. Sumner and Silver City turned his back on his promise to find the truth. This past week another letter, requiring an answer, came to the Sheriff requesting the information we have gathered in this investigation. **We have been told the letter from Dr. Gail [sic] Cooper's attorney is her attempt to gain the information we have spent years gathering to add to a book she is attempting to sell.**

[AUTHOR'S NOTE: Revealed is their new tactic to hide records by calling them private and immune to open records law for public documents. Also, accusing me as wanting their information for a book I am writing, is intended to mean that they had made spectacular new findings that I wanted to steal! That applied to open records law's "trade secret" exclusionary clause, which they would also misuse in litigation. It shields private businesses working for the state from revealing unrelated proprietary information in open records cases. The hoaxers were just public officials, generating public records.]

We will continue our investigation. Later, we shall make the decision if and when we will release the information. <u>Now, we choose to put an end to the harassment and political pressure by tendering our resignations as Deputies of Lincoln County Sheriff's Department, effective this date.</u>

[AUTHOR'S NOTE: Quitting as its Deputies, did not convert Case 2003-274's records from public to private!]

Respectively Submitted,
Steven M. Sederwall, Thomas T. Sullivan [written and typed]

THE RETURN OF THE "MEMORANDUM" AS A CONSPIRACY AGAINST HIMSELF

For his 2018 book, *Cold Case Billy the Kid*, W.C. Jameson gave Steve Sederwall a platform to rework his June 21, 2007 "Memorandum," in a chapter called "Politics v. Truth," to fabricate himself as a beleaguered, "cop"-hero martyr, seeking truth; with his fellow hoaxers becoming his betrayers. (Pages 168-171)

For this hoax, Sederwall secretly recycled the "Memorandum" as an elaborate conspiracy theory centered on himself as a lone Billy the Kid "investigator." So his duped narrator, Jameson wrote: "The government of New Mexico, from the governor on down to public officials, has fought to keep the myths and legends of Billy the Kid and Pat Garrett alive;" and initiated a number of attempts to thwart any quest for the truth." (Page 168) Sederwall's hallucinatory megalomaniacal fiction poured forth as follows.

As Mayor of Capitan, who happened to be a "reserve" deputy in the Lincoln County Sheriff's Department, he went to Santa Fe with Sheriff Tom Sullivan. There, for unstated reason, they met with Governor Bill Richardson and his communications director, Billy Sparks. Sparks immediately whisked Sederwall away to the "parking garage" and tell him that "[Billy the Kid historian] Fred Nolan had called the governor" and said the carpenter's bench was not real, and Richardson wanted Sparks to "talk with Sederwall about the situation."

Since the bench was just located, Sederwall suspected that a spy had gotten to Nolan in England. Since history professor, Paul Hutton, had been present, that spy must have been him! And, by chance, Hutton was Richardson's Billy the Kid legend history advisor! So there were a lot of politicians, employees, and sycophants in bed together! (Pages 169-170)

So Sparks, in the garage, needed Sederwall's help, since Fort Sumner officials, like its Mayor, Raymond Lopez, were upset that their "cash cow" would be ruined. (Page 170) And people feared carpenter's bench DNA would upset the legend. Sederwall, then still an idealist, thought Richardson would back the truth. But Sparks made clear that the governor had thought that Sederwall would merely "drive around, ask some questions, talk to the newspapers, and proudly declare that everything associated with the Billy the Kid legend was correct." But now it looked like intrepid Sederwall would do a DNA analysis that could "ruin the Billy the Kid legend." So idealist Sederwall abruptly realized, right in that garage, that this was all about politics and money, not truth. (Pages 170-171)

Billy Sparks then asked Sederwall to change *his* focus to a pardon for Billy the Kid. Sederwall, smelling a rat, got Sparks to admit the truth. The truth was that **Sederwall's "photograph and details about the ongoing investigation were showing up in 'every paper on the planet. [H]e was getting more publicity than Governor Richardson."** And they were afraid that Sederwall would find out that Pat Garrett had not killed Billy the Kid. And they wanted to hide this outcome. (Page 171)

Still in that fateful garage, Sederwall asked Sparks if the governor wanted to back out. Sparks said that Richardson wanted to be president of the United States, and wanted the publicity; and his attorney, Bill Robins III would file for the pardon for Billy the Kid "using Sederwall's investigations." So Sederwall could get "cop fun," and tourist dollars would flow in. Except they were now afraid of Sederwall's carpenter's bench. (Page 172)

Worse, Sparks knew about Sederwall's investigations into John Miller and "William Henry Roberts" as potential Billy the Kid's, as also risking the history. And Sparks admitted that they actually did not know where Billy the Kid was buried. (Page 172) **So Sederwall realized that he was doing such a good job as an investigator that they wanted him to stop, because it could interfere with Richardson being president of the United States.** (Page 172) Then Sparks shared a "heads-up": "they [unnamed] have you in their crosshairs and before this is over ... [y]ou guys are going to feel the heat." (Page 172)

Sederwall later learned that the opponent was Fort Sumner's Mayor Raymond Lopez, who had tried to get Richardson to stop the investigation. Evidence was that when Richardson's attorney, Bill Robins III, filed in Grant County to exhume Catherine Antrim to get her DNA **for Sederwall**, Lopez rushed there to stop officials from getting access. He feared her DNA "would not match the DNA from the workbench." (Pages 172-173)

GLITCH IN THE FABLE: In truth, Mayor Raymond Lopez had merely come to Silver City to sit in during a Catherine Antrim exhumation hearing and show solidarity with Silver City's Mayor, Terry Fortenberry, who was opposing

the mother's exhumation. And, for his fable to work, Sederwall hid that the bench had yielded no DNA.]

Sederwall then made up a Silver City Town Council meeting about the threat of *his* getting the mother's DNA; with fear he would show that Billy the Kid was not buried in New Mexico; and that "Brushy Bill" Roberts was Billy the Kid. So Sederwall realized they feared truth, and it was all for money. (Page 173)

Then Judge Henry Quintero, postponed exhumation of the mother, ruling: "Only if the petitioners are successful in locating the Kid's burial site and collecting his DNA, may they petition this court for a review of Catherine Antrim's matter." Sederwall claimed that meant Quintero knew the plan was to compare the mother's remains with Miller and "Brushy Bill," and also knew Fort Sumner's grave would be blocked; **so he wanted Sederwall to dig up Billy wherever he was buried.** (Pages 173-174)

FAKERY: Besides this bizarre rewrite of the case as his own, Sederwall misstated Judge Quintero's ruling of April 2, 2004, for "Sixth Judicial District Court, State of New Mexico, County of Grant. No. MS 2003-11, In the Matter of Catherine Antrim. Decision and Order." Quintero called the case "not ripe," meaning not ready for decision, until Billy the Kid's remains in Fort Sumner had been dug up and DNA extracted for matching; because there was no other reason to dig up the mother. Quintero was responding to digging up Billy in Fort Sumner in the February 26, 2004 filing by Attorneys Bill Robins III, David Sandoval, and Mark Acuña as "In the Matter of William H. Bonney, aka 'Billy the Kid.' Petition for the Exhumation of Billy the Kid's Remains." But Sederwall faked that Quintero's order meant digging up a "Billy the Kid" *anywhere*, **meaning he would accept John Miller in Arizona and "Brushy Bill" Roberts in Texas.**

Sederwall then made-up that Attorney Bill Robins III filed for the Fort Sumner Billy the Kid exhumation *after* Quintero ruled to interfere with Sederwall's digging up Miller and Roberts first as Quintero wanted. And he claimed surprise that his name had been included as a lawman petitioner by Robins. (Page 174)

FAKERY: To fake a conspiracy against the truth, Sederwall reversed the timing on the filings. In fact, first came the Robins filing on February 26, 2004 for the Fort Sumner

exhumation. That precipitated Judge Quintero's order of April 2, 2004, saying merely that he wanted the results of that exhumation before he would proceed in Silver City.

Also, Sederwall's claimed surprise at his name being on the petition is absurd; as lawmen petitioners for the exhumations, he, as Deputy Sheriff, and Tom Sullivan and Gary Graves, as Sheriffs, were on all the Case 2003-274 exhumation filings in Grant and De Baca Counties, because their standing as lawmen conducting the murder case against Pat Garrett was the *sole justification for exhumations.*

Sederwall claimed that three days before the Fort Sumner hearing, Billy Sparks called him and told him to drop the exhumation petition in Fort Sumner; and that it needed his permission because he was a listed petitioner. He gave permission, and then claimed the Fort Sumner politicos had a party to celebrate the news. (Page 174)

FAKERY: Sederwall is hiding that the withdrawal of the Fort Sumner exhumation petition was actually by Sheriff Tom Sullivan, who had just been threatened with potential recall by Lincoln County Commissioner Leo Martinez, for conducting a hoax in his department, and without permission of the County Commissioners. And Sullivan knew that fellow hoaxer, De Baca County Sheriff Gary Graves, was facing recall for unrelated malfeasances, but with added anger of his County Commissioners at his doing the "Billy the Kid Case" against their directive to stop.

The party was actually held by my lawyers opposing exhumation, and included Frederick Nolan, whom I had flown in to testify as to the history; Mayor Raymond Lopez, who stood for Fort Sumner; as well as local citizens like Billy the Kid Outlaw Gang founder, Marlyn Bowlin.

Sederwall next fabricated the response of the OMI for this figment of his imagination. He claimed that he then told Billy Sparks that he had reason to believe that Billy the Kid was not buried in Fort Sumner, and there was no body in its grave. (Pages 174-175) For proof, he stated that Governor Richardson had assigned the state medical investigators office to the case. And he, Sederwall, gave them his theories and plans. Then, state medical investigator, Debra Komar, investigated the Fort Sumner grave and the Arizona grave of John Miller. After that, she refused his calls. (Page 175)

So Sederwall concluded that this proved Komar found something in Fort Sumner or Arizona, and "the state of New Mexico wanted it covered up" from "the public." He said he was determined to find the truth. So on January 20, 2004, Komar appeared in court under a subpoena, to give a deposition. He stated that her going to Fort Sumner's cemetery upset local officials. And he stated that she had testified that she had been prevented from contacting him, and her attorney in the deposition prevented her from telling him what she found. (Pages 175-176) He concluded that her refusing to speak to him meant she "found something that would negate the legend of Billy the Kid if the information were released." (Page 176) He then lifted quotes from her deposition out of context: To the question, "You don't think Billy the Kid is buried at Fort Sumner, do you?" she answered: "I don't know. I have reason to suspect perhaps not." (Page 176)

FAKERY: Sederwall is making-up the OMI investigation, and Debra Komar's testimony; and implying falsely that he obtained her deposition.

The OMI investigation was not requested by Richardson, who had tried to block the OMI, since it opposed his hoped for exhuming Billy and his mother as forensically useless for DNA. (See pages 223-226 above)

The OMI did not evaluate the grave of John Miller, it being in another state, and not part of the New Mexico exhumation petitions it was opposing.

Debra Komar, as OMI forensic anthropologist, before her deposition, gave her January 9, 2004 Affidavit opposing the exhumations of Billy and his mother as forensically useless because of uncertainty of location of the remains in the Silver City and Fort Sumner cemeteries, and the risk of disturbing other remains. (See pages 223-226 above)

Komar's deposition was given to an attorney of the legal team I had brought in to oppose the exhumations, to document the OMI's opposition. She was cross-examined by Attorney Bill Robins III. (See pages 225-226 above) Komar had concluded: "So if you ask the opinion of myself and the Office of the Medical Investigator why is this being done or what scientifically valid conclusions can be drawn from it, I can't find any." (Deposition, Page 81)

But Sederwall was recycling his "Memorandum's" fakery, in which he had lifted her response to Attorney Robins about Billy's uncertain burial site out of context. (Deposition, Page 144) (See page 225 above) Komar's meaning was that Billy's buried body might no longer be present, with Fort Sumner's history of flooding, and possible accidental removal with soldiers' remains. She was merely repeating her Affidavit's contention that "[b]ased upon research performed by the OMI, the exact location of the Billy the Kid grave is not known." That meant location *within the Fort Sumner cemetery*. She was also referring to her earlier statements in her deposition, in which she said about Billy: "[T]he remains may no longer still be there. Even if they were buried there at one point." (Deposition, Page 69) She was citing references to Billy's remains being stolen to sell soon after burial, or past digging in the area finding no remains. (Deposition, Page 70) Or, in 1904, a Willie E. Griffin was hired to take soldiers' remains from that cemetery to move to Santa Fe's National Cemetery; and he knew that one was said to be buried in association with the contiguous graves of Billy, Charles Bowdre, and Tom O'Folliard. He found only two bodies, and took one. So he may have accidentally taken Billy! (Deposition, Page 71-72)

But Sederwall was faking that Komar said that Billy had never been buried in Fort Sumner, and was buried somewhere else - like Texas as "Brushy" or Arizona as John Miller! (See pages 225-226 above)

Sederwall concluded his fable with a claim that a David Bailey, a past Fort Sumner Mayor, had told De Baca County Sheriff Gary Graves that "Sederwall's investigation" had to be stopped, because he knew what was in the Billy the Kid grave, because he and a companion, on June 17, 2003, had dug it up and found nothing. And they had hidden their excavation by shoveling into adjoining graves. So Sederwall's concluding punch line was that there were no remains in Billy's grave. (Page 177)

HOAXING: Besides documenting a felonious crime by David Baily and an accomplice, Sederwall's claim merely substantiates the OMI's exhumation opposition based on no certain site for remains, if any still remained. And the 1962 blocked exhumation case of Lois Telfer repeated the same cite uncertainty.

But Sederwall's story does not hang together. The Billy the Kid grave is covered by a locked cage. Its surface is covered with concrete, and has three mounds to represent Billy, Charlie Bowdre, and Tom O'Folliard. And there are no adjoining graves to shovel into for cover-up. And the ground is hard-packed, since it is an inactive historical cemetery, with only a distant grave of Chino Silva, Jesus Silva's grandson, added in the 2000's. Furthermore, Marlyn Bowlin, then running the Old Fort Sumner Museum beside the cemetery, checked the graves daily, and would have seen David Baily's desecrations.

MEANINGLESS EVIDENCE: No remains available proves nothing. In fact, the poorly marked graves in the cemetery are described by a Leslie Traylor of Galveston, Texas, in his July, 1936 *Frontier Times* interview of a, titled "Facts Regarding the Escape of Billy the Kid." Traylor, a history buff, interviewed old-timers in Lincoln and Fort Sumner in 1933 and 1935. He wrote: "[T]he old cemetery near old Fort Sumner ... is now usually referred to as Hell's Half Acre. During the summer of 1935 I visited the old cemetery accompanied by Francisco Lovato, his son Pete, and a friend of theirs ... The old cemetery was originally surrounded by an adobe wall, but now is surrounded by a wire fence, the entrance being in the north side as before. Lucien B. Maxwell, the cattle king [sic] and father of Pete Maxwell, is buried in the old cemetery, but the exact site of his grave is unknown. His son Pete died in 1898 and there is a monument erected to his memory, supposedly near where is father is buried. The monument to Billy the Kid and his pals is badly defaced where Billy's name appears; the vandals still chipping off pieces of stone. I was told by Pete Lovato that his father helped Vincente Otero bury the remains of Thomas O'Folliard and Chas. Bowdre, who were killed in Dec., 1880, by Pat Garrett and his men, and that his father said that O'Folliard and Bowdre were not buried by the monument erected to the three pals, but were buried to the left of the entrance to the cemetery by the side of the old adobe wall, and now where the fence is ... Regardless of where the three pals were buried the monument serves its purpose just the same."

FORGING DR. HENRY LEE REPORTS

In 2010, when Steve Sederwall first published his unrelated "Billy Bonney's Bad Bucks" hoax, he was either feeling desperate or immune in my open records litigation against him and his fellow lawmen hoaxers, because he apparently decided to end my case by tricking the District Court Judge, George Eichwald, into believing that the "Billy the Kid Case's" forensic investigation by Dr. Henry Lee was done for him personally for his own private hobby; thus, having no public records to turn over to me. So he forged several Lee reports to dupe the judge about that.

HOAXING THE DISTRICT COURT JUDGE

The hoaxers well knew that the Dr. Henry Lee report I sought about his carpenter's bench investigation was fatal to their case, since it proved his report was a public record done for Case 2003-274, and they feared it would reveal that they never had the "bench-blood-of-Billy-the-Kid" to conduct exhumations. But the judge had Dr. Lee's May 1, 2006 response letter to me (through my proxy, Jay Miller) that he **"submitted my report [single] to the Lincoln County Sheriff's Department."**

So the lawmen defendants first claimed that they never got the report. But open records law requires also turning over records *not in direct possession*; so even if they "lost" it, they had to get me a copy from Lee. So the judge ordered them to turn over the Lee report. But unbeknownst to me and the judge, that started Sederwall's frenzy of forging Lee reports.

As it would turn out, Lee's actual report exposed their lying. But, at the start, it was still hidden, and forgeries were inconceivable.

FLOORBOARD REPORT ONE

On February 18, 2010, my then attorney called me to say that he had received *the* Lee report from Steve Sederwall's lawyer, Kevin Brown. I drove with pounding heart to his office, and was handed nine pages, with photos. **[FIGURE: 5]** Dated February 25, 2005, it was an official-looking report about *seeking "blood" at the old Lincoln courthouse upstairs landing for the Deputy Bell killing*. Attorney Brown's cover letter stated: "Our position is that the document Mr. Sederwall obtained from Dr. Lee is not a public record ... However to resolve this matter, I am enclosing the document Mr. Sederwall obtained from Dr. Lee. This should resolve all claims against both Mr. Sederwall and Mr. Sullivan ... If you do not believe all claims against both Mr. Sederwall and Mr. Sullivan are now resolved ... please return the document to me without making any copies."

The report's title was "Forensic Research and Training Center Forensic Examination Report: Examination of Lincoln County Courthouse. Forensic Examination Report" Its header stated its "Date of Request: May 22, 2004; and that it was "**Requested By: Steve Sederwall, and Bill Kurtis Productions;**" with "**Report To: Steven M. Sederwall.**" It stated: "On Sunday, August 1, 2004, the forensic investigation team examined the old Lincoln County Court House in Lincoln, New Mexico. **Present at the scene were Steve Sederwall,** Tom Sullivan, David Turk, Bill Kurtis, and Gary Wayne Graves. The target area of examination is located on the top landing of the stairs of the old courtroom." No mention was made of Case 2003-274! No one had an official title! And the case was done for "Steve Sederwall!"

Its **"Results and Conclusions"** section stated: "Various stains were observed on the surface and the underside of the floorboards. Chemical tests [with O-Tolidine] for the presence of blood were positive with some of those stains. These results indicate the presence of oxidas [sic - oxidase] activity with those stains tested positive, which suggests those stains could be bloodstains. Further DNA testing could reveal the nature and identity of that blood like stains [sic]."

Signers were "**Dr. Henry C. Lee**, Chief Emeritus, Connecticut State Forensic Laboratory, Distinguished Professor, University New Haven" and "**Calvin D. Ostler**, Forensic Consultant, Crime Scene Investigator" (Lee's business partner, and in the Utah Medical Examiner's Office).

I told my attorney to return it as unrequested. *I had asked for the carpenter's bench report.* Oddly, Sederwall had claimed in his deposition of August 18, 2008 that he had *a 12 page Lee bench report*, and had not mentioned this floorboard one. And he had refused turn-over as his private hobby. And, in this report, no one had titles, as if it was a hobby. But forgery never occurred to me.

A FLOORBOARD REPORT AS EXHIBIT F

On March 9, 2010, my attorney held a Presentment Hearing before the judge to demand the DNA records and to report that no requested records had been turned over. Sheriff Rick Virden lied through his attorney that he was not "required to produce documents that we are not in possession of."

Sederwall lied through his Attorney, Kevin Brown, that Lee's report met my request, and **was his only Lee report**. Brown stated: "I didn't want to disregard the Court's ruling, and so I obtained the particular document that Sederwall had that we were talking about. I presented it to [Dr. Cooper's attorney], and I said, I think this is going to resolve all the matter. If you disagree, return it back to me and we'll just go further. It was returned back to me, and I was told that this isn't what you requested ... **I will state to the Court, the document which I have here, which I would mark as an exhibit or do whatever, is the only document that Sederwall received**." It was marked **Exhibit F**. **[FIGURE: 6]** As an exhibit, it was part of the court record, but not shown to me in court. *But it seemed obvious that it would be the same floorboard report I had already been given and rejected.*

A FLOORBOARD REPORT AGAIN

On April 6, 2010, my attorney faxed me Virden's turn-over of the same floorboard report first given by Attorney Brown on February 18, 2010. The cover letter stated: "Attached is the Forensic Examination Report from Dr. Lee ... Please be advised that this report was never in Lincoln County's possession, and the only reason we have a copy of it is because Mr. [Kevin] Brown provided it to us."

On April 12, 2010, Virden's attorney sent a second letter: "This letter is to follow up my phone conversation with [Dr. Cooper's attorney] this morning regarding a document pertaining to the Billy the Kid investigation that he believes has not been produced. [In] Mr. Sederwall's deposition he testified that he received a copy of Dr. Lee's report 'about the workbench' ... Mr. Sederwall testified that it was perhaps 10 [sic - 12] pages in big font ... The report Mr. [Kevin] Brown produced seems to fit the above description, with one exception. It is a report authored by Dr. Lee that is 9 pages long in big font. However it appears to be an examination of floorboards rather than a workbench. Could Mr. Sederwall simply have been mistaken ... about the nature of the report? ... [I]f the only remaining dispute in this case is about whether there exists a second report ... we could either have an evidentiary hearing and allow Judge Eichwald to decide, or ... [Dr. Cooper's attorney] could subpoena Dr. Lee and have him produce any reports he authored dealing with Billy the Kid."

They were lying that Sederwall meant "floorboard" not "bench" report as his only record. Nevertheless, it seemed that the crooked lawmen were all talking about the same Lee floorboard report.

THE CARPENTER'S BENCH REPORT

On November 10, 2010, with my all-day Evidentiary Hearing looming, Steve Sederwall shockingly pulled another Dr. Lee report out of a hat - this time, the carpenter's bench report! **[FIGURE: 7]**

Its cover letter was to my attorney from his lawyer, Kevin Brown (keeping a straight face after telling the judge in the March 9, 2010 Presentment Hearing that Sederwall had *only one* report). Brown's letter stated: "Enclosed please find a copy of another report dated February 25, 2005 which deals with the examination of furniture by Dr. Lee ... It is our position that the documents produced are not public records. It is our position that if the documents are public records, they are protected by the trade secret privilege ... Nevertheless, these documents are being produced in attempt to resolve this matter."

Oddly, this report had very different font than the Lee floorboard report. One would assume a standard presentation by an expert. **And it lacked any "Results and Conclusions" section whatsoever - a forensic report's purpose!** It was titled "Forensic Research & Training Center Forensic Examination Report, Examination of furniture from Pete Maxwell's of July 15, 1881." It was 16 pages, and was signed by Lee and Calvin Ostler. Its header had no law enforcement information; and the "Requested by" section was expanded from the floorboard report's "Steve Sederwall, and Bill Kurtis Productions" to "**Steve Sederwall, Capitan, New Mexico, paid for by Investigating History Program, Kurtis Production.**"

Its "Introduction" stated: **At the request of Steve Sederwall of Lincoln County, New Mexico, Bill Kurtis and Jamie Schenk of Kurtis Production**, Dr. Henry Lee went to New Mexico on July 31, 2004 to assist in the re-investigation of the case of Billy the Kid. The forensic investigating team participating in re-investigation consist the [sic] following individuals: [listed as] **Steve Sederwall, Investigator;** Tom Sullivan, Investigator; Dr. Henry Lee, Chief Emeritus of the Connecticut State Police Forensic Laboratory; Calvin Ostler, Forensic Consultant, Riverton, Utah; Kim Ostler, Crime Scene Assistant, Riverton, Utah; David Turk, U.S. Marshall [sic], United States Marshall Service [sic]. In addition, Mike Haag, Firearm examiner from Albuquerque Police Department Crime Lab, also provided valuable technical assistance in the investigation. The forensic investigation team arrived at the Manny [sic - Mannie] Miller residence, located at (address removed), Albuquerque, New Mexico, at 18:20 hours on Saturday, July 31, 2004. Upon arrival we were presented with three pieces of evidence: a worktable, a washstand, and a headboard. Investigator Sullivan, Investigator Sederwall, and members of Bill Kurtis Productions had removed the three pieces of evidence from a storage building at the rear of the residence. Each item was inspected visually and macroscopically."

Listed were three separate investigations titled: "Item #1 Workbench," "Item # 2 Washstand," "Item # 3 Bed Headboard."

WORKBENCH: For the carpenter's bench, Lee's testing for "blood" on the top was listed on page 6 as by Phenopathlien and Ortho-tolidine. And page 9 listed testing the underside of the bench with Luminol. (All test for iron compounds - like blood or rust - with rust being more likely on a carpenter's bench.) And it had something fatal for the hoaxers on page 9; stating: "Swab samples of area number '3' and area number '4' were collected for DNA testing. Two swabs were taken from each area and placed in two separate swab boxes, one box was labeled for area number '3' and one box was labeled for area number '4'. **These two samples were transferred to Lincoln Sheriff Department.** In addition, scraping samples were also taken from these two areas. These samples were placed in two evidence envelopes [**the envelopes, when subpoenaed from Orchid Cellmark in 2012, were, labeled as for Case 2003-274] and the Lincoln Sheriff Department.**"

WASHSTAND: This had its photograph and had diagrams of the supposed bullet holes for the trajectory discussed by Lee in his press interviews at the time.

HEADBOARD: With no photograph or diagram, it merely stated: "A piece of headboard was examined. No bloodlike stains was observed. No bullet hole was found. No evidence of damage was noted." **[This hid that it was only an empty rim.]**

Though Sederwall had originally said the report was 12, not 16, pages, and although law enforcement titles were missing for requester Sederwall and the other investigators, the report did prove that the evidence samples went to the Lincoln County Sheriff's Department - contradicting the hoaxers' private hobby claim. There was no way of imagining that this revealing information was just careless rewriting for a forged document intended to prove the private hobbyists claim.

FLOORBOARD REPORT AS EXHIBIT F AND CARPENTER'S BENCH REPORT AS EXHIBIT E

For my January 21, 2011 Evidentiary Hearing, which had yielded the nervous flurry of turning over Lee reports to avoid contempt, Attorney Kevin Brown, for Sullivan and Sederwall, still called them "hobbyists."

Then Brown segued into his intended clinchers to the judge to show open records compliance and prove the amateur historian hobby. He said Sederwall's investigation with the carpenter's workbench was private, and its specimens were sent to Orchid Cellmark by report signer Calvin Ostler.

As proof, Brown then dramatically handed over to the Court the workbench report as Exhibit E and repeated hand-over of the floorboard report as Exhibit F.

Brown added, to address records hiding, in case the judge stuck to its being a public official case: "[O]nce we start talking about DNA, its existence or creation of documents, we are going to be getting into a recognized exception in the Public Records Act, which is trade secret privilege." The intent of this dishonest maneuver was to hide the fatally incriminating, also requested, Orchid Cellmark Lab records of DNA extraction and matching results as being Sederwall's and Sullivan's private "trade secrets."

THE LEE TURN-OVER REPORTS' SHOCKER

Complicating my case, was corrupt New Mexico politics, which made my own attorneys try to throw my case; and forced me to get new ones. Having fired the attorney who received the floorboard and carpenter's bench reports, I went to a meeting with my new attorneys to review the old attorney's boxes of my case's files.

As a layman, I was given just the court sessions' transcripts (for which I paid); but only an attorney got the Exhibits. So I wanted to review them to see what was entered into the record. In reviewing defense Exhibits from my January 21, 2011 Evidentiary Hearing, I was struck by their Exhibit E (for carpenter's bench) and Exhibit F (for floorboards). I had only seen the supposedly same ones given to my attorney before that hearing.

I have near-photographic memory. **I exclaimed, "This floorboard report is different from the one Sederwall gave my attorney on February 18, 2010, and gave to Virden's attorney on April 6, 2010!"** [Figure: 5 and Figure: 6]

This Exhibit F floorboard report had a different title font, which now matched the ornate one on the carpenter's bench report's title, which Sederwall had turned over on November 10, 2010 (and then gave to the Court as Exhibit E).

I thumbed through Exhibits E and F. Now *neither* had a "Results and Conclusions" section - though the originally turned-over Lee floorboard report had one!

From my own papers I took out that first Lee report to show these new attorneys the alterations from the first floorboard report, and the Exhibit F floorboard report given to the court. Noted were:

1) The "Requested by" phrase on the face of each report was different, showing on Exhibit 1 that Steve Sederwall and Bill Kurtis Productions requested the Report, while Exhibit F stated that it was requested by "Steve Sederall, Capitan, New Mexico, paid for by Investigation History Program, Kurtis Production."

2) The first paragraph had been changed in Exhibit F with additional descriptions of persons added as being present during the examination.

3) The photograph reference numbers had been changed, the text changed and some deleted.

4) The reference numbers on the diagrams had been changed throughout the report.

5) All of the "Results and Conclusions" on page 9 of the first floorboard report had been deleted from the Exhibit "F" floorboard report given to Court at the January 21, 2011 hearing.

Then, with all the reports laid out together, I realized that the Lee and Ostler signatures were superimposable - cut and pasted onto the reports. **SO SEDERWALL WAS FORGING LEE REPORTS!**

No wonder that since 2010 he had been pulling them like rabbits from a magician's hat. He was nervously re-working them in repeated fix-ups for court, while faking turn-over compliance, and thinking his scam would go unnoticed.

This was a bombshell. It proved Steve Sederwall was giving me and judge fake forged records as genuine, proved evidence tampering, and proved contempt of the judge's orders for turn-over. In fact, no real records whatsoever had been turned-over!

THE AUTHENTIC LEE REPORT

In his February 23, 2012 "Order" for my "First Motion to Supplement the Record and For Sanctions," requesting the authentic Lee Report and sanctions for the forgeries, the judge ordered: "Defendant Sederwall is to produce all original Reports received from Dr. Henry Lee with his original signature on them."

So Sederwall came up with another Lee report! On January 31, 2012, my attorney and I met in Attorney Kevin Brown's office. Brown kept a straight face when turning over yet another "only report" Sederwall had. **[FIGURE: 8]** This one had a different font, was 25 pages, with black-and white photos; and came with the same manila envelope Sederwall had been presenting since 2008 as holding his "one" Lee report - because it had his home mailing address for his claim of being a hobbyist!

Titled "Forensic Research & Training Center Forensic Examination Report," this report combined all investigations into one report - just as Lee had claimed in his letter to my proxy.

Its sections were: "Item #1 Workbench," "Item # 2 Washstand," "Item 3 (now labeled) **A piece of** Headboard," Item # 4 "Examination of Lincoln County Court House," and "Results and Conclusion." And it proved all the other reports were forgeries, rewritten by lifting, omitting parts, and changing parts.

The eye-opener was its heading and "Introduction." After giving the "Date of Report as February 25, 2005," **it gave the law enforcement information expurgated from the others, including case number and lawman titles.** It stated:

Requested By: **Lincoln County Sheriff's Office, New Mexico**
                      Investigating History Program, Kurtis Production
Local Case No. 2003-274
Date of Report: February 25, 2005
Report to: **Steve Sederwall**
                Lincoln County Sheriff's Office, New Mexico

Introduction

At the request of **Steve Sederwall of Lincoln County Sheriff's Office, Lincoln County**, Bill Kurtis and Jamie Schenk of Kurtis Production, [sic – and] Dr. Henry Lee went to New Mexico on July 31, 2004 to assist in the re-investigation of the case of Billy the Kid. The forensic investigation team participating in re-investigation consist [sic –of] the following individuals:

Dr. Henry Lee, Chief Emeritus of the Connecticut State Police Forensic Laboratory
Calvin Ostler, Forensic Consultant, Riverton, Utah
Kim Ostler, Crime Scene Assistant, Riverton, Utah
Tom Sullivan, Sheriff, Lincoln County New Mexico
Steve Sederwall Deputy Sheriff, Lincoln County New Mexico
David Turk, US Marshal, United States Marshall [sic] Service

In addition, Mike Haag, Firearm examiner from Albuquerque Police Department Crime Lab, also provided valuable technical assistance in the investigation.

The forensic investigation team arrived at the Manny [sic] Miller residence, located at (address given here, not removed like in Exhibit E version), Albuquerque, New Mexico, at 18:20 hours on Saturday, July 31, 2004. Upon arrival we were presented with three pieces of evidence: a worktable, a washstand, and a headboard. The three pieces of evidence had been removed from a storage building at the rear of the residence by **Sheriff Sullivan, Deputy Sederwall**, and members of Bill Kurtis Productions. Each item was inspected visually and macroscopically. The following were found [with findings given].

This report repeated Lee's giving his samples to the Lincoln County Sheriff's Department. **And it had the "Results and Conclusion" section which was removed from "Lee reports" Exhibits E and F.** It had only Lee's claim of "blood-like" stains (as far as Lee himself dared hoaxing in writing, though he had dishonestly left out rust as the likely source); **and did not claim actual blood - as the hoaxers had announced.**

Lee's "Results and Conclusion" section stated:

After a detail [sic] examination of the evidence and review of all the results of field testing, the following conclusion [sic] was reached.

1. Brownish dark stains were observed on different areas of the workbench. These areas were subjected to chemical presumptive blood tests. Some of those samples give a positive reaction. These results indicate the presence of Heme or Peroxidase like activity with those stains testing positive, which suggest that those stains could be bloodstains. Further DNA testing could reveal the nature and identity of these blood-like stains.

2. Two bullet holes were located on the side panels of the Washstand. The hole on the left panel is consistent with a bullet entry hole while the hole on the right side panel is consistent with a bullet exit hole. However, it is not possible to determine when those bullets were produced at this time. The angles produced in examination tell us two things:

First, the bullet was fired from no more than 41" from the floor given the reported limitations of the room. The room is reported to be 20' by 20'; the maximum distance is assumed to be 20'. If the firearm was a maximum of 41" off the floor it is unlikely that the shooter was standing. It is more likely that the shooter was kneeling, squatting, or close to the floor.

Second, the horizontal angle is such that if the Washstand was positioned so the back was against the wall, the shot could not have been fired from more than approximately 40 inches from the Washstand, because the wall would have been in the way. The angle of trajectory intersects the back plane of the Washstand at approximately 45 3/16", and no more than 46".

3. No bullet hole and no observable damage, no sign of bullet ricocheted type of defects were found on the Headboard.

4. The floor boards on the 2nd floor stair landing area of the court house have been repaired. Different types of wood and nails were used on this area.

5. Various stains were observed on the surface and underside of the floor boards. Chemical tests for the presence of blood were positive for some of those stains. These results indicate the presence of Heme or Peroxidase like activity with those stains tested positive, which suggests that those stains could be bloodstains. Further DNA testing could reveal the nature and identity of those blood-like stains.

The motive for forgeries was obvious: hiding the law enforcement case confirmation to fake a private hobby; and hiding Lee's non-committal conclusions about Billy the Kid's blood or DNA to fake legitimacy of the Arizona exhumations by lying that he got both.

This report also proved Lee's hoaxing. Recall that Bill Kurtis was filming a series about Garrett not having killed Billy the Kid. So Lee used unsubstantiated "crime scene" objects, like the washstand, and faking of no bullet hole in the headboard fragment. And Lee suggested blood, when rust was the obvious source of his reagents' iron-triggered reactions.

Nevertheless, Lee's report proved the hoaxers had lied that Case 2003-274 was their private hobby.

And when Lee gave his Affidavit for my case, on August 31, 2012, he swore that the work he did was for the Lincoln County Sheriff's Department for a case on the killing of William Bonney. He stated: "In approximately late July and early August of 2004, I assisted with the collection of samples from various locations thought to be locations where there may have been residue of biological material, which could be **relevant to an investigation into the death of William Bonney, a/k/a Billy the Kid, then being performed by the Lincoln County, New Mexico, Sheriff's Department**." That meant Henry Lee himself knew the courthouse floorboard investigation was connected to the "death of William Bonney" as its sub-investigation to claim that the location of Bell's bleeding would contradict Garrett's version, making him a liar; ergo, also future murderer of the innocent victim.

JUDGE'S RULING ABOUT THE FORGERIES

For Sederwall's June 26, 2012 deposition, my attorney asked about the forgeries: "Did you make up that report?" Glib con-artist Sederwall answered: "No, I did not make up the report. **The report has been massaged, it's been changed, it's been worked on. That's what's been done**." (Deposition Sederwall, 6/26/12; p. 561)

The District Court Judge, George Eichwald, was not fooled. For his May 15, 2014 "Findings of Fact and Conclusions of Law and Order of the Court" **[APPENDIX: 4]**, he ruled on Steve Sederwall's forgeries; though the monetary penalty for them that he awarded to me was removed by the corrupt higher courts in appeal to shield the lawmen (and Bill Richardson indirectly); though these courts did not deny that forgeries had been done.

Judge Eichwald wrote for his "Findings of Fact":

25. On May 31, 2012 a Hearing for Sanctions was conducted. The newest Lee report was presented as evidence of altering of the past Lee reports to conceal the law enforcement header, but was also called not original as lacking signatures. The subpoenaed Orchid Cellmark records were entered as evidence to prove records' existence. Sanctions included the ordering of new depositions of the Defendants.

26. In his June 26, 2012 deposition Sederwall admitted to: removing law enforcement information from later Lee reports; called the twenty-five (25) page Lee report he first received from Lee as original; and admitted to knowing that the Orchid Cellmark client was Calvin Ostler [the contact to send the records] ...

29. ... At an Evidentiary Hearing conducted on December 21 [sic – 18], 2012 and February 4, 2013 ... [w]itness Seterwall [sic], still calling Case 2003-274 his private hobby [in contempt of the judge's order that they were public records], admitted to altering the first Lee report's header to remove Case 2003-274 information; and admitted to creating the other report versions given to the Court and lacking law enforcement information.

Judge Eichwald wrote for his "Conclusions of Law":

18. In his June 26, 2012 deposition, Sederwall admitted to willful involvement in altering Lee reports by rewritings to remove the original law enforcement information in Lee's "first" report sent to him as Lincoln County Deputy Sheriff. Section 14-2-6(F) NMSA 1978 defines "public records" as "all documents, papers, letters, books, maps, tapes, photographs, recordings and other materials, regardless of physical form or characteristics, used, created, received, maintained or held by or on behalf of any pubic body and related to public business, whether or not the records are required by law to be created or maintained." The plain language implication is that the records are to be "originals" of [sic – or] true "duplicates" of the original. Under Rule 11-1001(D) NMRA 1978, "an original of a writing is the writing itself. Rile [sic –Rule] 11-101(E) NMRA 1978 states "a duplicate is a counterpart produced by the same impression as the original ... which accurately reproduces the original." Neither an "original" nor a "duplicate" report was presented, only altered records which do not comply with IPRA law.

19. The Defendants' actions and/or inactions in responding to Plaintiff's IPRA requests are in violation of IPRA law and subject to sanctions ...

26. Defendants' conduct in not providing the requested records enumerated in Findings of Fact 10, is willful, wanton, and in bad faith.

27. Defendants' conduct in providing altered records as discussed in Findings of Facts 25, 26, and 29 and Conclusions of Law 18 is wanton, willful, and in bad faith.

Forensic Research & Training Center

Forensic Examination Report

Date of Request: May 22, 2004

Requested By: Steve Sederwall, and Bill Kurtis Productions

Date of Report: February 25, 2005

Report to: Steven M. Sederwall

Examination of Lincoln County Court House:

On Sunday, 8/1/04, the forensic investigation team examined the old Lincoln County Court House in Lincoln, New Mexico. Present at the scene were Steve Sederwall, Tom Sullivan, David Turk, Bill Kurtis, and Gary Wayne Graves. The target area of examination is located on the top landing of the stairs of the old courtroom.

1. The staircase has been repainted several times over the years.

2. The 2nd floor hallway floor was recovered with wooden floor board. These floor boards were removed. The original floor was exposed. Photograph #1 shows an overall view of hall floor after the removal of new floor board.

3. Photograph #2 shows the target area, which is at the top landing of the stairs where presumptive blood tests were done. The area measured approximately 28 7/8" deep by 43 ½ "wide.

4. Figure 1 is a sketch diagram shows the general dimensions of this staircase.

5. Photograph # 3 depicts the location and condition of the floor boards in the target area.

FIGURE: 5. Title page of first forged Dr. Henry Lee floorboard report; titled "Examination of Lincoln County Court House;" dated February 25, 2005; 9 pages long

Forensic Research & Training Center

Forensic Examination Report ©

Date of Request: May 22, 2004

Requested By: Steve Sederwall, Capitan, New Mexico, paid for by
                     Investigation History Program, Kurtis Production

Date of Report: February 25, 2005

Report to: Steven M. Sederwall

Examination of Lincoln County Court House:

On Sunday, 8/1/04, the forensic investigation team examined the old Lincoln County Court House in Lincoln, New Mexico. Present at the scene were Steve Sederwall, Tom Sullivan, United States Marshal's Historian David Turk, Producer Bill Kurtis, and Gary Wayne Graves of De Baca County, New Mexico. The target area of examination is located on the top landing of the stairs of the old courtroom.

1. The staircase has been repainted several times over the years.
2. The 2nd floor hallway floor was recovered with wooden floorboard. These floor boards were removed. The original floor was exposed. Photograph #6 shows an overall view of hall floor after the removal of new floor board.

EXHIBIT F

FIGURE: 6. Title page of second forged Dr. Henry Lee floorboard report; titled "Examination of Lincoln County Court House;" dated February 25, 2005; 9 pages long; submitted to Court on January 21, 2011 as Exhibit F

Forensic Research & Training Center

Forensic Examination Report ©

Date of Request: May 22, 2004

Requested By: Steve Sederwall, Capitan, New Mexico paid for by Investigation History Program, Kurtis Production

Date of Report: February 25, 2005

Report to: Steven M. Sederwall

Examination of furniture from Pete Maxwell's of July 15, 1881:

Introduction

At the request of Steve Sederwall of Lincoln County, New Mexico, Bill Kurtis and Jamie Schenk of Kurtis Production, Dr. Henry Lee went to New Mexico on July 31, 2004 to assist in the re-investigation of the case of Billy the Kid. The forensic investigation team participating in re-investigation consist the following individuals:

    Steve Sederwall, Investigator
    Tom Sullivan, Investigator
    Dr. Henry Lee, Chief Emeritus of the Connecticut State Police Forensic Laboratory
    Calvin Ostler, Forensic Consultant, Riverton, Utah
    Kim Ostler, Crime Scene Assistant, Riverton, Utah
    David Turk, US Marshall, United States Marshall Service

FIGURE: 7. Title page of forged Dr. Henry Lee carpenter's bench report; titled "Examination of furniture from Pete Maxwell's of July 15, 1881," dated February 25, 2005; 16 pages long

Forensic Research & Training Center

Forensic Examination Report

Date of Request: May 22, 2004
Requested By: Lincoln County Sheriff's Office, New Mexico
Investigation History Program, Kurtis Production
Local Case No. 2003-274
Date of Report: February 25, 2005
Report to: Steve Sederwell
Lincoln County Sheriff's Office, New Mexico

Introduction

At the request of Steve Sederwell of Lincoln County Sheriff's Office, Lincoln County, Bill Kurtis and Jamie Schenk of Kurtis Production, Dr. Henry Lee went to New Mexico on July 31, 2004 to assist in the re-investigation of the case of Billy the Kid. The forensic investigation team participating in re-investigation consist the following individuals:

> Dr. Henry Lee, Chief Emeritus of the Connecticut State Police Forensic Laboratory
> Calvin Ostler, Forensic Consultant, Riverton, Utah
> Kim Ostler, Crime Scene Assistant, Riverton, Utah
> Tom Sullivan, Sheriff, Lincoln County, New Mexico
> Steve Sederwall Deputy Sheriff, Lincoln County, New Mexico
> David Turk, US Marshall, United States Marshall Service

In addition, Mike Haag, Firearm examiner from Albuquerque Police Department Crime Lab, also provided valuable technical assistance in the investigation.

FIGURE: 8. Title page of authentic and sole forensic report of Dr. Henry Lee for Lincoln County Sheriff's Department Case 2003-274; titled "Forensic Examination Report;" dated February 25, 2005; 25 pages long

THE RETURN OF MY LITIGATION AS MERELY AN ATTACK ON SEDERWALL

For his gullible dupe, W.C. Jameson, Steve Sederwall apparently gave a hoaxed version of my seven years of open records litigation in which he was a defendant - along with fellow Deputy and past Sheriff, Tom Sullivan, and Sheriff Rick Virden. As Jameson wrote in his 2018 *Cold Case Billy the Kid*: "[Sederwall was] hauled into court [for unstated cause] by one of the rabid embracers of the status quo" (Page x)

Jameson, never researching the litigation, missed seeing the Judge's May 15, 2014 "Findings of Fact and Conclusions of Law and Order of the Court" **[APPENDIX: 4]**; which stated:

> 4. The matter in controversy is for enforcement of the New Mexico Inspection of Public [Records] Act, Section 14-2-1 et seq. NMSA 1978 (IPRA) and **concerning the Defendants' refusal to turn over requested DNA records of Lincoln County Sheriff's Department Case No. 2003-274, "Billy the Kid Case,"** ("Case 2003-274").

CHAPTER 4
STEVE SEDERWALL'S OTHER BILLY THE KID HISTORY HOAXES

HOAXED "INVESTIGATIONS"

Showcasing Steve Sederwall in his 2018 *Cold Case Billy the Kid*, W.C. Jameson also narrated Sederwall's Billy the Kid hoaxes not in the "Billy the Kid Case, calling them "cop finds." Though many contradicted "Brushy Bill" as Billy the Kid by information "Brushy" never had, Jameson apparently decided that anything claiming history was not as written aided "Brushy's" cause.

HOAXING THE TUNSTALL MURDER

For the Tunstall period (Pages 4-10), Jameson claimed Tunstall's murder *had not been investigated*, so Steve Sederwall would do a crime scene investigation.

WRONG: The crime scene *was* investigated. Trackers, under John Newcomb, recovered Tunstall's corpse, described the two part crime scene (where he was murdered and where his body was hidden) and his wounds. One of the trackers was a law enforcement official: Probate Judge Florencio Gonzales, who likely provided their findings to the Coroner's Jury, and subsequently gave them in his June 8, 1878 deposition about the murder to Frank Warner Angel.

The trackers identified the murder site by blood, and located Tunstall's hidden body 100 yards off the trail, with his killed horse beside him, and his hat on its head. They called it a *"burlesque"* desecration. They located his revolver beside his corpse, with two empty chambers. but the lack of cartridge shells in them showed Tunstall had not fired. His skull was *"broken,"* there was a bullet entry at his breast, and a bullet entry at the back of his head, exiting the forehead. They also identified many fresh horse tracks, and concluded that the possemen passed by the horse herd just to kill Tunstall; thus, pointing to intentional murder, rather than stock retrieval.

Sederwall's so-called "crime scene investigation" involved using a metal detector to find an old rifle casing. Of course, he claimed it as the bullet that killed Tunstall! He also cited the Frank Warner Angel files, likely obtained from fellow hoaxer with easy access to the National Archives, U.S. Marshal's Service Historian David Turk (who had also helped him with the "Case 2003-274 Probable Cause Statement"); though Sederwall wrongly cited deposition quotes as being an Angel "report."

For his "investigation," Sederwall used an alleged Tunstall autopsy report, without given source, and allegedly by Fort Stanton Assistant Post Surgeon Daniel Appel. He excerpted quotes: "Wounded in the head, entered 3 in. behind and in the line with the superior border of the right ear, made its exit 1 ½ in. above the left orbit and ¼ in. left of the middle line of the forehead." (Page 14)

FLAWED EVIDENCE: Sederwall seemed unaware that Appel was a useless witness because of his Ring bias, shared by many at Fort Stanton. In addition, Appel was personally motivated to destroy Tunstall and McSween, in revenge for their exposing the Mescalero Indian Reservation frauds perpetrated by Appel's wife's father: Indian Agent Frederick Godfroy, in collusion with Lawrence Murphy, and his "House" partners, for their reservation contracts. Also, Godfroy, investigated after the Tunstall-McSween complaint, was caught stealing reservation supplies to be sold through "The House." And he was accepting rustled beef and mealy flour from "The House" for the Reservation. So biased Appel faked Tunstall's killing as self-defense by Brady's posse, making his descriptions useless for a crime scene reconstruction.

MISSED EVIDENCE: Sederwall missed Appel's official version in his July 1, 1878 deposition to Investigator Frank Warner Angel, which revealed his bias. [APPENDIX: 9]

In it, Appel fabricated a scene of Tunstall on the ground and attacking the possemen, while irrationally maddened by venereal disease; forcing them to shoot him in self-defense through the shoulder and head. Appel stated that the shoulder wound did not kill him immediately, but threw him off his horse. He described the second bullet as *"entering the head about one inch to the right of the median line almost on a line with the occipital protuberance of [and] the left orbit."* Slyly omitted is the entry point - as to that front-to-back line. Given only is the trajectory of *"about one inch to the right of the median line"* [which is opposite to the quote used by Sederwall]; but implied is Tunstall's being shot from the front, with the trajectory on level with the left eye across to the centered bump (occipital protuberance) at the base of the skull's back. Appel, noting the circumferential fracture, wrote snidely: *"In my opinion the skull both on account of its being very thin and from evidence of venereal disease was likely to be extensively fractured from such a wound and this fracture in this case resulted entirely from said wound."* But Appel hid that the head had been assaulted, a likely fracture contributor; lying *"There were no marks of violence or bruises on the body except the above two wounds."*

MISSED EVIDENCE: Sederwall was also apparently unaware that Alexander McSween, expecting cover-up for the Ring-backed Brady posse, got Lincoln's unbiased town doctor, Taylor Ealy, to participate in the autopsy. Ealy confirmed mutilation of Tunstall's *"broken"* head, noted by the first tracker investigators, which indicated malicious intent. That is why the verdict was murder, as found by Tunstall's Coroner's Jury Report of February 19, 1878; signed by George B. Barber, John Newcomb, Robert M. Gilbert, Samuel Smith, Frank Coe, Benjamin J. Ellis, John B. Wilson, Justice of the Peace. It stated:

> *We, the undersigned Justice of the Peace and Coroner's Jury who sat upon the inquest held this 19th day of February 1878 on the body of John H. Tunstall, here found in precinct No. 1. of the County of Lincoln, Territory of New Mexico, find that the deceased came to his death on or about the 18th day of February 1878 by means of diver bullets shot and sent forth out of*

> and from deadly weapons, and upon the head and body of said John H. Tunstall, which said deadly weapons were there and then held by one or more of the persons whose names are herewith written to wit, Jessie Evans, William Morton, Frank Baker, Thomas Hill, George Hindman, J.J. Dolan, and others not identified by the witnesses who testified before the Coroner's Jury.
>
> We, the undersigned, to the best of our knowledge and belied from the evidence of the Coroner's Inquest, believe the above statement to be a true and impartial verdict.

Sederwall also cited a few words of what he called "testimony provided by Billy the Kid," omitting that they were from Billy's deposition on June 8, 1878 to Frank Warner Angel.

HIDING EVIDENCE THAT "BRUSHY" WAS NOT BILLY: Billy Bonney's long articulate deposition (see pages 69-73 above) was another proof that coarse-spoken "Brushy" was not him; as well as the fact that "Brushy" and his hoaxing team were ignorant of that deposition; it being discovered in 1956 by Frederick Nolan. So "Brushy" never claimed to have given it as Billy. Sederwall seemed to avoid the problem by calling it "testimony."

Next, Sederwall, using his unspecified "autopsy report," and unaware of Appel's bias or lying, made-up trajectory paths of bullets, much like Dr. Henry Lee's fake forensics for the washstand claimed from the Maxwell bedroom.

Then, Sederwall, to feign a discovery, claimed a cover-up; accusing the Sheriff's posse of one - as had been obvious to all contemporaries and subsequent Billy the Kid historians! But Sederwall added: "**Judge Gonzales may also have been involved in the cover-up.**" (Pages 21-22) He cited Florencio Gonzales's eye-witness statement in his Angel deposition that the chest wound was from a rifle or carbine, and the head wound was from a pistol and traveled from back to front. So Sederwall accused him of making-up the firearms used.

HOAXING: Sederwall's accusing Florencio Gonzales of being in a "**cover-up**" (of what is uncertain) makes no sense. In fact, the real cover-up was blocking pursuit of Tunstall's

Ringite murderers, because Sheriff William Brady and Governor S.B. Axtell shielded them.

Sederwall had missed the point of Florencio Gonzales's June 8, 1878 Angel deposition, while merely trying to show-off firearms knowledge. Gonzales was, anti-Ring, and was himself blocking *cover-up of Tunstall's Ringite assassination*. Gonzales had been the elected Lincoln County Probate Judge since 1875, and was a Tunstall-McSween ally from San Patricio, who had mitigated their Ringite malicious prosecution by denying the fake claim of James Dolan's "House" on the Emil Fritz estate for $76,000.

As Gonzales said in his Angel deposition: *"[If anyone] undertook to oppose L.G. Murphy & Co., they were either killed or run out of the County ... I have no doubt that the murder of John H. Tunstall was premeditated and designed by L.G. Murphy, J.J. Dolan, and J.H, Riley, commonly known as "The House" and carried out by their tools."* As to the murder, he testified: *"It has been claimed that Mr. Tunstall fired upon the posse [by Appel and the Ring]... and that he fired two shots at them out of a Colt's Improved Revolver. We found his revolver quite close to the scabbard on the corpse. It must have been placed there by someone after Tunstall's death. We found two chambers empty, but there were no hulls or cartridge shells in the empty chambers [meaning no bullets shot from them] – the other four chambers had cartridges in them."* As to the corpse, he testified: *"On examination we found the skull broken. We found that a rifle or carbine bullet had entered his breast and a pistol bullet entered the back of his head coming out the forehead."* [Gonzales then described the hidden body, with the killed horse] *"over 100 yards off the trail."*

So Gonzales's deposition told Investigator Angel that the killing was like a coupe de grâce, with a shot at the back of the head (contradicting Tunstall as an aggressor, removing doubt about Dr. Appel's ambiguous Angel deposition, and proving murder). Appel had accidentally reinforced that scenario by claiming the chest strike would have thrown Tunstall off his horse, leaving him on foot for that final coupe de grâce shot. In addition, hiding the body, the killing of Tunstall's horse beside him, and the mocking *"burlesque"* of putting his hat on the horse's head, pointed to the viciousness of the murder. Sederwall missed it all by relying ignorantly on biased witness Appel with a malicious agenda, then faking Gonzales as a conspirator to fake a "discovery."

Sederwall then claimed *he* had discovered that Tunstall was murdered; that William Morton was the murderer; that the sheriff's pose was acting unlawfully; and did a cover-up!

HOAXING: All that may have been news to W.C. Jameson, but, with addition of more of Tunstall's historical killers, Sederwall's is the conventional version of Tunstall's assassination! In fact, knowing that Sheriff William Brady was complicit and was shielding the murderers, forced the Regulators to get murder warrants from Justice of the Peace John "Squire" Wilson to arrest the murderers, including William "Buck" Morton.

HOAXING THE MORTON AND BAKER KILLING

Known history of the William Morton, Frank Baker, and William McCloskey killings, yields a Sederwall "crime scene investigation." (Pages 32-34)

As expected, without anyone knowing the exact killing site in the vast open plain east of the Capitan Mountains, Sederwall found spent cartridges, though did not indentify them, or address the hunting going on for generations in the area.

He then gave versions of the killings, from Regulator Frank "McNab" [sic - MacNab], James Dolan, a Lucius Dills, and Pat Garrett. Using "what-if" fake reasoning, instead of evidence, he ruminated about *what if* Morton and Baker had their hands tied. *If* they had their hands tied, they could not snatch McCloskey's gun and kill him (as the Regulators claimed). And it is hard to ride a horse with tied hands. This makes Sederwall "discover" preposterously that the men were killed in revenge by Billy the Kid.

HOAXING: This is no investigation. It is just Sederwall fantasizing, and uses "Brushy Bill's" own guess about revenge as a killing motive. And finding cartridges proves no connection to the killings, and offers no information about them.

HOAXING THE SHERIFF BRADY KILLING

The Sheriff William Brady killing, called "the pivotal event of the Lincoln County War" by Jameson, is in "Blood and Mud." (Pages 41-51) Actually, the pivotal event was the killing of Tunstall, which yielded the Regulator movement freedom fight against the Santa Fe Ring, of which, the Brady killing was a part.

Claimed is that no investigation of the killings of Brady and Hindman occurred until "cop" Sederwall's (Pages 43-51); though cited is merely the known cold wet day, Brady coming into town on horseback from his ranch, and the claim that he was putting up a courthouse notice while accompanied by his four deputies.

But, like for "Brushy" and his original authors, the motive for Brady's murder was unknown. And Sederwall was unaware also. He used a Francisco Trujillo's 1937 Works Progress Administration hearsay statement that McSween told Billy to stop Brady from arresting him. "Brushy" himself had guessed: "Sheriff Brady was gunning for me with warrants for cattle stealing." (*Alias Billy the Kid*, Page 27) And Sederwall used historian, Robert Utley, to claim the Regulators wanted to get rid of Brady.

So Sederwall did a "crime scene" investigation, deciding killing in a town was a bad way to keep it secret; weather was too bad for socializing; it was better to kill Brady coming from his ranch (which he boasts "cops" call a "kill zone"). **So Sederwall claimed the Regulators were there to testify in the Grand Jury.** And when it was delayed, they got angry at Brady for "obstructing justice;" so abruptly killed him. Sederwall was possibly contriving a defense of non-premeditation by a "crime of passion."

HOAXING: Sederwall apparently lifted the in-town-to-testify error from a "Billy the Kid Case" hoax participant, Attorney Randi McGinn, who was one of Governor Richardson's own lawyers, who wrote a pardon petition for his scam to make "Brushy" Billy the Kid. In it, she wrote that the Regulators were "[p]resent to testify as witnesses before the grand jury about the killing of John Tunstall."

This was ignorant McGinn's bad error. In fact, the Regulators were outlawed by Governor S.B. Axtell's March 9, 1881 Proclamation, giving Brady absolute power. That same March 9th, they had killed "Buck" Morton and Frank Baker. To come to Lincoln that April 1, 1878, risked their lives, indicating their desperate motive. And they were not, as Sederwall used, witnesses in the Grand Jury - which had not begun. As outlaws, they dared not testify. And Tunstall's murder had adequate evidence for the murder indictments that finally resulted.

The Regulator's act was premeditated killing of Brady before he murdered McSween that day, when he returned to Lincoln for his upcoming Grand Jury trial for his Ring-concocted embezzlement case. Brady had hoped to kill him with guise of legal pursuit before his likely exoneration. The Regulators hid behind Tunstall's corral's adobe wall, and acted in unison when Brady and his deputies came into view in the brief time presented by the awkward position of the adobe wall and the blocking, long, eastward side of Tunstall's building. And Brady and his men walking abreast and armed, as Sederwall himself stated, was key: they were heading ominously to McSween's point of arrival to the east, confirming to the Regulators need to act.

MISSED CORRECT DEFENSE ARGUMENT: Sederwall seemed to argue non-premeditation by instantaneous "crime of passion" to mitigate the eventual first degree murder verdict Billy got in his Mesilla trial. But it was both incorrect and useless.

It would have been useless in Ringite Judge Bristol's Mesilla court, where his April 9, 1881 jury instructions for Billy trial for the Brady murder stated: *"If the design to kill is completely formed in the <u>mind but for a moment before inflicting the fatal wounds</u> it would be premeditated and in law the effect would be the same as though the design to kill had existed for a long time."* Bristol deemed it still first degree murder, meaning hanging as the sole penalty.

The correct argument for a lesser degree, was the Regulators' conviction that deadly force was the only way to stop Brady's murder of McSween. In fact, if their response had been to <u>immediate</u> threat - like seeing Brady attacking McSween - it would be a defense for exoneration - like self-defense. But the gap of about three hours before McSween's arrival, required a mitigating defense based on their *certainty* that Brady would then kill McSween.

So trial evidence had to show that Brady was a proven murderer of McSween's friend, John Tunstall, just 42 days earlier. And Brady had made a death threat to Tunstall in

McSween's presence, stating: "I won't shoot you now, you haven't long to run." Brady was also a rogue lawman, blocking arrest of Tunstall's killers, who were his own deputies and possemen. And he illegally imprisoned the Defendant, Billy Bonney, on February 20, 1878, to obstruct his arrest of Tunstall's killers in his capacity as a Deputy Constable appointed by Justice of the Peace John Wilson. And Brady was a known threat to McSween, having harassed him by property attachment in his embezzlement case far in excess of the $10,000 set by Judge Bristol for the trial. And McSween hid because of certainty of Brady's murderous intent, staying in protective custody of Deputy Sheriff Adolph Barrier, who was also certain of McSween's risk from Brady. On March 28, 1878, Brady, brought Fort Stanton soldiers to the ranch of John Chisum, in failed attempt to apprehend, and likely kill, McSween. And just four days later - the murder day - McSween would return to Lincoln for his eventual Grand Jury trial.

Also, on the murder day, Defendant Bonney had only a revolver, since Brady had confiscated his carbine; and all others had carbines. He could not attain the 60 yard range to Brady's position, so could not have been his killer. Furthermore, Defendant Bonney had no motive to kill Brady except in defense of McSween. To protect another from certain death is noble, and mitigates against a verdict of 1st degree murder, which is wanton and with malice aforethought. And it is the burden of the Territory, not the Defendant, to prove beyond reasonable doubt that the Defendant *did not* act in defense of another. The prosecution, using Brady's indicted fellow murderers as witnesses, failed to do that. So the jurors, with reasonable doubt as to whether the defendant acted justifiably in defense of another, could not find him guilty of 1st degree murder, and were free to find the him not guilty - or, at most, guilty of 2nd degree murder, which spared his life.

Sederwall also faked discovery of "discrepancies" in the Brady killing, stating reports that Brady and Deputies were on foot were false because it is unpleasant to walk in the mud; and Brady was old. Also, they were described as walking abreast, but *only horses walk abreast*! So he fabricated a scene with Brady riding his horse when shot, and falling off. And he cited a witness stating that "he saw "Brady 'fall into a sitting position.'" (Pages 49-50)

HOAXING: This is contrived for the history-is-not-as-written scam. In fact, walking on mud of unpaved streets was a part of Old West life. The word "abreast," means side by side - like Brady and the Deputies walked. It does not refer to horses; but Sederwall built his hoax around the claim of abreast horses, meaning being on horseback.

And Sederwall built his fakery on confusing Brady with shot and dying Deputy George Hindman, who did "**fall into a sitting position.**" In fact, Hindman landing upright, made Ike Stockton run to him from José Montaño's building for an attempted rescue.

The big picture here is that Sederwall's "crime scene investigation" is just fantasizing. No witness ever reported ridden horses in the scene.

Adding to his horseback scenario was Sederwall's claim that Billy stole Brady's horse. He then claimed that Billy sold Brady's horse to Henry Hoyt in the Bill of Sale.

HOAXING: Sederwall built on his own fakery that horses were involved; then used meaningless "what-ifs": *If* Billy stole the horse, he could have sold it to Hoyt in Tascosa, Texas. But this sale of an expensive sorrel for $75, on October 24, 1878, merely lifts conventional history of Billy's likely sale of Brady's sorrel horse, Dandy Dick, to Hoyt.

Missed by Sederwall is that, in the pre-Lincoln County War Battle period, Billy rode a gray horse; that the Hoyt sale was 206 days after the Brady killing; and in the post-Lincoln County War period of that sale Billy was doing guerilla rustling against Ringites, and was selling horses in Tascosa. Dandy Dick was likely stolen then, with other horses, from Catron's Carrizozo Ranch or the Ring-backing Charles Fritz ranch. As Billy had threatened in his July 13, 1881 "Regulator Manifesto" to Catron's ranch manager and brother-in-law, Edgar Walz: "*We are all aware that your brother-in-law, T.B. Catron sustains the Murphy-Kinney party ... Steal from the poorest or richest American or Mexican, and the full measure of the injury you do, shall be visited upon the property of Mr. Catron.*"

Noteworthy is the inadvertent "Brushy" discrediting, since "Brushy" did not claim this horseback-Brady ambush or horse theft by Billy the Kid - who he was supposed to be. (*Alias Billy the* Kid, Page 27)

HOAXING THE "BUCKSHOT" ROBERTS KILLING

Jameson claimed the Regulators' April 4, 1878 Blazer's Mill killing of "Buckshot" Roberts would be revisited "to demonstrate the difference between the manner in which this event has long been treated and what is more likely the truth as discerned by investigative analysis conducted by Steve Sederwall." The chapter is: "The Shooting at Blazer's Mill." (Pages 52-55)

First given is conventional history of the shooting at Joseph Blazer's building. But "Brushy's" fiction had left Jameson with a problem. Unaware of the Regulators, "Brushy" made-up the shooting as a culminating argument of himself, Charlie Bowdre, and "Buckshot, with his revenge shooting of "Buckshot" as Billy. (*Alias Billy the* Kid, Pages 27-28; using Pat Garrett's *The Authentic Life of Billy the Kid* fictional version, Pages 74-75) So left to Sederwall was making Billy as the killer. (Pages 54-55)

Admitted by Sederwall is that the building no longer exists. To cast doubt on the historical version, his only "evidence" was three letters by Joseph Blazer's son, A.N. Blazer, sent to historian, Maurice Garland Fulton, claiming himself an eye-witness at age 13. His non-historical claim was that "Buckshot" arrived **at night, and in minutes there was shooting**. But his three letters' dates reveal writing 52 years and 5 days after the scene, 53 years and 20 days after the scene, and 59 years, 4 months, and 23 days after the scene. Sederwall also used A.N.'s tale, told to him by his sister, that, Billy, coming back to Lincoln after his hanging trial, breakfasted at Blazer's Mill, and told her **he shot Roberts through the door of the room where Roberts retreated.** A.N. added "Buckshot's" wound as a **little up from the left hip.**

Using A.N., Sederwall made-up a "crime scene," with Billy sliding and falling at the room and firing through its door from a prone position! He even made-up the door having a bullet hole.

HOAXING: To fake a discovery, Sederwall used old-timer A.N. Blazer's malarkey a half-century later, plus hearsay by his sister to create his own fiction.

Sederwall hid the actual Regulator witnesses, with the scene given in participant, George Coe's, 1934 book, *Frontier Fighter*, showing A.N.'s lies. Written was: "[T]his battle [at Blazer's Mill] pitted ... Andrew "Buckshot" Roberts, bent on the reward money for the slayers of Brady and Hindman against the Regulator detachment led by Brewer, which included Bowdre, George and Frank Coe, the Kid, MacNab, Middleton, Waite ... Bowdre got the first shot, mortally wounding Roberts. [So "Buckshot" was killed by Bowdre.] [And Roberts later killed Brewer.] ... [And] Roberts severed Bowdre's gun belt with a single shot; 'another struck Coe's right thumb ... a third bullet went into Middleton's chest ... In the late afternoon [meaning the incident was early - not night] the army surgeon, Dr. Appel ... took off a thumb and [trigger] finger for [Coe].' " (Coe, Pages lix-ix)

Revealed also is A.N. Blazer's lie about "Buckshot's" left hip wound. In fact, he had a single abdominal one from Charlie Bowdre, as documented in U.S. Attorney Thomas Benton Catron's June 21, 1878 federal indictment of the Regulators for the killing and titled "The United States vs. Charles Bowdry [Bowdre], Doc Scurlock, Henry Brown, Henry Antrim alias "Kid," John Middleton, Stephen Stevens, John Scroggins, George Coe and Frederick Waite." It stated: "*[He was shot] in and upon the right side of the belly of him the said Andrew Roberts one mortal wound of the depth of ten inches and of breadth of one half of an inch* of which said mortal wound the Said Andrew Roberts then and there at the said [Mescalero] Reservation instantly died [sic - the next day]."

And Billy the Kid - if he had fired at all - was accused in Catron's indictment as firing in a group; not alone: "*[T]he Said Charles Bowdry, Doc Scurlock, Henry Brown, Henry Antrim – alias Kid – John Middleton, Stephen Stevens, John Scroggins, George Coe and Frederick Waite the Said Andrew Roberts in manner and form aforesaid feloniously, willfully, unlawfully of this malice aforethought and from a premeditated design to effect the death of the Said Andrew Roberts, did kill and murder.*"

The "Buckshot" Roberts killing is a well documented scene, and Sederwall gave no reason why an obviously faking old-timer should be believed instead.

Sederwall concluded his fake discrepancies by stating that "Buckshot" and Brewer were buried **in the same grave nearby**. So he did what he called "on-site examination;" and found two markers.

HOAXING: Sederwall mixed-up the burial issue. There are two graves, but not marked with certainty. When formal gravestones were finally added to this well-known tourist site, it was arbitrarily decided to make one grave Brewer's, and the other "Buckshot's." There is no discrepancy, just the irrelevant chance that that the corpses are reversed.

Sederwall may have lifted this error from a past William V. Morrison letter. On April 27, 1953, Morrison shared the same confusion with Paul A. Blazer (Joseph Blazer's son), writing: "I had heard that both of them were buried in the same grave. But your explanation that Brewer was buried the same day that he was killed and Roberts lived until the next day, being buried that afternoon ... convinced me that the legend is in error."

HOAXING THE LINCOLN COUNTY WAR BATTLE

The Lincoln County War chapter is titled "The Burning of the McSween House." (Pages 56-67) For it, Jameson presented names and events unknown to "Brushy;" thus, inadvertently discrediting his man, who made-up a "three day" "cattle war."

Error-filled, it plucks fix-ups from modern history books - including the name "Regulators;" the Frank Warner Angel files; and Dudley Court of Inquiry testimonies. At its end, Jameson revealed it was actually Steve Sederwall's "analysis of the 'war" (Page 67), inadvertently placing the blame.

The Jameson-Sederwall duo did not realize the War was a six month fight against the Santa Fe Ring that it began at Tunstall's assassination, had multiple skirmishes, and culminated in a six day battle in Lincoln.

In the Jameson-Sederwall fiction, the Regulators ride into Lincoln on July 14, 1878 for motives wrongly guessed as: they had warrants to arrest Tunstall's killers and to protect McSween.

HOAXING: In fact, July 14, 1878 began Attorney Alexander McSween's culminating show-down with the Ring, its local bosses at "The House," Ringite Sheriff George Peppin, and the Ring's allies of Seven Rivers boys and John Kinney's outlaw gang.

Ring terrorism had been escalating. On April 29, 1878, Seven Rivers boys, hiding in Charles Fritz's ranch ambushed Frank Coe and Regulator leader, Frank MacNab, murdering MacNab. On May 28, 1878, Governor Axtell made a Proclamation to remove unbiased Sheriff John Copeland, and replace him with Ringite George Peppin as Sheriff. And on July 3, 1878, just eleven days earlier, had been the retaliative terrorist massacre and property destruction at San Patricio by Sheriff George Peppin and John Kinney's outlaw gang to punish McSween's Hispanic sympathizers. Thus, most of the approximately 60 men who rode in for McSween were enraged, traumatized, Hispanic, and from San Patricio and Picacho; with a lesser number being Anglo Regulators. And the day before, Billy and the Regulators had sent the "Regulator Manifesto" to T.B. Catron's brother-in-law, Edgar Walz, making clear the anti-Ring intent.

Also, it was McSween's intention to take the town peacefully, and force James Dolan to move away. He was so confident of safety, that he kept his wife, her sister with five young children, and his law intern at the house. His men occupied positions throughout the town; which Jameson added to a list unknown to "Brushy" - though still missing the Tunstall store. Jameson also wrongly thought - using "Brushy" - that most of the men stayed with McSween, but they were distributed through the town and, initially, only Jim "Frenchie" French was with McSween.

Adrift, the Jameson-Sederwall duo create a bizarre fiction that the battle resulted from squabbling about trespassing on some McSween land in town, saying McSween got angry that Peppin's posseman were on his land in an old stone tower called the Torreon; and McSween also blamed Saturnino Baca, his tenant in a house on that land, and sent him an eviction notice. Claimed is that Baca, an "ex-sheriff," knew the law, so he sent for his friend, Fort Stanton Commander N.A.M. Dudley. And Dudley sent Post Surgeon Daniel Appel, who tried to negotiate as "a peacemaker," but the possemen would not leave the Torreon because it gave them "an advantage." So, according to the clueless duo, "the Regulators dug in for war."

HOAXING: This was simply made-up. In the Battle's first day of July 14th, the Torreon was of no advantage, since

McSween's men were positioned along Lincoln's single street, and could prevent attackers ascending the south foothills to shoot down at them. Saturnino Baca, McSween's tenant, but a Lincoln settler since 1867, was one of the few Hispanic Ringites, a traitor to his people; and McSween knew it. In a political alliance with T.B. Catron since 1868, Baca was also a hay supplier to "The House" in its earliest days in Lincoln in 1873, and a Murphy ally. And Baca had been a Probate Judge, not Sheriff. Lincoln's first Sheriff was William Brady; then came John Copeland; then George Peppin. But on the Battle's first day, Baca was not yet actively involved. And Ringite Appel did not come to town until later; and as a Ring-biased fact-finder to enable Commander Dudley's intervention, not as a peacemaker.

The duo thought shooting began when Deputy Jack Long tried to serve warrants on McSween for attempted murder. (Page 58)

HOAXING: Gunfire began with entry of shooting Ring-side Seven Rivers boys, joining the Peppin posse on the first day. That caused McSween's men, including Billy, to rush to his house as protectors.

Also, Sederwall-Jameson were unaware that Long's warrants for murder and attempted murder against McSween and Billy were invalid. They were written at Blazer's Mill on May 1, 1878 by then Justice of the Peace, David Easton, at James Dolan's and Billy Matthews's request after an April 30, 1878 Lincoln County War skirmish of Seven Rivers boys, coming to Lincoln to kill McSween, with McSween's men there to protect him.

Easton was T.B. Catron's Ring agent in Lincoln County. So Easton called the self-defense killings by the Regulators murder; though the Seven Rivers attackers had been arrested by then Sheriff, John Copeland. Easton's warrants named McSween, Billy, and others unknown, with murder and assault; with victims being four dead and one injured Seven Rivers men. But, fearing retribution, Easton then quit, invalidating his warrants!

The key point, missed by the duo, is that there was no legal reason for the Peppin posse to attack McSween. And he had been exonerated for embezzling by the Grand Jury three months earlier. That is why, on July 19th, when Commander Dudley marched on Lincoln, and realized this, he forced Justice of the Peace Wilson to write a warrant fabricating McSween's attempted murder of fact-finder, Private Berry Robinson on July 16th.

As to the duo's reference to evicting McSween's tenant Saturnino Baca, it occurred on July 15th, for his assisting Sheriff Peppin's possemen occupying the Torreon. Baca used that eviction notice for his pre-planned Ringite plot to evade the Posse Comitatus Act that barred military intervention in civilian matters, as passed the month before. The plot was to use its exception allowing intervention if women and children were in danger. So traitor to his people, Baca, wrote to Dudley that his pregnant wife and many children were in danger of McSween, and requested troops.

As to Post Surgeon Daniel Appel's coming to Lincoln, it was on July 15th, and he was no "peacemaker." A Ring tool, he had come at Dudley's orders for "fact finding," in further Ringite exploration of excuses to use troops to crush the winning McSween side.

It was at that point on July 15th, that the Ring side was adequately emboldened to send Jack Long to the McSween house with David Easton's invalid May 1st arrest warrants for McSween and Billy for the April 30th skirmish with the invading, Ringite Seven Rivers boys. But Long was repelled by shots from inside. This was the point that the ignorant duo faked the war as starting.

Still writing fiction, the Sederwall-Jameson duo next had departing failed "peacemaker" Daniel Appel encounter the John Kinney gang, whom they call "Seven Rivers Warriors" (confusing Kinney from Mesilla with the Seven Rivers boys). They add Jessie Evans, and say that Appel convinced Kinney to go to Lincoln - when Kinney and his Mesilla gang were there for the pre-planned attack - along with Seven Rivers boys from the Pecos valley.

For the next day (with no date, but with information compatible with July 16th), the duo have Sheriff Peppin station men on the south foothills to shoot unsuccessfully at "McSween's snipers." Claimed is that was when Peppin requested a howitzer cannon from Dudley.

HOAXING: This fiction missed the crucial point that McSween's plan for a peaceful take-over was working. The south foothills were unattainable, with his men able to fire at any attempted ascent. That was why Peppin tried to get military intervention to defeat the McSweens, in violation of the Posse Comitatus Act.

The duo then garble the next incident of July 16th. They state that Dolan and Kinney wrote Dudley making-up that McSweens had fired on his soldier in town. And that made Dudley come.

WRONG: In fact, that July 16th, responding to Peppin's cannon request, Dudley sent 9th Cavalryman Private Berry Robinson as another fact-finder. The McSweens, halting shooting for fear of hitting a soldier, enabled some Peppin men to ascend the south foothills. Robinson was then likely fired upon by the Dolan side, was uninjured but thrown from his horse, and returned to Fort Stanton. The Dolan side claimed Robinson was attacked by McSweens. But that did not cause Dudley's immediate intervention.

For that same July 16th, the duo have McSween-side Fernando Herrera shoot Charles Crawford, a Peppin posseman on the south foothills; with good surgeon Appel suddenly appearing in town to "risk his life" to give him aid - though Crawford died.

WRONG: The actual date was July 17th. And Appel was back in Lincoln in another "fact-finding mission," now with past Fort Stanton Commander George Purington, and five soldiers, with the excuse of Berry Robinson's shooting. Dudley was in a dilemma: afraid to act, but as an alcoholic incompetent, he was Ring-beholden, with T.B. Catron having already represented him for two prior court martials. He knew he was supposed to crush the uprising. So again Dudley's fact-finders recorded accusations against McSween, which he denied. It was in that context, that Appel - not risking his life because McSweens would not shoot at soldiers - retrieved dying Charles Crawford. But the crucial big picture missed by the duo was that it was now the fourth day of McSween's occupation, and he was holding the town, with Peppin's posse neutralized.

For July 18th, the duo have McSween side's Ben Ellis shot in the neck, though it occurred the day before. They then describe town doctor [Taylor] Ealy, going to assist Ben, making clear that Mrs. Ealy was there too. And an unidentified "Sue Gates" accompanies her to get water.

WRONG: The duo were unaware that there were also two young Ealy children, or that Susan Gates was a teacher living with the Shield family in McSween's house, but had taken shelter with the Ealy's. In fact, they missed the whole Shield family. Living in a wing of McSween's two part house, was Susan McSween's sister Elizabeth, her five children, and her husband David, who was McSween's law partner. There also was McSween's law student, Harvey Morris. The missed *big picture is women and children*. It was the obligation, under the Posse Comitatus Act, for Dudley to protect women and children. But he would instead enable their life-threatening attack by Ringites.

For the 19th, Sederwall-Jameson have Dudley arrive at Lincoln with troops. Showing-off, they digress, and declare, as if by discovery, that Dudley later lied in a court of inquiry that he had come to protect women and children! Noted also is the well known fact that, the day before, Dolan and John Kinney had visited Dudley at Fort Stanton, and had influenced him to intervene. As if shocked, the duo decide Dudley and Dolan were in a conspiracy(!) - which they define (!) - and decide they all lied!

HOAXING: The obvious is not discovery. In fact, Dolan's partner, John Riley, had been in Santa Fe; and one can presume he was strategizing Dudley's attack with T.B. Catron. The duo were unaware that the Lincoln County War was an uprising against the Ring, which was intentionally and ferociously crushed in the final battle.

But thinking they discovered Dudley's "lying," the duo give known examples of his outrages in Lincoln, like refusing aid to Susan McSween - an conclude the obvious: Dudley had refused aid to women and children! And they had Dudley pointing a cannon at McSween's front door. (Page 65)

WRONG: The cannon was pointed at José Montaño's house. Thus, the duo missed the key point: Dudley's intentional act of terror, which caused flight of McSween's men there and throughout the town. The strategy was to besiege McSween's house to kill him, and everyone else inside.

Now possessing the Dudley Court of Inquiry transcript (unlike "Brushy" and his authors), likely from Sederwall's fellow "Billy the Kid Case" hoaxer, U.S. Marshals Service David Turk, the duo had real   Billy's own   testimony, which they cite - though hiding how differently real Billy talked compared to grammatically impaired "Brushy." But they tried to use what Billy said to pretend the conducting of an "investigation." But Billy's crucial testimony for incriminating Dudley about taking sides - about three soldiers stationed at McSween's house by Dudley - is misunderstood as: "an attempt to draw fire."

WRONG: In fact, the key point that Billy was making was that the soldiers were stationed there to inhibit those inside from shooting, so as to give Sheriff Peppin's men the advantage. Billy had also stated that Dudley assigned three soldiers to accompany Peppin as a shield.

For the burning of the McSween house, the duo have Peppin order his posse to commit arson. They then identify an Andy Boyle as the fire-setter, but are unaware he was a Seven Rivers boy - calling him a "cattle rustler from Texas."

WRONG: Andy Boyle was not the only fire-setter, as proved by the May 23, 1879 eye-witness testimony of Susan McSween at the Dudley Court of Inquiry. She stated: *"I then said to Mr. McSween that I believe that I would go down to his camp and talk with [Dudley] myself ... [O]n my way to his camp I saw [Sebrian] Bates, he being a colored servant of mine ... just in the act of picking up some lumber. At the time I saw three of Murphy's men ... I then asked what they were doing, they said ... [t]hat Peppin and Col. Dudley had sent them to carry lumber to our house to set it on fire ... I then begged them not to do so."*

Also missed is a key point that Dudley enabled the fire to be set around the McSween family's women and children. And the duo were unaware of the catastrophic event that added to the fire: the house's keg of gunpowder for reloading cartridges exploded, ultimately leaving the men in the last remaining non-burning room, the kitchen.

The duo describe the nighttime escape from the room. They state that the "**Kid said they had to jump over the body of Harvey Morris,** then ran towards the Tunstall Store and then turned towards the river." (Page 66)

HOAXING: Jumping over Morris's body is invented here; and is not even in "Brushy's" own quote copying Billy's testimony on running towards the Tunstall store and river

(*Alias Billy the Kid*, Page 31), or Jameson's 1998 book (*Return of the Outlaw Billy the Kid*, Page 54), or in real Billy's testimony. It opens the possibility that Jameson simply published verbatim whatever Sederwall made-up.

FLAWED: Most importantly, even with Billy's transcript in hand, the confused duo missed Billy's key testimony about the escape. And it was fatal to "Brushy," who had no idea of it. Real Billy reported seeing three white soldiers (likely meaning officers) fire a volley at those escaping, including him; thus, making Dudley complicit with murder, as ordering his men to shoot at the escaping civilians, and in violation of the Posse Comitatus Act.

The duo then give the conventional killing of McSween and shooting of Yginio Salazar.

FLAWED: Missed from this conventional history are the murders of McSween-side Vincente Romero and Francisco Zamora. Even the friendly fire, fatal shooting of Ring-side Bob Beckwith is left out.

Unaware of the Battle's cause, the duo conclude feebly that Billy the Kid and his companions were disappointed because they did not get a chance to serve the warrants for Brady's murder, and had failed to protect McSween! And they floated this hoax's silly point that authorities cannot be trusted. Jameson narrated Sederwall's conclusion that "more violations of the law were committed by the men responsible for law enforcement than by those who were identified as outlaws." That was supposed to imply proof that lawman Pat Garrett killed the innocent victim, not Billy!

HOAXING PAT GARRETT AS LACKING AUTHORITY

To cast doubt on Pat Garrett - with usual hoax irrationality that anything bad about him, meant he did not kill Billy - a Sederwall "investigation" claimed that he had *illegally* tracked Billy the Kid in 1880, because he was only a "sheriff-elect" under Lincoln County Sheriff George Kimbrell, and not a Deputy U.S. Marshal as history claimed. (Page 81)

As "proof," used was one of Secret Service Operative Azariah Wild's reports stating that Wild had received paperwork for two Deputy U.S. Marshal commissions for a John Hurley from Santa

Fe's U.S. Marshal John Sherman. So he had crossed out one, and added Pat Garrett's name. Sederwall concluded that meant Garrett was not legally appointed, so had only authority in Lincoln County as a Deputy Sheriff. (Page 81) Thus, he could not make arrests in San Miguel County site of Fort Sumner, so was at the Billy the Kid death scene illegally.

HOAXING: Sederwall misstated Garrett's legitimacy in his Deputy U.S. Marshal appointment by Wild, whose intent was to empower him to head Territory-wide posses tracking the "Wilson & Kid gang."

Garrett's biographer, Leon Metz, in his 1974 *Pat Garrett: The Story of a Western Lawman*, gave the circumstance: "Since United States marshals and deputy marshals were too frightened to help him, Wild ... compiled a list of brave citizens ... Among them ... [was] Pat Garrett ... [He] wrote [U.S. Marshal] Sherman saying that these men would do the work if Sherman would simply sign United States deputy marshal commissions for all of them. Sherman happily complied, sending everything the Treasury man asked for, except that he mistakenly dispatched two commissions for Hurley and none for Garrett. Wild rectified this error by scratching Hurley's name from one of the papers and substituting Garrett's."

For his hoax, Sederwall omitted that Wild informed Secret Service Chief James Brooks, on January 3, 1881, of Garrett's appointment; and that, as one of only 40 Special Operatives in the country, he had power to make appointments and pursue investigations as he chose - including capturing and killing suspects. Wild had already reported his difficulty getting warrants and commissions. On October 13, 1880, he wrote: "*Complaints are made here against Marshal Sherman that he is a drunkard and inefficient. But as I am not investigating the Marshal [note that Wild had that power over him] I will not complain if he will arrest or commission men who will make the arrests I want.*" Also, Lincoln County citizens refused, as he wrote on October 29, 1880: "*There is no one who I can get to assist me here that I can trust as every one ... who resides here, and who would otherwise assist me is scared that he will be killed.*" Pat Garrett was one of the few willing to help, as Wild reported to Chief Brooks on November 11, 1880. And by November 21, 1880, Wild reported that Garrett had enlisted his friend, Barney Mason, to infiltrate the counterfeiting gang as a spy.

What Sederwall took out of context, was that Wild, back in his New Orleans home base, reviewing his New Mexico Territory case with Chief James Brooks to complain about problematic U.S. Marshal Sherman, and his sloppy paperwork. Wild's January 3, 1881 report stated:

> *I am disposed to believe U.S. Attorney Barnes will and has done all he could, but he had a man as Marshal who is but little or no assistance to him, and in fact I will state that had I gone there and found no U.S. Marshal I would have accomplished my work sooner and I believe more satisfactory to the government and to myself.*
>
> *I will respectfully state that I appealed to Marshal Sherman to appoint P.F. Garrett as Deputy Marshal to which he paid no attention. <u>I was in great need of Mr. Garrett's aid at that time and took one of the Commissions Sherman sent to John Hurley (he having sent two) and substituted the name of P.F. Garrett the very man who has rendered the Government such valuable service in killing and arresting these men who I was in pursuit</u>.*

So Garrett's Deputy U.S. Marshal appointment was proper. Chief Brooks acceptance confirmed its legitimacy.

In addition, further exposing Sederwall's hoaxing, was that he hid Wild's commendation letter for Garrett, included in his report to Chief Brooks of January 25, 1881:

> *Patrick F. Garrett Esq.*
>   *Sheriff of Lincoln County*
>   *New Mexico*
> *Dear Sir:-*
>   *Your letter dated Lincoln NM January 10th 1881 just received and noted.*
>   *1st Allow me to congratulate you, and your men for the success in bringing up, arresting and killing the worst band of outlaws in the United States ...*
>   *Your services to the Government have been of too great value to go unpaid or be treated in a miserly manner.*

> I have properly represented you and the services performed by you and your men to the Departments to which I belong, at Washington, and will continue to aid you all that is in my power until you are fully paid ...
> Very Respectfully
> Azariah F. Wild
> Operative

Garrett himself referenced his Deputy U.S. Marshal appointment in his 1882 *Authentic Life of Billy the Kid*: "[Bob] Olinger and myself were both commissioned as deputy United States marshals and held United States warrants for the Kid and Bowdre for the killing of ["Buckshot"] Roberts on an Indian Reservation." (Garrett, Page 145)

ATTACKING PAT GARRETT BY "BRUSHY BILL" AND "BILLY THE KID CASE" HOAXES

Defaming Pat Garrett as a murderer was the core of the "Brushy Bill" and "Billy the Kid Case" hoaxes. The Jameson-Sederwall duo continued attacks on him in chapters "A Liar and a Thief." (Pages 120-124) and "Reluctant Pursuit." (Pages 125-130) New Sederwall "cop investigation" hoaxes were toward that end.

So they accused Garrett of theft in handling Bob Olinger's estate, by keeping guns, and by giving his Whitney double-barrel shotgun to Garrett's friend, Joseph Lea. "Cop" Sederwall "discovers" in the list of clothes listed as valueless, Garrett's omission of hat, boots, and saddle. So he quoted Lilly Klasner from her book *My Girlhood Among Outlaws* (a posthumous memoir), saying after Olinger's death she got his six-shooter, field glasses and gauntlet. (Page 124) So Sederwall adds them to list Garrett's omissions; even though he had contended earlier in his text that Garrett should have given Olinger's possessions to Olinger's family (so Sederwall was possibly unaware that Klasner was Olinger's fiancé). This tomfoolery leads Sederwall to conclude that he had proved that Garrett was a liar and a thief. (Page 124) And presumably that made him a murderer too.

Garrett was next accused of not trying to capture Billy, since a May 12, 1881 *Las Vegas Gazette* article said Billy was near Fort

Sumner; even though Garrett was also cited as saying he was working out a plan of action. (Pages 125-126)

HOAXING: This mimics the Pat and Billy super-friendship of the "Billy the Kid Case" hoax. Omitted is that Billy's location was unknown and rumors were rife, as reflected by contemporary press. So it is reasonable that Garrett delayed, while using Azariah Wild-funded spies.

In Billy's fictional press, he had even been accused, in the May 4, 1881 *Santa Fe Daily New Mexican*, of murdering Billy Matthews in "More Killing by Kid, When But a Short Distance From Lincoln, He Meets one of His Old Enemies, and Kills Him and His Companion. Two More Victims." Here are other examples. On May 5, 1881 in the *Santa Fe Daily New Mexican's* "Anything that the imagination can concoct," had Billy seen in Albuquerque. On May 13, 1881, the *Santa Fe Daily New Mexican* reported Billy in Chloride City. On May 19, 1881, the *Santa Fe Daily New Mexican* printed, "The Kid is believed to be in the Black Range." On May 19, 1881, the *Santa Fe Daily New Mexican* printed "Billy the Kid was last seen in Lincoln County." And on June 13, 1881, the *Las Vegas Daily Optic* had " 'Billy the Kid,' He is Reported to Have Been Seen on Our Streets Saturday Night."

Claimed is that Garrett did not believe Billy was in Fort Sumner, and that his Deputy, John W. Poe, convinced to go there. And, to fake Garrett as unmotivated to capture Billy, Poe is portrayed as having to take the initiative.

HOAXING: Omitted is Garrett's explanation, in *The Authentic Life of Billy the Kid*, about using Poe for recognizance: "Poe was a stranger in the country, and there was little danger he would meet anyone at Sumner who might know him. So, after an hour or two spent in the hills, <u>I sent him to Fort Sumner to take observations. I advised him to go to Sunnyside,</u> seven miles above Sumner, and interview M. Rudulph, in whose judgment and discretion I had great confidence. It was understood that Poe would meet with us that night at moonlight." (Garrett, Pages 212-213)

Then, to portray Garrett as a liar, his approach to the Maxwell house with his deputies on the killing night is garbled from *The Authentic Life of Billy the Kid*, as to Garrett's seeing two figures in the peach orchard. The duo wrote: "As Garrett, Poe, and McKinney approached the houses, Garrett said, they 'heard the sound of voices conversing in Spanish,' though they were too far away to hear words distinctly. As they watched from hiding, 'a man rose from the ground in full view, but too fat away to recognize. He wore a broad-brimmed hat, dark vest and pants, and was in his shirt sleeves.' This man, claimed Garrett, was Billy the Kid, even though he previously stated he was too far away to recognize.' A few lines later, however, Garrett again wrote, 'The Kid by me unrecognized.' Did Garrett recognize the Kid or not?" This fake "discrepancy leads the conclusion that the incident never happened because Poe did not have it in his own book. So Garrett lied. (Page 129)

HOAXING: This is built on misstating Garrett from *The Authentic Life of Billy the Kid* about himself, Poe, and McKinney, on foot, secretly entering the Maxwell's peach orchard which extended to some houses "occupied by Mexicans, not more than sixty yards from Maxwell's house. We approached these houses cautiously, and when within earshot heard the voices of people conversing in Spanish [i.e., they heard the Spanish voices of the people in the houses]. We concealed ourselves quickly and listened, but the distance was too great to hear words or even distinguish voices [i.e., referring to a couple at a distance in the orchard, too far to make out their words]. Soon a man arose from the ground, close enough to be seen but too far away to be recognized [i.e., the distant man, whose words could not be made out, rose]. He wore a broadbrimmed hat, dark vest and pants, and was in his shirt sleeves ... [H]e went to the fence, jumped it, and walked toward the Maxwell house. Little as we suspected it, this man was the Kid." [i.e., after the killing, Garrett realized, likely by the corpse's outfit, that the man in shirt sleeves had been Billy] (Garrett, Page 214) Garrett makes clear he did not recognize Billy in the orchard: "**When the Kid, who had been thus unrecognized by me, left the orchard, I motioned to my companions.**" (Page 215)

And Poe merely omitted this insignificant scene in his book decades later. Sederwall was faking a "discrepancy."

HOAXING DEATH SCENE DOUBTS

The Jameson-Sederwall duo present their hoax's make-or-break July 14, 1881 death scene in chapters "Shooting at Fort Sumner" (Pages 131-134) and "Discrepancies." (Pages 135-163)

Concealed is that "Brushy's" tale is totally different from the "Billy the Kid Case's." He had a Billy Barlow accidentally killed in the dark night on the back porch. The "Billy the Kid Case" hoax had super-friend Pat Garrett shooting willing Billy to play dead on the carpenter's bench (to bleed for future fake DNA); then murdering the innocent victim to switch with Billy for burial.

Concealed also, is zero evidence supporting either hoax; and profuse evidence debunking them. So the duo rely on fake "discrepancies," fake "investigations," and Dr. Henry Lee's fake carpenter's bench and washstand forensics. The result is a megahoax, that disproves "Brushy" by its mismatch, and exposes Sederwall's and Jameson's fakery by its ridiculous lies.

Their hoaxed claim is that "researchers never noted the obvious and glaring discrepancies" in Pat Garrett's and John W. Poe's accounts of the shooting. There were none, but the Jameson-Sederwall duo propose to show them. (Page 135)

Since the only relevant fact is the profuse identification of the body as Billy Bonney's - obviously omitted here - the meaninglessness of their scam is obvious from the start. Important, however, are additions to the original hoaxes by Sederwall's new fake "cop investigations."

HOAXING "DISCREPANCIES"

Discrepancies are faked using Pat Garrett's 1882 *Authentic Life of Billy the Kid* and John W. Poe's *The Death of Billy the Kid*, to pretend they proved events did not occur. So the duo conclude that this "incident [shooting in the bedroom] as the two lawmen described it never took place." (Page 141) Examples follow:

1) DEPUTIES OUTSIDE: The duo claim it was suspicious for Garrett to enter the Maxwell's bedroom, while leaving his deputies outside, because it was too careless for searching for "the most dangerous outlaw in New Mexico." (Page 138)

HOAXING: Omitted is that Garrett did not believe that Billy was in Fort Sumner, and was merely checking with Maxwell. Omitted is another possibility, that a trap was being set, with Billy being sent to Maxwell's bedroom for ambush. In that case, it was strategic to have the deputies outside in case Billy escaped out of the room.

2) IN SOX AND BUTTONING PANTS: The approach of the stranger, in sox and buttoning his pants, is tackled by "cop" Sederwall, recycling his absurdity from his (concealed) Case No. 2003-274's "Probable Cause Statement" about it being too hard to hold a gun and a knife and button your pants; plus gravel would hurt your sensitive stockinged feet! (Page 139)

HOAXING: Billy apparently could multi-task! And apparently he could tackle gravel too! Sederwall's silliness in the "Probable Cause Statement" stated:

[Poe stated] *At this I stood up and advanced toward him, telling him not to be alarmed ... and still without the least suspicion that this was the very man we were looking for.*

This statement raises many questions with investigators. Poe says he sees a man *"partially dressed, and was bare-headed and bare-footed - or rather, had only socks on his feet, and it seemed to me that he was fastening his trousers as he came toward me art a very brisk walk."* Then the man covers him with his six shooter. Where did the man put the *"six-shooter"* when he was *"fastening his trousers"*?

He did not stop and lay it down because Poe says he *"he came toward me art a very brisk walk."*

3) SPEAKING SPANISH: Sederwall cogitated that if approaching Billy said, "Quien es?" and non-Spanish-speaking Poe responded in English to reassure him, then bi-lingual Billy would have reverted to English. So Sederwall concludes that left just two possibilities: it was not Billy, or Poe lied! (Page 140)

HOAXING: Omitted is that Billy was the most hunted man in the Territory. Speaking Spanish to a stranger was his disguise. Also, he probably used the language commonly, as he would with bi-lingual Peter Maxwell in the next a moment. And the disguise worked! Poe assumed he was a Maxwell worker. Sederwall's "just two" possibilities" are ridiculous.

4) LETTING BILLY ENTER THE BEDROOM: Sederwall claimed it was unimaginable that two deputies let a man with a knife and a gun walk into the bedroom with Garrett, without shouting a warning. And he imagines that Billy would have been more cautious, or even shot the deputies. (Pages 140-141)

HOAXING: Fantasizing is not evidence.

In fact, neither Poe nor McKinney knew Billy, and thought he was a Maxwell worker. Billy's gun was attributed to strangers alarming him, and could as easily be construed as a worker being protective of Maxwell, and rightly asking them in Spanish, "Who are you?" And none of the lawmen were expecting Billy to turn up at Maxwell's house, so were not alarmed. As Poe stated in his book: "**As Maxwell's was the one place in Fort Sumner I considered above suspicion of harboring the Kid, I was entirely off my guard.**" (Poe, Page 34)

As to Billy being incautious, he was known for fearlessness. That is how he ended up in Fort Sumner, instead of hightailing it to Old Mexico after his jailbreak. And Fort Sumner had strangers passing through. It is absurd to think that he would automatically shoot them!

5) ENTERING THE BEDROOM: Garrett's statement that the person "sprang quickly into the door" is contrasted with Poe describing Billy backing towards the door, to claim Billy never entered the room! (Page 132)

HOAXING: Actually, the manner of entering is merely vantage point. In his 1933 book, Poe described Billy as "**backed up into the doorway of Maxwell's room, where he halted for a moment, his body concealed by the thick adobe wall at the side of the doorway.**" (Poe, Page 35) So Poe could not have seen Billy's final turn to enter the room face-forward as Garrett saw. There is no discrepancy.

6) THE VICTIM'S IDENTITY: After the shooting, Maxwell is presented as running out; Garrett as doubtful, saying, "**I think I have got him;**" and Poe being doubtful. (Page 133)

HOAXING: Garrett did not say, "I think I have got him." In his book, he was certain: "I told my companions that **I had got the Kid**. They asked if I had not shot the wrong man. I told them I made no mistake, for I knew the Kid's voice too well."

He explained the Deputies' doubt: "Seeing a bareheaded, bare-footed man, in his shirt sleeves, with a butcher knife in his hand, and hearing his hail in excellent Spanish, they naturally supposed him to be a Mexican and an attaché of the establishment, hence their suspicion that I had shot the wrong man." (Garrett, Page 217)

As to Poe, *he* is the one who gave quote the duo called Garrett's: " 'I think I have got him' ... I said, 'Pat, the Kid would not come to this place; you have shot the wrong man ...' Upon my saying this, Garrett seemed to be in doubt himself as to whom he shot, but quickly spoke up and said, 'I am sure that was him, for I know his voice too well to be mistaken.' " (Poe, Pages 37-38) And Poe confirmed: "Upon examining the body, we found it to be that of Billy the Kid." (Page 41) There was no discrepancy.

7) POST-SHOOTING SCENES: The scene is given of "native people" taking the body "to a carpenter shop where it was laid out on a workbench." Poe is quoted about staying in Maxwell's house for fear of attack by "friends of the dead man." (Page 134) Then appears "cop" Sederwall to say it all seemed suspicious to him that Garrett would let women take the body of such a famous outlaw, or that he would "cower" in Maxwell's house. To him that means Garrett was a bad leader - or worse. (Page 134)

HOAXING: Sederwall's sexist fantasies are not evidence.

HOAXING NO MAXWELL BEDROOM DOOR

This new hoax by Steve Sederwall, of Peter Maxwell's bedroom having no outside door, was also used by W.C. Jameson in his 2016 *Pat Garrett: The Man Behind the Badge*. Its intent is to destroy the historical death scene in one fell swoop, since all participants recounted the outside door. That claim would lead to the claim that they were all lying in cahoots; ergo, everybody was covering up that Pat Garrett had not killed Billy the Kid.

Sederwall gave a diagram labeled "Floor plan of the Maxwell house;" and the alleged bedroom has no door. And the building itself is called a one-story adobe. (Page 137) **[FIGURE: 9]**

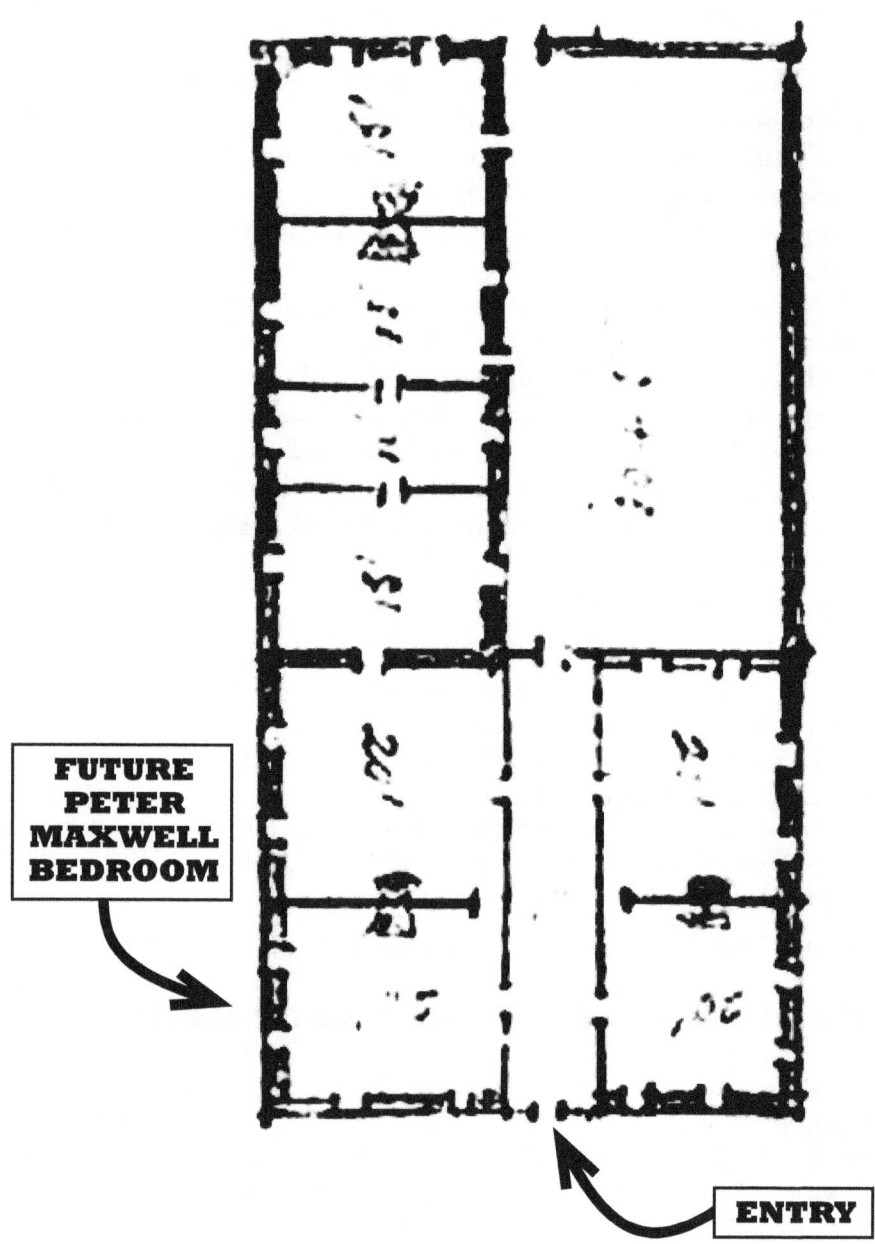

FIGURE: 9. Falsely used by the hoaxers as "Floor plan of Maxwell house" from the "National Archives" (Page 137), this diagram is from the National Archives as "Commanding Officer's Quarters, Fort Sumner, New Mexico Territory;" and its copy, so labeled, is at the Fort Sumner State Monument

To indicate that Garrett lied about the door, Sederwall claimed: "**Garrett wrote, '[Billy] 'stepped onto the porch and entered Maxwell's room through the open door left open on account of the extremely warm weather.'** " (Page 131) And Poe's witnessing Billy enter through that door is cited as to his lying also. (Page 140) Added is that if there was a door, it was not open, as Garrett said, because scary animals could get in. (Page 138) So the duo conclude that Garrett and Poe lied about the entire scene to conceal that Billy the Kid was never shot.

HOAXING: The claimed "floor plan" is not Maxwell's bedroom, but is the original Fort Sumner Commanding Officer's quarters for the Bosque Redondo Indian Reservation from 1863 to 1868. Since its sources in the National Archives and at Fort Sumner State Monument label it as such, the hoaxers are faking its identification.

Omitted is that in 1870, when Lucien Maxwell bought Fort Sumner, he rebuilt it as his family home. As Robert Mullin wrote on the back of the Maxwell house photo: *"Pete Maxwell's House Fort Sumner ... Originally 1 Story Flat Roof, Officers Quarters. 2nd Floor Added By Maxwell."*

The actual Maxwell house floor plan shows the outside door. [Figure: 10] And the Maxwell house photograph, also shows that door in Maxwell's bedroom. [Figure: 11]

And to claim, as did the hoaxing duo, that the door was not left open, is meaningless fantasizing.

And the Garrett quote is faked. He actually wrote: "When we reached the porch in front of the building, I left Poe and McKinney at the end of the porch, and about twenty feet from the door of Pete's bedroom, while I myself entered it." (Garrett, Page 215) The duo's quote is actually distorted from Poe's book; stating: "'You fellows wait here while I go in to talk to [Maxwell].' Thereupon he stepped onto the porch and entered Maxwell's room through the open door (left open on account of the extremely warm weather), while McKinney and myself stopped on the outside." (Poe, Page 31)

Also, Poe described the further role of that door when he almost shot Maxwell on the porch: "A moment after Garrett came out of the door, Pete Maxwell rushed squarely onto me in a frantic effort to get out of the room." (Poe, Page 38) There was no walking through the house.

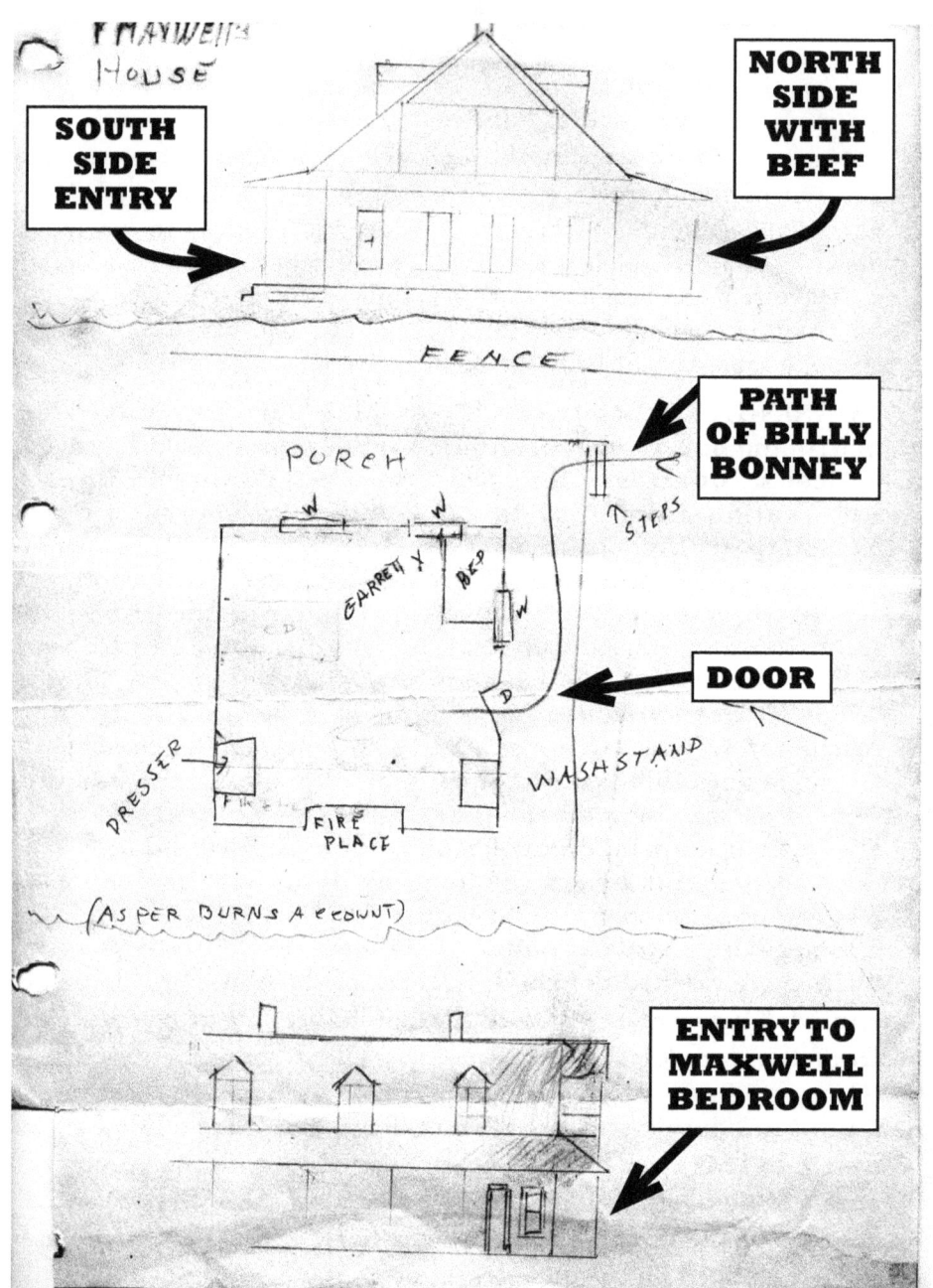

FIGURE: 10. Diagrams by Maurice Garland Fulton of the Maxwell's house, with Peter Maxwell's bedroom, and Billy Bonney's entry through its outside door. From the Midland, Texas, Haley Library, Robert N. Mullin Collection.

FIGURE: 11. Photograph of the Maxwell house showing Peter Maxwell's bedroom with a door to the outside. From the Midland, Texas, Haley Library, Robert N. Mullin Collection

CONCEALED SOURCE FOR NO OUTSIDE DOOR: This "investigation's" no door claim was lifted from an undated article by an unknown author (erroneously named as Gregory Scott Smith) titled "The Death of Billy the Kid: A New Scenario?" now in the Fort Sumner State Monument files. It used John L. McCarty papers of an October 22, 1942 interview titled "Kid Dobbs Interviews: An Interview with Garrett H. 'Kid' Dobbs at Farmington, New Mexico, on September 12, 1942, with Mel Armstrong and John McCarty, Thursday Morning, October 22, 1942, In the Presence of Mrs. Dobbs and Pat Flynn. J.D. White, Amarillo, Heard Part of the Final Statements of this Interview Re. Billy the Kid's Death."

Garrett H. "Kid" Dobbs merely spouted old-timer windbag malarkey. His fabrication, with the usual claim of knowing Billy the Kid, began with: "Billy told me ... he came from San Francisco, California, and had killed a chinaman out there for insulting his mother." Here is Dobbs's Lincoln County War Battle: "Once when a friend of Billy the Kid was killed, Billy went to Chisholm [sic] and volunteered to lead the Chisholm party at war ... They made a fight and Murphy's men set fire to McSwain's [sic] house ... Billy had killed four of Murphy's men during the fight ... [During the escape] McSwain [sic] was killed by Murphy. Mrs. McSwain [sic] yelled for her trunk in the house and Tom O'Folliard went back in and got it but burnt his whiskers."

For the death scene, Dobbs's fakery continued:

> Billy was hiding out in Pete Maxwell's house ...
>
> Maxwell wrote Garrett a letter saying he would turn over Billy to him. Garrett thought it might be a trick to trap him for Billy. <u>Pat had Frank Poe and Jim McIntosh, two deputies with him</u>. [Note ignorance of even of the famous deputies.] He told them he was afraid this was a trap and wasn't going up there until he spoke with Maxwell ... Garrett wrote a note to Maxwell and sent it to him by a Mexican boy telling him to meet them at the Mexican plaza 6 miles below Fort Sumner ...
>
> Garrett told Pete if it was a trap he would kill him too. He told Pete he was coming up that night.
>
> They arrived ay Maxwell's early before Billy came in from his daylight hiding and [Pat] told his deputies to bed down in one corner of Maxwell's yard. Pat went in to the house and waited in Maxwell's bedroom.

When Billy came in that night he saw the men in the yard and asked the cook who they were. The cook said they were some of Pete's sheepherders ...

In the meantime Maxwell had told the cook not to save any cold meat ... so the Kid would have to fix his own supper.

Billy asked the cook where the knife was ... Garrett could hear every word in the bedroom.

Then the Kid asked where the meat was and the cook said he guessed it was in the meat box. The Kid told him it wasn't. The cook told Billy it must be in Pete's bedroom then as Pete had brought some new meat out from town. [Note that Dobbs did not even know that Fort Sumner *was* the town.]

The Kid had the knife in his left hand and started to the bedroom to get some meat. [**Note that Billy walks through the house to get to the bedroom in this tall tale.**] There was a broken-rock walk way just large enough for two to pass in the hall way from the kitchen to the bedroom. There was a dining room between the kitchen and bedroom. Garrett could hear the Kid coming on those rocks. He was sitting on the foot of the bed [The interviewer here explains that the hall "ran east and west; and Pete's room was on the west] ...

It was warm weather and the bedroom window was open ... The door opened and Billy saw Pat move off the bed. Billy said: Como estes? (What's that) ...

Garrett ... fired and as Billy fell he fired over Pat's head and the bullet went in the ceiling ... Pat's shot went under Billy's heart ...

Pat and Pete ... told me how it happened many times as did the deputies.

For "The Death of Billy the Kid: A New Scenario?" the unknown author used this junk plus his/her ignorant attaching of the National Archives floor plan mislabeled as "the original layout of the officers' quarters buildings, one of which became the Maxwell house [**provided to show no outside door**]. Taken in conjunction with the Dobbs interview [**Billy walking through the house**], it raises a whole new series of questions as to exactly how Billy the Kid was killed on that July night in 1881." This author was unaware that Lucien Maxwell rebuilt the house as two stories and added the outside door to what would be Peter's bedroom. And the hoaxers lifted that diagram for *Cold Case Billy the Kid*. (Figure: 9, page 294 above). So the ignorant author concluded:

"We can posit an alternative scenario, based partly on what Dobbs said and partly on common sense. If the Kid was really after a hunk of steak he would have gone to the kitchen or the 'cool box' either in the storage or dining area or even outside in the courtyard, because it beggars belief that Maxwell would have a side of beef hanging in his bedroom. However, if the Kid was either going to or just leaving [his lover] Paulita either from the room next to Dona Luz - which would then require him to use the hallway just as Dobbs describes it – or alternatively from one of the two rooms on the northern side of the house, he would as he reached the front (eastern) doorway [believed by Smith, and used by the hoaxers, as the only entrance] – either from the inside or out – have seen the two strangers and acted just as Poe and Garrett described – skipping through the door [here an inside door] into Pete's bedroom to find out who they were – and Garrett was there waiting for him."

PAST NO DOOR GAMBIT: Sederwall had already used this fake "evidence" for the no door scam with fellow "Billy the Kid Case" hoaxer, Bob Boze Bell, for Bell's August, 2010's *True West's* "Caught with his Pants Down? Billy the Kid vs Pat Garrett, One Door Closes."

For it, Sederwall was a "retired lawman" giving "CSI" evidence that Billy was in Paulita's bedroom, "**across from Pete's, when he heard two men (Poe and McKinney) talking outside.**" Using Dobbs's no outside door, Sederwall has Billy enter the bedroom from the hall. And his "CSI" proof is none other than hoaxing Dr. Henry Lee's Case 2003-274 fake washstand forensics, with Sederwall making-up his own version that "**laser lines up perfectly with the hole [sic] in the washstand**" if Garrett shot Billy, then ran out the inside door, and on his knees fired back in, hitting the washstand!

So Bob Boze Bell concluded: "[C]onventional wisdom is often misinformed, which I found out when Gregory Smith [the erroneously listed author of the article] discovered the original 1863 floor plans ... Apparently, windows, not doors, were located alongside these rooms. Lucien ... might have created doorways when he and his family moved in. Yet if Pete's room did not have an outside door, historians will certainly be forced to look at the event with new eyes."

To be noted is that opportunistic Sederwall here backed the victim being Billy Bonney!

HOAXING SHOOTING SCENE DOUBTS

The historical shooting scene is given, with Garrett's sitting on Peter Maxwell's bed when Billy entered; with Maxwell identifying him; and with Garrett shooting twice. Doubts are presented about Garrett's claim that Billy had a gun and knife, and the possibility he was unarmed. (Pages 142-143)

HOAXING: Omitted are historical explanations for Garrett's description of the shooting. His telling of a surprise encounter with Billy was likely to shield Peter Maxwell from accusation of complicitness. It was possible that Maxwell played traitor, setting up the ambush with Garrett, who was hiding in the dark room, with his deputies outside to shoot in case Billy escaped. With Billy's popularity in the town, it would have been a great risk to Maxwell if this had been revealed. This is supported by Poe's book, in which he described almost shooting Maxwell when he ran out the door; which would have only occurred if Poe was anticipating an escaping Billy, and was prepared to shoot him. (Poe, Page 39) And Poe reported the danger from Billy's partisans: "**We spent the remainder of the night on the Maxwell premises, keeping constantly on our guard, was we were expecting to be attacked by friends of the dead man.**" (Poe, Page 44)

A further possibility is presented in Frederick Nolan's 1992 *The Lincoln County War: A Documentary History*. "Garrett found the Kid in bed with Paulita Maxwell and shot him *in flagrante delictu*; the authored version [given by Garrett] ... was then cooked up to protect the girl's reputation." (Nolan, Page 425)

Obviously, Garrett's concealing killing participants, is irrelevant to the corpse not being Billy's.

Questioned are whether two or three shots were fired.

HOAXING: The answer is known. Poe explained the sound of three shots in his book: "An instant later a shot was fired in the room, followed immediately by what everyone within hearing distance thought were two other shots. However, <u>there were only two shots fired</u>, the third report, as we learned afterward, being caused by the rebound of the second bullet, which had struck the adobe wall and rebounded against the headboard of a wooden bedstead." (Poe, Pages 36-37) Garrett also addressed it in his book as first thinking Billy had fired one shot to his two. But Billy's revolver showed no shot fired. Garrett stated: "We searched long and faithfully – found both my bullet marks but no other." (Garrett, Page 218) And eye-witness Peter Maxwell testified on July 15, 1881 for the Coroner's jurymen: "*Pat F. Garrett fired two shots at the said William Bonney and the said William Bonney fell near my fire place.*"

Omitting that the actual second strike involved Maxwell's headboard, given is Dr. Henry Lee's fake washstand forensics, with his positioning of Garrett on the floor and shooting. Added now is an unnamed Homeland Security "expert" to claim physiologic alterations in a shooter causing "fight or flight mode" and flinching, supposedly as confirmation of Lee's positioning of Garrett. So claimed is that Garrett lied. Also claimed is that he lied additionally by leaving out the washstand. (Pages 144-146)

HOAXING: This fakery uses the "Billy the Kid Case" hoax as evidence to call Garrett a liar, by its substitution of the unsubstantiated washstand for the shot headboard; and use of Dr. Henry Lee's fake crime scene reconstruction based on it. (See pages 197-198 above) And Poe had confirmed that: "[T]he second bullet, which had struck the adobe wall ... [had] rebounded against the headboard of a wooden bedstead." (Poe, Pages 36-37)

HOAXING THE BODY'S REMOVAL

Little is said about taking Billy's body from the bedroom to the carpenter's shop to avoid mentioning 200 townspeople's identifications of dead Billy Bonney.

Instead, a quote is taken from Garrett's July 15, 1881 "letter to the territorial governor": "It was my desire to have been able to take him alive, but his coming upon me so suddenly and unexpectedly led me to believe that he had seen me enter the room, or had been informed by someone of the fact, and that he had come there armed with pistol and knife expressly to kill me if he could." (Page 147) Trying to fake a discrepancy, there followed a convoluted rendition of Poe's stating that the room was too dark to make things out. And Poe is claimed to have had to go through the house to get to the bedroom to stick to the no-outside-door-to-Maxwell's-bedroom fakery. (Page 147)

HOAXING: Hiding numerous identifications of the corpse as Billy Bonney's, including the Coroner's Jury Report, this is mere blather about Garrett's description, and Poe's blocking entry based on the already faked lack of an outside door.

But Garrett's quoted letter of July 15, 1881 to Acting-Governor William Ritch (as reprinted in the Las Cruces *Rio Grande Republican* as "Kid the Killer Killed, Wm. Bonney alias Antrim, alias Billy the Kid, Fatally Meets Pat Garrett, the Lincoln County Sheriff" (see pages 107-108 above)) debunked the Sederwall-Jameson hoaxing by giving the shooting scene, and reprinting the Coroner's Jury report's identifying the body and confirming justifiable homicide. Written to initiate his receiving the promised reward, Garrett may have added his necessity of killing to address Lew Wallace's offers on December 22, 1880's Las Vegas *Daily Gazette*, and May 3, 1881's *Daily New Mexican*, which had both stated: "**I will pay $500 reward to any person or persons who will capture William Bonney, alias The Kid, and deliver him to any sheriff of New Mexico. Satisfactory proofs of identity will be required.**" It was not a dead-or-alive notice. So killing, instead of capture, had to be addressed. So Garrett did. Noteworthy is that this was also the letter confirming he had sent the original Coroner's Jury Report to First Judicial District Attorney William Breeden. And Breeden agreed to the justifiable homicide, and assisted in processing the reward through the Legislature. This alone destroyed the Sederwall-Jameson lies.

Next, in another hoaxed attempt to find "discrepancies," was quibbling about the body lying on its back or front, with Jesus Silva, Maxwell's foreman, quoted from Miguel Otero's **1936** book, *The Real Billy the Kid*, as the body being face down. So the duo questioned whether Silva entered first (Page 148) (with Jameson forgetting "Brushy" had a back porch, not a bedroom scene!).

HOAXING: With Garrett's shooting Billy from the front, Billy was likely thrust backwards, landing supine. And the hoaxers admit the room was next lit, and the body examined. And it could have been turned over then.

The Jesus Silva story came from an *Alias Billy the Kid* prompt footnote: a July, 1936 *Frontier Times* interview of a Leslie Traylor of Galveston, Texas, titled "Facts Regarding the Escape of Billy the Kid." Traylor, a history buff, interviewed old-timers in Lincoln and Fort Sumner in 1933 and 1935; including Jesus Silva about Garrett's shooting of Billy. He wrote: "Silva said he was at home when he heard the shot, and they sent for him, that when he arrived they were afraid to go into the room, and as he knew the Kid well and was not afraid, he went in with a light and found him dead, lying face downward with a pistol in one hand and a butcher knife in the other." So the real issue for the hoaxers to wrangle with is not face-up or down, but that Jesus Silva was yet another witness identifying the corpse as Billy Bonney's!

And Miguel Otero was a meaningless hearsay source, who wrote his book 55 years after the shooting!

There was no discrepancy.

HOAXING A "PETER MAXWELL" AS WITNESS

A key witness was Peter Maxwell, with his Coroner's Jury testimony stating: *"Pat F. Garrett fired two shots at the said William Bonney and the said William Bonney fell near my fire place and I went out of the room and when I came in again about three or four minutes after the shots the said William Bonney was dead."*

So Sederwall tried to discredit Maxwell's fatal testimony by citing a 1978 article by a Bundy Avants [sic] (in an unreferenced publication) titled "The Bundy Avants [sic] Story." The man claimed to have spoken to Maxwell years after the shooting, with Maxwell telling him: Billy was not shot; Poe was not there; the body was of a Mexican; and Garrett kept it all secret. (Page 136)

HOAXING: The Bundy Avant article is from a May-June, 1978 *True West* magazine interview with old-timer Avant, spouting malarkey. It is a good example of Sederwall's building a hoax with historical garbage as "evidence."

In 1894, as a child, Avant came, with his cattle ranching family, from Texas to Roswell, New Mexico; then moved to Capitan, when he was eight; then White Oaks in 1905 for farming. Avant's Billy the Kid-related tall tales begin with George Coe, who, he made-up, told him he had retrieved murdered John Tunstall's body. Name-dropping, Avant faked John Chisum's brand as the "Long S," when it was the "Long Rail." He babbled that "Colonel Henry Fountain" was a friend; when Fountain's name was Albert Jennings, and his little son, murdered with him, was Henry.

For his Peter Maxwell fabrication, <u>Avant had himself meeting an old man named "Pete," a cook at a ranch near the San Andres Mountains.</u> This pseudo-Pete says: "I've takin a likin' to you" ... I sensed he had something on his mind which had bothered him for a long time and he felt he had found someone to confide in." Avant says the man told him he was Pete Maxwell, and would tell Avant a secret, if he promised not to tell it "to a living sole as long as I'm alive." Pete then tells him, "Billy is not dead; I can take you to where he lives and has a nice family ... I'll tell you how it was ... There was no light in the house and Pat and I were in the dark when we heard someone come in. We both thought it was Billy. So when the man came in and sensed someone else was there beside me, he said, 'Quien es?' and Pat just fired. We heard the man fall. But when we struck a match and looked at him, we saw it was not the Kid ... Pat was pretty well shook up, as he didn't want it said he had killed the wrong man. It was a Mexican and we decided he was a drifter who would never be missed ... I agreed to keep quiet, too, as I could see it would give Billy a chance to slip away and start a new life, which he had been talking of doing." Avant says it must be true, because Maxwell would know.

In fact, Peter Maxwell lived near old Fort Sumner until his death on June 21, 1898. [FIGURE: 12] His death, as a "Las Vegas" item, in June 28, 1898's *The Albuquerque Citizen*; stated: "**By parties arriving from Fort Sumner it was learned Saturday that Peter Maxwell died at his home near that place, an the morning of the 21st, and was buried on the following day. He leaves a wife and one child. Peter Maxwell was the son of Lucien B. Maxwell, the original owner of the celebrated Maxwell land grant lying in Colorado and New Mexico. Peter Maxwell is well remembered in Las Vegas, where he was a frequent visitor in years past.**" Also, the coarse vernacular Avant faked for his pseudo-Pete mismatches sophisticated and bi-lingual Peter, son of Luz Trotier de Beaubien of Hispanic aristocracy, and Lucien Bonaparte Maxwell, of the prosperous and political Menard family.

Avant continued his Billy the Kid period lies with meeting John W. Poe at Roswell at a later date. Poe asks him what he thought of Garrett, and Avant "didn't think too highly of him." This pseudo-Poe, who was not present at the killing scene, tells Avant that he had been Garrett's deputy when Garrett killed Billy in Fort Sumner, but since "Pat Billy, and I were good friends at one time," he wanted to pay his last respects [with Avant unaware that Poe, not knowing Billy, had been there]. So pseudo-Poe used two horses to ride to Fort Sumner that night. Avant says Garrett refused to let Poe see the body; so Poe suspected foul play and turned in his badge. Avant concluded: "This made the second time in a period of three years that I had been told by two men, who of all people should know the facts, that Billy was not killed by Pat Garrett." (Avant, Pages 47-48)

FIGURE: 12. Peter Maxwell's house near Fort Sumner, where he lived after the town was sold; discrediting Bundy Avant's claim that he lived as a cook in a San Andres Mountains cow camp; from Midland, Texas, Haley Library, Robert N. Mullin Collection

HOAXING NO CORONER'S JURY REPORT

To counter the July 15, 1881 Coroner's Jury Report, the Jameson-Sederwall duo had only faked discrepancies, fake "investigations," and fake conspiracy theories.

Recycled was Steve Sederwall's "Billy the Kid Case" hoax's "Probable Cause Statement," with his made-up time discrepancies for Justice of the Peace Alejandro Segura's contacting Sunnyside's Milnor Rudulph to fabricate that the Jury never even convened. (See debunking in pages 165-166 above)

As in that "Probable Cause Statement," the body's location is questioned because the Report said: *"[T]he above jury convened in the home of Luz B. Maxwell and **proceeded to a room in the said house where they found the body of William Bonney alias "Kid."*** But the body was taken to the carpenter's shop vigil. So the location is called a lie. (Page 149)

HOAXING: It is obvious that, after that wake, the body was returned to the Maxwell house for the inquest.

Claimed is Justice of the Peace Segura "instructed Rudolph to assemble a coroner's jury and serve as foreman." (Page 149)

HOAXING: Segura himself appointed Rudulph and the five jurymen, as he stated in the Coroner's Jury Report: "*I, the undersigned, Justice of the Peace ... immediately upon receiving said information I proceeded to the said place and named Milnor Rudulph, Jose Silva, Antonio Saavedra, Pedro Antonio Lucero, Lorenzo Jaramillo and Sabal Gutierres a jury to investigate the case.*"

The Report, as written by Milnor Rudulph, about "gratitude of the community" being owed to Garrett, is called "suspicious" to "cop" Sederwall, because it praises Garrett, while Fort Sumner people were angry at the killing, not grateful. (Pages 150-151)

FALSE INTERPRETATION: Sederwall seems unaware that Rudulph, as discussed above, was a Ringite. (See page 66 above) Rudulph, who wrote the Report, would have praised Garrett for stamping out the last anti-Ring rebel. And the jurymen, presumably terrified by this Ring killing right in their town, would not have dared to object.

The Report's existence is next "doubted" by claiming its not being filed in San Miguel County; "Paco" Anaya claiming two reports; the inquest being speedy; William Keleher's photocopy in Spanish [in his 1957 *Violence in Lincoln County*] as the "second coroner's report;" his English translation meaning the victim spoke English; and that some signers misspelled names. So the duo doubt that the jurymen even saw the body. (Pages 150-151)

HOAXING: This is the "Brushy" hoax, with additions. As discussed above, the original Report was sent by Garrett to First Judicial District Attorney William Breeden, with a copy to Acting-Governor William Ritch. Breeden filed it in Santa Fe, where it was found in 1932 by state employee, Harold Abbott, in the capitol building. He made copies, eventually reproduced by historians, like William Keleher.

Windbag "Paco" Anaya's "two reports" was fabrication, as was the rest of his posthumous book's Billy the Kid history. But Anaya did know one thing: Billy was killed by Pat Garrett; hence the title, *I Buried Billy*.

As to viewing the body, the Coroner's Jury Report confirmed performing the inquest's legal duties: interviewing witness Peter Maxwell, identifying the body as Billy Bonney's, examining his fatal wound, and concluding that the homicide did not require prosecution by being justifiable self-defense.

For their conclusion, Sederwall-Jameson rely on their own fakery; and, of course, state that Pat Garrett killed an innocent man, rushed through the inquest process to hide the body of his non-Billy victim by burial, and wrote the "second" [i.e., real] Coroner's Jury Report himself. And 'cop' Sederwall intones that "somebody (or somebodies) are lying" to hide the truth. (Pages 151 -152)

HOAXING DISCOVERY OF "BILLY THE KID" MONIKER

Steve Sederwall pretended to have discovered that the name "Billy the Kid" was first used in the *Las Vegas Gazette* (Page 81), (which Jameson should have noticed debunks his man "Brushy," who made-up that it was his childhood alias because he was small!).

HOAX: This "find" came from Billy's December 12, 1880 letter to Lew Wallace, stating: "*I noticed in the Las Vegas Gazette a piece which stated that, <u>Billy "the" Kid</u>, the name by which I am known in the Country was the captain of a Band of Outlaws.*" But the showing-off was wrong.

In fact, the moniker "Billy the Kid" was first publicly used in the May 23, 1879 testimony of Susan McSween in the Dudley Court of Inquiry. She was being questioned by the prosecutor about requesting aid from Dudley by going to his camp. She stated: "*He said he ... did not intend to have anything to do with either party ... I then said it looked strange to me to see his men, or his soldiers I should say, guarding Peppin back and forth through town and sending soldiers around our house ... if he had nothing to do with it. He then got very angry and said it was none of my business, that he would send his soldiers where he pleased, that <u>I have no such business to have such men as Billy the Kid,</u> Jim French, and others of like character in my house. He then ... said that he had come to protect women and children. I then asked why he did not protect myself, my sister, and her children. He said I have no business, or we had no business, to be in that house, that he would not give us protection.*"

In fact, this testimony is so famous, that historian, Joel Jacobsen, used it to title his 1994 book <u>Such Men as Billy the Kid</u>: *The Lincoln County War Reconsidered.*

HOAXING DISCOVERY OF TOM O'FOLLIARD BEING TOM "FOLLIARD"

Indiscriminate W.C. Jameson, for his 2018 *Cold Case Billy the Kid* plugged a silly small Sederwall hoax claiming he had discovered that Tom O'Folliard's last name was really "Folliard."

Jameson had first used Sederwall's altered spelling in his 2012 book, *Billy the Kid: The Lost Interviews*, without citing Sederwall's hoax, and likely thinking it was real history. But the "Folliard" spelling was one of the give-aways in that book that Jameson was now forging "Brushy's" transcripts of his taped William V. Morrison interviews, in attempted fix-ups. In this case, trusting Sederwall yielded Jameson's revealing his fakery. Jameson had "Brushy" say: "**Folliard [sic]**, Salazar, and the rest of our boys started through." (Page 81) And Jameson apparently missed that this name change demolished "Brushy," who, as Billy, should know his good friend's name; and "Brushy" always used "O'Folliard;" stating, for example, in the actual quote that Jameson altered: "O'Folliard, Salazar, and the rest of our boys started through." (*Alias Billy the Kid*, Page 31)

For his *Cold Case Billy the Kid*," Jameson announced: "As a result of genealogical records and census records, detective Steve Sederwall learned [Tom O'Folliard's] **real name was Thomas O. Folliard**." (Page 82)

He "quotes" "Brushy," as if he used the "Folliard" name, when talking about "the winter of '79," **being with Tom "Folliard"** and meeting with J.J. Dolan and Jesse Evans "to talk about things," with a "fellow named Campbell along." (Page 86)

HOAXING: None of this is in *Alias Billy the Kid*, **where "Brushy" never used Dolan's initials or "Folliard." It appears made-up for this book. In** *Alias Billy the Kid*, **"Brushy" merely stated: "In the winter of '79 we got together with Dolan and Evans and agreed to quit fighting each other." (***Alias Billy the Kid***, Page 33)**

Sederwall enters the picture as an "investigator" who discovered that Tom's father, was "Tom Folliard," who emigrated from Ireland, married "Sarah Cook;" and had Tom after "**two and a half years**." (Page 82) They then moved to Monclova, Coahuila, Mexico, where the parents died of smallpox. John Cook (called Sarah's uncle) then took Tom to Uvalde, Texas.

Cited as evidence is that "[t]he Uvalde census for 1870 lists 'Thomas Folliard, 9 years old," and other family members. Claimed as Sarah's parents were David Cook and Eliza Jane Cook; and that **"[t]his would make Eliza Jane Cook, the woman who raised him, Tom's grandmother. Eliza Jane's married name was McKinney; she was Kip McKinney's cousin. Kip McKinney and Tom Folliard [sic] were related."** (Pages 82-83)

Sederwall concluded that with Tom raised in Uvalde, Kip McKinney being from there, and Garrett living there *from 1891 to 1900*, they were "all acquainted" (Page 83) [ignoring Tom being dead in 1880!]. Nevertheless, Sederwall presented, from *The Authentic Life of Billy the Kid*, dying O'Folliard's asking Garrett to put him out of his misery **as a friend**; and Garrett **denying he**

was his friend. That made Sederwall conclude absurdly that Garrett was "stressing the business of friends a bit to hard, as if he were trying to **cover up the fact that he and Folliard [sic] had been friends.**" (Page 84) This was a unstated nod to the "Billy the Kid Case" hoax, built on a faked super-friendship of Pat and Billy motivating the innocent victim murder.

Sederwall presented an anecdote of a Thalis Cook, as "Folliard's" uncle, writing about visiting him in New Mexico; but a Robert N. Mullin Collection letter by a Mrs. O.L. Shipman claimed Billy the Kid intercepted that letter, and told Thalis "he could not have Tom." (Page 83)

HOAXING: This is not a real genealogical investigation coordinating census reports, obituaries, and other kinship records. Sederwall just lifted from unsubstantiated sources; since O'Folliard's real genealogy is uncertain. Worse, Sederwall made-up information.

Only one relevant record exists, tentatively linked to Tom O'Folliard: the 1870 census on September 26, 1870 in Zavalla County, Uvalde, Texas, used by Sederwall. [FIGURE: 13]

Frederick Nolan cited it in his 2011 publishing of a 1940 manuscript by a Frank Clifford, titled *Deep Trails in the Old West: A Frontier Memoir*. But Nolan critiqued it as problematically listing Tom's age as 9 in 1870, which contradicted other claimed birthdays of 1854 and 1958. Also, the name used is "Folliard," making it not him or misspelled. Nolan concluded: "**[A] lot more work needs to be done before we have anything remotely like an acceptable biography.**" (*Deep Trails*, Nolan, Page 276)

But Sederwall used and modified unsubstantiated genealogies. He used a January, 1934 article by a Jack Shipman in *Voice of the Mexican Border* magazine, "Brief Career of Tom O'Folliard Billy the Kid's Partner," lacking sources and giving an Irish immigrant father named Tom O'Folliard. As Sederwall lifted for his own hoax, it made-up Tom's birth "**two and a half years**" after his parents' marriage. Shippman claimed, without proof, that Tom was raised by John Cook and his sister, Margaret Jane Cook, till she married; then his living with John, till his marriage in 1875. Then Tom was with grandmother, "**Mrs. David Cook.**" (Shipman, Page 216)

Philip J. Rasch's 1995 *Trailing Billy the Kid* (in *Cold Case Billy the Kid's* Bibliography) had "The Short Life of Tom O'Folliard," using Shipman's article. Rasch's Tom is born in Uvalde, Texas, to "Irish immigrant" Tom O'Folliard, and Sarah Cook; moves to Mexico, with the parents dying. Sarah's brother, John Cook, takes him to Uvalde to his sister Margaret Jane Cook, until her 1873 marriage. Then Tom lived with John Cook, until his marriage to "a Miss McKinney" in 1875; when he went to grandmother, "Mrs. James Cook." (Rasch, Page 77) The Thalis Cook tale is told, as Sederwall used. (Rasch, Page 81)

But these sources' Irish father was Tom O'Folliard. So Sederwall made-up his name as "Folliard" to match the census's misspelled "Folliard" to fabricate his "Folliard" discovery. And he made-up that the son's middle initial was "O," as: Thomas O. Folliard! (Page 82)

That "Folliard" is wrong, is proved by all contemporaries using O'Folliard. Even Operative Azariah Wild, who tracked him in the "Wilson & Kid gang," wrote in his report completed on October 18, 1880: *"Thomas O'Falliard: [Came] [f]rom Texas here."*

Pat Garrett, who knew and killed him, wrote in *The Authentic Life of Billy the Kid*: "[After the shooting] Mason came around the building just as O'Folliard was returning, reeling in his saddle. After we had laid him down inside, he begged me to kill him, saying that if I was a friend of his I would put him out of his misery. I told him I was no friend of his kind." (Garrett, Page 172) This quote also shows Sederwall's misstatement of the "friend" claim.

Sederwall made-up that Eliza Jane's married name was McKinney, when it was her *maiden name*, with *married name* Cook. And he made-up that she and David Cook were O'Folliard's grandparents.

It seemed that Sederwall was using "Brushy's" claim that Kip McKinney was his cousin, though Sederwall reduced it to "relative." "Brushy's" original team's prompt source for the claim had been the 1935 book by Frank M. King, titled *Wranglin' the Past: Reminiscences of Frank M. King*; stating: "Kip was also a cousin of Tom O'Folliard." (King, Page 173) Another prompt, was Garrett's O'Folliard death scene; stating: "He also asked [Barney] Mason to tell

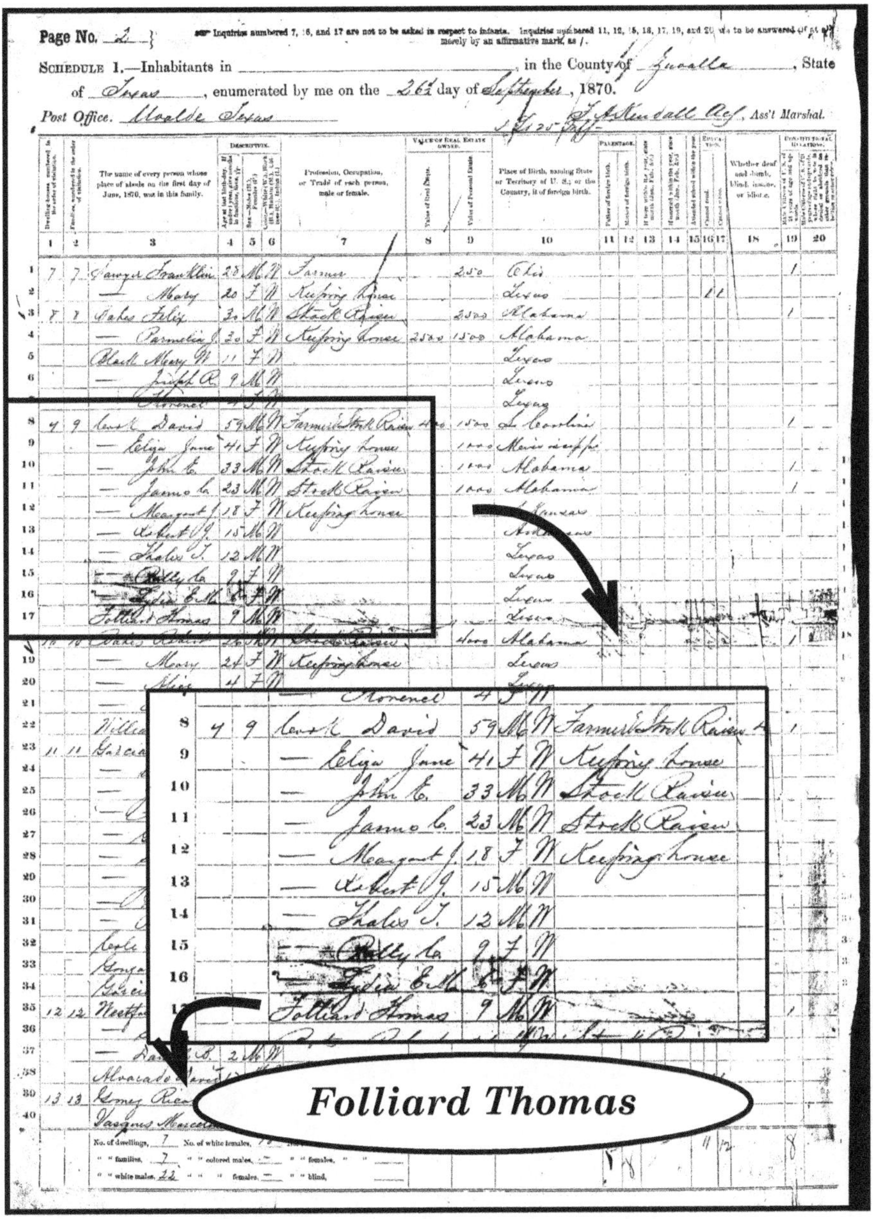

FIGURE: 13. U.S. Census Record 1870; recorded September 26, 1870; Zavalla County, Uvalde, Texas showing the possible Tom O'Folliard as "Folliard," but with questionable age of 9 years old. This spelling was used by the hoaxers to claim Tom O'Folliard's actual name was "Folliard."

McKinney to write to his grandmother in Texas and inform her of his death." (Garrett, Page 173) But that did not mean cousins, or even relatives.

Linking of Cook and McKinney families was explained in Frederick Nolan's note in Frank Clifford's *Deep Trials in the Old West*. He stated that, on April 4, 1875, Tom's uncle, John Enoch Cook married <u>Elizabeth Francis McKinney, a cousin of Kip McKinney</u>. Also, Tom's uncle, David Cook, had married, as second wife, <u>Eliza Jane McKinney Cook</u>. Nolan noted that possibly Eliza's father was a Collin McKinney, possibly Kip McKinney's grandfather, through Collin's son, Thalis McKinney. That would make her Kip's aunt. <u>None of this makes Tom and Kip blood cousins, but might explain dying Tom's knowing Kip could contact his Cook family</u>.

RECYCLED SCAM: Sederwall reused this faked genealogy for his "Billy the Kid's Bad Bucks" hoax, in which he made-up that an old-timer windbag author named "Lane <u>Cook</u>" was Tom O'Folliard's cousin (because of having the coincidental name "Cook"), and had done rustling and counterfeit money-laundering with Billy Bonney. (See pages 380, 391-397 below.)

CHAPTER 5
DAVID TURK AS A "BILLY THE KID CASE" HOAXER

U.S. MARSHALS SERVICE HISTORIAN DAVID TURK

U.S. Marshals Service Historian David Turk was hoaxing, along with Lincoln County Sheriff Tom Sullivan and Deputy Steve Sederwall, from the 2003 start of the "Billy the Kid Case," in which he helped prepare its "Probable Cause Statement," and added his own addendum, "The U.S. Marshals Service and Billy the Kid," to "prove" that Pat Garrett murdered an innocent victim. In the press, Turk also vouched for Dr. Henry Lee and "authenticated" the carpenter's bench. Noteworthy, is that his government position made him a subversive by defaming the Marshals Service's most famous, Old West Deputy U.S. Marshal. He was also the one to devise the hoax that Garrett had lacked authority to go to Fort Sumner on the July 14, 1881. In addition, he supplied National Archive records to assist the hoaxers.

Importantly, like Steve Sederwall, he was back for a hoaxing rerun, being cited in W.C. Jameson's 2018 *Cold Case Billy the Kid's* "Acknowledgments." And, by 2010, he had been active in devising the "Billy the Kid's Bad Bucks" hoax with Sederwall, which Jameson presented in that book.

IN THE "BILLY THE KID CASE" HOAX

David Turk was an active "Billy the Kid Case" hoaxer, participating in all aspects by using his title to fake expertise for the press, by supplying research, by writing his own hoax addendum and article, and by and being present to assist and to participate in a Dr. Henry Lee's fake forensic investigation.

FOR THE "PROBABLE CAUSE STATEMENT"

David Turk was the only "historian" to participate in production of Case 2003-274's "Probable Cause Statement," in which its author, Steve Sederwall, presented his input, as follows:

David S. Turk, Historian for the United States Marshals Service has discovered other such deceptions in his study of official records.

[AUTHOR'S NOTE: Referring to "other such deceptions" is fake. They are never given. And Turk, an active "Billy the Kid Case" hoaxer, contributed his own fake Probable Cause addendum to the hoax. (See pages 321-325 below)]

It is commonly believed

[AUTHOR'S NOTE: Misstatement: It is a *known*.]

that Lincoln County Sheriff Pat F. Garrett arrested the Kid in December of 1880 in Stinking Springs near Fort Sumner. But the records show that Garrett was elected in November of 1880 and did not take office until January of 1881.[5] ([5]Lincoln County Commissioners Records, November 8, 1880).

[AUTHOR'S NOTE: This leads to a fake claim that Garrett did not have proper authority to capture Billy.]

He went to Fort Sumner as a Deputy United States Marshall, but even that Commission and authority are now questioned. Secret Service Special Operative Azariah F. Wild of New Orleans writes in his daily logs "*I this day went to Lincoln to meet Capt. Lea & Garrett who are to organize the Posse Comatatus (sic) to make a raid on Fort Sumner to arrest counterfeiters.*"[6] ([6]Report of Azariah F. Wild, November 11, 1880, Record Group 87, National Archives) Garrett shot and killed Charles Bowdre and Tom O'Folliard during the chase and arrested the Kid. Later, Secret Service Special Operative Azariah F. Wild writes to his superior and admits he was deceptive in his commission of Garrett. "*I will respectfully state that I applied to Marshall Sherman to appoint P.F. Garrett as a Deputy Marshall to which he paid no attention. I was in great need of Mr. Garrett [sic – Mr. Garrett's aid] at that time and took one of the Commissions Sherman sent to John Hurley (he having sent two) and substituted P.F. Garrett the very man who has rendered the Government such a valuable service in killing and arresting these men who I was in pursuit."*[7] ([7]Report of Azariah F. Wild, January 4 [sic -3], 1881, Record Group 87, National Archives)

David Turk, Historian for the United States Marshal's Service has pointed out other documents

[AUTHOR'S NOTE: Just one document is presented; though Turk came to New Mexico in person in December of 2003, possibly to assist in writing the "Probable Cause Statement."]

bringing into question Garrett's involvement in the Kid's escape.

[AUTHOR'S NOTE: Note that Turk was, thus, involved in faking Garrett as assisting Billy the Kid's Lincoln jailbreak and helping Billy "escape" again by murdering the innocent victim in Fort Sumner.]

Mr. Turk has produced a Works Progress Administration, Federal Writer's Project interview where the following statement was taken:

The people around Lincoln

[AUTHOR'S NOTE: These are hearsay records that legitimate historians do not rely on as proof. In fact, the Fort Sumner killing was 150 miles from Lincoln, so any old-timer resident of Lincoln would have no direct knowledge of it.]

say Garrett didn't kill Billie (sic) the Kid. John Poe was with Garrett the night he was supposed to ... said that he didn't see the man that Garrett killed.

[AUTHOR'S NOTE: Besides the fact that Poe's statements all refer to seeing the victim, Poe did not know Billy.]

I can take you to the grave in Hell's High Acre, an old government cemetery, where Billie (sic) was supposed to be buried and show you the grave ...

[And Billie (sic) was seen by Bill Nicholi an Indian scout. Bill saw him in Mexico.[18] ([18]*Frances E. Tolly [Totty], comp. "Early Days in Lincoln County," Charles Remark Interview. February 14, 1938, Works Progress Administration, Federal Writer's Project, Folklore-Life Histories, Manuscript Division. Library of Congress.)*

[AUTHOR'S NOTE: This is more hearsay junk supplied as "proof" by Turk.]

FOR "AUTHENTICATIONS"

Turk's carpenter's bench "authentication" was to assist the "Billy the Kid Case" hoax by flashing his title for authority. On April 19, 2006, hoax-backing reporter, Julie Carter, in *RuidosoNews.com*, reported in "Digging up Bones": "UNM History professor Paul Hutton and **U.S. Treasury [sic - Marshals Service] historian Dave Turk have both authenticated the bench**." So, on August 8, 2006, I used my open records proxy, journalist, Jay Miller, to request from Turk's agency how he could do that. On August 31, 2006, a Nikki Cedric at Public Affairs answered: "Mr. Turk ... has seen the said workbench; *however, he did not state that any particular person was on the bench. This is for the lab to determine.* The bench does match descriptions given in other sources and he believes it to be the one described."

Turk was also listed as participating, in 2004, in Dr. Henry Lee's fake forensic investigation of the Deputy Bell killing at the Lincoln courthouse (where he was misrepresented as an actual U.S. Marshal in Lee's report, either by Lee's mistake or intentional misinformation).

HIDING INCRIMINATORY PUBLIC RECORDS

Turk must have known he was a subversive. He hid his participation in the "Billy the Kid Case" for years, while his irresponsible department covered up for him for my Freedom of Information Act requests through my journalist proxy, Jay Miller. Nevertheless, revealing information was supplied. On June 22, 2005, a William E. Bordley, Associate General Counsel/FOIPA Officer, sent Turk's job description: "Conducts historical research in order to prepare and edit historical articles for publications and exhibits on USMS history ... Develops fact sheets, brochures, pamphlets, and books on the history of the USMS. Research is conducted both on and off site." Participating in a filed, New Mexico, murder case stretched that job description; and its being a hoax topped off the impropriety!

As to Turk's hoax participation, Attorney William Bordley merely double-talked: "Regarding Item 6 of your request, Mr. Turk's role in this matter is to research and gather information relative to the Billy the Kid case to ascertain the historical accuracy of the U.S. Marshals Service involvement in the events relating to the Billy the Kid case."

So I wrote a records request, for Jay Miller to ask: "Did Turk author the "Probable Cause Statement?" (At that time, its authorship was still in question.) The shock answer came in a month from the U.S. Marshals Service. Turk had written a secret additional report as part of the "Probable Cause Statement!"

On August 24, 2005 a Mavis DeZulovich FOI/PA Liaison, Office of Public Affairs for the U.S. Marshals Service, had responded: "Mr. Turk is not the author of the Lincoln County Sheriff''s Department Probable Cause Statement 2003-274. **However, mention is made in that document to information contained in a research report authored by Mr. Turk entitled: "The U.S. Marshals Service and Billy the Kid."** So Turk's quote in the Statement was from *his own* research report! But he was hiding that incriminating document.

So, on August 18, 2004, I wrote, for Jay Miller to proxy, an open records request to Sheriff Tom Sullivan for all records in *his* files pertaining to David Turk. Sullivan refused to give any records, but claimed an exemption of their being part of his *ongoing criminal investigation* in Case 2003-274, the "Billy the Kid Case!" So he indirectly proved Turk's participation!

In April of 2006, I called Turk myself, terrified, since his division was part of Homeland Security, and he seemed like a crack-pot. I made up the name "Wilma Jordan" and a Polish accent, and requested a copy of his *The U.S. Marshals Service and Billy the Kid*. He said it was in "departmental revision."

On June 2, 2006, I called back as Wilma. He now claimed to be doing "revisions" himself, with indefinite delay. So I asked, "Zo, do you tink Pad Garred *did nod shood* Billy de Kid?" Bull's eye. "The facts do not fit together," said Turk. "Vy is dis your interest?" Wilma asked. Turk said because it involved murders of U.S. Marshals when Billy escaped in October of 1880. "Wilma," like Pandora, could not resist temptation. She said they were Garrett's *Deputy* Sheriffs (though Olinger was a Deputy U.S. Marshal), and it was *April* 28th of 18-*81*.

On June 15th, "Wilma" wrote Turk, wanting more information on why Garrett did not kill the Kid. And she wanted that report.

Turk's answer, on July 3, 2006, was intended to scare the stuffing out of nosy "Wilma Jordan": he had tracked her down, and supplied her address! Amazingly, there *really was a Wilma Jordan in New Mexico*! It was *her* address! (I hope she does not have a Polish accent.) This proves that some Homeland Security tax dollars go to employee research to protect their own backside's security. And Turk directed "Wilma" to a Steve Sederwall (!), with his telephone number provided! And, of course, there never came a copy of *The U.S. Marshals Service and Billy the Kid*.

I later learned that Sederwall himself had been asking around if anyone knew about a Polish woman who had called David Turk. At least I got confirmation that I had done the accent right!

On September 11, 2006, through Jay Miller, I tried Nikki Cedric again as: "Re. Follow-up to your August 31, 2006 response to my Freedom of Information Act request No. 2004USMS7634 in reference to David Turk, Historian for the U.S. Marshals Service; and request for clarification." I asked if he provided the sources for the "Probable Cause Statement." Responses ceased forever.

THE SECRET REPORT AS AN ARTICLE

February of 2007 brought hope. Turk had published "Billy the Kid and the U.S. Marshals Service" in hoax-promoting *True West* magazine! I got it. It proved his "revisions" were expurgations, leaving just U.S. Marshals in the Lincoln County War period.

But it had a telling peculiarity. After the conventional Billy the Kid death scene, Turk began spouting the familiar script of the "Brushy Bill" and "Billy the Kid Case" hoaxes. He faked Pat Garrett as the sole witness, claimed an innocent victim, and babbled about Billy's post July 14, 1881 survival. He wrote: "That traditional account [of the killing] - as told by Garrett himself (with the help of a ghostwriter) in the *Authentic Life of Billy, the Kid* - **has been questioned many times over the years with some accounts suggesting that the Kid got away to live another day or decades, and others indicating that somebody else besides the Kid died in Maxwell's bedroom**." So Turk was promoting that there had been "decades" of Billy's survival following Garrett's killing of an innocent victim!

GETTING TURK'S ACTUAL SECRET REPORT

Finally, on September 3, 2008, the Turk mystery was solved - as a part of my open records litigation against the hoaxer lawmen. For Sheriff Rick Virden's September 8, 2008 deposition, my attorney subpoenaed his Sheriffs Department file for Case 2003-274. Though Virden had expurgated the forensic DNA records I was after, its last 26 pages were *David Turk's actual "The U.S. Marshals Service and Billy the Kid!"*

The cover had a galloping Old West rider with a big marshal's badge. Its date was December 2003: the signing date of the "Probable Cause Statement!" It was titled: *United States Marshals Service Executive Services Division: Research Report, Submitted by David S. Turk.* Page one gave me what I wanted: "Research Report: The U.S. Marshals Service and Billy the Kid. **To Be Added in its Present Entirety, with Exhibits, to Lincoln County, New Mexico Case # 2003-274.**"

So David Turk had created an addendum for the "Billy the Kid Case's Probable Cause Statement," using his title and government money to defame a famous Deputy U.S. Marshal for a hoax! And he had contributed his own, major hoax document! And its style implied him as possibly assisting writing of the "Probable Cause Statement," besides his hearsay old-timer quote. And it showed that he was supplying National Archive documents for the hoax.

THE TURK ADDENDUM

Providing no historical evidence, David Turk backed the "Billy the Kid Case" hoax premise of Pat Garrett as murderer of an innocent victim. For filler, he discussed U.S. Marshals in the Lincoln County War period (including Garrett). But abruptly, based on a few WPA hearsay interviews from the 1930's (of people unconnected to the event), he concluded that Billy the Kid's killing "fueled speculation over the precise outcome."

Turk's *The U.S. Marshals Service and Billy the Kid* is called a "Research Report." It had a cover page, 9 pages of text; bibliographic "Endnotes;" and "Exhibits" consisting of a Turk article titled "How much did it cost to find Billy the Kid?"; a "National Police Gazette" May 21, 1881 article on Billy's escape; and a May 30, 1881 letter from Attorney Sidney Barnes (one of Billy's Mesilla prosecutors) about Billy's Mesilla trial and his later escape. (Turk's general and irrelevant information on U.S. Marshals is omitted here.)

The only parts of Turk's "Research Report" that also appear in the "Probable Cause Statement" are his Frances E. Totty, WPA quote about "Billie" being seen after the death date; and his "Endnote" sources, like Secret Service Operative Azariah Wild's reports. But Turk's report - that he tried so hard to hide - was part of the 2003-274 case file, as "probable cause" that Pat Garrett was a murderer of an innocent victim instead of Billy the Kid.

Below is the report that Turk knew should be hidden because it revealed him as a subversive incompetent.

Research Report: The U.S. Marshals Service and Billy the Kid

Submitted by David S. Turk, Historian
December 2003

"**Research Report: The U.S. Marshals Service and Billy the Kid**. To Be Added in its Present Entirety, with Exhibits, to Lincoln County, New Mexico Case # 2003-274."

Purpose of Research [Page 1]

There is renewed interest in examining the crimes and final resting place of William H. Bonney, also known as Henry Antrim, Henry McCarty, or Billy the Kid.

[AUTHOR'S NOTE: The only "renewed interest" was from the "Billy the Kid Case" hoax and loony conspiracy theorists.]

Two Sheriffs' Offices in New Mexico reopened an investigation, with the approval of the Governor of New Mexico. In September 2003 Steve Sederwall, Mayor of Capitan, and Deputy Sheriff, Lincoln County, New Mexico, contacted me on research matters relating to the Lincoln County War.

[AUTHOR'S NOTE: Turk claims Sederwall as his contact.]

Given the integral role of the U.S. Marshals Service, and the dual roles between our two institutions during the time of Billy the Kid, and further that Pat Garrett was a Deputy U.S. Marshal during the pursuit of the Kid, and that another Deputy U.S. Marshal (and Lincoln County officer), Robert Olinger, was shot and killed by the Kid during his escape, it is relevant to the agency's historical interest to research those portions of the case pertinent to it to ensure accuracy.

[AUTHOR'S NOTE: The report gives no information to doubt conventional history. It does not "ensure accuracy!"]

The primary investigation of Lincoln County, New Mexico State No. 2004-274 [sic] is being conducted by Lincoln County Sheriff Tom Sullivan, De Baca County Sheriff Gary Graves, and Steve Sederwall, but the following findings add significantly to the data being collected in revisiting Billy the Kid.

[AUTHOR'S NOTE: No reason is given for "revisiting Billy the Kid," except hearsay death rumors 56 years after the event.]

Overview of Research Focus [Page 1]

The following research relates to the prominent roles of the U.S. Marshals Service in the Lincoln County War ... Finally, there is a study on the deaths of Deputy Marshal Olinger and Lincoln County Officer J.W. Bell, followed by Billy the Kid's subsequent escape. The Works Progress Administration interviewed several Lincoln residents during the late 1930's in this regard ...

[AUTHOR'S NOTE: The oddness of this statement is easy to miss; but each part is irrelevant to the others. Out of nowhere, will come Turk's "suspicions" that the Kid was not Garrett's murder victim.]

Deputy U.S. Marshal Garrett and His Agency Status [Page 4]

[AUTHOR'S NOTE: This page, about Garrett's U.S. Marshal status has Secret Service Agent Azariah Wild's praise of Garrett to his Chief. All is irrelevant to Garrett's murder victim.]

Key Event: Billy the Kid's Escape and the Deaths of Bell and Olinger [Page 8]

On April 28, 1881, [sic - missing word] made his famous escape from Lincoln. Accounts of the events were recalled later by witnesses. A contemporary news account from *The National Police Gazette* dated May 21, 1881, followed a generally accepted recollection pattern with some minor inconsistencies. Deputy U.S. Marshal Olinger and guard J.W. Bell ... were holding the Kid in the jail. Olinger dined at a local establishment, and during his absence the shackled prisoner hit Bell with handcuffs. He then grabbed Bell's revolver and shot him in the chest ... Just as he [Olinger] entered a small gate leading through the jail fence, the Kid shot him with a double-barreled gun, filling his breast of shot and killing him.

[AUTHOR'S NOTE: Note that the *National Police Gazette*, published in New York, was merely a dime novel tabloid, and not a legitimate historical source. Also, Turk presents Billy the Kid's escape without Garrett's participation.]

Differing Accounts on Death of Billy the Kid [Pages 8 - 9.]

Deputy U.S. Marshal and Lincoln County Sheriff Pat Garrett pursued Billy the Kid for several months after the deaths

[AUTHOR'S NOTE: About 2 ½ months.]

of Deputy Olinger and J.W. Bell. The end of the chase appeared to be at Pete Maxwell's ranch on July 15 [sic], 1881.

[AUTHOR'S NOTE: This is hoaxer style sly innuendo of "suspicion" without evidence. And the date was July 14, 1881!]

What occurred at the Maxwell Ranch fueled speculation over the precise outcome. There appears [sic] to be many questions to answer.

[AUTHOR'S NOTE: This is full-blown, hoax conspiracy theory, with vague "suspicion." No evidence is given.]

According to the WPA interview of Francisco Trujillo in May 1937, Garrett was negotiating capture of the Kid with Pete Maxwell himself. Josh Brent's father was one of the Sheriff's deputies, stating that Garrett said "that he sure hated to kill the boy, but he knew it was either his life or the boy's life."

[AUTHOR'S NOTE: The "Billy the Kid Case" hoaxers omitted this hearsay from the "Probable Cause Statement." But they missed a great hoax quote – even though it is groundless! It was their chance to fake the Pat-Billy friendship.]

Yet another resident stated,

> The people around Lincoln say Garrett didn't kill Billie [sic] the Kid. John Poe was with Garrett the night he was supposed to ... [sic] said that he didn't see the man that Garrett killed. Ican [sic] take you to the grave in Hell's Half Acre, a old government cemetery [sic], where Billie [sic] was supposed to be buried to show you the grave.
>
> The cook at Pete Maxwell's was always putting flowers on the grave and praying at it. This woman thought a lot of Billie [sic], but after Garrett killed the man at Maxwell's home her grandson was never seen again and Billie [sic] was seen by Bill Nicoli? And indian scout. Bill saw him in old Mexico.

[AUTHOR'S NOTE: This hearsay was put in the "Probable Cause Statement" with attribution to Turk.]

The recollections took a legendary bent, even extending to events that occurred after those at the Maxwell ranch. Josh Brent stated that Garrett told his father that after he killed the Kid, "that a fellow from the east wrote him and said that he would pay $5000.00 for the trigger finger of the boy."

[AUTHOR'S NOTE: Irrelevant pseudo-historical filler like in the "Probable Cause Statement."]

Other Related Fact [Page 9.]

A sidelight from this period was the debunking of one widely-held story that Billy the Kid killed twenty-one men by the age of twenty-one. U.S. Attorney Barnes stated in a letter to the Attorney General, dated May 30, 1881, that while the Kid "has killed fifteen different men & is only twenty one years of age."

[AUTHOR'S NOTE: This irrelevant hearsay by one of Billy's Mesilla prosecutors, who had no way of knowing; was used to mimic historical savvy, as was done with name-dropping sources in the "Probable Cause Statement."]

So U.S. Marshals Service Historian David Turk was a "Billy the Kid Case" hoaxer, abusing the prestige of his federal title.

POISED FOR THE "BILLY THE KID'S BAD BUCKS" HOAX

U.S. Marshals Service Historian David Turk had been assisting the "Billy the Kid Case" hoaxers since 2003, and working with Steve Sederwall in particular. He and Sederwall would join forces again by 2010 for the "Billy the Kid's Bad Bucks" hoax, abandoning their usual defamation of Pat Garrett and attacking Billy Bonney himself as a fabricated counterfeiter.

CHAPTER 6
BOB BOZE BELL
AS A HOAXER

FAKING THE OLD WEST

The most hypocritical "Billy the Kid Case" hoaxer was Bob Boze Bell, an author-illustrator of a conventional Billy the Kid history book and the Editor-in-Chief of *True West* magazine.

In his 1996 edition of his *The Illustrated Life and Times of Billy the Kid*, before the advent of the "Billy the Kid Case" hoax, Boze Bell presented the conventional killing of Billy the Kid by Pat Garrett; writing:

> The Kid jumps back, but instead of firing he demands in Spanish one more time, "Quien es?"
> Big mistake. Garrett draws his revolver and fires twice. The Kid fell dead. (Boze Bell, Page 162)

For the Coroner's Jury Report, in that 1996 edition, he had no doubt it existed, the body was Billy's, and that Garrett was acquitted of murder. He wrote: "Justice of the Peace Alejandro Segura asks [Milnor] Rudolph [sic-Rudulph] to organize a coroner's jury and preside as foreman ... Rudolph agrees and assembles five men to convene proceedings in Pete Maxwell's bedroom ... The jurors acquit Garrett." (Boze Bell, Page 164)

And for Billy's burial, in that edition, he wrote: "Billy the Kid is buried in the old military cemetery next to his compadres." (Boze Bell, Page 164)

Seven years after his 1996 book, Bob Boze Bell was one of the main backers of the "Billy the Kid Case" hoax, using his *True West* magazine to disseminate its fakery and its connected "Brushy Bill" hoax: claiming that Pat never shot Billy, an innocent victim was murdered instead, and there was no Coroner's Jury Report. He was in league with his good friend, Paul Hutton, the University of New Mexico professor made official historian by Governor Bill Richardson for the "Billy the Kid Case Hoax."

So Boze Bell appeared in Hutton's 2004 TV "documentary," "Investigating History: Billy the Kid," backing the hoax and hoaxers, as they all pretended to be independent authorities assembled by Governor Richardson, and vouched for each other and "Brushy Bill." For his part, Boze Bell (subtitled on screen as "Editor, True West Magazine") stated snidely that: "Friends of Pat Garrett conducted what they called an autopsy. But there were no photographs." He added that those "friends" said that Garrett deserved the reward. **[The Coroner's jurymen were not Garrett's friends. The body was properly examined by the jurymen, who also heard witness Peter Maxwell. This was the Old West. People did not have cameras.]** Boze Bell added that Garrett did the killing in "secrecy," and buried the body the next day. **[Other than an ambush killing, there was no secrecy. There was a vigil for Billy open to the whole town. This fakery echoes W.C. Jameson's and Frederick Bean's "Brushy"-backing book:** *The Return of the Outlaw Billy the Kid.*] Boze Bell had to know he was hoaxing.

TRUE WEST MAGAZINE HOAX COVER-UP

In his *True West*, appealing to Old West aficionados, Bob Boze Bell backed the "Billy the Kid Case" hoax enough to rename that magazine *Fake West*.

But, at the start of my hoax opposition, I knew only that one of the magazine's owners, Bob McCubbin, was a wealthy Billy the Kid collector, who hosted Frederick Nolan when I brought Nolan from England to testify against the hoax.

McCubbin referred me to Bob Boze Bell in October of 2005, when I had relinquished my anonymity after the hoaxers secret Arizona exhumation of John Miller was revealed. I wanted *True West* to do a hoax exposé.

So on October 25, 2005, I called Bob Boze Bell. After my explanation, there was silence. He said: "But Sederwall and Sullivan are my friends. How could I write that?" I said I would be the author. He said: "Keep it short."

While waiting for a response to my article, I sent for *True West's* five magazines with "Billy the Kid Case" articles; four of which were by a Janna Bommersbach - and realized my mistake. *True West* had been backing the hoax all along!

Bommersbach's first article was at the hoax's start, in the August/September 2003 edition as: "Digging up Billy. If Pat Garrett didn't kill the Kid, who's buried in his grave?" The title was the message. Who said Garrett did not kill Billy? Who said there is a question about who is in Billy's grave? Like subliminal advertising, this was a month before the hoaxers descended on Silver City to petition for Catherine Antrim's exhumation. Bommersbach added, "And of course, *True West* will be there. Be there? Hell, we'll buy the shovels." She concluded:

> Most significantly, it's not some splinter or kooky group that wants to do the exhuming and genetic testing. It's the highest authority in New Mexico, Gov. Bill Richardson. Two other major driving forces are the current Lincoln County Sheriff Tom Sullivan and Capitan, New Mexico Mayor Steve Sederwall ... Gov. Richardson wants to know if the Kid deserves a pardon ... And all this adds up to not only a chance to clarify and perhaps correct American history, but also a great tourism boom for New Mexico.

One could respond: Why *aren't* a governor, a sheriff, and a mayor "kooky" for calling themselves historians?

In the next *True West* issue, October/November 2003, came "From Shovels to DNA: The inside story of digging up Billy." Richardson was again paraded: "Gov. Richardson said, 'By utilizing modern forensic, DNA and crime scene techniques, the goal of the investigation is to get to the truth. In the process, the reputation of Pat Garrett, still a hero to Lincoln County law enforcement, hangs in the balance.'"

By *True West*'s January/February 2005 magazine, Janna Bommersbach was pitching carpenter's bench DNA. She ended: "Let us not forget that Gov. Richardson endorsed the project, saying the search for the truth was a worthy cause and promising his office's cooperation."

Into *that* lions' den, I had gone! The lioness to whom I was assigned was named Meghan Saar. She e-mailed me on January 31, 2006 - wanting me to include the hoaxers too; writing:

"All parties in this article should be given the opportunity to respond; the article feels very biased and skewered toward one direction, and I feel this may be because not all parties were asked to comment."

I withdrew my article, citing *their* bias. Then I learned that Paul Hutton was their contributing editor, that he was Bob McCubbin's best friend, and that his "Investigating History: Billy the Kid" had been filmed in McCubbin's home library as background for narrating Hutton. When I confronted McCubbin, he denied having "editorial control."

By 2010, retaliatory Boze Bell painted a *True West* cover with me as a screaming harridan at Billy's open grave; and its article quoted Steve Sederwall's bizarre defamation that I came to Lincoln County to mutilate their horses!

HOAXING WITH W.C. JAMESON

In *True West*, Bob Boze Bell also promoted the "Billy the Kid Case" hoax's "Brushy Bill" thrust in a stacked debate titled "Was Brushy Bill Really Billy the Kid? Experts face off over new evidence." Set-up was Leon Metz, Pat Garrett's biographer, against W.C. Jameson, spouting "Brushy" fakery; as follows:

> On one side, passionate supporters of the historical status quo assert Roberts was a fraud, yet to date they have provided no logical, definitive proof ... Roberts was an illiterate man, yet he was astonishingly intimate with the people, geography, architecture and events of Lincoln County, New Mexico, in the late 1870s-early 1880s – an intimacy that could have come only from being present and involved ...
>
> After Roberts' image was compared to the only known photograph of Billy the Kid, one researcher concluded that William Henry Roberts was, in all likelihood, Billy the Kid, and as such, history needed to be rewritten ...

Jameson's *True West* interview, like his 1998 book, *The Return of the Outlaw Billy the Kid*, on which it was based, was fakery. "Brushy" had no special knowledge, using traceable prompts whose errors he parroted as "Billy the Kid memories." And the photoanalysis was a bogus 1990 study at the University of Texas, which altered the tintype and "Brushy's" face to fake a match.

Concealed is that, the year before the fake photoanalysis, a legitimate study had been done by the Lincoln County Heritage Trust: the Lincoln, New Mexico, museum which then housed the tintype. It was headed by famous forensic anthropologist, Clyde Snow, with a Thomas G. Kyle of the Los Alamos National Laboratory, and historical experts, comparing the tintype to the over 150 alleged Billy the Kid photos, along with a control of 100 photos of random men. Historian, Don Cline, in his unpublished *Brushy Bill Roberts: I Wasn't Billy the Kid*, referenced that study. It concluded that "Brushy" was not Billy based on eye position, nose, chin, and ears - namely everything on his head! And another pretender, John Miller, did as badly. (Cline, Page 169)

HOAXING WITH STEVE SEDERWALL

By 2010, Bob Boze Bell demonstrated that he was allied with Steve Sederwall for mutual promotion in *True West* magazine. This time, they backed Pat Garrett's killing of Billy, but claimed to have discovered a different death scene for Boze Bell's own hoax article in the August, 2010 edition, titled "Caught with his Pants Down? Billy the Kid vs Pat Garrett, One Door Closes."

They claimed that Peter Maxwell's bedroom did not have an outside door, as described by Pat Garrett and John W. Poe. That segued to claiming Garrett and Poe lied, because Billy Bonney's killing actually was in Paulita Maxwell's bedroom. The source for the no door claim was an article allegedly written by a Gregory Scott Smith, that referenced a faked Maxwell house floor plan with no outside door to the bedroom.

For this hoax, Sederwall, as a "retired lawman" giving "CSI" evidence that Billy was in Paulita's bedroom, "across from Pete's, when he heard two men (Poe and McKinney) talking outside." Using no outside door, he had Billy enter from the hall. And his proof was recycling Dr. Henry Lee's uncited Case 2003-274 fake washstand forensics, while making-up his own version that "laser lines up perfectly with the hole [sic] in the washstand" if Garrett shot Billy, then ran out the inside door, and on his knees fired back in, hitting the washstand!

Boze Bell claimed to have discovered that a "Gregory Smith discovered the original 1863 floor plans ... Apparently, windows, not doors, were located alongside these rooms ... [I]f Pete's room did not have an outside door, historians will certainly be forced to look at the event with new eyes." He concluded: "[C]onventional wisdom is often misinformed."

HOAXING: This was pure hoaxing.

The Paulita scenario came from Frederick Nolan's 1992 *The Lincoln County War: A Documentary History*. "Garrett found the Kid in bed with Paulita Maxwell and shot him *in flagrante delictu*; the authored version [given by Garrett] ... was then cooked up to protect the girl's reputation." (Nolan, Page 425)

The no bedroom door idea came from the duo's fake labeling of the National Archives diagram of the 1863 single-story Fort Sumner Commanding Officer's Quarters as the Maxwell house of 1870's when Lucien Maxwell rebuilt the building as two-story with bedroom door.

The diagram was lifted from an undated article in the Fort Sumner State Monument, erroneously attributed to a Gregory Scott Smith, and titled: "The Death of Billy the Kid: A New Scenario?" It relied on old-timer fakery of a Garrett H. 'Kid' Dobbs, interviewed on September 12, 1942. It had the diagram used by Boze Bell and Sederwall.

And Sederwall's forensic fakery using the washstand is even more preposterous than hoaxing Dr. Henry Lee's own fakery with it.

For W.C. Jameson's 2018 *Cold Case Billy the Kid*, Sederwall lifted this no door hoax for himself to claim that Pat Garrett could not have shot Billy the Kid, because he and Deputy John W. Poe described an outside door to Peter Maxwell's bedroom. And *he* had "discovered" that there was no outside door. Ergo: if Garrett lied about a door, he lied about the corpse, so he killed an innocent victim, not Billy Bonney! (See page 293-300 above for debunking of that no door hoax)

READY AND WILLING FOR THE "BILLY THE KID'S BAD BUCKS" HOAX

When Steve Sederwall was hawking his self-promoting hoax of Billy the Kid as a counterfeiter, his buddy Bob Boze Bell was there to help him pitch. *True West* magazine of June, 2015 published "Billy Bonney's Bad Bucks: Did the Kid Travel the Counterfeit Trail?" It took only three more years for their fellow hoaxer, W.C. Jameson, to make that hoax a centerpiece in his 2018 book: *Cold Case Billy the Kid*.

CHAPTER 7
AN ARMORY OF SMOKING GUNS

NOTHING BUT HOAXING

As seen, W.C. Jameson, had backed and done secret fix-ups for the most elaborate of the Billy the Kid imposter hoaxes: that of Oliver "Brushy Bill" Roberts. And, determined to win at any cost, he had turned hoaxer himself with disreputable secret fix-ups to "Brushy's" transcripts to better "match" Billy Bonney.

Steve Sederwall, as a Deputy Sheriff, had participated in the gigantic forensic DNA hoax of Lincoln County Sheriff's Department Case 2003-274's "Billy the Kid Case." In addition, backed in Jameson's 2018 book, *Cold Case Billy the Kid*, Sederwall had presented several other Billy the Kid hoaxes that he had manufactured. Furthermore, he had forged the forensic DNA reports of Dr. Henry Lee to trick the District Court judge in my open records litigation; and later, for Jameson, he had faked the "Billy the Kid Case" as his own private "investigation."

U.S. Marshals Service Historian David Turk aided and participated in the "Billy the Kid Case" hoax, bent on defaming Deputy U.S. Marshal Pat Garrett as killing an innocent victim, while lacking even the rudimentary historian's skill of differentiating hearsay sources from fact.

Their promoter and backer was the Editor-and-Chief of glossy *True West* magazine, Bob Boze Bell, indifferent that he himself had written and illustrated a history book in which Billy was killed by Pat Garrett and was no counterfeiter: his 1996 *The Illustrated Life and Times of Billy the Kid*.

These were the scammers who would present to the public the "Billy the Kid's Bad Bucks" hoax to accuse Billy Bonney of being a William Brockway gang counterfeiter, with their common denominator being cynical hijacking of the famous history for self-aggrandizement and profit.

PART III

HOAXING BILLY BONNEY AS A COUNTERFEITER

CHAPTER 1
FRAMING THE KID AS A COUNTERFEITER

A NEW DIRECTION IN HOAXING

Hoaxing Billy Bonney as a counterfeiter represented a new direction in hoaxing his history. The imposter hoaxes all distill to a defamatory attack on Pat Garrett as a murderer of the innocent victim, while aggrandizing Billy Bonney as leading a law-abiding life after the death scene. With this formula "Brushy Bill" Roberts and his promoting coach, William V. Morrison, had requested his gubernatorial pardon as Billy the Kid. And the "Billy the Kid Case" hoaxers had followed suit, seeking that pardon for "Brushy" posthumously.

But, by 2010, the balance tipped, as hoaxers' self-promotion and profiteering obscured their earlier goal of crowning one pretender or another as Billy the Kid. Instead, there was evolution to any attention-grabbing claim that might land a tabloid-level book or TV pseudo-documentary solving "history's mysteries."

In 2010, it was from this crass ambition, that focus changed to Billy Bonney himself as the hoaxers regrouped during my inhibitory open records litigation against the lawmen who did the "Billy the Kid Case's" fake forensics and exhumations. It appears that Steve Sederwall, while forging Dr. Henry Lee reports to trick that court, was also working with U.S. Marshals Historian David Turk to hoax Billy the Kid as an evil murderer-counterfeiter. They were backed by fellow "Billy the Kid Case" participants: *True West* magazine Editor-in-Chief Bob Boze Bell; reporter, Julie Carter at the *Ruidoso News*; and W.C. Jameson for his 2018 *Cold Case Billy the Kid: Investigating History's Mysteries.*

The hoaxers' goals were faking that the history was not as written, and that they were legitimate historians. Possibly Jameson hoped that this tactic opened the way to try again, in the future, with his own "Brushy Bill" quest.

RECYCLING A SEDERWALL HOAX

When W.C. Jameson partnered, as narrator, for Steve Sederwall's hoaxing in his 2018 book, *Cold Case Billy the Kid: Investigating History's Mysteries*, the real mystery was why he did it. As a "Brushy Bill"-believer - albeit with some 21st century hoaxing of his own to fix-up his man to match the modern history books - Jameson's goal was still crowning "Brushy" as Billy. And most of Sederwall's self-promoting hoaxes opposed "Brushy," since they made claims unknown to him as the supposed "Billy the Kid."

A dramatic example of this mismatch is Jameson's "Counterfeit Money" chapter (Pages 68-84), in which he recycled and expanded Sederwall's earlier fabrication of Billy the Kid as a counterfeiter and a cold-blooded murderer of an informer, in cahoots with famous Jesse James and famous William Brockway.

Jameson, slavishly adulating Sederwall, apparently missed that this scam demolished "Brushy," who, as supposed Billy Bonney, not only had no idea of these activities; but also was made so despicable, as Billy, that he deserved no sought pardons.

OVERVIEW OF THE COUNTERFEITING HOAX

Steve Sederwall's hoax was simple: tracking the famous William Brockway's gang's 1880 counterfeit bill distributions nationally, then faking its links to Billy Bonney, who was then being pursued by the Secret Service himself. It relied on readers not knowing obscure cited documents, which were then misstated; and on flaunting details of Brockway gang history, that even Billy the Kid aficionados would not know, because they were not part of that history.

But key was this hoax's throw-back to antiquated mythology of Billy the Kid. Jameson's book's back cover was a give-away; stating falsely: "Billy the Kid was a known cattle rustler and troublemaker who worked on ranches in southern New Mexico and the Texas Panhandle." This was a "Billy the Kid" of early cowboy movies. So if one was nostalgic for good ol' ignorance of the early 20th century, this was the hoax for them.

And its fake "Billy Bonney" hid real Billy's his grandeur, and the anti-Ring freedom fight for which he was the hero.

As will be seen, this simple hoax of fabricated links gained complexity by using obscure information related to Billy Bonney and the William Brockway gang. A summary provides a roadmap:

FROM BILLY BONNEY'S HISTORY

1) **JOHN CHISUM'S DEBT TO HIM:** In *The Authentic Life of Billy the Kid*, Pat Garrett claimed that in 1879, Billy rustled cattle from John Chisum because he considered him in debt by not paying the Tunstall era Regulators as promised.

HOAX: This incident is fictionalized to become part of a rustling-money-laundering scheme involving Billy Bonney and Brockway's gang.

2) **A SALE OF RUSTLED CATTLE TO COLORADO BUYERS:** In *The Authentic Life of Billy the Kid*, Pat Garrett related that Billy once sold rustled Chisum cattle to Colorado buyers at the Alamogordo, New Mexico, ranch of Alexander Grzelachowski. (Garrett, Page 86)

HOAX: Central to the hoax was lifting that non-specific Colorado location to fake "Colorado beef buyers" as being Brockway gang members, because some Brockway bill pushers lived in Colorado. Omitted was that they were *not* rustled cattle buyers, and the money-laundering by rustled stock was fabricated. Billy's sale was simply to get good money for the cattle to "settle" Chisum's debt.

3) **THE WHITE OAKS CONNECTION:** Billy sold rustled stock to the Dedrick brothers at their White Oaks livery.

HOAX: Billy's link to counterfeiting was made-up using White Oaks because the Dedrick brothers' counterfeiting business was centered there; along with Brockway bill courier W.H. West, and periodic presence of Brockway's pushers: James and Frank Doyle, Nate Foster, and John Hays. Billy had no connection to these Brockway men.

4) **THE SECRET SERVICE INVESTIGATION:** Special Operative Azariah Wild was in New Mexico Territory from mid-September through December of 1880 to investigate local counterfeiting. Though he found just a few counterfeit $100 bills passed by a Billy Wilson to local merchants, he was led by his Santa Fe Ring minders to believe that Billy Bonney headed huge a rustling-counterfeiting gang with Wilson, with the Ring's motive being the capture or killing of anti-Ring gadfly Billy.

HOAX: Obviously, this was a major hoax inspiration, since Wild himself linked Billy to the local counterfeiters. But Wild's reports reveal that he found no evidence, was persuaded by his Ringite minders to frame Billy for their murderous agenda, and abandoned his original and correct pursuit of the actual counterfeiters and plates. And he only linked the bills to Brockway when he was informed by his Chief, after leaving the Territory, that Brockway's pushers were in the Territory passing bills.

5) **AN OUTLAW MYTH ARTICLE:** As the Ring-assisting Secret Service pursued Billy, the Ring published its December 22, 1880 outlaw myth article: *New York Sun's* "Outlaws of New Mexico, The Exploits of a Band Headed by a New York Youth, The Mountain Fastness of the Kid and His Followers - War Against a Gang of Cattle Thieves and Murderers - The Frontier Confederates of Brockway, the Counterfeiter."

HOAX: This false linking of Billy Bonney and recently captured William Brockway seems a likely inspiration for the hoax, since lifted from it also was an outlaw myth fable about evil Billy Bonney murdering a freighter. The hoax expanded that lie to a fiction of Billy murdering the freighter because he had reported him as a counterfeiter to Secret Service Operative Azariah Wild.

6) **THE DEDRICK MONEY-LAUNDERING PROPOSAL:** The real rustling-money-laundering proposal, reported both by Azariah Wild and Pat Garrett in his *The Authentic Life of Billy the Kid*, was made by Dan Dedrick to Azariah Wild's spy, Barney Mason, Garrett's friend. In late November of 1880, Dedrick proposed to Mason for him to buy cattle in Mexico with $30,000 in counterfeit money, and bring them to New Mexico Territory for resale for good money.

HOAX: This scheme is concealed in the hoax, but it seems to have inspired the fiction of Billy's rustled cattle being sold to launder money. Since that technique makes no sense, an additional explanatory fabrication awkwardly added a made-up a Kansas bank accepting counterfeit money from Billy to exchange for good money.

7) **CONNECTION TO JESSE JAMES:** Dr. Henry Hoyt reported seeing Billy, in 1879, eating a meal with Jesse James at the Las Vegas, New Mexico Territory, Moore's Hotsprings Hotel; though Billy told him he and James were not engaged in business.

HOAX: Using that meeting, fabricated was that Billy and Jesse James were involved in counterfeiting together, though, in truth, Jesse did not do counterfeiting either.

8) **CONNECTION TO BILLY WILSON:** Billy Bonney used Billy Wilson for rustling.

HOAX: Bonney's association with accused counterfeiter Wilson was used to claim Bonney was a counterfeiter too. Hidden was that Wilson's legal defense was that he was *not a counterfeiter*, and that he had gotten bad bills from W.H. West when he sold him his White Oaks livery. This was accepted by 1896, and Wilson was pardoned.

9) **SECRET SERVICE PARDON PROPOSAL:** Billy made his second pardon attempt by offering to Azariah Wild to testify against the actual counterfeiters.

HOAX: Billy is fabricated as a unsavory snitch for turning on his counterfeiting fellows, though, in fact, they were not his fellows, and he was no counterfeiter. Built on this fabrication are fables of his being in a conspiracy with the mail carrier to read Wild's mail - when he made only one theft to check on Wild during the pardon negotiation.

FROM WILLIAM BROCKWAY HISTORY

1) **BROCKWAY'S MAIN PUSHERS:** From his New York City presses, Brockway distributed nationally to local buyers by his pushers: James Brace Doyle, Frank Doyle, Nate Foster, and John Hays. They resided in Illinois, Missouri, and Colorado. Local pushers receiving bills from them were Walter Greenway in Sherman, Texas, and W.H. West in White Oaks (with Dan Dedrick and his brothers intending money-laundering by cattle purchase with bad money with resale for good money).

HOAX: Because James Brace Doyle's wife's father had a Colorado ranch, and because Frank Doyle and Nate Foster also sometimes resided in Colorado, the hoax absurdly claimed that they *were* the "Colorado beef buyers" to whom Garrett had claimed Billy sold rustled stock. But they were not beef buyers, they were bill pushers. Their m.o. was to purchase for themselves businesses and mines with bad money, including in White Oaks. None of this had anything to do with Billy Bonney.

2) **BROCKWAY'S BILLS:** Found in New Mexico Territory by Azariah Wild were a few bills passed by Billy Wilson and obtained from W.H. West. It would only be after Wild left New Mexico Territory that he was informed that they were Brockway bills, likely brought to the Territory by James Doyle and W.H. West.

HOAX: Because they were Brockway bills in New Mexico Territory, made up was that they had a connection to Billy Bonney. Also made-up was locating one of them in the Secret Service archive.

3) **SHERMAN, TEXAS, OUTLET:** In the summer of 1880, before coming to New Mexico Territory, Azariah Wild investigated a local counterfeit bill passer named Walter Greenham, along with his family, and business associates. They were distributing Brockway bills, as Wild was only informed in 1881 by his Chief, after he left New Mexico Territory.

HOAX: Billy Bonney is fabricated as connected to those Texas counterfeiters by faking that he was connected to any Brockway counterfeiting nationally; when, in fact, he was connected to none.

4) **BROCKWAY'S SECRET SERVICE INVESTIGATION:** The Operatives investigating William Brockway were Andrew L. Drummond and Wallace W. Hall. They exposed him, his plate-maker, and his main bill distributors.

HOAX: Concealed is that they made no connection to Billy the Kid or Azariah Wild's investigation.

MISCELLANEOUS ADDED HOAXING

1) ADDING JESSE JAMES AS A COUNTERFEITER
2) ADDING JAMES DOLAN AS A COUNTERFEITER
3) CLAIMING BILLY BONNEY AS BEING IN A MAIL ROBBING CONSPIRACY
4) CLAIMING BILLY BONNEY AS MURDERING AN INFORMER OF HIM AS A COUNTERFEITER
5) CLAIMING BILLY AS DOING INTIMIDATION OF A POTENTIAL WITNESS AGAINST HIS COUNTERFEITING

CHAPTER 2
REALITY OF BILLY BONNEY AND WILLIAM BROCKWAY

BILLY BONNEY AS A RUSTLER

Billy Bonney was a not a counterfeiter. After the lost Lincoln County War Battle on July 19, 1878, he made money by gambling and rustling. And the historical context was that he was still hoping for the pardon for his Lincoln County War indictments as promised in 1879 by Governor Lew Wallace.

As to gambling, in his December 12, 1880 letter to Governor Lew Wallace, he stated: *"I had been at Sumner Since I left Lincoln making my living Gambling."*

As to rustling, he stayed true to his idealistic July 13, 1878 "Regulator Manifesto," which stated: *"We are all aware that your brother-in-law, T.B. Catron sustains the Murphy-Kinney party ... Steal from the poorest or richest American or Mexican, and the full measure of the injury you do, shall be visited upon the property of Mr. Catron."* One prize of his guerrilla rustling was dead Sheriff William Brady's sorrel horse, likely stolen from Lincoln County's Charles Fritz Ranch or T.B. Catron's Carrizozo Ranch, and "sold" in Texas to Henry Hoyt on October 24, 1878. And John Chisum got retaliative rustling for his betrayal of John Tunstall and Alexander McSween by refusing aid of his 80 cowboys, and not paying the Regulators' salaries as promised.

Billy's gave his Robin Hood self-image in the December 12, 1880 letter to Wallace: *"There is no Doubt but what there is a great deal of Stealing going on in the Territory ... **but so far as my being at the head of a Band there is nothing of it** in Several Instances I have recovered Stolen Property when there was no chance to get an Officer to do it. one instance for Hugo Zuber Post office Puerto de Luna. another for Pablo Analla Same Place."* And he never sold to Ringites, like rustler John Kinney.

For his rustling roundups, he used fellow Regulators - Tom O'Folliard, Charlie Bowdre, Josiah "Doc" Scurlock, and Jim "Frenchie" French (until Scurlock and French left the Territory) - as well locals. For non-Ring outlets, besides doing selling himself in Tascosa, Texas, he used New Mexico Territory's Pat Coghlan in Three Rivers and Dan Dedrick, owner of Bosque Grande ranch, near Fort Sumner. He also used Dedrick's brothers, Sam and Mose, all of whom were partners in a White Oaks livery.

Since Dedrick was also a counterfeiter, Billy's association with him and his livery put him in contact with actual counterfeiters.

Billy also got money with a gambling circuit from Fort Sumner, to Anton Chico, to Las Vegas; being charged in August of 1879 in a Las Vegas court for keeping a gaming table.

Home base was Fort Sumner, with "Doc" Scurlock and his wife living there, as well as Charlie Bowdre's wife Manuela; with Charlie himself working at the nearby ranch of Thomas Yerby. But Billy's location choice was weighed by friendliness of the Maxwell family and his secret liaison teenaged Paulita Maxwell.

To be noted is that the main Territorial rustling was by the Ring and from John Chisum, to meet beef contracts through "The House" for Fort Stanton and the Mescalero Indian Reservation.

SECRET SERVICE AND BILLY BONNEY

THE ROLE OF THE SANTA FE RING

The peculiar Secret Service investigation of alleged New Mexico Territory counterfeiting, from mid-September to the end of December of 1880, that eventually included pursuit of Billy Bonney, makes no sense without factoring in the Santa Fe Ring and its post-Lincoln County War agenda of eliminating the last remaining Regulators - Billy in particular. Shielded by partisan New Mexicans, they had been impossible to capture to kill. And bi-cultural Billy was capable of inspiring another Hispanic uprising - the actuality of the Lincoln County War Battle.

Those uprisings were Ring head, T.B. Catron's greatest fear, knowing the collective hatred inspired by his massive Hispanic land-grabs. When he became one of New Mexico's first two Senators, his anxiety was revealed in his response to the Spanish-American War. His biographer, Victor Westphall, in his 1973 book, *Thomas Benton Catron and his Era*, quoted his belief that

"Mexicans ... were perfectly equal to starting five new revolutions in five days ... He was convinced that intervention was inevitable and should have been carried out earlier." (Westphall, Page 375) And on May 28, 1911, Catron had written to his son Thom: *"[I]t is the disposition of most all of the Spanish-American people to indulge in revolutions."* (Vioalle Clark Hefferan, University of New Mexico doctoral thesis, Page 111)

Furthering the Ring's desire to eliminate Billy was his gadfly aggression. He not only rustled from Ringites, but also initiated pardon negotiations in 1879 with non-Ringite Governor Lew Wallace; which the Ring had barely managed to obstruct, but whose ominous and obvious intent was to free himself from its hold with its indictments of him from the Lincoln County War.

From this background, one can decipher the strange reports generated by the Secret Service Operative sent to New Mexico Territory: Azariah F. Wild. Adding complexity, is that he himself was apparently unaware of his mission, and may have been chosen by his Chief, James Brooks, for gullibility and laziness, since, throughout his stay, he did no legitimate investigation. He merely accepted input from his Ringite minders - local Ring "boss, James Dolan; Catron's brother-in-law, Edgar Walz; and Catron's Ringite replacement as U.S. Attorney, Sidney Barnes. He stayed with them in Fort Stanton, Lincoln, White Oaks, and Roswell, never even going to Fort Sumner where he eventually localized his fictional counterfeiting gang. He abandoned correct leads to actual counterfeiters; and let Ringites sabotage his pardon bargaining with Billy Bonney, who promised to expose real counterfeiters.

But the blame rests not just with Wild. Further proof of his manipulation, was that he was never informed by his Chief about links of Territorial counterfeiting to the national William Brockway gang - then in the process of being apprehended - until he had left the Territory and had effected Billy Bonney's attempted killing and capture through empowering Pat Garrett. And Chief Brooks had likely sent him at the request of Catron's Washington, D.C. co-boss, Stephen Benton Elkins, using local Lincoln County Ring boss, James Dolan, to act as the aggrieved local merchant passed four bad bills.

The hand of the Ring was also visible in leaked Azariah Wild reports used for its first, national and fictional article about "Billy the Kid," in the *New York Sun*, on December 22, 1880, titled "Outlaws of New Mexico, The Exploits of a Band Headed by a New York Youth, The Mountain Fastness of the Kid and His Followers,

War Against a Gang of Cattle Thieves and Murderers, The Frontier Confederates of Brockway, the Counterfeiter." There Billy was plastered with the Ring's outlaw myth; the Lincoln County War was hidden as a freedom fight; and Billy was gratuitously linked to just caught, famous William Brockway.

One can trace Wild's duping from his first obtaining from James Dolan, in company of Ringites Sidney Barnes and Edgar Walz in Santa Fe, a bill passed by a Billy Wilson. Wild correctly linked it to the actual counterfeiters, Dan Dedrick and W.H. West, with localization to their White Oaks livery and Dedrick's Bosque Grande Ranch, with possible printing plates. He also used a spy to determine the intended money laundering by buying cattle in Mexico with bad money, and reselling them for good money. But under Ringite influence, he abandoned reality and accepted the concoction that Billy Wilson and Billy Bonney actually headed a huge rustling-counterfeiting gang centered in Fort Sumner (where Billy and past Regulators Charlie Bowdre, Tom O'Folliard, and Josiah "Doc" Scurlock stayed). And, as Wild, who had discovered just a few counterfeit bills, became more defensive about his failing mission to his Chief, he inflated the "gang" to 60 rustlers, murderers, and counterfeiters, and became hysterically paranoid that they were after him. To capture this "gang," he empowered Pat Garrett, first likely backing him in the Lincoln County Sheriff's election, then making him a Deputy U.S. Marshal to track down and kill his fictional "Wilson & Kid gang" anywhere in the Territory, using spies and Texas posses that Wild backed.

Without Wild, the Ring would never have captured Bonney. One can say that duped Wild ultimately became an agent of an early Secret Service political murder.

WILD'S NEW MEXICO INVESTIGATION

New Orleans based, Azariah Wild, was required to write daily reports of his activities to his Chief, James Brooks, in Washington, D.C. Through them, one can trace his deviation from real counterfeiters to false accusation of Billy Bonney. And, as time went on with just a few bills found and no actual investigating done, Wild's defensive apologies to his Chief were bolstered by his fictional inflations of his made-up gang and its risk to citizens and himself.

Wild got his assignment on September 7, 1880, and responded to Chief Brooks on September 11th, as follows:

U.S. Treasury Department,
SECRET-SERVICE DIVISION,

<u>New Orleans</u> District

James J. Brooks,
  Chief U.S. Secret Service

Sir: I have the honor to submit the following, my report as <u>Special</u> Operative of this District for <u>Friday</u> the <u>10th</u> day of <u>September</u>, 18<u>80</u>, written at <u>New Orleans, Louisiana</u>, and completed at <u>9</u> o'clock <u>A.</u> M on the <u>11th</u> day of <u>September</u>, 18<u>80</u>
In New Orleans La.

    Engaged in and about the city the entire day.
    I have the honor to acknowledge the receipt of your letter of the 7th instant relative to my trip to New Mexico with your letters received by the Department from citizens of New Mexico enclosed therewith.
    I expect to start for New Mexico next Wednesday Sept 15th. I will endeavor to carry out your wishes in the matter.
    I have made arrangements for several Winchester rifles to take along with me in case they are wanted they are at hand.
    I also have spoken to the U.S. Marshal [John Sherman] for such articles as I may want in the shape of "bracelets etc" ...

                        Respectfully Submitted
                        Azariah F. Wild
                        Special Operative

    Wild's early reports show that he first identified as counterfeit bill distributors - whom he calls *"passers of the queer"* - William Wilson and a Thomas Cooper.
    For September 20th, he reported from Santa Fe, after meeting with Ringite U.S. Attorney Sidney Barnes and James Dolan, who came as the victimized Lincoln merchant who got four counterfeit $100 bills. They set Wild up by magnifying outlawry of counterfeiter, Dan Dedrick's, men. Wild wrote:

> *Engaged ... at the office of U.S. Attorney Barnes in consultation with him about the counterfeiting cases in White Oaks Lincoln County New Mexico ... [H]e will look more into the case, send for the U.S. Marshal [John Sherman] ... consult together and act in concert.*
>
> *The men (Thomas Cooper and William Wilson) are amongst the worst characters in Lincoln County where there have been over forty murders committed within the past two years, and not an arrest made.*
>
> *Judging from statements made by U.S. Attorney Barnes a bad state of affairs exists here in New Mexico. He informs me that there has not been a single arrest made here since last term of Court .... [and has] hopes of arresting Wilson and Cooper ...*
>
> **I met the post trader [James Dolan] here this day from Fort Stanton on whom one [of] these notes was passed. He has offered to render me any assistance possible,** *and has named several parties on whom I can rely to assist in making the arrests when we are ready to act.*
>
> *He repeats the information contained in the letters you sent me only a little more full in his details.*

[AUTHOR'S NOTE: That Chief Brooks was the Ring's contact, sending his unaware Special Operative to do the Ring's bidding, is indicated by "merchant James Dolan" – a main Ringite - being the contact to the Secret Service to get Wild assigned.]

For September 22, 1880, Wild wrote from Santa Fe, revealing his Ring manipulation; while confusing Lincoln residents' refusal to arrest their hero Regulators with White Oaks residents, who were unaware of Lincoln County War issues. Wild wrote dramatically:

> *I am going to have trouble in getting assistance to make arrests in White Oaks. The reputation of Lincoln County in which White Oaks is situated, that no one is willing to undertake the arrests or be known to have had anything to do with so far as I can find thus far, unless more money is paid than I believe the Division can afford to pay. I have come here to arrest or have these men arrested and am bound to do it if I have to attempt it by myself.*

For September 24, 1880, Wild, staying put in Santa Fe, met with Lincoln Ringites, vouched for as *"reliable"* by Ringite U.S. Attorney Barnes. He wrote:

I have this day seen and consulted in company with U.S. Attorney Barnes with several reliable men who are doing business in Lincoln County New Mexico [James Dolan; John Riley; Catron's brother-in-law, Edgar Walz] and who know the parties who I am after and all about them.

For September 25, 1880, writing from Santa Fe to get a free railroad pass - he stupidly revealed to *the railroad company* (!) his secret mission about a *"band of Counterfeiters and passers of the queer [who] are operating in the Territory ... I have been directed by the Department to visit this section of the country with a view to breaking them up and bring them to justice."*

For October 3, 1880, Wild wrote from Fort Stanton after meeting in Lincoln with James Dolan to see the counterfeit bill. But straying from Ring control in town, he also met with Attorney Ira Leonard - someone who could set him straight.

For October 4, 1880, Wild wrote from Fort Stanton documenting William Wilson's also passing a $100 counterfeit bill to Lincoln merchant José Montaño, and another to post trader firm Dowlin and Delaney. He described the bills, and stated that he would use those victims as witnesses against suspects, William Wilson and Thomas Cooper (whom misnames as "*Sam*").

On October 1, 1880, Wild reported that he met in Lincoln with James Dolan and was shown *"a counterfeit note which he had received from one William Wilson in exchange for merchandise and good money given in change."* He also met with Attorney Ira Leonard, who tried to keep him on course.

FIRST FOCUS ON BILLY BONNEY

For October 5, 1880, from Fort Stanton, Wild showed Ring manipulation, likely by Dolan, by expanding focus on Billy Wilson to rustling. Wild stated: *"[Wilson] is an American who has been here in Lincoln County for several years, and has the name of being engaged with others of his kind in stealing horses and cattle."*

That segued into linking him to Billy Bonney, Charlie Bowdre, and Tom O'Folliard at Fort Sumner, with whom Wilson did rustle. About Billy, Wild reported: *"William Antrom [sic -Antrim] alias W$\underline{m}$ Bonney alias Billy Kid"* is *"an outlaw in the mountains here who came here from Arizona after committing a murder there."* Using "Antrom" with an Arizona murder, implied Catron's usual use of investigators to ferret out past indictments of opponents for malicious prosecutions. So Wild had likely had been informed by Dolan of Billy's 1877 Cahill killing as Henry "Antrim."

Thus, Wild, 28 days after case assignment, had been told by Barnes, Dolan, and Walz - with Catron's Lincoln County agent, David Easton, to be added - that Billy was a murderous counterfeiter outlaw *"with whom these cattle thieves meet, and by many it is believed that they (the cattle thieves and shovers of the queer) receive the counterfeit money."* Though Wild still doubted, he inflated his investigation to men of *"notorious character [acting] in concert in their hellish deeds."* He wrote for that October 5th report :

> *In tracing up the history and character of William Wilson known here as Billy Wilson I found that he is an American who has been here in Lincoln County for several years, and has the name of being engaged with others of his kind at stealing horses and cattle. A few weeks ago he and several of his clan stole 38 head of beef cattle from a ranch near Fort Bascom, and brought them here to Lincoln County where they found their way into the hands of the United States and are now on the Mescalero Indian Reservation **as I am informed by David Easton, one of the men in charge.** The evidence is conclusive against Wilson as being the party who stole them and sold them here ...*

[AUTHOR'S NOTE: Easton hid Catron's rustling from John Chisum to meet beef contracts by blaming it on what Wild calls the "clan" - which he soon updated to Western lingo of "gang." And citing rustling at Fort Bascom, at the Texas border, shows Wild was blaming all rustling on this "clan."]

> *There is an outlaw in the mountains here who came here from Arizona after committing a murder there named William Antrom alias W<u>m</u> Bonney alias Billy Kid with whom these cattle thieves meet, and by many it is believed that they (the cattle thieves and shovers of the queer) receive the counterfeit money. <u>I have found no evidence so far to support their suspicions</u>. The people here as a general thing do not know good money from bad.*

The following is a copy of a letter this day [October 5, 1880] written to U.S. Attorney Barnes ...

    S.M. Barnes Esq.
        U.S. Attorney
            Santa Fe New Mexico

Dear Sir:

On or about the 5th day of August 1880 in the town of Lincoln (Lincoln County) New Mexico one William Wilson now residing at White Oaks did pass on James J. Dolin [sic] a $100 counterfeit national bank note on the Merchants National Bank of New Bedford Massachusetts dated February 14, 1865 ...

In connection with the passing of this note I will state that at the time William Wilson passed the note on Dolin he (Wilson) gave him (Dolin) three $100 notes of the same kind and as he believes of the same character with a $50 note ...

I will respectfully state from information that [Thomas] Cooper and [William] Wilson are both employed at a livery & sales stables at White Oaks [owned by counterfeiter, Dan Dedrick's brothers, Mose and Sam] kept by James [sic – W.H.] West a notorious character recently from Texas.

When they go out they generally travel together, and are supposed to act in concert in their hellish deeds.

I have this far been unable to find only one man who is willing to step forward, and assist in the arrest of these men not out of any fear they have of their resistance but assassination afterwards ...

I expect to go to White Oaks the last of this week & expect to remain some days ...

    Very Respectfully Yours
      Azariah Wild
      Special Operative

The letter of which the foregoing is a copy has been written as per agreement with the U.S. Attorney [Ringite Sidney Barnes] before leaving Santa Fe.

He (the U.S. Attorney) there proposed that he would swear out warrants himself on information I would send him [from Ring informants], and have Deputy Marshals sent from Santa Fe provided men could not be found in Lincoln County to make the arrests.

I expect to go to Lincoln at 7 A.M. Wednesday the 6th to meet Judge Leonard and the Clerk of Court who went to White Oaks Sunday morning after which I will go to the Oaks myself - the first conveyance I can get.

[AUTHOR'S NOTE: Leonard, with usual poor strategizing, never explained the Ring or Billy's Regulator role.]

On October 5, 1880, Wild reported that he was shown a counterfeit note from the Merchants National Bank of New Bedford passed by Wilson on August 15, 1880 to Jose Montaño. With his typical lazy misspellings, he reported that *"William Dowling"* [sic – Dowlin] of "Delaney & Dowling" [sic- Dowlin and Delaney] got a *"$100- Counterfeit National Bank Note on the Revere National Bank of Boston Massachusetts."* Wild did no further follow-up investigation of the bills.

A SECRET SERVICE PARDON

Wild had correctly stated about his Ringite input on Billy: *"I have found no evidence so far to support their suspicions."* And since he was not intentionally aiding the Ring, he accepted Ira Leonard's help to investigate the counterfeiting. So Leonard, as Billy's lawyer, engineered a second pardon bargain in exchange for Billy's testimony against the real counterfeiters (like Dan Dedrick). He also disclosed the first pardon bargain with Lew Wallace, explaining Billy's Amnesty Proclamation exclusion; as Wild reported: *"Gov. Wallace has issued a proclamation granting immunity to those not indicted but as Antrom has been indicted the proclamation did not cover his (Antrom's) case."* So Wild was now poised to save Billy's life by a pardon which Wallace might have backed, since it freed him of its responsibility and Ring attack.

And Billy's knowledge of the Territorial underworld had already been demonstrated in his March 23, 1879 interview with Lew Wallace which yielded "Statements by Kid," in which he reported Santa Fe Ring-associated rustlers and murderers.

Wild described the new pardon option in his report for October 8, 1880, written in Fort Stanton; stating:

I left Fort Stanton at 7 o'clock A.M. on the stage and reached Lincoln the County seat at 8:30 A.M. a distance of 9 miles.

The object of my visit to Lincoln was to see Judge Ira Leonard and the Clerk of the County Court who went to White Oaks Sunday and returned Tuesday.

They inform me that Tom Cooper is at White Oaks. That William Wilson left White Oaks some time since and was at Bosque Grande N.M. [counterfeiter Dan Dedrick's ranch] on the Rio Pecos above [sic- 12 miles below] Fort Sumner

353

In my report of October 5th I spoke of an outlaw whose name was Antrom alias Billy Bonney. During the Lincoln Co. War he killed men on the Indian Reservation for which he has been indicted in the Territorial and the United States Court.

[AUTHOR'S NOTE: Wild garbled the "Buckshot" Roberts 1878 federal indictment by U.S. Attorney Catron as killing men on the Mescalero Reservation.]

Gov. Wallace has issued a proclamation granting immunity to those not indicted but as Antrom has been indicted the proclamation did not cover his (Antrom's) case and he (Antrom) has been in the mountains as an outlaw ever since a space of about two years time.

Governor Wallace has since written Antrom's attorney on the subject saying he should be let go but has failed to put it on shape that satisfied Judge Leonard Antroms attorney.

[AUTHOR'S NOTE: This is Wild's garbling of Wallace's not filing the pardon in a court of law.]

It is believed, and in fact is almost known that he (Antrom) is one of the leading members of this gang.

[AUTHOR'S NOTE: Wild here entangles his Ringite input, and is clearly confused about Billy's counterfeiting role. And it seems that Leonard forgot to describe Billy's anti-Ring role or testimonies. In fact Wild, an honest man, might have been sympathetic, since he himself was likely forced into retirement in 1893 for exposing New Orleans political corruption. But the toxic seed had been planted in Wild's mind that Billy was "*one of the leading members of this gang.*" And with increasing Ringite input, Wild would soon claim Billy as the gang's leader.]

Antrom has recently written a letter to Judge Leonard which has been shown to me in confidence that leads me to believe that we can use Antrom in these cases provided Gov. Wallace will make good his written promises and the U.S. Attorney [Barnes] will allow the case pending in the U.S. Court to slumber and give him (Antrom) one more chance to reform.

[AUTHOR'S NOTE: Wild is prepared to get Billy's pardon granted. He is convinced Wallace made the pardon promise, and believes he could get Wallace to issue the pardon affidavit. But Wild also realized that Catron's federal indictment for the "Buckshot" Roberts killing would block Territorial gubernatorial pardon unless "*the U.S. Attorney [Barnes] will allow the case pending in the U.S. Court to slumber.*" In fact, Wild's

identifying that federal indictment obstacle may have helped Leonard formulate the most clever argument of his career to get it quashed in Billy's 1881 hanging trial.]

I have promised nothing and will not except to receive any propositions he (Leonard) and his client see fit to make and submit them to U.S. Attorney Barnes.

Judge Leonard has written Antrom to meet him (Leonard) at once for consultation.

The chances are that the conversation will take place within the next week when I will report fully to you and submit whatever propositions they see fit to make to US. Attorney Barnes for such action as he deems proper to take.

[AUTHOR'S NOTE: Leonard's pardon plan was doomed, since Wild naively planned to reveal it to the Ring via Barnes.]

While it may appear to you that I am working up this case slowly I will respectfully ask you to take into consideration that I am where there is no telegraphic communications with any point [apparently the Ring concealed the Fort Stanton telegraphic option], and the mail facilities next to nothing so that I have not received a letter since I left New Orleans even from my own family, also that I am in a place where the better citizens are afraid of their lives should they be known to give information against the gang, and the officers are more or less linked in and connected with the outlaws. ***In my candid judgment I have struck the worst nest of counterfeiters in the United States, one that I believe will lead to the headquarters of the gang and the long looked for [money printing] plates if continuously worked.***

If you will have patience with me I am willing to remain here and will work these cases although the change of climate is great between this and that in my District proper [New Orleans]. We have had snow in the mountains since I arrived, and I have been compelled to get heavy clothing throughout.

[AUTHOR'S NOTE: Wild's anxiety about justifying his mission after finding almost no counterfeit bills and apprehending no counterfeiters or presses, made him exaggerate his quarry as "*the worst nest of counterfeiters in the United States.*" He was also confused by Ring input which made him think citizens were afraid to give evidence against the "gang" (instead of against the Ring), and which accused Lincoln County Sheriff George Kimbrell as being in cahoots with Billy. Also, soft and miserable Wild was further curtailing his activities because of cold weather, leaving himself open to more Ring control.

All these variables would add up to his solution: the invention of "the gigantic Kid gang."]

For October 7, 1880, from Fort Stanton, Wild reported Ira Leonard's apparent attempt to also educate him on Ring frauds - here land grants - possibly as lead-in to explaining Billy's freedom fighting role. Wild was uninterested in the big picture, and Leonard did not pursue it. Instead, he informed Wild about counterfeiters - Dan Dedrick, W.H. West, Billy Wilson, and Thomas Cooper - as a "gang." But he carelessly did not exclude Billy, leaving Wild open to Ringite's inclusion of Billy in it.

Wild's report for October 8, 1880, from Fort Stanton, made clear that Catron's brother-in-law, Edgar Walz, had been in Wild's first meeting with U.S. Attorney Barnes. Walz was now acting as Wild's minder (probably with James Dolan) by setting up "informers." One was a William Delaney. Wild wrote: *"Post Master and post trader here [with Will Dowlin], and he believes there is just such a gang working the frontier ...* **He also thinks Antrom alias Billy Bonney to be one of the gang**.*"* Demonstrated is a ricochet technique of Ringite cronies to trick Wild - with Delaney and Dowlin in with Walz and Dolan. Likely aware of a new pardon promise, they were linking Billy to the "gang" to end Wild's plan.

Reporting for October 9, 1880, still at Fort Stanton, in his letter to Ringite U.S. Attorney Sidney Barnes - recopied in his report - Wild revealed his new pardon bargain for Billy. He also revealed that Ira Leonard had given information about the counterfeiters in White Oaks and at Dan Dedrick's ranch - likely obtained by Leonard from Billy to advertise Billy's value to justify the new pardon bargain. In addition, Billy wrote himself. Wild stated: *"I have recently seen a letter written by him [Billy] in which he expresses himself as being tired of dodging the officers &c. The letter has been answered and the chances are that I will meet him."* But Wild added derogatory Ringite input about Billy, and located him at Fort Sumner, making clear that well-meaning but slow-witted Leonard, had failed to counteract Ring sabotage. So Wild was influenced against Billy, and informed the Ring, via Barnes, about Billy's new pardon possibility with his testifying (the last thing Ringites wanted to hear after Billy's Frank Warner Angel Deposition on their murdering Tunstall; testimony against James Dolan himself, and Billy Campbell and Jessie Evans for murdering Huston Chapman; and testimony against commander N.A. M. Dudley for treason). Wild wrote:

The following is a copy of a letter written to U.S. Attorney Barnes this day: Fort Stanton NM Oct 9th 1880

Hon Sidney N Barnes
    U.S. Attorney Santa Fe N.M. –

Dear Sir.
    Since I wrote you last Judge Leonard and the Clerk of Court have been to White Oaks, and on their return inform me that West with whom Cooper and Wilson have been making their headquarters at White Oaks left there around the 24th of September to go to Deadwood to look after a drove of cattle supposed to have been stolen by the clan.
    William Wilson is reported to be at Bosque Grande at Dedrick's ranch. Dedrick is reported as being one of the leaders of the clan, and partners with West in the Corral at White Oaks.

[AUTHOR'S NOTE: Wild is on the right track for counterfeiting, likely getting the information from Ira Leonard via Billy.]

    William Antrom alias Billy Kid is at Fort Sumner and is a member of the clan. I have recently seen a letter written by him in which he expresses himself as being tired of challenging the officers. The letter has been answered and the chances are that I will meet with him under circumstances which may bring about good results the particulars of which I will communicate should they be worthy of mention ...
    While I am waiting for the necessary papers to arrest Wilson and Cooper I am working to catch other fish in my net, and if able to use Antrom alias Billy Kid on reasonable terms with the party referred to as being willing to give information for a consideration I am satisfied full fifty arrests will follow.

[AUTHOR'S NOTE: Leonard's careless strategy for a meeting, left Billy open to capture; which Wild's revelation to Barnes now ensured. And Wild had inflated the "gang" to 50 strong!]

                            Respectfully Yours
                              Azariah F. Wild

At 2 o'clock P.M. I received through the mail a letter from Ira E. Leonard Esq. of Lincoln dated Oct 9th giving information relative to a meeting of 14 of the clan at [Beaver] Smith's Saloon at Fort Sumner ... I wrote out a copy of this letter and forwarded it to U.S. Attorney Barnes ... I will respond to Judge Leonards request and go to Lincoln Monday A.M. [October 11, 1880].

[AUTHOR'S NOTE: Leonard's eagerness to help made Wild connect a "gang" to Fort Sumner, where he also located Billy.]

On October 10, 1880, Wild reported key information about real counterfeiters: Ira Leonard had informed him that W.H. West and William Wilson's headquarters was White Oaks. And Wilson was also reported to be at the Bosque Grande ranch of the Dedricks. Wild wrote: "*Dedrick is reported as being one of the leaders of the clan [gang], and partners with West in the coral [sic] at White Oaks.*" So by October 10th, Wild had correctly localized counterfeiting to White Oaks and Bosque Grande: "*William Wilson is reported to be at Bosque Grande at Dedricks ranch.* ***Dedrick is reported as being one of the leaders of the clan [gang], and partners with [W.H.] West in the coral [sic] at White Oaks.***" But Wild never did the follow-up investigation.

Reporting for October 11, 1880, Wild wrote from Lincoln requesting from Barnes arrest warrants for Regulators. So Ringite input had scuttled Leonard's pardon plan: Wild intended to arrest Billy, Bowdre, Scurlock, and O'Folliard. To Barnes, Wild wrote: "*It may be well to send down warrants for the other parties who stand indicted in U.S. Court [by T.B. Catron as No. 411], and who are making Fort Sumner their headquarters.*"

For October 14, 1880, still in Lincoln, Wild demonstrated that he had been manipulated to merge counterfeiters with Billy's group in Fort Sumner. He wrote: "*William Wilson is at present with eighteen other desperados at Fort Sumner one hundred and sixty miles from here, and 125 miles from Las Vegas. He has with him three men who were indicted in the U.S. Court.* ***They are a terror to the whole country*** *... I think I will have trouble in making the arrests.*"

Since October 6, 1880, Billy's pardon chance awaited the Wild meeting. But Billy was wary, having experienced the treacherous murders of John Tunstall, Dick Brewer, Frank MacNab, Alexander McSween, Harvey Morris, Francisco Zamora, Vincente Romero, and Huston Chapman; and near assassination of Ira Leonard. So he robbed the mail-coach between Fort Sumner and Sunnyside on October 16, 1880 to check Wild's reports. With him was Billy Wilson, later indicted for that mail theft. Learning of the arrest plan by reading Wild's October 11th report about arresting those who "*were indicted in the U.S. Court*" and in Fort Sumner. Billy recognized the trap, and backed out of the testifying offer.

And Wild, having accomplished nothing, now needed "the Kid" to fake his own outlaw myth to feign action.

WILD'S IMAGINARY OUTLAW GANG

Wild was unaware of Billy's mail theft for four days. Reporting on October 15, 1880, still from Lincoln, he gave inadvertent evidence of Catron as his mission's puppeteer. Writing a garbled rendition of Tom Cooper's helping John Chisum round up rustled cattle, Wild stopped calling the Carrizozo ranch Edgar Walz's, and correctly called it *"Catron's ranch."* Telling, is Wild's familiarity by omitting the full name, as required. And he even knew that Chisum's rustled cattle were at *"Catron's ranch!"* He wrote: *"I have received reliable information that Tom Cooper was in White Oaks Thursday morning and left to go to Catron's ranch ten miles distant to assist John Chisum 'round up' his cattle."*

[AUTHOR'S NOTE: Befuddled Wild apparently misunderstood the reference to Ring-rustled Chisum cattle, which were kept at Catron's Carrizozo Ranch and his Pecos Cow Camp to meet Fort Stanton and Mescalero Reservation beef contracts. This information may have further confused Wild about a link of Billy's rustling to counterfeiters and rustling.]

Reporting for October 16, 1880, still in Lincoln, Wild blamed his inactivity on awaiting arrest warrants, and on lawmen not arresting men with federal indictments (like Billy). Ringite input is evident in his fictions: He reported a big gang in Fort Sumner; Lincoln County Sheriff George Kimbrell as playing cards with Billy; and Catron's brother-in-law, Edgar Walz, offering him his employee as a "witness" about the gang. Also, Wild, was getting paranoid in his isolated situation, stating: *"I am led to believe that many people here mistrust my business."* He wrote:

These men (outlaws) have centered at and make Fort Sumner their headquarters, and at the present time there are about eighteen notorious characters there who are engaged in stealing stock, passing counterfeit money, and robbing the mails all of which they do with impunity and as I am told in open daylight.

There are four of the men who I number amongst the eighteen who are indicted in the U.S. Court (one for murdering the Indian Agent) *[Billy with garbled Blazer's Mill killing of "Buckshot" Roberts]* ***and for whom warrants are out for and no attempt has been made to arrest them although I am reliably informed he*** *[Billy]* ***comes into the towns nearby and plays cards with the Sheriff of this county***

[George Kimbrell]. I have endeavored to get warrants of arrest from the territorial courts for these parties but find the witnesses unwilling to appear. I also find that should the arrests be made that the lives of the court officers would be in danger ... To place them in jail we could not do as we have none ...

[AUTHOR'S NOTE: Garrett had to use Texans to hunt Billy.]

I am led to believe that many people here mistrust my business ... I have traced up another $100 – note and trace it back to William Wilson ... I have not yet seen the note ...

In a recent report I spoke of a man who claimed he could give valuable information who was in the employ of E.A. Waltz [Walz]. I have just received a note from Walz [about that].

Wild's report for October 17, 1880, from Lincoln, focused on random "outlaws" and Regulators, whose histories he garbled:

As I have learned the names of several of the outlaws now congregated at and near Fort Sumner I will give them with their history so far as I have it which is about as follows:

Charles Bowdre: Hails from Va. Indicted by the U.S. Grand Jury in 3rd Dist. of this Territory for murder.

William Antrom alias Billie Bonnie alias "Billie Kid": Indicted in 3rd District of U.S. Court for the murder of the Indian Agent. Comes from Kansas here.

Dr Joseph G. Scurlock [Josiah "Doc" Scurlock]: Indicted for same offense. He claims Georgia as his native place. He is indicted for murder in 3rd Dist. U.S. Court. He killed one man each in Louisiana and Texas ...

James French: From Texas. Indicted in U.S. Court for murdering Maj Brady Sheriff of Lincoln County ...

There are many more men connected with this gang whose names I have not learned but are making Fort Sumner and vicinity their headquarters.

Wild's report for October 18, 1880, still from Lincoln, documented contact with Edgar Walz about his witness employee, a James DeVours, who, refused to *"make any written proposition"* but will *"tell you all he knows about the gang of counterfeiters."* DeVours, supposedly a ranch hand, was in the long Ring tradition of fake testifiers, adding, according to Walz, that he would *"leave it to your Chief to say what he shall receive [be paid] provided that his name can be kept secret."* So this supposed ranch hand knew about the Secret Service "Chief!" DeVours claimed, according to Walz, that *"their presses and plates are in this county ... [and] they have near $200,000 struck ... [T]here are a large number of persons engaged in passing [the counterfeit bills].* Wild added officiously: *"I do not fully credit his story but I think enough of it to probe it to the bottom."*

[AUTHOR'S NOTE: Wild made no follow-up on the presses.]

But Wild's Ring minders diverted him. For his report completed on October 18th in Lincoln, under the influence of Dolan and Walz, he listed *"outlaws"* [past Regulators] indicted federally by Catron for the "Buckshot" Roberts killing [which Wild garbled as *"the Indian Agent"*], and now based in Fort Sumner. And Wild turned from real counterfeiters in White Oaks and Dan Dedrick's Bosque Grande ranch with possible plates, to focus on *"Charles Bowdre ... Billie Kid ... Dr. Joseph G. Scurlock ...Henry Brown ... Thomas O'Folliard [and] James French."* Adding Billy Wilson, he called them a rustling-counterfeiting gang; and applied the unlimited lethality permitted by the Secret Service.

For his report for October 20, 1880, still in Lincoln, Wild finally admitted to Chief Brooks Billy's October 16th mail theft. He muffled that fiasco by adding mail theft to his fabricated gang's crimes, and claiming need of a posse to seize them in Fort Sumner:

In this mail I had several reports which if taken and read as they must have been as both mail pouches were cut open and the contents scattered about the ground. If this is as I believe it must be the plans of our capture and my mission here is as well known to them as it is to myself.

I have respectfully notified the U.S. Attorney [Sidney Barnes] of this gang of men, and of their headquarters being at Fort Sumner. I have also asked for warrants to arrest these men and for Commissions for such men as are willing to assist me in the making of the arrests ...

I have organized secretly a "Posse Comitatus" of thirty men here to go and assist me in making these arrests. Not only those who are wanted for murder & robbing the U.S. mail and are indicted in the U.S. Courts ...

So far as having arrests made by the Territorial officers I have explained the many difficulties. **The Sheriff of this county**

[George Kimbrell] has since he had the warrants in his possession for their arrest for murder under the hand of the Territory played cards and drank with him [Billy] repeatedly ...

The parties Kid, Wilson, O'Follier [O'Folliard] and Picket who are undoubtedly the ones who robbed the mail on the 17th [sic – 16th] are out at a ranch twelve miles from Fort Sumner. Tom Cooper and Dedrick are at White Oaks, and can be taken at any time unless my reports taken from the mail frighten them away.

[AUTHOR'S NOTE: Billy is now listed first, as Wild lumps Regulators with Dan Dedrick's few counterfeiters]

For October 22, 1880, still in Lincoln, Wild now accepted any Ringite input to inflate his *"Wilson and Kid gang,"* and attributed to it any rustling in the Territory. He wrote:

Wilson and his gang have within the past four days stolen sixty-eight head of cattle from a man named Ellis – 400 head from another party and seven horses from John Chisum ...

The man who was driving the mail [Fred Weston] back at the time it was robbed says (so I am informed by the mail carrier who arrived at this post [Fort Stanton] this morning) recognized several of the gang as being the Wilson and Kid gang who done the robbing of the mail on the night of the 16th inst.

I am informed that the Sheriff of San Miguel County [including Fort Sumner] went to their headquarters near Fort Sumner to arrest some one of the gang and was repulsed and left without making arrests.

For October 27, 1880, still in Lincoln, Wild included a copy of his response letter to Edgar Walz's "ranch hand witness," James DeVours - who had written with suspiciously legalese sounding like Catron - to confirm payment for information.

For October 28, 1880, still in Lincoln, Wild was back on track with local counterfeiters; reporting: **"*I am perfectly confident that <u>there is a counterfeit gang here who are making counterfeit $100- and $50- notes</u> as I am of anything that I do not know absolutely certain, and that I have not seen with my own eyes.*"** And he correctly named the counterfeiters: '*The leading man of this gang is W.H. West ... He left here before I came ... and is now in Topeka Kansas. He is one of the proprietors of a coral [sic] or stable at White Oaks.*

He has as partners several brothers named Dedrick who own a ranch near Fort Sumner. <u>It is at this ranch that it is believed the plates and tools are at the present time.</u>"

[AUTHOR'S NOTE: Wild never investigated Dedrick's ranch for the plates and press.]

But for that October 28th, Wild also inflated his imaginary gang to a *"force,"* writing:

The <u>force</u> of desperados now at Fort Sumner the headquarters of the gang numbers <u>twenty six.</u> They openly say that they number sixty two in Lincoln County and defy the authorities.

Captain Conrad now commanding at Fort Stanton said to me "You might as well go. You never will be able to make the arrests. You have not, and in my judgment cannot get a sufficient force to handle the men you have to contend with."

[AUTHOR'S NOTE: Here gullible Wild reveals himself also being fed Ringite information by colluding Fort Stanton officers. It should be recalled that Ringite Commander N.A.M Dudley had marched on Lincoln from there, and his Ring-beholden Court of Inquiry (with his representation by T.B. Catron's law firm member) had occurred there.]

I replied I believed I would but at the same time was in doubt.

I especially call your attention to the location: **All the outlaws or nearly all have been driven out of Texas and Arizona, and concentrated at Fort Sumner. They have two ranches. One seventy five miles the other twelve miles from Fort Sumner. They have a band of their men out stealing horses, cattle, robbing mails ... whilst the balance of their force remain at the ranch guarding stock they have stolen ...**

[AUTHOR'S NOTE: This shows that Wild has fused Dan Dedrick's counterfeiting to Billy's petty rustling and any other Territorial rustling – adding himself to the Ring's and Wallace's outlaw myth-making!]

This is a case that requires time to work but I candidly believe I can work it successfully by taking time. If I had a good man with me it would be of great service.

The leading man of the gang is W.H. West ... He is one of the proprietors of a coral or stable at White Oaks. He has as partners several brothers named Dedrick [Dan, Mose, Sam] who own a ranch near Fort Sumner. It is at this ranch that it is believed the plates and tools &c are at the present time.

I am informed this day by Judge Leonard that a lady passenger who was along at the time the stage was robbed near Fort Sumner that she recognized No. 80 and William Antrom alias "Billy Bony" as two of the robbers who robbed her and the mails.

By his October 31, 1880 report, still from Lincoln, Wild hysterically decided he was in another Lincoln County War [with his Ringite input making that an outlaw insurrection]! Additionally, he revealed his intent and power to "*arrest or kill the whole business.*" Noteworthy, however, is that he never made clear how he thought Billy connected to counterfeiting, or how rustling connected to counterfeiting. He wrote:

If things are not looked to [by arrests] ... **soon it will end in another "Lincoln County War."** *I have on two occasions stopped a disturbance between the stockmen and the outlaws by asking them to delay until I could get warrants for my parties when we would take the eleven warrants now here and* **arrest or kill the whole business***. They now say as soon as the election is over they are going to delay no longer.*

[AUTHOR'S NOTE: Revealed is that Wild was exaggerating the situation into a "Lincoln County War," and was agitating White Oaks miners (here called "stockmen") about "outlaws."]

ADDING PAT GARRETT

The person picked by the Ring to kill Billy Bonney with guise of legality was Patrick Floyd Garrett: a 30 year old, marginally employed, ex-buffalo hunter living in Fort Sumner. To replace anti-Ring Sheriff, George Kimbrell, Garrett was advertised as a law-and-order candidate to White Oaks men, misled by Azariah Wild's hunt for a rustling and counterfeiting gang headed by Billy Bonney and Billy Wilson.

Garrett was elected Sheriff on November 2, 1880. Wild immediately made him a Deputy U.S. Marshall to add Territorial jurisdiction, and also forced Sheriff Kimbrell to deputize him.

Garrett likely knew that the "Kid gang" was a fabrication. He had been acquainted with Billy in Fort Sumner since 1878 when he came off the buffalo range. But he knew that killing Billy was a life-changing chance; and he took it.

WITCH-HUNTING BILLY BONNEY

After enlisting Pat Garrett, for November 4, 1880, duped Wild reported his intent to attack Fort Sumner to capture William Wilson and "*William Antrom [sic] alias 'Billy Bony' [sic] alias 'Billy Kid'* "as gang leaders.. He stated: "*I am now engaged in making preparations to get fifty men together to go to Fort Sumner and arrest this gang of men.*"

Reporting for November 6, 1880, still in Lincoln, Wild was in a paranoid tizzy about his swelling "gang," with its "leaders": "*William Wilson and ... 'Billy Kid.'* " And Ringite District Judge Warren Bristol happily issued arrest warrants. Wild wrote:

From every indication there is no scare amongst this gang or they are calculating to make a stand at Fort Sumner and fight. They are known to be twenty nine in number ...

Judge Bristol is now here and in an interview with him yesterday he said he would issue warrants for parties who have been engaged in violating the United States law ...

I will soon be in readiness to go to Fort Sumner after certain parties ... The parties who robbed the mail or who were the leaders of it was William Wilson and **William Antrom alias "Billy Bony" alias "Billy Kid."**

Reporting for November 10, 1880, still in Lincoln, Wild had met with Garrett "*to make a raid on Fort Sumner to arrest the counterfeiters.*" Wild, declared the "gang" "*the worst (organization) gang of men that this country has;*" writing:

[W]e have organized a force in the "Pan Handle" (Texas) to cooperate with us in this raid with a aim of acquiring a huge number of these outfits who are from that state. By doing this there will be but little chance of their escaping and if captured ***will probably break up the worst (organization) gang of men that this country has. John Kinney has qualified as Deputy U.S. Marshal*** *so I have a man to represent the U.S. Marshal [Garrett] while the other parties will act as a 'Posse Comitatus.' "*

[AUTHOR'S NOTE: Still relying on Ringites, Wild appointed as a Deputy U.S. Marshal outlaw, John Kinney: Ringite rustler and San Patricio massacre perpetrator with Sheriff Peppin, and posseman in the Lincoln County War Battle! This added to making Seven Rivers rustler Robert Olinger a Deputy U.S.

Marshal, as he reported on October 13, 1880. Even Lew Wallace had called Olinger *"amongst the most bloody of the "Bandits of the Pecos"* in a September 15, 1879 letter to Carl Schurz.]

For November 14, 1880, still in Lincoln, Wild described using a White Oaks man, James Bell, *"to make a deal with [a counterfeiter] if possible."* [Bell would be a posseman involved in killing Jim Carlyle in friendly fire at Greathouse's ranch, then blaming Billy. He was later deputized by Pat Garrett as Billy's pre-hanging guard, and was killed by Billy in his April 28, 1881 jailbreak.]

For November 18th and 20th, 1880, still in Lincoln, Wild reported hiring Garrett's friend, Barney Mason, Peter Maxwell's Fort Sumner foreman, to spy there. Then spying Mason reported an important real counterfeiting discovery: Dan Dedrick planned to money-launder $30,000 in counterfeit bills by buying cattle in Mexico with it, then reselling them for good money. Wild wrote:

It appears from the statements of Garrett and Mason that he (Mason) is an experienced stockman and is now and has been for some time past in the employ of a man named Maxwell who resides at Fort Sumner. He (Mason) states that a few days ago one Daniel Dedrick who resides at Bosque Grande, and who has an interest with his brother Samuel Dedrick & West in a livery stable at White Oaks came to him and proposed [to hire him to take $30,000 counterfeit money to Texas, buy cattle there, take them to a place near Mexico to Dedrick and West, then leave the country] ...

[And] Mason states that William Wilson boards at his house when at Fort Sumner ...

[And Mason states] [t]hat William Wilson and Billy Kid left about the 15th inst with sixty head of stolen horses and went down the Canadian River to be gone two or three weeks. That on their return they would probably return to his house when he would turn them over to Patrick F. Garrett Deputy U.S. Marshall and Sheriff.

[AUTHOR'S NOTE: Manipulated by colluding Garrett and Mason, Wild mingled Billy's petty rustling with a concocted Wilson-Kid gang to feign accomplishment for his failed mission. And, once again, he failed to follow-up a real counterfeiting lead: the Dedrick money-laundering scheme or source of the $30,000.]

In his report for November 27, 1880, Wild wrote that W.H. West and Dan Dedrick told Mason that they were holding off the deal until the *"excitement and trouble"* ended - meaning that loose-lipped Wild had revealed is mission to too many people, and they were warned. So James DeVours had *"left the country for safety,"* as had W.H. West. And Dan Dedrick moved permanently to California. And Wild had made no attempt to apprehend them.

COYOTE SPRING AND GREATHOUSE AMBUSHES

Having elected Pat Garrett as Sheriff by their majority voting to eliminate "the Kid gang," White Oaks men were primed for action; though Billy was unaware and still bringing rustled horses to the Dedrick's livery there. The residents formed the White Oaks posse, under Deputy Sheriff Will Hudgens, to capture him.

On November 22, 1880, they ambushed Billy and his companions near White Oaks at their Coyote Spring campsite; but firing wildly, they merely killed two of their quarry's horses.

Billy's group made it to "Whiskey Jim" Greathouse's ranch, about 40 miles to the north. There, at November 28, 1880's dawn, the posse attacked them again. When Billy offered to negotiate, they sent in Jim Carlyle. But Carlyle panicked, fleeing through a window, and being killed in friendly fire when mistaken for Billy. The posse then retreated. But Billy finally realized his danger.

From Pat Garrett's Roswell home, Azariah Wild reported his fables. For November 23, 1880, he related to Chief Brooks the Coyote Spring ambush. His "Billy Kid" was now leader of the *"Kid force,"* magnified to outnumber White Oaks men, with exaggerated casualties of horses. He wrote: *"The [Deputy] Sheriff at White Oaks with his Posse went out ... and attempted to arrest Billy Kid, William Wilson and others on Monday the 22nd instant and have return to town empty handed. **Kid force out numbered that of the Sheriffs**. Each party had several horses killed ... There is talk of "Judge Lynch" trying them at last account."*

Wrongly dating as November 26th, still at Garrett's house, very agitated Wild reported the Greathouse ranch attack: *"Information has just reached me through a reliable source that Billy Kid had been driven out of the Canadian River country and was now at Greathouse's ranch with twenty five armed men and a bunch of stolen horses ...The citizens went out to capture them but they made their escape after about forty shots were exchanged."*

Reporting for November 26, 1880, still at Garrett's house, Wild invented a near-war, and described Garrett's posse; implying Garrett's lying about the "Kid gang" as being Texas rustlers to get the Panhandle Cattleman's Association involved. Wild wrote:

Information has reached me here this day that William Wilson with about twenty five others are near White Oaks, and that every man able to bear arms at that place is under arms to protect the place ... Barney Mason has not yet returned [from making his counterfeit money deal with Dan Dedrick]. We would start from here (Roswell) with a force only nearly every horse in this section of the country is sick at present with distemper.

Deputy U.S. Marshal [Frank] Stewart from Texas [actually a Panhandle Cattleman's Association detective] is reported to be at Puerta de Luna with 40 men and after several of the men who are in this gang for crimes committed in Texas. I shall communicate with him soon as I can get a reliable man to send, and then press the "Rustlers" from White Oaks back into Fort Sumner and then surround the place with forces from above and below.

Wild reported for November 27, 1880, still at Garrett's Roswell home, and by then in paranoid terror of his imaginary gang; though his sole fact was that his spy, Barney Mason, had related that Dan Dedrick had backed out of the cattle-for-counterfeit-money deal. And Mason had given Dedrick's counterfeiting associates as only William Wilson, W.H. West, and Tom Cooper. Apparently Mason, like Garrett, was just duping Wild for personal profit, knowing that no "gang" existed. Wild wrote: *"I will respectfully state that I am very impatient to get away from here but the shape things have taken I feel it my duty to remain ... At the present time I am entirely cut off from reaching the rail road by these outlaws and will have to employ a guard unless I remain until arrests are made and go along to Santa Fe with them."*

For November 28, 1880, Wild wrote more misinformation from Garrett's Roswell house, stating that *"the Kid with seventeen men were [at the Greathouse ranch]."*

For November 29, 1880, Wild, still at Garrett's house, wrote that he was setting out with *"an armed and mounted force of twenty men under command of Deputy U.S. Marshals Olinger and Garrett."* With feverish paranoia, he added certainty that *"there will be blood shed."* He wrote: *"We have at the present time between one and two hundred armed men out scouting for this gang of outlaws and counterfeiters ... It is believed that there will be blood shed when ever our men come up with the main gang if ever we are able to do so."*

For November 30, 1880, still at Garrett's house, Wild added more to the Greathouse ambush, with usual fabrications; writing:

"Information has reached me this day that William Wilson et al of their gang numbering 17 were run into Greathouses Ranch. That the house was surrounded by a Deputy Sheriff [Will Hudgens] and a posse numbering in all 13. One of the posse named Carlisle [Jim Carlyle] ... was one of the leaders ... and after a little talk with the parties on the inside of the house he was induced to go in. Soon as he was inside of the house he was murdered. Soon after Carlisle was murdered William Wilson and his gang made a rush out of the house, and made their escape under cover of the night."

For December 1, 1880, Wild reported that he had stayed in Roswell, but Garrett had left *"with a Posse to go to Fort Sumner."*

Writing for December 2, 1880, Wild hysterically decided that the gang had come to Roswell after him! He wrote: *" Several of W$^{\underline{m}}$ Wilson gang of men have been seen near this place this day. It is feared trouble is brewing near at this place and I am now writing my report in the post office of this place which is filled with men arrived to resist any attack that may be made ... I am unable to get out of this place with safety."*

On December 3, 1880, Wild, still in Garrett's house, reported ludicrously that Garrett *"had divided his force"* and was apparently arresting random people - like ones in *"a cave some twenty miles from Fort Sumner."* Lacking any real arrests - or even a real gang - Wild whined to his Chief: *"There has been cold weather and snow since the 20th of September to say nothing of being away from my family and almost severed from civilization. I have felt it my duty to do as I have and hope you will consider this and not place the blame of the delay on me."* Wild added that his work was appreciated locally, unaware that the appreciation was by the Ring, now poised to kill Billy Bonney.

For December 5, 1880, Wild, still in Garrett's house, reported his arrests of random murderers. For Chief Brooks, Wild rationalized failure as: *"The outlaws have divided up and have men on every road leading from Lincoln County to the Rail Road. You need not feel any anxiety as to my getting out of here safe as there are good citizens enough to protect me when I start."*

For December 7, 1880, Wild, still in Garrett's house, tracked his phantom and migratory gang to Lincoln. *"They left going in the direction of the Capitan Mountains where it is believed their main force is."*

For December 9, 1880, he wrote that Garrett had captured *"a large number of stolen horses and cattle."* This was his distortion of what Billy reported to Wallace on December 12th: that two of his mules had been robbed by Garrett from the Fort Sumner area ranch of a Thomas Yerby. Garrett, unlike Wild, knew his job was to hunt just one man.

For the same December 9th, still in Garrett's house, flagrantly paranoid Wild reported: *"I am very anxious to get away from here ... [T]he "rustlers" a (name given to Wilson and his band) have men on two out of three roads ... I am going to leave here for headquarters first occasion that presents itself to get away with safety.* " By December 23, 1880, Wild was departing New Mexico Territory, and reporting from Santa Fe en route to New Orleans.

In his report for December 24, 1880, Wild wrote murderously: *"I have this day received information of an almost positive nature that Deputy U.S. Marshal P.F. Garrett had the Kid and Wilson at his mercy and that **he will either kill or arrest them**."* So, by empowering Garrett with Texan posses, Wild had achieved killings of Tom O'Folliard, Charlie Bowdre; and, in a little over six and a half months, would indirectly ensure Billy Bonney's death.

So, in 3 months and 13 days from case assignment to departure from New Mexico Territory, Azariah Wild had collected a few counterfeit bills passed by Billy Wilson, and had captured no real counterfeiters. But, without realizing it, he had succeeded in his Ring mission by enlisting a lawman, Pat Garrett, to track Billy Bonney, and give a gloss of legitimacy to intended murder. And he had inadvertently added himself to the long list of the Santa Fe Ring's hired killers of opponents.

AFTERMATH OF AZARIAH WILD

A year after leaving New Mexico Territory, and with input from Chief James Brooks, Wild finally was informed of the link of his New Mexico Territory investigation to counterfeiter, William Brockway. It was through Brockway's bill distributor, Frank Doyle, a source of bills in New Mexico Territory, as well as bills found in his summer of 1880 Sherman, Texas, investigation.

From New Orleans, for October 16, 1881, Wild reported to Brooks: *"I have the honor to acknowledge the receipt of your letter of the 13th instant in which you state that James B. Doyle the notorious counterfeiter has a brother who has just returned home to Bradford Ill from Santa Fe, Las Vegas and White Oaks New Mexico. I shall without delay make the necessary inquiries as directed."* Defensively, Wild cited his Sherman investigation of counterfeiter, Walter B. Greenham, who had committed suicide, but had met with a "stranger" named "Kibby," who then went to Kansas City (as Wild had reported on June 11, 1880); and whom he now saw as James Doyle's brother, Frank Doyle. Wild wrote:

> "*[Being in Texas] was at a time when I had not the least idea of going to New Mexico. On or soon after my arrival in New Mexico* **I learned [W.H.] West of White Oaks ... whose place was the headquarters of William Wilson, Tom Cooper and William Antrom, alias "Billy the Kid"** *had gone to Kansas and Colorado on business and that on his return he brought back with him to White Oaks a man who claimed to hail from New York and that his name was* Duncan. *From the best description I could get at the time, this man answered the description well enough to have been the same man who called himself Kibby at Sherman Texas. It was after West returned to White Oaks in company with this man that an effort was made to employ Barney Mason to go into Texas with $30,000 counterfeit money to purchase cattle &c. ... Soon as I get a description or photograph of [Frank] Doyle I will have no trouble in tracing him in New Mexico provided he is known there and is the man who accompanied West back from Kansas to White Oaks.*"

Defensive about his erroneously focused investigation, Wild had kept Billy in his counterfeiters' list as self-justification. In fact, he had collected no evidence implicating Billy as a counterfeiter. And, in reality, from Texas to New Mexico Territory, Wild had merely encountered William Brockway's local counterfeit bill distribution sites to pushers like Walter Greenham, W.H. West, and Dan Dedrick. None of this connected to Billy or the other Regulators.

And, as will be seen, none of it even connected to Billy Wilson - the only person who ended up indicted and prosecuted for the counterfeiting, since there was no actual gang. Wilson was eventually exonerated for his counterfeiting sentence and got a presidential pardon in 1896. But Billy was by then dead, as intended, for 15 years.

Tellingly, however, Azariah Wild's obvious incompetence received no Secret service criticism. The reason was that Chief Brooks had purposefully withheld the Brockway gang information that could have put Wild on the right track. Wild had been the right man for his peculiar job, and he had gotten it done as intended.

WILLIAM BROCKWAY
AND HIS COUNTERFEITING GANG

William E. "Long Bill" Brockway alias Edward W. Spencer, who died in 1920 at 97, was the most famous bill counterfeiter ("coneyman") of the second half of the 1800's, starting before the Civil War; and already featured as the master in George P. Burnham's *American Counterfeiters* in 1875. Working from Brooklyn, New York, he was an engraver trained in electrotyping transfer of images to metal plates. He worked with another engraver named Charles H. Smith. His main distributor ("shover of the queer") was Illinois-based James Brace Doyle. With Doyle's brother, Frank Doyle, brother-in-law, Nathan B. "Nate" Foster, and a John W. Hays, this gang provided near-perfect counterfeit bills around the country to local pushers.

The March, 1882 *Government Counterfeiter Detector*, featuring pusher, James Doyle, in "The Boss of the Boodle and King of 'Outside Men,'" hypothesized that Brockway might have put into "circulation all the counterfeits of the National Bank Hundreds, which for several years have bothered the experts," with some even "sent to Europe."

By October 21, 1880, Secret Service Operatives Andrew L. Drummond, focusing on Brockway and Charles Smith, and Wallace W. Hall, tracking James Brace Doyle, had achieved their arrests.

During Azariah Wild's New Mexico Territory investigation, that apprehension made the news, along with the outcome being Brockway's once again going unpunished. On November 25, 1880, Brockway turned over his plates in exchange for no jail time. This slick solution was reported in December 3, 1880's *New York Times* as "The Crimes of Brockway, Story of the Notorious Counterfeiter's Career, Clemency Extended to Him by the Government in 1867 – He Soon Resorts to His Former Life – What a Secret Service Officer Says." It stated: "The release of Brockway, the counterfeiter, on condition of his turning over to the Government all the plates and materials used by him, is only a repetition of similar clemency which was accorded him in 1867."

The *Government Counterfeiter Detector's* June 30, 1881 "Annual Report of the Secret Service Division of the United States Treasury Department" by Chief James J. Brooks, reported that Brockway had turned over "twenty-two finely executed counterfeit plates for printing United States bonds and state National bank notes, two expensive ruling machines, one press; $40,000 in counterfeits notes, much fiber paper and other property." Engraver Charles Smith likewise got immunity. With postponements, James Doyle started a 12 year sentence in 1882.

The gang's counterfeit $100 notes were listed in the *Secret Service Currency Reference Information: 1860's-1880's,* and John S. Dye's *Government Counterfeiter Detector* of February, 1882 as being made from skeleton plates, to which Smith added title plates for six banks: Merchants National Bank of New Bedford, Massachusetts; Second National Bank of Wilkes Barre, Pennsylvania; National Exchange Bank of Baltimore, Maryland; National Revere Bank of Boston, Massachusetts; Pittsfield National Bank of Pittsfield, Massachusetts; and Pittsburgh National Bank of Commerce, Pittsburgh, Pennsylvania.

On August 4, 1895, Brockway was rearrested for counterfeiting. Sentenced to 10 years, he was released early; and apparently continued to dabble in his criminal craft.

BROCKWAY'S PUSHERS

Brockway's main bill distributors, traveling from New York, to the mid-West and Southwest, were James and Frank Doyle, Nate Foster, John Hays and William H. West. They sold to locals, who passed bills or money-laundered them; as intended by the Dedricks by stock-buying.

To enrich themselves, the Doyles, Foster, and Hays purchased stores, a farm, saloons, and mines. **Despite their insertion in the Billy the Kid counterfeiting hoax, these distributors did not do Dedrick-style money-laundering with cattle; nor were they "cattle buyers" in Colorado, nor were they involved in rustling.**

Secret Service Operative Wallace Hall followed Brockway's main distributors. About the Doyle brothers, he reported for October 10, 1881 that they had been associated with Brockway since he and Charles Smith had visited them in Bradford, Illinois in 1875. Hall traced their bill-distributing travels. For October 10, 1881, he reported Frank Doyle, then in Bradford, had returned that July *"from a year absence in the south-west,"* with cited places as *"Las Vegas, Santa Fe and White Oaks New Mexico."* And Nate Foster, then in Blakely's Mills, Colorado, had been in *"Las Vegas and Santa Fe, New Mexico, also Colorado Springs, Colorado."*

About John Hays, Hall reported on February 24, 1881 that a "boodle" (bunch of counterfeit bills) was found in his Moundville, Missouri, farm's haystack. Hays also passed bills in Missouri; and, in 1880, fellow distributor, W.H. West, stayed at his farm and store. And James Doyle's wife, once he was apprehended, moved to Deer Trail, Colorado, where her father had a cattle ranch. **[Note that both Colorado and this ranch were misstated for the Billy the Kid counterfeiting hoax, to fake a cattle-buying-rustling-money-laundering site.]**

Hall's report for May 19, 1882 recorded their purchases. In about May of 1881, Nate Foster *"had a saloon in White Oaks New Mexico. That Hays Frank Doyle, and others ... were with him. Hays was engaged in mining ... in the vicinity of White Oaks, N.M. That Hays about a year ago [May, 1881] passed a cft hundred on a clothing merchant in Denver ... in payment of a clothing account of Nate Foster's."* And West passed the counterfeit hundreds in New Mexico (with real name William Budd). All were in Nevada, Missouri in 1880, before going to White Oaks. And Hall concluded that they had stored the bills in Hays's Moundville haystack.

For July 1, 1882, Hall traced James Doyle's wife's brother, Nate Foster, to Deer Trail, Colorado; thence to New York to get $20,000 in counterfeit $100 bills; with James Doyle, taking bills to Colorado and Frank Doyle. They passed some bills in Colorado. Then Frank Doyle, Nate Foster, and John Hays *"went to New Mexico and Texas where more of the notes were passed. Hays and some of the party later located in Nevada, Missouri. Eventually, however, again all went to New Mexico, and Texas, where they engaged in the saloon business, mining speculations, &c,&c."*

For October 7, 1882, Hall reported that *"young Doyle – James B's son – and Nathan Foster were in Colorado."* Thus, Brockway's "passers of the queer" were untouched, and now were in a new generation with "young Doyle."

As to the Brockway gang's bill distribution in New Mexico, from W.H. West in White Oaks, they went to the Dedricks; with Dan possibly also having plates and press at his Bosque Grande ranch. Their cattle-buying-money-laundering scheme was uncovered by Azariah Wild's spy, Barney Mason, and described in Wild's report completed on November 21, 1880. (See pages 340, 365, 370, 388-390 above and below) They apparently used local pushers for smaller quantities of bills: men identified by Wild in his report completed on November 28, 1880: *"[My spy, Mason] saw* **William Wilson** *on last Sunday night have a long talk with*

*[W.H.] West, [Dan] Dedrick & **[Tom] Cooper**. That it was agreed that Cooper was to go to El Paso and return by the 16th of December. That Cooper had just purchased a fine horse at San Marical for which he (Cooper) paid $150 ... That he (Mason) was given to understand the horse was paid for in counterfeit money."*

Azariah Wild unwittingly linked the local counterfeiters to Brockway's gang by identifying the banks on notes when describing a defect of printing press pin-holes in the paper. In his report for October 4, 1880, he listed them as the National Revere Bank of Boston, Massachusetts passed to William Dowlin, and the Merchants National Bank of New Bedford, paid to José Montaño. He also stated that a $100 bill passed by Wilson on August 5, 1880 to James Dolan was from the Merchants National Bank of New Bedford, Massachusetts. And he reported that Cooper passed to the clerk of Dowlin & Delaney a counterfeit National Revere Bank of Boston Massachusetts. For October 10, 1880, Wild reported that past Indian Agent, Frederick Godfroy, got a $100 counterfeit bill from Wilkes Barre Second National Bank of Wilkes Barre, Pennsylvania, which traced to its recipient: the banker husband of John Chisum's niece.

The big picture was that William Brockway's gang - James B. Doyle, Frank Doyle, Nate Foster, and John W. Hays – were reported as distributing counterfeit bills in Illinois, Missouri, Colorado, Texas, and New Mexico Territory. For New Mexico, the courier was William Budd, alias William H. West, whose partners, the Dedrick brothers, planned to launder bills by stock purchase and resale; and, in turn, used minor pushers, like Tom Cooper.

None of this involved Billy Bonney. But the outcome was that none of the real counterfeiters got significant punishment. And non-counterfeiter Billy got death.

CHAPTER 3
STEVE SEDERWALL'S COUNTERFEITING HOAX ARTICLES

A BACK-UP BY FELLOW "BILLY THE KID CASE" HOAXERS

Steve Sederwall first presented his "Billy the Kid's Bad Bucks" hoax in 2010 and 2015 articles fabricating a link between Brockway's counterfeiting and Billy Bonney's rustling as a national money-laundering scheme. Cited was U.S. Marshals Service Historian David Turk as participating with him.

In 2010, Sederwall was also forging Dr. Henry Lee reports for my open records litigation in the "Billy the Kid Case." On March 9, 2010, he had turned-over his first forged Lee floorboard report. On November 10, 2010, he gave me his forged Lee carpenter's bench report. At January 21, 2011's Evidentiary Hearing, he gave the Court a second forged Lee floorboard report as Exhibit F, and the forged Lee carpenter's bench report as Exhibit E.

And it was on July 16, 2010 that he presented to the *Ruidoso News* his "discovery" that Billy the Kid was actually a national-level counterfeiter. Since the hoax was expanded in 2018's *Cold Case Billy the Kid*, it is more extensively debunked there.

HOAXING ARTICLE: "COUNTERFEIT BANK NOTE REWRITES CHAPTER OF BILLY THE KID"\

On July 16, 2010, "Billy the Kid Case" hoax-backing, reporter, Julie Carter, published "Counterfeit Bank Note Rewrites Chapter of Billy the Kid" in the *Ruidoso News*. A $100 bank note was captioned: "**The front view of a counterfeit bank note passed in Lincoln County by Billy the Kid and his gang. William Brockway ... printed it from the plate the Secret Service recovered the day before Thanksgiving in 1880. The plate had been engraved by Charles Smith, a government employee whose job was engraving Federal currency plates. The note was located by the United States Secret Service in their vault in Washington, D.C., January 2010**." Added was Sederwall's helper: U.S. Marshals Service Historian David Turk. This was Sederwall's tale:

> In January of 2010, Sederwall called the Secret Service and spoke with Michael Sampson, of the public affairs office [sic – archivist].
>
> "I told him I was looking for evidence that they might have in their vault from a case in the 1880's," Sederwall said. "He politely laughed, but after telling him why I was looking, I gave him the dates [sic- of] the counterfeit that Wilson had passed had been recovered, the name of the bank, along with the serial numbers of both notes that we found documented in [Billy] Wilson's [counterfeiting] indictments.
>
> Sampson returned the call a day later with good news. "The notes were in a file with no paperwork," he said. Until now, no one had any idea what the notes were or why they were there." [So David Turk, being local, picked them up. And Sampson then helped them sort it all out "working the case backwards."]

HOAXING: The title of the article summarized the hoax, since it was a fabricated claim.

For this exposé, I called Secret Service archivist, Michael Sampson. He told me what actually happened. In 2010, Sederwall contacted him requesting counterfeit bills obtained by Azariah Wild in New Mexico Territory. Sampson told him <u>there were none in the files</u>. So Sederwall requested <u>any counterfeit bill from the period</u>. He was given a random bill. It had no documented connection in the Secret Service to Wild or to Billy Bonney; and it was not filed as a Brockway bill, though it is from a bank used in Brockway's plates. So Sederwall's claim about Brockway's engraver, Charles Smith, was irrelevant. But this fakery set the pattern of the entire hoax: faking links between William Brockway and Billy Bonney.

So Sederwall and David Turk built this counterfeiting hoax on lying that the bill they located connected to Azariah Wild's New Mexico investigation and to Billy Bonney, and that it represented evidence that Billy was a counterfeiter.

Sederwall next made-up that Wild found no plates in New Mexico, because there were 22 plates found for "three different Eastern banks;" which meant "organized crime ... much bigger than recorded by historians." So David Turk, like in his fake carpenter's bench authentication (see page 189 above), stated that the bills were made in New York, went to Chicago, "then branched out into Texas, Missouri, Colorado, New Mexico, and Mexico."

HOAXING: This fakes a link between the turned-over Brockway plates and Billy Bonney. And it hides that Wild had been informed by an employee named James DeVours at T.B. Catron's Carrizozo ranch that the plates were in the Territory, with Wild deciding they were at the Bosque Grande Ranch of counterfeiter, Dan Dedrick. But, diverted by his Ringite minders to pursue Billy Bonney, Wild never investigated the local plates.

Turk then made-up that the counterfeiters intended to "buy stolen cattle and use fake bills of sale to launder the money."

HOAXING: This garbles Wild's report from spy, Barney Mason, of Dan Dedrick's cattle-buying money-laundering plot. Rustling was not involved. But this hoax adds rustling for money-laundering to fake a link to Billy's rustling.

Next came disjointed claims. James Dolan, who reported getting counterfeit bills to the Secret Service, is called a counterfeiter himself, from an alleged August, 1880 letter to the Secret Service by a woman in Chicago. A non sequitor to 1878, claims the Secret Service was investigating counterfeiter William Brockway, and plate maker, Charles Smith. That leapt to: **"[The Secret Service] knew about the cattle theft operation run by the Kid and his gang used to launder some of the money."**

HOAXING: Dolan as a counterfeiter came from a misstating Operative Wallace W. Hall's report for August 24, 1880 about a Miss N.M. Ferguson of Chicago and her reporting a counterfeit bill involving New Mexico Territory merchant Will <u>Dowlin</u>, not James <u>Dolan</u>.
Made-up is that the Secret Service claimed Billy had a rustling-money-laundering gang. Wild's late 1880 investigation accused Billy of having a rustling gang, which he linked to local counterfeiters. That accusation, was repeated in John H. Koogler's *Las Vegas Morning Gazette* in his December 3, 1880 article titled "Desperadoe's

Stronghold, An Organized Gang Assisted by Nature and Defiantly Reckless, Who Terrorize the Country to the East of Us." It motivated Billy to write a letter of denial on December 12, 1880 to Governor Lew Wallace; stating: *"I noticed in the Las Vegas Gazette a piece which stated that, Billy "the" Kid, the name by which I am known in the Country was the captain of a Band of Outlaws who hold Forth at the Portales. There is no such Organization in Existence. So the Gentleman must have drawn very heavily on his Imagination."*

Next thrown in was that in November of 1880, the Secret Service caught Brockway, Charles Smith, and James Doyle; and found the 22 plates. **Sederwall stated: "Brockway provided answers to the Secret Service's questions, including how the bank notes were getting in to New Mexico and Colorado. Simply put, they were buying cattle from a group of cattle thieves in White Oaks, N.M.: Billy the Kid and his gang."** So Sederwall claimed his "investigation" proved the Brockway counterfeiting gang was arrested by the Secret Service before Garrett even pursued them. So, he claimed, Garrett deserved no credit.

HOAXING: Made-up is that Brockway did rustling-counterfeit-money-laundering. He printed and sold bills. It was the Dedricks' group that passed bills, and intended to buy cattle for money-laundering. Rustling played no part. Billy Bonney played no part.

Added is usual hoaxers' maligning of Garrett, by faking that capturing Brockway meant capturing his "gang" in New Mexico; and Garrett had not done that. But Garrett's mission was to capture Billy and his fellow Regulators. He did that. And he never claimed Billy was a counterfeiter.

Cited is a January 6, 1881 article of the Long Port, Indiana, *Long Port Journal* about Brockway's bills there. But Sederwall adds: "The information that enabled the Government officers to fix the handling of counterfeit money upon the Kid's gang came from a freighter named Smith. Soon afterward, while Smith was on his way from Las Vegas to Fort Sumner, with a load of freight, he was waylaid and murdered by some of the gang."

HOAXING: Murdered freighter Smith is a fable Sederwall lifted and expanded from fake news press. It is exposed in Sederwall's recycling of it in *Cold Case Billy the Kid*. (See pages 416-417 below)

The *Ruidoso News* article ended with Sederwall's blather about the carpenter's bench, the shot washstand, and Billy's not taking a "rifle" from dead Brady's body; adding that he was "shedding new light on the story of Billy the Kid," and was making a website titled www.billythekidcase.com.

BLOWING SMOKE: Sederwall was advertising Sederwall, the motive for this entire hoax. And his website was outrageously selling Case 2003-274's public documents, while he was hiding them in my open records litigation. That impropriety helped me win. The Judge stated in his May 15, 2014 "Findings of Fact": "In their June 21, 2007 "Memorandum" to Virden, Sullivan and Sederwall admitted to having Case 2003-274 records, but called them private property ... Furthermore, from 2010 to 2012, Sederwall offered Case 2003-274 records for sale on his own billythekidcase.com website."

HOAXING ARTICLE: "BILLY BONNEY'S BAD BUCKS"

Five years later, Sederwall expanded his counterfeiting fiction in fellow "Billy the Kid Case" hoaxer and editor, Bob Boze Bell's *True West* magazine of June, 2015, as "Billy Bonney's Bad Bucks: Did the Kid Travel the Counterfeit Trail?" For it, Sederwall proclaimed in his ongoing self-promotion: "With all we know about Billy the Kid, most do not know that he was part of a counterfeiting ring."

For illustration, oddly, was not the $100 bill used in Sederwall's 2010 *Ruidoso News* article, but a **$5.00 one** captioned: "Both sides of an actual counterfeit bill from the New Mexico ring. Courtesy of Steve Sederwall." **[To be noted is that Brockway printed $100 bills, and Azariah Wild located only $100 counterfeit bills in the Territory; further adding to the fakery that this $5 bill was connected to Billy Bonney, New Mexico Territory counterfeiters, or the Azariah Wild investigation there.]**

For this rerun, Sederwall faked additionally that Billy was in counterfeiting cahoots with Jesse James. **[Concealed was that the source was a possible 1879 sighting of Billy <u>eating a meal</u> with James in a Las Vegas, New Mexico, hotel. And James was not a counterfeiter.]**

Sederwall also made-up that Billy was in a cattle rustling-counterfeit money-laundering scheme with Brockway's pusher, John Hays. **[The fake reasoning was that Hays was in the Civil War, as was Jesse James; so that meant that Hays was connected to Billy via James. But Hays was not connected to James or to Billy. And James was no counterfeiter.]**

Then Sederwall claimed that Billy "had stolen cattle in the Panhandle for John Chisum's ranch, and the rancher had not paid him as promised. The Kid stole the cattle back." **[This fakery garbled Billy's claim that Chisum had not paid him and the Regulators promised wages in the Lincoln County War period, and may have rustled from him to settle the debt.]** As proof, Sederwall cited a Lane Cook, called Tom Folliard's [sic] cousin, as stealing Chisum's cattle to sell to Hays for counterfeit money, which Lane laundered in Kansas City, Missouri. **[This fakery was built on two separate lies: misstating old-timer Jim (Lane) Cook's 1936 book,** *Lane of the Llano's* **different tall tale (see pages 391-397 below); and fabricating Tom O'Folliard's name and genealogy (see pages 309-314 above), then connecting it to Jim Cook.]**

To get his hoax to New Mexico Territory, Sederwall made-up an elaborate fable with merchant, James Dolan, as a "cattleman" passing counterfeit bills in Tularosa in 1880, which brought in Secret Service Operative Azariah Wild, who caught him; making Dolan lie that he got the bills from Billy Wilson. **[This re-ran Sederwall's original hoaxing garbling a Miss N.M. Ferguson reporting to the Secret Service of a counterfeit bill connected to New Mexico's Will <u>Dowlin</u> [not James Dolan] & Company, with one letter about it from M.J. <u>Dowlin</u> being from <u>Tularosa</u>. (See pages 427-430 below)]**

This fakery was Sederwall's lead-up to his faked find of a Wild investigation bill. This version had U.S. Marshals Service Historian David Turk "locate the sample of counterfeit that matched the bill described in [Billy] Wilson's 1881 indictment." **["Match" hides its being a random bill provided by Secret Service archivist, Michael Sampson, to trick the reader into thinking it was connected to Wild and Billy Bonney.]**

Then made-up is that "**four days** after Dolan pointed the finger at Wilson, the Kid offered to be a government snitch." **[There was no connection. Wild reported to Chief Brooks for September 20, 1880 that he had met in Santa Fe with

U.S. Attorney Sidney Barnes and James Dolan, who reported getting four bad bills from Wilson. Billy's pardon bargain of testifying against the counterfeiters was initiated by his attorney, Ira Leonard, weeks later, as Wild reported on October 8, 1880. And demeaning Billy as a "snitch" is part of this new direction in hoaxing: attacking Billy himself rather than Pat Garrett.]

Sederwall alleged that Billy's "snitching" was because a "man named Smith [told Wild that] the Kid was reading his reports while they were in possession of mail carrier Mike Cosgrove." [This fable lifted the fake report of Smith's murder in a December 22, 1880 *New York Sun* article. The Kid's reading reports came from Wild's reporting, on October 21, 1880, Billy's single October 16, 1880 mail coach theft during the pardon negotiation, in which cautious Billy checked Wild's reports, learned his arrest plan, and stopped the negotiation. And Mike Cosgrove, a mail contractor, not a mail carrier, was not connected, except for giving captured Billy a new suit, as described in a December 27, 1880 *Las Vegas Daily Gazette* article by Lucius "Lute" Wilcox about the Stinking Springs capture titled 'The Kid. Interview with Billy Bonney The Best Known Man in New Mexico."

But Sederwall, using Cosgrove's giving suits, and wrongly claiming him as the mail carrier, made-up that it was a ploy to get Billy alone to plead with him not to reveal that he had let Billy read Wild's reports! [**This is Sederwall's wild fictionalizing.**]

Sederwall ended with his 2010 fakery that Garrett had not broken "the counterfeit ring in Lincoln County," because it was broken by Brockway's arrest. He added that Billy's bad bills had bought Lincoln County businesses, livestock, and mining claims. [**This claim is apparently lifted and altered from the Secret Service report by Operative Wallace Hall for July 1, 1882, with his tracing of Brockway's pushers Frank Doyle, Nate Foster, and John Hays** *"to New Mexico and Texas where more of the notes were passed ... Eventually, however, again all went to New Mexico, and Texas, <u>where they engaged in the saloon business [and] mining speculations</u>."* **None of this had anything to do with cattle-buying or Billy Bonney.]**

CHAPTER 4
THE RETURN OF THE COUNTERFEITING HOAX IN A BOOK

PARTNERING WITH W.C. JAMESON

For *Cold Case Billy the Kid*, Sederwall, narrated by W.C. Jameson, expanded his hoax; declaring: "For reasons not understood ... every writer who treated the Lincoln County War and Billy the Kid either completely ignored or provided all too brief attention to the issue of counterfeit money." He named the counterfeiters as "Billy Wilson ... W.W. West [sic], James J. Dolan ... Billy the Kid ... and Jesse James." (Pages 68-69)

HOAXING: Counterfeiting was not a Lincoln County War event; the War being in 1878. Operative Azariah Wild came at 1880's end. And Sederwall falsely linked Billy, Dolan, and Jesse James to counterfeiters W.H. West and Wilson.

Sederwall's growing hoax now had Billy Bonney partnering Jesse James in national counterfeiting with the Brockway gang in a money-laundering racket involving cattle rustled from John Chisum, sold in Colorado to Brockway's gang; with Billy's murdering informer Sam Smith, who told Azariah Wild the plot.

PULP FICTION INSPIRATION

Though not cited in the Bibliography, Sederwall's obvious source was the Ring's key Billy the Kid outlaw myth article in Billy's lifetime: the December 22, 1880 *New York Sun's* "Outlaws of New Mexico, The Exploits of a Band Headed by a New York Youth, The Mountain Fastness of the Kid and His Followers - War Against a Gang of Cattle Thieves and Murderers - The Frontier

Confederates of Brockway, the Counterfeiter." (See pages 13-19 above) Sederwall's use is proved by his lifting its error of Billy the Kid gang's murdering a freighter named Smith.

The article was mere pulp-fiction, as illustrated by its fictional Billy the Kid and Lincoln County War. It stated: "About three years ago a difficulty arose in Lincoln County, New Mexico, between the stockmen and the Indian agent on the reservation. The trouble arose in regard to some cattle that had been purchased for the Indians. Nearly every man in the county was under arms, and the troops were called out by Gov. Wallace to quell the disturbance. The Kid was mixed up in the affair, and had some narrow escapes. On one occasion he was hotly pursued and was obliged to take refuge in a house in Lincoln, which was surrounded by sixty solders. To the demand to surrender, he only laughed and shot down a soldier just to show that he was game. The house was set on fire, when the Kid, after loading up his Winchester Rifle, leaped from the burning building and made a dash for liberty. All the while he was running he kept firing from his Winchester, bringing down a number of his pursuers. Bullets whistled over his head, but he made his escape, and leaping on a horse was soon laughing at his pursuers. There is no telling how many men he has killed. He sets no value on human life, and has never hesitated at murder when it would serve his purpose."

Tacked on were William Brockway and his accomplice, James Doyle: "Government officials are now interested in the campaign [to catch the Wilson-Kid gang], for, in addition to their other crimes, the outlaws have put in circulation a large quantity of the counterfeit money manufactured by William Brockway, the forger. The bills were obtained by one of the gang named Doyle who formerly operated in Chicago, and counterfeit $100 bills in large numbers have been put in circulation among the stockmen and merchants in all that region."

HOAX: This article likely inspired Sederwall's hoax. But its use of New Yorker, Brockway - not claimed as complicit in the New Mexico gang by Azariah Wild - was likely just added as a local New York hook, with Brockway's gang having just been arrested there in late October.

HOAXING A LINK TO A COUNTERFEIT BILL

Sederwall repeated his July 16, 2010 *Ruidoso News* article's photo of a $100 bill which he had labeled as "a counterfeit bank note passed in Lincoln County by Billy the Kid and his gang." Now it was labeled as "[a] counterfeit hundred-dollar bill passed in Lincoln County, New Mexico, during the 1880's." (Page 77)

HOAXING: This is the random bill from Secret Service archivist, Michael Sampson, with faked connection to Lincoln County, Azariah Wild, and Billy Bonney.

HOAXING SOURCES AS EVIDENCE FOR A BROCKWAY LINK

Cold Case Billy the Kid's Bibliography cites three Brockway articles and some Secret Service reports, misleadingly implying that they were sources linking Billy to Brockway. They were not.

An October 24, 1880 *New York Times* article, "Old Counterfeiters Caught, Brockway and Two Others Arrested as J.B. Doyle's Accomplices," was about the Brooklyn, New York, arrests of Brockway as king-pin; Jasper Owens as printer; and William H. Smythe [sic - Charles Smith] as engraver. J.B. Doyle was the passer, apprehended at his transport of a valise of Brockway bills from New York to Chicago. That was it.

A May 6, 1882 *New York Times's* "Brockway's Forged Bonds: The Counterfeiter Telling How Doyle Got the Bonds - Curious Statements in Court," had Doyle's Chicago trial, with Brockway testifying that Doyle did not know the bills were bad. That was it.

Lastly, was syndicated "True Detective Stories," by Operative Andrew L. Drummond, as "A Genius Who Went Wrong," from the December 20, 1908 *New York Herald* about his capturing Brockway; Operative Wallace W. Hall's tracking of James Doyle; Brockway and Smith getting no jail time by surrendering plates; and Doyle getting 12 years in prison. That was it.

Cited also were some Secret Service reports; again, as if indicating the link claimed by the hoax. They did not.

Those of Andrew L. Drummond and Wallace W. Hall were about the Brockway case, with tracing his bills westward to Illinois, Missouri, Colorado, Texas and New Mexico Territory. Focus was on James Doyle as the major pusher, who, as Drummond stated in his report for June 3, 1881, *"traveled East and West quite often."*

Hall, most involved in tracing bill distribution, was cited in the Bibliography for his report of August 24, 1880 about a Miss N.M. Ferguson reporting a counterfeit bill gotten in New Mexico Territory; for his report for January 24, 1881 about counterfeit bills being found in a Moundville, Missouri, haystack on John W. Hay's farm, along with Hays's association with W.H. West and

White Oaks; his report for October 10, 1881 which traced the Brockway-associated Doyle brothers to Las Vegas, Santa Fe and White Oaks, New Mexico; his report for May 19, 1882 referencing Frank Doyle, Nate Foster, and John W. Hays as in Deer Trail, Colorado, and White Oaks, New Mexico, with linking their bills from the Moundville, Missouri, haystack to the one gotten by Miss Ferguson in Santa Fe; his report for June 17, 1882 announcing that James Doyle had finally started his prison term; his report for July 8, 1885 revealing that William Doyle, son of James Doyle, had counterfeit plates in the Bradford, Illinois, area; and his June 30, 1885 report stating that $100 counterfeit notes being passed in Denver, Colorado, were likely old *"Foster-Doyle notes."*

And Azariah Wild's reports citing his Sherman, Texas, and New Mexico findings of local pushers, later linked by him to Frank Doyle, were listed.

HOAXING: The sources were used for name-dropping Brockway's history and gang members to fake links to Billy the Kid. In fact, they showed no link to Billy Bonney.

HOAXING A LINK TO BILLY'S BONNEY'S RUSTLING

Sederwall's centerpiece in framing Billy Bonney as a counterfeiter, was his convoluted fabrication that Billy's rustling was actually a multi-state counterfeit money-laundering scheme, making Billy central to the Brockway gang's bill distribution.

HOAXING PAT GARRETT AS A SOURCE

Sederwall's hoax was built on faking one Pat Garrett quote. He claimed that, in *The Authentic Life of Billy the Kid*, Garrett stated that John Chisum owed Billy money for services in the Lincoln County War, so Billy and his "gang" accepted cattle in trade; then rebranded them and sold them "to a group of 'Colorado beef buyers" with Billy telling them "he was working for John Chisum;" but Chisum took them back. (Page 68) Sederwall asked why Billy changed brands if he worked for Chisum; and claimed that the Colorado beef buyers bought the cattle with counterfeit money, which was why they could not go to the law when Chisum took them back. (Page 69)

HOAXING: Garrett's quote was faked for the hoax's key lie: that "Colorado beef buyers" meant Brockway's pushers!

Also, Billy was not employed by Chisum. In 1878, when Chisum was in business with John Tunstall and was his Lincoln Bank president, Chisum offered to pay Tunstall's employees - like Billy. But he never did - even though they fought in the Lincoln County War. And Chisum never traded cattle to Billy as payment. That is why Billy did retaliative rustling against him.

Pat Garrett's actual quotation in *The Authentic Life of Billy the Kid* about Billy's "settling up" the Chisum debt was: "In April [of 1879], they returned to Fort Sumner and resumed depredations on loose stock ... In October of 1879, the Kid with O'Folliard, Bowdre, Scurlock, and two Mexicans rounded up and drove away from Bosque Grande ... one hundred and eighteen head of cattle, which were the property of Chisum. They drove them to Yerby's ranch in his absence, branded them, and turned them lose on the range ... They said Chisum owed them $600 each, for services rendered during the War. They afterwards drove those cattle to Grzelachowski's ranch at Alamo Gordo, and sold them to Colorado beef buyers, telling them they were employed in settling up Chisum's business. Chisum followed the cattle up, recovered them, and drove them back to his range." (Garrett, Page 118)

First of all, Garrett and ghostwriter Ash Upson were not historians. In April of 1879, Billy was still jailed in Juan Patrón's Lincoln house for his Lew Wallace pardon bargain, and he did not leave until June. But Garrett made clear that Billy's retaliative rustling was for Chisum's debt, and not getting cattle in trade. Thus, Billy rebranded them as his own. Sederwall's claiming that Billy told the Colorado buyers that he **"was working for"** Chisum, built falsely on Garrett's text of **"settling up Chisum's business,"** which meant taking care of the debt his own way.

As to the unnamed "Colorado beef buyers," Sederwall based his hoax in pretending they were Brockway's Colorado pushers. But *they* were not beef buyers! And Billy's deal was made through Alexander Grzelachowski, the possible actual connection to the buyers. And Chisum's recovery shows only that he proved ownership. Also, for Sederwall's fable, if Colorado buyers paid in counterfeits,

Billy was a victim, not a counterfeiter! And either way, money-laundering was not involved.

Sederwall had lifted and fictionalized the real money-laundering of counterfeits from the unrelated plot of real counterfeiter, Dan Dedrick, as told to Azariah Wild by his Fort Sumner spy, Barney Mason. Reporting from Lincoln for November 20, 1880 on November 21st, Wild revealed the scheme <u>to buy cattle with bad money, with resale for good money</u>. To note, is that the bill courier was W.H. West, accompanied by a New Yorker, likely Brockway's pusher, Frank Doyle, as Wild decided a year later. All this had no <u>connection to Billy or to rustling</u>. Wild reported:

> *He (Mason) states that a few days ago one Daniel Dedrick who resides at Bosque Grande, and who has an interest with his brother Samuel Dedrick & West in a livery stable at White Oaks came to him and proposed as follows:*
>
> *"I (Daniel Dedrick) want to employ you (Barney Mason). That after a short conversation with Dedrick he (Dedrick) stated that he wanted me (Mason) to take a lot of counterfeit money down to the Rio Grande on Texas and buy up all the cattle. I (Mason) could bring them to a point near New Mexico turn them over to him (Dedrick) and West give them a square bill of sale of the same and I (Mason) to then leave the country and go to Mexico and from there wheresoever I pleased."*
>
> <u>*That when West returned a few days since he brought with him $30,000 in counterfeit* *money which had been made from a new plate, and from which had not yet been "spotted."*</u>
>
> <u>*Mason goes on to state that Daniel Dedrick informed him that when West recently returned to White Oaks that one man who hailed from New York came with him and was there at the time.*</u> *"To the best of his memory he (Dedrick) called the man Duncan and that he was pretending to represent J.H. Hardin of New York."*
>
> <u>*Mason stated that Dedrick informed him that they could get all the counterfeit money they desired from West, and that he was given to understand that the*</u>

money came from the New York stranger who came with West on his return to White Oaks.

Mason states that William Wilson boards at his house when at Fort Sumner. That he has seen him [with] counterfeit money at various times. That he (Mason) knows he Wilson passed a $100- on a saloon keeper named [Beaver] Smith at Fort Sumner. That he (Smith) sent it to the bank and had it returned as counterfeit. That Wilson laughed at Smith and agreed to redeem it with good money although Wilson told him (Mason) that he was only letting the old man (Smith) down easy.

In that same report for November 20, 1880, Wild made clear Billy's separate rustling, using Billy Wilson; writing: "*That William Wilson & Billy Kid left about the 15th inst with sixty head of stolen horses and went down the Canadian River to be gone two or three weeks. That on their return they would probably return to his [Mason's] house when he would turn them over to Patrick F. Garrett Deputy U.S. Marshal and Sheriff elect.*"

On November 28, 1880, for November 27th, Wild reported that the Mason deal was put on hold, with the gang apparently spooked by his investigation. Wild wrote: "[Mason] *saw West and Dedrick about the sending of him to purchase cattle on the Rio Grande with counterfeit money. That they say they will not do anything in the matter until the present excitement and trouble is over.*"

Garrett, knowledgeable, with Barney Mason being his friend, confirmed that money-laundering scheme, making clear it had no connection to Billy or rustling, in his 1882 *The Authentic Life of Billy the Kid*:

> [Mason] told me that he had stopped at Bosque Grande ... at the ranch of Dan Dedrick and that Dan had read him a letter from W.H. West, partner of his brother, Sam Dedrick, in the stable business in White Oaks. The gist of the letter was that West has $30,000 in counterfeit greenbacks and that he intended to take this money to Mexico, there buy cattle with it, and then drive them back across the state line. He wanted to secure the services of a reliable assistant whose business would be to accompany

him to Mexico, makeham purchases of the cattle as fast as they were bought, receive bills of transfer so that in case of detection the stock would be found in the legal possession of the apparently innocent party. West's letter went on to suggest Barney Mason as just the man to assume the role of scapegoat in these nefarious traffickings. (Garrett, Page 140)

But Sederwall added Brockway's gang members; making-up: "The Secret Service learned that four men living in Colorado - James and Frank Doyle, John Hays, and Nate Foster - were **buying cattle with counterfeit money**." Then he made-up: "**They were the Colorado beef buyers mentioned by Pat Garrett** who paid for cattle delivered to them by Billy the Kid." (Pages 76-77)

HOAXING: Sederwall's house-of-cards hoax was built on his making-up that Brockway's gang bought "**cattle with counterfeit money**" and were the "**Colorado beef buyers**" Garrett mentioned.

In fact, Operative Wallace W. Hall traced the Doyles, Hays, and Foster to Colorado, among many places. But they were pushers. To frame Billy, Sederwall made-up a connection of cattle buying to rustling (unlike Dedrick's buying-with-bad-selling-for-good plot); used the pushers' "Colorado" location; and faked it made them "**Colorado beef buyers**" cited by Garrett. Made-up is that Billy delivered the cattle. And how rustled cattle could launder money is unexplained. In fact, Sederwall showed no link to Billy.

HOAXING BILLY IN BROCKWAY'S GANG

To fake Billy the Kid as operating on a national level, Sederwall cited Azariah Wild's summer of 1880 Sherman, Texas, investigation; and claimed Wild knew the counterfeiting extended beyond Texas. Sederwall added New Mexico, and said the counterfeiting ranged from New York to the Southwest. (Page 71)

HOAXING: **Sederwall was merely describing Brockway's national bill distributions to local pushers, unrelated to Billy. And rustling-money-laundering was not present.**

Azariah Wild's Sherman, Texas, investigation, in summer of 1880, was of local counterfeit bill pusher, Walter Greenham, his family, and local business associates. There was no cattle-rustling-money-laundering plot. Wild's going to New Mexico Territory at the end of that year for the West-Dedrick counterfeiting case was unrelated, in his mind, to his Sherman investigation.

A year later, however, with input about the Brockway gang finally provided by Chief James Brooks, Wild linked Greenham's Texas bills to Brockway's pushers, James Doyle and his brother Frank. He then decided that Frank Doyle was also providing counterfeit bills to White Oaks's W.H. West, and thus to the Dedricks.

Sederwall cited Operative Wallace W. Hall's reports about John Hays's "boodle" in his Missouri farm's haystack, with his connections to Frank Doyle, Nate Foster, and New Mexico.

HOAXING: This is just more Brockway history, without any link to Billy Bonney.

HOAXING BILLY AS A "MONEY-LAUNDERING RUSTLER" FOR BROCKWAY'S GANG

Since no evidence existed that Billy's rustling connected to counterfeiting, money-laundering, or Brockway's gang, Sederwall made it up in a convoluted fiction. His hoax depended on it.

First used in his June 2015 *True West's* "Billy Bonney's Bad Bucks," Sederwall's rustling-money-laundering claim had an alleged "eye witness" named **Lane Cook**. (Pages 71-72) **[For that article, Sederwall faked Lane Cook as Tom O'Folliard's cousin. That recycled his O'Folliard is "Folliard" hoax, in which he faked a genealogy for O'Folliard with Cook relatives. (See pages 309-314 above) Since this author Lane, had the last name Cook, Sederwall simply made-up the cousin relationship. And he made-up Lane Cook selling rustled Chisum cattle to a man named Hays to money-launder in Kansas City, Missouri.]**

For this rerun, Sederwall rewrote his fable, accidentally revealing how he had constructed it. He had Billy and Tom O'Folliard, in 1879, riding to the South Llano River ranch of a **Jim Cook** in "Texas Hill Country," and telling "old friend" Cook that John Chisum owed him and O'Folliard money, "and how they planned to collect." Cook is quoted as saying that Billy and Tom would go to the Pecos and round up 3,200 "of Uncle Johnny's steers," and give him a bill of sale for them. Cook was to drive them to Kansas to sell, pay himself, and return with the remaining money for Billy. Sederwall adds: **"The Kid specifically told Cook to sell the cattle in Honeywell, Kansas; take the money to Kansas city and deposit it; wait for three days; and then return to the bank and withdraw it."** Cook did this and paid Billy $9,000.

Sederwall claimed that, to him, this is a "tell," because Kansas City was far away, and waiting three days was strange. So that meant "to have the money laundered;" meaning Cook had deposited bad money from the sale and gotten back good money.

That segued to Sederwall claiming: "Later the Secret Service pieced together the details of the criminal enterprise;" adding that it found "John Hays, [no first name] Doyle, and [no first name] Foster "at Deer Trail, Colorado, when the gang were operating in the counterfeit hundreds." He added it was Colorado because **"Hays's father-in-law owned a cattle ranch in Deer Trail ... Foster lived in Colorado ... [and] [t]hey were the 'Colorado beef buyers.** Buying and selling cattle was yet another way of laundering counterfeit money."

That segued to Sederwall's claim that on June 8, 1880, the plot unraveled when the Vernon County bank in Nevada, Missouri, caught John Hays passing a counterfeit bill, which Hays admitted came from the "**Mastin Bank** in Kansas City." Tying this to his Cook tale, Sederwall adds: "It was the **same bank** where Jim Cook deposited the money he received from the sale of John Chisum's cattle that had been stolen by Billy the Kid." (Page 72)

That segued to claiming the Mastin brothers founded the bank "with money from the Confederacy and that it catered to the beef industry." And the **Mastins**, as "Confederate sympathizers," were still trying "to collapse the Union's financial system" by saturating with bogus money. "Cook and Hays were laundering money at the **Mastin Bank** in Kansas City." (Page 73)

That segued to claiming the Secret Service exposed this when they found counterfeit money in John Hays's haystack. Added is that "Agent Wallace Hall learned from Nevada County residents that Hays had been shipping cattle from the west to Missouri. He also learned that Hays traveled to Kansas City on a number of occasions to deposit large sums of money at the **Mastin Bank**. It was determined that this was counterfeit money and the intention was to have it laundered at the bank." And the people doing it were in Deer Trail, Colorado. (Page 73)

That segued to claiming [no first name] Doyle and Foster fled to White Oaks. (Page 73)

HOAXING: This very complex flimflam is a con-artistry pinnacle. It needs dissection to reveal that it showed no connection to Billy, rustling, money-laundering, or reality. It was just fiction to link rustling and counterfeiting.

1) EYE-WITNESS COOK: On "eye-witness," Jim (Lane) Cook, the fiction is built. The Bibliography cites James L. Cook's 1936 *Lane of the Llano: Being the Story of Jim (Lane) Cook as Told to T.M. Pearce.*

Cook was an old-timer windbag. A 1936 review of his book by a J. Frank Dobie in *Southwest Review* called it "**puerile invention.**" The Texas State Historical Society called it: "a bunch of the worst lies that would make Bill Burns, Zane Grey, and John Cook green with envy;" adding that historian, J. Evetts Haley, said Cook "**failed to distinguish truth from fiction.**" Haley also wrote "Jim Cook: On the Frontiers of Fantasy" for Spring, 1964's *The Shamrock*, stating Cook wrote in the "**frontiers of fantasy.**"

As examples, Cook claimed he worked for John Chisum, who stole cattle and horses *from him*. (Cook, Page 87) His Lincoln County War fiction, adding himself, stated: "**It was while I was working for Uncle John that trouble between rival cattle gangs started over at Lincoln. A band was stealing from Uncle John, and Chisum hired Billy the Kid to fight for him ... He promised Billy fifteen dollars a day as a fighter. The Kid rode in to Uncle John one day and said, 'Come on and go up to Lincoln with us. We're going to shoot up the town.' He had O'Folliard and five or six others with him ... Uncle John didn't go, but Billy and the rest of us did. When we got into Lincoln, the soldiers came in there with orders to get Billy dead or alive. We had to barricade ourselves in the McSween house. Mrs. McSween wasn't there. The boys played her piano and sang during the day while the bullets were coming into her house. McSween was killed when he stepped out the door to talk to the** commander of the soldiers. Eventually the soldiers set fire to the roof, and at about twilight the Kid decided to make a break. There was a long adobe wall which ran to the house and down to the creek. We broke out along this wall – Billy, Tom O'Folliard, myself, and some others. The Negro soldiers had placed themselves around two sides of the wall, and they couldn't fire at us without shooting each other ... After this fight ... [Chisum] sold out everything he had to some St. Louis merchants." (Pages 88-89)

Cook's fiction, lifted and altered by Sederwall, stated:

[My wife and I] had not been long at home [at his ranch on the South Llano] when Billy the Kid and Tom O'Folliard came to see us. They said they believed they had a plan how we could get our money out of Chisum ... Billy said he and Tom would go back on the Pecos and round up thirty-two hundred of Uncle Johnny's big steers, bringing them across to Paint Rock Crossing on South Llano River; close to our ranch. He would give me a bill of sale for them; I was to drive them to Kansas and sell them, pay myself, and bring him and Tom what was left ...

In about thirty days Billy came back and said the thirty-two hundred big steers were at Paint Rock Crossing ready for me. He handed me a bill of sale. It had a signature on it and the name was Uncle John's. ...

I drove the steers to Honeywell, Kansas, and sold them without a hitch. I put the money in the <u>Master Bank of Kansas City</u>. [My wife] and I sewed nine thousand dollars in big bills up in our clothing ... We met the boys at Portales Springs ... I said to Billy and the others: "Now when you get this money, you go out of the country ... and settle down. You know I'm your friend. I'm the best friend you boys have got." They didn't take my advice. I never saw Billy again. He was killed at Fort Sumner two years later." (Pages 91-92)

So Cook's tale - besides being made-up - was about <u>selling rustled Chisum cattle to give Billy $9,000.</u> It was not about counterfeiting. And the bank was the "<u>Master</u> Bank of Kansas City; not Sederwall's "<u>Mastin Bank</u>."

To create his money-laundering fable, Sederwall had made-up that: "The Kid specifically told Cook to sell the cattle in Honeywell, Kansas; take the money to Kansas city and deposit it; wait for three days; and then return to the bank and withdraw it;" which was not in Cook's tale.

In fact, Cook's own faking tale was likely built on Pat Garrett's *The Authentic Life of Billy the Kid's* rendition of selling rustled Chisum cattle for money to meet Chisum's debt.

2) THE MONEY-LAUNDERING LEAP: Having himself made-up the Cook-Kansas-City-Mastin-deposit, Sederwall claimed *it* proved money-laundering!

3) IMAGINARY SECRET SERVICE CONNECTION: Building on his fable, Sederwall added a non sequitor: "**Later the Secret Service pieced together the details of the criminal enterprise,**" to feign the Secret Service as revealing that Cook-Billy-rustling-laundering; instead of just its actual, and unrelated, exposure of the Brockway gang.

4) IMAGINARY CONNECTION TO BROCKWAY'S AGENTS: Having falsely thrown in the Secret Service, Sederwall switched to the Secret Service's Brockway investigation, changed the scene to Colorado, added Brockway's agents, a Doyle [Frank or James unspecified] and Nate Foster, and quoted without citation: "at **Deer Trail, Colorado, when the gang were operating in the counterfeit hundreds;**" as if this tracked Billy to Colorado. But the quote was lifted from Operative Wallace Hall's report for May 13, 1882 stating that James B. Doyle was with Frank Doyle, Nate Foster, John W. Hays and others at Deer Trail, Colorado *"when the gang were operating in the cft hundreds."* It had nothing to do with Billy.

5) IMAGINARY CONNECTION TO A COLORADO CATTLE RANCH: Building on "Colorado," Sederwall made-up that "Hays's father-in-law owned a cattle ranch in Deer Trail ... Foster lived in Colorado ... [and] [t]hey were the 'Colorado beef buyers.' Buying and selling cattle was yet another way of laundering counterfeit money." But the father-in-law is faked. The real father-in-law with the ranch was James Doyle's wife's father. After Doyle's arrest, she had

gone home to wait out the proceedings. And the statement that cattle transactions were to launder money, was lifted from the unrelated Dan Dedrick-Barney Mason plot reported by Azariah Wild for November 18th and 20th, 1880.

Most deceitful, is Sederwall's lie that Hays and Doyle "**were the "Colorado beef buyers"** - going back to the starting point of his hoax with faking Pat Garrett's *The Authentic Life of Billy the Kid*, about Billy selling rustled Chisum cattle to "Colorado beef buyers" at Grzelachowski's ranch (Garrett, Page 118) - as meaning Billy sold to Brockway's agent John Hays! Except Brockway's agents were not beef buyers. And "Colorado" did not mean it had to be them!

So faked was: Billy as a counterfeiter, Jim Cook's Kansas sale, and a link to Brockway's men in Colorado.

6) IMAGINARY MASTIN BANK LINK: Continuing his money-laundering fiction, Sederwall added the "Mastin Bank in Kansas City," with a long-winded anti-Union conspiracy adding Cook and Hays: as "**the same bank where Jim Cook deposited the money**" from Billy's cattle." The problem here was reading: Cook's tale used Master Bank not Mastin Bank – toppling Sederwall's house of cards.

7) IMAGINARY LINK TO HAYS'S HAYSTACK: Pretending he had linked Billy through Cook, Sederwall gave the Secret Service's find of counterfeit bills in John Hays's haystack. Faking cattle-selling as central to the Brockway gang, to link to Billy's rustling, he claimed that "**Agent Wallace Hall learned from Nevada County residents that Hays had been shipping cattle from the west to Missouri [and that he deposited] sums of money at the Mastin Bank;**" then fled with Nate Foster to White Oaks.

First of all, the "Mastin Bank" was faked, with its elaborate money-laundering by Confederates fable being invented by Sederwall from misreading of Jim Cook's, "Master Bank." And Operative Hall, expert on the gang, did not claim a west to east sale of cattle; instead reporting for May 13, 1882 on Nate Foster's having a **saloon in White Oaks, and John Hays** "*engaged in mining or some mining speculations at or in the vicinity of White Oaks.*" For July 1, 1882, he traced Frank Doyle, Foster, and Hays "*to New Mexico and Texas where more of the notes were passed ... Eventually, however, again all went to New*

Mexico, and Texas, where they engaged in the saloon business, mining speculations" – not cattle-buying. And none of it had to do with Billy Bonney.

HOAXING A LINK OF AZARIAH WILD'S SHERMAN, TEXAS, INVESTIGATION TO BILLY

Sederwall cited Azariah Wild's summer of 1880 Sherman, Texas, investigation, claiming a man named "Kirby [sic - Kibby] from New York" met with a man named "Walter Graham [sic – Greenham]" for a deal to supply money to buy cattle for resale with a percentage of the profits. But Wild learned that Kirby [sic] was James Doyle "linked to New York counterfeiters." Sederwall stated that Wild learned that "Grahm" [sic] was being sent packages of counterfeit notes from Chicago, to buy cattle "to be herded into Missouri and placed on a ranch in Vernon County owned by John Hays." So, Sederwall claimed, Wild realized the "counterfeiting enterprise he was investigating was not limited to Texas and New Mexico, but rather turned out to be a widespread activity ranging from New York across the country into the American Southwest." (Page 71)

HOAXING: This was another faked linking of Billy, rustling, and Brockway's gang; this time by misstating Azariah Wild's Sherman, Texas, investigation from June 6, 1880 to July 10, 1880. It was unconnected to Wild's New Mexico Territory investigation from September to the end of December 1880, except that he was unwittingly witnessing different distribution sites of Brockway's bills through local passers. Wild himself reported for October 16, 1881 about Sherman: *"[It] was at a time when I had not the least idea of going to New Mexico."*

When in Sherman, Wild depicted the gang as local wagon factory owners, Walter B. Greenham, who had just committed suicide, his partner, Calvin Jackson, their wives, the firm of M. Schneider Bros., the Planters and Merchants Bank, and Greenham's counterfeiting family in Maine and New Hampshire. They passed bills gotten by Greenham when in New York in the winter of 1879 (report for June 7, 1880) or from a New Yorker courier calling himself Kibby or Kibbey alias Murphy [Frank Doyle].

Contrary to Sederwall's claim, Wild did not claim that Kibby made a deal with Greenham to supply money to buy cattle for resale with profit sharing. What Wild stated for his report for June 4, 1880 was about another Texas case, separate from Greenham's; writing: *"Information has reached me of there being a man in Foces Co. buying up cattle and paying in part or all in counterfeit money ... That after taking them they dispose of them for what they can get."* And for June 22, 1880, Wild wrote about *"two brothers named John and Clive Merchant down in the neighborhood of Brown County engaged in the cattle business who are reported as men who handle counterfeit money when there is any in circulation."*

But Greenham used that money-laundering technique for cotton. For his report of June 11, 1880, Wild wrote that "Kibby" accompanied Greenham in his buggy out to look at a cotton patch; the implication being its purchase with bogus money for resale for good money.

As to the Greenham counterfeiters' connection to cattle, for June 12, 1880, Wild reported *"that Greenham just a short time before his death was at his place [in Pilot Grove, Texas] and purchased some cattle ... That Greenham said he was going to start a stock ranch in the Indian Territory."* And for June 14, 1880, Wild quoted the informer who reported that small deal Greenham had made: "He either sent over 108 or 110 head [to Indian Territory] before he killed himself." And the informer had seen his pickle jar in which he kept his 71, $100, presumably counterfeit bills.

Likewise, in that report, Wild wrote that the Schneider brothers' business was both mercantile and in cattle. Important to note, however, is that, like in the Dedrick-Mason plot, rustling was not involved.

And contrary to Sederwall's fiction that Greenham was being mailed packages of counterfeit bills from Chicago, to buy cattle **"to be herded into Missouri and placed on a ranch in Vernon County owned by John Hays;"** for his report for June 12, 1880, Wild had merely checked with the local postmaster about *any* registered mail, and learned: *"The postmaster remembered a registered mail package a Quimby & Co. from Chicago, Ill."* Sederwall had made-up the rest to link Greenham with Brockway's agent, John Hays - something never stated by Wild.

It was not until Wild's October 16, 1881 report (a year after his time in New Mexico), that Chief James Brooks finally filled him in on the Brockway gang, and that Frank Doyle had been in Santa Fe, Las Vegas, and White Oaks. Then Wild decided "Kibby" was Frank Doyle, and surmised that when W.H. West from White Oaks had traveled *"to Kansas and Colorado on business and that on his return he brought back with him to White Oaks a man who claimed to hail from New York and that his name was Duncan."* Wild now decided that he was Frank Doyle also; and was the likely bill courier, because soon afterward *"an effort was made to employ Barney Mason to go into Texas with $30,000 counterfeit money to purchase cattle."*

Though Wild still persisted in that October 16, 1881 report to join incorrectly Billy's name to the West-Dedrick counterfeiters, he was, in fact, merely describing the New Mexico outlet of some Brockway bills.

And Sederwall's statement that Wild realized the "counterfeiting enterprise" was not just in "Texas and New Mexico, but from New York across the country," just pertained to the Brockway gang, not Billy or rustling; though Sederwall's intent was to fake a connection.

HOAXING A LINK TO BILLY THROUGH JOHN HAYS TO LEA BROTHERS AND PAT GARRETT

Sederwall then linked John Hays to White Oaks, New Mexico, where, on February 23, 1881 Hays quitclaimed his Missouri farm (with the once 'boodle' containing haystack) to an A. Kahn, with deed notarized by a Frank Lea at the Lincoln County courthouse.

Sederwall added that Lea's brother Joseph, from Roswell, New Mexico, had ridden - along with Frank and Jesse James - with William Quantrill. (Page 73)

HOAXING: Name-dropping Brockway's pusher John Hays, is an attempt to link him with Joseph Lea, and Jesse James. But Joseph Lea did not ride with the James brothers. William Pennington's 1998 "Roster of Quantrill's, Anderson's and Todd's Guerrillas and Other 'Missouri Jewels,' " lists Lea as fighting only on August 21, 1863 for William Quantrill's pro-Confederate "bushwacker" massacre in Lawrence, Kansas. Frank James joined Quantrill in 1862, at 19, but did not fight in that battle. And Jesse James joined a year after the battle, in 1864, at 17.

Faked too is linking Joseph's brother, Frank Lea, to John Hays. Frank Lea's notarizing of Hays's quitclaim, only means Frank did a professional service.

Building on his fake linking of Frank or Joseph Lea to Jesse James, Sederwall then contended that Frank Lea was Pat Garrett's friend; implying Garrett was in on the counterfeiting too.

HOAXING: Garrett's friend was Frank's brother, Joseph Lea, as documented by Garrett's biographer, Leon Metz, in his 1973 *Pat Garrett: The Story of a Western Lawman*. And Joseph Lea was an upstanding citizen. As Metz wrote: "News of [Garrett's] bravery and perseverance so impressed the Roswellians that John Chisum and <u>Captain Joseph C. Lea, the latter a prominent local resident who commanded universal local respect in Lincoln County</u>, approached Pat Garrett and induced him to move to Roswell in time to qualify for the election [as Lincoln County Sheriff]." (Metz, Pages 54-55)

And none of this has anything to do with Billy Bonney.

HOAXING A LINK TO JESSE JAMES AND COUNTERFEITING

To his Billy-Brockway "counterfeiting gang," Sederwall added Jesse James to prove "historians were wrong." (Page 70)

His "proof" was Henry Hoyt's, book: *A Frontier Doctor*. Hoyt was part of Billy the Kid history by receiving, from Billy, on October 24, 1878, in Tascosa, Texas, a bill of sale for an expensive horse. In his book, Hoyt related that he subsequently encountered Billy with Jesse James at Moore's Hotsprings Hotel in Las Vegas, New Mexico Territory. On that meeting, Sederwall built his claim.

HOAXING: In fact, Hoyt merely claimed that, in late 1879, he saw Billy and James *eating together* at the Hotsprings Hotel. His publisher denied his claim of James in a footnote, though Hoyt stuck to it. (Hoyt, Page 111) But eating together does not mean counterfeiting together!

In fact, Hoyt described the whole encounter. Teenaged Billy was in Las Vegas for an boyish adventure of seeing passenger trains. Hoyt wrote: "I ... found at a corner table the only vacant seat in the room. Glancing at the three guests already there, I was perfectly amazed to recognize that the one to my left was Billy the Kid, urbane and smiling as ever. We shook hands, but neither mentioned a name. We were chatting away of old times in Texas [Tascosa in October of 1878] ... when the man on Bonney's left made a comment ... Whereupon Billy said, 'Hoyt, meet my friend Mr. Howard from Tennessee' ... Mr. Howard had noticeable characteristics. He had piercing steely blue eyes with a peculiar blink, and the tip of a finger on his left hand was missing. I mentally classed him as a railroad man ... After dinner we separated and Billy, taking me to his room, gave me, after pledging me to secrecy, one of the surprises of my life. Mr. Howard was no other than the bandit and train robber, Jesse James." (Hoyt, Pages 110-111)

And Hoyt confirmed no business relationship; writing: "Jesse James had been in seclusion for some time; [hotel owners] Mr. and Mrs. Moore were former friends whom he could trust, so he came out to size up the situation in a new territory. Billy also knew the Moores, and as he had not seen a passenger train since he was a youngster, he had slipped into Las Vegas, discarded his cowboy togs for an entire new city outfit of clothing, and was having the time of his life for a few days at the Hot Springs ... Jesse James was prospecting and preparing to make a move, and after meeting Billy and sizing him up made a tentative offer to join forces and hit the trail together. <u>Although both were outlaws ... their lives and activities were entirely different. Billy was never a train or bank robber ... His only peculations had been rounding up cattle and horses carrying someone else's brand ... His offences, for which he was now an outcast, were entirely traceable to the now historic Lincoln County War ... On account of the differences in their status and of the fact that a union with Jesse James would carry him away from the magnet at Fort Sumner [Paulita Maxwell], Billy turned down his proposal.</u>" (Hoyt, Pages 112-113)

Sederwall added that future New Mexico Territory Governor, Miguel Otero, claimed that Moore's Hotsprings Hotel owner told him that Jesse James came there. (Page 70)

HOAXING: Hoyt made that claim too, but denied criminal collusion of Jesse and Billy. And Otero made no connection of Billy to Jesse James.

Sederwall cited a June 24, 1880 *Sacramento Daily Record-Union* article about a William Ralston being a counterfeiter, as well as being Frank James's brother-in-law. Sederwall adds that Secret Service agent P.S. Tyrell [sic - P.D. Tyrrell], in July 8, 1881, stated that Frank James sold counterfeit coins. (Pages 70-71)

HOAXING: This has nothing to do with Billy or Jesse James. And Wild's case was for was counterfeit bills, not coins. Operative Patrick D. Tyrell stated for his report for July 8, 1881, completed July 10th, that an informer told him *"that Frank James had a large amount of counterfeit coin, and that he [the informer] could get all he wanted from James."* **No link was made to Jesse James.**

And Operative Wallace W. Hall, expert on Brockway's pushers in the West, referenced Jesse James in a September 1, 1882 report as only a *"robber and bandit."*

Sederwall then claimed that Frank James lived in Nevada, Missouri; that the population had ex-Confederates; that it was good for holding stolen cattle bought with counterfeit money; and that is why John W. Hays, a known counterfeiter, like Frank James, lived there. And in the Civil War, Hays and Frank James rode with William Quantrill. (Pages 71).

HOAXING: Lumping unconnected people with his made-up rustled cattle bought with counterfeit money is to trick the reader into believing a relationship existed with Brockway's pusher, John Hays, in Moundville, Missouri, and Frank James (with hoped-for implication of Jesse James). But William Pennington's 1998 "Roster of Quantrill's, Anderson's and Todd's Guerrillas and Other 'Missouri Jewels,' " lists only a John Hays (with no W.) and no dates of service or battles. Frank James joined Quantrill in 1862, at 19, but had minimal service. There is no evidence that the two would have met, if Brockway's Hays was actually among Quantrill's hundreds of men.

Sederwall quoted Azariah Wild's report of January 2, 1881: "Information on [sic - of] the arrest of William Wilson, William Antrim [sic- Antrom] alias Billy the Kid, with several members of their gang by Deputy U.S. Marshal Patrick F. Garrett has reached me." Sederwall said the report also stated: **"There is no trouble in arresting Jesse James if he is not already arrested. I have put several men on his track who have been** assisting me and would have arrested or caused his arrest when in New Mexico had I known he was wanted for any crime against the U.S. Government." (Pages 73-74) Sederwall claimed that Billy's and Jesse James's names being in the same report meant they were in cahoots in counterfeiting.

HOAXING: Wild did not link Billy and Jesse James. After leaving New Mexico, he reported this James rumor. And the Secret Service never made a case against James. In fact, Wild confirmed James was not *"wanted for any crime against the U.S. Government"* - meaning counterfeiting.

REALITY: Jesse James had no criminal connection to Billy the Kid; and no source accuses James of counterfeiting.

Azariah Wild mentioned James twice.

For his December 23, 1880, report about Stinking Springs capture of what the called the *"Kid & Wilson gang;"* he garbled him with Jessie Evans and Billy Campbell of Huston Chapman's murder notoriety; stating that Pat Garrett *"is still in pursuit of the balance of the outlaws: Jessie James is surely here under the name of Campbell."*

Wild's second mention was in that report of January 2, 1881, when he was back in New Orleans; but it was a rumor not pursued.

Lew Wallace also switched Jesse James for Jessie Evans in his Billy the Kid outlaw myth articles. On June 18, 1881 and June 23, 1900, for respective interviews published in the Crawfordsville *Saturday Evening Journal* and *The Indianapolis Press* - with respective titles, "Billy the Kid, General Wallace Tells Why the Young Desperado of New Mexico Wanted to Kill Him" and "Gen. Wallace's Feud with Billy the Kid," he fabricated: **"A young lawyer named Chapman was murdered in Lincoln county, and for this were arrested four men, among whom was the notorious Jesse James, under one of his many names."** Wallace's June 8, 1902 *New York World Magazine's* "General Lew Wallace Writes a Romance of 'Billy the Kid'" had: **"[A] young attorney in Lincoln, had been murdered. Half a dozen men were arrested, accused of the crime. Among them was Jesse James."** And since Wallace had conferred with Wild in New Mexico, he may have been the one to confuse Wild about the two men.

HOAXING A LINK OF BILLY BONNEY TO BILLY WILSON FOR COUNTERFEITING

For guilt by association, Sederwall linked Billy Bonney to Azariah Wild's accused counterfeiter, William "Billy" Wilson, to claim that proved Bonney was a counterfeiter too. Hidden was that his own sources in the Bibliography showed that Wilson was eventually cleared of counterfeiting, making the claim moot.

For his ploy, Sederwall called Wilson Billy's "close associate" and "a member of the Regulators."(Page 74) As evidence, he cited Wilson's "March 30, 1881" counterfeiting trial.

HOAXING: Wilson was neither a "close associate" of Billy's nor a "Regulator." He was accused by Secret Service Operative Azariah Wild of passing a few counterfeit bills and being part of Wild's fictional "Wilson & Kid gang." In fact, Wilson was merely used by Billy for rustling and a one-time mail theft of Wild reports during Billy's pardon negotiation with Wild.

And Sederwall's own cited sources not only make no counterfeiting connection of Wilson and Billy the Kid, but they even deny that Wilson was a counterfeiter!

The *Cold Case Billy the Kid* Bibliography lists the source for Wilson's trial as the National Archives in Broomfield, Colorado. But that file, in actuality, has no trial of "March 30, 1881." Its Cases against Wilson were archived as No. 1-757, for passing counterfeit money; No. 1-760 for assault on Fred Weston, mail carrier; No. 1-761 for counterfeiting; and No. 1-762 for motion for change of venue; and numbered on his own filings as 438 and 439. But most pages are missing. There is no mention of Billy Bonney. Recorded is that Wilson was indicted by a grand jury on February 22, 1881 of *"passing, uttering, publishing, selling and attempting to pass &c Counterfeit National Bank Notes."* He was defended by Catron & Thornton - meaning T.B. Catron's law firm; Catron's his partner, William T. Thornton, doing the defense. The prosecution witnesses were James J. Dolan, Jose Montaño, David Easton, Pat Garrett, Ira Leonard, and William Robert. In his Affidavit of April 4, 1881, Wilson claimed innocence for his appearance before Judge Warren Bristol in Mesilla.

It stated: *"[H]is defense is that he is not guilty of the offense charged ... that he did not pass said counterfeit money knowingly."* When he requested a continuance on July 27, 1881, that defense was expanded in his deposition: *"[D]efendant expects to prove by the testimony of David Easton, and of James Dolan, and of Jose Montaño, that the defendant is a person of good character, that by the testimony of Dan Dedrick, and of Samuel Dedrick, and of the said W.H. West, deponent expects to prove that the money in the indictment herein, against deponent, described and charged by this deponent to have been passed as counterfeit money, came to the hands of, and was received by, deponent honestly and in good faith and in due course of business, and without any knowledge on the part of the deponent that the same was counterfeit [being received as payment from W.H. West for his White Oaks livery."* By March 1, 1882, through Attorney Thornton, Wilson filed an appeal; though Wilson did not succeed until 1896, when Thornton got him a presidential pardon.

The other Wilson source in the Bibliography is Philip J. Rasch's 1995 *Trailing Billy the Kid*, in his chapter titled "Amende Honorable: The Life and Death of Billy Wilson" (written in 1958). This early historian described Wilson as a "**gunfighter**" who "**rode with William Bonney**" (Rasch, Page 58), possibly inspiring Sederwall's fable of Wilson as a "close associate" and a "Regulator." Rasch, using Wilson's transcripts and his 1896 presidential pardon, denied Wilson was a counterfeiter, and repeated Wilson's claim that his sale of his White Oaks livery in late 1879 to W.H. West was the innocent source of bad bills, and that he was wrongly accused by Azariah Wild. (Rasch, Page 59) And Rasch linked Wilson to "Billy the Kid and his gang" <u>as a rustler</u>. (Rasch, Page 58) Documented also was Wilson's being with Billy Bonney at capture attempts at Coyote Spring, the Greathouse ranch, and Stinking Springs. (Rasch, Pages 59-62) As to Wilson's Mesilla counterfeiting trial, Rasch stated that his attorney was William T. Thornton, with James Dolan and Pat Garrett testifying for the prosecution - though he admitted that much of the record is lost (that means by 1958). Rasch stated that Wilson's trial in Santa Fe was for passing bills and mail theft. He was convicted of passing on

February 28, 1882, and sentenced to seven years in the penitentiary; but he escaped on September 9, 1882. (Rasch, Page 64) He then assumed the alias David L. Anderson, and lived in Texas, where he held public jobs. In 1896, he applied for and got a pardon, with support of Pat Garrett, James Dolan, and his past attorney, then Governor, William Thornton. The argument was that his "association with Billy the Kid had been the cause of prejudice against him" (Rasch, Page 66); that prejudice being for outlawry, not counterfeiting - since Wilson's defense was denial of counterfeiting. As Thornton argued: "I believed at that time and I still believe that this boy was absolutely innocent ... I could not conceive how it was possible for a man of ordinary sense to pass a counterfeit $100 bill and place the remaining counterfeit bills in the safe of the man [James Dolan] upon whom he had passed the money." (Rasch, Pages 66-67) On August 25, 1896, President Grover Cleveland granted Wilson a pardon, based on: "this convict was very young when convicted and developments upon his trial and representations now made to me cause very grave doubts as to his guilt." (Rasch, Page 67) Wilson went on to become a Sheriff, and was killed on June 4, 1918 trying to apprehend a criminal. (Rasch, Page 68) So Rasch, Sederwall's cited source, made no claim that Wilson was a counterfeiter or that Billy Bonney was one!

Furthermore, it should be noted that during Wilson's court appearances before Judge Warren Bristol in Mesilla for counterfeiting, Billy Bonney was in jail with him, since both were captured at Stinking Springs, and Billy was to be tried on his Lincoln County War indictments for the "Buckshot" Roberts, William Brady, and George Hindman killings. But no indictment was made in Mesilla on Billy Bonney for counterfeiting. Since Wilson listed Pat Garrett as a prosecution witness, and since Garrett was involved in the Azariah Wild tracking and capture of Billy, it is clear that Garrett, as thoroughly knowledgeable, did not consider Billy a counterfeiter - because he was not one.

Importantly, when Wilson petitioned for a pardon from Grover Cleveland in 1896 through his past attorney, William Thornton, then Governor of New Mexico Territory, his main accusers, Pat Garrett and James Dolan then denied his counterfeiting, and blamed his association with outlaw-murderer "Billy the Kid" for prejudicing them and his jury. <u>Noteworthy, is that they did not accuse Billy of being a counterfeiter, but merely tainting Wilson with his outlaw reputation.</u>

On May 24, 1896, Pat Garrett wrote to Attorney William Thornton, then Governor, in his capacity as Acting Sheriff of Doña Ana County, to request Wilson's pardon. He wrote:

Dear Sir –

I write you for the purpose of stating the facts with reference to Billy Wilson who was convicted in 1881 for passing counterfeit money & afterward escaped from the jail at Santa Fe –

I was the principal witness in the case & Jimmy Dolan was the other important witness against him – I worked hard for his conviction, from the fact that I believed him guilty, but from positive evidence since that time, I am now fully convinced that he was innocent – I have made it an object to fully investigate every thing pertaining to Wilson, & while <u>I must admit, that I was somewhat prejudiced against him from the fact that he was arrested with "Billy the Kid'</u> –

He was at the time quite young, & engaged in the Livery Stable business at White Oaks, when a <u>man by the name of West undoubtedly brought the counterfeit money into the County & bought Wilson's stable, paying him therefore with this money</u> –

I have since 1891 known Billy Wilson in Texas as D.L. Anderson, where he has enjoyed the reputation of being a good, honest, & straight forward citizen, has occupied many positions of trust & for a long time employed as manager of the Dolores Cattle co. in Kinney Co Texas – I know of nothing he has done which would be dis credited to him since his escape – He is a man of family, all of whom command the respect of all the people with whom they come in contact -

Yours Very Truly
P.F. Garrett

On June 30, 1896, main prosecution witness, James Dolan, wrote to Attorney William Thornton, then Governor; stating:

Dear Governor:
I write you in behalf of Billy Wilson, who was convicted some years ago at Santa Fe of the crime of passing counterfeit money, and who, from information which has come to me since his conviction, I believe has been wrongfully convicted. You were his Attorney at the time, and Pat Garrett, who at the time was the Sheriff of Lincoln County and myself were the principal witnesses against Wilson. The circumstances connected with his trial and conviction are about as follows: <u>He had sold just prior to that time a Livery Stable at White Oaks to a man by the name of West</u>. A few days afterward he came to Lincoln and came into my store with several one hundred dollar bills; he asked me to change one of them, which I did; the other bills he put in my safe, and left them there some time; when he took them out he wanted me to change another one of them, but I could not make the change, and he took it to Jose Montaña [sic], bought a few articles there, and received the balance in change for the bill; he then stayed around Lincoln for some time after which he went up to Sumner, where I understand one of the other bills was passed. He remained in Sumner until Pat Garrett went to arrest 'Billy the Kid', a noted desperado who had killed several men, and whom Garrett killed in arresting him. <u>And Wilson was arrested at the same time in company with the Kid. I am ready to admit that the fact that Wilson was in company with this outlaw prejudiced me against him and did much to induce me at the time to believe he knew the character of the money he passed. I feel certain that it was this prejudice existing in the minds of the jurors, and the excitement in the County, owing to his association with this outlaw, for several weeks prior to his arrest that tended to his conviction</u>. I now have grave doubts as to Wilson's knowledge of the character of the money passed. And I have information

which I consider very reliable that he has lived a life of an honorable and upright citizen ever since his escape from jail a few days after his conviction, and I write you this letter to ask you to aid me in securing his pardon, and also to forward this letter or statement of the case to the Attorney General for his consideration.

Wilson at the time was but a boy, I think perhaps about eighteen years of age – certainly not over twenty. I have never heard of his committing any other crime either before or since this, and [he] had many friends in this County up to the time he was found in company of the 'Kid'

Hoping that you may be able to secure this pardon. I remain

Yours Very Respectfully
Jas J. Dolan
Ex Member of Territorial Council

On July 7, 1896, Governor William Thornton wrote to Attorney General Judson Harmon in Washington, D.C., to request Wilson's pardon; stating:

Sir:
I have the honor to call your attention to the case of 'Billy Wilson", who was convicted in the District Court in the Territory of New Mexico sitting at Santa Fe, N.M. in the year 1881, of the crime of passing counterfeit money, and beg leave to make application for pardon; I was his attorney and desire to state to you the following facts: Mr. Wilson at the time was young, and a cowboy about 18 years of age, who had but newly come to this territory, and had very little experience except upon the range. He was the owner of a livery stable in the then new town of White Oaks; <u>he sold this stable to a man by the name of West, and received in payment therefore four $100.00 new greenback bills</u>. Shortly after

this, he went to the county seat, and passed one of these bills upon a merchant by the name of James J. Dolan, placing the other three in an envelope and putting it in the safe of this merchant, Mr. Dolan, where he left them for some weeks. He afterwards drew out one of the bills and passed it upon a man named Montoya [sic], and a few days later went to Ft. Sumner, in an adjoining county, where he remained for four or five months, when he was arrested in company with a notorious outlaw known as "Billy the Kid", whose real name, I cannot at this time give you. This outlaw had just [prior to this time killed a deputy marshal and sheriff of Lincoln County, and there was great indignation felt towards him by the people of the territory. This prejudice extended to all parties in his company and naturally reached Wilson. I believed at that time and I still believe that this boy was absolutely innocent that the money he received from the same of the livery stable, and passed upon Mess. Dolan and Montoya, was counterfeit. I could not conceive how it was possible for a man of ordinary sense to pass a counterfeit $100 bill, and place the remaining counterfeit bills in the safe of the man upon whom he had passed the money. The prejudice against him arising from his association with this outlaw was so great that the conviction was obtained upon evidence showing the above state of facts. An appeal was taken to the Supreme Court, but a few weeks after the conviction there was a jail delivery at Santa Fe when Wilson made his escape and has ever since remained at lodge. I have followed his course for a number of years, and am able to state upon information and belief, that he has during the past 15 years, since his conviction, lived an honest and honorable life … and enjoys the respect and esteem of the community in which he lives ... H now lives in Texas under the name of D.L. Anderson, and I herewith submit to you for your consideration the letters of about twenty-five of the most responsible citizens who have known him during the many years he has lived amongst them, and showing the character which he has borne. I also enclose letters of the two principal witnesses against him, Sheriff Pat. F. Garrett and Hon. J.J. Dolan, the last named being the person upon whom he passed the money; <u>each of these witnesses upon investigation, have concluded that he was wrongly convicted.</u> I also submit a letter from Chief Justice Prince, late Governor of this Territory, before whom Wilson was tried and convicted, recommending his pardon. Mr. Wilson, at my suggestion has agreed to surrender himself to the authorities, and submit his case upon its merits, and either receive executive clemency or submit to the punishment which has been adjudged against him.

<u>This is one of the few cases where I have been interested in which I would feel perfectly justified in saying that from the beginning to the end, I have always felt and I still feel and believe implicitly in the innocence of Billy Wilson, and that his punishment would be an outrage</u> ...

Hoping you will give this matter your prompt attention, and thanking you in advance, I remain,

> Respectfully,
> *W.T. Thornton*
> Governor

On August 25, 1896, President Grover Cleveland granted Billy Wilson the following pardon, as quoted in full in Philip J. Rasch's 1995 *Trailing Billy the Kid* - and listed in the *Cold Case Billy the Kid* Bibliography; and also available in the National Archives file also listed in that Bibliography:

Whereas Billy Wilson, alias D.L. Anderson, in the United States District Court for the Territory of New Mexico, in the year 1881 or 1882, was convicted of passing counterfeit money; and

Whereas, this convict was convicted about fifteen years ago, and escaped from jail pending an appeal from his conviction, and since his escape he has established a new home and has by reputable conduct gained the respect and good will of his neighbors, who numerously testify to his good character and standing; and

Whereas this convict was very young when convicted and <u>developments upon his trial and representations now made to me cause very grave doubts in my mind as to his guilt</u>; and

Whereas I am entirely satisfied that the ends of justice will be answered and a desirable citizen saved to society by the act of clemency, I have determined upon and it is my wish that the pardon in this case be sent to the Governor of New Mexico in order that the condition upon which it is granted may be complied with:

Now therefore let it be known that I, Grover Cleveland, President of the United States of America, in consideration of the premises, hereby grant to the said Billy Wilson, alias D.L. Anderson, a pardon upon the condition that the pardon of convict shall take effect immediately and after his personal appearance and sentence in the proper courts or if sentence has been pronounced, upon his surrender to proper authorities under such sentence.

In testimony whereof I have hereunto signed my name and caused the seal of the Department of Justice to be affixed.

Done in the city of Washington this twenty-fifth day of August, A.D. 1896, and of the Independence of the United States the one hundred and twenty-first.

Thus, Sederwall hid that Billy Wilson was not a counterfeiter. So linking him to Billy Bonney had nothing to do with counterfeiting. And Garrett, Dolan, and Thornton considered Billy Bonney an outlaw-murderer, with no mention of counterfeiting.

Sederwall next rolled out, yet again, his random counterfeit $100 bill, with his claim that his call to "Secret Service public affairs officer Michael Sampson ... led to the discovery in the secret Service Archives of **one of the bank notes passed by Billy Wilson.** A close examination of the bill by the Secret Service yielded the information that it had been the work of ace counterfeiter William E. Brockway." And, he added, that Brockway's bills had ended up in Lincoln County. (Pages 74-75)

HOAXING: This repeats Sederwall's lie about the random bill he got from Secret Service archivist, Michael Sampson, which was not connected in their records to Wild's investigation, to Lincoln County, to Billy Bonney, to Billy Wilson, or to Brockway; though it had a bank Brockway's bills used. It is, thus, not one "passed by Billy Wilson."

Building on his faked friendship of Billy Bonney to Billy Wilson, Sederwall again tried to link Billy to Brockway's pushers by name-dropping them. He said Nate Foster and W.H. West used counterfeit money to buy White Oaks property. And "West bought the stable from **the Kid's friend Billy Wilson**," and Wilson was also living with Samuel Dedrick who "was also paying for cattle using counterfeit bills that he obtained from West." (Page 77)

HOAXING: Using his made-up friendship of Billy Bonney and Wilson, Sederwall faked a link to Brockway pushers - Foster, West, and Sam Dedrick - at White Oaks. And he threw in the Dedrick-Barney Mason cattle buying plot, though it was by Dan, not Sam; and was unconnected to Billy Bonney or to rustling, being merely buying cattle with bad money and reselling them for good money.

This fiction used sources for name-dropping:

Operative Wallace Hall's report for May 19, 1882 recorded that in about May of 1881, Nate Foster "*had a saloon in White Oaks New Mexico. That Hays Frank Doyle, and others ... were with him. Hays was engaged in mining or some mining speculations at or in the vicinity of White Oaks, N.M.* For July 1, 1882, Hall described Nate Foster and Frank Doyle passing bills in Colorado, then going to

"New Mexico and Texas where more of the notes were passed. Hays and some of the party later located in Nevada, Missouri. Eventually, however, again all went to New Mexico, and Texas, where they engaged in the saloon business, mining speculations, &c,&c."

Even Pat Garrett was aware of the counterfeiters' investments. In *The Authentic Life of Billy the Kid*, he wrote: "Billy Wilson had sold some property to W.H. West and received in payment $400 in counterfeit money." (Garrett, Page 141)

None of this had anything to do with Billy the Kid. None of this was a Sederwall "discovery." None of this indicated that Billy Bonney participated in counterfeiting.

HOAXING BILLY AS AN SECRET SERVICE "SNITCH," INFORMER MURDERER, AND CONSPIRATOR TO ROB MAIL

Though one wonders why Sederwall's fiction of evil Billy the Kid (ergo, evil "Brushy" as Billy) is in "Brushy"-backing W.C. Jameson book, he repeated it from his June, 2015 *True West* article: "Billy Bonney's Bad Bucks," in which **Billy offered to "snitch" against fellow counterfeiters to Azariah Wild because a "man named Smith" told Wild that "the Kid was reading his reports while they were in possession of mail carrier Mike Cosgrove."** So Billy murdered Smith. (Pages 78-79)

Sederwall built this fiction from unrelated parts: Billy's October of 1880 Secret Service pardon bargain attempt, an April of 1880 murder of freight hauler named Sam Smith, and a December of 1880 Las Vegas jail visit to Billy of mail contractor, Mike Cosgrove.

HOAXING BILLY'S SECRET SERVICE PARDON BARGAIN

Billy's pardon bargain for testifying against counterfeiters was made-up as connecting him to Brockway's gang. Sederwall claimed: "In truth, all the Kid knew about the counterfeit ring involved Doyle and Hays, the Colorado beef buyers." (Page 78) Furthermore, to construct his evil Billy, Sederwall painted his testimony offer as being a "snitch" against compatriots.

HOAXING: Billy was not a counterfeiter, so testifying against them violated no loyalty among thieves. And Sederwall made-up that Billy's one time selling of cattle to *Colorado* buyers, meant that he sold to Brockway's men: Frank and James Doyle and John Hays - though they were just sometimes in Colorado, and were bill pushers, not cattle buyers for money-laundering. So, in reality, Billy would have had no knowledge of "Doyle and Hays."

Wild's reports indicate Billy's pardon bargain testimony was to be against Wild's suspects: the Dedricks, W.H. West, and their apparent pushers, Billy Wilson and Tom Cooper. At that time, Wild, saw the counterfeiting as local. And these would have been men Billy knew.

In his report for October 6, 1880, Wild presented a pardon option for Billy in exchange for that testimony. For October 9, 1880, he included a copy of his letter to U.S. Attorney Sidney Barnes about it. He also stated that Billy's attorney, Ira Leonard, had revealed the counterfeiters in White Oaks and at Dan Dedrick's ranch - likely obtained by Leonard from Billy to advertise his testimony's value. And Billy wrote too, as he had to Lew Wallace, about *"being tired of dodging the officers."*

But Barnes was a Ringite, likely alerting Wild's minders, James Dolan and Catron's brother-in-law, Edgar Walz; because Wild abruptly changed direction, claiming that Billy was in the counterfeiting gang, and it centered in Fort Sumner. So his report of October 11, 1880 documented his requesting from Barnes arrest warrants for Regulators: Billy, Bowdre, Scurlock, and O'Folliard.

By October 16, 1880, savvy Billy checked on Wild himself. He robbed the mail-coach, would have read Wild's report for October 11th stating: *"It may be well to send down warrants for the other parties who stand indicted in U.S. Court, and who are making Fort Sumner their headquarters."* Billy apparently decided that meeting with Wild would be a trap, refused the meeting; but lost his second chance at a pardon.

For his report for October 20, 1880, Wild admitted the mail theft to his Chief, and stated: *"In this mail I had several reports which if taken and read as they must have been as both mail pouches were cut open and the contents scattered about the ground. If this is as I believe it must be the plans of our capture and my mission here is as well known to them as it is to myself. I have respectfully notified the U.S. Attorney [Sidney Barnes] of this gang of men, and of their headquarters being at Fort Sumner."*

HOAXING SAM SMITH'S MURDER

Confusing dates, Sederwall continued his fiction of monster Billy the counterfeiter. For Billy as the murderer of Sam Smith, he cited a supposed *Santa Fe New Mexican* article of May 21, 1880 about Billy and his gang **murdering "a freighter named Smith"** because **Smith snitched to Wild about his counterfeiting gang.** Sederwall gave its alleged quote: "The information that enabled the Government officers to fix the handling of counterfeit money upon the Kid's gang came from a freighter named Smith. Soon afterward, while Smith was on his way from Las Vegas to Fort Sumner with a load of freight, he was waylaid and murdered by some of the gang." (Pages 78-79)

HOAXING: First of all, Wild was not in New Mexico Territory until late September of 1880; first meeting with U.S. Attorney Sidney Barnes and counterfeiting victim, James Dolan, on September 20, 1880. So he was not there in May of 1880 to be snitched to by Sam Smith.

And Sam Smith's April of 1880 murder had nothing to do with Billy Bonney. Sederwall's quote was lifted from the December 22, 1880 *New York Sun's* "Outlaws of New Mexico, The Exploits of a Band Headed by a New York Youth" (See pages 17-18 above), which likely inspired his hoax. But it was fake news. Smith was killed by Apaches.

Sam Smith's killing was well publicized in this period of Indian Wars in which Native American retaliations were feared. Though there was no *Santa Fe New Mexican* article of May 21, 1880 about the incident, as Sederwall claimed; there was May 21, 1881's *The Santa Fe Daily New Mexican's* "Mescalero Marauders," that reported Smith's murder by Mescalero Apaches. It stated: "**Last Thursday the stock ranch of Hon. T.B. Catron, of this city, known as the Carizoso [sic] ranch, was taken in by <u>a party of the [Mescalero Apache] Indians</u> ... The Indians were seen by the herders while killing the cattle, but the latter dared not attack them being outnumbered. As this ranch is only ten miles from the camp of White Oaks and thirty-five miles west of Fort Stanton, <u>it is</u>**

more than probable that this party was the same which murdered Sam Smith, the freighter, near Pato Springs."

The Pato Springs Apache murder of Sam Smith was also recorded in the 1880 *Annual Report of the Secretary of War* as on April 15, 1880; though that date varied in the press. *The Las Vegas Daily Gazette* of April 27, 1880 reported from Lincoln: "I am sorry to state to you that the Indians from the agency and also Victorio's band are a bad racket. They killed Sam Smith, our freighter, who left Las Vegas loaded for us on the 8th and arrived at Patos on the 20th in the evening; and on the 21st he was killed at Dry Lake. The goods were taken, harness and all, also sheets of wagon." The May 4, 1880 *Sacramento Daily Record-Tribune's* front page had "Indian Depredations in Colorado and Dakota;" stating: "A freighter, Samuel Smith by name, was killed at Patos Springs on the 19th ultimo, by nine Indians, supposed to be Mescalero Apaches or Comanches.

HOAXING A "MAIL CARRIER" MIKE COSGROVE CONSPIRACY

Recycling his June, 2015 *True West* article, "Billy Bonney's Bad Bucks," building on his meaningless May 21, 1880 date for faking Billy's "murder of freighter Smith," and aware that Wild had reported a mail theft by Billy (though it was October 16, 1880), Sederwall made-up that "around this time" (i.e. May of 1880), Wild became aware that Billy "was stopping the mail coach and reading his reports." Sederwall then claimed this proved Billy was in a conspiracy with the "mail carrier" "in the tampering;" though Sederwall now omitted his prior use of Mike Cosgrove's name. (Page 79)

HOAXING: This elaborate fakery had several fictions.

Firstly, the May of 1880 date is fake, since Wild was not there until September of 1880. Also, Billy robbed the mail coach just once: On October 16, 1880 to check on Azariah Wild's intentions, as written in his reports, during their pardon negotiation that month.

And the mail-theft conspiracy was just another part of Sederwall's evil Billy fabrication. The Mike Cosgrove Sederwall accused was not a "mail deliverer," but a large-scale "mail contractor." Sederwall was using the famous December 27, 1880 *Las Vegas Daily Gazette* article by Lucius "Lute" Wilcox about the Stinking Springs capture titled 'The Kid. Interview with Billy Bonney The Best Known Man in New Mexico;" in which Cosgrave gave new suits to Garrett's prisoners, including Billy. It stated: "**Mike Cosgrove, the <u>obliging mail contractor</u>, who has met the boys frequently while on business down the Pecos, had just gone in with four large bundles [of suits].**" Mail contractor was a political appointment, and Cosgrove was likely publicizing himself. But in his *True West* article, Sederwall had fabricated that Cosgrave's suit gift "proved" his conspiracy to let Billy read Wild's mailed reports, because he was getting Billy alone to ask him to keep it secret from Wild!

That Cosgrave was a mail contractor was presented in October 19, 1881's *Las Vegas Daily Optic*, for "Cosgrove's Contract," describing that his brother, Cornelius Cosgrove, on July 1, 1878, with a bid of $14,900, got the 442½ mile mail route contract from Las Vegas to Las Cruces; then added a route along the Pecos River to Roswell for an additional $2,517. In about July of 1879, Cornelius turned over the route to Mike. Since this was the period of Star Route scandals, the pay increase that the Cosgroves got of $73,997 was scrutinized. But Mike Cosgrove retained the route. The *Official Register of the United States Containing a List of the Officers and Employees in the Civil, Military, and Naval Service on the First of July, 1881, Volume II*, on page 209 lists his Star Service contract. And the 1888 *Miscellaneous Documents of the Senate of the United States for the First Session of the Fiftieth Congress. Volume II* confirms, on page 190, that a mail contractor was a political position, with appointment by the Second Assistant Postmaster-General.

As to <u>Mike Cosgrave's mail carrier</u>, an April 26, 1882 *Las Vegas Daily Optic* article, in the section "Optic Oracle," named Cosgrove's "buckboard driver" as hairy "Dutchy," who made news when he was shaved by a barber.

But accused counterfeit bill pusher, Billy Wilson, had participated in that mail theft. So the name of the actual mail carrier involved was given in his own 1881 Case No. 1-760 for mail theft in "U.S. vs William Wilson, U.S. Territorial Court, First Judicial District, Santa Fe, Assault on <u>Fred Weston</u>, mail carrier." Stated was that on October 16, 1880, "*together with others whose names are to the jurors aforesaid unknown with force and arms, guns and pistols did then and there within the jurisdiction of this court ... did make an assault upon said* Fred Weston, *he ... being ... the Carrier and Agent of the Mail of the United States of America ... there being conveyed upon a buckboard by said Carrier and Agent* Fred Weston *... between Fort Sumner and Sunnyside."* To be noted is that this Billy Wilson case is cited in the Bibliography with its National Archives location. That means Sederwall knew that Mike Cosgrove was not the "mail carrier," and hid Fred Weston to build his hoax.

To be notes is just one mail theft, on October 16, 1880, against mail carrier, Fred Weston, to check Wild's reports, as confirmed by Wilson's indictment for it. None of this has anything to do with Billy Bonney as a counterfeiter.

HOAXING A LINK OF BILLY'S TESTIFYING OFFER AS PROOF OF HIS BEING A COUNTERFEITER

Sederwall claimed that Billy's willingness to be a prosecution witness against the counterfeiters, meant he *was* a counterfeiter.

HOAXING: This hid that Wild had identified the New Mexico Territory counterfeiters before Ring influence.

New to the Territory, Wild correctly focused on White Oaks, reporting for September 22, 1880: *"I am going to have trouble in getting assistance to make arrests in White Oaks."* Reporting for October 4, 1880, Wild identified William Wilson and Tom Cooper as passing $100 counterfeit bills to Lincoln merchant José Montaño, and to post trader firm Dowlin and Delaney, in addition to James Dolan. For October 5, 1880, from Fort Stanton, Wild reported: *I will respectfully state from information that [Thomas] Cooper and [William] Wilson are both employed at a livery & sales stables at White Oaks kept by James West a notorious character recently from Texas."* For October 10, 1880, Wild wrote: *"William Wilson is reported to be at Bosque Grande at Dedrick's ranch. Dedrick is reported as being one of the leaders of the clan, and partners with West in the Corral at White Oaks."*

And Billy had gotten his information not from being a counterfeiter, but from associating with them: selling stock to Dan Dedrick and his brothers at the White Oaks livery, and using Billy Wilson for rustling.

Also, Pat Garrett, working with Wild, did not accuse Billy of counterfeiting; instead naming the same New Mexico Territory suspects in his *The Authentic Life of Billy the Kid* as Dan Dedrick, W.H. West, and Billy Wilson. (Garrett, Pages 140-142)

HOAXING BILLY AS A COUNTERFEITER DOING WITNESS INTIMIDATION

Building on his fiction of evil Billy revenge murdering Sam Smith for informing on him, Sederwall added that Billy scared-off another witness named James DeVours, who was referenced in Azariah Wild's report of October 9, 1880; and who Sederwall called the "manager of the Carriso [sic] Ranch." (Page 78-79)

HOAXING: The manager of T.B. Catron's Carrizozo Land and Cattle Company ranch was his Ringite brother-in-law, Edgar Walz.

Sederwall misstated Devours. As Wild reported, he was a low level counterfeiter and ranch employee. Wild's report for October 18, 1880, documented Walz's relating that DeVours would give information about the *"gang of counterfeiters"* if paid. But, by his report for November 28, 1880, Wild admitted that the counterfeiters had gotten wind of his activities, and halted their Mason-cattle buying plot *"until the present excitement and trouble is over."* Dan Dedrick and W.H. West fled, as did Walz's counterfeiting workers. DeVours, Wild noted, *"left the country for safety."* All this was unrelated to Billy Bonney.

HOAXING A LINK TO A.P. ANAYA'S COUNTERFEITING CLAIM

Sederwall concluded his case for Billy as a counterfeiter with A.P. "Paco" Anaya, a mainstay in "Brushy Bill" and "Billy the Kid Case" hoaxes for his windbag malarkey. Here used was his claim that Billy had a lot of cash because it was "spurious." (Page 79)

INVALID SOURCE: Anaya's book, *I Buried Billy*, published in 1991, is windbag malarkey, except for confirming that Billy Bonney's killing. (See pages 421-422 below) He wrote:

"Billy and his pals always had a lot of money ... but this money was spurious money that Billy Wilson had stolen in Washington when he was employed by the government [and they] printed about $5000." (Anaya, Pages 70-71)

Hidden are Anaya's other tall tales. For example, about John Chisum's debt to Billy, he made-up a bizarre scene in which he witnessed Billy meeting Chisum in a bar, and making him bite a pistol. ("You could hear the sound the teeth made on the barrel.") Then Billy beat up Chisum to make him pay. (Anaya, Pages 84-86)

HOAXING A COUNTERFEITING LINK TO STINKING SPRINGS

Steve Sederwall topped-off his Billy the Kid as a counterfeiter hoax in W.C. Jameson's chapter "The Stinking Springs Incident," (Pages 85-91) in which Pat Garrett tried to kill Billy.

Noteworthy is Sederwall's cynical opportunism, since he had spent years promulgating the "Billy the Kid Case" hoax with the claim that Pat Garrett was Billy's super-friend, who was the accessory to murdering his own deputies so Billy could escape the Lincoln jail (risking hanging himself), and then murdered the innocent victim to save Billy in Fort Sumner (risking hanging again). And "Brushy" was demolished too, since this Stinking Springs tale has counterfeiting claims unknown to him as "Billy."

To build the Stinking Springs fiction, it seems that the Jameson-Sederwall duo never visited the site, since omitted is its most dramatic feature: the huge arroyo near the front of the rock house shelter in which Garrett and his posse hid. Instead, the scene was lifted from old-timer "Paco" Anaya's windbag malarkey in his posthumous 1991 book, *I Buried Billy*.

As with the rest of the counterfeiting hoax, Sederwall was faking a "discovery" by himself. His intent was to use that counterfeiting hoax as "evidence" for a hoaxed "discovery" about Stinking Springs.

INVALID SOURCE: No legitimate historian or lawman would use A.P. "Paco" Anaya as a reliable witness. Totally ignorant of the historical events, Anaya simply spouted windbag malarkey.

Anaya's book, *I Buried Billy*, was printed posthumously in 1991 by founders of the Billy the Kid Outlaw Gang, Joe and Marlyn Bowlin, as an old-timer document given to them by his nephew, Sam Anaya in 1989. It had input from Paco's son, Louis Anaya, from a 1937 article in *Personal Adventure Stories* magazine titled "I Hid Out Billy the Kid." (*I Buried Billy*, Page 17) Sam stated it was completed in Spanish in 1930 when Paco was **"seventy less nine days."** The Bolins had it translated. (*I Buried Billy*, Page 10)

The book's punch line is that "Paco" Anaya witnessed Billy Bonney's burial, as well as knowing him in Fort Sumner after his great escape; though Paco was two years younger (born January 25, 1862). (*I Buried Billy*, Page 68) Besides that, the book is merely Anaya's, often ludicrous, fiction; though he claimed to know Billy since August of 1878, when he was a teenaged sheep herder in the Fort Sumner area. (*I Buried Billy*, Page 23)

An example of Anaya's tall tales is the Lincoln County War Battle. He stated that one day in August of 1878, Bob Beckwith came with 48 armed men to Alexander McSween, telling him he had come to fix things with him and the Murphys. **"Bob followed McSween and Billy the Kid followed both into McSween's office. When McSween sat down he turned his back to Bob and then Bob drew his gun and shot him in the back. At the same moment Billy shot Bob in the head and he fell dead. At the same time, the other Texans outside started a fire in several parts of the house."** (*I Buried Billy*, Page 30)

Another example of Anaya's tall tales is that for Billy's Lincoln jailing, Billy's food is **"very well cooked by the black cook, Gus, which was the cook's name."** (*I Buried Billy*, 51) [Gottfried Gauss was white, German, the building's caretaker, and John Tunstall's past cook.] And about Stinking Springs, for which Anaya would be used as Sederwall's source, he thought it was December of 1879, and Billy was being pursued by Sheriff Pepen [sic- Peppin] and 40 men. (*I Buried Billy*, Page 88)

But "cop" Sederwall based his "investigation" on Anaya's malarkey to fake a Stinking Springs "discovery."

For the capture, Sederwall has the lawmen wait outside for daylight. A Garrett quote is given, based on his knowing that Billy wore a distinctive hat: "I told the posse that should the Kid make his appearance, it **was my intention to kill him**, and the rest would surrender." And Garrett's fatal shooting of Bowdre, mistaken for Billy, is given. (Pages 86-87)

ANAYA'S FAKERY: Again proving himself a useless historical source, Anaya lifted the historical hat incident to make-up his own hat story. He put Billy at a mail stop between Pinos and White Oaks, where Billy traded his hat with a Mexican. So the Pepen [sic] Posse [confused from the 1878 Lincoln County War Battle] saw it and killed the Mexican as Billy. (*I Buried* Billy, Page 90) Then Billy and his group flee to the Wilcox ranch, but Garrett and 40 Texans [from the 1880 posse] have a run-in with Tom O'Folliard and Tom Pickett; and Billy sent them smoke signals so they could meet-up again. (Anaya, Pages 94-97) And Anaya has no killing of O'Folliard!

For the surrender, Sederwall claimed that he "discovered" that Billy had **urinated on the piled-up weapons** in the rock house before surrendering as the last person out (Page 88); with Tom Pickett as first out waving a white cloth. (Page 87)

HOAXING USING ANAYA'S FAKERY OF BODILY WASTE: Sederwall relied on "Paco" Anaya's malarkey for his "urinating" discovery, but misread Anaya's text. Anaya wrote: "[W]hen Billy gave up, and as soon as Billy was secure, Pat went into the house to bring what they had there, and found that Billy had piled up all the rifles and pistols, as well as the gunbelts, and did his business on them and got them all covered. When Pat saw them he said to Billy, 'What did you do that to the weapons for?' And Billy answered, 'That's all they're good for when you can't use them.' " (*I Buried Billy*, Page 107)

But Anaya's dirty joke is about *defecation* to ruin the weapons. Urination, actually, was used by buffalo hunters, like Garrett, to cool hot barrels of their Sharps Big Fifties during multiple shootings into a herd, and would not have been seen as disgusting.

More important is that the real witness, Pat Garrett, gave no such scene with a urinating Billy last out, with first-out as white-flag-bearing Tom Pickett. Garrett stated in *The Authentic Life of Billy the Kid*: "[Dave] Rudabaugh stuck out from the window a handkerchief that had once been white ... In a few minutes all of them - the Kid, Wilson,

Pickett, and Rudabaugh – came out." (Garrett Pages 181-182)

But Sederwall was setting-up his fake "cop discoveries" that history is not as written.

Sederwall added to his fable, from an uncited source, never reported information that the possemen heard the sound of porthole-making. (Page 88) So Sederwall called the sound of "porthole-making" a "tell" because "writers and historians missed [that] in addition to pursuing the man who was convicted of killing Sheriff Brady and gunning down two of his deputies, Garrett was sent by the United States Secret Service in pursuit of counterfeiters." (Page 88)

HOAXING A "DISCOVERY": First of all, Billy was accused of killing *one* Brady deputy: George Hindman. The other indictment, besides Brady, was for posseman, Andrew "Buckshot Roberts." Sederwall seems to be confusing Billy's April 28, 1881 Lincoln jailbreak with killings of Deputies Bell and Olinger, with the December 22, 1880 Stinking Springs capture.

Also, Stinking Springs's line cabin was a windowless, solid, stacked-rock house. Portholes could not be cut out, like they had been in the adobe McSween house in the Lincoln County War Battle (a possible inspiration for this hoaxing); casting doubt on the porthole-cutting claim.

Also, Garrett's working with the Secret Service on a counterfeiting case is known history. His participation was given by himself, 137 years before Sederwall claimed he discovered it. In *The Authentic Life of Billy the Kid*, Garrett stated: "In October [of 1880], Azariah F. Wild, a detective in the employ of the Treasury Department. hailing from New Orleans, La., visited New Mexico to glean information in regard to the circulation of counterfeit money, some of which had certainly been passed in Lincoln County." (Garrett, Page 139) But Garrett made clear in his book that his warrants, and consequent pursuit, were for Billy's murder indictments: "[Bob] Olinger [commissioned also through Azariah Wild] and myself were both commissioned as deputy United States marshals and held United States warrants for the Kid and Bowdre for the killing of ["Buckshot"] Roberts on an Indian Reservation." (Garrett, Page 145) And Garrett never claimed Billy as a counterfeiter.

Sederwall was just building on his own Billy-as-counterfeiter hoax.

So Sederwall, pretending he discovered a connection to Garrett's pursuit and counterfeiting, and pretending that Billy was a counterfeiter, pretended that Billy worried that Garrett would find counterfeit bills on him; which, Sederwall stated, would make Garrett file "federal counterfeiting charges" against him. (Page 88) Sederwall added that the porthole-making sound was really burying counterfeit money along with a Colt .45! (Page 90)

HOAXING: This is Sederwall's usual fake reasoning by "what-ifs." He had not proved Billy was a counterfeiter - or a urinater, or a hole digger! Also, on December 22, 1880, Billy already had a bigger federal indictment to worry about: past U.S. Attorney T.B. Catron's 1878 federal indictment No. 411 for the murder of "Buckshot" Roberts - with hanging as outcome.

Furthermore, the switcheroo from porthole-making to digging, is even more absurd as being heard from a windowless solid rock house by men at a distance and hiding in a deep ravine.

But, building on thin air, Sederwall quoted John Meadows from Billy's post-jailbreak, as saying Billy told him he could not yet leave the Territory for lack of money. So Sederwall made-up that this meant that Billy was referring to lack of counterfeit money, because it was stored in the Stinking Springs rock house! (Page 89)

HOAXING: This is Sederwall's "what-ifs" fakery to preposterous lengths: *if* Billy was a counterfeiter, *if* he hid counterfeit money in the Stinking Springs rock house, *if* he dug a hole to hide it, *if* he urinated on it, *if* he needed cash, *then* he might want to go back and get it!

Of course, missing is the reality that Billy misled his friend, John Meadows, about excuses for staying in the Territory. Kept secret from Meadows, was Billy's romance with Paulita Maxwell. Meadows's ranch was south of the Lincoln jailbreak, with Billy possibly intending to go to Old Mexico. But Billy then apparently decided he could not leave the Territory and Paulita, and turned northeast to her and Fort Sumner and almost certain death.

Sederwall then made-up that Billy piled the guns on the hole with counterfeit money to "camouflage" it; and added "urine" supposedly to repel squeamish Garrett. (Page 90) He added that historian Philip Rasch claimed that in 1932, Tom Pickett, sent an Ed Coles to dig up the money. But none was found. (Page 90) So Sederwall spewed "what-ifs": What if after the jailbreak Billy had retrieved the counterfeit money and gun? What if the gun got rusty after being in the ground? What if it was then useless?

Now guess if Sederwall claimed a found a gun? He stated that in 1910, a child named Ralph Camp dug inside the rock house and found a rusted Colt .45 (with photo provided).

HOAXED "INVESTIGATION": Revealed is that Sederwall had built his "discovery" backwards by meaningless "what ifs" using the 1910 gun finding and "Paco" Anaya's Billy defecating fable, which Sederwall had confused as urinating.

Used also to construct the hoax was Philip Rasch's 1995 *Trailing Billy the Kid*, **cited in the Bibliography, which gave the Pickett-Cole tale of seeking money in the Stinking Springs cabin, but in that tale it is real money, and skeptical Rasch emphasized Tom Pickett's reputation for telling tall tales. (Rasch, Page 108)**

Also, no serial number is given to check the gun's dating. And the rock house was a Maxwell sheep herders' line cabin, likely built after Maxwell bought Fort Sumner. So from 1870 to 1910, anyone could leave the gun there. No link is established to Billy, to counterfeiting, to urinating, to defecating, or to real history.

CHAPTER 5
HOAXING JAMES DOLAN AS A COLLUDING COUNTERFEITER

ADDING ANOTHER CHARACTER TO THE FICTION

A separate hoax was attached to the Billy the Kid as counterfeiter hoax. It involved fabricating James Dolan as a counterfeiter too, presumably in the Brockway gang. It arose from Sederwall's misstating Operative Wallace Hall's reports.

Sederwall stated that on October 2, 1880, Wild got a counterfeit bill from James Dolan, allegedly from Billy Wilson; and Dolan was also holding three more bills for him. But Sederwall claimed that Wilson and Dolan were enemies; thus, Dolan framed Wilson, and was their counterfeiter himself. (Pages 77- 78) This recycled his 2010 *Ruidoso News* counterfeiting article about a **Miss N.M. Ferguson from Chicago** writing an August of 1880 letter to the Secret Service **accusing** <u>Dolan</u>.

Claimed now was that on August 8, 1880, Miss Ferguson wrote to Operative Wallace Hall reporting that counterfeit bills were being passed in New Mexico, and enclosed a note from "Fort Stanton, New Mexico, resident J.C. Delaney" which had a counterfeit bill enclosed. Hall's report of August 24, 1880 was quoted: *"[T]he Delaney letter, if true in its statements, gives some light as to who are operating in the counterfeit hundreds in that region."* But Sederwall added: **"Hall learned from Ferguson the name of the suspect who had passed the counterfeit bill to Delaney:** <u>**James J. Dolan of Lincoln**</u>**."** (Page 76)

HOAXING: Sederwall's fable was built on misreading or willfully faking Operative Wallace Hall's reports of August 3, 1880, August 24, 1880, October 10, 1880, and July 1, 1882 about a Miss N.M. Ferguson of Chicago getting a counterfeit $100 bill when in New Mexico Territory. But the letters were <u>from</u> merchant <u>Dowlin</u>, not <u>about</u> merchant <u>Dolan</u>! And <u>she had written a letter to John C. Delaney at Fort Stanton</u>. She also <u>enclosed response letters</u> she had received about that counterfeit bill. One was from merchant, John C. Delaney, to her, and one was from merchant, M.J. Dowlin, to Will Dowlin and Co. <u>Importantly, none of them now exist in the Secret Service files; so there is no known content about *"who [were] operating in the counterfeit hundreds in that region.*"</u> Sederwall made-up that "Hall learned from Ferguson the name of the suspect who had passed the counterfeit bill to Delaney: James J. Dolan of Lincoln."

Hall's actual conclusion was merely that Miss Ferguson had gotten a Brockway bill, then being passed in New Mexico by his gang members. There was no connection to Billy the Kid or to James Dolan in his reports; as follows:

1) For August 3, 1880, from Chicago, Hall tried to find out if a Miss M.M. [sic - later wrote N.M.] Ferguson had gotten an answer to her letter to a John C. Delaney in Fort Stanton, New Mexico, in which she had enclosed the counterfeit bill. [Delaney ran the Fort Stanton post store with Will Dowlin.] For August 4th, Hall reported his meeting with Ferguson, who had gotten no reply *"to her letter returning the cft $100 note to J.C. Delaney."* <u>So the sole Ferguson letter had merely informed Delaney about her getting the bad bill.</u>

2) Hall's report for August 24, 1880, stated that he received from Ferguson a cover note with two enclosed response letters. <u>So there was a Ferguson note accompanying enclosed letters</u>. Hall stated that one letter was dated Fort Stanton, New Mexico, August 8, 1880, and was *"addressed to Miss Ferguson and signed J.C. Delaney. It referenced a $100 Revere Bank of Boston note and speaks of some persons in that section supposed to be 'shoving' them"* <u>So one letter was from J.C. Delaney to Ferguson.</u> Hall stated: *"Enclosed with this Delaney letter, I received a letter <u>dated Tularosa Aug 5th, 1880</u>, addressed to Messrs. Will Dowlin & Co and signed M.J. Dowlin. It also refers to the Ferguson cft hundred ... <u>The Delaney letter, if true in its statements, gives some light as to who are operating in the counterfeit hundreds in that region.</u>"* So the second enclosed letter was from M.J. Dowlin to Will Dowlin & Co.

But it was the apparent source of Sederwall's lifted location of <u>Tularosa</u> for his fable, and his lifted *"light"* given *"as to who are operating in the counterfeit hundreds in that region;"* though it is lost, so any specific accusations it might have had are unknown.

3) Hall's report for October 10, 1881, followed-up for Chief Brooks about Ferguson's matter: *"You will remember that almost one year ago cft $100 were put in circulation about Santa Fe, New Mexico, and one of these cft hundreds was received from there by Miss N.M. Fergusson of this city [Chicago]. I forwarded you, on Aug 24, 1880 letters of J.C. Delaney and Will Dowlin & Co and M.J. Dowlin of New Mexico concerning cft $100 shovers, etc. etc."* Hall now connected Fergusson's bill to the Brockway gang, hypothesizing they came from the "boodle" in John Hays's haystack; writing: *"Frank Doyle, brother of James [Doyle] is now in Bradford, Ill. Had returned in July, this year, from a year absence in the south-west. Mentioned Las Vegas, Santa Fe and White Oaks New Mexico as some of the places where [Frank] Doyle had spent a portion of his time. You will remember that almost one year ago cft $100 were put in circulation about Santa Fe, New Mexico, and one of these cft hundreds was received from there by Miss N.M. Fergusson of this city. I forwarded you, on Aug 24, 1880 letters of J.C. Delaney and Will Dowlin & Co and M.J. Dowlin of New Mexico concerning cft $100 shovers, etc. etc. ... [and] Frank Doyle was ... in that section at that time. again it might have been his 'boodle' found in the haystack near Nevada, Mo."* <u>So Hall now filled in *"who [were] operating in the counterfeit hundreds in that region"*: Brockway's pusher, Frank Doyle</u>; who likely got the bad bill from Brockway's pusher, John Hays, from his stock of bills in his Missouri haystack. None of this had to do with Billy Bonney or James Dolan.

4) Hall's report for July 1, 1882 referenced the Ferguson matter: *"With my report of August 24, 1880 I sent you two letters. One dated Fort Stanton Texas [sic] Aug 24, 1880, addressed to Miss N.M. Ferguson, signed J.C. Delaney; the other dated Tularosa Aug 5, 1880, addressed to Will Dowlin & Co, and signed by M.J. Dowlin. The cft [counterfeit] $100* <u>*referred to in these letters was no doubt passed by some of the Hays Foster party.*</u> *I think you never returned these*

letters to me. I cannot find them in my files." So Hall now added Brockway pusher, Nate Foster. None of this had to do with Billy Bonney or James Dolan.

Thus, the men involved in the Ferguson matter were merchants who were passed the bad bill. William "Will" Dowlin, with his brother Paul, had a mill on the Ruidoso River since about 1869, operating as Paul Dowlin & Co. In 1873, when L.G. Murphy & Co. were kicked out from their sutler store in Fort Stanton after James Dolan tried to murder a soldier, Paul took it over as post-trader, and Will operated the mill; becoming, by 1876, Paul Dowlin & Brother. When Paul died in 1877, Will sold the mill, and kept the store. In about 1878, Will partnered with John C. Delaney for the store. In 1879, they bought "The House" in Lincoln by mortgage from T.B. Catron - who had claimed it in the bankruptcy of J.J. Dolan & Co. But Dowlin and Delaney defaulted on their mortgage from Catron in December of 1880; and Catron sold then sold "The House" in January of 1881 to Lincoln County for its new courthouse and jail.

Azariah Wild, for October 4, 1880, had reported that William Dowlin had received a National Revere Bank of Boston, Massachusetts passed by William Wilson; also demonstrating Dowlin & Delaney's getting bad bills; like Wallace Hall reported for Miss N.M. Ferguson. But Wild never linked the bill to Brockway's gang when he was in New Mexico Territory. And there was no link to Billy Bonney in any of this.

And none of this had anything at all to do with indicating that James Dolan was a counterfeiter.

CHAPTER 6
A NON-EXISTENT CASE

SMOKE AND MIRRORS AND THE WILLIAMS BONNEY AND BROCKWAY

No evidence was presented by Steve Sederwall - as assisted by U.S. Marshals Service Historian David Turk, and narrated by W.C. Jameson - to indicate that Billy Bonney was a counterfeiter; was connected to William Brockway or his gang members; did counterfeiting with Jesse James; rustled to launder counterfeit money; murdered freighter, Sam Smith; intimidated potential witness, James Devours; or plotted with a mailman to read Azariah Wild's reports.

Sederwall's only "achievement" by his flaunted fakery was demeaning the "Brushy Bill" and "Billy the Kid" hoaxes by creating an evil Billy in contradiction to their positive portrayal of him as pardon-worthy. And, obviously, all Sederwall's claims knocked "Brushy" out of the running by his being unaware of them for his own Billy the Kid impersonation.

And one has to guess that W.C. Jameson missed all that in his dazzled hero-worship of "cop" Steve Sederwall and his knee-jerk acceptance of any history-is-not-as-written gambit.

PART VII

SUMMARY AND CONCLUSIONS

CHAPTER 1
A RETURN TO ANTIQUE MALARKEY

MASQUERADE

On April 21, 1980, a woman named Rosie Ruiz briefly won the female category in the 84th Boston Marathon with a time of 2:31:56: the fastest for a woman in its history, and third fastest for a woman in any marathon. But she was not sweaty, not muscular, and not seen by other runners. Then a freelance photographer recalled seeing her, the year before, shortcutting the New York Marathon by subway. After eight days, she was stripped of her title. Later a friend claimed she had admitted to sneaking into the race from the crowd less than a mile from the finish.

The hoaxers covered in this book are the Rosie Ruizes of Billy the Kid history, trying to cheat their way to acclaim, while accomplishing nothing whatsoever. It takes a sociopathic scorn of one's fellows to perform these masquerades. They all had it.

By the "Billy the Kid's Bad Bucks" hoax in W.C. Jameson's 2018 *Cold Case Billy the Kid*, the cheaters had 15 years of hoaxing under their belts as practice for this masterpiece of chicanery; and they felt untouchable. With impunity, Jameson had re-written "Brushy's" words to better fake him as Billy the Kid. And the "Billy the Kid Case" hoaxers had escaped ransacking John Miller's and William Hudspeth's graves, escaped forensic records forgeries, and escaped monetary penalties in my open records case. Instead, they were extolled in press, a magazine, and in TV documentaries.

So, after years of defaming Pat Garrett as a murderer, they had turned to attacking Billy Bonney, in a throw-back to his earliest outlaw myths, from when he was still alive to deny them.

The blame goes to corrupt, past, New Mexico Governor, Bill Richardson, who had resuscitated the old imposter hoaxes, and had empowered and emboldened these charlatans. This book is a step toward countering their collective lies with truth.

ANNOTATED APPENDIX

APPENDIX: 1. Original Spanish Coroner's Jury Report of July 15, 1881 for William H. Bonney aka Kid (Courtesy of Indiana Historical Society, Lew Wallace Collection)

> Territorio de Nuevo Méjico
> Condado de San Miguel } Precinto N° 27.
> Del 4eino y Distrito judicial
> Al Procurador ~~General~~ del Territorio de Nuevo Méjico — Salud.
>
> Este dia 15 de Julio, A.D. 1881, recivi yo, el abajo firmado, Juez de Paz del Precinto arriba escrito, informacion que habia habido una muerte en Fuerte Sumner en dicho precinto é immediatamente al recivir la informacion procedí al dicho lugar y nombré á Milnor Rudulph, José Silva, Antonio Saavedra, Pedro Antonio Lucero, Lorenzo Jaramillo y Sabal Gutierres un j[urado] do para averiguar el asunto y venir. El dicho jurado en la casa de Luz 10. axwell procedieron á un cuarto en dicha casa donde hallaron el cuerpo de William Bonney alias "Kid" con un balazo en el pecho en el lado yzquierdo del pecho y habiendo ecsaminado el cuerpo ecsaminaron la evidencia de Pedro Maxwell cuya evidencia es como sigue " Estando yo acostado en

mi cama en mi cuarto a cosa de media noche
El dia 14 de Julio entró á mi cuarto Pat. F.
Garrett y se sentó en la orilla de mi cama á
platicar conmigo. A poco rato que Garrett
se sentó entró William Bonney y se arrimó
á mi cama con una pistola en la mano y
me preguntó "Who is it? Who is it?" y Entónces
Pat. F. Garrett le tiró dos balazos á dicho
William Bonney y se cayó el dicho Bonney
en un lado de mi fogon y yo sali del cuarto
cuando volví á entrar yá en tres ó cuatro
minutos despues de los balazos estaba muerto dicho Bonney."

  El jurado há hallado el siguiente
dictámen "Nosotros los del jurado u-
nanimente hallamos que William Bonney há sido muerto por un balazo en el
pecho yz quierdo en la region del Corazon
tirado de una pistola en la mano de Pat.
F. Garrett y nuestro dictámen es que
el hecho de dicho Garrett fué homicidio
justificable y estamos unániones en
opinion que la gratitud de toda la

comunidad es devida á dicho Garrett por su hecho y que es digno de ser recompensado."

M. A. Lucero
Presidente

Antº Saavedra
Pedro Antº Lucero
Jose + Silba
Vidal + Gutierrez
Lorenso + Jaramillo

Todo cuya informacion pongo á conocimiento de V.

Alejandro Segura
Juez de Paz

APPENDIX: 2. NO DNA FROM CARPENTER'S BENCH: Orchid Cellmark's October 15, 2004's "Laboratory Report, Forensic Identity, Mitochondrial Analysis, Results and Conclusions" for its Case 4444-001B-004B (for Case 2003-274's bench results).

[AUTHOR'S SUMMARY: Lee's carpenter's bench underside swabbings and shavings were labeled as evidence numbers 4444-001B, 4444-002B, 4444-003B, and 4444-004B. <u>"Results" showed the specimens "failed to yield amplifiable DNA." "Conclusions" recorded: "no mitochondrial [DNA] sequence data were generated.</u>"

LABORATORY REPORT - FORENSIC IDENTITY – MITOCHONDRIAL ANALYSIS

CASE DATA:

Referring Agency:	Calvin D. Ostler
Cellmark Case #:	FOR 4444B
Agency Contact:	Calvin D. Ostler
Report Date:	October 15, 2004

1. **Evidence Received:**

Accession #	Sample Description	Receipt Date/ Method of Delivery
4444-001A	Wood shavings "Lincoln County Courthouse #1"	8/4/04 - FedEx
4444-002A	Wood shavings "Lincoln County Courthouse #2"	
4444-001B	Swabbing from "underside of bench #3"	
4444-002B	Swabbing from "underside of bench #4"	
4444-003B	Wood shavings "underside of bench #3"	
4444-004B	Wood shavings "underside of bench #4"	

DR. HENRY LEE'S CARPENTER'S BENCH SAMPLES:
4444-001B
4444-002B
4444-003B
4444-004B

2. Results:

Sequence data obtained from the swabbing from the underside of the bench (4444-001B) are inconclusive. As a result, no data from this sample are reported.

The swabbing from the underside of the bench (4444-002B) and wood shavings from the underside of the bench (4444-003B and 4444-004B) were extracted according to accepted mitochondrial extraction protocol; however, the swabbing and wood shavings (4444-002B, 4444-003B, 4444-004B) failed to yield amplifiable DNA. Therefore, no sequence data were generated for comparison to a reference specimen.

Procedures used in the analysis of this case adhere to the standards adopted by the DNA Advisory Board on DNA analysis methods.

3. Conclusions:

Sample 4444-001B provided an inconclusive mtDNA profile; therefore, no conclusions can be reached with regard to the origin of this sample.

Samples 4444-002B, 4444-003B and 4444-004B did not provide sufficient human mitochondrial DNA for sequencing. Since no mitochondrial sequence data were generated, no conclusions with regard to this sample can be reached.

4. Disposition of Evidence:

All evidence received in this case will be returned to the submitting agency.

Orchid Cellmark has maintained complete chain of custody documentation from receipt of evidence to disposition.

NO DNA RECOVERED:

3. Conclusions

Sample 4444-001B provided an <u>inconclusive mtDNA profile</u>; therefore, no conclusions can be reached with regard to the origin of this sample.

Samples 4444-002B, 4444-003B and 4444-004B did not provide sufficient human mitochondrial DNA for sequencing. Since <u>no mitochondrial sequence data were generated</u>, no condlusions with regard to this sample can be reached.

---

5. Case Review:

The individuals below have reviewed the results and conclusions described in this report.

Joseph Warren
Forensic Supervisor

Rick W. Staub, Ph.D.
Laboratory Director

Kristina Paulette
Forensic Analyst

S I G N E D under oath before me this 15th day of October, 2004.

Notary Public

APPENDIX: 3. Lincoln County Deputy Sheriff Steve Sederwall's "Supplemental Report for the Exhumation of John Miller for Case No. 2003-274"

LINCOLN COUNTY SHERIFF'S DEPARTMENT
SUPPLEMENTAL REPORT

Case #:   2003-274
Date: Thursday, May 19, 2005
Subject: Exhumation of John Miller,
Location: Arizona Pioneers' Cemetery, Prescott, Arizona
Report By: Steven M. Sederwall

On Thursday, May 19, 2005, at approximately 1:00 pm the following met at the Arizona Pioneers' Cemetery in Prescott, Arizona.

Investigators:

Steven M. Sederwall; Lincoln County Sheriff's Deputy
DOB- 09/02/52
Capitan, New Mexico

Tom Sullivan; Sheriff of Lincoln County, Retired
DOB- 04/10/40
Capitan, New Mexico

Dale Tunnell; Arizona State Investigator
DOB-
Phoenix, Arizona

Stephen W. McGregor; Ex-Lincoln County Sheriff's Deputy
DOB- 07/16/57
Hannibal, Missouri

Dr. Rick Staub; Orchid Cell Mark, DNA
DOB- 02/15/52
Dallas, Texas

Mike Poline; Yavapi County Sheriff's Deputy
DOB- 06/29/62
Prescott, Arizona

Laura Fulginiti; Forensic Scientist – Anthropologist
DOB – 11/09/62
Phoenix, Arizona

Kristen Hartnett; Forensic Scientist – Archeologist
DOB – 10/30/77
Phoenix, Arizona

Misty Rodarte; Arizona Pioneers' Administration
DOB – 01/29/74
Prescott, Arizona

George Tomsen; Arizona Pioneers' Cemetery Manager
DOB- 07/07/42
Prescott, Arizona

Others Present:

Pearl Tenney Romney
DOB- 01/12/24
Prescott, Arizona

Anthony Rodarte
DOB- 01/11/71
Prescott, Arizona

Diana Shenefield
DOB- 01/09/59
Prescott, Arizona

Jesse Shenefield
DOB- 03/08/90
Prescott, Arizona

Russ Hadley
DOB- 02/24/35
Prescott Arizona

Toby Deherrera Jr.
DOB- 10/11/70
Prescott, Arizona

Pat Sullivan
DOB- 07/23/41
Capitan, New Mexico

Linda Fischer
DOB- 04/29/60
Prescott Valley, Arizona

Billie Martin
DOB- 04/27/37
Prescott, Arizona

Dale Sams
DOB 02/26/57
Prescott Valley, Arizona

Clara Enest
DOB- Unknown
China Valley, Arizona

Bill Kurtis Production - these people no longer paid by BKP - complaint being done by them

Joel Saptori; Cameraman
DOB- 06-13-69
Oak Park, Illinois

Greg Gricus; Soundman
DOB- 11/16/65
Oak Park, Illinois

RELEASED TO:
BY PRESCOTT POLICE DEPT

444

APPENDIX: 4. Judge George P. Eichwald. "Findings of Fact and Conclusions of Law and Order of the Court." May 15, 2014.

THIRTEENTH JUDICIAL DISTRICT COURT
COUNTY OF SANDOVAL
STATE OF NEW MEXICO

GALE COOPER and DE BACA COUNTY NEWS,
a New Mexico Corporation,
          Plaintiffs,
v.   No. D-1329-CV-2007-1364

RICK VIRDEN, LINCOLN COUNTY SHERIFF and CUSTODIAN OF THE RECORDS OF THE LINCOLN COUNTY SHERIFF'S OFFICE; and STEVEN M. SEDERWALL, FORMER LINCOLN COUNTY DEPUTY SHERIFF; and THOMAS T. SULLIVAN, FORMER LINCOLN COUNTY SHERIFF AND FORMER LINCOLN COUNTY DEPUTY SHERIFF,
                                          Defendants.

FINDINGS OF FACT AND CONCLUSIONS OF LAW AND ORDER OF THE COURT

All requested Findings of Fact and Conclusions of Law are denied except such as are herein incorporated by the Court.

FINDINGS OF FACT

1. This Court has jurisdiction over the parties and subject matter of this litigation.

2. Plaintiff De Baca County News is no longer a party to this litigation as it has settled all matters in controversy with Defendants.

3. On January 14, 2014 Plaintiff Gale Cooper (hereinafter Cooper) filed a voluntary dismissal against Defendant Thomas Sullivan as Defendant Sullivan is now deceased.

4. The matter in controversy is for enforcement of the New Mexico Inspection of Public [Records] Act, Section 14-2-1 et seq. NMSA 1978 (IPRA) and concerning the Defendants' refusal to turn over requested DNA records of Lincoln County Sheriff's Department Case No. 2003-274, "Billy the Kid Case," ("Case 2003-274").

5. Case 2003-274 is a murder case, filed in 2003 in the Lincoln County Sheriff's Department by Sheriff Tom Sullivan (hereinafter Sullivan) and his commissioned Deputy Steve Sederwall (hereinafter Sederwall) to be solved by forensic DNA acquisitions and matching, and accusing the suspect Pat Garrett of murdering an innocent victim instead of Billy the Kid; with a sub-investigation of Billy the Kid's double homicide of Deputies James Bell and Robert Olinger.

6. From 2003 to 2004, Case 2003-274's New Mexico exhumation attempts on Billy the Kid and his mother for matching DNA were legally blocked so no DNA was obtained.

7. In 2004 Billy the Kid's DNA was allegedly obtained for Case 2003-274 by Dr. Henry Lee (hereinafter Lee) from an old carpenter's bench on which Billy the Kid [was] laid after being shot. Lee's specimens were sent for DNA processing to Orchid Cellmark Lab (hereinafter Orchid Cellmark) in Texas.

8. In 2005 newly elected Lincoln County Sheriff Rick Virden (hereinafter Virden) deputized Sullivan and Sederwall to continue Case 2003-274 by exhuming Billy the Kid's identity claimants John Miller and "Brushy Bill" Roberts for DNA match[ing] with Lee's bench DNA to solve the Garrett murder.

9. On May 19, 2005, for Case 2003-274, John Miller and William Hudspeth were exhumed in Arizona and their bones were taken to Orchid Cellmark for DNA extractions and for DNA matching to the carpenter's bench DNA.

10. From April 24, 2007 to June 26, 2007 Plaintiff Cooper made IPRA records requests from Sheriff Virden for Case 2003-274 through her then attorney Mickey Barnett ("request phase"). Requested records were for:

    A. Lee's DNA recoveries from the carpenter's bench;
    B. Orchid Cellmark's DNA extractions from Lee's specimens;
    C. Orchid Cellmark's DNA extractions for the two Arizona bodies; and
    D. Orchid Cellmark's DNA matchings for the carpenter's bench [DNA] to the bodies [DNA].

11. In the request phase, no records were given and their denials were improper: without valid IPRA exceptions; with Sullivan and Sederwall after having resigned their deputyship on June 21, 2007 admitting to records possession, but calling them private hobby "trade secrets;" with Virden denying having any Case 2003-274 records; and with Virden not attempting to recover records from Sullivan, Sederwall, Lee, or Orchid Cellmark.

12. The case at hand for enforcement of IPRA was filed on October 15, 2007.

13. In their August 18, 2008 depositions Sullivan and Sederwall admitted knowing that the requested records existed, and admitted that Sederwall possessed Lee's carpenter's bench report.

14. On September 3, 2007 [sic – 2008], by subpoena duces tecum, Virden turned over his Case 2003-274 file of one hundred ninety-three (193) pages; lacking requested records, but with documents confirming the DNA investigation and having contact information for records recovery.

15. In his September 8, 2008 deposition Virden denied knowledge of requested records.

16. On November 20, 2009 Partial Summary Judgment was issued in favor of Plaintiffs and against Defendants declaring the records requested were public, were created in official capacities, and should be turned over.

17. On February 18, 2010 Sederwall turned over to the Plaintiffs an unrequested nine (9) page Lee report on courthouse floorboards. Its header had no link to Case 2003-274. It was signed by Lee and Calvin Ostler. In the March 9, 2010 Presentment Hearing, the Court was told that this floorboard report was the only Lee report in Sederwall's possession.

18. On October 26 2010 Virden first made records requests to Lee and Orchid Cellmark but never followed up to recover the records after Lee responded that he had one report, and Orchid Cellmark responded that it would send the records if released by their client.

19. On November 10, 2010 Sederwall turned over to the Plaintiffs a sixteen (16) page Lee report on the carpenter's bench but [it] was lacking a link to Case 2003-274.

20. An Evidentiary Hearing was held on January 21, 2011 and Virden argued that he could not turn over records that were not in his direct possession and which he did not know existed. Sederwall's Lee courthouse floorboard report was entered as Exhibit "F," and the carpenter's bench report was entered as Exhibit "E." At this hearing the Court reminded the parties that the Partial Summary Judgment previously entered on November 20, 2009 found that the Defendants and the investigation were official and connected to the Lincoln County Sheriff and that all evidence was public record and that all information should be turned over to Plaintiffs.

20. [sic – numbering incorrect] In July, 2011 Cooper recognized that the Lee courthouse floorboard report (entered as Exhibit "F") was a rewrite of the alleged same floorboard report given on November 10, 2010, and that this rewriting also put in doubt the authenticity of the carpenter's bench report (Exhibit "E").

21. At a September 23, 2011 Presentment Hearing Cooper alerted the Court of the discrepancies in the Lee reports.

22. On January 17, 2012 a Hearing on Sanctions was conducted and Plaintiffs stated that there were no records productions and allegations of altered Lee reports. Production of the original Lee report was ordered. Plaintiff De Baca County News requested attorney's [sic – attorneys'] fees which were granted.

23. On January 31, 2012 Sederwall turned over a twenty-five (25) page "original" Lee report combining the courthouse floorboard and the carpenter's bench. Its header identified Lee's work as for Case 2003-274.

24. On March 20, 2012 Plaintiff De Baca County News subpoenaed the Orchid Cellmark records for Case 2003-274, receiving one hundred thirty-three (133) pages on April 20, 2012. The records included DNA results from Lee's specimens and from the two exhumed Arizona bodies.

25. On May 31, 2012 a Hearing for Sanctions was conducted. The newest Lee report was presented as evidence of altering of the past Lee reports to conceal the law enforcement header, but was also called not original as lacking signatures. The subpoenaed Orchid Cellmark records were entered as evidence to prove records' existence. Sanctions included the ordering of new depositions of the Defendants.

26. In his June 26, 2012 deposition Sederwall admitted to: removing law enforcement information from later Lee reports; called the twenty-five (25) page Lee report he first received from Lee as original; and admitted to knowing that the Orchid Cellmark client was Calvin Ostler.

27. In his June 27, 2012 deposition Virden admitted to: waiting three (3) years into litigation to write record requests to Lee and Orchid Cellmark; not requesting from Lee the report when Lee wrote back that he had one; and not trying to find out the client's name after Orchid Cellmark wrote back that it was required to send Virden the requested records.

28. Cooper challenged De Baca County News standing which the Court denied.

29. At an Evidentiary Hearing conducted on December 21 [sic – 18], 2012 and February 4, 2013 Virden admitted: that the subpoenaed Orchid Cellmark DNA records were from Case 2003-274 but gave no valid explanation for waiting three (3) years to begin records recovery or for not following up on the resulting responses to get the records. Witness Seterwall [sic], still calling Case 2003-274 his private hobby, admitted to altering the first Lee report's header to remove Case 2003-274 information; and admitted to creating the other report versions given to the Court and lacking law enforcement information.

30. Court ordered mediation between Cooper and Defendants was unsuccessful.

CONCLUSIONS OF LAW

1. Section 14-2-5 NMSA 1978 states, "The intent of the legislature in enacting the Inspection of Public Records Act is to ensure as the policy of the State of New Mexico, that all persons are entitled to the greatest possible information regarding the affairs of government and the official acts of public officers and employees."

2. Section 14-2-8© NMSA 1978 states, "No person requesting records shall be required to state the reason for inspecting records."

3. Cooper's status as an author is irrelevant in requesting records under IPRA and [she] is entitled to receive document[s] which were requested.

4. Without statutory justification, no requested records were produced by the Defendants.

5. The requested records exist, and have been recoverable from the time of the request phase.

6. After De Baca County News' subpoena outside IPRA requirement, the requested Lee report and the Orchid Cellmark DNA matchings remain unrecovered.

7. Section 14-2-5 NMSA 1978 states, "To provide persons with such information is ... an integral part of the routine duties of public officers and employees. Virden produced no requested records and gave no statutory justification for non-recovery, in violation of IPRA.

8. Virden did not comply with Section 14-2-11(B)(1-3) NMSA 1978, "Procedure for Denied Requests: by providing the requester with a written explanation of the "denial" listing: "the records sought", "each person responsible for the denial," and "mailed to the person requesting the records within fifteen days after the request." Improper denial under Section 14-2-11(C) subjects the custodian to monetary [up to $100 per day] damages.

9. In both the request and enforcement phases, Virden's records recovery refusal[s] have been misplaced and ignored IPRA by arguing that recovery pertains only to records in direct physical possession. Section 14-2-6(A) NMSA 1978 states enforcement custodial responsibility "regardless of whether the records are in that person's actual physical custody and control." Section 14-2-6(F) NMSA 1978 repeats that "public records" can be held "on behalf of any public body." *Toomey v. Truth or Consequences,* N.M. Ct. Ap. No. 30,795, P.4. (2012) clearly stated "public agencies must produce all record[s], even those held by or created by a private entity 'on behalf of' the public agency.["] The DNA records of Lee and Orchid Cellmark were held on behalf of Lincoln Sheriff's Office by Lee and Orchid Cellmark, and are intrinsic to solving its Pat Garrett murder Case 2003-274.

10. Virden was obligated to recover records from it [sic- his] deputy agents. *Ronald A. Coco, Inc. v. St Paul's Methodist Church of Las Cruces, N.M., Inc.*, 78, N.M. 97, 99, 428 P.2d 636, 638 (1967), states, in part, "Unquestionably, insofar as an agent's acts are with the agent's authority they are in legal contemplation of the acts of the principal."

11. Ignorance of records existence was argued by Virden to refuse recovery. Ignorance is not an IPRA exception under Section 14-2-1(A) (1-8) NMSA 1978. Virden's lack or [sic - of] knowledge of records is disingenuous, since his deputies admitted to records possession, his Case 2003-274 file showed DNA investigations and recovery options, Lee responded to Virden and Lee had the record, and Orchid Cellmark responded to Virden that it had the records. Virden's questioning the existence of records burdens the requester with proof, contrary to the decision in *State of New Mexico ex Re.* [sic – *rel.*] *Newsome v. Alarid*, 90 N.M. 790, 568 P.2d 1236 (1977), which held that the burden is placed upon the custodian to justify why the records sought to be examined should not be furnished. See also, *City of Farmington v. The Daily Times*, 2009-NMCA-057, 146, N.M. 349, 210 P.3d 246.

12. Virden ignored Section 14-2-7(E)(5) NMSA 1978, "the responsibility of a public body to make available public records for inspection." Virden waited three (3) years into litigation to seek records, then did not actually try to recover them from Lee and Orchid Cellmark. To prevent stonewalling, IPRA has time based damages in NMSA Section 14-2-11. IPRA damage provisions are intended to encourage public entities' prompt compliance with records requests. *Derringer v. State*, 133 N.M. 721, 68 P.3rd 691 9(Ct. App. 2003).

13. As public officials, under Section 14-2-5 NMSA 1978, Sullivan and Sederwall had to provide records as, "an integral part of the routine duties of public officers and employees."

14. As commissioned deputies, under Section 13[sic - 14]-2-11(B)(2) NMSA 1978, along with Virden, they were "responsible for the denial of records." As Virden's deputies, they were his agents. "A person may appoint an agent to do the same acts and achieve the same legal consequences by performing of an act as if he or she had acted personally." 3 Am. Jur. 2d Agency Section 18, at 422 (2002). Section 4-41-9 NMSA 1978 states, "The said deputies are hereby authorized to discharge all the duties which belong to the office of sheriff, that may be placed under their charge by their principals, with the same effect as though they were executed by the respective sheriffs."

15. Sullivan and Sederwall said they were hobbyists and the records were private property. Sullivan's and Sederwall's argument of being "unsalaried "reserve deputies" is irrelevant to the records responsibility, since "an agent is a person who, by agreement with another called the principal, represents the principal in dealings with third persons or transacts some other business ... for the principal, with or without compensation. UJI 13-401, NMRA.

16. In their June 21, 2007 "Memorandum" to Virden, Sullivan and Sederwall admitted to having Case 2003-274 records, but called them private property, while at the same time resigning their public official positions as deputies. Furthermore, from 2010 to 2012, Sederwall offered Case 2003-274 records for sale on his own billythekidcase.com website.

17. After being court-ordered, Sederwall made a non-specific records request for Orchid Cellmark on February 3 [sic – 5], 2011; later admitting in his June

26, 2012 deposition, that he knew Calvin Ostler was the Orchid Cellmark client contact for getting records released.

18. In his June 26, 2012 deposition, Sederwall admitted to willful involvement in altering Lee reports by rewritings to remove the original law enforcement information in Lee's "first" report sent to him as Lincoln County Deputy Sheriff. Section 14-2-6(F) NMSA 1978 defines "public records" as "all documents, papers, letters, books, maps, tapes, photographs, recordings and other materials, regardless of physical form or characteristics, used, created, received, maintained or held by or on behalf of any pubic body and related to public business, whether or not the records are required by law to be created or maintained." The plain language implication is that the records are to be "originals" of [sic – or] true "duplicates" of the original. Under Rule 11-1001(D) NMRA 1978, "an original of a writing is the writing itself. Rile [sic –Rule] 11-101(E) NMRA 1978 states "a duplicate is a counterpart produced by the same impression as the original ... which accurately reproduces the original." Neither an "original" nor a "duplicate" report was presented, only altered records which do not comply with IPRA law.

19. The Defendants' actions and/or inactions in responding to Plaintiff's IPRA requests are in violation of IPRA law and subject to sanctions.

20. Damages for enforcement of a denied request to inspect records are governed by Section 14-2-12(D) NMSA 1978, not Section 14-2-11(C) NMSA 1978. [**NOTE: This is untrue.**] The statutory maximum per-day penalty of Section 14-2-11(C) NMSA 1978 does not create any standard for an amount of damages under Section 14-2-12 (D) NMSA 1978. *Faber v. King*, 2013-NMCA-080, 306 P.3d 519, cert. granted, 2013-NMCERT-007.

21. Section 14-2-12(D) provides for damages, "which we hold must be somehow specified as to their true nature by the district court." *Faber v. King*, 2013-NMCA-080 {15}.

22. Punitive damages cannot be recovered in absence of compensatory or nominal damages. *Madrid v. Marquez*, 2001-NMCA-087 pp. 3, 131, N.M. 132, 33 P.3d 683.

23. UJI 13-1832, NMRA reads in part, "Nominal damages are a trivial sum of money ... awarded to a party who has established right to recover, but has not established that she is entitled to compensatory damages."

24. Plaintiff Cooper has established that she has a right to recover but has not established that she is entitled to compensatory damages and is awarded one thousand dollars ($1,000.00) as nominal damages against Defendants.

25. UJI 13-1827, NMRA allows the award of punitive damages if the conduct of the Defendants is malicious, willful, reckless, wanton, or in bad faith.

26. Defendants' conduct in not providing the requested records enumerated in Findings of Fact 10, is willful, wanton, and in bad faith.

27. Defendants' conduct in providing altered records as discussed in Findings of Facts 25, 26, and 29 and Conclusions of Law 18 is wanton, willful, and in bad faith.

28. Based on Defendants' conduct, Plaintiff Cooper is entitled to punitive damages in the amount of one hundred thousand dollars ($100,000.00) against Defendants.

29. Section 14-2-12(D) allows for an award of attorney's fees and costs.

30. Plaintiff Cooper is awarded attorney's [sic – attorneys'] fees which have not been previously paid.

31. Plaintiff Cooper is awarded her costs.

ORDER

IT IS THEREFORE ORDERED Judgment be entered in favor of Plaintiff Cooper against Defendants as follows:

1. Nominal Damages in the amount of thousand dollars ($1,000.00);
2. Punitive Damage in the amount of one hundred thousand dollars ($100,000.00);
3. Attorney's fees which have not been previously paid;
4. Plaintiff is awarded costs and shall provide the Court with an affidavit supporting her costs within ten (10) days of the filing of these Findings of Fact and Conclusions of Law and Order of the Court;
5. Interest shall accrue at the rate of 8.75 percent per annum commencing from the date of the filing of the Judgment in this matter.
6. Plaintiff shall prepare the Judgment reflecting the Court's decision, approved as to form by counsel for Defendants, within fifteen (15) days of the filing of these Findings of Fact, Conclusion[s] of Law and Order of the Court.

George P. Eichwald
GEORGE P. EICHWALD
District Judge

APPENDIX: 5. FULGINITI REPORT: Dr. Laura Fulginiti. "Re: Exhumation, Pioneer Home Cemetery, Prescott, Arizona for Dale L. Tunnell, Ph.D. [sic], Forensitec. June 2, 2005.

RE: EXHUMATION PIONEER HOME CEMETERY, PRESCOTT, ARIZONA FOR DALE L. TUNNELL, PhD, FORENSITEC. JUNE 2, 2005

On May 19, 2005 at approximately 1230 hours I am asked to assist in the exhumation of the remains of an individual known as Mr. John Miller by Dr. Dale Tunnell, President, Forensitec. The purpose of my involvement is to aid in the exhumation process as well as to assess any skeletal remains recovered. The exhumation takes place at the Arizona Pioneer [sic] Home Cemetery, Iron Springs Road in Prescott Arizona in the presence of Dr. Tunnell, several of his associates, members of the Arizona Pioneer Home staff and Kristen Harnett M.A., AMSU graduate student.

Dr. Tunnell located the alleged gravesite of Mr. Miller prior to our arrival on the scene. The gravesite was located using the line of headstones to the West of the target grave. A standard reference point was established as the headstone of Michael Clancy. At approximately 1400 hours, a backhoe began to remove the sod overlying the alleged grave, which was oriented in an East-West direction, with the head to the West. When fragments of wood began to be removed, the grave was excavated using a shovel. Once the top of the casket and a portion of femur were unearthed, the excavation relied on digging with trowels and by hand. The position of the femur indicated that the remains were supine, with the feet to the East and the skull to the West. The left femoral shaft, minus the head, was removed, examined, and packaged for DNA analysis.

Dr. Tunnell, in consultation with the cemetery staff and his other associates determined that the adjacent grave to the   North was likely that of Mr. Miller and excavation shifted to that gravesite.

[AUTHOR'S NOTE: This unmarked North Grave was not John Miller's, as Dr. Fulginiti later proved; and was that of random man, William Hudspeth. His exhumation was a multi-felony crime, later covered-up by the Maricopa County prosecutor.]

The backhoe removed the overlying sod until fragments of wood began to be unearthed. The excavation shifted to shovels and the top of the casket was identified. Excavation proceeded using trowels and hand tools until various aspects of the skeleton were identified and cleared. The skeleton in this grave was also lying supine, head to the West and feet to the East. The casket had collapsed onto the body at some point prior to the exhumation process. **A metal detector on loan from the Yavapai County Sheriff's Office and operated by Det. Mike Poling, YCSO, was used to locate metal items, including nails and casket fittings.** (These items were donated to the Arizona Pioneer Home for their museum).

[AUTHOR'S NOTE: Poling was accidentally present to deliver specimens to Laura Fulginiti; but the hoaxers later lied that he was the lawman responsible for the exhumation.]

Minimal historical artifacts, such as buttons, a possible rivet, portions of wood from the casket and casket fittings were identified as they were unearthed. Skeletal elements were measured for depth and location, removed from the grave and examined (see Forensitec report). Pathological conditions such as osteoarthritis, healed fractures and markers of occupation were noted as follows. The vertebrae exhibited signs of extreme osteoarthritis in the form of lipping of the vertebral bodies, collapse of some of the bodies and osteophytic activity. **There were extensive healed traumata on the right scapula**

[AUTHOR'S NOTE: So the damaged right scapula was in North Grave of William Hudspeth, and was not a shot left scapula of John Miller as the hoaxers later lied.]

and the left clavicle, a healed Colles' fracture of the right distal radius, a healed fracture of the second rib and a healed fracture of the left fourth metacarpal. The bone was dark brown in color, friable and dry. There was postmortem damage, both from the collapse of the lid of the casket onto the remains as well as from the removal process. The remains were photographed, samples were harvested for DNA (tooth and femur) and the remains were returned to the grave and reburied.

Anecdotal historical information suggested that Mr. John Miller had died from complications of a fractured hip while recuperating in the Arizona pioneer Home. The individual in the north grave, while having extensive pathological conditions, particularly in the upper body, did not have discernible pathology of the *os coxae*.

[AUTHOR'S NOTE: That the North Grave's remains lacked John Miller's broken hip; so the scapula was not his. So the South Grave is Miller's; and it had the broken hip.]

At this point in the exhumation, a decision was made to exhume the *os coxae* of the individual in the south grave to confirm that we had indeed excavated the remains of Mr. John Miller from the north grave. The south grave was excavated by shovel to the point where the remnants of the casket lid were identified. Excavation resumed using trowels and hand tools until the left femoral head was identified.

The head of the femur was misshapen with bony remodeling, suggesting an antemortem [before death] injury. Additional excavation revealed the left innominate, which also had extensive remodeling of the acetabulum, ischium and pubis. The ischium tapered to a point with lack of union to the pubis, suggesting a healing fracture of the ischiopubic ramus. **This evidence led the team to believe that the individual in the south grave was, in fact, more consistent with the known facts regarding the Medical history of Mr. John Miller and additional DNA samples were recovered (femur, scalp?, matter from inside the braincase).**

[AUTHOR'S NOTE: Confirmation of South Grave as John Miller's because of broken hip.]

The maxillae and mandible were recovered but were edentulous.

[AUTHOR'S NOTE: Miller had NO TEETH AT ALL. The Hoaxers later lied that he had buck teeth like Billy the Kid's!]

There was limited pathology of the vertebrae, ribcage, clavicles and scapulae of the individual from the south grave. Mild osteoarthritis of the vertebral bodies was the only pathology of note. Photographs of the cranium and mandible were taken and the remains were returned to the grave and reburied.

Biological profiles of the two individuals are similar. Both were adult males, consistent with individuals of European (White) descent, and of advancing years. The nasal apertures on both were tall and narrow, with a sharp nasal sill, the malars were retreating and the cranial shape, while fragmentary, was round. The pubic symphyses exhibited characteristics of Suchey-Brooks Phase IV (36-86 years, mean 61.2 years).The symphyseal faces were flat and eroded with marked ventral ligaments. The sternal ends of the ribs; while fragmentary, exhibited long bony extensions, consistent with an Iscan, Loth stage 8 (65 plus). **The individual in the south grave was edentulous.**

[AUTHOR'S NOTE: Repeated is that Miller had NO TEETH.]

The scene was returned to a state approximating that prior to our arrival and was cleared shortly after sundown. Items of evidence collected were distributed to members of the Arizona Pioneer Home Cemetery staff and to Dr. Richard Staub (see Forensitec report).

Laura C. Fulginiti, Ph.D., D-ABFA
Forensic Anthropologist

[AUTHOR'S NOTE: Fulginiti Report Summary.]

1) DALE TUNNELL: "located the alleged gravesite of Mr. Miller prior to [her] arrival on the scene."

2) MILLER'S SOUTH GRAVE: "The left femoral shaft, minus the head," was taken by DR. Staub "for DNA."

3) HUDSPETH'S NORTH GRAVE: "Dr. Tunnell, in consultation with the cemetery staff and his other associates determined that the adjacent grave to the North was likely that of Mr. Miller and excavation shifted to that gravesite."

4) HUDSPETH'S NORTH GRAVE: "A metal detector on loan from the Yavapai County Sheriff's Office and operated by Det. Mike Poling, YCSO, was used to locate metal items, including nails and casket fittings."

5) HUDSPETH'S REMAINS: "There were extensive healed traumata on the right scapula and the left clavicle, a healed Colles' fracture of the right distal radius, a healed fracture of the second rib and a healed fracture of the left fourth metacarpal."

6) THE NORTH GRAVE IS IDENTIFIED AS NOT MILLER'S:: "Anecdotal historical information suggested that Mr. John Miller had died from complications of a fractured hip while recuperating in the Arizona pioneer Home. The individual in the north grave ... did not have discernible pathology of the *os coxae*."

7) THE SOUTH GRAVE IS IDENTIFIED AS MILLER'S: "The head of the femur was misshapen with bony remodeling, suggesting an antemortem injury ... The ischium tapered to a point with lack of union to the pubis, suggesting a healing fracture of the ischiopubic ramus. This evidence led the team to believe that the individual in the south grave was, in fact, more consistent with the known facts regarding the Medical history of Mr. John Miller and additional DNA samples were recovered ... The maxillae and mandible were recovered but were edentulous."

APPENDIX: 6. GRAVE-ROBBED REMAINS OF JOHN MILLER AND WILLIAM HUDSPETH:
Orchid Cellmark Laboratory's May 19, 2005 "Chain of Custody" for the taken skeletal remains.

[AUTHOR'S SUMMARY: Stolen from Miller's South grave were his "skull and mummified brains," "jawbone," "pelvis," "left femur," and part of his casket. Stolen from Hudspeth's North grave were his "mandible and teeth," and "right femur."]

APPENDIX: 7. DNA EXTRACTIONS FROM JOHN MILLER AND WILLIAM HUDSPETH: Orchid Cellmark Laboratory's January 26, 2009 "Laboratory Report - Forensic Identity – Mitochondrial Analysis," for Case 4444 (for Case No. 2003-274)

[AUTHOR'S SUMMARY: Under "Results," DNA is listed for Miller's South grave's left femur, as specimen 4444-011, as "a mitochondrial DNA profile obtained; and "for Hudspeth's North Grave's right femur, as specimen 4444-013, as "mitochondrial DNA profile obtained." Useless mixed DNA profile is listed under "Results" from Hudspeth's "mandible and teeth" as specimen 4444-012; and from Dr. Lee's courthouse floorboard sample for the Deputy Bell's killing as specimen 4444-002A.]

LABORATORY REPORT - FORENSIC IDENTITY – MITOCHONDRIAL ANALYSIS

CASE DATA:

Referring Agency:	Calvin D. Ostler
Cellmark Case #:	FOR 4444
Cellmark Report #:	FOR 4444C
Agency Contact:	Calvin D. Ostler
Report Date:	January 26, 2009

4444. Evidence Received:

Accession #	Sample Description	Receipt Date/Method of Delivery
4444-001A	Wood shavings "Lincoln County Courthouse #1"	8/4/04 FedEx
4444-002A	Wood shavings "Lincoln County Courthouse #2"	
4444-001B	Swabbing from "underside of bench #3"	
4444-002B	Swabbing from "underside of bench #4"	
4444-003B	Wood shavings "underside of bench #3"	
4444-004B	Wood shavings "underside of bench #4"	
4444-005	Reference hair - BTK?	1/31/05 USPS
4444-006	Jaw bone from south grave	5/19/05 Hand delivered to Orchid Cellmark (Stemmons Frwy) by Rick W. Staub (RWS)
4444-007	Casket wood from south grave	
4444-008	Paper/cloth material from south grave	
4444-009	Skull and mummified brains from south grave	
4444-010	Pelvis from south grave	NOTE: HAND-DELIVERED BY DR. STAUB
4444-011	Left femur from south grave	
4444-012	Mandible and teeth from north grave	
4444-013	Right femur from north grave	

SOUTH GRAVE = JOHN MILLER

NORTH GRAVE = WILLIAM HUDSPETH

2. **Results:**

Mitochondrial DNA from specimen 4444-002A, 4444-005, 4444-011, 4444-012, and 4444-013 was amplified and sequenced at Hypervariable Regions I and II of the Mitochondrial Control Region. Sequence data are presented as variations from the Revised Cambridge Reference Sequence (rCRS). Bases not specifically listed are consistent with rCRS.

	HVI (16024 – 16365)			
	16153	16223	16266	16292
4444-011	•	T	•	T
4444-013	A	•	G	•
rCRS	G	C	C	C

(•) consistent with rCRS

4444-013: RANDOM MAN WILLIAM HUDSPETH'S FEMUR YIELDED MEANINGLESS DNA

	HVII (73-340)						
	73	189	204	207	263	309.1	315.1
4444-011	G	G	C	A	G	C	C
4444-013	•	•	•	•	G	303-340 INC	
rCRS	A	A	T	G	A	-	-

(•) consistent with rCRS (INC) inconclusive (-) no base present at this position

Samples 4444-002A, and 4444-012 indicate a mixture of two or more mitochondrial DNA profiles. Consequently, no sequence data are reported.

Specimen 4444-005 was extracted according to the accepted Mitochondrial DNA Extraction Protocol. No mitochondrial DNA was detected following amplification. Therefore, no sequence data were generated for comparison to reference specimens.

Procedures used in the analysis of this case adhere to the standards adopted by the DNA Advisory Board on DNA analysis methods.

4444-012: HUDSPETH MANDIBLE GAVE USELESS MIXED DNA

APPENDIX: 8. Debra Komar, PhD. "Sixth Judicial Court, State of New Mexico, County of Grant. No. MS 2003-11 "In the Matter of Catherine Antrim. Affidavit of Debra Komar, PhD." January 9, 2004.

AFFIDAVIT OF DEBRA KOMAR, PhD.

The undersigned Debra Komar, PhD. upon oath, states:

1. My name is Debra Komar, PhD. I am a forensic anthropologist employed by the Office of the Medical Investigator (OMI) at the Health Sciences Center (HSC) at the University of New Mexico in Albuquerque, New Mexico. A copy of my resume is attached as Exhibit A. My training, education and background qualifies me to make the statements contained in this Affidavit.

2. In my capacity as a forensic anthropologist for the OMI, I was asked to investigate the following questions related to the bodies of William Bonney aka "Billy the Kid" and Catherine Antrim, the mother of William Bonney: (a) whether the bodies could be located; (b) whether the bodies could be recovered; and (c) whether the bodies would be in a state such that a positive identification could be made. The stated purpose of the request was to aid in a criminal investigation of the circumstances behind the death of Billy the Kid and any involvement by Pat Garrett.

3. Based on research of Silver City cemetery records, the location of the body of Catherine Antrim may not be known to a reasonable degree of scientific probability. According to cemetery records, Catherine Antrim was buried in 1874 in Silver City in a cemetery within the City limits. In 1877, the cemetery in which she was buried flooded. Records indicate that the floodwaters could have disturbed the burial sites within the cemetery. In 1882, as a result of a change in the city ordinance requiring burials outside the city limits, Catherine Antrim's body was removed to a new burial site. It is not certain to a reasonable degree of scientific probability that the body, which was exhumed and moved in 1882, was that of Catherine Antrim. **Accordingly, if the purpose of exhuming Catherine Antrim is to provide a "known" standard for DNA testing, the fact that she cannot be positively identified renders all DNA tests suspect to a reasonable degree of scientific probability.**

4. If attempt is made to exhume the supposed body of Catherine Antrim from the burial site with her name, it is probable with a reasonable degree of scientific probability that **the remains of other individuals will be disturbed**. The burial site with Catherine Antrim's name is Plot D-27 at Memory Lane Cemetery. **This plot is the resting place of twelve (12) other known individuals**. See Exhibit B to Zumwalt Affidavit. In addition to the known individuals within Plot D-27, present cemetery records list two hundred seventy six (276) other individuals known to be buried in Memory Lane Cemetery but whose exact location within the cemetery is listed in the records as

"unknown." See Exhibit C to Zumwalt Affidavit. Similarly, cemetery records also indicate that there are **at least four hundred fifty five (455) additional individuals who are buried within the Memory Lane Cemetery in "unmarked graves."** See Exhibit D to Zumwalt Affidavit. Given the uncertainty of the original location of the aforementioned burials and the fact that the cemetery flooded in 1877; July 1899; July-August 1895, 1892 (twice); August 1904; October 1909, 1913, and 1915; it is impossible to say to a reasonable degree of scientific probability that the remains of some other individual(s) will not be encountered in the process of exhuming the supposed remains of Catherine Antrim.

5. Should the exhumation uncover remains, the process of DNA collection will destroy portions of the remains. The process of DNA collection involves cutting and destroying large portions of bone. The amount of bone and the extent of the destruction is dependent upon the number of extractions per test and the extent of preservation of the remains. If independent tests of DNA are performed, which is generally considered to be scientifically sound, or if preservation of the remains is poor, which given the history is expected to be the case, significant destruction of the recovered remains is scientifically probable.

6. Should the exhumation uncover the supposed remains of Catherine Antrim and DNA samples can be obtained, prior studies show that the probability of successfully extracting mitochondrial DNA (mtDNA) from remains interred in excess of 120 years is extremely low. Support for this principle is found at Stone et al, 2001; Ivanov et al, 1966; Jeffreys et al, 1992; and Gill et al, 1994 (see references). Accordingly, given the age of the remains at this date, it is not certain to a reasonable degree of scientific probability that any DNA will be usable as a standard for comparison to any individual.

7. Because of these technical problems, it has been the long-standing practice of the OMI to decline to disturb any remains that have been buried in an excess of 50 years. Ms. Antrim's remains, as well as those of Billy the Kid, both greatly exceed this threshold period.

8. **If the purpose of the exhumation of the remains of Catherine Antrim is to compare her DNA to the remains of the believed Billy the Kid, those remains are not likely to be obtained in my opinion. Based upon research performed by the OMI, the exact location of the Billy the Kid grave is not known, in my opinion, to a reasonable degree of scientific probability.**

9. If the purpose of exhuming Catherine Antrim is to compare her DNA to individuals claiming to be potential living descendents of Billy the Kid, it is not possible, to a reasonable degree of scientific probability to do so. The only DNA sample that may be successfully extracted from Catherine Antrim would be mitochondrial DNA (mtDNA). This mtDNA sample provides proof of matrilineal lineage only - in other words, it only passes from mother to child and not from father to child. Billy the Kid would carry his mother's mtDNA; however, <u>his</u> biological children would

have received their mtDNA from their own mother and not Billy.

10. **If the purpose of extracting mtDNA from the supposed remains of Catherine Antrim is to obtain a sample to compare against Brushy Bill Roberts in Texas, such a comparison, in my opinion, is also scientifically flawed. Based on research to date, I am unaware that Mr. Roberts ever claimed to be the biological child of Catherine Antrim. Thus, a test between his mtDNA and the putative remains of Catherine Antrim would have no scientific basis to a reasonable degree of scientific probability.**

11. **Based on the fact that DNA testing of the supposed remains of Catherine Antrim would have no probative value and the fact that an exhumation would likely disrupt other burial sites, an exhumation of Catherine Antrim is scientifically unsound in my opinion.**

FURTHER AFFIANT SAYETH NOT.

Debra Komar, PhD.

APPENDIX: 9. Deposition to Frank Warner Angel of Fort Stanton Assistant Post Surgeon Daniel M. Appel on his official autopsy on John H. Tunstall. July 1, 1878.

Territory of New Mexico)
County of Lincoln   )

Daniel M. Appel being duly sworn says that he is Assistant Surgeon U.S. Army and have been and am now stationed at Fort Stanton New Mexico.

That on or about the 21st day of February 1878 [sic- February 19, 1878] I made a postmortem examination of John H. Tunstall. I found that there were two wounds in his body, one in the shoulder passing through and fracturing the right clavicle near its centre coming out immediately over the superior border of the right scapula passing through in its course the right subclavian artery, this would have caused his death in a few minutes and would have been likely to have thrown him from his horse. It would not have produced immediate insensibility. The other wound entered the head about one inch to the right of the median line almost on a line with the occipital protuberance and passed out immediately above the border of the left orbit. There was a fracture of the skull extending around the whole circumference from the entrance to the exit of the ball – and a transverse fracture across the middle portion of the base of the skull extending from the line of fracture on one side to that of the other. In my opinion the skull both on account of its being very thin and from evidences of venereal disease was very likely to be extensively fractured from such a would and the fractures in this case resulted entirely from said wound. A wound of this kind would cause instantaneous death passing as it did through the most vital portion of the brain. There were no marks of violence on the body except the two above wounds – nor was the body or skull mutilated, The cap of the skull was not at all fractured.

It is my opinion that both of the wounds could be caused at one and the same time – and if made at the same time were made by different persons from different directions and were both most likely made while Tunstall was on horseback in as much as the direction of the wounds were slightly upwards.

There being no powder marks on the body to indicate that the wounds were made at a short distance – and the further fact that the edges of the wounds of exit were not very ragged I am of the opinion that they were both made by rifles.

Powder marks would be shown on the body of the gun or pistol was fired within about six feet of the body.

D.M. Appel, Asst. Surgeon U.S. Army

ANNOTATED BIBLIOGRAPHY

RELEVANT 19th CENTURY HISTORY

COMPREHENSIVE REFERENCES

Nolan, Frederick. *The War: A Documentary History.* Norman: University of Oklahoma Press. **1992.**
_____. *The West of Billy the Kid.* Norman: University of Oklahoma Press. **1998.**

HISTORICAL ORGANIZATIONS (PERIOD)

SANTA FE RING, 19th CENTURY

MODERN SOURCES

Brown, Richard Maxwell. *Strain of Violence: Historical Studies of American Violence and Vigilantism.* New York: Oxford University Press. 1975. (**New Mexico unique for assassination as part of political system**)
Caffey, David L. *Chasing the Santa Fe Ring: Power and Privilege in Territorial New Mexico.* Albuquerque, New Mexico: University of New Mexico Press. 2014.
_____. *Frank Springer and New Mexico: From the Colfax County War to the Emergence of Modern Santa Fe.* Texas A and M. University Press. 2007.
Cleaveland, Agnes Morley. *No Life for a Lady.* Boston: Houghton Mifflin. 1941.
_____. *Satan's Paradise: From Lucien Maxwell to Fred Lambert.* Boston: Houghton Mifflin Company. 1952.
Cleaveland, Norman, *Colfax County's Chronic Murder Mystery.* Santa Fe: New Mexico. The Rydel Press. 1977.
_____. *A Synopsis of the Great New Mexico Cover-up.* Self-printed. 1989.
_____. *Some Comments Norman Cleveland May Make to the Huntington Westerners on Sept. 19, 1987.* Unpublished.
_____. *Some Highlights of William R. Morley's Contribution to the Pioneer Development of the Southwest.* Self-printed. No Date.
_____. *The Great Santa Fe Cover-up.* Based on a Talk given Before the Santa Fe Historical Society on November 1, 1978. Self-printed. 1982.
Cleaveland, Norman and George Fitzpatrick. *The Morleys - Young Upstarts on the Southwest Frontier.* Albuquerque, New Mexico: Calvin Horn Publisher, Inc. 1971.
Cooper, Gale. *The Santa Fe Ring Versus Billy the Kid: The Making of An American Monster.* Albuquerque, New Mexico: Gelcour Books. 2018.
Klasner, Lilly. Eve Ball. Ed. *My Girlhood Among Outlaws.* Tucson, Arizona: The University of Arizona Press. 1972. Klasner, Lilly. Eve Ball. Ed. *My Girlhood Among Outlaws.* Tucson, Arizona: The University of Arizona Press. 1972. (**John Chisum's in jail write-up about Santa Fe Ring injustices to himself**)
Lamar, Howard Robert N. *The Far Southwest 1846 – 1912: A Territorial History.* New Haven and London: Yale University Press. 1966. (**Chapter 6 covers the Santa Fe Ring**)
Meinig, D. W. *The Shaping of America. A Geographical Perspective on 500 Years of History. Vol. 3. Transcontinental America 1850 - 1915.* New Haven and London: Yale University Press. 1998. (**Pages 127 and 132 are on the Santa Fe Ring.**)
Montoya, María E. Translating Property. The Maxwell Land Grant and the Conflict Over Land in the American West, 1840-1900. Berkeley and Los Angeles: University of California Press. 2002.

Naegle, Conrad Keeler. *The History of Silver City, New Mexico 1870-1886.* University of New Mexico Bachelor of Arts thesis. Pages 30-60. Unpublished. 1943. Collection of the Silver City Museum, Silver City, New Mexico. (**Grant County rebellion**)

_____. "The Rebellion of Grant County, New Mexico in 1876." *Arizona and the West: A Quarterly Journal of History.* Autumn, 1968. Volume 10. Number 3. Tucson, Arizona: The University of Arizona Press. 1968. Pages 225-240. (**Grant County rebellion against Santa Fe Ring**)

Newman, Simeon Harrison III. "The Santa Fe Ring." *Arizona and the West.* Volume 12. Autumn 1970. Pages 269-288.

Otero, Miguel A. *My Life on the Frontier, 1882-1897: Incidents and Characters of the period when Kansas, Colorado, and New Mexico were Passing Through the Last of their Wild and Romantic Years.* New York: The Press of the Pioneers. 1935. Pages 232-233. (Quoted by Victor Westphall, *Thomas Benton Catron and His Era.* Page 188*)* (**Quote: "the 'Santa Fe Ring,' the real machine controlling the political situation in New Mexico."**)

Pearson, Jim Berry. *The Maxwell Land Grant.* Norman: University of Oklahoma Press. 1961.

Taylor, Morris F. *O.P. McMains and the Maxwell Land Grant Conflict.* Tucson, Arizona: The University of Arizona Press. 1979. (**Traces origins of the Santa Fe Ring**)

Theisen, Lee Scott. "Frank Warner Angel's Notes on New Mexico Territory, 1878." *Arizona and the West: A Quarterly Journal of History.* Winter 1976. Volume 18. Number 4. Pages 333-370. (**About the Angel notebook given to Lew Wallace and listing names of Santa Fe Ring members**)

Westphall, Victor. *Thomas Benton Catron and His Era.* Tucson, Arizona: University of Arizona Press. 1973. (**Ring-denier, who cites sources exposing the Ring**)

CONTEMPORARY SOURCES (CHRONOLOGICAL)

A.C.L. Editorial. "New Mexico, A Sorry Showing for a Would-be State, Tweed's Disciples Preying on the Populace, How the Territorial Ring is Run, Why the Territory Should Not Be Made a State. **March 13, 1876.** *The Boston Daily Globe.* Volume IX, Number 62. Newspaperarchive.com.

No Author. "A Contemplated Political Change." Grant County *Herald.* **September 16, 1876.** Quoted by Conrad Keeler Naegle in *The History of Silver City, New Mexico 1870-1886* doctoral thesis. Pages 39-40. (**Listing reasons to escape the Ring by annexing to Arizona Territory**)

Wallace, Lew. "Our mutual friend, M. Hinds, who will hand you this ..." Letter to A.H. Markland. **November 14, 1878.** Indiana Historical Society. Lew Wallace Collection. M0292. Box 3. Folder 17. (**Ring tries to remove him as governor**)

Leonard, Ira E. "When you left here I promised to write you concerning events transpiring here ..." Letter to Lew Wallace. **May 20, 1878 [sic - 79].** Indiana Historical Society. Lew Wallace Collection. M0292. Box 4. Folder 10. (**Quote: "Santa Fe ring ... so long an incubus on the government."**)

Wallace, Lew. "I have the honor to inform you that the Legislature of this Territory adjourned ..." **February 16, 1880.** Letter to Carl Schurz. Indiana Historical Society. Lew Wallace Collection. M0292. Box 4. Folder 14. (**Key documentation of Catron as head of the Santa Fe Ring, and Wallace's Ring opposition**)

No Author. "White Cap's Proclamation." *Las Vegas Optic.* March 12, 1880. (**Manifesto against land-grabbing Catron and the Ring**)

No Author. "The Santa Fe Ring is the most corrupt combination that ever cursed any country or community." Las Cruces *Thirty-Four Newspaper.* **October 27, 1880.** From Victor Westphall, *Thomas Benton Catron and His Era.* Page 186. (**Article on Santa Fe Ring abuses urging voters to oppose Ring candidates**)

No Author. "The Ring must soon discover that the time has passed in New Mexico when men can be herded like so many sheep ..." *Albuquerque Daily Democrat.*

March 4, 1884. (Quoted by Victor Westphall, *Thomas Benton Catron and His Era*. Page 191.) (**About Santa Fe Ring control of appointments to legislature**)

No Author. *Santa Fe Weekly New Mexican Review*. **March 13, 1884.** *Santa Fe Weekly New Mexican Review*. (**Accusation of Catron and the Ring of controlling grand juries and** bribery)

No Author. *Albuquerque Daily Democrat*. **March 15, 1884.** (**Oscar P. McMains "Memorial" against land-grabbing Ring**)

Valdez, Jose and Enrique Mares. "Scorching Letter, The Knights of Labor Send a Communication to Powderly! Politicians Arraigned! The Boldest Document Ever Issued in the Territory." **August 18, 1890.** *Las Vegas Democrat*. Volume 1. Center for Southwest Studies. Thomas B. Catron Papers, MSS 29, Series 102, Box 8, Folder 4. (**Gives history of Santa Fe Ring with T.B. Catron as head**)

No Author. *Los Angeles Times*. **1899**. Undated clipping, Laughlin Papers, State Records Center, Santa Fe, New Mexico. Quoted by Victor Westphall, *Thomas Benton Catron and His Era*. Page 285. (**Joking article about the Santa Fe Ring**)

EXPOSÉS Of (CONTEMPORARY)

COMPLAINT ABOUT TO PRESIDENT RUTHERFORD B. HAYES

Matchett, W.B. and Mary E. McPherson. " W.B. Matchett and Mary E. McPherson 'Make certain charges against the U.S. Officials in the Territory of New Mexico.' " Letter to President Rutherford B. Hayes. Received and filed **May 1, 1877**. Interior Department Papers 1850-1907; Appointments Division and Subsequent Actions. Microfilm File Case Number 44-4-8-3. Record Group 48. Microfilm No. M750. Roll 1. National Archives and Records Administration. U. S. Department of Justice. Washington, D.C. (**Sent to President Rutherford B. Hayes and Secretary of the Interior Carl Schurz.**)

McPherson, Mary and W.B. Matchett. "To the President. Please make the enclosed a part of the evidence in the case of "Charges Against New Mexican Officials" Letter to President Rutherford B. Hayes. **May 3, 1877**. McPherson, Mary E. Letters and Petitions to President Rutherford B. Hayes re: Removal Governor Axtell and the Santa Fe Ring. Interior Department Papers 1850-1907; Appointments Division and Subsequent Actions. Microfilm File Case Number 44-4-8-3. Record Group 48. Microfilm Roll M750. National Archives and Records Administration. U.S. Department of Justice. Washington, D.C. (**Addendum to their May, 1877 "Certain Charges Against U.S. Officials in New Mexico Territory."**)

_____. "The Secretary of the Interior, Sir – Accompanying please find copy of charges, &c., against S.B. Axtell, Governor, and Other New Mexican Officials ..." "Charges Against New Mexican Officials." Letter to Secretary of the Interior Carl Schurz. **May 5, 1877**. McPherson, Mary E. Letters and Petitions to President Rutherford B. Hayes re: Removal Governor Axtell and the Santa Fe Ring. Interior Department Papers 1850-1907; Appointments Division and Subsequent Actions. Microfilm File Case Number 44-4-8-3. Record Group 48. Microfilm Roll M750. National Archives and Records Administration. U.S. Department of Justice. Washington, D. C.

_____."*In the Matter of Charges vs. Gov. S.B. Axtell and Other New Mexico Officials*. Submitted to the Departments of the Interior and Justice. **August, 1877.** Printed as a 31 page booklet. No publisher listed. Indiana Historical Society. Lew Wallace Collection. M0292. Box 3. Folder 20. (**About the Santa Fe Ring, Catron, and Elkins; in Lew Wallace's personal possession**)

McPherson, Mary. "Please place before the Attorney General ..." Letter to President Rutherford B. Hayes. **August 23, 1877**. Interior Department Papers 1850-1907; Appointments Division and Subsequent Actions. Microfilm File Case Number 44-4-8-3. Record Group 48. Microfilm No. M750. Roll 1. National Archives and Records Administration. U. S. Department of Justice. Washington, D.C.

Springer, Frank. Deposition to Investigator Frank Warner Angel for the Departments of Justice and the Interior. **August 9, 1878.** Frank Warner Angel report titled *In the Matter of the Investigation of the Charges Against S.B. Axtell Governor of New Mexico.* October 3, 1878. Interior Department Papers 1850-1907; Appointments Division and Subsequent Actions. Microfilm Case File No. 44-4-8-3. Record Group 48. Microfilm Roll M750. National Archives and Records Administration. U.S. Department of Interior. Washington, D.C.

(SEE: Thomas Benton Catron; Frank Warner Angel, Legislature Revolt, Grant County Rebellion, Colfax County War, Lincoln County War)

SECRET SERVICE, 19th CENTURY (CHRONOLOGICAL)

Bowen, Walter S. and Harry Edward Neal. *The United States Secret Service.* Philadelphia and New York: Chilton Company Publishers. **1960.**

Brooks, James J. *1877 Report on Secret Service Operatives.* (**September 26, 1877**). "On Azariah Wild." Page 392. Department of the Treasury. United States Secret Service. Washington, D.C.

Johnson, David R. *Illegal Tender. Counterfeiting and the Secret Service in Nineteenth Century America.* Washington and London: Smithsonian Institution Press. **1995.**

OPERATIVE ANDREW L. DRUMMOND

Drummond, Arthur L. "Daily Reports of U. S. Secret Service Agents, 1875-1937. Record Group 87. ." Microfilm T-915. Rolls: 91, 92. (January 1, 1880 – September 30, 1880). 92 (October 1, 1880 - June 30, 1881)). National Archives and Records Department. Department of the Treasury. Secret Service Division. Washington, D.C. (**Reports in *Cold Case Billy the Kid's* counterfeiting hoax against Billy Bonney: September 14, 1880, November 30, 1880) (Additional reports for debunking *Cold Case Billy the Kid* hoaxers: September 18, 1880, December 2, 1880, (Pages 660-661) June 10, 1881, June 29, 1881)**

OPERATIVE WALLACE W. HALL

Hall, Wallace W. "Daily Reports of U. S. Secret Service Agents, 1875-1937." Microfilm T-915. Record Group 87. Microfilm Rolls: 153 (January 1, 1879 – December 31, 1880), 154 (January 1, 1881 - December 31, 1881; February 24, 1881), 155: (January 1, 1882 – July 31, 1883; January–June 1882, July 1, 1882). National Archives and Records Department. Department of the Treasury. Secret Service Division. Washington, D.C. (**Reports cited in *Cold Case Billy the Kid's* fake counterfeiting claim against Billy Bonney: May 19, 1880, August 4, 1880, February 24, 1881, February 26, 1881, October 11, 1881, May 9, 1882, May 19, 1882, May 27, 1882; though they have no link to Billy Bonney) (Additional reports for debunking *Cold Case Billy the Kid* hoaxers: August 3, 1880, August 24, 1880, October 10, 1880, January 24, 1881, January 27, 1881, February 27, 1881, October 10, 1881, October 11, 1881, May 19, 1882, June 6, 1882, June 17, 1882, July 1, 1882, September 1, 1882, October 7, 1882, July 10, 1885)**

Dye, John S. *Government Counterfeiter Detector.* **March, 1881.** Volume XXIX. Number 10. From Secret Service Library, Counterfeit Division via Archivist Michael Sampson. (**Applies to Wallace Hall's report of January 24, 1881 about counterfeit currency in Moundville, Missouri**)

OPERATIVE PATRICK D. TYRRELL

Tyrell, Patrick D. Report of July 8, 1881. "Daily Reports of U. S. Secret Service Agents, 1875-1937." Record Group 87. Microfilm T-915. Roll 285. National Archives and Records Department. Department of the Treasury. Secret Service Division. Washington, D.C. (**Cited in** *Cold Case Billy the Kid*)

OPERATIVE AZARIAH F. WILD

BIOGRAPHICAL SOURCE

Nolan, Frederick. "Biography of Azariah Wild." Unpublished and personal communications, June 11, 2005 and October 9, 2005.

CONTEMPORARY SOURCES (CHRONOLOGICAL)

Brooks, James J. *1877 Report on Secret Service Operatives.* "On Azariah Wild." **September 26, 1877.** Page 392. Department of the Treasury. United States Secret Service. Washington, D.C.

Wild, Azariah F. "Daily Reports of U. S. Secret Service Agents, 1875-1937." Record Group 87. Microfilm T-915. Microfilm Rolls 306 (June 15, 1877 - December 31, 1877), 307 (January 1,1878 - June 30, 1879), 308 (July 1, 1879 - June 30, 1881; October 4, 1880, Pages 330-333; October 5, 1880, Pages 336-339; November 11, 1880, Pages 484-488), 309 (July 1, 1881 - September 30, 1883), 310 (October 1, 1883 - July 31, 1886). National Archives and Records Department. Department of the Treasury. Secret Service Division. Washington, D.C. (**Reports cited in W.C. Jameson's 2018 book,** *Cold Case Billy the Kid* **Bibliography for that book's counterfeiting claim against Billy Bonney: June 11, 1880, June 12, 1880, October 28, 1880, November 10, 1880, November 30, 1880, January 3, 1881, October 4, 1881, October 6, 1881, October 16, 1881) (Other reports relevant to** *Cold Case Billy the Kid's* **counterfeiting claim against Billy Bonney: May 1, 1880-July 31, 1880; October 4, 1880, October 5, 1880, November 11, 1880, November 21, 1880, November 28, 1880)**

Wild, Azariah. Telegraph on counterfeit bills. **January 4, 1881.** Herman B. Weisner Papers, ca. 1957-1992. New Mexico State University Library at Las Cruces. Archives and Special Collections Department. Accession No. Ms 0249. Box 11. Folder O-1. Folder Name: "Olinger, Robert and James W. Bell."

NEW MEXICO TERRITORY REBELLIONS AGAINST THE SANTA FE RING (CHRONOLOGICAL)

LEGISLATURE REVOLT (1872)

No Author. *Journal of the House of Representatives of the Territory of New Mexico, Session of 1871-1872.* Santa Fe: A.P. Sullivan. **1872.** Pages 144-154. (**Confirms troops used by Ring to suppress the Legislature Revolt of 1872**)

No Author. "Our Own Dear Steve, How Elkins Made His Influence Felt in New Mexico – The Ring in Which a Judge Figured – Politics in 1870. *Las Vegas Daily Optic.* **September 2, 1884.** (Reprinted from the *Omaha Herald*) Front Page. Volume V, Number 258, Column 4. Newspaperarchive.com. (**Exposing the Santa Fe Ring in the 1872 Legislature Revolt**)

GRANT COUNTY REBELLION (1876)

MODERN SOURCES

Naegle, Conrad Keeler. *The History of Silver City, New Mexico 1870-1886*. University of New Mexico Bachelor of Arts thesis. Pages 30-60. Unpublished. 1943. Collection of the Silver City Museum, Silver City, New Mexico.

_____. "The Rebellion of Grant County, New Mexico in 1876." *Arizona and the West: A Quarterly Journal of History*. Autumn, 1968. Volume 10. Number 3. Tucson, Arizona: The University of Arizona Press. 1968. Pages 225-240. (**Rebellion against Santa Fe Ring**)

CONTEMPORARY SOURCES (CHRONOLOGICAL)

No Author. "Diario del Consejo der Territorio de Neuvo Mejico, Session de 1871-1872." *Santa Fe New Mexican*. **January 8, 1872**. Santa Fe: A.P. Sullivan. 1872. Pages 144-154. New Mexico Supreme Court Library. Santa Fe, New Mexico. (**A Ring expurgated document, with a copy found in 1942 by Conrad Naegle; confirming troops used by Ring to suppress Territorial legislature**)

No Author. "Diario del Consejo der Territorio de Neuvo Mejico, Session de 1871-1872. Las Cruces *Borderer*. **January 24, 1872**. Pages 110-113. (**Don Diego Archuleta, President of the Council, gives speech objecting to troops in legislature**)

No Author. "Ring influence [in the Territorial legislature is] being actively used against every measure that tends to do justice" [in Grant and Doña Ana Counties]." *Grant County Herald*. **August 8, 1875**. Quoted by Conrad Keeler Naegle in *The History of Silver City, New Mexico 1870-1886*, doctoral thesis. Page 39.

No Author. "A Contemplated Political Change." Grant County *Herald*. **September 16, 1876**. Quoted by Conrad Keeler Naegle in *The History of Silver City, New Mexico 1870-1886* doctoral thesis. Pages 39-40. (**Listing reasons to escape the Ring by annexing to Arizona Territory**)

No Author. [Grant County should not] "sort o' wait and hear from Santa Fe ... before taking action." Tucson *Arizona Citizen*. **September 23, 1876**. Quoted by Conrad Keeler Naegle in *The History of Silver City, New Mexico 1870-1886* doctoral thesis. Page 41. (**Arizona encourages escape from Santa Fe Ring**)

No Author. Grant County *Herald*. **September 23, 1876**. (**Need for school system stressed.**)

No Author. Grant County *Herald*. **September 30, 1876**. (**"Annexation Meeting" announced**)

No Author. "Proceedings of Grant County Annexation Meeting." Grant County *Herald*. **Saturday October 7, 1876**. Page 2. Columns 1 and 2. Collection of the Silver City, New Mexico, Museum. (**"Grant County Declaration of Independence"**)

No Author. Grant County *Herald*. " 'Petition to Remove Judge Bristol. We the undersigned citizens of the Third Judicial District of the Territory of New Mexico, without regard to party, would respectfully request and petition for the removal of Judge Warren Bristol ...' " No date. **1876 or 1877**.(Quoted in "W.B. Matchett and Mary E. McPherson 'Make certain charges against the U.S. Officials in the Territory of New Mexico.' " Letter to President Rutherford B. Hayes. Received and filed May 1, 1877. Interior Department Papers 1850-1907; Appointments Division and Subsequent Actions. Microfilm File Case Number 44-4-8-3. Record Group 48. Microfilm No. M750. Roll 1. National Archives and Records Administration. U.S. Department of Justice. Washington, D.C.) (**Anti-Santa Fe Ring article**)

(SEE: Santa Fe Ring; Thomas Benton Catron; Stephen Benton Elkins)

COLFAX COUNTY WAR (1877)

MODERN SOURCES

Caffey, David L. *Frank Springer and New Mexico: From the Colfax County War to the Emergence of Modern Santa Fe*. Texas A and M. University Press. 2007.

Cleaveland, Norman. *The Morleys - Young Upstarts on the Southwest Frontier*. Albuquerque, New Mexico: Calvin Horn Publisher, Inc. 1971.

Dunham, Harold H. "New Mexican Land Grants with Special Reference to the Title Papers of the Maxwell Grant." *New Mexico Historical Review*. (January 1955) Vol. 30, No. 1. pp. 1 - 23.

Keleher, William A. *The Maxwell Land Grant. A New Mexico Item*. Albuquerque, New Mexico: University of New Mexico Press. 1964.

Lamar, Howard Roberts. *The Far Southwest 1846 - 1912. A Territorial History*. New Haven and London: Yale University Press. 1966.

Montoya, María E. *Translating Property. The Maxwell Land Grant and the Conflict Over Land in the American West, 1840-1900*. Berkeley and Los Angeles, California: University of California Press. 2002.

Murphy, Lawrence R. *Lucien Bonaparte Maxwell. Napoleon of the Southwest*. Norman: University of Oklahoma Press. 1983.

Pearson, Jim Berry. *The Maxwell Land Grant*. Norman: University of Oklahoma Press. 1961.

Poe, Sophie. *Buckboard Days*. Albuquerque, New Mexico: University of New Mexico Press. 1964.

Taylor, Morris F. *O.P. McMains and the Maxwell Land Grant Conflict*. Tucson, Arizona: The University of Arizona Press. 1979.

CONTEMPORARY SOURCES (CHRONOLOGICAL)

No author. "Anarchy at Cimarron." *Santa Fe Weekly New Mexican*. **November 16, 1875**. (**Ringite backing of Axtell's use of troops in the Colfax County War**)

Dawson, Will. Editorial. *Cimarron News and Press*. **December 31, 1875**. (**Ring-biased editorial by temporary editor blaming citizens for unrest**)

No Author. Report on murder trial for Franklin Tolby. Pueblo, *Colorado Chieftain*. **May 25, 1876**. Quoting *Daily New Mexican*, May 1, 1876. From Morris F. Taylor. *O.P. McMains and the Maxwell Land Grant Conflict*. Tucson, Arizona: The University of Arizona Press. 1979. Page 49. (**Ring-biased jury instructions by Judge Henry Waldo to protect Ring murderers of Tolby**)

No Author. "Rejoicing at Cimarron," "Axtell's Head Falls at Last," "General Lew. Wallace Appointed Governor." *Cimarron News and Press*. **September 6, 1878**.

No Author. *Santa Fe Weekly New Mexican*. **September 21, 1878 and October 19, 1878**. (**Ring-biased accolades for removed Gov. Axtell**)

(SEE: Santa Fe Ring; Thomas Benton Catron; Stephen Benton Elkins)

LINCOLN COUNTY WAR (1878)

MODERN SOURCES

Cramer, T. Dudley. *The Pecos Ranchers in the Lincoln County War*. Orinda, California: Branding Iron Press. 1996.

Fulton, Maurice Garland. Robert N. Mullin. Ed. *History of the Lincoln County War*. Tucson, Arizona: The University of Arizona Press. 1997.

Jacobsen, Joel. *Such Men as Billy the Kid. The Lincoln County War Reconsidered*. Lincoln and London: University of Nebraska Press. 1994.

Keleher, William A. *The Fabulous Frontier: Twelve New Mexico Items*. Albuquerque, New Mexico: The University of New Mexico Press. 1962.

_____. *County 1869-1881.* Albuquerque, New Mexico: University of New Mexico Press. 1957.
Mullin, Robert N. Re: Frank Warner Angel Meeting with President Hayes. August, 1878. Binder RNM, VI, M. Midland, Texas: Nita Stewart Haley Memorial Library and J. Evetts Haley History Center. (Unpublished).
Nolan, Frederick W. *The Life and Death of John Henry Tunstall.* Albuquerque, New Mexico: The University of New Mexico Press. 1965.
_____. *The Lincoln County War: A Documentary History.* Norman: University of Oklahoma Press. 1992.
_____. *The West of Billy the Kid.* Norman: University of Oklahoma Press. 1998.
Rasch, Philip J. *Gunsmoke in Lincoln County.* Laramie, Wyoming: National Association for Outlaw and Lawmen History, Inc. with University of Wyoming. 1997.
_____. Robert K. DeArment. Ed. *Warriors of Lincoln County.* Laramie: National Association for Outlaw and Lawmen History, Inc. with University of Wyoming. 1998.
Utley, Robert M. *High Noon in Lincoln. Violence on the Western Frontier.* Albuquerque, New Mexico: University of New Mexico Press. 1987.
Wilson, John P. *Merchants, Guns, and Money: The Story of Lincoln County and Its Wars.* Santa Fe, New Mexico: Museum of New Mexico Press. 1987.
No Author. "Disturbances in the Territories, 1878 - 1894. Lawlessness in New Mexico." Senate Documents. 67th Congress. 2nd Session. December 5, 1921 - September 22, 1922. pp. 176 - 187. Washington, D.C.: Government Printing Office. 1922.

CONTEMPORARY SOURCES (CHRONOLOGICAL)

No Author. "Brady Inventory McSween Property." **February, 1878.** Herman B. Weisner Papers, ca. 1957-1992. New Mexico State University Library at Las Cruses. Rio Grande Historical Collections. Accession No. Weisner Ms 0249. Box 10. Folder M15. Folder Name. "Will and Testament A. McSween."
No Author. "Amnesty for Matthews and Long in the Third Judicial Court April Term 1879." **April, 1879.** Herman B. Weisner Papers, ca. 1957-1992. New Mexico State University Library at Las Cruses. Rio Grande Historical Collections. Accession No. Ms 0249. Box 1. Folder 4. Folder Name. "Amnesty."
No Author. "Charges against Jessie Evans and John Kinney." Doña Ana County Civil and Criminal Docket Book. **August 18, 1875 to November 7, 1878.** Herman B. Weisner Papers, ca. 1957-1992. New Mexico State University Library at Las Cruses. Rio Grande Historical Collections. Accession No. Ms 0249. Box 13. Folder V 3. Folder Name. "Venue, Change Of."
No Author. "Dismissal of Cases Against Dolan, Matthews, Peppin, October 1879 District Court." **October, 1879.** Herman B. Weisner Papers, ca. 1957-1992. New Mexico State University Library at Las Cruses. Rio Grande Historical Collections. Accession No. Ms 0249. Box 13. Folder V3. Folder Name: "Venue, Change Of."
No Author. "Killers of Tunstall. February 18, 1879." Herman B. Weisner Papers, ca. 1957-1992. New Mexico State University Library at Las Cruses. Rio Grande Historical Collections. Accession No. Ms 0249. Box 12. Folder T1. Folder Name: "Tunstall, John H."
No Author. "Lincoln County Indictments July 1872 - 1881." Herman B. Weisner Papers, ca. 1957-1992. New Mexico State University Library at Las Cruses. Rio Grande Historical Collections. Accession No. Ms 0249. Box 8. Folder L11. Folder Name. "Lincoln Co. Indictments."

(SEE: William H. Bonney, John Henry Tunstall, Alexander McSween, Samuel Beach Axtell, Frank Warner Angel, Nathan Augustus Monroe Dudley)

HISTORY OF WILLIAM HENRY BONNEY (WILLIAM HENRY McCARTY, HENRY ANTRIM, AKA BILLY THE KID)

BIOGRAPHICAL SOURCES

Abbott, E.C. ("Teddy Blue") and Helena Huntington Smith. *We Pointed Them North: Recollections of a Cowpuncher.* Norman, Oklahoma: University of Oklahoma Press. 1955. (**Billy the Kid's multi-culturalism, Page 47.**)

Anaya, Paco. *I Buried Billy.* College Station, Texas: Creative Publishing Company. 1991.

Ball, Eve. *Ma'am Jones of the Pecos.* Tucson, Arizona: The University of Arizona Press. 1969.

Boze Bell, Bob. *The Illustrated Life and Times of Billy the Kid.* Cave Creek, Arizona: Boze Books. **1992**. (Frank Coe quote about the Kid's cartridge use, Page 45.)

Boze Bell, Bob. *The Illustrated Life and Times of Billy the Kid.* Second Edition. Phoenix, Arizona: Tri Star-Boze Publications, Inc. **1996**.

Burns, Walter Noble. *The Saga of Billy the Kid.* Stamford, Connecticut: Longmeadow Press. 1992. (Original printing: 1926, Doubleday.)

_____. "I also know that the Kid and Paulita were sweethearts." Unpublished letter to Jim East. June 3, 1926. Robert N. Mullin Collection. File RNM, IV, NM, 116-117. Nita Stewart Haley Memorial Museum, Haley Library. Midland, Texas.

Coe, George with Doyce B. Nunis, Jr. Ed. *Frontier Fighter. The Autobiography of George Coe Who Fought and Rode With Billy the Kid.* Chicago: R. R. Donnelley and Sons Company. 1984.

Cooper, Gale. *Billy the Kid's Writings, Words, and Wit.* Gelcour Books: Albuquerque: New Mexico. 2012.

_____. *Billy and Paulita: The Saga of Billy the Kid, Paulita Maxwell, and the Santa Fe Ring.* Gelcour Books: Albuquerque: New Mexico. 2012.

_____. *The Lost Pardon of Billy the Kid: An Analysis Factoring in the Santa Fe Ring, Governor Lew Wallace's Dilemma, and a Territory in Rebellion.* Gelcour Books: Albuquerque: New Mexico. 2017.

_____. *The Santa Fe Ring Versus Billy the Kid: The Making of an American Monster.* Gelcour Books: Albuquerque: New Mexico. 2018.

Garrett, Pat F. *The Authentic Life of Billy the Kid The Noted Desperado of the Southwest, Whose Deeds of Daring and Blood Made His Name a Terror in New Mexico, Arizona, and Northern Mexico.* Santa Fe, New Mexico: New Mexico Printing and Publishing Co. 1882. (Edition used: Edited by Maurice Garland Fulton. New York: The Macmillan Company. 1927)

Hendron, J. W. *The Story of Billy the Kid. New Mexico's Number One Desperado.* New York: Indian Head Books. 1994.

Hoyt, Henry. *A Frontier Doctor.* Boston and New York: Houghton Mifflin Company. 1929. (**Describes Billy's superior abilities. Pages 93-94, including fluency in Spanish.**)

Jacobsen, Joel. *Such Men as Billy the Kid. The Lincoln County War Reconsidered.* Lincoln and London: University of Nebraska Press. 1994.

Kadlec, Robert F. *They "Knew" Billy the Kid. Interviews with Old-Time New Mexicans.* Santa Fe, New Mexico: Ancient City Press. 1987.

Keleher, William A. *The Fabulous Frontier: Twelve New Mexico Items.* Albuquerque, New Mexico: The University of New Mexico Press. 1962.

_____.*Violence in Lincoln County 1869-1881.* Albuquerque, New Mexico: University of New Mexico Press. 1957.

Koop, W.E. *Billy the Kid: The Trail of a Kansas Legend.* Self Published. **1965**.

McFarland, David F. Reverend. *Ledger: Session Records 1867-1874. Marriages in Santa Fe New Mexico.* "Mr. William H. Antrim and Mrs. Catherine McCarty."

March 1, 1873. (Unpublished). Santa Fe, New Mexico: First Presbyterian Church of Santa Fe.
Meadows, John P. "Billy the Kid to John P. Meadows on the Peñasco, May 1-2, 1881." *Roswell Daily Record.* February 16, 1931. Page 6.
_____. Ed. John P. Wilson. *Pat Garrett and Billy the Kid as I Knew Them: Reminiscences of John P. Meadows.* Albuquerque: University of New Mexico Press. 2004.
Mullin, Robert N. *The Boyhood of Billy the Kid.* Monograph 17, Southwestern Studies 5(1). El Paso, Texas: Texas Western Press. University of Texas at El Paso. 1967.
Poe, John W. *The Death of Billy the Kid.* (Introduction by Maurice Garland Fulton). Boston and New York: Houghton Mifflin Company. 1933.
_____. "The Killing of Billy the Kid." (a personal letter written at Roswell, New Mexico to Mr. Charles Goodnight, Goodnight P.C., Texas) July 10, 1917. Earle Vandale Collection. 1813-946. No. 2H475. Center for American History. University of Texas at Austin.
Rakocy, Bill. *Billy the Kid.* El Paso, Texas: Bravo Press. 1985.
Rasch, Phillip J. *Trailing Billy the Kid.* Laramie, Wyoming: National Association for Outlaw and Lawman History, Inc. with University of Wyoming. 1995.
Russell, Randy. *Billy the Kid. The Story - The Trial.* Lincoln, New Mexico: The Crystal Press. 1994.
Scanland, John M. (Foreword) using Patrick F. Garrett, Patrick F. *Billy the Kid: The Outlaw. Authentic Story of Billy the Kid by Pat F. Garrett. Greatest Sheriff of the Old Southwest.* New York: Atomic Books Inc. **1946**. Oberlin College Library Special Collections, Pop Culture. Walter F. Tunks Collection. Number 2344. (**Pirated edition of Pat Garrett's** *Authentic Life of Billy the Kid* **featuring apocryphal outlawry of Billy the Kid**)
Siringo, Charles A. *The History of Billy the Kid.* Santa Fe: New Mexico. Privately Printed. 1920.
Tuska, Jon. *Billy the Kid. His Life and Legend.* Westport, Connecticut: Greenwood Press. 1983.
Utley, Robert M. *High Noon in Lincoln. Violence on the Western Frontier.* Albuquerque, New Mexico: University of New Mexico Press. 1987.
_____. *Billy the Kid. A Short and Violent Life.* Lincoln and London: University of Nebraska Press. 1989.
Weddle, Jerry. *Antrim is My Stepfather's Name. The Boyhood of Billy the Kid.* Monograph 9, Globe, Arizona: Arizona Historical Society. 1993.
No Author. "The Prisoners Who Saw the Kid Kill Olinger." April 28, 1881. Herman B. Weisner Papers, ca. 1957-1992. New Mexico State University Library at Las Cruces. Rio Grande Historical Collections. Accession No. Ms 0249. Box 30 T. Folder 8.

WORDS OF (CHRONOLOGICAL)

HOYT BILL OF SALE

Bonney, W H. "Know all persons by these presents ..." Thursday, **October 24, 1878**. Indiana Historical Society. Lew Wallace Collection. M0292. Box 14, Folder 11.

LETTERS TO LEW WALLACE

Bonney, W H. "I have heard you will give one thousand $ dollars for my body which as I see it means alive ..." **March 13(?), 1879**. Fray Angélico Chávez Historical Library, Santa Fe, New Mexico. Lincoln County Heritage Trust Collection. (AC481).
_____. "I will keep the keep the appointment ..." **March 20, 1879**. Indiana Historical Society. M0292.

_____. "... on the Pecos." ("Billie" letter fragment). **March 24(?), 1879**. Indiana Historical Society. Lew Wallace Collection. M0292. Box 4. Folder 7.

_____. "I noticed in the *Las Vegas* Gazette a piece which stated that 'Billy the Kid' ..." **December 12, 1880**. Indiana Historical Society. Lew Wallace Collection. M0292.

_____. "I would like to see you ..." **January 1, 1881**. Indiana Historical Society. Lew Wallace Collection. M0292.

_____. "I wish you would come down to the jail and see me ..." **March 2, 1881**. Fray Angélico Chávez Historical Library, Santa Fe, New Mexico. Lincoln County Heritage Trust Collection. (AC481).

_____. "I wrote you a little note day before yesterday ..." **March 4, 1881**. Indiana Historical Society. Lew Wallace Collection. M0292.

_____. "For the last time I ask ..." **March 27, 1881**. Indiana Historical Society. Lew Wallace Collection. M0292.

LETTER TO SQUIRE WILSON

Bonney, W H. "Friend Wilson ..." **March 18, 1879**. Indiana Historical Society. Lew Wallace Collection. M0292. (**For pardon negotiation with Lew Wallace**)

LETTER TO EDGAR CAYPLESS

Bonney, W H. "I would have written before ..." **April 15, 1881**. Copy in William Kelleher's *Violence in Lincoln County;* originally reproduced in Griggs *History of the Mesilla Valley*. (**Original lost**)

"REGULATOR MANIFESTO" LETTER

Regulator. "Mr. Walz. Sir ..." Letter to Edgar Walz. **July 13, 1878**. Adjutant General's Office. File 1405 AGO 1878. (Quoted in Maurice Garland Fulton, *History of the Lincoln County War*. Tucson: University of Arizona Press. 1975. Pages 246-247.)

DEPOSITION OF

Bonney, William Henry. Deposition to Frank Warner Angel. **June 8, 1878**. Frank Warner Angel report, Pages 314-319 from *In the Matter of the Examination of the Causes and Circumstances of the Death of John H. Tunstall a British Subject*. Report filed October 4, 1878. Angel Report. Records of the Justice Department. Record Group 60. Class 44 Litigation Files. Container 21. National Archives and Records Administration. U.S. Department of Justice. Washington, D.C. or Angel Report in Interior Department Papers 1850-1907; Appointments Division and Subsequent Actions. Microfilm File Case Number 44-4-8-3. Record Group 48. Microfilm No. M750. Roll 1. National Archives and Records Administration. U.S. Department of Justice. Washington, D.C.

COURT TESTIMONY OF

Rynerson, William. "The Grand Jurors for the Territory of New Mexico taken from the body of the good and lawful men of the County of Lincoln ..." Indictments of the April, Lincoln County Grand Jury. **April 28, 1879**. Herman B. Weisner Papers, ca. 1957-1992. New Mexico State University Library at Las Cruces. Rio Grande Historical Collection. Accession No. Ms 0249. Box 4/39. Folder E-Z. Folder Name: "Jessie Evans Accessory to Murder." (**Billy's testimony for pardon bargain**)

Bonney, William Henry. Testimony in Court of Inquiry for N.A.M. Dudley. **May 28-29, 1879**. *Proceedings of a Court of Inquiry in the Case of Lt. Col. N.A.M. Dudley (May 2,1879 – July 5, 1879)*. File No. QQ1284. (Boxes 3304, 3305, 3305A); Court Martial Files 1809-1894. Records of the Office of the Judge Advocate General - Army. Record Group 153. Old Military and Civil Branch. National Archives and Records Administration. Washington, D. C.

Waldo, Henry. "Then was brought forward William Bonney, alias "Antrim," alias "the Kid," a known criminal of the worst type ..." Closing argument on Billy Bonney's testimony in Court of Inquiry for N.A.M. Dudley. **July 5, 1879**. *Proceedings of a Court of Inquiry in the Case of Lt. Col. N.A.M. Dudley (May 2,1879 – July 5, 1879)*. File No. QQ1284. (Boxes 3304, 3305, 3305A); Court Martial Files 1809-1894. Records of the Office of the Judge Advocate General – Army. Record Group 153. Old Military and Civil Branch. National Archives and Records Administration. Washington, D. C.

INTERVIEW WITH LEW WALLACE OF

Wallace, Lew. "Statements by Kid, made Sunday night **March 23, 1879**." (Cover sheet reads: "Fort Stanton, March 20, 1879. William Bonney ("Kid") relative to arrangement with him." Indiana Historical Society. Lew Wallace Collection. M0292. Box 4. Folder 6.

NEWSPAPER INTERVIEWS BY

Wilcox, Lucius "Lute" M. (city editor, owner, J.H. Koogler). "The Kid. Interview with Billy Bonney The Best Known Man in New Mexico." *Las Vegas Gazette*. **December 27, 1880.**
_____. Interview, at train depot. *Las Vegas Gazette*. **December 28, 1880**. **(Has Billy Bonney's "adios" quote.)**
No Author. "Something About the Kid." *Santa Fe Daily New Mexican*. **April 3, 1881**. **(With quotes Billy Bonney's "this is the man" and "two hundred men have been killed ... he did not kill all of them.")**
No Author. "I got a rough deal ..." *Mesilla News*. **April 15, 1881**.
Newman, Simon N. Ed. Interview with "The Kid." *Newman's Semi-Weekly*. **April 15, 1881.**
_____. Departure from Mesilla. *Newman's Semi-Weekly*. **April 15, 1881**.
No Author. "Advise persons never to engage in killing." *Mesilla News*. **April 16, 1881.**

FEDERAL INDICTMENT OF

Catron, Thomas Benton. "Case No. 411. The United States vs. Charles Bowdry [Bowdre], Doc Scurlock, Henry Brown, Henry Antrim alias "Kid," John Middleton, Stephen Stevens, John Scroggins, George Coe and Frederick Waite." **June 21, 1878**. Herman B. Weisner Papers, ca. 1957-1992. New Mexico State University Library at Las Cruces. Rio Grande Historical Collections. Accession No. Ms 0249. Box 1. B-Folder 4. Name: Andrew Roberts Indictment.

GENERAL LETTERS ABOUT

Kimbrell, George. "I have the honor to request that you will furnish me a posse ..." Letter to Lieutenant Millard Filmore Goodwin. **February 20, 1879**. Indiana Historical Society. Lew Wallace Collection. Box 4, Folder 3. **(For pursuit of William Bonney and Yginio Salazar)**
Goodwin, Millard Filmore. ""I have the honor to submit the following report regarding my duties performed ..." Letter to Fort Stanton Post Adjutant John Loud. **February 23, 1879**. Indiana Historical Society. Lew Wallace Collection. Box 4. Folder 3. **(Assisting pursuit of William Bonney and Yginio Salazar)**
Dudley, Nathan Augustus Monroe. "I enclose herewith report of 2nd Lieut. M.F. Goodwin ..." Letter to Acting Assistant Adjutant General at Headquarters. **February 24, 1879**. Indiana Historical Society. Lew Wallace Collection. M0292. Box 4, Folder 3. **(Documents military pursuit of William Bonney)**
Leonard, Ira. "The air is filled tonight with 'rumors of wars ... Letter to Lew Wallace. **April 20, 1879**. Indiana Historical Society. Lew Wallace Collection. M0292. Box 4. Folder 9. **(About DA Rynerson: "He is bent on going for the Kid")**

Hoyt, Henry F. "This time it is me who is apologizing for the long delay in answering ..." (Letter to Lew Wallace Jr.) **April 27, 1927.** Indiana Historical Society. Lew Wallace Collection. M0292. Box 14, Folder 11.

_____. "Copy of a bill of sale written by W$\underline{m}$ H. Bonney ..." Letter to Lew Wallace Jr. **April 27, 1927.** Indiana Historical Society. Lew Wallace Collection. M0292. Box 14, Folder 11. (**Calls Billy Bonney "a natural leader of men"**)

SECRET SERVICE REPORTS ABOUT

Wild, Azariah F. "Daily Reports of U. S. Secret Service Agents, Azariah F. Wild." Microfilm T-915. Record Group 87. Rolls 308 (July 1, 1879 - June 30, 1881) National Archives and Records Department. Department of the Treasury. United States Secret Service. Washington, D. C.

LEW WALLACE WRITINGS TO AND ABOUT

WALLACE'S LETTERS TO (CHRONOLOGICAL)

Wallace, Lew. "Come to the house of Squire Wilson ..." Letter to W H. Bonney. **March 15, 1879.** Indiana Historical Society. Lew Wallace Collection. M0292. Box 4. Folder 6.

_____. "The escape makes no difference in arrangements ..." Letter to W.H. Bonney. **March 20, 1879.** Indiana Historical Society. Lew Wallace Collection. M0292. Box 4. Folder 6.

WALLACE'S LETTERS ABOUT (CHRONOLOGICAL)

Wallace, Lew. "I have just ascertained that 'The Kid' is at a place called Las Tablas ..." Letter to Edward Hatch. **March 6, 1879.** Indiana Historical Society. Lew Wallace Collection. Box 9, Folder 10. (**Written on dead John Tunstall's stationery**)

_____. "I beg to submit to you a list of persons whom it is necessary, in my judgment, to arrest ..." Letter to Henry Carroll. **March 11, 1879.** Indiana Historical Society. Lew Wallace Collection. M0292. Box 4. Folder 5. (**Sherman outlaw list with "The Kid" – William Bonney**)

_____. "I enclose a note for Bonney." Letter to John "Squire" Wilson. **March 20, 1879.** Indiana Historical Society. Lew Wallace Collection. M0292. Box 4. Folder 6.

_____. "My time has been so constantly occupied in getting my work into operation ..." Letter to Carl Schurz. **March 21, 1879.** Indiana Historical Society. Lew Wallace Collection. M0292. Box 4. Folder 7. (**Listing the Kid -William Bonney in anti-outlaw campaign of "taking the head off the evil."**)

_____. "To day I forwarded a telegram to you, with another to the President ..." Letter to Carl Schurz. **March 31, 1879.** Indiana Historical Society. Lew Wallace Collection. M0292. Box 4. Folder 7. (**Mention of "precious specimen nicknamed 'The Kid' "**)

REWARD NOTICES FOR

Wallace, Lew. "Be good enough to prepare a draft of proclamation of reward $500 for the capture and delivery of William Bonney, alias the Kid ..." Letter to Territorial Secretary William Ritch. **December 13, 1880.** Herman B. Weisner Papers, ca. 1957-1992. New Mexico State University Library at Las Cruces. Rio Grande Historical Collections. Accession No. Ms 0249. Box W3. Folder 13. Folder Name: "Wallace, Gov. N.M." From Lew Wallace Papers. New Mexico State Records Center. Santa Fe, New Mexico. (**Wallace's first reward for Billy the Kid**)

_____. "Billy the Kid: $500 Reward." *Las Vegas Gazette.* **December 22, 1880.**

_____. "Billy the Kid. $500 Reward." **May 3, 1881.** *Daily New Mexican.* Vol. X, No. 33. Page 1, C 3.

REWARD POSTERS FOR

Greene, Chas. W. "To the New Mexican Printing and Publishing Company." **May 20, 1881.** Indiana Historical Society. Lew Wallace Collection. M0292. Box 4, Folder 17. (**Printer's bill to Lew Wallace for Reward posters for "Kid"**)

_____. "I enclose a bill ..." Letter to Lew Wallace for "Kid" wanted posters. **June 2, 1881.** Indiana Historical Society. Lew Wallace Collection. M0292. Box 4, Folder 18.

DEATH WARRANT FOR

Wallace, Lew. "To the Sheriff of Lincoln County, Greeting ..." **April 30, 1881.** Indiana Historical Society. Lew Wallace Collection. M0292. Box 9, Folder 11.

CORONER'S JURY REPORT FOR

Rudulph, Milnor, Pedro Lucero, Jose Silba, Sabal Gutierrez, Lorenso Jaramillo. Coroner's Jury Report for William Bonney alias "Kid." **July 15, 1881.** Original in Spanish. Indiana Historical Society. Lew Wallace Collection. M0292. Box 9. Folder 11. (**Certified photocopy donated by Maurice Garland Fulton in 1951 of Spanish Coroner's Jury Report, July 15, 1881 - matches photo in William Kelleher's** *Violence in Lincoln County,* **Pages 306-307**)

Rudulph, Milnor, Pedro Lucero, Jose Silba, Sabal Gutierrez, Lorenso Jaramillo. Coroner's Jury Report for William Bonney alias "Kid." **July 15, 1881.** English translation. The Mullin Collection, RNM, VI, J - Legal Papers and Documents. Midland, Texas: Nita Stewart Haley Memorial Library and J. Evetts Haley History Center.

Rudulph, Milnor, Pedro Lucero, Jose Silba, Sabal Gutierrez, Lorenso Jaramillo. Coroner's Jury Report for William Bonney alias "Kid." **July 15, 1881.** English translation. William A. Keleher. *Violence in Lincoln County 1869-1881.* Pages 343-344.

Ritch, William G. "In the matter of the application by Patrick F. Garrett for a reward claimed to have been offered May-1881 for the capture of Wm Bonney alias "the Kid." *Executive Record Book Number 2.* July 25, 1867-November 8, 1882. **July 21, 1881.** Pages 533-535. New Mexico Secretary of State Records. Collection 1971-001, Series 1; Records of the Secretary of the Territory. (Accessed from Albuquerque Public Library Microfilm, Territorial Archives of New Mexico, Roll 21.) (**Presentation of Garret's bill for the reward and demonstrating that Acting-Governor Ritch agreed with the reward, and citing the Coroner's Jury Report's identification of William Bonney**)

No Author. *Executive Record Book Number 2.* July 25, 1867-November 8, 1882. **July 21, 1881.** Pages 533-535. New Mexico State Records Center and Archives, Santa Fe. New Mexico Secretary of the State Records Series 1. Records of the Secretary of the Territory. (**About granting Garrett's reward, citing copy of Coroner's Jury Report**)

No Author. "Kid the Killer Killed, Wm. Bonney alias Antrim, alias Billy the Kid, Fatally Meets Pat Garrett, the Lincoln County Sheriff." Las Cruces *Rio Grande Republican.* **July 23, 1881.** Page 2. Volume 1, Number 10. NewspaperArchive.com. (**Copy of Pat Garrett's letter to Acting Governor William Ritch confirming that the original Coroner's Jury Report was sent to District Attorney of the First Judicial District, and copy of it was included in this letter to the Governor**)

King, Frank M. *Wranglin' the Past: Reminiscences of Frank M. King.* "Chapter xix, The Kid's Exit." Pasadena, California: Trail's End Publishing Company. **1935 and 1946.** (**Describes recent location of Pat Garrett's report to the Governor about the killing of Billy the Kid, with confirmation of Coroner's Jury Report, Page 171**)

Keleher, William A. *Violence in Lincoln County 1869-1881*. Albuquerque, New Mexico: University of New Mexico Press. **1957**. (**Photocopy of Spanish Coroner's Jury Report, July 15, 1881. Pages 306-308; Kelleher's English translation, Pages 343-344.**)

Cooper, Gale. *The Coroner's Jury Report of Billy the Kid: An Inquest That Sealed the Fame Of Billy Bonney and Pat Garrett*. Albuquerque, New Mexico: Gelcour Books. **2019**.

OUTLAW MYTH ARTICLES ABOUT (CHRONOLOGICAL)

GENERAL ARTICLES (CHRONOLOGICAL)

No Author. Grant County *Herald*. **May 10, 1879**. Results of the Lincoln County Grand Jury. (**Also published in the Mesilla** *Thirty Four*. **Confirmation of the William Bonney testimony and James Dolan and Billy Campbell murder indictments, from Page 224 of William Kelleher,** *Violence in Lincoln County*.)

Koogler, John H. Editorial. "Desperadoe's Stronghold, An Organized Gang Assisted by Nature and Defiantly Reckless, Who Terrorize the Country to the East of Us." *Las Vegas Morning Gazette*. **December 3, 1880**. Volume 2, Number 120. https://chroniclingamerica.loc.gov. (**Calling Billy Bonney an outlaw leader; motivating his denial letter of December 12, 1880 to Governor Lew Wallace.**)

No Author. "Outlaws of New Mexico, The Exploits of a Band Headed by a New York Youth, The Mountain Fastness of the Kid and His Followers - War Against a Gang of Cattle Thieves and Murderers - The Frontier Confederates of Brockway, the Counterfeiter." *The Sun*. New York. **December 22, 1880**. Vol. XLVIII, No. 118, Page 3, Columns 1-2.

No Author. "A Big Haul! Billy Kid, Dave Rudabaugh, Billy Wilson and Tom Pickett in the Clutches of the Law." *The Las Vegas Daily Optic*. Monday, **December 27, 1880**. Volume 2, Number. 45. Page 4, Column 2. chroniclingamerica.loc.gov.

No Author. "A Bay-Mare. Everyone who has heard of Billy 'the kid' has heard of his beautiful bay mare." *Las Vegas Morning Gazette*. Tuesday, **January 4, 1881**.

No Author. "The Kid. Billy 'the Kid' and Billy Wilson were on Monday taken to Mesilla for Trial." *Las Vegas Morning Gazette*. Tuesday, **March 15, 1881**.

Newman, Simon. "In the Name of Justice! In the Case of Billy Kid." *Newman's Semi-Weekly*. Saturday, **April 2, 1881**.

No Author. "Billy the Kid. Seems to be having a stormy journey on his trip Southward." *Las Vegas Morning Gazette*. Tuesday, **April 5, 1881**.

No Author. "The Kid." *Santa Fe Daily New Mexican*. **May 1, 1881**. Volume X, Number 32, Page 1, Column 2.

No Author. "Billy Bonney. Advices from Lincoln bring the intelligence of the escape of 'Billy the Kid.'" *Las Vegas Daily Optic*. Monday, **May 2, 1881**.

No Author. "The Kid's Escape." *Santa Fe Daily New Mexican*. Tuesday Morning, **May 3, 1881**. Volume X, Number 33, Page 1, Column 2.

No Author. "The above is the record of as bold a deed ..." *Santa Fe Daily New Mexican*. **May 4, 1881**. (**About Billy's great escape jailbreak**)

No Author. "Dare Devil Desperado. Pursuit of 'Billy the Kid' has been abandoned." *Las Vegas Daily Optic*. **May 4, 1881**.

No Author. "More Killing by Kid, When But a Short Distance From Lincoln, He Meets one of His Old Enemies, and Kills Him and His Companion. Two More Victims." Editorial. *Santa Fe Daily New Mexican*. **May 4, 1881**. Volume X, No. 34, Page 1, Column 2. Newspaperarchive.com. (**Claims Kid killed Billy Matthews**)

No Author. No headline. "Anything that the imagination can concoct ..." *Santa Fe Daily New Mexican*. **May 5, 1881**. Volume X. Page 4, Column 1. Newspaperarchive.com. (**Claims Kid was in Albuquerque**)

No Author. No headline. Mr. Richard Dunham says ..." *Santa Fe Daily New Mexican*, **May 5, 1881**, Volume X. Page 4, Column 3. Newspaperarchive.com. (**Claims Kid was in Stinking Springs**)

No Author. "Richard Dunham's May 2, 1881 encounter with Billy the Kid.", *Santa Fe Daily New Mexican*, **May 5, 1881**, Page 4, Column 3. (private collection)

No Author. "The question if how to deal with desperados who commit murder has but one solution - kill them." *Las Vegas Daily Optic*. Tuesday, **May 10, 1881**.

No Author. "Billy 'the Kid.' " *Las Vegas Gazette*. Thursday, **May 12, 1881**.

No Author. "The Kid was in Chloride City ..." *Santa Fe Daily New Mexican*. **May 13, 1881**. Page 4, Column 3.

No Author. "Billy 'the Kid' is in the vicinity of Sumner." *Las Vegas Gazette*. Sunday, **May 15, 1881**.

No Author. "The Kid is believed to be in the Black Range ..." *Santa Fe Daily New Mexican*. **May 19, 1881**. Page 4, Column 1.

No Author. "Billy the Kid was last seen in Lincoln County ..." *Santa Fe Daily New Mexican*. **May 19, 1881**. Page 4, Column 1.

No Author. (O.L. Houghton's Conversation with Lew Wallace, before May 26, 1881), *The Las Vegas Daily Optic*, **May 26, 1881**, p.4, c.4. Indiana Historical Society. Lew Wallace Collection. M0292.

No Author. " 'Billy the Kid' has been heard from again." *Las Vegas Daily Optic*. Friday, **June 10, 1881**.

No Author. " 'Billy the Kid,' He is Reported to Have Been Seen on Our Streets Saturday Night." *Las Vegas Daily Optic*. Monday Evening, **June 13, 1881**. Vol. 2, No. 188, Page 4, Column 2.

Wilcox, Lute, Ed. "Billy the Kid would make an ideal newspaper-man in that he always endeavors to 'get even' with his enemies." *Las Vegas Daily Optic*. Monday Evening, **June 13, 1881**. Volume 2, Number 188, Page 4, Column 1.

No Author. "Land of the Petulant Pistol, "Scenes" where Life and Land are Cheap ... 'Billy the Kid' as a Killer." *Las Vegas Daily Optic*. Wednesday Evening, **June 15, 1881**. Front Page. 1, Volume 2, Number 190, Columns 1-2. (Possibly contributed to by Lew Wallace, who published with a similar title in the Crawfordsville *Saturday Evening Journal* on June 18, 1881)

No Author. "Barney Mason at Fort Sumner states the 'Kid' is in Local Sheep Camps." *Las Vegas Morning Gazette*. **June 16, 1881**.

No Author. "The Kid." *Santa Fe Daily New Mexican*. **June 16, 1881**. Volume X, Number 90, Page 4, Column 2.

No Author. "Billy the Kid." *Las Vegas Daily Optic*. Thursday, June 28, 1881.

No Author. " 'The Kid' Killed." *Las Vegas Daily Optic*. **July 18. 1881**.

No Author. No title. **Thursday, July 28, 1881.** Pueblo, Colorado, *Colorado Chieftain*. www.coloradohistoricnewspapers.org. (**Quoting from the New York *Tribune* on killing of "Tiger in human form known as "Billy the Kid"**)

Gauss, Gottfried. Interview with *Lincoln County Leader*. **November 21, 1889. (About Billy Bonney's Lincoln jailbreak)**

LEW WALLACE'S ARTICLES

Koogler, John H. "Interview with Governor Lew Wallace on 'The Kid.'" *Las Vegas Gazette*. **April 28, 1881**.

No Author. "The Thug's Territory. Stage Robbers and Cut-Throats Have Things Their Own Way in New Mexico. Gen. Lew Wallace Anxious to Punish the Crime That is So Prevalent – A Chapter About 'Billy the Kid' – The Governor has a Narrow Escape From Being Spanked." *St. Louis Daily Globe-Democrat*. Monday Morning, **May 16, 1881**. Page 2, Columns 5 and 6. (private collection)

No Author. (Lew Wallace interview) "Billy the Kid. General Wallace Tells Why the Young Desperado of New Mexico Wanted to Kill Him, A Dashing and Daring Career in the Land of the Petulant Pistol." (Lew Wallace interviewed on June 13,

1881), Crawfordsville *Saturday Evening Journal*, **June 18, 1881**. Indiana Historical Society. The Papers of Lew and Susan Wallace. Microfilm Edition. Indianapolis, Indiana: Indiana Historical Society Press. 2008.

No Author. (Lew Wallace interview) "Lew Wallace's Foe. Threatened by 'Billy the Kid.' The Writing of 'Ben Hur' Interrupted. An Incident of the Soldier-Author's Career in New Mexico. *San Francisco Chronicle.* December 10, 1893. Indiana Historical Society. Lew Wallace Collection. M0292. Box 14. Folder 11. (Lew Wallace creating outlaw myth of outlaw Billy the Kid")

No Author. "Street Pickings," Weekly *Crawfordsville Review - Saturday Edition*, **January 6, 1894**. Indiana Historical Society. The Papers of Lew and Susan Wallace. Microfilm Edition. Series I. Reel 27. Indianapolis, Indiana: Indiana Historical Society Press. 2008.

No Author. "An Old Incident Recalled." Crawfordsville *Weekly News-Review*. **December 20, 1901**. Indiana Historical Society. The Papers of Lew and Susan Wallace. Microfilm Edition. Series I. Reel 27. Indianapolis, Indiana: Indiana Historical Society Press. 2008.

Lewis, E.I. "Gen. Wallace's Feud with Billy the Kid, When the General Was Governor of New Mexico and Billy Bonne Was the Most Dangerous Western Outlaw. He Was a Waif and Was Reared in Indiana. *The Indianapolis Press.* Saturday, **June 23, 1900**. Page 7. Lew Wallace Collection. Indiana Historical Society. M0292. Box 14. Folder 11. (photocopy) (Original article is in OMB 23, Box 1. Folder 5) **(Creating self-serving myth of outlaw Billy the Kid")**

Wallace, Lew. "General Lew Wallace Writes a Romance of 'Billy the Kid' Most Famous Bandit of the Plains: Thrilling Story of the Midnight Meeting Between Gen Wallace, Then Governor of New Mexico, and the Notorious Outlaw, in a Lonesome Hut in Santa Fe." *New York World Magazine.* Sunday, **June 8, 1902**. Lew Wallace Collection. Indiana Historical Society. M0292. . Box 14. Folder 11.

OTHER HISTORICAL FIGURES (PERIOD)

ANGEL, FRANK WARNER

PRESIDENT HAYES MEETING BY

Mullin, Robert N. Re: Frank Warner Angel Meeting With President Hayes August, 1878. Binder RNM, VI, M. (Unpublished). Midland, Texas: Nita Stewart Haley Memorial Library and J. Evetts Haley History Center. (Undated).

LETTERS BY

Angel, Frank Warner. "I am in receipt of your favor of the 12th ..." Letter to Samuel Beach Axtell. **August 13, 1878**. Interior Department Papers 1850-1907; Appointments Division and Subsequent Actions. Microfilm Roll M750. National Archives and Records Administration Record Group 48. Microfilm Case Number 44-4-8-3. U.S. Department of Interior. Washington D.C.

_____. "I enclose copies of letters received by me from Gov Axtell ..." Letter to Secretary of the Interior Carl Schurz. **August 24, 1878**. (Enclosing copy of letter to him from Governor S.B. Axtell of August 12, 1878; and Angel's response to Axtell of August 13, 1878.) Microfilm File Case Number 44-4-8-3. Record Group 48. Microfilm No. M750. Roll 1. National Archives and Records Administration. U.S. Department of Justice. Washington, D.C.

_____. "I have just been favored by a call from W.L. Rynerson ..." Letter to Secretary of Interior Carl Schurz. **September 6, 1878**. Microfilm File Case Number 44-4-8-3. Record Group 48. Microfilm No. M750. Roll 1. National Archives and Records Administration. U.S. Department of Justice. Washington, D.C.

REPORTS BY

Angel, Frank Warner. *Examination of charges against F. C. Godfroy, Indian Agent, Mescalero, N. M.* **October 2, 1878.** (Report 1981, Inspector E.C. Watkins; Cited as Watkins Report). M319-20 and L147, 44-4-8. Record Group 075. National Archives and Records Administration. U.S. Department of Justice. Washington, D. C.

_____. *In the Matter of the Investigation of the Charges Against S.B. Axtell Governor of New Mexico. Report and Testimony.* **October 3, 1878.** Angel Report. Interior Department Papers 1850-1907; Appointments Division and Subsequent Actions. Microfilm Case File No. 44-4-8-3. Record Group 48. Microfilm Roll M750. National Archives and Records Administration. U.S. Department of Interior. Washington, D.C. (**Mentions Santa Fe Ring**)

_____. *In the Matter of the Examination of the Causes and Circumstances of the Death of John H. Tunstall a British Subject.* Report filed **October 4, 1878.** Angel Report. Interior Department Papers 1850-1907; Appointments Division and Subsequent Actions. Microfilm File Case Number 44-4-8-3. Record Group 48. Microfilm No. M750. Roll 1. National Archives and Records Administration. U.S. Department of Justice. Washington, D.C.

_____. *In the Matter of the Lincoln County Troubles. To the Honorable Charles Devens, Attorney General.* **October 4, 1878.** Angel Report. Microfilm Case File No. 44-4-8-3. Record Group 48. Microfilm Roll M750. National Archives and Records Administration. U.S. Department of Justice. Washington, D.C.

NOTEBOOK ON SANTA FE RING MEMBERS BY

Angel, Frank Warner. "To Gov. Lew Wallace / Santa Fe, N. M., 1878." Notebook. **1878.** Indiana Historical Society. Lew Wallace Collection. M0292. Microfilm No. F372. (**Original missing, copy on microfilm; Notebook prepared for Lew Wallace listing names of Santa Fe Ring members**)

Theisen, Lee Scott. "Frank Warner Angel's Notes on New Mexico Territory, 1878." *Arizona and the West: A Quarterly Journal of History.* Winter 1976. Volume 18. Number 4. Pages 333-370. (**About the Angel notebook**)

AXTELL, SAMUEL BEACH

CONTEMPORARY SOURCES (CHRONOLOGICAL)

No author. "Anarchy at Cimarron." *Santa Fe Weekly New Mexico.* **November 16, 1875.** (**Ring-biased article justifying Governor S.B. Axtell calling in troops in the Colfax County War after murder of Reverend Franklin Tolby**)

Axtell, Samuel B. "The Legislature to Assess Property. *Message of Gov. Samuel B. Axtell to the Legislative Assembly of New Mexico, Twenty-second Session.* Page 4. Manderfield & Tucker, Public Printers: Santa Fe, New Mexico. **1875 or 1876.** Interior Department Papers 1850-1907; Appointments Division and Subsequent Actions. Microfilm File Case Number 44-4-8-3. Record Group 48. Microfilm No. M750. Roll 1. National Archives and Records Administration. U.S. Department of Justice. Washington, D.C.

Elkins, Stephen B. "I trouble you to say a word in behalf of Gov. Axtell ..." Letter to President Rutherford B. Hayes. **June 11, 1877.** Interior Department Papers 1850-1907; Appointments Division and Subsequent Actions. Microfilm Roll M750. National Archives and Records Administration Record Group 48. Microfilm Case Number 44-4-8-3. U. S. Department of Interior. Washington D. C. (**Trying to prevent Axtell's removal as governor**)

Axtell, Samuel B. "I have today mailed to you a reply to the charges on file in your Dept against me." Letter to Secretary of the Interior Carl Schurz. **June 15, 1877.** Interior Department Papers 1850-1907; Appointments Division and Subsequent

Actions. Microfilm Roll M750. National Archives and Records Administration Record Group 48. Microfilm Case Number 44-4-8-3 U.S. Department of Interior. Washington D.C. (**Refuting charges made in Colfax County**).

Isaacs, I. and G.N. Coe. "Charges Against S.B. Axtell, Governor of New Mexico." **June 22, 1878**. Interior Department Papers 1850-1907; Appointments Division and Subsequent Actions. Microfilm File Case Number 44-4-8-3. Microfilm No. M750. Roll 1. National Archives and Records Administration. Record Group 48. U.S. Department of Justice. Washington, D.C.

Routt, John C. "I am here on a visit to my daughter and have more by accident than otherwise heard statements ..." Letter to President Rutherford B. Hayes. **August 29, 1878**. Interior Department Papers 1850-1907; Appointments Division and Subsequent Actions. Microfilm File Case Number 44-4-8-3. Microfilm No. M750. Roll 1. National Archives and Records Administration. U.S. Department of Justice. Washington, D.C. (**Ringite letter opposing removal of Governor Axtell and U.S. Attorney Catron.**)

Schurz, Carl. "I transmit herewith an order from the President ..." **September 4, 1878**. Letter to Lew Wallace. Indiana Historical Society. Lew Wallace Collection. M0292. Box 3. Folder 14. (**Suspension of Governor S.B. Axtell and Wallace's appointment as new Governor**)

Elkins, Stephen Benton. "To the President. Referring to a conversation had with you last week ..." Letter to President James Abram Garfield. **March 17, 1881**. (Received Executive Mansion April 6, 1881). Interior Department Papers 1850-1907; Appointments Division and Subsequent Actions. Microfilm Roll M750. National Archives and Records Administration Microfilm Roll M750. National Archives and Records Administration Record Group 48. Microfilm Case Number 44-4-8-3. U.S. Department of Interior. Washington D.C. Microfilm Case Number 44-4-8-3. U.S. Department of Interior. Washington D.C. (**Request for re-appointment of Axtell as Territorial New Mexico Governor**)

Bradstreet, George P. "Referring to the nomination of Sam'l B. Axtell of Ohio to be Chief Justice of the Supreme Court of New Mexico ... he is alleged to have been removed by President Hayes ..." Letter to Judiciary Committee of the U.S. Senate. **June 22, 1882**. Interior Department Papers 1850-1907; Appointments Division and Subsequent Actions. Microfilm Roll M750. National Archives and Records Administration Microfilm Roll M750. National Archives and Records Administration Record Group 48. Microfilm Case Number 44-4-8-3. U.S. Department of Interior. Washington D.C.

No Author. " 'Chief Justice Axtell' is a bitter pill for the Raton *News and Press*." *Santa Fe New Mexican*. **July 18, 1882**. (**Santa Fe Ring instatement of S.B. Axtell as Chief Justice**)

BACA, SATURNINO

BIOGRAPHICAL SOURCES

Charles, Tom. (Edited by Mrs. Tom Charles) "The Father of Lincoln County." *More Tales of Tularosa*. 1961. (unpublished manuscript)

Jonathan (no last name given). "About Saturnino Baca." July 23, 2001. http://www.genealogy.com/forum/surnames/topics/baca/509/

Nolan, Frederick. "New and Updated Biographies." *The Lincoln County War: A Documentary History. Revised Edition*. .Santa Fe: Sunstone Press. 2009.

LETTERS FROM AND ABOUT (CHRONOLOGICAL)

Baca, Saturnino. "When I sent in my bid for the hay contract ..." Letter to Quartermaster Captain A.J. McGonigle. **July 19, 1871.** University of New Mexico Library. Center for Southwest Studies. Thomas B. Catron Papers, MSS 29, Series 803, Box 1, Folder 25. (**About hay contract to Fort Stanton**)

Kantz, August V. "I learn from Col. Fritz that you are under the impression ..." Letter to Quartermaster Captain A.J. McGonigle. **July 20, 1871.** University of New Mexico Library. Center for Southwest Studies. Thomas B. Catron Papers, MSS 29, Series 803, Box 1, Folder 25. (**Emil Fritz pressures Fort Stanton to take bottom hay - which would make contract for Baca fillable - and Kantz warns that Fritz and Murphy will get hay monopoly**)

Carey, A.B. "Letter of Saturnino Baca, dated Fort Stanton ..." Letter to Quartermaster Captain A.J. McGonigle. **July 20, 1871.** University of New Mexico Library. Center for Southwest Studies. Thomas B. Catron Papers, MSS 29, Series 803, Box 1, Folder 25. (**Baca declines his contract to supply grama hay**)

McGonigle, A.J.M. "I have the honor to forward enclosed herewith ..." Letter to Quartermaster General M.C. Meigs. **September 24, 1871.** University of New Mexico Library. Center for Southwest Studies. Thomas B. Catron Papers, MSS 29, Series 803, Box 1, Folder 25. (**Wants Baca barred from hay contracts**)

BONNEY, WILLIAM HENRY

(See History of William Henry Bonney)

BOWDRE, CHARLES

CONTEMPORARY SOURCES (CHRONOLOGICAL)

Wallace, Lew. "Please select ten of your Rangers ..." Letter to Juan Patrón. **March 3, 1879.** Indiana Historical Society. Lew Wallace Collection. M0292. Box 4. Folder 4. (**To arrest "Scurlock and Bowdre"**)

_____. Lew. "I have reliable information that J.G. Scurlock and Charles Bowdre are now at a ranch called Taiban ..." Letter to Edward Hatch. **March 6, 1879.** Indiana Historical Society. Lew Wallace Collection. Box 4, Folder 4.

BRADY, WILLIAM

BIOGRAPHICAL SOURCE

Lavash, Donald R. *Sheriff William Brady. Tragic Hero of the Lincoln County War.* Santa Fe, New Mexico: Sunstone Press. 1986.

CONTEMPORARY SOURCES (CHRONOLOGICAL)

Brady, William. Affidavit of **July 2, 1876** concerning appointment as Administrator for the Emil Fritz Estate. Copied from the original District Court Record. (private collection)

_____. Affidavit of **August 22, 1876** documenting business debts to L. G. Murphy and Co. pertaining to the Emil Fritz Estate. Copied from the original District Court Record. (private collection)

_____. Affidavit of **July _, 1876** of Resignation as Emil Fritz Estate Administrator. Copied from the original District Court Record. (private collection.)

_____. Affidavit of **August 22, 1876** confirming giving Alexander McSween the books of the L.G. Murphy Company for the purpose of making business debt collections. Copied from the original District Court Record. (private collection)

Tunstall, John Henry. "A Taxpayer's Complaint ... January 18, 1878." Mesilla *Independent.* **January 26, 1878.** (**Exposé of William Brady embezzling tax money to buy cattle for "The House;" and Catron then paid that bill**)

Dolan, James J. "Answer to A Taxpayer's Complaint." Mesilla *Independent.* **January 29, 1878.** (**Response to J.H. Tunstall's exposé**)

Bristol, Warren. "Action of Assumpsit to command Sheriff Brady of Lincoln County to attach goods of Alexander A. McSween." **February 7, 1878.** District Court Record. (private collection).

_____. Preprinted form for "Writ of Attachment" (Printed and sold at the office of the Mesilla News) filled out to command the Sheriff of Lincoln County to attach goods of Alexander McSween for a suit of damages for ten thousand dollars. **February 7, 1878**. District Court Record. (private collection).

Brady, William. "List of Articles Inventoried by Wm Brady sheriff in the suit of Charles Fritz & Emilie Scholand vs A.A. McSween now in the dwelling house belonging to A.A. McSween." (undated, but in **February of 1878**) (private collection)

BRISTOL, WARREN HENRY

CONTEMPORARY SOURCES (CHRONOLOGICAL)

Bristol Warren. "From sources of information that I deem perfectly reliable I am satisfied that there are public disorders in Lincoln County ..." Letter to Governor Marsh Giddings. **January 10, 1874.** Herman B. Weisner Papers, ca. 1957-1992. New Mexico State University Library at Las Cruces. Rio Grande Historical Collections. Accession No. Weisner Ms 0249. Box 4/39. Folder D-4. Folder Name: "Judge Bristol's letter." (**Creating Ring's outlaw myth and proposing military intervention**)

_____. "Writ of Embezzlement." **December 21, 1877**. Herman B. Weisner Papers, ca. 1957-1992. New Mexico State University Library at Las Cruces. Rio Grande Historical Collections. Accession No. Ms 0249. Box 10. Folder M-13. Folder Name. "Will and Testament A. McSween." (**Emilie Fritz Scholand's sworn complaint against Alexander McSween**)

_____. "Action of Assumpsit to command Sheriff Brady of Lincoln County to attach goods of Alexander A. McSween." **February 7, 1878**. District Court Record. (private collection).

_____. Preprinted form for "Writ of Attachment" (Printed and sold at the office of the Mesilla News) filled out to command the Sheriff of Lincoln County to attach goods of Alexander McSween for a suit of damages for ten thousand dollars. **February 7, 1878**. District Court Record. (private collection).

_____. "My reasons for not holding October term of Court ..." Telegram to U.S. Marshal John Sherman. **October 4, 1878**. Indiana Historical Society. Lew Wallace Collection. M0292. Box 3. Folder 15.

_____. *Instructions to the Jury*. District Court 3rd Judicial. District Doña Ana. Filed **April 9, 1881**. Writ of Embezzlement. New Mexico State University Library at Las Cruces. Rio Grande Historical Collection. Accession No. Ms 0249. Box 1. Folder 14C. Folder Name: "Billy the Kid Legal Documents."

CATRON, THOMAS BENTON

BIBLIOGRAPHICAL SOURCES

Cleaveland, Norman, *A Synopsis of the Great New Mexico Cover-up*. Self-printed. 1989.

_____. *The Great Santa Fe Cover-up*. Based on a Talk given Before the Santa Fe Historical Society on November 1, 1978. Self-printed. 1982.

_____. *The Morleys - Young Upstarts on the Southwest Frontier.* Albuquerque, New Mexico: Calvin Horn Publisher, Inc. 1971. (**Page 93 gives Catron's vindictive indictment of Cleaveland's grandmother, Ada Morley, for mail theft as revenge denying him use of a Maxwell Land Grant buggy.**)

Dodge, Andrew R., and Betty K. Koed, eds. *Biographical Directory of the United States Congress 1774-2005*. Washington, D.C.: United States Government Printing Office. 2005

Dunham, Harold H. "New Mexican Land Grants with Special Reference to the Title Papers of the Maxwell Grant." *New Mexico Historical Review*. (January, 1955) Vol. 70. No. 1. pp. 1 - 23.

Hefferan, Vioalle Clark. *Thomas Benton Catron*. Albuquerque, New Mexico: University of New Mexico. Zimmerman Library. Unpublished Thesis for the Degree of Master of Arts. 1940. .(**In praise of Catron; includes railroad involvement, Page 35; First National Bank stockholder from 1871 to 1907, Page 28**)

Keleher, William A. *The Maxwell Land Grant. A New Mexico Item*. Albuquerque, New Mexico: University of New Mexico Press. 1964.

Klasner, Lilly. Eve Ball. Ed. *My Girlhood Among Outlaws*. Tucson, Arizona: The University of Arizona Press. 1972.

Lamar, Howard Robert N. *The Far Southwest 1846 – 1912: A Territorial History*. New Haven and London: Yale University Press. 1966. (**Chapter 6 covers the Santa Fe Ring**))

Montoya, María E. *Translating Property. The Maxwell Land Grant and the Conflict Over Land in the American West, 1840-1900*. Berkeley and Los Angeles: University of California Press. 2002.

Mullin, Robert N. "A Specimen of Catron's Dirty Work. Sworn Affidavit of Samuel Davis." October 1, 1878. Binder RNM IV, EE. (Unpublished). Midland, Texas: Nita Stewart Haley Memorial Library and J. Evetts Haley Historical Center.

_____. "Catron Embarrassed Throughout His Life by an Affliction." (Date Unknown). Binder RNM, IV, M. (Unpublished). Midland, Texas: Nita Stewart Haley Memorial Library and J. Evetts Haley Historical Center. Robert Mullin Papers. Binder RNM IV, EE (Unpublished).

_____. "Prior to Lincoln County War Catron Had Defended Colonel Dudley." (No Date). Notes from "Lincoln County War Cast of Characters." Midland, Texas: Nita Stewart Haley Memorial Library and J. Evetts Haley Historical Center.

Murphy, Lawrence R. *Lucien Bonaparte Maxwell. Napoleon of the Southwest*. Norman: University of Oklahoma Press. 1983.

Otero, Miguel A. *My Life on the Frontier, 1882-1897: Incidents and Characters of the period when Kansas, Colorado, and New Mexico were passing through the last of their Wild and Romantic Years*. New York: The Press of the Pioneers. 1935. Pages 232-233. (Quoted by Victor Westphall, *Thomas Benton Catron and His Era*. Page 188*)* (**Quote: "the 'Santa Fe Ring,' the real machine controlling the political situation in New Mexico."**)

Pearson, Jim Berry. *The Maxwell Land Grant*. Norman: University of Oklahoma Press. 1961.

Sluga, Mary Elizabeth. *Political Life of Thomas Benton Catron 1896-1912*. Albuquerque, New Mexico: University of New Mexico. Zimmerman Library. Unpublished Thesis for the Degree of Master of Arts. 1941. (**Thesis in praise of Catron for an M.A.**)

Taylor, Morris F. *O.P. McMains and the Maxwell Land Grant Conflict*. Tucson, Arizona: The University of Arizona Press. 1979. (**Traces origins of the Santa Fe Ring with T.B. Catron and S.B. Elkins**)

Westphall, Victor. *Thomas Benton Catron and His Era*. Tucson, Arizona: University of Arizona Press. 1973.

_____. "Fraud and Implications of Fraud in the Land Grants of New Mexico." *New Mexico Historical Review*. 1974. Vol. XLIX, No. 3. 189 - 218.

Wooden, John Paul. *Thomas Benton Catron and New Mexico Politics 1866-1921*. Albuquerque, New Mexico: University of New Mexico. Zimmerman Library. Unpublished Thesis for the Degree of Master of Arts. 1959. (**M.A. thesis praising Catron**)

GENERAL CONTEMPORARY EXPOSÉS OF(CHRONOLOGICAL)

Middaugh, Asa F. Deposition. **March 31, 1876**. "Exhibit B" in the August 9, 1878 deposition of Frank Springer to Investigator Frank Warner Angel. Frank Warner Angel report titled *In the Matter of the Investigation of the Charges Against S.B. Axtell Governor of New Mexico*. October 3, 1878. Interior Department Papers

1850-1907; Appointments Division and Subsequent Actions. Microfilm Case File No. 44-4-8-3. Record Group 48. Microfilm Roll M750. National Archives and Records Administration. U.S. Department of Interior. Washington, D.C. (**About Catron's malicious prosecution of Ada McPherson Morley**)

Springer, Frank. Deposition to Investigator Frank Warner Angel. **August 9, 1878**. Frank Warner Angel report titled *In the Matter of the Investigation of the Charges Against S.B. Axtell Governor of New Mexico*. October 3, 1878. Interior Department Papers 1850-1907; Appointments Division and Subsequent Actions. Microfilm Case File No. 44-4-8-3. Record Group 48. Microfilm Roll M750. National Archives and Records Administration. U.S. Department of Interior. Washington, D.C. (**Mentions Catron, Elkins, and the Santa Fe Ring, and provided Exhibits of letters exposing Catron's evil.**)

No Author. "The Santa Fe Ring is the most corrupt combination that ever cursed any country or community." Las Cruces *Thirty-Four Newspaper*. **October 27, 1880**. From Victor Westphall, *Thomas Benton Catron and His Era*. Page 186. (**Article summarizing Ring abuses in urging voters to oppose Ring candidates**)

No Author. "The Ring must soon discover that the time has passed in New Mexico when men can be herded like so many sheep ..." *Albuquerque Daily Democrat*. **March 4, 1884**. Quoted by Victor Westphall, *Thomas Benton Catron and His Era*. Page 191. (**About Santa Fe Ring control of appointments to legislature**)

Valdez, Jose and Enrique Mares. "Scorching Letter, The Knights of Labor Send a Communication to Powderly! Politicians Arraigned! The Boldest Document Ever Issued in the Territory." **August 18, 1890**. *Las Vegas Democrat*. Volume 1. Center for Southwest Studies. Thomas B. Catron Papers, MSS 29, Series 102, Box 8, Folder 4. (**Gives history of Santa Fe Ring with T.B. Catron as head**)

No Author. "Catron and the Laboring Men." Unknown newspaper. **1892?** University of New Mexico Library. Center for Southwest Studies. Thomas B. Catron Papers, MSS 29, Series 401, Box 1, Folder 3. (**Opposition to Catron as Delegate to Congress as "the biggest corporation man in New Mexico"**)

Victory, John P. "No Consistent Democrat Should Vote for T.B. Catron, John P. Victory in Forcible and Cogent Language Gives Answerable Reasons." **No month, 1895**. Printed broadside. University of New Mexico Library. Center for Southwest Studies. Thomas B. Catron Papers, MSS 29, Series 409, Box 1, Folder 3.

Wallace, Lew. "I have your several letters, including the last one of the 3rd inst." Letter to Eugene Fiske. **November 6, 1897**. Indiana Historical Society. Lew Wallace Collection. AC233. Box 1. Folder 7. (part of 1981 addition) (**About Catron's control over New Mexicans**)

Cutting, Bronson. "Catron was the boss of the Territory ..." Letter to James Roger Addison. **December 11, 1911**. Cited by Victor Westphall in *Thomas Benton Catron and His Era* from his citation: Lincoln County Manuscripts Division. Box 12. Courtesy of David Stratton. (**Catron as head of the Santa Fe Ring**)

Johnson, E. Dana. "[H]e ruled with a rod of iron ..." Editorial. *Santa Fe New Mexican*. **May 16, 1921**. Catron Papers 801, Box 1. Quoted by Victor Westphall, *Thomas Benton Catron and His Era*. Pages 394-395. (**Tactics of "boss" Catron without using the words Santa Fe Ring**)

(SEE: Santa Fe Ring; Frank Warner Angel)

FEDERAL INDICTMENT OF REGULATORS BY

Catron, Thomas Benton. "Case No. 411. The United States vs. Charles Bowdry [Bowdre], Doc Scurlock, Henry Brown, Henry Antrim alias "Kid," John Middleton, Stephen Stevens, John Scroggins, George Coe and Frederick Waite." **June 21, 1878**. Herman B. Weisner Papers, ca. 1957-1992. New Mexico State University Library at Las Cruces. Rio Grande Historical Collections. Accession No. Ms 0249. Box 1. Folder B-4. Folder Name: Andrew Roberts Indictment.

RESIGNATION AS TERRITORIAL U.S. ATTORNEY BY

Elkins, Stephen Benton. "Elkins – Telegraph Cipher, Cipher with Catron." Sent to T.B. Catron. ___ 1878? University of New Mexico Library. Center for Southwest Studies. Thomas B. Catron Papers, MSS 29, Series 108, Box 1, Folder 4. (**Ring code-cipher key about T.B. Catron's resignation as U.S. Attorney**)

_____. "Asking delay of action upon charges against U.S. Atty. Catron ..." **September 24, 1878.** Angel Report. Microfilm File Case No. 44-4-8-3. Record Group 48. National Records and Archives Administration. Microfilm No. M750. Roll 1. U.S. Department of Justice. Washington, D. C.

_____. "Regarding Attorney General's decision on T.B. Catron." Letter. **September___, 1878.** Angel Report. Microfilm File Case No. 44-4-8-3. Record Group 48. National Records and Archives Administration. Microfilm No. M750. Roll 1. U.S. Department of Justice. Washington, D.C.

Catron, Thomas Benton. "In accordance with a purpose long entertained ...." Letter to Charles Devens. **October 10, 1878.** Angel Report. Microfilm File Case No. 44-4-8-3. Record Group 48. National Records and Archives Administration. Microfilm No. M750. Roll 1. U.S. Department of Justice. Washington, D.C. (**Resignation as U.S. Attorney**)

Devens, Charles. "Your resignation of the office of United States Attorney ..." Letter to T.B. Catron. **October 19, 1878.** Angel Report. Microfilm File Case No. 44-4-8-3. Record Group 48. National Records and Archives Administration. Microfilm No. M750. Roll 1. U.S. Department of Justice. Washington, D. C.

Catron, Thomas Benton. "Please change my resignation ...." **November 4, 1878.** Telegram to Charles Devens. Angel Report. Microfilm File Case No. 44-4-8-3. Record Group 48. National Records and Archives Administration. Microfilm No. M750. Roll 1. U.S. Department of Justice. Washington, D. C. (**Resignation as U.S. Attorney**)

Devens, Charles. "Your resignation of the office of United States Attorney ..." Letter to T.B. Catron. **November 12, 1878.** Angel Report. Microfilm File Case No. 44-4-8-3. Record Group 48. National Records and Archives Administration. Microfilm No. M750. Roll 1. U.S. Department of Justice. Washington, D.C.

Elkins, Stephen Benton. "Relative to resignation of T. B. Catron U. S. Attorney." Letter to Charles Devens. **November 10, 1878.** Angel Report. Microfilm File Case No. 44-4-8-3. Record Group 48. National Records and Archives Administration. Microfilm No. M750. Roll 1. U.S. Department of Justice. Washington, D.C.

Devens, Charles. "To honorable S. B. Elkins re. T. B. Catron continuing to act as U.S. Attorney ..." Letter to Stephen B. Elkins. **November 12, 1878.** Angel Report. Microfilm File Case No. 44-4-8-3. Record Group 48. National Records and Archives Administration. Microfilm No. M750. Roll 1. U.S. Department of Justice. Washington, D.C.

Barnes, Sidney M.. "I Sidney M. Barnes do solemnly swear ..." Swearing in as U.S. Attorney. **January 20, 1879.** Angel Report. Microfilm File Case No. 44-4-8-3. Record Group 48. National Records and Archives Administration. Microfilm No. M750. Roll 1. U.S. Department of Justice. Washington, D.C. (**Catron replaced by Ringite attorney Sidney Barnes**)

Elkins, Stephen Benton. "I have waited some time to reply to your lengthy letter ..." Letter to T.B. Catron. **August 15, 1879.** West Virginia & Regional History Center. West Virginia University Libraries, Morgantown, W. Va. Stephen B. Elkins Papers (A&M 53). Box 1. Folder 1. (**Reveals he prevented Catron's dismissal and indictment from Angel's report**)

Clancy, Frank W. "From something I have heard ..." Letter to T.B. Catron. **September 20, 1892.** University of New Mexico Library. Center for Southwest Studies. Thomas B. Catron Papers, MSS 29, Series 102, Box 16, Folder 2. (**Warning Catron that opponents are seeking the Angel Report to use against his campaign for Delegate, but Elkins is making obstacles**)

_____. "I am much surprised at what you say in your letter ..." Letter to T.B. Catron. **December 2, 1896.** University of New Mexico Library. Center for Southwest Studies. Thomas B. Catron Papers, MSS 29, Series 106, Box 1, Folder 6. **(Surprise that Catron now wants to be U.S. Attorney again)**

PECOS RIVER COW CAMP OF (CHRONOLOGICAL)

Riley, John H. Letter to N.A.M. Dudley. **May 19, 1878. (Fabricated Regulator theft of Catron's cattle from the Dolan Pecos Cow Camp)** Cited by Victor Westphall, Page 87.

Catron, Thomas Benton. Catron letter to Governor S. B. Axtell to intervene in Lincoln County. **May 30, 1878.** Midland, Texas: Nita Stewart Haley Memorial Library and J. Evetts Haley Historical Center. Robert Mullin Papers. Binder RNM IV, EE (Unpublished). **(Fabricated attack of Regulators on his cow camp workers)** Cited by Victor Westphall, Page 89-90.

OWNERSHIP FILING ON CARRIZOZO CATTLE COMPANY BY

Catron, Thomas Benton.. Statement of Sole ownership of Carrizozo Ranch in Tax Dispute Case. No date. Herman B. Weisner Papers, ca. 1957-1992. New Mexico State University Library at Las Cruces. Rio Grande Historical Collections. Accession No. Ms 0249. Box. 2. Folder C-8. Folder Name "T.B. Catron Tax Troubles." **(One of Catron's Lincoln County holdings)**

CHAPMAN, HUSTON INGRAM

CONTEMPORARY SOURCES (CHRONOLOGICAL)

Wallace, Lew. "I enclose you a copy of a letter from Las Vegas ..." Letter to Edward Hatch. **October 28, 1878.** Indiana Historical Society. Lew Wallace Collection. M0292. Box 3. Folder 16. **(Forwards Chapman's letter to Hatch)**

_____. "In a communication, dated October 28. inst., I requested, for reasons stated, a safe-guard for Mrs. McSween ..." Letter to Edward Hatch. **November 9, 1878.** Indiana Historical Society. Lew Wallace Collection. M0292. Box 3. Folder 17.

No Author. (signed E.). "Death of Chapman." *Las Vegas Gazette.* **March 1, 1879.** From *Proceedings of a Court of Inquiry in the Case of Lt. Col. N.A.M. Dudley (May 2,1879 – July 5, 1879).* File No. QQ1284. (Boxes 3304, 3305, 3305A); Court Martial Files 1809-1894. Records of the Office of the Judge Advocate General – Army. Record Group 153. Old Military and Civil Branch. National Archives and Records Administration. Washington, D. C.

No Author. "Wallace and Lincoln County." Grant County *Herald.* **March 1, 1879.** Indiana Historical Society. The Papers of Lew and Susan Wallace. Microfilm Edition. Indianapolis, Indiana: Indiana Historical Society Press. 2008. **(Ridicule about Huston Chapman's murder)**

Chapman, W.W. "Yours of the 1st inst. came ..." Letter to Ira E. Leonard. **March 20, 1879.** Indiana Historical Society. Lew Wallace Collection. M0292. Box 4. Folder 6.

Rynerson, William. "The Grand Jurors for the Territory of New Mexico taken from the body of the good and lawful men of the County of Lincoln ..." Indictments of the April, Lincoln County Grand Jury. **April 28, 1879.** Herman B. Weisner Papers, ca. 1957-1992. New Mexico State University Library at Las Cruces. Rio Grande Historical Collection. Accession No. Ms 0249. Box 4/39. Folder E-Z. Folder Name: "Jessie Evans Accessory to Murder." **(Billy's testimony indicts J.J. Dolan, Billy Campbell, and Jessie Evans fulfilling his pardon bargain)**

Chapman, W.W. "Since receiving yours of the 1st March ..." Letter to Ira Leonard. **May 8, 1879.** Indiana Historical Society. Lew Wallace Collection. M0292. Box 4. Folder 10.

LETTERS BY

Chapman, Huston I. "You will please pardon me for presuming so much upon your kindness ..." Letter to Lew Wallace. **October 24, 1878.** Indiana Historical Society. Lew Wallace Collection. M0292. Box 3. Folder 16. (**Makes clear N.A.M. Dudley's danger to Susan McSween**)

_____. 'You attach much importance to the awe-inspiring influence of the military ..." Letter to Lew Wallace. **November 25, 1878.** From Frederick Nolan, *The Lincoln County War,* p. 359.

_____. "You must pardon me for so often presuming upon your kindness ..." Letter to Lew Wallace. **November 29, 1878.** Indiana Historical Society. Lew Wallace Collection. M0292. Box 3. Folder 18.

CHISUM, JOHN SIMPSON

Hinton, Harwood P., Jr. "John Simpson Chisum, 1877-84." *New Mexico Historical Review* 31(3) (July 1956): 177 - 205; 31(4) (October 1956): 310 - 337; 32(1) (January 1957): 53 - 65.

Klasner, Lilly. Eve Ball. Ed. *My Girlhood Among Outlaws.* Tucson, Arizona: The University of Arizona Press. 1972. (**Contains John Chisum's in jail write-up about Santa Fe Ring injustices to himself**)

COE FAMILY

BIOGRAPHICAL SOURCES

Coe, George. Doyce B. Nunis, Jr. Ed. *Frontier Fighter. The Autobiography of George Coe Who Fought and Rode With Billy the Kid.* Chicago: R. R. Donnelley and Sons Company. 1984.

Coe, Wilbur. *Ranch on the Ruidoso. The Story of a Pioneer Family in New Mexico, 1871 - 1968.* New York: Alfred A. Knopf. 1968.

DEDRICK BROTHERS

BIOGRAPHICAL SOURCES

Upham, Elizabeth. (Related by marriage to Daniel Dedrick). Personal interviews. 1998.
Upham, Marquita. (Relative by marriage to Daniel Dedrick). Personal interview. 1998.

CONTEMPORARY SOURCES (CHRONOLOGICAL)

Dedrick, Dan. "I have been under an arrest for six days ..." **April 5, 1879.** Letter to Lew Wallace. Indiana Historical Society. Lew Wallace Collection. M0292. Box 4. Folder 8. (**Says he was not told his arrest charges**)

No Author. "Arrests of Dedricks. Legal Documents." Herman B. Weisner Papers, ca. 1957-1992. New Mexico State University Library at Las Cruces. Rio Grande Historical Collections. Accession No. Ms 0249. Box 1. Folder B-8. Folder Name: "Lincoln County Bonds."

DOLAN, JAMES JOSEPH

BIOGRAPHICAL SOURCE

Slates, Thomas. "The James J. Dolan House, Lincoln New Mexico." *New Mexico Architecture* 11. 8/9 (1969). pp. 17-20.(**With Dolan biography**)

CONTEMPORARY SOURCES BY AND ABOUT (CHRONOLOGICAL)

Tunstall, John Henry. "A Tax-payer's Complaint, Office of John H. Tunstall, Lincoln, Lincoln Co., N.M., January 18, 1878, 'The Present Sheriff of Lincoln County Has Paid Nothing During His Present Term of Office.' Governor's Message for 1878." Mesilla *Independent.* **January 26, 1878.** Volume 1, Number 32. NewspaperArchive.com. **(Exposé of William Brady and John Riley for embezzling tax money to buy cattle; T.B. Catron then paid that bill)**

Dolan, James J. "Answer to A Taxpayer's Complaint." Mesilla *Independent.* **January 29, 1878. (Response to J.H. Tunstall's exposé of embezzlement of tax money to buy cattle)**

McSween, Alexander. "It looks as though the agent were the property of J.J. Dolan & J.H. Riley, known here as Dolan & Co." Letter to Secretary of Interior Carl Schurz. **February 11, 1878.** From Frederick Nolan. *The Life and Death of John Henry Tunstall.* Albuquerque, New Mexico: The University of New Mexico Press. 1965. Page 266.

Rynerson, William. "Friends Riley & Dolan, Lincoln N.M. I have just received letters from you mailed 10th inst." **February 14, 1878.** Letter to James Dolan and John Riley. Copy as Exhibit B in June 6, 1878 deposition of Alexander McSween. Frank Warner Angel report. *In the Matter of the Examination of the Causes and Circumstances of the Death of John H. Tunstall a British Subject.* Report filed October 4, 1878. Frank Warner Angel report. Interior Department Papers 1850-1907; Appointments Division and Subsequent Actions. Microfilm File Case Number 44-4-8-3. Record Group 48. Microfilm No. M750. Roll 1. National Archives and Records Administration. U.S. Department of Justice. Washington, D.C. (James J. Dolan Deposition. June 20, 1878. Pages 235-247.) **(Implying planned killing of J.H. Tunstall)**

Wilson, John, George B. Barker, Robert M. Gilbert, John Newcomb, Samuel Smith, Benjamin Ellis. "We the undersigned Justice of the Peace and Coroners Jury who sat upon the inquest held this 19th day of February 1878 on the body of John H. Tunstall ..." Coroner's Jury Report for John Tunstall. **February 19, 1878. (Naming as murderers, among others, James Dolan, Frank Baker, Jessie Evans, William Morton, and George Hindman)**

Rynerson, William. "The Grand Jurors for the Territory of New Mexico taken from the body of the good and lawful men of the County of Lincoln ..." Indictments of the April, Lincoln County Grand Jury. **April 28, 1879.** Herman B. Weisner Papers, ca. 1957-1992. New Mexico State University Library at Las Cruces. Rio Grande Historical Collection. Accession No. Weisner MS 249. Box 4/39. Folder E-Z. Folder Name: "Jessie Evans Accessory to Murder." **(Billy Bonney's testimony indicts J.J. Dolan, Billy Campbell, and Jessie Evans for pardon bargain)**

Purington, George Augustus. "The District Court adjourned on Thursday ..." **May 3, 1879.** Indiana Historical Society. Lew Wallace Collection. M0292. Box 4. Folder 10. **(Letter to Adjutant General on Grand Jury indictments of the Murphy-Dolans - including Dolan for the H.I. Chapman murder - and N.A.M. Dudley; copy sent to Lew Wallace)**

Wild, Azariah F. "Daily Reports of U. S. Secret Service Agents, Azariah F. Wild." Microfilm T-915. Record Group 87. Rolls 307 (January 1,1878 - June 30, 1879) and 308 **(July 1, 1879 - June 30, 1881).** National Archives and Records Department. Department of the Treasury. United States Secret Service. Washington, D. C. **(Dolan as an informer against "the Kid gang")**

DUDLEY, NATHAN AUGUSTUS MONROE

BIOGRAPHICAL SOURCES

Kaye, E. Donald. *Nathan Augustus Monroe Dudley: Rogue, Hero, or Both?* Parker, Colorado: Outskirts Press, Inc. 2007.

Oliva, Leo E., *Fort Union and the Frontier Army in the Southwest*. Southwest Cultural Resource Center, Professional Papers No. 41, National Park Service, 1993, Pages 488-489, 550, 574, 624-626, 656-659 are on Dudley. (**Quoted to E. Donald Kaye from the now-lost letter of Amos Kimball: "I guess you heard that Dudley made Colonel. The army bureaucracy is like a giant cesspool, where the biggest chunks rise to the top."**)

MILITARY COURT OF INQUIRY FOR

Leonard, Ira E. *"Charges and specifications against Lieutenant Colonel N.A.M. Dudley, Commander at Fort Stanton, New Mexico."* **March 4, 1879**. Letter to Secretary of War George McCrary. *Proceedings of a Court of Inquiry in the Case of Lt. Col. N.A.M. Dudley (May 2,1879 - July 5, 1879)*. File No. QQ1284. (Boxes 3304, 3305, 3305A); Court Martial Files 1809-1894. Records of the Office of the Judge Advocate General - Army. Record Group 153. Old Military and Civil Branch. National Archives and Records Administration. Washington, D. C. (**Charges against Dudley for murders of A.A. McSween and H.I. Chapman and arson of McSween's house**)

No Author. *Proceedings of a Court of Inquiry in the Case of Lt. Col. N.A.M. Dudley (May 2,1879 - July 5, 1879)*. File No. QQ1284. (Boxes 3304, 3305, 3305A); Court Martial Files 1809-1894. Records of the Office of the Judge Advocate General - Army. Record Group 153. Old Military and Civil Branch. National Archives and Records Administration. Washington, D. C.

ELKINS, STEPHEN BENTON

BIOGRAPHICAL SOURCES (CHRONOLOGICAL)

Lambert, Oscar Doane. *Stephen Benton Elkins. American Foursquare*. Pittsburgh, Pennsylvania: University of Pittsburg Press. **1955**.

Cleaveland, Norman, *The Morleys - Young Upstarts on the Southwest Frontier*. Albuquerque, New Mexico: Calvin Horn Publisher, Inc. **1971**.

Westphall, Victor. *Thomas Benton Catron and His Era*. Tucson, Arizona: University of Arizona Press. **1973**.

Taylor, Morris F. *O.P. McMains and the Maxwell Land Grant Conflict*. Tucson, Arizona: The University of Arizona Press. **1979**. (**Traces origins of the Santa Fe Ring with T.B. Catron and S.B. Elkins**)

Cleaveland, Norman. *The Great Santa Fe Cover-up. Based on a Talk given Before the Santa Fe Historical Society on November 1, 1978*. Self-printed. **1982**.

_____. *A Synopsis of the Great New Mexico Cover-up*. Self-printed. **1989**.

ARTICLE ABOUT

No Author. " 'The Territory of Elkins.' Assassination of Supposed Sun Correspondent. The Murder of the Rev. F.J. Tolby in New Mexico. A Probate Judge Accused of Complicity in the Crime. Indignation Meeting." *New York Weekly Sun*. **December 22, 1875**. Interior Department Papers 1850-1907; Appointments Division and Subsequent Actions. Microfilm Roll M750. National Archives and Records Administration. Record Group 48. Microfilm Case File Number 44-4-8-3. U. S. Department of Interior. Washington, D.C. (**In May 1, 1877 complaint to President Hayes as "Mary E. McPherson and W.B. Matchett 'Make certain charges**

(SEE: Santa Fe Ring, Thomas Benton Catron)

EVANS, JESSIE

BIOGRAPHICAL SOURCE

McCright, Grady E. and James H. Powell. *Jessie Evans: Lincoln County Badman.* College Station, Texas: Creative Publishing Company. 1983.

CONTEMPORARY SOURCES (CHRONOLOGICAL)

Wilson, John, George B. Barker, Robert M. Gilbert, John Newcomb, Samuel Smith, Benjamin Ellis. "We the undersigned Justice of the Peace and Coroners Jury who sat upon the inquest held this 19th day of February 1878 on the body of John H. Tunstall ..." Coroner's Jury Report for John Tunstall. **February 19, 1878.** (**Naming as murderers, among others, James Dolan, Frank Baker, Jessie Evans, William Morton, and George Hindman**)

Wallace, Lew. "I have information that William Campbell, J.B. Matthews, and Jesse Evans were of the party engaged in the killing ..." Letter to Edward Hatch. **March 5, 1879.** Indiana Historical Society. Lew Wallace Collection. M0292. Box 4, Folder 4. (**Murder of Huston Chapman**)

Rynerson, William. "Indictments of the April, Lincoln County Grand Jury." **April 28, 1879.** Herman B. Weisner Papers, ca. 1957-1992. New Mexico State University Library at Las Cruces. Rio Grande Historical Society Collection. Accession No. Ms 0249. Box 4/39. Folder E-Z. Folder Name: "Jessie Evans Accessory to Murder." (**Billy's testimony indicts Dolan, Campbell, and Evans for his pardon**)

Purington, George Augustus. "The District Court adjourned on Thursday ..." **May 3, 1879.** Indiana Historical Society. Lew Wallace Collection. M0292. Box 4. Folder 10. (**Letter to Adjutant General on Grand Jury indictments of the Murphy-Dolans - including Evans for the H.I. Chapman murder - and N.A.M. Dudley; copy sent to Lew Wallace**)

FOUNTAIN, ALBERT JENNINGS

BIBLIOGRAPHICAL SOURCE

Gibson, A. M. *The Life and Death of Colonel Albert Jennings Fountain.* Norman: University of Oklahoma Press. 1965.

CONTEMPORARY SOURCE

Fountain, Albert Jennings, Attorney and J.D. Bail. "Instructions Asked for by Defendants Counsel. April 9, 1881. Herman B. Weisner Papers, ca. 1957-1992. New Mexico State University Library at Las Cruces. Rio Grande Historical Society Collection. Accession No. Ms 0249. Box 1. Folder 14-D. Folder Name: "Billy the Kid Legal Documents."

FRITZ FAMILY (EMIL AND CHARLES FRITZ AND EMILIE FRITZ SCHOLAND)

Fritz, Charles. Affidavit of **September 18, 1876** claiming that Emil Fritz had a will. Probate Court Record. (private collection)

_____. Affidavit of **September 26, 1876** Authorizing Alexander McSween to Receive Payments for the Emil Fritz Estate. Probate Court Record. (private collection)

Scholand, Emilie and Charles Fritz. Affidavit of **September 26, 1876** appointing McSween to collect debts for the Emil Fritz Estate. Copied from the original District Court Record. (private collection)

Fritz, Charles. Affidavit of **December 7, 1877** to order Alexander McSween to pay the Emil Fritz insurance policy money. Probate Court Record. (private collection)

Scholand, Emilie. Affidavit of **December 21, 1877** Accusing Alexander McSween of Embezzlement. Copied from the original District Court Record. (private collection)

Bristol Warren. "Writ of Embezzlement." **December 21, 1877.** Herman B. Weisner Papers, ca. 1957-1992. New Mexico State University Library at Las Cruces. Rio Grande Historical Collections. Accession No. Ms 0249. Box 10. Folder M-13. Folder Name. "Will and Testament A. McSween." **(Emilie Fritz Scholand's sworn complaint against Alexander McSween)**

Fritz, Charles. Affidavit sworn before John Crouch, Clerk of Doña Ana District Court, for Writ of Attachment issued against property of Alexander A. McSween. Probate Court Record. **February 6, 1878.** (private collection)

_____ and Emilie Scholand. Attachment Bond sworn before John Crouch, Clerk of Doña Ana District Court, against Alexander A. McSween for indebtedness to them. **February 6, 1878.** (private collection).

No Author. Diagram showing parcels of land to each of the heirs of Emil Fritz. Herman B. Weisner Papers, ca. 1957-1992. New Mexico State University Library at Las Cruces. Rio Grande Historical Collections. Accession No. Ms 0249. Box P1. Folder 11. Folder Name. "Charles Fritz Estate."

GARRETT, PATRICK FLOYD

BIBLIOGRAPHICAL SOURCES

Metz, Leon C. *Pat Garrett. The Story of a Western Lawman.* Norman: University of Oklahoma Press. 1974.

Mullin, Robert N. "Killing of Joe Briscoe." Letter to Eve Ball. January 31, 1964. (Unpublished). Binder RNM, VI, H. Nita Stewart Haley Memorial Museum. Haley Library. Midland, Texas.

_____. "Pat Garrett. Two Forgotten Killings." *Password.* X(2) (Summer 1965). pp. 57 - 65.

_____. "Skelton Glen's Manuscript Entitled 'Pat Garrett As I Knew Him on the Buffalo Ranges.'" (1890, Unpublished). Binder RNM, III B, 20. Nita Stewart Haley Memorial Museum. Haley Library. Midland, Texas. **(The killing of Joe Briscoe is recounted)**

AUTOBIOGRAPHICAL SOURCES

Garrett, Pat F. *The Authentic Life of Billy the Kid The Noted Desperado of the Southwest, Whose Deeds of Daring and Blood Made His Name a Terror in New Mexico, Arizona, and Northern Mexico.* Santa Fe, New Mexico: New Mexico Printing and Publishing Co. 1882. (Edition used: Edited by Maurice Garland Fulton. New York: The Macmillan Company. 1927)

REWARD FOR KILLING BILLY THE KID

No Author. No title. *Santa Fe Daily New Mexican.* **July 21, 1881.** Volume X, Number 120, Page 4. Column 1. NewspaperArchive.com. **(Pat Garrett's meeting with Acting Governor Ritch about the Billy the Kid reward.)**

Ritch, William G. "In the matter of the application by Patrick F. Garrett for a reward claimed to have been offered May-1881 for the capture of Wm Bonney alias "the Kid." *Executive Record Book Number 2.* July 25, 1867- November 8, 1882. **July 21, 1881.** Pages 533-535. New Mexico Secretary of State Records. Collection 1971-001, Series 1; Records of the Secretary of the Territory. (Accessed from Albuquerque Public Library Microfilm, Territorial Archives of New Mexico, Roll 21.) **(Presentation of Garret's bill for the reward, showing that Acting-Governor Ritch agreed with the reward, but legal opinion from Attorney General William Breeden necessitated getting a legislative act to convert Wallace's private reward to Territorial)**

No Author. "Kid the Killer Killed, Wm. Bonney alias Antrim, alias Billy the Kid, Fatally Meets Pat Garrett, the Lincoln County Sheriff." Las Cruces *Rio Grande Republican*. **July 23, 1881.** Page 2. Volume 1, Number 10. NewspaperArchive.com. (**Copy of Pat Garrett's letter to Acting Governor William Ritch confirming that the original Coroner's Jury Report was sent to District Attorney of the First Judicial District, and copy of it was included in this letter to the Governor**)

Sheldon, Lionel. "In the Matter of the Claim of Sheriff Pat Garrett." Letter to the Legislature. **February 14, 1882.** Territorial Archives of New Mexico. Microfilm Roll 5, Frame 765. (**As Governor, approving Garrett's reward and stating he would have granted it outright had it not already been sent to the Legislature by Acting-Governor Ritch for an act**)

No Author. "An Act for the Relief of Pat. Garrett." *1882 Acts of the Legislative Assembly of the Territory of New Mexico, Twenty-Fifth Session. Convened at the Capitol, at the City of Santa Fe, on Monday, the 2d day of January, 1882, and adjourned on Thursday, the 2d day of March, 1882.* **February 18, 1882.** Chapter 101. Page 191. (**Granting Pat Garrett's reward for Billy the Kid, confirming it had been withheld on a technicality**)

Fulton, Maurice Garland. "I think I have solved the puzzle of the reward offers ..." October 28, 1951. Letter to Robert N. Mullin. Nita Stewart Haley Memorial Library and J. Evetts Haley History Center, Midland, Texas. Mullin Collection. Series RNM, VI, J, Legal Papers and Documents. "William Bonney, Reward for Death, Lincoln Notes." (**Confirming Attorney General's opinion to Acting Governor William Ritch about conversion of reward by legislative act**)

_____. "The rewards for the Kid give a clue to Catron's participation ..." **November 26, 1951.** Letter to Robert N. Mullin. Nita Stewart Haley Memorial Library and J. Evetts Haley History Center, Midland, Texas. Mullin Collection. Series RNM, VI, J, Legal Papers and Documents. "William Bonney, Rewards." (**Contemplating Catron's participation for the reward**)

_____. "Ritch was governor for the time-being ..." **March 15, 1953.** Letter to Robert N. Mullin. Nita Stewart Haley Memorial Library and J. Evetts Haley History Center, Midland, Texas. Mullin Collection. Series RNM, VI, J, Legal Papers and Documents. "William Bonney, Rewards." (**Confirming Attorney General's opinion to Acting Governor William Ritch about conversion of reward by legislative act**)

OTHER CONTEMPORARY SOURCES (CHRONOLOGICAL)

No Author. "Garrett Exonerates Maxwell." *Santa Fe Daily New Mexican.* **July 21, 1881.** Volume X, Number 120. NewspaperArchive.com. (**Confirming Pat Garrett's killing of Billy the Kid**)

Wild, Azariah F. "Daily Reports of U. S. Secret Service Agents, Azariah F. Wild." Microfilm T-915. Record Group 87. Roll 308 (**July 1, 1879 - June 30, 1881**). National Archives and Records Administration. Department of the Treasury. United States Secret Service. Washington, D. C. (**Using Garrett to capture Billy Bonney**)

GAUSS, GOTTFRIED

Gauss, Gottfried. Interview with *Lincoln County Leader.* **November 21, 1889.** (**About Billy Bonney's Lincoln jailbreak**)

HOYT, HENRY F.

AUTOBIOGRAPHICAL SOURCE

Hoyt, Henry. *A Frontier Doctor.* Boston and New York: Houghton Mifflin Company. 1929. (**Describes Billy Bonney's superior abilities, pp. 93-94.**)

CONTEMPORARY SOURCES (CHRONOLOGICAL)

Bonney, William H. Bill of Sale to Henry Hoyt. **October 24, 1878**. Collection of Panhandle-Plains Historical Museum. Canyon, Texas. (Item No. X1974-98/1)

Hoyt, Henry F. "This time it is me who is apologizing ..." Letter to Lew Wallace Jr. (Lew Wallace's grandson) **April 27, 1927**. Indiana Historical Society. Lew Wallace Collection. M0292. Box 14, Folder 11.

_____. "Copy of a bill of sale written by Wm H. Bonney ..." Letter to Lew Wallace Jr. **April 27, 1927**. Indiana Historical Society. Lew Wallace Collection. M0292. Box 14, Folder 11.

KINNEY, JOHN

BIOGRAPHICAL SOURCE

Mullin, Robert N. "Here Lies John Kinney." *Journal of Arizona History*. 14 (Autumn 1973). Pages 223 - 242.

LEONARD, IRA E.

BIOGRAPHICAL SOURCE

Nolan, Frederick. Biography and photograph of Ira Leonard. Unpublished. personal communication. July 29, 2005.

COURT OF INQUIRY OF N.A.M. DUDLEY BY (SEE: Nathan Augustus Monroe Dudley Court of Inquiry)

LETTERS TO AND FROM

LEW WALLACE TO AND FROM

Leonard, Ira E. "Dear Gov. You have undoubtedly learned ere this of the assassination ..." Letter to Lew Wallace. **February 24, 1879**. Indiana Historical Society. Lew Wallace Collection. M0292. Box 4. Folder 3. (**On Chapman murder.**)

Wallace, Lew. "It is important to take steps to protect the coming court ..." Letter to Ira Leonard. **April 6, 1879**. Indiana Historical Society. Lew Wallace Collection. M0292. Box 4. Folder 8.

Leonard, Ira. "The air is filled tonight with 'rumors of wars ... Letter to Lew Wallace. **April 20, 1879**. Indiana Historical Society. Lew Wallace Collection. M0292. Box 4. Folder 9. (**About District Attorney Rynerson: "He is bent on going for the Kid"**)

_____. "When you left here I promised to write you concerning events transpiring here ..." Letter to Lew Wallace. **May 20, 1878 [sic - 79]**. Indiana Historical Society. Lew Wallace Collection. M0292. Box 4. Folder 10. (**Has quote on the Murphy-Dolan party as: "part and parcel of the Santa Fe ring that has been so long an incubus on the government of this territory."**)

_____. "I write to you with pencil because I am laboring for breath ..." Letter to Lew Wallace. **May 23, 1879**. Indiana Historical Society. Lew Wallace Collection. M0292. Box 4. Folder 11. (**With quote "we are pouring the 'hot shot' into Dudley." (With enclosed letter of May 20, 1879)**)

_____. "Dudley commenced on the defense Thursday afternoon ..." Letter to Wallace. **June 6, 1879**, Indiana Historical Society. Lew Wallace Collection. M0292. Box 4. Folder 11. (**About disgust at corrupt Court.**")

_____. "Yours of the 7th inst reached me ..." Letter to Lew Wallace. **June 13, 1879**. Indiana Historical Society. Lew Wallace Collection. M0292. Box 4. Folder 11. (**about Court of Inquiry corruption**)

MATTHEWS, JACOB BASIL "BILLY"
BIOGRAPHICAL SOURCE
Fleming, Elvis E. *J.B. Matthews. Biography of a Lincoln County Deputy.* Las Cruces, New Mexico: Yucca Tree Press. 1999.

MAXWELL, DELUVINA
Maxwell, Deluvina. "I came here after Lucien Maxwell was already here...." Letter to J. Evetts Haley. June 24, 1927. Nita Stewart Haley Memorial Library and J. Evetts Haley History Center, Midland, Texas. J. Evetts Haley Collection, JEH, J-I – Maxwell, Deluvina. (**Debunking "Billy the Kid Case" hoax and *Cold Case Billy the Kid* claims that Peter Maxwell's bedroom had no door to the outside, and that Pat Garrett did not kill Billy the Kid**)

MAXWELL FAMILY
Cleaveland, Agnes Morley. *No Life for a Lady.* Boston: Houghton Mifflin. 1941.
_____. *Satan's Paradise: From Lucien Maxwell to Fred Lambert.* Boston: Houghton Mifflin Company. 1952.
Cleaveland, Norman. *The Morleys - Young Upstarts on the Southwest Frontier.* Albuquerque, New Mexico: Calvin Horn Publisher, Inc. 1971.
Dunham, Harold H. "New Mexican Land Grants with Special Reference to the Title Papers of the Maxwell Grant." *New Mexico Historical Review.* (January 1955) Vol. 30, No. 1. pp. 1 - 23.
Freiberger, Harriet. *Lucien Maxwell: Villain or Visionary.* Santa Fe, New Mexico: Sunstone Press. 1999.
Keleher, William A. *The Maxwell Land Grant. A New Mexico Item.* Albuquerque, New Mexico: University of New Mexico Press. 1964.
Lamar, Howard Roberts. *The Far Southwest 1846 - 1912. A Territorial History.* New Haven and London: Yale University Press. 1966.
Miller, Kenny. Descendant of Lucien Bonaparte Maxwell. Personal communication. 2011 to 2012.
Montoya, María E. *Translating Property. The Maxwell Land Grant and the Conflict Over Land in the American West, 1840-1900.* Berkeley and Los Angeles, California: University of California Press. 2002.
Murphy, Lawrence R. *Lucien Bonaparte Maxwell. Napoleon of the Southwest.* Norman: University of Oklahoma Press. 1983.
Pearson, Jim Berry. *The Maxwell Land Grant.* Norman: University of Oklahoma Press. 1961.
Poe, Sophie. *Buckboard Days.* Albuquerque, New Mexico: University of New Mexico Press. 1964.
Taylor, Morris F. *O. P. McMains and the Maxwell Land Grant Conflict.* Tucson, Arizona: The University of Arizona Press. 1979. (**Origins of Santa Fe Ring**)
No Author. "Mrs. Paula M. Jaramillo, 65 Died Here Tuesday." *The Fort Sumner Leader.* Official Newspaper County of De Baca. December 20, 1929. No. 1158, Page 1, Column 1. (**Billy Bonney's sweetheart, Paulita Maxwell**)

COMMANDING OFFICER'S QUARTERS BEFORE MAXWELL FAMILY CONVERSION
Diagram. "Commanding Officer's Quarters Fort Sumner, New Mexico Territory." National Archives, Microfilm RG 98, Consolidated Files Quartermaster General; with copy in Fort Sumner, New Mexico, State Monument. (**Faked in *Cold Case Billy the Kid* as being the Maxwell house itself**)

MAXWELL FAMILY HOUSE IN FORT SUMNER

Drawing. "As per Burns account." Maxwell family house, and diagram of Peter Maxwell's bedroom with external door. Nita Stewart Haley Memorial Library and J. Evetts Haley History Center, Midland, Texas. Mullin Collection. Series RNM, IV, Y, Notebook: Places and Events, A-O. (**Debunking** *Cold Case Billy the Kid* **hoax that Peter Maxwell's bedroom had no door to the outside**)

Photograph. "Pete Maxwell's House Fort Sumner." Annotated on back by Robert N. Mullin. **Undated.** Nita Stewart Haley Memorial Library and J. Evetts Haley History Center, Midland, Texas. Mullin Collection. Series RNM, IV, A, 161.0. (**Maxwell family house showing external door in Peter Maxwell's bedroom debunking** *Cold Case Billy the Kid* **that the Maxwell house was one story and that Maxwell's bedroom had no door to the outside**)

Mullin, Robert N. "Pete Maxwell's House Fort Sumner, Prior to Erection of New Home 2 ½ Mi. S.E.[after sale of town]; Originally 1 Story Flat Roof, Officers Quarters. 2nd Floor Added By Maxwell." Annotation on back of photograph of Maxwell house. **Undated.** . Nita Stewart Haley Memorial Library and J. Evetts Haley History Center, Midland, Texas. Mullin Collection. Series RNM, IV, A, 161.0. (**Making clear the distinction between the Officer's Quarters and the later Maxwell house**)

PETER MAXWELL'S HOUSE OUTSIDE OF FORT SUMNER

Photograph. "Peter Maxwell's home near Fort Sumner, post Lincoln County War, presented to Robert N. Mullin by Maurice Garland Fulton, who obtained it from Mrs. Susan McSween Barber. Nita Stewart Haley Memorial Library and J. Evetts Haley History Center, Midland, Texas. Mullin Collection. Series RNM, IV, A-161. (**For debunking** *Cold Case Billy the Kid* **hoax that Peter Maxwell lived as a cook in a San Andres Mountain cow camp because he moved from Fort Sumner**)

No Author. "Las Vegas." Death Notice of Peter Maxwell. **June 28, 1898.** *The Albuquerque Citizen*. Page 2, Column 3. NewspaperArchive.com. (**Peter Maxwell death notice about Fort Sumner area residence and death**)

MAXWELL FAMILY FURNITURE

Blythe, Dee. "Billy the Kid Landmarks Fast Vanishing: Historic Spots Hard to Find; Markers Needed." *Clovis, New Mexico Evening News-Journal.* **May 31, 1937** Volume 9. Number 2. Section E. Monday,. (**Photo and article about Maxwell family furniture**)

Weddle, Jerry. "The Kid at Old Fort Sumner." *The Outlaw Gazette: Billy the Kid Outlaw Gang New Mexico.* **December, 1992.** (**Louisa Beaubien Barrett, Luz Maxwell's niece, error-filled history as recorded by her daughter Marian Barrett, including the claim that Pat Garrett's second shot went through a washstand; later used in the "Billy the Kid Case" hoax**)

_____. Statement that he interviewed Stella Abreu Maxwell in Albuquerque in her old age, and she stated she got the carpenter's bench from a man in Fort Sumner for her 1925 Billy the Kid Museum. Author's interview. February 5, 2018. (**The bench had not been kept by the family**)

McSWEEN, ALEXANDER

Bristol Warren. "Writ of Embezzlement." **December 21, 1877**. Writ of Embezzlement. New Mexico State University Library at Las Cruces. Rio Grande Historical Collections. Lincoln County Papers. New Mexico State University Library at Las Cruces. Rio Grande Historical Collections. Accession No. Ms 0249. Box No. 10. Folder M-13. "Will and Testament A. McSween." (**Emilie Fritz Scholand's sworn complaint against Alexander McSween**)

Fritz, Charles. Affidavit sworn before John Crouch, Clerk of Doña Ana District Court, for Writ of Attachment issued against property of Alexander A. McSween. Probate Court Record. **February 6, 1878.** (private collection).

Bristol, Warren. Action of Assumpsit to command Sheriff of Lincoln County to attach goods of Alexander A. McSween. **February 7, 1878.** District Court Record. (private collection).

_____. Preprinted form in his name for "Writ of Attachment" (Printed and sold at the office of the Mesilla News) filled out to command the Sheriff of Lincoln County to attach goods of Alexander McSween for a suit of damages for ten thousand dollars. **February 7, 1878.** (private collection).

McSween, Alexander. "It looks as though the agent were the property of J.J. Dolan & J.H. Riley, known here as Dolan & Co." Letter to Secretary of Interior Carl Schurz. **February 11, 1878.** From Frederick Nolan. *The Life and Death of John Henry Tunstall.* Albuquerque, New Mexico: The University of New Mexico Press. 1965. Page 266.

_____. "Will and Testament A. McSween." **February 25, 1878.** Herman B. Weisner Papers, ca. 1957-1992. New Mexico State University Library at Las Cruces. Rio Grande Historical Collections. Accession No. Ms 0249. Box 10. Folder M15. Folder Name. "Will and Testament A. McSween."

_____. and B.H. Ellis. Secretaries. "The undersigned have the Honor of transmitting you, as requested, a copy of the proceedings of a meeting held by the citizens of Lincoln County ..." Letter to President Rutherford B. Hayes; with attached proceedings of the April 1878 Lincoln Grand Jury. **April 26, 1878.** Microfilm File Case Number 44-4-8-3. Record Group 48. Microfilm No. M750. Roll 1. National Archives and Records Administration. U.S. Department of Justice. Washington, D.C.

_____. Deposition to Frank Warner Angel. **June 6, 1878.** Pages 5-183 of Frank Warner Angel report *In the Matter of the Examination of the Causes and Circumstances of the Death of John H. Tunstall a British Subject.* Report filed **October 4, 1878.** Angel Report. Microfilm File Case Number 44-4-8-3. Record Group 48. Microfilm No. M750. Roll 1. National Archives and Records Administration. U.S. Department of Justice. Washington, D.C. (**Reports secret**

Angel, Frank Warner. *In the Matter of the Lincoln County Troubles. To the Honorable Charles Devens, Attorney General.* **October 4, 1878.** Angel Report. Microfilm File Case Number 44-4-8-3. Record Group 48. Microfilm No. M750. Roll 1. National Archives and Records Administration. U.S. Department of Justice. Washington, D.C.

McSWEEN, SUSAN

BIOGRAPHICAL SOURCE FOR

Chamberlain, Kathleen P. *In the Shadow of Billy the Kid: Susan McSween and the Lincoln County War.* Albuquerque: University of New Mexico Press. 2013.

CONTEMPORARY SOURCES ABOUT (CHRONOLOGICAL)

Dudley, Nathan Augustus Monroe. "I am in receipt of a copy of letter written by one H.I. Chapman, calling himself the Attorney ..." **November 9, 1878.** Letter to Lew Wallace. From *Proceedings of a Court of Inquiry in the Case of Lt. Col. N.A.M. Dudley (May 2,1879 – July 5, 1879).* File No. QQ1284. (Boxes 3304, 3305, 3305A); Court Martial Files 1809-1894. Records of the Office of the Judge Advocate General - Army. Record Group 153. Old Military and Civil Branch. National Archives and Records Administration. Washington, D.C. (**Answer to charges, with attached defamatory affidavits against Susan McSween**)

McSween, Susan. Testimony in Court of Inquiry for Lieutenant Colonel N.A.M. Dudley. **May 23-24, 26, 1879.** *Proceedings of a Court of Inquiry in the Case of Lt. Col. N.A.M. Dudley (May 2,1879 – July 5, 1879).* File No. QQ1284. (Boxes 3304, 3305,

3305A); Court Martial Files 1809-1894. Records of the Office of the Judge Advocate General – Army. Record Group 153. Old Military and Civil Branch. National Archives and Records Administration. Washington, D.C.

No Author. Verdict on Civil Cause 298 for arson of Susan McSween's house. *Mesilla News*. **December 6, 1879**. Unpublished. personal communication from Frederick Nolan. July 29, 2005. (**Dudley exonerated**)

MEADOWS, JOHN P.

Meadows, John P. "Billy the Kid to John P. Meadows on the Peñasco, May 1-2, 1881." *Roswell Daily Record*. February 16, 1931. Page 6.

Meadows, John P. Ed. John P. Wilson. *Pat Garrett and Billy the Kid as I Knew Them: Reminiscences of John P. Meadows*. Albuquerque: University of New Mexico Press. 2004.

MURPHY, LAWRENCE GUSTAV

Murphy, Lawrence G. "Will of Lawrence G. Murphy." Herman B. Weisner Papers, ca. 1957-1992. New Mexico State University Library at Las Cruces. Rio Grande Historical Collections. Accession No. Ms 0249. Box 11. Folder P15. Folder Name: "Murphy, Lawrence G."

O'FOLLIARD, THOMAS "TOM"

GENEALOGY SEARCHES (NO CERTAIN MATCH TO HISTORICAL TOM O'FOLLIARD, OR TO PROOF OF KIN RELATIONSHIP WITH THOMAS "KIP" McKINNEY)

Kendall, F.A. "U.S. Census Record 1870. Year: 1870. Census place Zavalla County, Uvalde, Texas." **September 26, 1870.** United States Federal Census. Roll 593_1597, Page 551 B, Family History Library Film 553096. Ancestry.com. 1870 United States Federal Census. Provo, Utah. (**With O'Folliard misspelled as Folliard, but claimed by hoaxers as discovering it as his real name**)

Find A Grave, database and images (https://www.findagrave.com: accessed 27 January 2019), memorial page for Elizabeth Jane "Eliza" McKinney Cook (1829–1901), Find A Grave Memorial no. 100551036, citing Marathon Cemetery, Marathon, Brewster County, Texas, USA ; Maintained by Jim McKinney.

"Mississippi Marriages, 1800-1911," database, FamilySearch (https://familysearch.org/ark:/61903/1:1:V28W-VB6: 10 February 2018), David Cook and Eliza Jane Mc Kinney, 24 Sep 1846; citing Monroe, Mississippi; FHL microfilm 866,906.

Find A Grave, database and images (https://www.findagrave.com: accessed 17 February 2019), memorial page for Collin "Cullen" McKinney (1795–1845), Find A Grave Memorial no. 70869601, citing Old Stand Cemetery, Franklin County, Alabama, USA ; Maintained by Jim McKinney (contributor 47510435).

Find A Grave, database and images (https://www.findagrave.com: accessed 17 February 2019), memorial page for Thalis Newton McKinney, Sr (1 Mar 1817–12 Nov 1886), Find A Grave Memorial no. 67306306, citing Uvalde Cemetery, Uvalde, Uvalde County, Texas, USA ; Maintained by Jim McKinney (contributor 47510435).

Thomas C. McKinney is listed in the 1870 U.S. Census for Uvalde as the son of Thalis McKinney: Source Citation: Year: 1870; Census Place: Uvalde, Texas; Roll: M593_1597; Page: 541B; Family History Library Film: 553096. Source Information: Ancestry.com. 1870 United States Federal Census [database on-line]. Provo, UT, USA: Ancestry.com Operations, Inc., 2009. Images reproduced by FamilySearch.

"Texas, County Marriage Index, 1837-1977," database, FamilySearch (https://familysearch.org/ark:/61903/1:1:QK8B-F35P : 22 December 2016), Stephen Folliard and Sarah Rop Cook, 06 May 1859; citing Uvalde, Texas, United States, county courthouses, Texas; FHL microfilm 1,017,584. https://www.wikitree.com/wiki/Folliard-1.

PATRÓN, JUAN

Wallace, Lew. "Be good enough to send word to all your men to turn out soon as possible …" Letter to Juan Patrón. **March 19, 1879**. Indiana Historical Society. Lew Wallace Collection. M0292. Box 4. Folder 6. (**Reports escape of Jessie Evans and Billy Campbell from Fort Stanton**)

Patrón, Juan. First letter to Lew Wallace on **March 29, 1879**. Indiana Historical Society. Lew Wallace Collection. M0292. Box 4, Folder 7.

_____. Second letter to Lew Wallace on **March 29, 1879**. Indiana Historical Society. Lew Wallace Collection. M0292. Box 4, Folder 7.

PEPPIN, GEORGE

No Author. "Old Citizen Gone." *Capitan News.* **September 23, 1904.** Volume 5. Number 29. Page 4. Center for Southwest Research. Microfilm AN2.L52a.

POE, JOHN WILLIAM

Poe, John W. "The Killing of Billy the Kid." (a personal letter written at Roswell, New Mexico to Mr. Charles Goodnight, Goodnight P.C., Texas) July 10, 1917.

_____. *The Death of Billy the Kid.* (Introduction by Maurice Garland Fulton). Boston and New York: Houghton Mifflin Company. 1933.

Poe, Sophie. *Buckboard Days.* Albuquerque, New Mexico: University of New Mexico Press. 1964.

RILEY, JOHN HENRY

CONTEMPORARY SOURCES ABOUT

Tunstall, John Henry. "A Tax-payer's Complaint, Office of John H. Tunstall, Lincoln, Lincoln Co., N.M., January 18, 1878, 'The Present Sheriff of Lincoln County Has Paid Nothing During His Present Term of Office.' Governor's Message for 1878." Mesilla *Independent.* **January 26, 1878**. Volume 1, Number 32. NewspaperArchive.com. (**Exposé of William Brady and John Riley for embezzling tax money to buy cattle; and T.B. Catron then paid that bill**)

Dolan, James J. "Answer to A Taxpayer's Complaint." Mesilla *Independent.* **January 29, 1878**. (**Response to J.H. Tunstall's exposé**)

McSween, Alexander. "It looks as though the [Indian] agent were the property of J.J. Dolan & J.H. Riley, known here as Dolan & Co." Letter to Secretary of Interior Carl Schurz. **February 11, 1878**. From Frederick Nolan. *The Life and Death of John Henry Tunstall.* Albuquerque, New Mexico: The University of New Mexico Press. 1965. Page 266.

RUDULPH, MILNOR

Keleher, William A. *Violence in Lincoln County 1869-1881.* Pages 350-351. Albuquerque, New Mexico: University of New Mexico Press. 1957.

RYNERSON, WILLIAM LOGAN

BIOGRAPHICAL SOURCES

Miller, Darlis A. "William Logan Rynerson in New Mexico. 1862-1893." *New Mexico Historical Review* 48 (April 1973) pp. 101-131.

No Author. "A Brief History of the Rynerson House." Las Cruces: Del Valle Design & Imaging. No copyright. https://delvalleprintinglc.com/rynerson-house/.

CONTEMPORARY SOURCES BY AND ABOUT (CHRONOLOGICAL)

Rynerson, William L "Indictments of the April, Lincoln County Grand Jury." **April 28, 1879.** Herman B. Weisner Papers, ca. 1957-1992. New Mexico State University Library at Las Cruces. Rio Grande Historical Society Collection. Accession No. Ms 0249. Box 4/39. Folder E-Z. Folder Name: "Jessie Evans Accessory to Murder." **(Indictments of Dolan, Campbell, and Evans)**

_____. "Friends Riley & Dolan, Lincoln N.M. I have just received letters from you mailed 10th inst." Letter to James Dolan and John Riley. **February 14, 1878.** Copy as Exhibit B in June 6, 1878 deposition of Alexander McSween. Frank Warner Angel report. *In the Matter of the Examination of the Causes and Circumstances of the Death of John H. Tunstall a British Subject.* Report filed October 4, 1878. Interior Department Papers 1850-1907; Appointments Division and Subsequent Actions. Microfilm File Case Number 44-4-8-3. Microfilm No. M750. Roll 1. National Archives and Records Administration. U.S. Department of Justice. Washington, D.C. (James J. Dolan Deposition. June 20, 1878. Pages 235-247.) **(Planned killing of J.H. Tunstall)**

Angel, Frank Warner. "I have just been favored by a call from W.L. Rynerson ..." Letter to Secretary of Interior Carl Schurz. **September 6, 1878.** Microfilm File Case Number 44-4-8-3. Record Group 48. Microfilm No. M750. Roll 1. National Archives and Records Administration. U. S. Department of Justice. Washington, D.C.

Rynerson, William. Venue Change. **April 21, 1879.** Herman B. Weisner Papers, ca. 1957-1992. New Mexico State University Library at Las Cruces. Rio Grande Historical Collection. Accession No. Ms 0249. Box 1. Folder 14-D. Folder Name: "Billy the Kid Legal Documents." **(Change of Billy Bonney's trial venue from Lincoln County to Doña Ana County to insure a hanging trial by prevent Lincoln County citizens knowledgeable about the War being jurors)**

SALAZAR, YGINIO

Wallace, Lew. "I beg to submit to you a list of persons ... to arrest ..." Letter to Henry Carroll. **March 11, 1879.** Indiana Historical Society. Lew Wallace Collection. M0292. Box 4. Folder 5. **(Lists Ygenio Salazar and "the Kid)**

Salazar, Joe. (Grandson of Yginio Salazar). Personal Interviews 1999-2001. **(My interviews about Ygenio)**

TUNSTALL, JOHN HENRY

BIOGRAPHICAL SOURCES

Nolan, Frederick W. *The Life and Death of John Henry Tunstall.* Albuquerque, New Mexico: The University of New Mexico Press. 1965.

CONTEMPORARY SOURCES (CHRONOLOGICAL)

Tunstall, John Henry. "A Tax-payer's Complaint, Office of John H. Tunstall, Lincoln, Lincoln Co., N.M., January 18, 1878, 'The Present Sheriff of Lincoln County Has Paid Nothing During His Present Term of Office.' Governor's Message for 1878." Mesilla *Independent.* **January 26, 1878.** Volume 1, Number 32. NewspaperArchive.com. **(Exposé of William Brady and John Riley for embezzling tax money to buy cattle; and T.B. Catron then paid that bill)**

Dolan, James J. "Answer to A Taxpayer's Complaint." Mesilla *Independent.* **January 29, 1878. (Response to J.H. Tunstall's exposé of embezzlement of tax money to buy cattle)**

Rynerson, William. "Friends Riley & Dolan, Lincoln N.M. I have just received letters from you mailed 10th inst." Letter to James Dolan and John Riley. **February 14, 1878.** Copy as Exhibit B in June 6, 1878 deposition of Alexander McSween. Frank Warner Angel report. *In the Matter of the Examination of the Causes and Circumstances of the Death of John H. Tunstall a British Subject.* Report filed October 4, 1878. Interior Department Papers 1850-1907; Appointments Division and Subsequent Actions. Microfilm File Case Number 44-4-8-3. Record Group 48. Microfilm No. M750. Roll 1. National Archives and Records Administration. U. S. Department of Justice. Washington, D.C. (James J. Dolan Deposition. June 20, 1878. pp. 235-247.) **(Planned killing of J.H. Tunstall)**

Wilson, John, George B. Barker, Robert M. Gilbert, John Newcomb, Samuel Smith, Benjamin Ellis. "We the undersigned Justice of the Peace and Coroners Jury who sat upon the inquest held this 19th day of February 1878 on the body of John H. Tunstall ..." Coroner's Jury Report for John Tunstall. **February 19, 1878.** **(Naming Tunstall's murderers)**

Springer, Frank. "I hope you have received a full account of the Troubles in Lincoln County from your nephew ..." Letter to Senator Rush Clark. **April 9, 1878.** Herman B. Weisner Papers, ca. 1957-1992. New Mexico State University Library at Las Cruces. Rio Grande Historical Collections. Accession No. Ms 0249. Box 4/39. Folder D-6. Folder Name "Frank Springer Letter to Rush Clark." **(Links Santa Fe Ring to murder of J.H. Tunstall)**

(SEE: Frank Warner Angel)

WALLACE, LEW

AUTOBIOGRAPHICAL AND BIOGRAPHICAL SOURCES

Governor of Territorial New Mexico. 1878-81." *New Mexico Historical Review. 59(1)* (January, 1984).

Morsberger, Robert E. and Katherine M. Morsberger. *Lew Wallace: Militant Romantic.* New York: McGraw-Hill Book Company. 1980.

Wallace, Lew. *An Autobiography. Vol. I.* New York and London: Harper and Brothers Publishers. 1997.

_____. *An Autobiography. Vol. II.* New York and London: Harper and Brothers Publishers. 1997.

COLLECTED PAPERS OF

Wallace, Lew. Collected Papers. Microfilm Project Sponsored by the National Historical Publications Commission. Microfilm Roll No. 99. Santa Fe, New Mexico: State of New Mexico Records Center and Archives. 1974.

_____. Lew and Susan Wallace Collection. Indiana Historical Society. M0292.

_____. Collected Papers. Lilly Library. Bloomington, Indiana.

SECRET ANGEL NOTEBOOK ON SANTA FE RING FOR

Angel, Frank Warner. "To Gov. Lew Wallace, Santa Fe, N. M., 1878." Notebook. **1878.** Indiana Historical Society. Lew Wallace Collection. M0292. Microfilm No. F372. **(Original missing, copy on microfilm; secret notebook prepared for Lew Wallace listing names for Lincoln County and the Santa Fe Ring)**

Theisen, Lee Scott. "Frank Warner Angel's Notes on New Mexico Territory, 1878." *Arizona and the West: A Quarterly Journal of History.* Winter 1976. Volume 18. Number 4. Pages 333-370. **(About the Angel notebook)**

AMNESTY PROCLAMATION OF

Wallace, Lew. "Proclamation by the Governor." **November 13, 1878**. Indiana Historical Society. Lew Wallace Collection. M0292. Box 3. Folder 17. (**Amnesty Proclamation for Lincoln County War fighters, but excluding those already indicted, like Billy Bonney**)

DUDLEY COURT OF INQUIRY TESTIMONY BY

Wallace, Lew. Testimony in Court of Inquiry for Lieutenant Colonel N.A.M. Dudley. **May 12-15, 1879**. *Proceedings of a Court of Inquiry in the Case of Lt. Col. N.A.M. Dudley (May 2,1879 – July 5, 1879)*. File No. QQ1284. (Boxes 3304, 3305, 3305A); Court Martial Files 1809-1894. Records of the Office of the Judge Advocate General – Army. Record Group 153. Old Military and Civil Branch. National Archives and Records Administration. Washington, D.C.

INTERVIEW NOTES ON BILLY BONNEY BY (SEE: William H. Bonney)

REWARD NOTICES AND POSTERS FOR WILLIAM BONNEY BY
(SEE: William H. Bonney)

LETTERS BY AND TO

TO AND FROM WILLIAM BONNEY
(SEE: History of William H. Bonney)

TO SHERIFF PATRICK F. GARRETT

Wallace, Lew. "To the Sheriff of Lincoln County, New Mexico, Greeting ..." **April 30, 1881**. Indiana Historical Society. Lew Wallace Collection. M0292. Box 9. Folder 11. (**Death Warrant for William Bonney after his Mesilla trial and before his Lincoln jailbreak**)

TO AND FROM IRA E. LEONARD (SEE: Ira Leonard)

TO AND FROM JUSTICE OF THE PEACE JOHN B. WILSON

Wallace, Lew. "I hasten to acknowledge receipt of your favor of the 11th Jan. ult. ..." **January 18, 1879**. Indiana Historical Society. Lew Wallace Collection. M0292. Box 4. Folder 1. (**Lincoln County as carrying on a revolution**)

Wallace, Lew. "I enclose a note for Bonney." Letter to John "Squire" Wilson. **March 20, 1879**. Indiana Historical Society. Lew Wallace Collection. M0292. Box 4. Folder 6. (**The pardon negotiation for Billy Bonney**)

Wilson, John B. Signed JBW. **April 8, 1879**. Indiana Historical Society, Lew Wallace Collection. M0292. Box 4, Folder 8. (**Notes on rustling**)

_____. Letter to Lew Wallace. **May 18, 1879**. Indiana Historical Society. Lew Wallace Collection. M0292. Box 4, Folder 5.

ARTICLES ABOUT WILLIAM BONNEY BY (SEE: William H. Bonney)

WALZ, EDGAR A.

No Author. *The American Book of Biography: Men of 1912*. Chicago: American Publishers Association. 1913. Page 614.

No Author. "Edgar A. Walz Dead: Expert on credit, Founder of The Travelers Hotel Credit Corporation – Managed New Mexico Ranch in Youth." *The New York Times*. **April 5, 1935**. Volume LXXXIV, Number 28,195. Page 24.

WILD, AZARIAH (SEE: Secret Service)

WILSON, WILLIAM "BILLY"

BIBLIOGRAPHIC SOURCES

O'Neal, Bill. "Anderson, D.L. 'Billy Wilson.' " *Encyclopedia of Western Gunfighters.* Norman: University of Oklahoma Press. 1979.

Rasch, Philip J. *Trailing Billy the Kid.* "Chapter 8: Amende Honorable: The Life and Death of Billy Wilson." The National Association for Outlaw and Lawman History, Inc. Stillwater, Oklahoma: Western Publications. 1995.

COUNTERFEITING TRIAL OF

U.S. vs William Wilson. U.S. Territorial Court. First Judicial District. Santa Fe. 1881. National Archives at Broomfield, Colorado. Including:

Case No. 1-757, passing counterfeit money **(Denied by Wilson)**
Case No. 1-760, assault on Fred Weston, mail carrier
Case No. 1-761, counterfeiting **(Denied by Wilson)**
Case No. 1-762, motion for change of venue

Barnes, Sidney W. "Requesting certified copies of charters of certain banks for use in case of Billy Wilson." **July 12, 1881.** Letter to Attorney General Wayne McVeigh. National Archives. Records of the Department of Justice. **(Bills claimed as passed by Wilson were from the 2nd National Bank of Wilkesbarre, Pennsylvania and the National Bank of New Bedford, Massachusetts)**

PARDON OF

Application for Executive Clemency. National Archives, College Park, Maryland. Record Group 204. Entry 1a. Pardon Case files 1853-1946. Box 324. Record P. Pages 716-756.

Letters for Petition for Pardon. 1896. National Archives, College Park, Maryland. Record Group 204. Entry 1a. Pardon Case files 1853-1946. Box 324.

Pardon Advised. December 5, 1883. National Archives, College Park, Maryland. Record Group 204. Entry 1a. Pardon Case files 1853-1946. Record J. Box No. 161. Pages 228-254.

Garrett, Patrick Floyd. "I write you for the purpose of stating the facts ..." **May 24, 1896.** Letter to William Thornton as "Acting Sheriff of Doña County." National Archives, College Park, Maryland. Record Group 204. Entry 1a. Pardon Case files, Billy Wilson. Box 324. **(Garrett now denies Wilson was a counterfeiter and recommends pardon)**

Dolan, James J. "I write you on behalf of Billy Wilson ..." **June 30, 1896.** Letter to William Thornton as "Principal Prosecuting Witness against Wilson." National Archives, College Park, Maryland. Record Group 204. Entry 1a. Pardon Case files, Billy Wilson. Box 324. **(Dolan now denies Wilson was a counterfeiter and recommends pardon)**

Thornton, William T. "I have the honor to call your attention to the case of 'Billy Wilson.' " **July 7, 1896.** Letter to Attorney General Judson Harmon. National Archives, College Park, Maryland. Record Group 204. Entry 1a. Pardon Case files, Billy Wilson. Box 324. **(Requesting Wilson's pardon, denying counterfeiting)**

Conditional Pardon granted. **August 25, 1896.** National Archives, College Park, Maryland. Record Group 204. Records of the Office of the Pardon Attorney, Billy Wilson. Docket of Pardon Cases 1853-1923. Volume 17. PI-87. Entry 7.

Grover Cleveland's Presidential Pardon Number 756. **August 25, 1896.** Volume 17, Page 354. National Archives. Record Group 204, Records of the Pardon Attorney, Pardon Application File Number P-756, Billy Wilson. **(Cited as above and quoted in Philip Rasch's 1995 *Trailing Billy the Kid*)**

WILSON, JOHN B. "SQUIRE"

CORONER'S JURY REPORT FOR JOHN H. TUNSTALL BY

Wilson, John, George B. Barker, Robert M. Gilbert, John Newcomb, Samuel Smith, Benjamin Ellis. "We the undersigned Justice of the Peace and Coroners Jury who sat upon the inquest held this 19th day of February 1878 on the body of John H. Tunstall ..." Coroner's Jury Report for John Tunstall. **February 19, 1878.** **(Naming as murderers, among others, James Dolan, Frank Baker, Jessie Evans, William Morton, and George Hindman)**

LETTERS FROM

Wilson, John B. Letter to Lew Wallace. Unsigned but noted as from "Sqr. Wilson by Wallace. Undated, but likely **March, 1879.** Indiana Historical Society. Lew Wallace Collection. M0292. Box 4, Folder 7. **(On Lady Liberty stationery)**
_____. Affidavit of John Wilson. **March ?, 1879.** Indiana Historical Society. Lew Wallace Collection. M0292. Box 4, Folder 7.
_____. Signed JBW. **April 8, 1879.** Indiana Historical Society, Lew Wallace Collection. M0292. Box 4, Folder 8. **(Notes on rustling)**
_____. Letter to Lew Wallace. **May 18, 1879.** Indiana Historical Society. Lew Wallace Collection. M0292. Box 4, Folder 5.

LETTERS TO

Bonney, W H. "Friend Wilson ..." **March 18, 1879.** Indiana Historical Society. Lew Wallace Collection. M0292. **(For mediating his pardon negotiation with Lew Wallace)**
Wallace, Lew. "I enclose a note for Bonney." Letter to John "Squire" Wilson. **March 20, 1879.** Indiana Historical Society. Lew Wallace Collection. M0292. Box 4. Folder 6. **(The pardon negotiation for Billy Bonney)**

OLIVER "BRUSHY BILL" ROBERTS BILLY THE KID IMPOSTER HOAX

SOURCES TO DEBUNK CLAIMS IN "BRUSHY BILL" HOAX, IN ADDITION TO CITED SOURCES FOR WILLIAM BONNEY'S REAL HISTORY (CHRONOLOGICAL)

No Author. Roberts family members. Federal Census for Arkansas, Sebastian County, Bates Township. **June 1, 1880.** Lines 27-33. (Cited in Don Cline's *Brushy Bill Roberts: I Wasn't Billy the Kid* to show "Brushy" was 10 months old at the census – 20 years too young to be Billy Bonney)

Wilcox, Lucius "Lute" M. (city editor, owner, J.H. Koogler). "The Kid. Interview with Billy Bonney The Best Known Man in New Mexico." *Las Vegas Gazette.* **December 27, 1880. (Mentions that Billy Bonney has squirrel-like incisors; that contradicts "Brushy's" tusk-like extracted canine teeth)**

Rudulph, Milnor. Coroner's Jury Report for William Bonney alias "Kid." **July 15, 1881.** Indiana Historical Society. Lew Wallace Collection. M0292. Box 9. Folder 11. Accession Number 1951.0104 from Maurice G. Fulton. **(Photostatic copy of original Spanish Coroner's Jury Report, certified on January 18, 1951, donated by Maurice Garland Fulton - matches photo in William Kelleher's *Violence in Lincoln County* copy; identifying body of Billy Bonney)**

Ritch, William G. "In the matter of the application by Patrick F. Garrett for a reward claimed to have been offered May-1881 for the capture of Wm Bonney alias "the Kid." *Executive Record Book Number 2.* July 25, 1867- November 8, 1882. **July 21, 1881.** Pages 533-535. New Mexico Secretary of State Records. Collection 1971-001, Series 1; Records of the Secretary of the Territory. (Accessed from Albuquerque Public Library Microfilm, Territorial Archives of New Mexico, Roll 21.) **(Presentation of Garret's bill for the reward and demonstrating that Acting-Governor Ritch agreed with the reward, but legal opinion from Attorney General William Breeden necessitated getting a Legislative act to convert Wallace's private reward to Territorial; also shows that Charles Greene was the printer of the reward notice, not Garrett's attorney as C.L. Sonnichsen wrongly claimed)**

No Author. "Kid the Killer Killed, Wm. Bonney alias Antrim, alias Billy the Kid, Fatally Meets Pat Garrett, the Lincoln County Sheriff." Las Cruces *Rio Grande Republican.* **July 23, 1881.** Page 2. Volume 1, Number 10. NewspaperArchive.com. **(Copy of Pat Garrett's letter to Acting Governor William Ritch confirming that the original Coroner's Jury Report was sent to District Attorney of the First Judicial District, and copy of it was included in this letter to the Governor)**

No Author. " 'The Kid' Killed! He Meets His Death at the Hands of Sheriff Pat Garrett, of Lincoln County. The Particulars of the Affair as Poured into the Ears of Eager Reporters. *The Las Vegas Daily Optic.* **July 18, 1881.** Volume 2, Number 217. Newspaperarchives.com. **(Confirming Pat Garrett's killing of Billy the Kid)**

No Author. *Executive Record Book Number 2.* July 25, 1867-November 8, 1882. **July 21, 1881.** Pages 533-535. New Mexico State Records Center and Archives, Santa Fe. New Mexico Secretary of the State Records Series 1. Records of the Secretary of the Territory. **(About granting Garrett's reward; source used by Sonnichsen to fabricate irregularity)**

No Author. "Garrett Exonerates Maxwell." *Santa Fe Daily New Mexican.* **July 21, 1881.** Volume X, Number 120. Newspaperarchives.com. **(Confirming Pat Garrett's killing of Billy the Kid)**

No Author. No title. *Santa Fe Daily New Mexican.* **July 21, 1881.** Volume X, Number 120, Page 4. Column 1. (**Pat Garrett's presentation to Acting Governor Ritch of his reward request, with Ritch willing to pay but needed to go through procedures.**)

No Author. "Words of Commendation and Encouragement." *Las Vegas Daily Gazette.* **July 22, 1881.** Volume 3. Number 15. Newspapers.com. (**Confirming Pat Garrett's killing of Billy the Kid**)

Ashenfelter, Singleton M. "Exit 'The Kid', The Fugitive Murderer Hunted Down and Killed by Sheriff Garrett." *The New Southwest, And Grant County Herald.* **July 23, 1881.** Number 30. Page 2. Column 3. University of New Mexico. Zimmerman Library. Microfilm AN2 G71. (**Ashenfelter's apocryphal description of Billy the Kid's body lifted by the "Brushy Bill" hoax, but confirmation of the killing**)

No Author. "The Life of Billy the Kid. His Name Was Billy McCarthy, and He was Born in New York." *The New York Sun.* (From *The St. Louis Globe-Democrat*) **August 10, 1881.** Volume XLIII, Number 314. Newspapers.com. (**Confirming Pat Garrett's killing of Billy the Kid**)

Glen, Skelton. "Pat Garrett As I Knew Him on the Buffalo Ranges." (**1890**, Unpublished). Binder RNM, III B, 20. Nita Stewart Haley Memorial Museum. Haley Library. Midland, Texas. (**The killing of Joe Briscoe is recounted, but was unknown to "Brushy" who garbles it from a John Meadows article**)

No Author. "Death of T.C. McKinney." *The Carlsbad Current.* **September 24, 1915.** Front page. Column 5. ChroniclingAmerica.loc.gov/. (**With no claim that Kip McKinney and Tom O'Folliard were cousins**)

Taeger, Mary Nell. "Severo Gallegos Tells His Story and of His Family's Friend, 'Billy the Kid.'" *Ruidoso News.* **July 30, 1948.** Front page, Page 6. Volume II, Number 11. NewspaperArchive.com. (**A Billy the Kid history confabulator, used by Morrison as a prompt for "Brushy's" jailbreak tale. Gallegos was then used give a fake affidavit that "Brushy" was Billy**)

_____. No Author. "Severo Gallegos Tells His Story and of His Family's Friend, 'Billy the Kid.'" (continued) *Ruidoso News.* **August 6, 1948.** Page 3. Volume II, Number 12. NewspaperArchive.com. (**A Billy the Kid history confabulator, with this part 2 article used by Morrison as a prompt for "Brushy's" jailbreak tale. Gallegos was then used give a fake affidavit that "Brushy" was Billy**)

Roberts, Oliver Pleasant. ("Brushy" writing as O.L. Roberts) "Dear Uncle Kit Carson, We got here O.K. ..." Letter to Oran Ardious Woodman. **April 1, 1949.** From Roy L. Haws, *Brushy Bill: Proof His Claim to Be Billy the Kid Was a Hoax.* **2015.** (Pages 113-117) (**"Brushy Bill's" possibly modeling himself as Billy the Kid based on this Kit Carson imposter**)

No Author. "Cornering Jesse James." *Hico News Review.* **February 3, 1950.** Front Page. Volume LXIV, Number 38. Texas Tech University Library. Southwest Collections/Special Collections Library. Microfilm H626 Hico (Texas) News Review 1929-1974 Reel 8. (**"Brushy" claiming J. Frank Dalton as Jesse James**)

Holford, Carolyn. "'Brushy Bill' Is Back From Gotham." *Hico News Review.* **February 20, 1950.** Front Page. Volume LXIV, Number 36. Texas Tech University Library. Southwest Collections/Special Collections Library. Microfilm H626 Hico (Texas) News Review 1929-1974 Reel 8. (**Reporting on Morrison-backed radio show on January 3, 1950 with J. Frank Dalton as Jesse James and "Brushy" backing him and having "wild west" tales**)

No Author. "Fort Sumner Jury Thought the Kid Had Been Killed." *Alamogordo News.* **November 30, 1950.** Volume 53, Number 48. .NewspaperArchive.com. (**Finding the Coroner's Jury Report; ignored in *Alias Billy the Kid***)

No Author. Will A. Keleher, History Student, Sure Kid Was Shot." *Albuquerque Journal.* **December 1, 1950.** Volume illegible, Number 61. Newspaperarchive.com. (**Debunking "Brushy's" claim to be Billy the Kid**)

No Author. "Notorious Character is Buried." *Hico News Review.* **January 5, 1951.** Front Page. Volume LXV, Number 34. Texas Tech University Library. Southwest Collections/Special Collections Library. Microfilm H626 Hico (Texas) News Review 1929-1974 Reel 8. (**Obituary of "Brushy Bill" Roberts**)

Morrison, William V. Letter to Carl Breihan. **March 17, 1954.** (**Cited in Don Cline's** *Brushy Bill Roberts: I Wasn't Billy the Kid* **to show Morrison's attempt to sell "Brushy's" story for movies or TV**)

_____. Letter to Philip Rasch. **April 12, 1954.** Rio Grande Historical Collections./Hobson Huntslinger University Archives. New Mexico State University, Las Cruces. (**Lying that he was being backed for "Brushy" by many people, including William Keleher**)

Sonnichsen, C.L. and William V. Morrison. *Alias Billy the Kid.* Albuquerque, New Mexico: University of New Mexico Press. **1955.** (**Backing Roberts as Billy the Kid**)

Keleher, William A. *Violence in Lincoln County 1869-1881.* Albuquerque, New Mexico: University of New Mexico Press. **1957.** (**Photocopy of Spanish Coroner's Jury Report, July 15, 1881. Pages 306-308; Kelleher's English translation, Pages 343-344.**)

Walker, Dale L. *C.L. Sonnichsen: Grassroots Historian.* El Paso: Texas Western Press. **1972.** (**About co-author of Roberts in the Billy the Kid hoax**)

Pittmon, Geneva Roberts. "Dear Sir: the reason you are not finding my family ..." **December 16, 1987.** Letter to Joe Bowlin. In collection of Old Fort Sumner Museum, Fort Sumner, New Mexico. (**Roberts's niece using family Bible to prove Roberts was not Billy the Kid**)

_____. "I don't know of any job he held ..." Letter to Don Cline. **April 27, 1988.** (**Cited in Don Cline's** *Brushy Bill Roberts: I Wasn't Billy the Kid* **to show "Brushy" was a mentally disabled farm hand in his real life.**)

Sonnichsen, C.L. "I believe, without evidence, that Bill Morrison had a law degree ..." Letter to Don Cline. **June 30, 1988.** (**About believing that Morrison was a lawyer**)

Metz, Leon. "I met William V. Morrison in the early 1970's ..." Letter to Don Cline. **July 2, 1988.** (**Cited in Don Cline's** *Brushy Bill Roberts: I Wasn't Billy the Kid* **to show that Morrison denied being a lawyer**)

Tunstill, William A. *Billy the Kid and Me Were the Same: A Documentary on the Life of Billy the Kid.* Roswell, New Mexico: Western History Research Center. 1988. (**"Brushy"-backer faking a genealogy using duped Eulaine Emerson Haws's approval, and debunked by "Brushy's" relative Roy L. Haws, Eulaine Emerson Haws's son, in his 2015** *Brushy Bill: Proof That His Claim to Be Billy the Kid Was a Hoax*)

Cline, Don. *Brushy Bill Roberts: I Wasn't Billy the Kid.* **Undated [1988 or 1989?].** Unpublished manuscript. New Mexico Commission of Public Records. State Records Center and Archives. Santa Fe. MS Donald Cline Collection. Subseries 5.2, Folder 138. Box 10421. Serial No. 9560 Santa Fe NMSRCA. (**Debunking "Brushy's" Billy the Kid claims**)

_____. Interview with "Brushy's" brother, Tom's daughter, Mary June Roberts. **January 28, 1988.** (**Denying "Brushy's" genealogical claims**)

Anaya, Paco. *I Buried Billy.* College Station, Texas: Creative Publishing Company. 1991. (**Eye-witness claim of burying Billy Bonney**)

Jameson, W.C. and Frederic Bean. *The Return of the Outlaw Billy the Kid.* Plano, Texas: Republic of Texas Press. **1998.** (**Backing Roberts as Billy the Kid**)

Walker, Dale L. *Legends and Lies: Great Mysteries of the American West.* New York: A Tom Doherty Associates Book. **1997.** (**Backing Roberts as Billy the Kid**)

Nolan, Frederick. *The West of Billy the Kid.* Norman: University of Oklahoma Press. **1998.** (**See Page 7 for quote on the Eugene Cunningham hoaxed photo of Catherine Antrim, which "Brushy" confabulated as his aunt, Kathleen Bonney**)

Johnson, Jim. *Billy the Kid: His Real Name Was ...*" Denver, Colorado: Outskirts Press, Inc. **2006**. (**Debunking Roberts as Billy the Kid**)

Haws, Roy L. *Brushy Bill: Proof That His Claim to Be Billy the Kid Was a Hoax.* Santa Fe: Sunstone Press. **2015**. (**Roberts relative debunking him as Billy the Kid**)

Jameson, W.C. *Cold Case Billy the Kid: Investigating History's Mysteries.* Guilford, Connecticut: Twodot. **2018**. (**Recycling the "Billy the Kid Case" hoax to argue for Roberts as Billy the Kid**)

No Author. "Memorials." *El Paso Post-Herald.* **September 9, 1977**. Volume XCVII, Number 216. Page 24, Column 5. Newspaperarchive.com (**Obituary for William V. Morrison, showing he was not an attorney**)

Caperton, Thomas J. *Historic Structure Report. Lincoln State Monument. Lincoln New Mexico.* Santa Fe, New Mexico: Office of Cultural Affairs, Department of Finance and Administration, Historic Preservation Division. **1983**. (**With floor plan of the Lincoln court-house proving "Brushy's" faked armory location**)

Nolan, Frederick. *The West of Billy the Kid.* Norman: University of Oklahoma Press. **1998**. (**Seven Rovers boy's tintype with Marion Turner identified by Eve Ball, but claimed to be himself as 17 as Billy the Kid by "Brushy Bill;" Page 157**)

Salazar, Joe. (Grandson of Yginio Salazar). Interviews **1999-2001**. (**My interviews about Ygenio Salazar, cited by the hoaxers as believing Billy had survived the Garrett shooting**)

Cox, Jim. *The Great Radio Soap Operas.* Jefferson, North Carolina: McFarland & Company, Inc. Publishers. **1999**. (**About "We the People" radio show, in which "Brushy" appeared to vouch for J. Frank Dalton as Jesse James**)

No Author. "We the People." https://www.otrcat.com/p/we-the-people. **2019**. (**About "We the People" radio show, in which "Brushy" appeared to vouch for J. Frank Dalton as Jesse James**)

(See William H. Bonney's Coroner's Jury Report)

ARTICLES ON REJECTED PARDON (CHRONOLOGICAL)

Humphreys, Sexton. "Pardon Me, I'm Alive," Says Billy the Kid." *Indianapolis News.* **November 25, 1950**. Page 9. Indiana Historical Society. Lew Wallace Collection. M0292. Box 14. Folder 12.

Morgan, Art. "Billy the Kid Only a Phony It Turns Out." *Santa Fe New Mexican.* **November 30, 1950**. Issue 6. Front page, Page 3. NewspaperArchive.com.

No Author. "Mabry Terms "Billy" Outright Imposter." *Clovis News Journal.* **November 30, 1950**. Volume 22, Number 208. Newspaperarchive.com. (**Thursday, when interview was held**)

Smylie, Vernon. "Billy the Kid Flunks in Talk With Governor." *El Paso Herald Post.* **November 30, 1950**. Volume LXX, Number 285. Front Page, Page 13. Newspaperarchive.com. (**Thursday, when interview was held**)

United Press. "Pardon Mt 6-Shooters. Billy the Kid? Governor to Decide." *The Indianapolis News.* **November 30, 1950**. Indiana Historical Society. Lew Wallace Collection. M0292. Box 14. Folder 12.

No Author. " 'Billy the Kid' Bubble Bursts as Gov. Mabry Rejects Oldster's Claim." *Albuquerque Journal.* **December 1, 1950**. Volume [illegible], Number 61. Front Page, Page 4. Newspapers.com.

No Author. "Will A. Keleher, History Student, Sure Kid Was Shot." *Albuquerque Journal.* **December 1, 1950**. Volume [illegible], Number 61. Front Page. Newspaperarchive.com. (**Supports Governor Mabry calling "Brushy Bill" a Billy the Kid imposter**)

No Author. "Billy the Kid is Called Imposter by New Mexico Chief." *Lubbock Morning Avalanche.* **December 30, 1950**. Page 12. Newspaperarchive.com.

JOHN MILLER
BILLY THE KID IMPOSTER HOAX

No Author. Obituary of John Miller. *Prescott Courier*. **November 8, 1937**. **(Gives date of birth as December, 1850)**

Huff, J. Wesley. "Did Pat Garrett Kill Billy the Kid? Herman Tecklenburg Says No; Billy Lived on Ranch at Ramah 35 Years Ago and Visited Him. *The Gallup Independent*. **August 9, 1944**. Volume 55, Number 185. Newspapers.com. **(Tecklenburg's Billy the Kid confabulations)**

Airy, Helen L. *Whatever Happened to Billy the Kid?* Santa Fe, New Mexico: Sunstone Press. **1993**. **(John Miller as Billy the Kid)**

Johnson, Jim. *Billy the Kid: His Real Name Was ...* Denver, Colorado: Outskirts Press, Inc. **2006**. **(Debunking evidence for John Miller as Billy the Kid, and providing his dates of arrival and death at the Arizona Pioneers' home cemetery, and his obituary)**

Sams, Dale. Arizona Pioneers' Home and Cemetery Administrator. Personal communication. January 12, 2010. **(Confirmed that records list John Miller's DOB as December – 1850; and birthplace as Fort Sill, Texas)**

"BILLY THE KID CASE" HOAX, LINCOLN COUNTY SHERIFF'S DEPARTMENT CASE NO. 2003-274

RELEVANT BOOKS

Althouse, Bill. *Frozen Lightening: Bill Richardson's Strike on the Political Landscape of New Mexico*. Buckman, New Mexico: Thinking Out Loud Press. **2006**.

Bugliosi, Vincent. *Outrage: The Five Reasons Why O.J. Simpson Got Away With Murder*. New York and London: W.W. Norton & Company. **1996**. **(Exposé of Dr. Henry Lee faking forensics in legal cases, Pages 47-49)**

Cline, Donald. *Alias Billy the Kid: The Man Behind the Legend*. Santa Fe: New Mexico: Sunstone Press. **1986**. **(Historian cited by the hoaxers as backing them; apparently unaware of his 1988 manuscript:** *Brushy Bill Roberts: I Wasn't Billy the Kid* **)**

Cooper, Gale. *Billy the Kid's Pretenders: Brushy Bill and John Miller*. Albuquerque, New Mexico: Gelcour Books. **2012**.

_____. *Billy the Kid's Writings, Words, and Wit*. Albuquerque, New Mexico: Gelcour Books. **2012**.

_____. *MegaHoax: The Strange Plot to Exhume Billy the Kid and Become President*. Albuquerque, New Mexico: Gelcour Books. **2012**.

_____. *Cracking the Billy the Kid Case Hoax: The Strange Plot to Exhume Billy the Kid, Convict Sheriff Pat Garrett of Murder, and Become President of the United States*. Albuquerque, New Mexico: Gelcour Books. **2014**.

_____. *The Billy the Kid Imposter Hoax of Brushy Bill Roberts*. Albuquerque, New Mexico: Gelcour Books. **2019**.

_____. *Billy the Kid's Pretender John Miller*. Albuquerque, New Mexico: Gelcour Books. **2019**.

_____. *The Cold Case Billy the Kid Megahoax: The Plot to Steal Billy the Kid's Identity and Defame Sheriff Pat Garrett as a Murderer*. Albuquerque, New Mexico: Gelcour Books. **2019**.

_____. *The Coroner's Jury Report of Billy the Kid: An Inquest That Sealed the Fame Of Billy Bonney and Pat Garrett.* Albuquerque, New Mexico: Gelcour Books. **2019**.

Garcia, Elbert A. *Billy the Kid's Kid 1875-1964, The Hispanic Connection.* Santa Rosa, New Mexico: Los Products Press. **1999**. **(Early participant in "Billy the Kid Case" as unsubstantiated kin of Billy the Kid)**

Garrett, Pat F. *The Authentic Life of Billy the Kid The Noted Desperado of the Southwest, Whose Deeds of Daring and Blood Made His Name a Terror in New Mexico, Arizona, and Northern Mexico.* Santa Fe, New Mexico: New Mexico Printing and Publishing Co. **1882**. (Edition used: Edited by Maurice Garland Fulton. New York: The Macmillan Company. 1927)

Metz, Leon C. *Pat Garrett. The Story of a Western Lawman.* Norman: University of Oklahoma Press. **1974**.

Nolan, Frederick. *The West of Billy the Kid.* Norman: University of Oklahoma Press. **1998**. **(Page 7 for quote on the Eugene Cunningham hoaxed photo of Catherine Antrim)**

Palast, Greg. *Armed Madhouse.* New York: Penguin Group USA. **2007**. **(Bill Richardson exposé)**

Poe, John W. *The Death of Billy the Kid.* (Introduction by Maurice Garland Fulton). Boston and New York: Houghton Mifflin Company. **1933**. **(Pages 22 and 25-26 have Milnor Rudulph quote with the part omitted by hoaxers' from their Probable Cause Statement)**

Richardson, Bill, with Michael Ruby. *Between Worlds: The Making of an American Life.* New York: G.P. Putnam's Sons. **2005**. **(Bill Richardson autobiography)**

Siringo, Charles. *The History of Billy the Kid.* Santa Fe: New Mexico. Privately Printed. **1920**. **(Reproduces the Jim East letter on pages 96-107)**

(SEE: William H. Bonney; Oliver "Brushy Bill" Roberts Billy the Kid Imposter Hoax; John Miller Billy the Kid Imposter Hoax; *Cold Case Billy the Kid* Megahoax

CORONER'S JURY REPORT FOR WILLIAM H. BONNEY (SEE WILLIAM H. BONNEY)

PAT GARRETT'S PROSECUTION IMMUNITY "BILLY THE KID CASE" BY STATUTE OF LIMITATIONS

No Author. "An Act to Provide the Limitation of Criminal Actions." *Acts of the Legislative Assembly of the Territory of New Mexico, Twenty-Second Session, Convened at the Capitol. at the City of Santa Fe on Monday the 6th Day of December, 1875, and Adjourned on Friday the 14th day of January, 1876.* Santa Fe, New Mexico: Manderfield & Tucker, Public Printers. **1876**. Hathitrust Digital Library. **(Providing for a 10 year statute of limitations on murder; so Garrett could not be prosecuted in 2003 for the 1881 killing of Billy Bonney, since that expired in 1891)**

No Author. Ed. L. Bradford Prince. *The General Laws of New Mexico.* "Limitations of Criminal Actions. "Limitation of Criminal Actions, Acts of the Legislative Assembly of the Territory of New Mexico, Twenty-Second Session, Convened at the Capitol, at the City of Santa Fe on Monday the 6th day of December, 1875, and Adjourned on Friday the 14th day of January, 1876." Chapter 13, Section 1. **1882**. **(Providing for a 10 year statute of limitations on murder; so Garrett could not be prosecuted in 2003 for the 1881 killing of Billy Bonney)**

PAMPHLETS FOR (CHRONOLOGICAL)

Turk, David S. Historian U.S. Marshals Service. "Research Report: The U.S. Marshals Service and Billy the Kid. To Be Added in its Present Entirety, with Exhibits, to Lincoln County, New Mexico Case # 2003-274." U.S. Marshals Service Executive

Services Division." **December, 2003. (a major hoax document by "Billy the Kid Case" participant as an addendum to the "Probable Cause Statement")**

Madrid, Patricia A. Attorney General. *Inspection of Public Records Act Compliance Guide. Fourth Edition. The "Inspection of Public Records Act" NMSA 1978, Chapter 14, Article 2: A Compliance Guide for New Mexico Public Officials and Citizens.* Santa Fe: Office of the Attorney General. **January, 2004. (For open records compliance and litigation)**

PRESS RELEASE FOR (GOVERNOR BILL RICHARDSON)

Richardson, Bill. "Governor Bill Richardson Announces State Support of Billy the Kid Investigation." **June 10, 2003. (Announcement at State Capitol of state backing of case # 2003-274 and listing of the participants: Tom Sullivan, Steve Sederwall, Gary Graves, Sherry Tippett, and Paul Hutton)**

_____. "Gov. Bill Richardson Appoints Criminal Defense Lawyer to NM Supreme Court." **November 2, 2007. (Corrupt Charles Daniels, husband of Richardson's attorney Randi McGinn)**

_____. "Governor Bill Richardson to Consider Billy the Kid Pardon Petition." Press release. **December 16, 2010. (The Randi McGinn pardon petition for "Billy the Kid")**

_____. "Governor Richardson to Announce his decision on Billy the Kid Pardon Request Tomorrow." Press release. **December 30, 2010.**

LETTERS ABOUT

Kurtis, Bill. "This letter is provided as official verification ..." Letter to Steve Sederwall. **October 4, 2010.** Entered by Sederwall's Defense Attorney as Exhibit A in Sandoval District Court Case No. D-1329-CV-2007-1364 Hearing on January 17, 2012. **(Paying for Dr. Henry Lee's forensics)**

E-MAILS ABOUT

Saar, Meghan. To Gale Cooper. "BTK Hoax Article." E-Mail To Gale Cooper. **January 31, 2006. (Hoax-backing *True West* magazine rejecting my article proposal to expose the "Billy the Kid Case" hoax)**

Ford, Simon. "Subj. Questions regarding Orchid-Cellmark." E-mail to Gale Cooper. **January 31, 2011. (Consultation on mixed DNA samples and DNA separation costs)**

Miller, Kenny. Personal communication to author about family history and showing Maxwell family objects - including the carpenter's bench, bedstead, and wash stand - and providing photos of them to author. **2011 to 2012. (Information from Maxwell family descendant)**

BLOGS ABOUT

No author. "Fraud Alleged at Cellmark, DNA Testing Firm. TalkLeft: The Politics of Crime. http://www.talkleft.com./new_archives/008809.html. **November 18, 2004.**

Boze Bell, Bob. "The Wild is back in the West." BBB's Blog. **April 24, 2006. (Announcement of invitation of Sullivan and Sederwall to Cannes Film Festival.)** http://www.truewestmagazine.com/weblog/blogger1.htm

WEBSITE FOR:

Sederwall, Steve. "billythekidcase.com" Website. From **October (?) 2010 to 2012(?). (For $25.00 membership selling Case 2003-274 records)**

TELEVISION DOCUMENTARIES PERPETRATING

History Channel. "Investigating History: Billy the Kid." Week **of April 24, 2004 and May 2, 2004**.(Co-Producer, writer, narrator was "Billy the Kid Case" hoaxer Paul Hutton)

National Geographic International Discovery ID Channel. "History Mysteries." **2010**. **(Sederwall presenting the fake Dr. Lee Deputy James Bell top-of-the-stairs murder "investigation")**

ARTICLES ABOUT (CHRONOLOGICAL)

Humphreys, Sexson. "Pardon My 6-Shooters: Billy the Kid? Governor to Decide; 'Pardon Me, I'm Alive,' Says Billy the Kid." *The Indianapolis News*. Thursday, **November 30, 1950**. Indiana Historical Society. Lew Wallace Collection (M292). Box 14. Folder 12.

Hutton, Paul Andrew. "Dreamscape Desperado." *New Mexico Magazine*. Volume 68. Number 6. Pages 44-58. **June, 1990**.

Janofsky, Michael. "122 Years Later, the Lawmen Are Still Chasing Billy the Kid." *The New York Times*. **June 5, 2003**. Vol. CLII, No. 52,505. Pages 1 and A31. **(First national announcement of Billy the Kid Case)**

No Author. "Lincoln County deputy sheriff sends his own letter to governor." *Silver City Daily Press*. **June 25, 2003**. Pages 1, 13.

DellaFlora, Anthony. "State Not Kidding Around: Governor won't mind if probe of the notorious 19th century N.M. outlaw boosts tourism." *Albuquerque Journal*. **June 11, 2003**. No. 162. Pages 1 and A1. **(First big New Mexico announcement of Billy the Kid Case)**

Bommersbach, Jana. "Digging Up Billy: If Pat Garrett didn't kill the Kid, who's buried in his grave?" *True West*. **August/September 2003**. Volume 50. Issue 7. P. 42-45.

No Author. AP. "Authorities call for exhumation of Billy the Kid's mother to solve mystery." *Silver City Sun News*. **October 11, 2003**.

Bommersbach, Jana. "From Shovels to DNA: The inside story of digging up Billy." *True West*. **October/November, 2003**. Volume 50. Issue 7. Pages 42-45.

Jameson, W.C. and Leon Metz. "Was Brushy Bill Really Billy the Kid? Experts face off over new evidence." *True West*. **November/December, 2003**. Volume 50. Issue 10. Pages 32-33.

Murphy, Mary Alice. "Billy the Kid 'Hires' a Lawyer." *Silver City Daily Press Internet Edition*. http://www.thedailypress.com/NewsFolder/11.17.2.html. **November 17, 2003**.

Boyle, Alan. "Billy the Kid gets a lawyer: 122 years after shootout, attorney to gather information for a pardon." msnbc.com. **November 18, 2003**.

Fecteau, Loie. "No Kidding: Governor Taps Lawyer For Billy." *Albuquerque Journal*. Page 1, A6. **November 19, 2003**.

No Author. AP. "Lawyer Appointed to Represent Dead Outlaw." *Silver City Sun News*. http://www.krqe.com/expanded.asp?RECORD_KEY%5bContent. **November 19, 2003**. **(Bill Robins III's appointment by Richardson)**

No Author. "Lawmakers Consider Posthumous Pardon for Billy the Kid." *abqtrib.com News*. **November 21, 2003**.

Boyle, Alan. "Billy the Kid's DNA Sparks Legal Showdown: Sheriffs and mayors face off over digging up remains from the Old West." *msnbc.com*. **November 21, 2003**.

Romo, Rene. "Kid's Mom May Stay Buried: Silver City wins round to block exhumation for outlaw's DNA." *Albuquerque Journal*. **December 9, 2003**. Section D3.

Janna Bommersbach. "Breaking Out More Shovels: Fort Sumner's Sheriff Gary Graves commits to digging up Billy the Kid's Grave." *True West*. **January/February, 2004**. Volume 51. Issue 1. Pages 46-47. **(Hoax-backing article)**

Benke, Richard. AP. "N.M. Re-Opens Case of Billy the Kid." Yahoo! News. **January 13, 2004**.

_____. "Billy the Kid's Life and Death May Be Put to DNA Test: Officials want to examine the body of the outlaw's mother to test a Texas man's claim that he was Bonney. If so, Pat Garrett didn't kill the Kid." *The Nation.* **January 18, 2004. (Uses fake Overton Affidavit given by Attorney Sherry Tippett)**
No Author. AP. "Billy the Kid hearing delayed for months: Sheriffs need more time to prepare arguments for exhuming remains of outlaw's mother." **January 23, 2004.**
Miller, Jay. "Digging Up the Latest on Billy the Kid." *Las Cruces Sun-News.* **February 3, 2004.**
Gonzales. Carolyn. "Hutton writes wild frontier stories for History Channel." *University of New Mexico Campus News.* **February 16, 2004.** Volume 39. No. 12. **(Hoaxer Hutton's TV program announced)**
Miller, Jay. "The Billy the Kid Code." *Las Cruces Sun-News.* **March 29, 2004.**
Nathanson, Rick. "Grave Doubts: 'Investigating History' series tries to clear up the mysteries surrounding Billy the Kid." *Albuquerque Journal Weekly TV Guide: Entertainer.* **April 24, 2004.** Pages 3, 5.
Garrett, Wm. F. "Letters to the Editor." *De Baca County News.* Page 4. **May 6, 2004. (Garrett family member objects to hoax)**
Murphy, Mary Alice and Melissa St. Aude. "Sederwall, Sullivan uninvited to ball." *Silver City Daily Press Internet Edition.* **June 10, 2004.**
Hill, Levi. "Billy the Kid Stirring Up Dust in Silver City." *Las Cruces Sun-News.* **June 12, 2004.** Section 5A. Pages 1, A2.
No Author. "Attorney Refuses Judge's statements concerning exhumation." *thedailypress.com.* **June 15, 2004. (Attorney Tippett lies about the OMI)**
Richardson, Bill. "Verbatim: I have to decide whether to pardon him. But not right away – after the investigation, after the state gets more publicity." *Time.* **June 21, 2004.** Vol. 163. No. 25. Page 17.
Romo, Rene. "Back off on Billy, Gov. Asked: Silver City says inquiry into death of Kid would harm state tourism. *Albuquerque Journal.* **June 23, 2004.** Section B-1, B-5.
No Author. "Lincoln county deputy sheriff sends his own letter to governor." *Silver City Daily Press.* **June 25, 2004.** Pages 1, 13. **(Letter from Steve Sederwall)**
No Author. "Editorials: New Racing Schedule Tramples Horseman." *Albuquerque Journal.* **June 26, 2004.**
Miller, Jay. "Inside the Capitol. Bizarre case of Billy the Kid." *Roswell Daily Record.* **July 2, 2004.** Page A4.
Romo, Rene. "Forensic Expert on Billy's Case: Questions Remain on Outlaw's Fate." *Albuquerque Journal.* **August 2, 2004.** Page 1. **(Falsely claims blood on bench; says "trace blood")**
No Author. "Forensic expert joins Billy the Kid inquiry in New Mexico." *AP SignOnSanDiego.com.* **August 2, 2004. (Announcing Dr. Henry Lee)**
Miller, Jay. "Inside the Capitol. Sheriffs slippery on Billy the Kid Case." *Roswell Daily Record.* **August 9, 2004.** Page A4.
Cherry, Doris. "Forensics 101 for 'Billy'." *Lincoln County News.* **August 12, 2004.** Pages 2, 10. **(Quotes Sullivan's lie: "a lot" of blood on bench)**
Miller, Jay. "Inside the Capitol. Expert questions Kid probe." *Roswell Daily Record.* **August 20, 2004.** Page A4.
_____. "Inside the Capitol. Hat dance on probe funding." *Roswell Daily Record.* **September 1, 2004.** Page A4.
_____. "Inside the Capitol. Three sheriffs push Kid Case." *Roswell Daily Record.* **September 5, 2004.** Page A4.
_____. "Inside the Capitol. Sheriffs hoax is world-class." *Roswell Daily Record.* **September 8, 2004.** Page A4.
_____. "Inside the Capitol. Kid gets day in court Sept. 27." *Roswell Daily Record.* **September 12, 2004.** Page A4.
_____. "Inside the Capitol. Kid probe making us think." *Roswell Daily Record.* **September 13, 2004.** Page A4.

Stinnett, Scot. "De Baca County Citizens' Committee Files Petition for Recall of Sheriff Gary Graves." *De Baca County News.* **September 14, 2004.**

Miller, Jay. "Inside the Capitol. Who is Attorney Bill Robins?" *Roswell Daily Record.* **September 15, 2004.** Page A4.

Green, Keith. "Mountain Asides: Billy's restless bones are stirred up once again. *RuidosoNews.com.* **September 16, 2004.**

Miller, Jay. "Inside the Capitol. Kid Case: David fights Goliath." *Roswell Daily Record.* **September 17, 2004.** Page A4.

_____. "Inside the Capitol. Many reasons to dig up Kid." *Roswell Daily Record.* **September 19, 2004.** Page A4.

_____. "Inside the Capitol. Nothing to worry about." *Roswell Daily Record.* **September 20, 2004.** Page A4.

Stallings, Dianne. "Showdown in the County Seat." *RuidosoNews.com* **September 21, 2004. (Commissioner Leo Martinez's meeting threatening recall of Sheriff Sullivan for perpetrating a hoax)**

Miller, Jay. "Inside the Capitol. Who speaks for Pat Garrett?" *Roswell Daily Record.* **September 22, 2004.** Page A4.

Stallings, Dianne. "Showdown in the County Seat: shouting match erupts at County Commissioners meeting Tuesday over investigation of Billy the Kid." *Ruidoso News.* **September 22, 2004.**

Cherry, Doris. "Lincoln County 'War' Heats Up Over 'Billy: Capitan Mayor Tracks His Kind of '---' To County Commission Meeting. Tells Jay Miller where to go: wonders why commissioner has his panties in a wad." *Lincoln County News.* **September 23, 2003.** Vol. 99. No. 38. Pages 1-3. **(Commissioner Martinez stops the hoaxers' exhuming Billy the Kid)**

Miller, Jay. "Inside the Capitol. Is there a new Santa Fe Ring?" *Roswell Daily Record.* **September 24, 2004.** Page A4.

Stinnett, Scott. "Rest in Peace, Billy! Exhumation case dismissed." *De Baca County News.* **September 30, 2004.** Vol. 104. No. 2. Pages 1, 5, 6.

Miller, Jay. "Inside the Capitol. Fort Sumner celebrates win." *Roswell Daily Record.* **October 1, 2004.** Page A4.

No author. "Fraud Alleged at Cellmark, DNA Testing Firm. TalkLeft: The Politics of Crime. http://www.talkleft.com./new_archives/008809.html. **November 18, 2004. (Dr. Henry Lee's lab commits DNA faking)**

Jana Bommersbach. "Kid Exhumation Nixed: Billy and his mom to rest in peace. *True West.* **January/February 2005.** Volume 52. Issue 1. Pages 68-69.

Massey, Barry. "Casinos, contracting lawyers fund Madrid." The New Mexican. http://www.freenewmexican.com/news/13746.html **May 14, 2005.**

Stinnett, Scott. "Judge rules Graves recall can proceed: Parker finds probable cause after two-day hearing." *De Baca County News.* **August 25, 2005.** Vol. 104. No. 49. Pages 1, 4, 10. **(The Recall Hearing of Sheriff Gary Graves)**

_____. "Testimony paints Graves as 'above the law': Recall probable cause hearing emotional, contentious." *De Baca County News.* **September 1, 2005.** Vol. 104. No. 50. Pages 1, 5, 6, 8, 9, 10.

Carter, Julie. "Follow the Blood: In the Billy the Kid Case, Miller Exhumed." *RuidosoNews.com.* **October 6, 2005. (Sederwall lies about blood on bench; gives "dead men don't bleed" quote; has the Lonnie Lippman photo of him holding John Miller/William Hudspeth skull)**

Sullivan, Tom. "Letters: Your Opinion." *RuidosoNews.com.* **October 21, 2005. (Sullivan letter to the editor: "Why are they so afraid of the truth?")**

Carter, Julie. "Billy the Kid in Prescott? *New Mexico Stockman.* **November, 2005.** Pages 38, 39, 76.

Romo, Rene. "Billy the Kid Probe May Yield New Twist. *Albuquerque Journal. ABQ Journal.com.* **November 6, 2005. (Claims Sullivan and Sederwall have John Miller's DNA)**

Struckman, Robert. "Bitterroot man hopes to uncover truth about Billy the Kid." http://www.helenair.com/articles/2006/03/13/montana/a05031306_01.txt (Missoulian) **March 13, 2006. (Hoaxer Dale Tunnell backing John Miller as Billy the Kid**

Dodder, Joanna. "Officials could face charges for digging up alleged Billy the Kid." *The Daily Courier of Prescott Arizona.* **April 12, 2006. (Sullivan claims DNA in "two months," and fakes Hudspeth skeleton as John Miller's and makes up a left scapula bullet wound)**

Banks, Leo W. "The New Billy the Kid? The mad search for the bones of an American outlaw icon has come to Arizona." *Tucson Weekly.* http://www.tucsonweekly.com/gbase/Currents/Content?oid=oid:81013 **April 13, 2006. (Sullivan lies that bench is "saturated with blood; Dr. Rick Staub says DNA extracted from William Hudspeth not John Miller)**

Carter, Julie. "Digging up bones, Arizona may protest Miller exhumation." jcarter@tularosa.net. **April 19, 2006.**

Dodder, Joanna. "Officials could face charges for digging up alleged Billy the Kid." *The Daily Courier of Prescott Arizona.* **April 12, 2006. (Sullivan claims DNA in "two months," and fakes Hudspeth skeleton as John Miller's with buck teeth and a left scapula bullet wound)**

Banks, Leo W. "The New Billy the Kid? The mad search for the bones of an American outlaw icon has come to Arizona." *Tucson Weekly.* http://www.tucsonweekly.com/gbase/Currents/Content?oid=oid:81013 **April 13, 2006. (Sullivan lies that bench is "saturated with blood; Dr. Rick Staub says DNA extracted from William Hudspeth not John Miller)**

Carter, Julie. "Digging up bones, Arizona may protest Miller exhumation." jcarter@tularosa.net. **April 19, 2006.**

Carter, Julie. "Culture Shock: The cowboys and the Kid go to France." jcarter@tulerosa.net. **May 5, 2006. (Sullivan worked on movie 9 months)**

Shafer, Mark. "N.M. pair may face charges in grave case." **May 13, 2006.** markshafer @ArizonaRepublic.com. http://www.azcentral.com/arizonarepublic/local/articles/0513billythekid0513.html

Myers, Amanda Lee. "New Mexicans Dig Up Trouble in Arizona." *Albuquerque Journal, New Mexico and the West.* **May 14, 2006.** Page B4. **(Also in gulfnews.com; states Dallas lab" is doing DNA comparisons)**

_____."Billy the Kid Still 'Wanted.' " **May 16, 2006.** gulfnews.com. http://archive.gulfnews.com/articles/06/05/16/10040234.html.

No author. "Festival de Cannes, **May 17-28, 2006.** Requiem for Billy the Kid." http://www.festival-cannes.fr/films/fiche_film.php?langue=4355535. **(Cannes Film Festival synopsis)**

No author. "Out of Competition/Cannes Classics: Requiem for Billy the Kid. Festival de Cannes May 17-28, 2006." http://www.festival-cannes.fr/films/fiche_film.php?langue=4355535. **May 20, 2006. (Sullivan and Sederwall called two sheriffs)**

McCarthy, Todd. "Requiem for Billy the Kid." **May 21, 2006.** Variety.com. http://www.variety.com/review/VE1117930570?categoryid=2220&cs=1&nid=2562.

McCoy, Dave. "L 'Ouest Américain." **May 25, 2006.** MSN Movies. http://movies.msn.com/movies/canneso6/dispatch8.

Bennett, Ray. "Requiem for Billy the Kid." TheHollywoodReporter.com. **May 26, 2006. (Demonstration of hoax damage to history)**

Carter, Julie. "The cowboys are back in town, film in six months." jcarter@tulerosa.net. **June 9, 2006. (Describes plans for more programs)**

Valdez, Jannay. "Digging Up the Truth About Billy." *RuidosoNews.com.* http://ruidosonews.com/apps/pbcs.dll./article?AID=/2006069/OPINION03/6060903 51/101 **June 9, 2006.**

Dodder, Joanna. "Back at Rest: Bones of Billy the Kid return to Prescott." *The Daily Courier.* **July 9, 2006.**

http://prescottdailycourier.com/print.asp?ArticleID=40353&Section ID=1&SubSectionID=1

No Author. AP. "Prescott, Ariz. - Prosecutors won't seek charges against two men who exhumed the remains of a man who claimed to be the outlaw Billy the Kid." AOL News. **October 23, 2006.**

_____. AP. "Billy the Kid Case Dropped." *Albuquerque Journal.* Metro. D3. **October 24, 2006.**

_____. AP. "Men Who Exhumed Billy the Kid Won't Be Charged." **October 24, 2006.** *New York Sun.* http://www.nysun.com/article/42176. **(Claims Sullivan and Sederwall did Arizona exhumation, have Miller DNA, and sent to Orchid for matchings to bench DNA)**

_____. AP. "Arizona: No Charges Sought for Exhuming Remains." *New York Times.* A-26. **October 24, 2006.** http://www.nytimes.com/2006/10/24/us/24brfs-002.html?r=1&oref=slogin. **(Cover-up of illegal John Miller/William Hudspeth exhumations)**

Martínez, Tony and Alison. "Better Days Ahead for New Mexico Highlands University?" *The Hispanic Outlook in Higher Education.* **December 4, 2006.**

Turk, David S. "Billy the Kid and the U.S. Marshals Service." *Wild West.* **February, 2007.** Volume 19. Number 5. Pages 34 – 41. **(Turk's expurgated "U.S. Marshals Service and Billy the Kid")**

Jason Strykowski. "A Tale of Two Governors … And one Kid." *True West.* **May, 2007.** Vol. 54. Issue 5. Page 64.

No Author. AP. "Billy the Kid Exhumation a Possibility." *Roswell Daily Record.* **May 2, 2007. From Stephenville, Texas AP on "Brushy Bill" exhumation attempt; Sederwall claims has John Miller's DNA)**

Carter, Julie. "Brushy Bill targeted for DNA testing; Billy the Kid workbench goes on display." *Ruidoso News.* **May 3, 2007.**

_____. AP. "Manhunt for Real Billy the Kid Goes On: Deputy hopes DNA will finally reveal outlaw's true identity." *Albuquerque Journal.* **May 4, 2007.** B3.

Zorosec, Thomas. "DNA could solve mystery of Billy the Kid." Chron.com - Houston Chronicle. **May 5, 2007. (From Hamilton, Texas; "Brushy Bill" exhumation attempt)**

Carter, Julie. AP. "Texas town denies request to exhume Billy the Kid claimant." *Houston Chronicle.* **May 11, 2007.**

_____. "Evidence Hidden in Spector Trial." BBC Internet News. May 24, 2007. **(Dr. Henry Lee alleged as destroying evidence)**

_____. AP. "Famed experts credibility takes a hit at Spector trial." CNN.com law center. **May 25, 2007. (Dr. Henry Lee allegedly destroyed evidence)**

Stallings, Dianne. "Billy the Kid case straps county for insurance." *RuidosoNews.com.* **August 13, 2008.**

Carter, Julie. "Lincoln County deputies resign commissions for Kid case." *Ruidosonews.com.* **August 16, 2007. (Start of ploy calling Case 2003-274 a "hobby")**

Romo, Rene. "Seeking the Kid, Minus Badges. Deputies Resign to Hunt for Billy." *Albuquerque Journal.* **August 18, 2007.** No. 230. pp. 1-2.

Concerned Citizens of Lincoln County. "Should Lincoln County Have Grave Concerns Over A Person Like Steve Sederwall Running for Sheriff? *Lincoln County News.* **October 16, 2008.** Page 6.

Miller, Jay. "Kid's Pardon a Publicity Stunt." "Inside the Capitol" syndicated column "Inside the Capitol" and blog, insidethecapitol.blogspot.com. **June 23, 2010.**

Stinnett, Scot. "Billy the Kid historian says pardon all part of the hoax." *De Baca County News.* Pages 3, 9. **June 24, 2010. (Reprint of my Jay Miller article without commentary)**

No Author. "Billy the Kid 'to be pardoned.' " *Press Trust of India* (*Hindustan Times*) and Pakistan *Daily Express.* **July 11, 2010. (Pardon for "Brushy Bill")**

Romo, Rene. "Gov. Weighs Pardon for Billy the Kid." *Albuquerque Journal. Saturday,* No. 205. Front page, and A6. **July 24, 2010.**

Licón, Adriana Gómez. "Pardon form New Mexico governor unlikely for Billy the Kid." *El Paso Times.* **July 29, 2010.**

Massey, Barry. Associated Press. Santa Fe. "Billy the Kid To Be Pardoned, 130 Years Later? Lawman's Grandchildren Outraged; 'Would You Issue A Pardon For Someone Who Made His Living As A Thief?' National, international, and internet publications. **July 30, 2010.**

Gardner, David. Los Angeles. "Pat Garrett's family plan showdown over plans to finally pardon Billy the Kid." London's *Daily Mail Online.* **July 31, 2010.**

Boardman, Mark. "The Lunacy of Billy the Kid." *True West.* **August, 2010.** Volume 57. Issue 8. Pages 42-47. **(Defamatory article about me)**

Massey, Barry. Associated Press. Santa Fe. "NM gov meets with lawman Pat Garrett's descendants." **August 4, 2010.** www.wthr.com/global/story.asp?s=12926188.

Vaughn, Chris. "Texas Town seeks New Mexico pardon for Billy the Kid." *Fort Worth Star-Telegram.* **August 14, 2010. (Bid for "Brushy Bill" Roberts pardon.)**

Lacey, Marc. "Old West Showdown Is Revived. *New York Times.* **August 15, 2010. (Richardson shape-shifted to "amateur historian.")**

No Author. "A Tale of Two Billys." *New English Review: The Iconoclast.* (Internet). **August 15, 2010.**

Gordon, Bea. "Examining Legend: The Pardoning of Billy the Kid.. New Mexico Gov. Bill Richardson's talking about exonerating the state's most famous outlaw. But at what cost?" www.newwest.net/topic/article/29850/C37/L37/ **August 17, 2010.**

Massey, Barry. Associated Press. Santa Fe. " 'Billy the Kid' pardon effort draws Wild West showdown." Wilkes-Barre, Pennsylvania. *The Times Leader.* **August 21, 2010. (Introduction of William N. Wallace and Indiana Historical Society opposition. In starpress.com of east central Indiana as "Should Billy the Kid Be Pardoned?")**

Miller, Jay. "When is a promise not a promise?" *Inside the Capitol.* **August 30, 2010.** (Sides, Hampton. "Not-So-Charming Billy." *NY Times Opinion Section Op-Ed Contributor.* September 6, 2010.

Richardson, Bill. "Governor Bill Richardson to Consider Billy the Kid Pardon Petition." Press release. **December 16, 2010. (Floating the Randi McGinn petition)**

Martinez, Edecio. "Billy the Kid to be Pardoned 130 Years Later." CBSNEWS.com. **December 27, 2010.**

Guarino, Mark. "Outgoing New Mexico Gov. Bill Richardson is considering a pardon for celebrated outlaw Billy the Kid. An informal e-mail poll shows support. But time is running out." Associated Press. **December 29, 2010.**

Levy, Glen. "Will Billy the Kid Be Pardoned? Governor Has Until Friday." TIME NewsFeed.com. **December 29, 2010.**

Richardson, Bill. "Governor Richardson to Announce his decision on Billy the Kid Pardon Request Tomorrow." Press release. **December 30, 2010.**

Burke, Kelly David. "Billy the Kid Pardon?" FoxNews.com. **December 30, 2010.**

Hopper, Jessica. "Gov. Bill Richardson: 'I've Decided Not to Pardon Billy the Kid.' " ABCNEWS.com. **December 31, 2010.**

Rojas, Rick. "No Pardon for Billy the Kid. New Mexico Gov. Bill Richardson says, 'The Romanticism appealed to me ... but the facts and evidence did not support it." *Los Angeles Times.* **December 31, 2010.**

Watson, Kathryn. "Alas, no pardon for Billy the Kid: New Mexico's Richardson says close call." washingtontimes.com. **December 31, 2010.**

No Author. "Richardson Declines to Pardon Outlaw Billy the Kid." FoxNews.com. **December 31, 2010.**

Lacey, Marc. "For 2nd Time in 131 Years, Billy the Kid is Denied Pardon." *New York Times.* Page A10. **January 1, 2011.**

Todd, Jeff. "Trial seeks truth in Billy the Kid case." KRQE. **February 17, 2011.**

Romo, Rene. "Fight Won, Questions Remain: Billy the Kid DNA Report Released." *Albuquerque Journal.* Front Page and Page B1. **April 29, 2012.**

Sandlin, Scott. "Billy the Kid case costs taxpayers nearly $200K: Billy the Kid lives on in battle of public records." *Albuquerque Journal.* Front Page, Page A2, Page A8. No. 162. **June 11, 2013. (Fakes blood on carpenter's bench)**

Cherry, Doris. "Modern Billy the Kid 'Cases' Cost Public Plenty: County Shells Out Bucks for Failing to Release Information." *Lincoln County News.* **June 27, 2013.** Volume 109. Number 6. Front Page and Pages 7-8. **(Based on my June 18, 2013 letter to the Lincoln County Commissioners)**

Stallings, Dianne. "Former Lincoln County sheriff dies in Texas: Tom Sullivan died Saturday in Texas." **October 22, 2013.** ruidosonews.com.

"BILLY THE KID CASE" LEGAL DOCUMENTS (BY LOCATION)

CAPITAN, NEW MEXICO
(FIRST ANNOUNCEMENT OF CASE NO. 2003-274)

Sederwall, Steve, "Mayor's Report, **May 5, 2003**." *Village of Capitan: Capitan Village Hall News.* Capitan, New Mexico. **(Announces filed Case 2003-274)**

ALBUQUERQUE, NEW MEXICO
(OPPOSITION OF THE OMI TO EXHUMATIONS)

Zumwalt, Ross E. "Affidavit of Ross E. Zumwalt, MD. In the Matter of Catherine Antrim. Case No. MS 2003-11 Sixth Judicial Court, County of Grant, State of New Mexico. **January 9, 2004. (Exhumation refused based on invalid DNA)**

Komar, Debra. "Affidavit of Debra Komar, PhD. In the Matter of Catherine Antrim. Case No. MS 2003-11 Sixth Judicial Court, County of Grant, State of New Mexico. **January 9, 2004. (Exhumation refused based on invalid DNA)**

Snead, William E. Attorney for Office of Medical Investigator." "In the Matter of Catherine Antrim: Response of Office of Medical Investigator to Petition to Exhume Remains of Catherine Antrim." Case No. MS 2003-11. Sixth Judicial Court, Grant County. **January 13, 2004. (Opposition of OMI to exhumation)**

Komar, Debra. "Deposition of Debra Komar, Ph.D. In the Matter of Catherine Antrim. Case No. MS 2003-11." Sixth Judicial Court, County of Grant, State of New Mexico. Taken by Adam S. Baker, Attorney for Town of Silver City. Signed: Debra Komar, Ph.D. **January 20, 2004. (Exhumation refused based on invalid DNA in Billy the Kid's and mother's graves)**

LINCOLN COUNTY, NEW MEXICO
(LINCOLN COUNTY SHERIFF'S DEPARTMENT
CASE NO. 2003-274, "BILLY THE KID CASE")

Virden, R.E. Lincoln County Undersheriff report. "I participated in the investigative reconstruction ..." **April 28, 2003. (Participation in Case # 2003-274.)**

Sullivan, Tom. Lincoln County Sheriff. "Lincoln County Sheriff's Department is currently conducting an investigation ..." Letter to Charles Ryan, Director Arizona Department of Corrections. **April 30, 2003. (Describes Garrett as murderer and planned exhumations of John Miller and "Brushy Bill" Roberts)**

_____. "Denial Letter." Pre-printed form to my attorney, Randall M. Harris. **October 8, 2003. (Open records denial for the Probable Cause Statement using exception of ongoing law enforcement investigation.)**

Sullivan, Tom. Sheriff, Lincoln County Sheriff's Office, and Steven M. Sederwall. Deputy Sheriff, Lincoln County Sheriff's Office. "Lincoln County Sheriff's Office, Lincoln County, New Mexico, Case: William H. Bonney, a.k.a. William Antrim, a.k.a. The Kid, a.k.a. Billy the Kid: An Investigation into the events of April 28,

1881 through July 14, 1881 – seventy-seven days of doubt." **No Date. (Rejected Probable Cause Statement for Case No. 2003-274. In Lincoln County Sheriff's Department case file for 2003-274.)**

_____. "Lincoln County Sheriff's Department Case #2003-274 Probable Cause Statement." Filed in Lincoln County Sheriff's Department. Carrizozo, New Mexico. **December 31, 2003. (Became publicly available as "Plaintiff Exhibit 1 in Petitioner's Attorney Sherry Tippett's Silver City "Brief in Chief in Support of the Exhumation of Catherine Antrim." Case No. MS 03-011." Sixth Judicial Court, County of Grant, State of New Mexico." January 5, 2004)**

Overton, Homer D. aka Homer D. Kinsworthy. "Affidavit for Lincoln County Sheriff's Department Case #2003-274 Probable Cause Statement." **December 22, 2003. (Fake swearing that Garrett's widow –dead in 1936 - told him in 1940 that Garrett did not kill the Kid. Became publicly available as "Plaintiff Exhibit 1 in Petitioner's Attorney Sherry Tippett's Silver City "Brief in Chief in Support of the Exhumation of Catherine Antrim." Case No. MS 03-011." Sixth Judicial Court, County of Grant, State of New Mexico." January 5, 2004)**

No Author. "Contact List, William H. Bonney Case # 2003-274, Lincoln County Sheriff's Office & Investigators." No Date. **Probably 2003. (In Lincoln County Sheriff's Department Case file for 2003-274)**

Virden, Rick, Lincoln County Sheriff. "Deputy Sheriff Commission [Card] to Tom Sullivan." **January 1, 2005.**

_____. "Deputy Sheriff Commission [Card] to Steven Sederwall." **February 25, 2005.**

Sederwall, Steven M., Lincoln County Sheriff's Deputy Investigator. "Lincoln County Sheriff's Department Supplemental Report, Case #2003-274. Subject: Exhumation of John Miller. Location: Arizona Pioneers' Cemetery, Prescott, Arizona." **May 19, 2005. (Arizona exhumations John Miller and William Hudspeth)**

Virden, R.E. Lincoln County Sheriff. letter to Jay Miller. "We are interested in the truth surrounding Billy the Kid and are continuing the investigation ..." **November 28, 2005. (Virden confirms continuing Billy the Kid case and deputizing Sullivan and Sederwall for it.)**

Virden, R.E. Lincoln County Sheriff. To Hamilton, Texas, Mayor Roy Ramsey [sic]. "This letter will inform you that Tom Sullivan and Steve Sederwall are both commissioned deputies ..." **No date, but around May 2007. (Virden's attempt to exhume "Brushy" with Sullivan and Sederwall as the Deputies)**

Lee, Henry, Dr. Letter to Jay Miller. "In response to your letter dated March 27, 2006 ..." **May 1, 2006. (Lee confirms sending his carpenter's bench and floorboard report to Lincoln County Sheriff's Department.)**

"Jordan, Wilma" aka Gale Cooper. To David Turk, Historian U.S. Marshals Service. "Looking for the truth is good ..." **June 15, 2006. (Attempt to get the Turk's "U.S. Marshal's Service and Billy the Kid " pamphlet for Case 2003-274.)**

Turk, David. Historian U.S. Marshals Service. To "Wilma Jordan." "Thank you for your thoughtful and thorough letter ..." **July 3, 2006. (Tracked "Wilma's" address; refuses to give his "U.S. Marshal's Service and Billy the Kid "pamphlet.)**

Sederwall, Steve. "billythekidcase.com." Sederwall's pay for view website with Case 2003-274 records. **October, 2010. (Selling public records online.**

SILVER CITY, NEW MEXICO
(EXHUMATION ATTEMPT ON CATHERINE ANTRIM)

Tippett, Sherry. Attorney. To Richard Gay, Assistant to the Chief of Staff, Governor Richardson's Office. "Memorandum, RE: Exhumation of Catherine Antrim." **July 11, 2003. (Tippett's lie of OMI backing exhumation.)**

Tippett, Sherry. Attorney for Petitioners Sullivan, Sederwall, and Graves. "In the Matter of Catherine Antrim: Petition to Exhume Remains." Case No. MS 03-011. Sixth Judicial Court, County of Grant, State of New Mexico. **October 3, 2003.** **(Start of exhumation attempts; perjury about permission from OMI)**

Kennedy, Paul J., Adam S. Baker, Thomas F. Stewart, Robert L. Scavron, Attorneys for Mayor Terry Fortenberry on Behalf of the Town of Silver City. "In the Matter of Catherine Antrim: Motion to Intervene." Case No. MS 03-011. Sixth Judicial Court, County of Grant, State of New Mexico. **October 31, 2003. (Start of my exhumation opposition)**

_____. "In the Matter of Catherine Antrim: Response in Opposition to the Petition to Exhume Remains." Case No. MS 03-011. Sixth Judicial Court, County of Grant, State of New Mexico. **October 31, 2003.**

Tippett, Sherry J. Attorney for Petitioners. "State of New Mexico, County of Grant, Sixth Judicial District Court, In the Matter of Catherine Antrim, No. MS. 2003-11. Petitioner's Response in Opposition to the Town of Silver City's Motion to Intervene." (Unfiled) **No Date.**

Baker, Adam S. Attorneys for Mayor Terry Fortenberry on Behalf of Silver City. "In the Matter of Catherine Antrim: Request for Hearing." Case No. MS 03-011. Sixth Judicial Court, County of Grant, State of New Mexico. **November 4, 2003.**

Foy, Jim, District Judge. "In the Matter of Catherine Antrim: Notice of Recusal." Case No. MS 03-011. Sixth Judicial Court, County of Grant, State of New Mexico. **November 14, 2003. (Honest Judge Foy removes himself)**

Miranda, Velia C., District Court Clerk. "In the Matter of Catherine Antrim: Notice of Assignment/Designation of District Judge H.R. Quintero." Case No. MS 03-011. Sixth Judicial Court, County of Grant, State of New Mexico. **November 14, 2003. (Entry of Richardson appointee judge)**

Tippett, Sherry J. Attorney for Petitioners Sullivan, Sederwall and Graves. "In the Matter of Catherine Antrim: Petitioner's Response in Opposition to the Town of Silver City's Motion to Intervene." No. MS. 2003-11. State of New Mexico, County of Grant, Sixth Judicial District Court. (Unfiled) **No Date.**

Robins, Bill III and David Sandoval, Attorneys for Billy the Kid. "In the Matter of Catherine Antrim: Billy the Kid's Unopposed Motion for Intervention and Request for Expedited Disposition." Case No. MS 2003-11. Sixth Judicial Court, County of Grant, State of New Mexico. **November 26, 2003. (First petition with dead Billy the Kid as co-Petitioner to Sullivan, Sederwall, and Graves.)**

Amos-Staats, Joani. "In the Matter of Catherine Antrim: Joani Amos-Staats' [sic] Response in Opposition to the Petition to Exhume." Case No. MS 2003-11. Sixth Judicial Court, County of Grant, State of New Mexico. **December 5, 2003. (Adjacent grave opposition based on disturbing remains)**

_____. "In the Matter of Catherine Antrim: Joani Amos-Staats' [sic] Motion to Intervene and Request for Expedited Hearing." Case No. MS 2003-11. Sixth Judicial Court, County of Grant, State of New Mexico. **December 8, 2003.**

_____. "In the Matter of Catherine Antrim: Joani Amos-Staats' [sic] Response in Opposition to the Petition to Exhume Remains." Case No. MS 2003-11. Sixth Judicial Court, County of Grant, State of New Mexico. **December 8, 2003.**

Kennedy, Paul J., Adam S. Baker, Thomas F. Stewart, Robert L. Scavron, Attorneys for Mayor Terry Fortenberry on Behalf of the Town of Silver City. "In the Matter of Catherine Antrim: Reply in Support of the Town of Silver City's Motion to Intervene." Case No. MS 2003-11. Sixth Judicial Court, County of Grant, State of New Mexico. **December 8, 2003. (Justifying need to protect Antrim grave)**

Tippett, Sherry J. Attorney for Petitioners Sullivan, Sederwall and Graves. "In the Matter of Catherine Antrim: Petitioners Response in Opposition to the Town of Silver City's Motion to Intervene." Case No. MS 2003-11. Sixth Judicial Court, County of Grant, State of New Mexico. **December 8, 2003. (Tippett lies by saying town has no "legal interest" to intervene)**

Quintero, H.R. District Judge. "In the Matter of Catherine Antrim: Order." Case No. MS 03-011. Sixth Judicial Court, County of Grant, State of New Mexico. **December 9, 2003. (Rescheduling hearing from January 6, 2004 to January 27, 2004.)**

Baker, Adam S. Attorneys for Mayor Terry Fortenberry on Behalf of the Town of Silver City. "In the Matter of Catherine Antrim: Intervenor Town of Silver City's Brief on Petition to Exhume." Case No. MS 03-011. Sixth Judicial Court, County of Grant, State of New Mexico. **January 5, 2004. (Arguing 1962 precedent case of Lois Telfer blocking exhumation)**

Tippett, Sherry J. Attorney. To Mayor Steve Sederwall, Sheriff Tom Sullivan, Sheriff Gary Graves. "In the Matter of Catherine Antrim: Petitioners Brief in Chief in Support of Exhumation." Case No. MS 2003-11. Sixth Judicial Court, County of Grant, State of New Mexico. **January 5, 2004. (Using Probable Cause Statement and Homer Overton Affidavit as Plaintiff exhibits)**

Robins, Bill III and David Sandoval. Attorneys for Billy the Kid. "In the Matter of Catherine Antrim: Billy the Kid's Pre-Hearing Brief." Case No. MS 2003-11. Sixth Judicial Court, Grant County. **January 5, 2004. (Linking exhumation and pardon with "Brushy Bill" Roberts as Billy – CRACKED THE HOAX as a "Brushy Bill" scam by using "Brushy's" dark night for July 14, 1881)**

Tippett, Sherry. Attorney for law enforcement Petitioners Tom Sullivan, Steve Sederwall, Gary Graves. "In the Matter of Catherine Antrim: Petitioner's [sic] Brief in Chief in Support of Exhumation." Case No. MS 2003-11. Sixth Judicial Court, Grant County. **January 5, 2004.**

Amos-Staats, Joani. "In the Matter of Catherine Antrim: Intervenor Joani Amos-Staats' [sic] Brief on Petition to Exhume." Case No. MS 2003-11. Sixth Judicial Court, County of Grant, State of New Mexico. **January 6, 2004.**

Kennedy, Paul J., Adam S. Baker, Thomas F. Stewart, Robert L. Scavron, Attorneys for Mayor Terry Fortenberry on Behalf of the Town of Silver City. "In the Matter of Catherine Antrim: Response in Opposition to Petitioners' Brief in Chief." Case No. MS 2003-11. Sixth Judicial Court, County of Grant, State of New Mexico. **January 21, 2004.**

_____. "In the Matter of Catherine Antrim: Silver City's Response in Opposition to Petitioners' Motion for Continuance." Case No. MS 2003-11. Sixth Judicial Court, County of Grant, State of New Mexico. **January 21, 2004.**

Tippett, Sherry J. Attorney. To Mayor Steve Sederwall, Sheriff Tom Sullivan, Sheriff Gary Graves. "Attached is a copy of Judge Quintero's Order of December 9, 2003, ruling on our Hearing ..." **December 17, 2003. (States that they will win on January 27, 2004; urges completing the Probable Cause Statement)**

Quintero, H.R. District Judge, Division 1. "Order of Continuance. In the Matter of Catherine Antrim. Case No. MS 03-011." Filed **January 23, 2004.** Sixth Judicial Court, County of Grant, State of New Mexico. Filed January 23, 2004. **(Tippett sanctioned to pay airfare for witness, Frederick Nolan for changing the hearing date on short notice)**

Robins, Bill III and David Sandoval. Attorneys for Billy the Kid. "In the Matter of Catherine Antrim: Billy the Kid's Brief on the Question of Ripeness." Case No. MS 2003-11. Sixth Judicial Court, Grant County. **February 24, 2004. (Setting up Quintero's sending the exhumation to Fort Sumner)**

Acúna, Mark Anthony and Sherry J. Tippett. Attorneys for Petitioners Sullivan, Sederwall and Graves. "In the Matter of Catherine Antrim: Petitioners' Brief on the Question of Ripeness." Case No. MS 2003-11. Sixth Judicial Court, Grant County. **February 24, 2004.**

Baker, Adam S. and Thomas F. Stewart, Robert L. Scavron, Attorneys for Silver City and Joani Amos-Staats. "In the Matter of Catherine Antrim: Silver City's and Joani Amos-Staats' [sic] Joint Motion to Dismiss on Grounds of Ripeness." Case No. MS 2003-11. Sixth Judicial Court, County of Grant, State of New Mexico. **February 24, 2004.**

Acúna, Mark Anthony. Attorney for Petitioners Sullivan, Sederwall and Graves. "In the Matter of Catherine Antrim: Entry of Appearance." Case No. MS 03-011. Sixth Judicial Court, County of Grant, State of New Mexico. **February 26, 2004.** **(Replacing Tippett for law enforcement Petitioners)**

Robins, Bill III and David Sandoval. Attorneys for Billy the Kid. "In the Matter of Catherine Antrim: Response to Motion to Dismiss." Case No. MS 2003-11. Sixth Judicial Court, Grant County. **March 10, 2004.**

Quintero, Henry R. "In the Matter of Catherine Antrim: Decision and Order." Case No. MS 03-011." Sixth Judicial Court, County of Grant, State of New Mexico. **April 2, 2004. (Stipulation that case is not ripe, and requires DNA from Fort Sumner Billy the Kid grave first before trying to exhume Catherine Antrim)**

Fortenberry, Terry D, Mayor; Thomas A. Nupp Councilor District 2; Steve May, Councilor District 4; Gary Clauss, Councilor District 3; Judy Ward, Councilor District 1; Alex Brown, Town Manager; Cissy McAndrew, Executive Director Chamber of Commerce; Frank Milan, Director Silver City Mainstreet Project; Susan Berry, Director Silver City Museum. "Open Letter to Governor Bill Richardson." **June 21, 2004. (Request to cease "Billy the Kid Case" exhumations)**

Kemper, Lisa. Kennedy Han, PC. Controller, (via fax). To Gale Cooper. "*In the Matter of Catherine Antrim, 6th Judicial Dist. Ct. Case No. MS 2003-001,* 'This is to confirm our receipt of payment ...'" Baker, Adam. Confirmation of payment of Attorney Sherry Tippett's Judge Henry Quintero sanction by Attorney Bill Robins III. **September 1, 2004.** (See "Order of Continuance. In the Matter of Catherine Antrim. Case No. MS 03-011.") Filed January 23, 2004. Sixth Judicial Court, County of Grant, State of New Mexico. Signed: H.R. Quintero, District Judge, Division 1." April 28, 2004, **(Court sanctions Tippett, and secret donor to case, Bill Robins III pays her sanction.)**

FORT SUMNER, NEW MEXICO
(EXHUMATION ATTEMPT ON WILLIAM H. BONNEY)

De Baca County Commissioners Special Meeting." Minutes. (Powhatan Carter III, Chairman; Joe Steele; Tommy Roybal; Nancy Sparks, County Clerk. To whom it may concern. "The De Baca County Commissioners are in full support of Village of Fort Sumner's stand against exhuming the body of Billy the Kid." **September 25, 2003. (Voted against exhumation of Billy the Kid)**

Robins, Bill III and David Sandoval, Mark Acuña, Attorneys for Co-Petitioner Billy the Kid and Sheriff-Petitioners. "In the Matter of William H. Bonney, aka 'Billy the Kid': Petition for the Exhumation of Billy the Kid's Remains." Case No. CV-04-00005. Tenth Judicial District, County of De Baca, State of New Mexico. **February 26, 2004. (Robins joins Acuña to exhume the Kid)**

Robins, Bill III and David Sandoval, Attorneys for Co-Petitioner Billy the Kid. "In the Matter of William H. Bonney, aka 'Billy the Kid': Notice of Excusal." Case No. CV-2004 [sic]-00005. Tenth Judicial District, County of De Baca, State of New Mexico. **March 5, 2004. (Petitioners' removal of honest Judge Ricky Purcell from hearing the case.)**

Jimenez Maes, Petra, Chief Justice. "In the Matter of William H. Bonney, aka 'Billy the Kid': Order Designating Judge." Case No. CV-2004-00005. Tenth Judicial District, County of De Baca, State of New Mexico. **April 1, 2004. (Richardson's corrupt judge appointee, Ted Hartley, is appointed to case)**

Baker, Adam S. and Herb Marsh, Jr., Attorneys for the Village of Fort Sumner. "In the Matter of William H. Bonney, aka 'Billy the Kid': Village of Fort Sumner's Unopposed Motion to Intervene." Case No. CV-04-00005. Tenth Judicial District, County of De Baca, State of New Mexico. **April 12, 2004.**

_____. "In the Matter of William H. Bonney, aka 'Billy the Kid': Response in Opposition to the Petitioners for the Exhumation of Billy the Kid's Remains. In the Matter of William H. Bonney, aka 'Billy the Kid.' " Case No. CV-04-00005. Tenth Judicial District, County of De Baca, State of New Mexico. **April 12, 2004.**

Hartley, Teddy L. "In the Matter of William H. Bonney, aka 'Billy the Kid': Order." Case No. CV-04-00005. Tenth Judicial District, County of De Baca, State of New Mexico. **April 20, 2004. (Intervention of Village of Fort Sumner granted)**

Baker, Adam S. and Herb Marsh, Jr., Attorneys for the Village of Fort Sumner. "In the Matter of William H. Bonney, aka 'Billy the Kid': Response in Opposition to the Petition for the Exhumation of Billy the Kid's Remains." Case No. CV-04-00005. Tenth Judicial District, County of De Baca, State of New Mexico. **May 6, 2004.**

_____. "In the Matter of William H. Bonney, aka 'Billy the Kid': Village of Fort Sumner's Motion For Proof of Attorneys' Authority To Act On Behalf Of William H. Bonney." Case No. CV-04-00005. Tenth Judicial District, County of De Baca, State of New Mexico. **June 24, 2004. (Confronting Attorney Bill Robins III's fakery of representing Billy the Kid based on dead Billy not being real so he cannot have a lawyer)**

_____. "In the Matter of William H. Bonney, aka 'Billy the Kid': Village of Fort Sumner's Motion to Dismiss Against Petitioners Sullivan, Sederwall, and Graves for Lack of Standing." Case No. CV-04-00005. Tenth Judicial District, County of De Baca, State of New Mexico. **June 24, 2004. (Invalid murder case because Pat Garrett properly killed Billy the Kid)**

Hartley, Teddy L. District Judge. "Notice of Hearing. "In the Matter of William H. Bonney, aka 'Billy the Kid': Notice of Hearing." Case No. CV-04-00005. Tenth Judicial District, County of De Baca, State of New Mexico. **July 6, 2004. (Hearing set for September 27, 2004)**

Acuña, Mark Anthony, Attorney for the Petitioners Sullivan, Sederwall and Graves. "In the Matter of William H. Bonney, aka 'Billy the Kid': Petitioner's Response to the Village of Ft. Sumner's Motion to Dismiss." Case No. CV-04-00005." Tenth Judicial District, State of New Mexico, County of De Baca. **July 29, 2004.(Acuña argues Sheriff-petitioners' Sullivan, Graves, and Sederwall's standing based on law enforcement as Sheriffs and Deputy Sheriff; later Sullivan and Sederwall would lie that they had done the case as private hobbyists to avoid the open records act for public officials to hide their fake DNA documents)**

Robins, Bill III and David Sandoval; Attorneys for the Billy the Kid; and Adam S. Baker and Herb Marsh, Jr., Attorneys for the Village of Fort Sumner. "In the Matter of William H. Bonney, aka 'Billy the Kid': Stipulation of Dismissal." Case No. CV-04-00005. Tenth Judicial District, County of De Baca, State of New Mexico. **August 23, 2004. (Fake dead Billy the Kid petition dismissed with prejudice)**

"In the Matter of De Baca County Sheriff Gary Graves. Petition for Order Allowing Recall Vote." Case No. CV-04-00019. Tenth Judicial District Court, State of New Mexico, County of De Baca. **September 13, 2004. (Recall starts against Sheriff Gary Graves, separate from the exhumation case.)**

Acuña, Mark Anthony and Adam S. Baker, Attorneys for Petitioners Graves, Sullivan and Sederwall; and the Village of Fort Sumner. "In the Matter of William H. Bonney, aka 'Billy the Kid': Stipulation of Dismissal With Prejudice." Case No. CV-04-00005. Tenth Judicial District, County of De Baca, State of New Mexico. **September 24, 2004. (Petitioners withdraw with prejudice at Fort Sumner. Definitive victory against Billy the Kid exhumation.)**

ARIZONA: YAVAPAI (PRESCOTT) AND MARICOPA COUNTIES (EXHUMATIONS OF JOHN MILLER AND WILLIAM HUDSPETH)

Sederwall, Steven M., Lincoln County Sheriff's Deputy Investigator. "Lincoln County Sheriff's Department Supplemental Report, Case #2003-274. Subject: Exhumation of John Miller. Location: Arizona Pioneers' Cemetery, Prescott, Arizona." **May 19, 2005. (Arizona exhumations John Miller and William Hudspeth)**

Cahall, Anna, Detective Prescott Police Department. "CASE REPORT 0600012767." **April 5, 2006. (Concerning the John Miller exhumation)**

Tunnell, Dale. To Jeanine Dike. "Subject: RE: Disinterment of Wm Bonney." **May 3, 2005.**

Dike, Jeanine. To Dale Tunnell. "Subject: Disinterment of Wm Bonney." **May 3, 2005.**

_____. To Dale Sams. "Subject: FW: Disinterment Wm Bonney." **May 3, 2005.**

_____. To Dale Sams. "Subject: FW: Disinterment Wm Bonney." **May 4, 2005.**

Sams, Dale. To George Thompson. "Subject: Disinterment." **May 4, 2005. (Confirms Sams has no idea where the Miller grave is located.)**

Sederwall, Steven M., Lincoln County Sheriff's Deputy Investigator. "Lincoln County Sheriff's Department Supplemental Report, Case #2003-274. Subject: Exhumation of John Miller. Location: Arizona Pioneers' Cemetery, Prescott, Arizona." **May 19, 2005. (Arizona exhumations John Miller and William Hudspeth)**

Fulginiti, Laura C. Ph.D., D-ABFA. Forensic Anthropologist. To Dale L. Tunnell, Ph.D. "RE: Exhumation, Pioneer Home Cemetery, Prescott, Arizona." **June 2, 2005. (Report of the Miller-Hudspeth exhumations revealing fake hoaxer claims of buck teeth and bullet wound to left scapula of John Miller.)**

Sederwall, Steven. To Misty Rodarte. "Subject: Billy the Kid." **July 6, 2005.**

Winter, Anne. "To: Tim Nelson; Alan Stephens. Subject: Pioneer Home, Grave, Billy the Kid and DNA." **August 18, 2005. (Has attachment of Pioneers' Home Supervisor Gary Olson's cover-up letter to her and implied internal cover-up. Also states that Sullivan paid for the exhumation.)**

_____. "To: Tim Nelson; Alan Stephens. Subject: Billy the Kid." **September 8, 2005. ("80% DNA match" with Miller claimed)**

Olson, Gary. Superintendent Arizona Pioneers' Home. To David Snell. "You recently asked the Arizona Pioneers' Home if a body in its cemetery had been exhumed ..." **October 3, 2005. (Confirms original cover-up of John Miller exhumation.)**

Winter, Anne. "To Gary Olson. Subject: RE: the kid." **October 17, 2005. (Requesting any DNA results yet to him.)**

Olson, Gary. "To Anne Winter. Subject: RE: the kid." **October 17, 2005. (Reporting on no DNA results yet to him.)**

Winter, Anne. "To: Jeanine L'Ecuyer. Subject: FW: the kid." **October 17, 2005. (Reporting on no DNA results yet to Olson.)**

Olson, Gary. "To: Anne Winter. Subject: FW: re. John Miller." **October 20, 2005. (Cover-up `planned for Romo. "I thought you and the Governor may want to know about this request.")**

Winter, Anne. "To: Tim Nelson; Alan Stephens. Subject: FW: re. John Miller. October 20, 2005. (Cover-up plan for Romo presentation: "Remember there was the legal issue that they dug up two bodies.")**

_____. "To: Jeanine L'Ecuyer. Subject: FW: re. John Miller." **October 25, 2005. (Planning cover-up for media requests.)**

Sederwall, Steven. "To: Barbara J. Miller; Steve McGregor; Rick Staub; Misty Rodarte; Emily Smith; Bob Boze Bell. Subject: in the Albuquerque Journal." **November 6, 2005. (Copy Romo article.)**

Olson, Gary. "To Anne Winter, Mark Wilson. Subject: FW: in the Albuquerque Journal." **November 7, 2005. (Copy Romo article.)**

Winter, Anne. "To: Jeanine L'Ecuyer; Tim Nelson; Alan Stephens. Subject: Billy the Kid. **November 7, 2005. (About Gary Olson's cover-up in KPNX interview.)**

Snell, David. To Shiela Polk. Yavapai County Attorney. "I feel it is my duty to report to you that graverobbers are plying their trade ..." **March 11, 2006. (Arizona citizen starting criminal investigation of Miller/Hudspeth exhumations.)**

Jacobson, Marcia. "To Anne Winter, Policy Advisor for Health, Office of the Governor, and Chief Randy Oaks, Prescott Police Department. Re: Disinterment of bodies at Arizona Pioneer's [sic] Home Cemetery." **March 30, 2006. (Attempted cover-up of John Miller and William Hudspeth exhumations.)**

Cahall, Anna, Detective Prescott Police Department. "CASE REPORT 0600012767." **April 5, 2006. (Concerning the John Miller exhumation; interviews with Sullivan, Sederwall, Tunnell)**

Savona, Glenn A. Prescott City Prosecutor. To Shiela Sullivan Polk, Yavapai County Attorney. "Re: Police Department DR# 2006-12767 Arizona Pioneers' Home Cemetery." **April 13, 2006. (Calls exhumations potential felonies)**

Cooper, Gale. To Detective Anna Cahall. Prescott Police Department. "Re: Exhumation of John Miller and adjacent grave for pursuing the New Mexico Billy the Kid Case." **April 13, 2006.**

_____. To Detective Anna Cahall. Prescott Police Department. "Re: Pertinent articles regarding exhumation of John Miller and remains from adjacent grave for alleged promulgation of the New Mexico Billy the Kid Case, a murder investigation." **April 17, 2006.**

_____. To Deputy County Attorney Steve Jaynes and County Attorney Dennis McGrane. (via fax) "Re: Information on the New Mexico Billy the Kid Case pertinent to the Arizona John Miller exhumations." **May 2, 2006.**

Sederwall, Steve. To confidential recipient. "Well we have the governor reaching out to the Arizona to stop this investigation." **May 16, 2006.**

Cooper, Gale. To Attorney Jonell Lucca (via fax). "Re: Case # CA20006020516. Follow-up to our telephone conversation of June 9, 2006, to address the issue of Permit for the exhumations of John Miller and the remains from an adjacent grave for promulgation of the New Mexico Billy the Kid Case, a murder investigation." **June 12, 2006.**

_____. To Attorney Jonell Lucca (via fax). "Re: Case # CA20006020516. Follow-up to my fax of June 12, 2006, to address additional issues pertinent to the exhumations of John Miller and William Hudspeth, done for promulgation of the New Mexico Billy the Kid Case, an alleged murder investigation." July 11, 2006.

Sams, Dale. Arizona Pioneers' Home Administrator. To Gale Cooper. Confirming approximate date of John Miller's birth as 1850. **August 8, 2006.**

Cooper, Gale. To Attorney Jonell Lucca (via fax). "Re: Case # CA20006020516. Follow-up to my fax of July 11, 2006, to address issues pertinent to the promulgators of the New Mexico Billy the Kid Case (which resulted in the exhumations of John Miller and William Hudspeth); with added focus on its alleged forensic experts and co-participants." **August 11, 2006.**

_____. To Attorney Jonell Lucca. "Re: Enclosed reference copy of Freedom of Information Act (FOIA) to Governor Janet Napolitano regarding her possible participation in the Prescott, Arizona exhumations of John Miller and William Hudspeth, and their legal issues related to Maricopa County Prosecutor's Office Case # CA20006020516." **September 22, 2006.**

_____. To Attorney Jonell Lucca. "Re: Information pertaining to Case # CA20006020516 (exhumations of John Miller and William Hudspeth) - American Academy of Forensic Science Ethics and Conduct Complaint against Dr. Henry Lee." **October 2, 2006.**

Lucca, Jonell L. To Dr. Gale Cooper. "This letter is to inform you that the Maricopa County Attorney's Office has declined to file charges ..." **October 17, 2006. (Corrupt claim that the only suspects were Jeanine Dike and Dale Tunnell to shield Sullivan and Sederwall)**

Cooper, Gale. To Attorney Jonell Lucca. "Re: Maricopa County Case # CA20006020516." **October 30, 2006. (Confirmation of getting Lucca's** case termination letter, and asking why she changed suspects. **Never answered.**)

Cooper, Gale. To Detective Anna. Prescott Police Department. "Re: Freedom of Information Act Request for Records of Prescott Police Department Case No. 06-12767. **September 11, 2008.** (**No response**)

HAMILTON, TEXAS
(EXHUMATION ATTEMPT ON "BRUSHY BILL" ROBERTS)

Cooper, Gale. "Billy the Kid Case in a Nutshell." Faxed letter to Hamilton, Texas, Mayor Roy Rumsey. **May 3, 2007.** (**About hoax to dig up "Brushy Bill"**)

Virden, R.E. Lincoln County Sheriff. To Hamilton, Texas, Mayor Roy Ramsey [sic]. "This letter will inform you that Tom Sullivan and Steve Sederwall are both commissioned deputies ..." **No date, but around May 2007.** (**Virden's attempt to exhume "Brushy Bill" Roberts.**)

Cooper, Gale. "RE: Lincoln County Sheriff's Department's 2007 attempt to exhume Oliver "Brushy Bill" Roberts. Faxed letter to Hamilton, Texas, Mayor Roy Rumsey. **September 11, 2008.**

Rumsey, Roy. Hamilton Mayor. "RE: Lincoln County Sheriff's Department's 2007 attempt to exhume Oliver Roberts." Faxed letter to Gale Cooper. **September 12, 2008.** (**Confirmation that the case is closed**)

PAST ATTEMPT TO EXHUME WILLIAM H. BONNEY

"Motion to Intervene. In Re Application of Lois Telfer, Petitioner for the Removal of the Body of William H. Bonney, Deceased, From the Ft. Sumner Cemetery in Which He is Interred for Reinterment in the Lincoln, New Mexico, Cemetery. Case No. 3255." **December 5, 1961.** In the District Court of the Tenth Judicial District Within and For the County of De Baca. Signed: Victor C. Breen and John Humphrey, Jr., Attorneys for Louis A Bowdre. (**Louis Bowdre was the relative of Charles Bowdre whose grave is contiguous to William Bonney's.**)

Breen, Victor C. and John Humphrey, Jr., Attorneys for Louis A Bowdre. "Motion to Intervene. In Re Application of Lois Telfer, Petitioner for the Removal of the Body of William H. Bonney, Deceased, From the Ft. Sumner Cemetery in Which He is Interred for Reinterment in the Lincoln, New Mexico, Cemetery." Case No. 3255. In the District Court of the Tenth Judicial District, County of De Baca. **December 5, 1961.** (**Louis Bowdre was the relative of Charles Bowdre whose grave is contiguous to William Bonney's.**)

Kinsley, E.T. District Judge. "Decree. In Re Application of Lois Telfer, Petitioner for the Removal of the Body of William H. Bonney, Deceased, From the Ft. Sumner Cemetery in Which He is Interred for Reinterment in the Lincoln, New Mexico, Cemetery." Case No. 3255." In the District Court of the Tenth Judicial District Within and For the County of De Baca. **April 6, 1962.** (**Petition for exhumation Billy the Kid denied on basis that his grave could not be located and the search would disturb Bowdre's remains. That precedent was ignored by the current Petitioners and their attorneys.**)

MY OPEN RECORDS REQUESTS (CHRONOLOGICAL)

RECORDS REQUESTS BY JAY MILLER AS MY PROXY

Miller, Jay. To Steve Sederwall, Mayor of Capitan and Deputy Sheriff of Lincoln County. "FOIA/IPRA." **May 13, 2004.**

_____. To Village of Capitan Records Custodian. "I would like to inspect and copy the following documents of Steve Sederwall ..." **May 13, 2004.**

_____. To County Clerk of Lincoln County/Records Custodian, Lincoln County Courthouse. "Re: I would like to inspect the following documents of Tom Sullivan, elected Sheriff of Lincoln County." **May 13, 2004.**

_____. To County Clerk of DeBaca County/Records Custodian. "Freedom of Information Act Request: Inspect and copy records pertaining to Gary Graves, elected sheriff ..." **May 13, 2004.**

Morel, Alan P. Lincoln County Attorney. To Jay Miller. "RE: Freedom of Information Act Request dated May 13, 2004." **May 19, 2004.**

Grassie, Anna Gail. (For Village of Capitan and Mayor Steve Sederwall). To Jay Miller. "Reference: Freedom of Information Request from Jay Miller dated May 13, 2004." **May 25, 2004.**

Miller, Jay. To Michael Cerletti, Secretary, Department Tourism. "RE: FOIA/IPRA on Billy the Kid Case promulgators and Department of Tourism." **May, 28, 2004.**

_____. To Attorney Alan P. Morel. "Re: Response to your letter dated May 19, 2004 on behalf of the County Clerk of Lincoln County and Lincoln County Sheriff Tom Sullivan." **June 1, 2004.**

_____. To Mayor Steve Sederwall. "FOIA/IPRA on Steve Sederwall as Mayor of Capitan and Deputy Sheriff of Lincoln County." **June 1, 2004.**

Morel, Alan P. Lincoln County Attorney. To Jay Miller. "RE: Response to your letter dated May 19, 2004 on behalf of the County Clerk of Lincoln County and Lincoln County Sheriff Tom Sullivan. **June 1, 2004.**

Sederwall, Steven: Mayor. To Jay Miller. "I am in receipt of your letter dated June 1, 2004." **June 3, 2004.**

Morel, Alan P. Lincoln County Attorney. To Jay Miller. "RE: Freedom of Information Act Request June 1, 2004." **June 4, 2004.**

Cerletti, Mike.. To Jay Miller. "Reply to your freedom of information request." **June 7, 2004. (Denied participation of Tourism Department in Billy the Kid Case)**

Miller, Jay. To Lincoln County Attorney Alan Morel. "Copy all documents relevant to David Turk, historian for the U.S. Marshals Service ..." **June 9, 2004.**

_____. To Mayor of Capitan and Deputy Sheriff of Lincoln County Steve Sederwall. "Evade response by claiming that you were being addresses solely in your capacity as Mayor ..." **June 9, 2004.**

_____. To Sheriff Gary Graves and Nancy Sparks, De Baca County Clerk. "Freedom of Information Act Request: I would like to inspect any and all documents relevant to David Turk ..." **June 9, 2004.**

Sederwall, Steven M. To Jay Miller. "This office has no records ..." **June 10, 2004.**

Miller, Jay. To Mayor Steve Sederwall. "FOIA/IPRA on Steve Sederwall as Mayor of Capitan and Deputy Sheriff of Lincoln County." **June 10, 2004.**

_____. To Attorney General Patricia Madrid. "Re: Follow-up on FOIA/IPRA Request to Lincoln County Sheriff Tom Sullivan." **June 14, 2004. (This was stonewalled. No response ever came.)**

Sparks Nancy. (Clerk for Sheriff Gary Graves). To Jay Miller. "Re: FOIA/IPRA request for records of De Baca County Sheriff Gary Graves." **June 14, 2004.**

Miller, Jay. To Mayor of Capitan and Deputy Sheriff of Lincoln County Steve Sederwall. "Thank you for your prompt response to my letter of June 1, 2004 ... " **June 21, 2004.**

_____. To Attorney General Patricia Madrid. RE: Follow-up on FOIA/IPRA Requests to Steve Sederwall, Mayor of Capitan and Deputy Sheriff of Lincoln County." **June 21, 2004.**

_____. To Lincoln County Attorney Alan Morel. "I would like to inspect and copy any and all documents relevant to your client Tom Sullivan, Sheriff of Lincoln County with regard to a statement made by his attorney Sherry Tippett ..." **June 23, 2004.**

_____. To Mayor of Capitan and Deputy Sheriff of Lincoln County Steve Sederwall. "To inspect and copy all records relevant to your attorney, Sherry Tippett's, claims ..." **June 23, 2004.**

_____. To Michael Cerletti, Secretary Tourism. "Thanks for your response ..." **June 23, 2004.**

Lama, Albert J. Assistant Attorney General. To Jay Miller. "Concerning an alleged violation of the Inspection of Public Records Act by the Lincoln County, De Baca County, and Village of Capitan." **June 24, 2004. (This was sent to corrupt Assistant AG Mary Smith, who later covered-up for Sederwall.)**

Miller, Jay. To Attorney General Patricia Madrid. "Re: Follow-up on FOIA/IPRA Requests to Steve Sederwall, Mayor of Capitan and Deputy Sheriff of Lincoln County." **June 21, 2004. (Instead of answering, they closed the case)**

Graves, Gary W. De Baca County Sheriff. To Jay Miller. "I am writing in response to your request ..." **June 22, 2004. (Denies information on David Turk)**

Miller, Jay. To Sheriff Gary Graves. "Freedom of Information Act Request: Inspect and copy all records relevant to your attorney, Sherry Tippett ..." **June 23, 2004.**

_____. To Sheriff Gary Graves and Nancy Sparks. "Re: FOIA/IPRA request for records." **June 25, 2004.**

Graves, Gary W. De Baca County Sheriff. To Jay Miller. "I do not maintain requests for travel reimbursements ..." **June 29, 2004. (His clerk did send records!)**

_____. To Jay Miller. "As per your FOIA/IPRA Request on **June 23, 2004** ..." June 29, 2004. **(Denies records on Attorney Sherry Tippett.)**

_____. To Jay Miller. "I do not maintain or have any records in reference to Sherry Tippett ..." **June 29, 2004.**

Miller, Jay. To Attorney Alan Morel. "Re: Deputizing of Capitan Mayor Steve Sederwall as referenced in your letter dated June 4, 2004 on behalf of Lincoln County Sheriff Tom Sullivan." **July 1, 2004.**

Morel, Alan P. Attorney for Lincoln County. To Jay Miller. "Re: Deputizing of Capitan Mayor Steve Sederwall as referenced in your letter dated June 4, 2004 on behalf of Lincoln County Sheriff Tom Sullivan." **July 1, 2004.**

_____. To Jay Miller. "RE: Freedom of Information Act/Inspection of Public Records Act Request dated June 23, 2004." **July 2, 2004.**

Sparks, Nancy. De Baca County Clerk. "I have sent you everything I have on Sheriff Graves ..." July 2, 2004.

Prelo, Marc. Attorney for Village of Capitan. To Jay Miller. "RE: Village of Capitan/Freedom of Information Act - Inspection of Public Records Request. **July 5, 2004. (Response for Sederwall to Jay Miller)**

Miller, Jay. To Assistant AG Mary Smith. "Re: Response to your letter of June 24, 2004." **July 8, 2004.**

_____. To Sheriff Gary Graves. "Re: Follow-up on your responses to my prior FOIA/IPRA requests." **July 8, 2004.**

Morel, Alan P. Lincoln County Attorney. To Jay Miller. "RE: Freedom of Information Act Request dated July 1, 2004." **July 9, 2004. (Statutes justifying deputizing Sederwall)**

Smith, Mary H., Assistant Attorney General. To Jay Miller. "Re: Determination of Inspection of Public Records Act Complaint v Village of Capitan." **August 3, 2004. (Corrupt rejection of open records complaint.)**

_____. To Jay Miller. "Re: Determination of Inspection of Public Records Act complaint v De Baca County." **August 3, 2004. (Corrupt rejection of open records complaint.)**

Miller, Jay. To Sheriff Tom Sullivan. "Re: David Turk, Historian for the U.S. Marshals Service." **August 5, 2004.**

_____. To Office of General Counsel - FOIA REQUEST, Attn. Arleta Cunningham, U.S. Marshal's Service. "Re. David Turk, historian for U.S. Marshal's Service, FOIA on Sederwall/Sullivan/Graves/ Billy the Kid Case." **August 5, 2004.**

_____. To Assistant AG Mary Smith. "Re. Response to your letter of August 3, 2004 about determination of my IPRA complaint v Mayor of Capitan Steve Sederwall, who also represents himself as Deputy Sheriff of Lincoln County; and the Village of Capitan." **August, 10, 2004.**

Sullivan, Tom, Lincoln County Sheriff. "In response to your 'Inspection of Public Records Act" request dated August 5, 2004." **August 18, 2004. (Denies open records request on David Turk based on ongoing criminal investigation)**

Morel, Alan P. Lincoln County Attorney. To Jay Miller. "In response to your "Information Act Request dated August 5, 2004." **August 18, 2004.**

Miller, Jay. To Deputy Attorney General Stuart Bluestone. "Re: Complaint and appeal for assistance with regard to non-compliance with FOIA/IPRA requests made to Capitan Mayor Steve Sederwall, who represents himself as Deputy Sheriff of Lincoln County and the Village Clerk of Capitan." **August 28, 2004. (No response)**

_____. To Deputy Attorney General Stuart Bluestone. "Re: Complaint and appeal for assistance with regard to non-compliance with FOIA/IPRA requests made to Lincoln County Sheriff Tom Sullivan and Lincoln County Clerk." **September 4, 2004. (No response)**

Utley, Robert M. "Billy Again." **September 16, 2004. (Sent to Jay Miller and forwarded to me regarding Paul Hutton in Billy the Kid Case.)**

Smith Mary. Assistant Attorney General. To Jay Miller. "Re: Inspection of Public Records Act complaint v Steve Sederwall, Mayor of Capitan and Lincoln County Deputy Sheriff." **May 17, 2005. (Nine months later: Rejection of complaint)**

Bordley, William E. To Jay Miller. "Freedom of Information/Privacy Act Request No. 2004USMS7634, Subject: David Turk, Historian U.S. Marshals Service, FOIA on Sederwall/Sullivan/Graves/Billy the Kid Case." June 22, 2005.

Miller, Jay. To William E. Boardley, Associate General Counsel/FOIPA Officer, U.S. Marshal's Service. "Follow-up on your response titled Freedom of Information Act Request No. 2004USMS7634 Subject: David Turk, Historian U.S. Marshal's Service, FOIA on Sederwall/Sullivan/Graves/Billy the Kid Case." **July 25, 2005.**

DeZulovich, Mavis. FOI/PA Liaison, Office of Public Affairs. To Jay Miller. "This letter is in response to your Freedom of Information/Privacy Act Request No. 2004USMS7634 in reference to David Turk. **August 24, 2005. (States Turk is not Probable Cause Statement author, but references his pamphlet.)**

Virden, R.E. Lincoln County Sheriff. Letter to Jay Miller. "We are interested in the truth surrounding Billy the Kid and are continuing the investigation ..." **November 28, 2005. (Confirms deputizing Sullivan and Sederwall for "Billy the Kid Case")**

Miller, Jay. To Paul Hutton. "As a journalist following the Billy the Kid Case ..." **February 6, 2006.**

_____. To Attorney General Patricia Madrid. "Re: Follow-up on non-response by Attorney General to my September 4, 2004 Complaint and Appeal for assistance with regard to non-compliance by past Lincoln County Sheriff Tom Sullivan with my FOIA/IPRA Requests." **March 20, 2006.**

_____. To Paul Hutton. "Repeat of one sent to you on February 6, 2006, because I received no response to it." **March 20, 2006.**

_____. To Sheriff Rick Virden. "Inspection of Public Records Act/Freedom of Information Act request." **March 27, 2006.**

_____. To Attorney Marc Prelo. "Re: Follow-up on Freedom of Information Request response dated July 5, 2004." **March 27, 2006. (Requests information on taxpayer money for Sederwall's Billy the Kid Case participation)**

Prelo, Marc Attorney. To Jay Miller. "RE: Village of Capitan/Freedom of Information Act – Inspection of Public Records Request." **Match 31, 2006. (Confirms his use of taxpayer money for Sederwall's Billy the Kid Case participation)**

Morel, Alan P. Lincoln County Attorney. To Jay Miller. "RE: Freedom of Information Act/Inspection of Public Records Act request dated March 27, 2006, to Lincoln County Sheriff Rick Virden. **April 3, 2006.**

_____. To Jay Miller. "Re: Follow-up on Freedom of Information Act Request Responses Dated May 19, 2004 and June 4, 2004." **April 17, 2006. (Confirms his use of taxpayer money for Sullivan's Billy the Kid Case participation)**

Miller, Jay. To Attorney General Patricia Madrid. "Re: Follow-up on FOIA/IPRA Request to Lincoln County Sheriff Tom Sullivan." **May 6, 2006**. **(No response)**

_____. To Assistant Attorney General Mary Smith. "Re. Response to your letter of May 17, 2005 rejecting my IPRA complaint against then Mayor of Capitan Steve Sederwall, who also represented himself as Deputy Sheriff of Lincoln County." **May 6, 2006**. **(No response.)**

Miller, Jay. To Assistant Attorney General Mary Smith. "Re. Response to your letter of May 17, 2005 rejecting my IPRA complaint against then Mayor of Capitan Steve Sederwall, who also represented himself as Deputy Sheriff of Lincoln County." **June 13, 2006**. **(Repeat complaint with new information. No response.)**

_____. To Paul Hutton. "Re. Clarification of my letter to you dated March 20, 2006, and reframing of it as a FOIA/IPRA Request." **June 13, 2006**.

_____. To Attorney Mark Acuña. "Re. Follow-up on your legal participation in the New Mexico Billy the Kid Case and participation of the Jaffe Law Firm in the New Mexico Billy the Kid Case." **June 22, 2006**. **(No response.)**

_____. To Attorney General Patricia Madrid. "Re. FOIA/IPRA Request with regard to your relationship with Attorney Bill Robins III and/or his law firm Heard, Robins, Cloud, Lubel & Greenwood LLP." **August 8, 2006**.

_____. To Attorney Mark Acuña.. "Re. Follow-up on my unanswered letter of June 22, 2006 with regard to your legal participation in the New Mexico Billy the Kid Case and the participation of your Jaffe Law Firm in the New Mexico Billy the Kid Case." **August 8, 2006**. **(No response).**

_____. To Mavis DeZulovich. FOIA/PA Liaison U.S. Department of Justice. "Re: Follow-up to your August 24, 2005 response to my Freedom of Information Act request No. 2004USMS7634 in reference to David Turk, Historian for the U.S. Marshals Service." **August 8, 2006**. **(Request for Turk's pamphlet)**

Hutton, Paul "I was never the 'state historian' ..." . Letter to Jay Miller. **June 20, 2006**. **(Central "Billy the Kid Case" hoaxer lies about his role)**

Miller, Jay. To Attorney Mark Acuña. "Re. Follow-up on your legal participation in the New Mexico Billy the Kid Case and participation of the Jaffe Law Firm in the New Mexico Billy the Kid Case." **June 22, 2006**. **(No response.)**

_____. To Attorney General Patricia Madrid. "Re. FOIA/IPRA Request with regard to your relationship with Attorney Bill Robins III and/or his law firm Heard, Robins, Cloud, Lubel & Greenwood LLP." **August 8, 2006**.

_____. To Attorney Mark Acuña.. "Re. Follow-up on my unanswered letter of June 22, 2006 with regard to your legal participation in the New Mexico Billy the Kid Case and the participation of your Jaffe Law Firm in the New Mexico Billy the Kid Case." **August 8, 2006**. **(No response).**

_____. To Mavis DeZulovich. FOIA/PA Liaison U.S. Department of Justice. "Re: Follow-up to your August 24, 2005 response to my Freedom of Information Act request No. 2004USMS7634 in reference to David Turk, Historian for the U.S. Marshals Service." **August 8, 2006**. **(Requesting copy of David Turk's pamphlet on Billy the Kid and U.S. Marshals Service)**

_____. To Dr. Rick Staub, Director Orchid Cellmark Lab. "Re: The participation by you and Orchid Cellmark in the New Mexico Billy the Kid Case." **August 8, 2006**. **(No response.)**

Kupfer, Elizabeth, Records Custodian. To Jay Miller. "Need additional time ..." **August 14, 2006**.

Miller, Jay. To Attorney General Patricia Madrid. "RE: FOIA/IPRA request regarding Attorney Bill Robins III and/or his law firm Heard, Robins, Cloud, Lubel, and Greenwood." **August 24, 2006**.

Cedrick, Nikki. FOIA/PA Liaison U.S. Department of Justice. "Per your FOI request No. 2004USMS7634." **August 31, 2006**. **(Refuses to send copy of David Turk's pamphlet on Billy the Kid)**

Miller, Jay. To Attorney General Patricia Madrid. "Re: Second FOIA/IPRA Request with regard to documentation of financial relationship of Attorney General

Patricia Madrid and/or her Office, and Attorney Bill Robins III and/or his law firm Heard, Robins, Cloud, Lubel, and Greenwood LLP." **September 1, 2006.**

_____. To Assistant Attorney General Mary Smith. "Re. Response to your letter of May 17, 2005 rejecting my IPRA complaint against then Mayor of Capitan Steve Sederwall, who also represented himself as Deputy Sheriff of Lincoln County." **September 1, 2006. (No response)**

_____. To Deputy Attorney General Stuart Bluestone. "Re: Follow-up on your recent telephone call to me about my current, repeated, FOIA/IPRA non-compliance complaints to Attorney General Patricia Madrid with regard to Tom Sullivan's and Steve Sederwall's participation in the Billy the Kid Case in their capacities as public officials." **September 1, 2006. (No response)**

Bordley, William E. Associate General Counsel/FOIPA Officer for U.S. Department of Justice. To Jay Miller. "Re: Freedom of Information/Privacy Act Request No. 2006USMS9782 Subject: Copy of Report Entitled *The U.S. Marshals Service and Billy the Kid.*" **September 5, 2006. (Refuses to send copy of David Turk's pamphlet on Billy the Kid)**

Kupfer, Elizabeth, Records Custodian. To Jay Miller. "Need additional time ..." **September 6, 2006.**

Miller, Jay. To Nikki Cedrick, FOIA/PA Liaison U.S. Department of Justice. "Re: Follow-up to your August 31, 2006 response to my Freedom of Information Act request No. 2004USMS7634 in Reference to David Turk, Historian for the U.S. Marshals Service; and request for clarification." **September 11, 2006.**

Smith, Glenn R., Deputy Attorney General and Elizabeth Kupfer, Custodian of Public Records. (For Attorney General Patricia Madrid). To Jay Miller." RE: Inspection of Public Records Request." **September 20, 2006.**

Bordley, William E. Associate General Counsel/FOIPA Officer for U.S. Department of Justice. To Jay Miller. "Re: Freedom of Information/Privacy Act Request No. 2006USMS9782 Subject: Copy of Report Entitled *The U.S. Marshals Service and Billy the Kid.*" **September 5, 2006. (Refuses copy of David Turk's pamphlet on Billy the Kid.)**

Kupfer, Elizabeth, Records Custodian. To Jay Miller. "Need additional time ..." **September 6, 2006.**

Miller, Jay. To Nikki Cedrick, FOIA/PA Liaison U.S. Department of Justice. "Re: Follow-up to your August 31, 2006 response to my Freedom of Information Act request No. 2004USMS7634 in Reference to David Turk, Historian for the U.S. Marshals Service; and request for clarification." **September 11, 2006.**

Smith, Glenn R., Deputy Attorney General and Elizabeth Kupfer, Custodian of Public Records. (For Attorney General Patricia Madrid). To Jay Miller." RE: Inspection of Public Records Request." **September 20, 2006.**

RECORDS REQUESTS BY GALE COOPER

"Jordan, Wilma" aka Gale Cooper. To David Turk, Historian U.S. Marshals Service. "Looking for the truth is good ..." **June 15, 2006. (Attempt to get the Turk's "U.S. Marshal's Service and Billy the Kid " pamphlet for Case 2003-274.)**

Turk, David. Historian U.S. Marshals Service. To "Wilma Jordan." "Thank you for your thoughtful and thorough letter ..." **July 3, 2006. (Creepy Turk traced a "Wilma Jordan's" address; refused to send his Billy the Kid pamphlet)**

Cooper, Gale. To Governor Bill Richardson and Records Custodian for FOIA/IPRA Requests. "Re: Freedom of Information Act (FOIA)/Inspection of Public Records Act (IPRA) request concerning participation of Governor Bill Richardson in the New Mexico Billy the Kid Case and related issues." **September 22, 2006.**

_____. To Governor Janet Napolitano. "Re: Freedom of Information Act (FOIA) request pertaining to the Prescott, Arizona exhumations of John Miller and William Hudspeth at the Arizona Pioneers' Home Cemetery on May 19, 2005." **September 22, 2006.**

_____. To Sheriff Rick Virden. "Re: Freedom of Information Act (FOIA)/New Mexico Inspection of Public Records Act (IPRA) request pertaining to Lincoln County Sheriff's Department Case # 2003-274 ("Billy the Kid Case") and to its May 19, 2005 Prescott Arizona exhumations of John Miller and William Hudspeth." **September 22, 2006.**

Morel, Alan P. Lincoln County Attorney. To Gale Cooper. "Re: Freedom of Information Act/Inspection of Public Records Act Request dated September 22, 2006, to Lincoln County Sheriff Rick Virden." **September 29, 2006.**

Sullivan, Tom and Steve Sederwall. To Lincoln County Attorney Alan Morel. "The Dried Bean. 'You Believin' Us or Them Lyin' Whores.' " **September 30, 2006. (Exhibit 4 in IPRA response to me of October 11, 2006 from Sheriff Rick Virden through Lincoln County Attorney Alan Morel.)**

Maestas, Marcie. Records Custodian for Governor Bill Richardson. To Gale Cooper, M.D. "Received your request to inspect certain records ..." **October 3, 2006.**

Morel, Alan P. Lincoln County Attorney. To Gale Cooper. "RE: Freedom of Information Act (FOIA)/New Mexico Inspection of Public Records Act (IPRA) to Lincoln County Sheriff Ricky [sic] Virden and the Lincoln County Records Custodian, dated September 22, 2006." **October 11, 2006.**

Maestas, Marcie. Records Custodian for Governor Bill Richardson. To Gale Cooper, M.D. "Response to your Inspection of Public Records request received by our office on September 28, 2006 ..." **October 13, 2006. (Denial of each item, but miscellaneous documents provided)**

Michael R. Haener. Deputy Chief of Staff to Governor Janet Napolitano. "Enclosed records responsive to your request ..." **November 13, 2006.**

Cooper, Gale. To Governor Janet Napolitano. "Re: Repeated Freedom of Information Act (FOIA) request pertaining to the Prescott, Arizona exhumations of John Miller and William Hudspeth at the Arizona Pioneers' Home Cemetery on May 19, 2005." **March 20, 2007. (Repeated because of no response)**

_____. To Governor Janet Napolitano's Records Custodian. "Re: Repeat submission of incompletely answered Freedom of Information Act request dated September 22, 2006. **March 21, 2007.**

Shilo Mitchell, Deputy Press Secretary for Governor Janet Napolitano. To Gale Cooper, M.D. ""We have no responsive documents from your last request ..." **August 2, 2007.**

Cooper, Gale. To January Contreras, Policy Advisor for Health for Governor Janet Napolitano. "Re: Non- response to my Freedom of Information Act request dated June 29, 2007." **August 10, 2007.**

_____. "Re: Freedom of Information Act request pertaining to New Mexico Governor Bill Richardson's Grand Jury investigation(s) concerning CDR Financial Products, Inc." To Attorney General Eric Holder. **May 25, 2010.**

_____. "Re: Freedom of Information Act request pertaining to New Mexico Governor Bill Richardson's Grand Jury investigation(s) concerning CDR Financial Products, Inc." To President Barak Obama. **May 25, 2010.**

_____. "Re: Freedom of Information Act request pertaining to New Mexico Governor Bill Richardson's Grand Jury investigation(s) concerning CDR Financial Products, Inc." To New Mexico U.S. Attorney Greg Fouratt Obama. **May 25, 2010.**

Hardy, David M. Section Chief, Record/Information Dissemination Section. "Subject: Bill Richardson, January 2008 – Present, FOIPA Request No.: 1149852-000." To Gale Cooper. U.S. Department of Justice, Federal Bureau of Investigation. **June 28, 2010. (Refused records as being on a "third party")**

Stewart, William G. II. Assistant Director. "Subject of Request: Gov. Bill Richardson (grand jury investigation), Request Number 2010-2058." To Gale Cooper. U.S. Department of Justice. **July 14, 2010. (Refused based on "personal privacy")**

_____. "Subject of Request: Gov. Bill Richardson (grand jury investigation), Request Number 2010-2045." To Gale Cooper. U.S. Department of Justice. **July 28, 2010. (Refused information based on "personal privacy")**

INVESTIGATIONS OF DR. HENRY LEE AND ORCHID CELLMARK LAB (CHRONOLOGICAL)

BACKGROUND

Bugliosi, Vincent. *Outrage: The Five Reasons Why O.J. Simpson Got Away With Murder.* New York and London: W.W. Norton & Company. **1996.** (**Exposé of Dr. Henry Lee forensic scams, Pages 47-49.**)

No author. "Fraud Alleged at Cellmark, DNA Testing Firm." TalkLeft: The Politics of Crime. http://www.talkleft.com./new_archives/008809.html. **November 18, 2004.**

Bailey, James A. and Margaret B. Bailey. "Billy the Kid Death Scene: Reviewing Ballistic Evidence. *Wild West History Association.* **September, 2016.** Volume 9, Number 3, Pages 30-46. (**Using Lee's forensic fakery of the washstand to create a death scene; also traces is furniture 's provenance (Pages 31-32)**)

Shen, Maxine. "CBS and the brother of JonBenet Ramsey settle their $750m defamation lawsuit to the 'satisfaction of both parties' after he claimed their documentary implied he killed his sister." **January 5, 2019.** DailyMailOnline.com. (**Defamation case involving Dr. Henry Lee's forensics**)

RECORDS REQUESTS BY JAY MILLER AS MY PROXY

Miller, Jay. To Dr. Henry Lee. "Re: Forensic consultation in the New Mexico Billy the Kid Case." **March 27, 2006.** (**Included all the articles with Lee's forensic claims**)

Lee, Henry, Dr. To Jay Miller. "In response to your letter dated March 27, 2006 ..." **May 1, 2006.** (**Says sent his single forensic report for Case No. 2003-274 to the Lincoln County Sheriff's Department directly**)

Miller, Jay. To Dr. Henry Lee. "Re: Follow-up on your letter of May 1, 2006 responding to my request of March 27, 2006 for information on your forensic consultation in the New Mexico Billy the Kid Case." **June 15, 2006.**

_____. To Dr. Henry Lee. "Re: Follow-up to my letter of June 15, 2006 with regard to your forensic consultation in the New Mexico Billy the Kid Case." **August 8, 2006.**

_____. To Dr. Rick Staub. "Re: The participation by you and Orchid Cellmark in the New Mexico Billy the Kid Case." **August 8, 2006.** (**No response**)

ETHICS COMPLAINT AGAINST

Cooper, Gale. To Haskell Pitluck, AAFS Ethics Committee Chairman and members of the AAFS Ethics Committee. "Re: Formal Ethics Complaint against Dr. Henry Lee for his work as a forensic expert in Lincoln County, New Mexico, Sheriff's Department Case # 2003-274 ('the Billy the Kid Case')." **October 2, 2006.**

Cooper, Gale. To Haskell Pitluck, AAFS Ethics Committee Chairman. "Re: Follow-up on my October 2, 2006 complaint on Dr. Henry Lee to the Ethics Committee of the American Academy of Forensic Sciences." **March 5, 2007.**

_____. To Dr. Bruce Goldberger. President AAFS. "Re: Informing of non-action to date on my American Academy of Forensic Sciences Ethics Committee complaint filed October 2, 2006 against Dr. Henry Lee." **April 10, 2007.**

Goldberger, Bruce. Dr. and President AAFS. To Gale Cooper. (via fax) "I have received the complaint today ..." **April 12,, 2007.**

_____. To Gale Cooper. (via fax) "You should receive a letter from Mr. Pitluck in the coming week or two ..." **May 4, 2007.**

Pitluck, Haskell M. AAFS Ethics Committee Chairman. To Gale Cooper, M.D. "Ethics Committee has completed its investigation ..." **May 9, 2007.** (**Corrupt denial**)

Cooper, Gale. To Haskell Pitluck, AAFS Ethics Committee Chairman. "Re: Follow-up on the May 9, 2007 AAFS response to my October 2, 2006 Ethics Complaint on Dr. Henry Lee. **May 30, 2007.**

_____. To Dr. Bruce Goldberger. President AAFS. "Re: Need for clarification in the May 9, 2007 AAFS Ethics Committee response to my AAFS Ethics and Conduct Complaint of October 2, 2006 against Dr. Henry Lee." **May 30, 2007.**

Pitluck, Haskell M. AAFS Ethics Committee Chairman. To Gale Cooper, M.D. "Ethics Committee has completed its investigation ..." **June 2, 2007. (Denial of any responsibility by Dr. Lee for "actions or statements of others.")**

Cooper, Gale. To Rene Romo. *Albuquerque Journal*. "Re: Attributions made by you in your August 2, 2004 *Albuquerque Journal* article titled 'Forensic Expert on Billy's Case: Questions Remain on Outlaws Fate.'" **June 19, 2007.**

_____. To Haskell Pitluck, AAFS Ethics Committee Chairman. "Re: Requested clarification of your responses of May 9, 2007 and June 2, 2007 to my October 2, 2006 AAFS Ethics Complaint against Dr. Henry Lee." **June 19, 2007.**

_____. To Den Slaney. Albuquerque Museum of Art and History. "Re: Information request for Dreamscape Desperado exhibit." **June 29, 2007. (Using fake carpenter's bench blood claim)**

Pitluck, Haskell M. AAFS Ethics Committee Chairman. To Gale Cooper, M.D. "Ethics Committee has completed its investigation ..." **July 6, 2007.**

Cooper, Gale. To Albuquerque Museum of Art and History Director Cathy Wright. "Re: Information request concerning past Dreamscape Desperado exhibit." **July 30, 2007. (Concerning their labeling of the carpenter's bench as having blood according to Dr. Henry Lee)**

Slaney, Deborah. Curator of History at the Albuquerque Museum of Art and History. To Gale Cooper. "Re: Information request concerning past Dreamscape Desperado exhibit." **August 6, 2007. (Claim Paul Hutton verified bench blood)**

Walz, Kent. Editor-in-Chief *Albuquerque Journal*. To Gale Cooper. "Response to your letter concerning Rene Romo's story of August 2, 2004." **August 13, 2007. (Stated Lee never denied the claims attributed to him)**

OPEN RECORDS VIOLATION CASE:

Sandoval County District Cause No. D-1329-CV-2007-1364, Gale Cooper and De Baca County News, a New Mexico Corporation, PLAINTIFFS, vs. Rick Virden, Lincoln County Sheriff and Custodian of Records; and Steven M. Sederwall, Former Lincoln County Deputy Sheriff; and Thomas T. Sullivan, Former Lincoln County Sheriff and Former Lincoln County Deputy Sheriff, DEFENDANTS. (CHRONOLOGICAL)

INSPECTION OF PUBLIC RECORDS ACT STATUTE

Madrid, Patricia A. Attorney General. *Inspection of Public Records Act Compliance Guide. Fourth Edition. The "Inspection of Public Records Act" NMSA 1978, Chapter 14, Article 2: A Compliance Guide for New Mexico Public Officials and Citizens.* Santa Fe: Office of the Attorney General. **January, 2004.**

King, Gary, Attorney General. "IPRA Guide: The Inspection of Public Records Act NMSA 1978, Chapter 14, Article 2; A Compliance Guide for New Mexico Public Officials and Citizens. Seventh Edition. **2012.**

RECORDS REQUEST PHASE

Cheves, Philip W. Barnett Law Firm. To Sheriff Rick Virden. "Re: Request for Inspection of Public Records." **April 24, 2007. (Start of my records requesting for the Dr. Henry Lee and Orchid Cellmark forensic DNA records)**

Morel, Alan P., Lincoln County Attorney. To Barnett Law Firm. "Re: Freedom of Information Act/Inspection of Public Records Act Request Dated April 24, 2007." **April 27, 2007. (Fakes Case 2003-274 as only deputy murder investigation.)**

Cheves, Philip W. Barnett Law Firm. To Sheriff Rick Virden. "Re: Request for Inspection of Public Records." **May 9, 2007.**
_____. To Alan P. Morel, Esquire. "Re: Request for Inspection of Public Records." **May 9, 2007.**
Morel, Alan P., Lincoln County Attorney. To Barnett Law Firm. "RE: Freedom of Information Act/Inspection of Public Records Act Request to Sheriff Rick Virden Dated May 9, 2007." **May 11, 2007. (Lies that Lincoln County have no Case 2003-274 records "whatsoever")**)
_____. To Barnett Law Firm. "RE: Freedom of Information Act/Inspection of Public Records Act Request to Alan P. Morel, Esq., Dated May 9, 2007." **May 14, 2007. (Fakes "deputies too records" excuse)**
Cheves, Philip W., Barnett Law Firm. To Alan P. Morel, Esquire. "Re: Request for Inspection of Public Records." **June 8, 2007.**
Cheves, Philip W., Barnett Law Firm. "Re: Request for Inspection of Public Records" to Tom Sullivan. **June 14, 2007.**
_____. "Re: Request for Inspection of Public Records" to Steve Sederwall. **June 14, 2007.**
Morel, Alan P., Lincoln County Attorney. Thomas Stewart, Lincoln County Manager, and Rick Virden, Lincoln County Sheriff. To Tom Sullivan and Steve Sederwall. "Re: Request for Inspection of Public Records." **June 21, 2007. (This was attached to Morel's letter of June 22, 2007 as feigned records recovery attempt from Sullivan and Sederwall.)**
Sederwall, Steven M. and Thomas T. Sullivan. To Rick Virden, Lincoln County Sheriff. "Memorandum. Subject: Billy the Kid Investigation." **June 21, 2007. (Key hoax document attached to the Morel letter of June 22, 2007, blames Richardson and Robins for case, attaches $6,500 in "bribery" checks to Sullivan, and quitting as deputies)**
Morel, Alan P. Lincoln County Attorney. To Barnett Law Firm. "RE: Freedom of Information Act/Inspection of Public Records Act Request to Alan Morel, Esq., Dated June 8, 2007." **June 22, 2007. (Attached was the Sullivan-Sederwall June 21, 2007 "Memorandum.")**
Morel, Alan P., Lincoln County Attorney. To Barnett Law Firm. "RE: Freedom of Information Act/Inspection of Public Records Act Request to Alan P. Morel, Esq., dated June 8, 2007." **June 26, 2007. (Last response before litigation)**

RECORDS LITIGATION PHASE

Barnett, Mickey. "Verified Complaint for Declaratory Judgment Ordering Production of Certain Records and Information." **October 15, 2007. (Start of litigation for Cause No. D-1329-CV-2007-1364, repeats records in first request)**
_____. "Verified First Amended Complaint for Declaratory Judgment Ordering Production of Certain Records and Information." **November 1, 2007. (Removes Lincoln County as defendant, repeats records in first request)**
Zimitski, Dewayne. Process server for Steve Sederwall and Tom Sullivan. "Affidavit of DeWayne Zimitski for Cause No. D 1329 CV 2007-01364." **December 27, 2007. (Thuggish evasion by cursing Sullivan)**
Cooper, Gale. To Attorney General Gary King. "Re: Informing about an IPRA violation case: Sandoval County Thirteenth Judicial District Cause No. D1329-CV2007-1364." **January 22, 2008.**
_____. To Attorney Leonard DeLayo for FOG. "Re: Sandoval County Thirteenth Judicial District Court Cause No. D 1329 CV2007-1364; an IPRA violation case." **January 22, 2008.**
Werkmeister, Nicole. Attorney for Narvaez law firm. Cause No. D1329-CV-07-1364." Thirteenth Judicial District Court, State of New Mexico, County of Sandoval. March 5, 2008. "Motion to Dismiss Based on Improper Venue and Failure to State a Claim." **March 5, 2008. (Attorney for Rick Virden)**

Brown, Kevin M. Attorney for defendants Sullivan and Sederwall. To Barnett Law Firm. "Thomas T. Sullivan's Responses to Request for Production of Documents, No. D-1329-CV-2007-01364." **March 17, 2008.** (**Claims not public records, and defendant does not have them..**)

_____. To Barnett Law Firm. "Steven M. Sederwall's Responses to Request for Production of Documents." **March 17, 2008.** (**Claims not public records, and defendant does not have them..**)

Barnett, Mickey. "Plaintiffs' Response to the Motion of Defendant Rick Virden to Dismiss For Improper Venue and Failure to State Claim." **March 24, 2008.**

Shandler, Zachary. (For Attorney General Gary King). To Gale Cooper M.D. "RE: Gale Cooper and De Baca County News vs. Lincoln County et al., Cause No. D-1329-CV2007-1364." **April 3, 2008.**

Kent, Kerry. ML Claims Examiner. "Tom, I'm sending you a letter advising that the IJ $10,000 limit for attorneys fees is gone ..." E-Mail. **August 9, 2008.** (**Proving huge taxpayer costs of my IPRA litigation**)

Stewart, Tom. Lincoln County Manager. "Subject: FW: IJ 20282/Billy the Kid File. County Commissioners, For the first time I can recall as county manager, we have run out of insurance coverage on a case." E-Mail. **August 9, 2008.** (**Though proving taxpayer costs of my IPRA litigation, the defendants ignored the liability and ultimately incurred the huge plaintiffs' bill**)

Stinnett, Scot. To Gale Cooper. (via e-mail). "IPRA Case Updates." **August 12, 2008.** (**About FOG probably joining IPRA case.**)

Sullivan, Thomas T. "Deposition." **August 18, 2008.** (**Taken by Mickey Barnett**)

Sederwall, Steven M. "Deposition." **August 18, 2008.** (**Taken by Mickey Barnett**)

Barnett, Mickey. Attorney. To Gale Cooper. (via e-mail). "FOG is in." August 22, 2008.

Virden, Rick. "Deposition." **September 8, 2008.** (**Taken by David Garcia**)

Werkmeister, Nicole. "Re" Gale Cooper, et al, v. Rick Virden, et al. Thirteenth Judicial District Court Cause No. D-1329-CV-2007-01364." Attorney. Letter to Attorney Mickey D. Barnett. **September 3, 2008.** (**Virden turn-over by subpoena duces tecum of Sheriff's Department file for Case # 2003-274**)

Virden, Rick. Case 2003-274 file Turn-over. **September 3, 2008.** (**By subpoena duces tecum; 193 pages**)

Rogers, Patrick J. Attorney. "Docs for editing. To: Mickey Barnett; David A. Garcia." (via e-mail). Monday, **September 22, 2008.** (Forwarded to Gale Cooper on September 25, 2008.) (**Threat FOG to pressure for dismissing Virden**)

Cooper, Gale. From Attorney David Garcia. (via e-mail). "Re: FW: Docs for editing." **September 25, 2008.**

_____. "Subj. IPRA Case Communication for Review. To Attorneys Barnett and Garcia and Scot Stinnett." (via e-mail). **September 28, 2008.** (**Case overview, our legal relationship, and responses to the Rogers e-mail.**)

_____. To Attorney Leonard DeLayo. "Fwd: Response regarding IPRA Case." **September 29, 2008.** (**Case overview for Barnett of September 28, 2008 with responses to the Rogers e-mail.**)

Rogers, Patrick. Forwarded from Scot Stinnett. (via e-mail). "No Subject." **September 30, 2008.** (**A copy of an e-mail from corrupt Attorney Rogers to Attorney DeLayo pushing falsely for Sederwall as Records Custodian.**)

_____. "Re: Second Response To Your FOG Proposal." To Gale Cooper. (via e-mail) **October 1, 2008** 4:40:27 AM.. (**Attorney Rogers tries to coerce me by Sederwall as Records Custodian or he will withdraw FOG**)

Barnett, Mickey D. Attorney. "Re: Sullivan Sederwall Depositions. To Gale Cooper." (via e-mail). **October 1, 2008.**

Brown, Kevin M. Attorney. "Re: Cooper v. Lincoln County, et al. No. D-1329-CV-07-1364. To Patrick J. Rogers**." October 16, 2008.**

Cooper, Gale. To Attorney Pat Rogers. "Re: Response documents forwarded to me by e-mail on October 20, 2008 concerning NMFOG's actions in relation to my IPRA case No. D-1329-CV-1364." **October 27, 2008.**

Rogers, Patrick J. Attorney. Letter of withdrawal as the FOG attorney pertaining to my IPRA case. **November 10, 2008.** (**Corruptly trying to throw my case**)

Cooper, Gale. "Re: My response to your letter of October 16, 2008 to Attorney Pat Rogers, and my dissociation from the referenced Foundation For Open Government communications." Letter to Brown. **November 17, 2008.**

Threet, Martin E. Attorney and Attorney A. Blair Dunn." Plaintiffs' Motion for Summary Judgment. Gale Cooper and De Baca County News, a New Mexico Corporation, Plaintiffs, vs. Lincoln County and Rick Virden, Lincoln County Sheriff and Custodian of Records; and Steven M. Sederwall, Former Lincoln County Deputy Sheriff; and Thomas T. Sullivan, Former Lincoln County Sheriff and Former Lincoln County Deputy Sheriff, Defendants. No. D-1329-CV-07-1364." County of Sandoval, Thirteenth Judicial District Court. **July 31, 2009.**

Werkmeister, H. Nicole. Attorney. Defendant Rick Virden's Response to Plaintiff's [sic] Motion for Summary Judgment and Cross-Motion for Summary Judgment. Gale Cooper and De Baca County News, a New Mexico Corporation, Plaintiffs, vs. Lincoln County and Rick Virden, Lincoln County Sheriff and Custodian of Records; and Steven M. Sederwall, Former Lincoln County Deputy Sheriff; and Thomas T. Sullivan, Former Lincoln County Sheriff and Former Lincoln County Deputy Sheriff, Defendants. No. D-1329-CV-07-1364." County of Sandoval, Thirteenth Judicial District Court. **August 29, 2009.**

Brown, Kevin. Attorney. "Defendants Sederwall and Sullivan's Response to Motion for Summary Judgment. Gale Cooper and De Baca County News, a New Mexico Corporation, Plaintiffs, vs. Lincoln County and Rick Virden, Lincoln County Sheriff and Custodian of Records; and Steven M. Sederwall, Former Lincoln County Deputy Sheriff; and Thomas T. Sullivan, Former Lincoln County Sheriff and Former Lincoln County Deputy Sheriff, Defendants. No. D-1329-CV-07-1364." County of Sandoval, Thirteenth Judicial District Court. **September 2, 2009.**

Threet, Martin E. Attorney and Attorney A. Blair Dunn. "Plaintiffs' Reply and Motion to Exceed Page Limit For Exhibits. Gale Cooper and De Baca County News, a New Mexico Corporation, Plaintiffs, vs. Lincoln County and Rick Virden, Lincoln County Sheriff and Custodian of Records; and Steven M. Sederwall, Former Lincoln County Deputy Sheriff; and Thomas T. Sullivan, Former Lincoln County Sheriff and Former Lincoln County Deputy Sheriff, Defendants. No. D-1329-CV-07-1364." County of Sandoval, Thirteenth Judicial District Court. **September 29, 2009.** (**Attempt to enter my extensive evidence into court record**)

_____. Motion for Summary Judgment. **January, 2010.**

Eichwald, George P. Hearing for "Plaintiffs' Motion for Summary Judgment." Transcript. **November 20, 2009.** (**Plaintiffs' Motion for Summary Judgment Granted.**)

_____. "Summary Judgment" granted for Plaintiffs. January, 2010.

Brown, Kevin. "I am enclosing the document Mr. Sederwall received from Dr. Lee ..." Letter. **February 18, 2010.** (**Unrequested Lee floorboard report**)

Lee, Henry and Calvin Ostler. "Forensic Research and Training Center Forensic Examination Report: "Examination of Lincoln County Court House." **February 25, 2005.** (**Given to Plaintiffs on February 18, 2010 by Brown and on April 6, 2010 by Werkmeister as a requested Lee report – but was the fake Version I (9 pages) of an unrequested floorboard report**)

Threet, Martin E. "I am returning the Lee report ..." Letter to Brown. (Rejecting and returning the Lee floorboard report) **February 25, 2010.**

"Presentment Hearing." Transcript. **March 9, 2010.** (**Defendants give unrequested Lee floorboard report as fulfilling records turn-over; and lying that it is only the record in Sederwall's possession**)

Eichwald, George P., District Judge. "Order Granting Plaintiff's Motion for Summary Judgment and Denying Defendant Virden's Cross Motion for Summary Judgment and Order Granting Leave to File Interlocutory Appeal" **March 12, 2010.** (**Grants evidentiary hearing.**)

Werkmeister, Nicole. "Attached is the Forensic Examination Report From Dr. Henry Lee ..." Fax cover letter. **April 6, 2010. (Copy faxed of same unrequested (fake) Lee floorboard report from Brown was enclosed)**

Eichwald. George P., District Judge. "Order Granting Plaintiffs' Motion for Summary Judgment and Denying Defendant Virden's Cross-Motion for Summary Judgment and Order Granting Leave to File Interloculatory Appeal." **March 12, 2010. (Major Plaintiff victory)**

Threet, Martin E. "Take a look at this letter ..." Fax cover letter to me. **April 13, 2010. (Werkmeister sending fake floorboard Lee report to us)**

Threet, Martin E. "The time for interloculatory appeal having passed ..." Letter to Werkmeister and Brown. **May 3, 2010.**

Hearing for "Mandatory Order of Disclosure and Production Hearing." Transcript. **September 9, 2010.**

Threet, Martin E. "Re: Billy the Kid. "Henry Narvaez has again repeated his assurance to me that if we will agree to dismiss Virden ..." Fax to me. **September 14, 2010. (Threet's attempt to trick me into dismissing Virden)**

_____. "Re: Plaintiff's response to letter from Sheriff Rick Virden. It is the position of my clients ..." Letter. **September 27, 2010.**

Virden, Rick. "It is my understanding that on May 22, 2004, Steve Sederwall ..." Letter to Henry Lee. **October 26, 2010. (sham recovery attempt to Dr. Henry Lee)**

_____. "It is my understanding that in the spring or summer of 2004, Steve Sederwall sent a blood sample(s) to Orchid Cellmark ..." Letter "To Whom It May Concern." **October 26, 2010. (Sham recovery attempt to Orchid Cellmark)**

Narvaez Law Firm. Billing to New Mexico County Insurance Authority. **October 31, 2010. (Listing secret meetings with Attorney Threet to dismiss Virden)**

Gulliksen, Joan., Orchid Cellmark Customer Liaison, Forensics. "Orchid Cellmark is in receipt of your letter requesting DNA documents ..." Letter to Virden. **November 2, 2010. (Orchid Cellmark response requesting client name to release records; Virden did not get the records)**

_____. "Orchid Cellmark, this is Joan ..." Transcript of telephone call from Virden. **November 2, 2010. (Virden did no follow-up)**

_____. "Orchid Cellmark, this is Joan ..." E-mail to Virden. **November 2, 2010. (Virden did no follow-up)**

Brown, Kevin. "Enclosed please find a copy of another report dated February 25, 2005 which deals with the examination of furniture by Dr. Lee." Letter to Threet. **November 10, 2010. (Sending Lee's forged bench report; different font than the first forged floorboard report)**

Lee, Henry and Calvin Ostler. "Forensic Research and Training Center Forensic Examination Report: "Examination of furniture from Pete Maxwell's of July 15, 1881." February 25, 2005. **(Given to Plaintiffs on November 10, 2010 as Lee bench report (16 pages) – but was its forged Version I)**

Werkmeister, Nicole. Letter to Threet. **November 4, 2010. (Shaming Virden recovery of Orchid Cellmark records; saying Lee did not respond)**

Lee, Henry. "This letter is in response to your letter ..." Letter to Virden. **November 12, 2010. (Lee confirms report; Virden never asked for it!)**

Werkmeister, Nicole. Letter to Threet. **November 22, 2010. (copies of Virden's sham Lee and Orchid Cellmark requests sent to Threet)**

Robins, Bill III. Deposition taken by Attorney Martin E. Threet. **January 6, 2011.**

"Evidentiary Hearing on Plaintiff's Motion for Mandatory Order of Disclosure and Production." Transcript. **January 21, 2011. (Defendants gave forged Lee Floorboard report (9 pages) Version II entered as Exhibit F; forged Lee bench report (16 pages) Version I entered as Exhibit E)**

Lee, Henry and Calvin Ostler. "Forensic Research and Training Center Forensic Examination Report: "Examination of furniture from Pete Maxwell's of July 15, 1881." February 25, 2005. **(Given to Court on January 21, 2011 as Lee bench report (16 pages), Exhibit E – but was its fake Version 1)**

Lee, Henry and Calvin Ostler. "Forensic Research and Training Center Forensic Examination Report: "Examination of Lincoln County Court House." February 25, 2005. **(Given to Court on January 21, 2011 as Lee floorboard report (9 pages), Exhibit F – but was its forged Version II)**

Brown, Kevin. "I represent Steve Sederwall ..." Letter to Dr. Staub. **February 3, 2011. (Sederwall's court-ordered bogus Orchid Cellmark recovery attempt)**

Cooper, Gale. "Re: Termination of legal services for Gale Cooper and the *De Baca County News* vs Lincoln County Sheriff Rick Virden et al case." Letter to Attorney Martin E. Threet. **February 12, 2011. (Termination of Threet)**

_____. "Subj: Change of Legal Representation for Virden et al." E-mail to Attorney Blair Dunn. **April 13, 2011. (Termination of Dunn)**

Brown, Kevin. Letter. **June 7, 2011. (Follow-up to Sederwall's court-ordered Dr. Lee report turn-over)**

"Presentment Hearing." Transcript. **September 23, 2011. (Plaintiffs presenting discrepancies in the Lee reports)**

Eichwald, George P., District Judge. "Order on Hearing of January 21, 2011." **September 28, 2011. (Joined the deputy killings and Kid killing investigations; calling them and records public)**

Riordan, William and Patrick Griebel. "Plaintiffs' Requested Findings of Fact and Conclusions of Law." **November 4, 2011.**

Cooper, Gale. "Re: Immediate termination of services for Sandoval District Court Cause No. D-1329-CV-07-1364." Letter to Attorney Griebel. **November 21, 2011.**

Griebel, Patrick and Jeremy Theoret. "Plaintiff's Motion for Payment of Damages, Costs and Fees." **December 12, 2011.**

_____. "Plaintiff's Reply in Support of Motion for Payment of Damages, Costs and Fees." **January 13, 2012.**

Hearing on "Plaintiffs' Motion to Supplement the Record and a Request for Sanctions, and Co-Plaintiff's Motion For Attorney Fees." **January 17, 2012. (Lee reports presented for sanctions as forged; and co-plaintiff Stinnett requests fees for past attorneys. Judge grants 100% fees)**

Brown, Kevin. Court-ordered turn-over of 25 page, "original" Lee report. **January 31, 2012. (Turn-over of the authentic, 25 page, Lee report)**

Eichwald, George P., District Judge. "Order on Plaintiffs Motion to Supplement the Record and Request for Award of Sanctions against Defendants." **February 23, 2012. (Ordered Sederwall to produce original Lee report)**

Lee, Henry and Calvin Ostler. "Forensic Research and Training Center Forensic Examination Report." February 25, 2005. **(Court-ordered turn-over to Plaintiffs on January 31, 2012 as "original" Lee report (25 pages) combining bench, floorboards, and wash stand)**

Griebel, Patrick J. Attorney for Scot Stinnett. "Subpoena for Production or Inspection to Laboratory Corporation of America." **March 29, 2012. (Non-IPRA subpoena of records from Orchid Cellmark parent company)**

_____. "Reply in Support of Plaintiff's Motion for Order to Show Cause." **April 11, 2012. (Co-Plaintiff's attempt to get Sullivan and Sederwall "Private Donor Fund" checking account information))**

Hearing on "Plaintiffs' Second Motion to Supplement the Record and a Request for Sanctions." **May 31, 2012 (Forged Lee reports for sanctions)**

Brown, Kevin. Court-ordered turn-over of another 25 page, "original" Lee report. **June 7, 2012. (CD of same report as given on January 31, 2012, but with color photos and no signatures)**

Sederwall, Steven. Deposition. **June 26, 2012. (Admitted forgery as "massaging!")**

Virden, Rick. Deposition. **June 27, 2012.**

"Status Conference." Transcript. **September 21, 2012.**

Eichwald, George P., District Judge. "Order." For Status Conference of **September 21, 2012. (Court-ordered mediation and Evidentiary hearing)**

STEVE SEDERWALL'S FORGED DR. HENRY LEE REPORTS

Brown, Kevin. "I am enclosing the document Mr. Sederwall received from Dr. Lee ..." Letter. **February 18, 2010. (Unrequested Lee floorboard report which was a forgery)**

Lee, Henry and Calvin Ostler. "Forensic Research and Training Center Forensic Examination Report: "Examination of Lincoln County Court House." February 25, 2005. **(Given to me on February 18, 2010 by Kevin Brown and on April 6, 2010 by Nicole Werkmeister as a requested Lee report – but was Version I (9 pages) of an unrequested and forged floorboard report)**

Threet, Martin E. "I am returning the Lee report ..." Letter to Brown. (Rejecting and returning the Lee floorboard report) **February 25, 2010. (Not knowing it was a forgery, I returned it merely as unrequested)**

"Presentment Hearing." Transcript. **March 9, 2010. (Defendants gave the judge the unrequested (forged) Lee floorboard report as fulfilling records turn-over; and lied that was the only record in Sederwall's possession)**

Werkmeister, Nicole. "Attached is the Forensic Examination Report From Dr. Henry Lee ..." Fax cover letter. **April 6, 2010. (Copy faxed of same unrequested (forged) Lee floorboard report from Brown)**

Brown, Kevin. "Enclosed please find a copy of another report dated February 25, 2005 which deals with the examination of furniture by Dr. Lee." Letter to Threet. **November 10, 2010. (Sending Lee's (forged) bench report; different font than the (forged) floorboard report)**

Lee, Henry and Calvin Ostler. "Forensic Research and Training Center Forensic Examination Report: "Examination of furniture from Pete Maxwell's of July 15, 1881." February 25, 2005. **(Given to me on November 10, 2010 as Lee bench report (16 pages) – but was forged)**

"Evidentiary Hearing on Plaintiff's Motion for Mandatory Order of Disclosure and Production." Transcript. **January 21, 2011. (Defendants gave forged Lee Floorboard report (9 pages) Version II as Exhibit F; and forged Lee bench report (16 pages) as Exhibit E)**

Lee, Henry and Calvin Ostler. "Forensic Research and Training Center Forensic Examination Report: "Examination of furniture from Pete Maxwell's of July 15, 1881." February 25, 2005. **(Given to Court on January 21, 2011 as Lee bench report (16 pages), Exhibit E – but was a forgery)**

Lee, Henry and Calvin Ostler. "Forensic Research and Training Center Forensic Examination Report: "Examination of Lincoln County Court House." February 25, 2005. **(Given to Court on January 21, 2011 as Lee floorboard report (9 pages), Exhibit F – but was its forged Version II)**

"Presentment Hearing." Transcript. September 23, 2011. **(I realized forgery was taking place and presented discrepancies in the Lee reports)**

Hearing on "Plaintiffs' Motion to Supplement the Record and a Request for Sanctions, and Co-Plaintiff's Motion For Attorney Fees." January 17, 2012 **(Sanctions against Defendants requested for forged reports; and co-plaintiff requested fees for past attorneys. Judge granted 100% fees)**

Eichwald, George P., District Judge. "Order on Plaintiffs Motion to Supplement the Record and Request for Award of Sanctions against Defendants." February 23, 2012. **(Ordered Sederwall to produce authentic Lee report)**

Lee, Henry and Calvin Ostler. "Forensic Research and Training Center Forensic Examination Report." February 25, 2005. **(Court-ordered turn-over to Plaintiffs on January 31, 2012 as "original," authentic, sole Lee report (25 pages) combining bench, floorboards, and wash stand)**

Hearing on "Plaintiffs' Second Motion to Supplement the Record and a Request for Sanctions." **May 31, 2012 (Sanctions requested for forged Lee reports)**

ORCHID CELLMARK RECORDS SUBPOENAED
(RECEIVED 133 PAGES ON APRIL 20, 2012)

Griebel, Patrick J. Attorney for Scot Stinnett. "Subpoena for Production or Inspection to Laboratory Corporation of America." **March 29, 2012. (Non-IPRA subpoena of records from Orchid Cellmark parent company; got 133 pages of results of Lee's floorboards and bench, and Arizona exhumations; missing DNA matching results of bench to remains)**

SELECT RECORDS

Evidence Bag Photo. Chain of Custody Label: "Case No. 2003-274, Underside Bench 4. Date: 07,31,04." Below is written Orchid Cellmark Case and Specimen No. 4444-002B. **July 31, 2004. (Case 2003-274 was made Orchid Cellmark Case No. 4444)**

Ostler, Calvin D. "FedEx Mailing Envelope and tracking information to "Rick Staub, Orchid Cellmark." **August 3, 2004. (Specimens delivered August 4, 2004)**

"Orchid Cellmark Evidence Evaluation Worksheet Case No. 4444 A and B." **August 16, 2004. (Identifying Calvin Ostler as client; listing Lee's floorboard and bench specimens)**

"Orchid Cellmark Evidence Evaluation Worksheet Case No. 4444." **April 13, 2006. (Listing specimens from John Miller-William Hudspeth exhumations.**

"Orchid Cellmark Chain of Custody for Case No. 4444." **May 19, 2005. (On date of John Miller exhumation and signed by Orchid Cellmark Director Rick Staub with the south and north grave specimens he collected listed)**

"Orchid Cellmark Laboratory Report - Forensic Identity - Mitochondrial Analysis for 4444." **January 26, 2009. (Listing specimens for reports requested by me: Lee's from bench and Orchid Cellmark's from the Arizona graves.)**

GALE COOPER AS PRO SE

Cooper, Gale. "Plaintiff Gale Cooper's Court Ordered Request for Evidentiary Hearing Already Scheduled for December 18, 2012." **November 1, 2012.**

Cooper, Gale. "Plaintiff Gale Cooper's Entry of Pro Se Appearance." **November 13, 2012.**

_____. "Plaintiff Gale Cooper's Pre-Evidentiary Hearing Brief." **November 14, 2012.**

_____. "Plaintiff Gale Cooper's Pre-Evidentiary Hearing Brief." **November 14, 2012.**

Narvaez, Henry, Attorney for Virden. "It is our position that those deposition [sic] and exhibits are not relevant to the subject matter of the hearing..." Letter to Gale Cooper. **November 20, 2012. (Trying to keep out June 26-27, 2012 incriminating depositions of Sullivan and Sederwall)**

Cooper, Gale. "Plaintiff Gale Cooper's Witness List for Evidentiary Hearing on December 18, 2012." **December 10, 2012.**

"Evidentiary Hearing." Transcript. **December 18, 2012. (Virden testifies)**

Cooper, Gale. "Plaintiff Gale Cooper's Motion to Compel Defendants' Production of the Requested Forensic DNA Records of Lincoln County Sheriff's Department Case No. 2003-274." **January 3, 2013.**

_____. "Plaintiff Gale Cooper's Motion for Expedited Hearing on Her Filed Motions for the February 4, 2013 Evidentiary Hearing." **January 14, 2013.**

"Evidentiary Hearing." Transcript. February 4, 2013. **(Sederwall and Morel testify)**

Cooper, Gale. "Notice of Filing of Attached Plaintiff Gale Cooper's Proposed Findings of Fact and Conclusions of Law." **February 27, 2013.**

_____. "Plaintiff Gale Cooper's Proposed Findings of Fact and Conclusions of Law." **February 27, 2013.**

Cooper, Gale. "Plaintiff Gale Cooper's Motion to Request Award of Her Costs and Damages From Defendants and to Request Award of Sanctions Against Defendants." **May 23, 2013**.

_____. "Affidavit of Gale Cooper." **May 22, 2013. (Sworn costs)**

_____. "Plaintiff Gale Cooper's Request for Hearing." **May 23, 2013**.

Cooper, Gale. "Re: Open letter to Lincoln County Commissioners about Lincoln County Sheriff's Department **Case No. 2003-274** and Sandoval County District Court **Cause No. D-1329-CV-1364**, Gale Cooper and De Baca County News vs. Rick Virden, Lincoln County Sheriff and Custodian of the Records of the Lincoln County Sheriff's Office; and Steven M. Sederwall, Former Lincoln County Deputy Sheriff; and Thomas T. Sullivan, Former Lincoln County Sheriff and Former Lincoln County Deputy Sheriff." **June 18, 2013. (Summary of "Billy the Kid Case" hoax, its litigation, and its costs; no response)**

_____. "Plaintiff Gale Cooper's Notice of Briefing Completion with Repeated Request for Hearing." **July 1, 2013**.

_____. "Addendum to Plaintiff Gale Cooper's Motion to Request Award of Her Costs and Damages From Defendants and to Request Award of Sanctions Against Defendants." **July 1, 2013**.

_____.Hearing for Plaintiff Gale Cooper's Motion to Request Award of Her Costs and Damages From Defendants and to Request Award of Sanctions Against Defendants." Transcript. December 18, 2013. **(I won!)**

Eichwald, George P. Judge. "Findings of Fact and Conclusions of Law and Order of the Court." **May 15, 2014. (Plaintiff Gale Cooper prevailed)**

_____ "Final Judgment." **March 8, 2017. (Plaintiff Gale Cooper prevailed)**

COLD CASE BILLY THE KID MEGAHOAX OF W.C. JAMESON'S 21ˢᵗ CENTURY BOOKS

THE JAMESON BOOKS (CHRONOLOGICAL)

Jameson, W.C. *Billy the Kid: Beyond the Grave.* Boulder, Lanham, Maryland: Taylor Trade Publishing. **2005. (A repeat of the "Brushy Bill" imposter hoax)**

_____. *Billy the Kid: The Lost Interviews.* Clearwater, Florida: Garlic Press Publishing. **2012.** (Reprint 2017). **(Forged rewriting of the 1949 Morrison transcript of "Brushy" to fake dialogue to update the hoax)**

_____. *Pat Garrett: The Man Behind the Badge.* Boulder, Colorado: Taylor Trade Publishing. **2016. (Defamation of Pat Garrett, "Brushy Bill" as a quoted authority, and "Billy the Kid Case" hoaxing as evidence to claim Garrett murdered an innocent victim instead of Billy the Kid)**

_____. *Cold Case Billy the Kid: Investigating History's Mysteries.* Guilford, Connecticut: Twodot. **2018. (Fusing the "Brushy" hoax and "Billy the Kid Case" hoax to argue for "Brushy" as Billy the Kid)**

KEY SOURCES CITED BY HOAXERS (CHRONOLOGICAL)

(SEE: "Brushy Bill" Robert's hoax sources; Secret Service Operatives in Historical Organizations; and counterfeiting framing of Billy Bonney)

Bonney, William Henry. Deposition to Frank Warner Angel. **June 8, 1878.** Depositions, Pages 314-319. National Archives and Records Administration. Records of the Justice Department. Record Group 60. Class 44 Litigation Files. Container 21. Washington, D.C. (**A quote was used, but the deposition was hidden, since "Brushy" was unaware of it**)

Garrett, Pat F. *The Authentic Life of Billy the Kid*. Santa Fe, New Mexico: New Mexico Printing and Publishing Co. **1882.** (Edition used by me: Edited by Maurice Garland Fulton. New York: The Macmillan Company. 1927)

Hoyt, Henry F. "Copy of a bill of sale written by Wm H. Bonney ..." Letter to Lew Wallace Jr. **April 27, 1927.** Indiana Historical Society. Lew Wallace Collection. M0292. Box 14, Folder 11. (**Provided a copy of the Bill of Sale of October 24, 1878**)

Poe, John W. *The Death of Billy the Kid*. (Introduction by Maurice Garland Fulton). Boston and New York: Houghton Mifflin Company. **1933.**

Otero, Miguel, *The Real Billy the Kid*. New York: Rufus Rockwell Wilson. **1936.** (**Claim that Jesus Silva for shot Billy Bonney face down. But Otero had no first-hand knowledge, and the book was 55 years after the event.**)

Poe, Sophie. *Buckboard Days*. Albuquerque, New Mexico: University of New Mexico Press. **1964.**

Klasner, Lilly. Eve Ball. Ed. *My Girlhood Among Outlaws*. Tucson, Arizona: The University of Arizona Press. **1972.**

Avant, Bundy. (Told to Arthur Clements). "The Bundy Avant Story: New Mexico in the days when a thin population was intent on bettering itself and each man could devise his own method for 'getting' while getting' was good.' " (Part One) *True West*. **May-June, 1978,** Volume 25, Number 5. (**Old-timer malarkey about a "Peter Maxwell" in the San Andres Mountains telling Avant that Garrett did not kill Billy the Kid; plus other apocryphal Billy the Kid tales**)

Anaya, Paco. *I Buried Billy*. College Station, Texas: Creative Publishing Company. **1991.**(**Cited as claiming counterfeiting for Billy**)

Rasch, Philip J. *Trailing Billy the Kid*. National Association for Outlaw and Lawman History, Inc. **1995.** Page 108. (**Used as source about Tom O'Folliard false genealogy; Page 77; misstated 1932 tale by Tom Pickett of failing to get *counterfeit money* hidden in the Stinking Springs rock cabin; when Rasch wrote that it was *real money*; Page 108**)

Lee, Henry and Calvin Ostler. "Forensic Research and Training Center Forensic Examination Report: "Examination of Lincoln County Court House." February 25, 2005. (**Apparently the forged "Billy the Kid Case's floorboard report**)

Lee, Henry. "Forensic Examination Report (Examination of Furniture From Pete Maxwell's of July 15, 1881) 22 May 2004." From W.C. Jameson, *Cold Case Billy the Kid*. Page 187. (**Apparently the forged "Billy the Kid Case's" carpenter's bench, washstand, and headboard report**)

FOR DEBUNKING HOAXING OF WILLIAM BONNEY'S CORONER'S JURY REPORT'S NON-EXISTENCE

(SEE: William H. Bonney, Coroner's Jury Report; and Patrick F. Garrett, Reward)

FOR DEBUNKING HOAXING OF "INVESTIGATION" OF JOHN TUNSTALL'S MURDER

Gonzales, Florencio. Deposition to Frank Warner Angel. **June 8, 1878.** Frank Warner Angel report, Pages 314-319 from *In the Matter of the Examination of the Causes and Circumstances of the Death of John H. Tunstall a British Subject.* Report filed October 4, 1878. Angel Report. Records of the Justice Department. Record Group 60. Class 44 Litigation Files. Container 21. National Archives and Records Administration. U.S. Department of Justice. Washington, D.C. or Angel Report in Interior Department Papers 1850-1907; Appointments Division and Subsequent Actions. Microfilm File Case Number 44-4-8-3. Record Group 48. Microfilm No. M750. Roll 1. National Archives and Records Administration. U.S. Department of Justice. Washington, D.C. (**Showing that Steve Sederwall's claim that Gonzales was involved in a cover-up of Tunstall's murder was wrong**)

Appel, Daniel M. Deposition to Frank Warner Angel. **July 1, 1878.** Frank Warner Angel report, Pages 314-319 from *In the Matter of the Examination of the Causes and Circumstances of the Death of John H. Tunstall a British Subject.* Report filed October 4, 1878. Angel Report. Records of the Justice Department. Record Group 60. Class 44 Litigation Files. Container 21. National Archives and Records Administration. U.S. Department of Justice. Washington, D.C. or Angel Report in Interior Department Papers 1850-1907; Appointments Division and Subsequent Actions. Microfilm File Case Number 44-4-8-3. Record Group 48. Microfilm No. M750. Roll 1. National Archives and Records Administration. U.S. Department of Justice. Washington, D.C. (**Contradicting Steve Sederwall's description of Appel's autopsy report on John Tunstall**)

Nolan, Frederick W. *The Life and Death of John Henry Tunstall.* Albuquerque, New Mexico: The University of New Mexico Press. **1965.** (**With Tunstall's Coroner's Jury Report, page 285; and Daniel Appel's autopsy report, pages 286-287; and with Dr Taylor Ealy's; to counter hoaxer claims about their "investigation" of Tunstall's murder**)

FOR DEBUNKING HOAXING OF "BUCKSHOT" ROBERTS KILLING "INVESTIGATION"

Catron, Thomas Benton. "Case No. 411. The United States vs. Charles Bowdry [Bowdre], Doc Scurlock, Henry Brown, Henry Antrim alias "Kid," John Middleton, Stephen Stevens, John Scroggins, George Coe and Frederick Waite." **June 21, 1878.** Herman B. Weisner Papers, ca. 1957-1992. New Mexico State University Library at Las Cruces. Rio Grande Historical Collections. Accession No. Ms 0249. Box 1. B-Folder 4. Name: Andrew Roberts Indictment. (**Describes the "Buckshot" Roberts killing and his single fatal would, contradicting the fabrication used of A.N. Blazer**)

FOR DEBUNKING HOAXING OF PAT GARRETT AS A NON-LEGITIMATE DEPUTY U.S. MARSHAL

Wild, Azariah F. "Daily Reports of U. S. Secret Service Agents, 1875-1937." Microfilm T-915. Record Group 87. Microfilm Roll 308 (July 1, 1879 - June 30, 1881; October 13, 1880; October 21, 1880; October 29, 1880; January 3, 1881 (replacing his name with crossed-out John Hurley); January 25, 1881 (letter praising Garrett's service). National Archives and Records Department. Department of the Treasury. Secret Service Division. Washington, D.C. (**Showing legal appointment**)

FOR DEBUNKING HOAXING OF TOM O'FOLLIARD'S NAME AND GENEALOGY

No Author. "Death of T.C. McKinney." *The Carlsbad Current.* **September 24, 1915.** Page 1. Column 5. ChroniclingAmerica.loc.gov/. **(With no claim that Kip McKinney and Tom O'Folliard were cousins)**

Shipman, Jack. "Brief Career of Tom O'Folliard, Billy the Kid's Partner." No Author. *Voice of the Mexican Border.* Volume 1, Number 5. **January, 1934.** Pages 216-219. **(Gives unsubstantiated genealogy of Tom O'Folliard (Page 216) with no mention that he and Kip McKinney were cousins)**

King, Frank M. *Wranglin' the Past: Reminiscences of Frank M. King.* "Chapter xix, The Kid's Exit." Pasadena, California: Trail's End Publishing Company. **1935 and 1946. (False claim that Tom O'Folliard and Kip McKinney were cousins, Page 173)**

Rasch, Philip J. *Trailing Billy the Kid.* National Association for Outlaw and Lawman History, Inc. **1995.** Page 108. **(Used as source for Tom O'Folliard's false genealogy; Page 77)**

Clifford, Frank. Ed. Frederick Nolan. *Deep Trails in the Old West: A Frontier Memoir.* Norman: University of Oklahoma Press. **2011.** Page 276. (From original unpublished manuscript written in 1940) **(Explaining "cousin" error linking Tom O'Folliard to Kip McKinney as a marriage of a McKinney *cousin* into the O'Folliard family; which does not make Tom and Kip cousins; and stating Tom O'Folliard's genealogy is uncertain)**

FOR DEBUNKING HOAXING OF PETER MAXWELL'S EXTERNAL BEDROOM DOOR AS ABSENT

Armstrong, Mel and John McCarty. "Kid Dobbs Interviews: An Interview with Garrett H. 'Kid' Dobbs at Farmington, New Mexico," on September 12, 1942, with Mel Armstrong and John McCarty [with] Garrett H. Kid Dobbs in his Home in Farmington, New Mexico, Thursday Morning, October 22, 1942, In the Presence of Mrs. Dobbs and Pat Flynn. J.D. White, Amarillo, Heard Part of the Final Statements of this Interview Re. Billy the Kid's Death." **October 22, 1942.** John L. McCarty Papers. Amarillo Public Library. **(Old-timer malarkey claiming no outside door in Maxwell bedroom used as a source)**

Author Unknown. (Falsely attributed to Gregory Scott Smith). "The Death of Billy the Kid: A New Scenario?" Using "Kid Dobbs Interviews: An Interview with Garrett H. 'Kid' Dobbs at Farmington, New Mexico," on September 12, 1942, with Mel Armstrong and John McCarty" with undated commentary attributed incorrectly to Gregory Scott Smith, Monument Manager at the Fort Sumner State Monument, and using mislabeled diagram of Fort Sumner Commanding Officer's Quarters as the Maxwell house. Fort Sumner, New Mexico, State Monument files. **(Article using Kid Dobbs's fakery with added mislabeled diagram of Fort Sumner's Commanding Officer's Quarters as being the Maxwell house, to fabricate no outside door to the Maxwell bedroom)**

Boze Bell, Bob. (With Steve Sederwall) "Caught With His Pants Down? Billy the Kid Vs Pat Garrett. One Door Closes." **August, 2010.** *True West.* Volume 57. **(Using wrongly alleged author, Gregory Scott Smith's, "Death of Billy the Kid" article to claim no outside door, plus Sederwall hoaxing "CSI" proof of it by Dr. Henry Lee's fake washstand investigation. It was recycled by Sederwall in W.C. Jameson's *Cold Case Billy the Kid*)**

FOR DEBUNKING HOAXING OF FACE DOWN CORPSE

Traylor, Leslie. "Facts Regarding the Escape of Billy the Kid." *Frontier Times.* **July, 1936.** Pages 506-513 (on Page 509). FrontierTimesMagazine.com. (**About his Jesus Silva interview on identifying Billy's body**)

Otero, Miguel, *The Real Billy the Kid.* New York: Rufus Rockwell Wilson. **1936.** (**Claim that Jesus Silva saw shot Billy Bonney face down.**)

FOR DEBUNKING HOAXING OF OLD PETER MAXWELL AS A COOK DENYING GARRETT SHOT BILLY

Avant, Bundy. (Told to Arthur Clements). "The Bundy Avant Story: New Mexico in the days when a thin population was intent on bettering itself and each man could devise his own method for 'getting' while getting' was good.' " (Part One) *True West.* **May-June, 1978**, Volume 25, Number 5. (**Old-timer malarkey about a "Peter Maxwell" in the San Andres Mountains telling Avant that Garrett did not kill Billy the Kid**)

No Author. "Las Vegas." *The Albuquerque Citizen.* **June 28, 1898.** Page 2, Column 3. NewspaperArchive.com. (**Peter Maxwell death notice about Fort Sumner area residence and death**)

FOR DEBUNKING HOAXING OF BILLY BONNEY AS A BROCKWAY GANG COUNTERFEITER

(See Historical Organizations: Secret Service, Operatives)

No Author. "Crimes of Brockway, Story of the Notorious Counterfeiter's Career, Clemency Extended to Him by the Government in 1867 – He Soon Resorts to His Former Life – What a Secret Service Officer Says." *New York Times.* **December 3, 1880.** Volume XXX. Number 9122. Page 2. www.newspapers.com. (**Possible inspiration for the faked link in the December 22, 1880** *The Sun's* **"Outlaws of New Mexico"**)

No Author. "Outlaws of New Mexico, The Exploits of a Band Headed by a New York Youth, The Mountain Fastness of the Kid and His Followers - War Against a Gang of Cattle Thieves and Murderers - The Frontier Confederates of Brockway, the Counterfeiter." *The Sun.* New York. **December 22, 1880.** Vol. XLVIII, No. 118, Page 3, Columns 1-2. (**Apparent inspiration for faking a counterfeiting connection between Billy Bonney and William Brockway**)

Carter, Julie. "Counterfeit Bank Note Rewrites Chapter of Billy the Kid." **July 16, 2010.** *Ruidoso News.* Pages 1A, 9A. http://archives.lincolncountynm.gov/. (**Steve Sederwall linking Billy the Kid to national counterfeiting; then recycled in** *Cold Case Billy the Kid* **without this reference**)

Sederwall, Steve. "Billy Bonney's Bad Bucks: Did the Kid Travel the Counterfeit Trail?" **June, 2015.** *True West.* Volume 62. Number 6. Page 29. (**Sederwall's repeat of his 2010 counterfeiting claim to "Billy the Kid Case" hoax-backing** *True West*; **later in** *Cold Case Billy the Kid* **without this reference**)

BROCKWAY SOURCES CITED BY HOAXERS

No Author. "Old Counterfeiters Caught, Brockway and Two Others Arrested as J.B. Doyle's Accomplices." **October 24, 1880.** *New York Times.* Volume XXX, Number 9087. Page 5. National Archives. Secret Service Library, Counterfeit Division, via Archivist Michael Sampson.

No Author. "Brockway's Forged Bonds: The Counterfeiter Telling How Doyle Got the Bonds – Curious Statements in Court." **May 6, 1882.** *New York Times.* Volume XXXI, Number 9567. Column 2, Page 5. ProQuest.

Drummond, A.L. "True Detective Stories: A Genius Who Went Wrong." **December 20, 1908.** *New York Herald.* Page 7. National Archives. Secret Service Library, Counterfeit Division, via Archivist Michael Sampson.

OTHER BROCKWAY COUNTERFEITING REFERENCES

Dye, John S. *Dye's Government Counterfeiter Detector.* "The Boss of the Boodle and King of the 'Outside Men.' " **March, 1881.** Volume XXIX. Number 10, Pages 4-6. National Archives, Secret Service Library, Counterfeit Division via Archivist Michael Sampson. (**On James Brace Doyle as passing Brockway's counterfeit $100 bills nationally; case of Operative Andrew L. Drummond**)

_____. *Dye's Government Counterfeiter Detector.* "Quotations From the Record." **March, 1881.** Volume XXIX. Number 10, Pages 2-3. National Archives, Secret Service Library, Counterfeit Division via Archivist Michael Sampson. (**On finding some Brockway counterfeit bills in the Moundville, Missouri, haystack of John Hays; case of Operative Wallace W. Hall**)

Brooks, James J. "Annual Report of the Secret Service Division of the United States Treasury Department." **June 30, 1881.** *Government Counterfeiter Detector.* National Archives, Secret Service Library, Counterfeit Division, via Archivist Michael Sampson. (**About apprehension of Brockway gang**)

No Author. *Secret Service Currency Reference Information: 1860's-1880's.* Pages 160-165. National Archives, Secret Service Library, Counterfeit Division, via Archivist Michael Sampson. (**Banks used for Brockway's counterfeits**)

Dye, John S. "The Smith Plates." *Government Counterfeiter Detector.* **February, 1882.** Volume XXX. Number 9. National Archives, Secret Service Library, Counterfeit Division, via Archivist Michael Sampson. (**Description of Charles Smith's plates for William Brockway**)

_____. *Government Counterfeiter Detector.* **November, 1882.** Volume XXXI. Number 6. National Archives, Secret Service Library, Counterfeit Division, via Archivist Michael Sampson. (**General description of how counterfeit currency and skeleton plates are made**)

No Author. "Notes." The American Law Review (1866-1906) Volume 38. **1904.** Pages 576-577. Proquest. (**Biography of William Brockway**)

FOR DEBUNKING HOAXING OF A COUNTERFEIT BILL AS FROM BILLY THE KID

Sampson, Michael. Interviews and Consultation with Gale Cooper. **February and March of 2019.** National Archives at College Park. Secret Service Library, Counterfeit Division. 8601 Adelphi Road, College Park, Maryland. (**Statement that National Archives counterfeit bank note provided to Steve Sederwall was random, and not connected to Azariah Wild, Billy Bonney or documented as by William Brockway as claimed by Sederwall**)

FOR DEBUNKING HOAXING OF RUSTLING AS COUNTERFEIT MONEY-LAUNDERING

Haley, J. Evetts. *The XIT Ranch of Texas and the Early Days of the Llano Estacado.* Chicago: Lakeside Press. **1929.** (**Confirming James Cook as a liar in his *Lane of the Llano*, used as an "eye witness" source by Sederwall**)

Cook, James L. *Lane of the Llano: Being the Story of Jim (Lane) Cook as Told to T.M. Pearce.* Pages 91-92 Boston: Little Brown & Company. **1936.** (**Old-timer malarkey about selling Billy the Kid's cattle rustled from John Chisum; faked by Steve Sederwall as an "eye witness" source for Billy's rustling-counterfeit money-laundering scheme**)

Dobie, J. Frank. "Son-of-a-Gun Stew." Review. *Southwest Review.* **July, 1936.** Volume 21, Number 4. Pages 444-445. jstor.org. (**Calling Jim Cook's** *Lane of the Llano* **"puerile invention"**)

Haley, J. Evetts. "Jim Cook: On the Frontiers of Fantasy." *The Shamrock.* Spring, 1964. Pages 4-7. (**Stating Cook wrote in "fantasy"**)

No Author. *Deaf Smith County: The Land and its People.* Hereford, Texas: Deaf Smith County Historical Society. **1982.** (**Cook as liar in his** *Lane of the Llano*)

No Author. Biography of James L. Cook. Texas State Historical Association. https://tshaonline.org/handbook/online/articles/fco49. (**Cook as liar in his** *Lane of the Llano*)

FOR DEBUNKING HOAXING OF BILLY BONNEY IN A COUNTERFEITING CONSPIRACY WITH JESSE JAMES

Hoyt, Henry. *A Frontier Doctor.* Boston and New York: Houghton Mifflin Company. **1929. (Billy Bonney eating a meal with Jesse James (Pages 110-113) used to claim counterfeiting partnership.)**

Settle, William A. *Jesse James Was His Name.* Columbia, Missouri: University of Missouri Press. **1966. (No mention of Jesse James as a counterfeiter)**

Ross, James R. *I, Jesse James.* Dragon Publishing Corp. **1988. (Great-grandson of Jesse James as author. No mention of counterfeiting, William Brockway, or Billy Bonney)**

Pennington, William. "Roster of Quantrill's, Anderson's and Todd's Guerrillas and Other 'Missouri Jewels.' " **1998.** pennington.tripod.com/roster.htm . (**Showing times of service of Joseph Lea, and Frank and Jesse James, and that they did not serve together with Quantrill; also with John Hays with no dates**)

Stiles, T.J. *Jesse James: Last Rebel of the Civil War.* New York: Vintage Books. **2003. (No mention of counterfeiting, William Brockway, or Billy Bonney)**

James, Eric F. *Jesse James Soul Liberty: Behind the Family Wall of Stigma and Silence.* Danville, Kentucky: Cashel Cadence House. **2012. (No mention of counterfeiting, William Brockway, or Billy Bonney)**

Sederwall, Steve. "Billy Bonney's Bad Buck's: Did the Kid Travel the Counterfeiting Trail." *True West.* June, 2015. Volume 62. Number 6. Page 29. (**Contention that Billy the Kid and Jesse James were in cahoots in counterfeiting**)

Sampson, Michael. Interviews and Consultation with Gale Cooper. **February and March of 2019.** National Archives at College Park. Secret Service Library, Counterfeit Division. 8601 Adelphi Road, College Park, Maryland. (**Confirming no Secret Service investigation of Jesse James as a counterfeiter**)

FOR DEBUNKING HOAXING OF JAMES DOLAN AS A COUNTERFEITER (FAKING WITNESS MISS N.M. FERGUSON)

Hall, Wallace W. "Daily Reports of U. S. Secret Service Agents, 1875-1937." Microfilm T-915. Record Group 87. Microfilm Rolls: 153 (January 1, 1879 – December 31, 1880); 155: (January 1, 1882 – July 31, 1883; January–June 1882, July 1, 1882). National Archives and Records Department. Department of the Treasury. Secret Service Division. Washington, D.C. (**Reports misstated as being letters by an N.M. Ferguson reporting a counterfeit bill concerning Will Dowlin, not James Dolan: for August 3, 1880, completed August 4, 1880 (questioning Ferguson about if she got a response from J.C. Delaney about getting a counterfeit bill); for August 24, 1880 completed August 30, 1880 (refers to undated cover note from Ferguson with two enclosed letters: one dated August 8, 1880 from Fort Stanton, which she got from J.C. Delaney; one dated August 5, 1880 from Tularosa, which was from M.J. Dowlin to Will Dowlin & Co.); for October 10, 1880, completed October 11, 1880 (reminding Chief Brooks about his Ferguson reporting); and for July 1, 1882, completed July 7, 1882, reporting that he had sent Chief Brooks the** letters on the Ferguson case, but Brooks had not returned them. So Hall's reports have no actual Ferguson letters)

No Author. National Archives and Records Administration, College Park, Maryland. RG 87, Records of the Secret Service, Entry A1-9 Register of letters received, 1863-1903, Volume 5. (**No actual letters referenced by Wallace Hall on the N.M. Ferguson case are present'**)

No Author. National Archives and Records Administration, College Park, Maryland. RG 87, Records of the Secret Service, Entry A1-7 Register of letters received, 1863-1903, Volume 9. (**No actual letters referenced by Wallace Hall on the N.M. Ferguson case are present**)

FOR DEBUNKING HOAXING OF PAT GARRETT AS CONNECTED TO COUNTERFEITING

Metz, Leon C. *Pat Garrett. The Story of a Western Lawman.* Norman: University of Oklahoma Press. 1974. (**Contradicts Steve Sederwall's fakery that that Frank Lea was connected to counterfeiting and was Garrett's friend, giving instead a Captain Joseph C. Lea, his brother, as Garrett's friend**)

FOR DEBUNKING HOAXING OF FREIGHTER SAM SMITH'S KILLING AS CONNECTED TO BILLY THE KID AND COUNTERFEITING

Secretary of War. "Samuel Smith, killed by Mescaleros at Pato Spring, April 15, 1880. *Annual Report of the Secretary of War for the Year 1880.* Volume 1. Washington: Government Printing Office. **1880**. Page 106. Google books. (**Listing Sam Smith as killed by Mescaleros; contradicting hoaxers' tale that Smith was killed by Billy the Kid gang in revenge for revealing their counterfeiting**)

No Author. "The Indian News." **April 27, 1880.** *Las Vegas Daily Gazette.* chroniclingamerica.loc.gov. (**Confirming Smith was killed by Victorio's band, contradicting hoaxers' claim that he was killed by Billy the Kid gang in revenge for revealing their counterfeiting**)

No Author. "Indian Depredations in Colorado and Dakota." **May 4, 1880.** *Sacramento Daily Record-Union.* Front page. Volume XLIX, Number 477, Column 6. chroniclingamerica.loc.gov. (**Confirming Smith was killed by Mescalero Apaches, contradicting hoaxers' claim that he was killed by Billy the Kid gang in revenge for revealing their counterfeiting**)

No Author. "Mescalero Marauders." *Santa Fe Daily New Mexican.* **May 21, 1880.** Page 4, Column 1. NewspaperArchives.com. (**Confirming Smith was killed by Mescalero Apaches, contradicting hoaxers' claim that he was killed by Billy the Kid gang in revenge for revealing their counterfeiting**)

No Author. "Outlaws of New Mexico, The Exploits of a Band Headed by a New York Youth, The Mountain Fastness of the Kid and His Followers - War Against a Gang of Cattle Thieves and Murderers - The Frontier Confederates of Brockway, the Counterfeiter." *The Sun.* New York. **December 22, 1880.** Vol. XLVIII, No. 118, Page 3, Columns 1-2. (**Actual source of quote by Steve Sederwall, wrongly attributed to the May 21, 1880** *Santa Fe New Mexican,* **with this Santa Fe Ring outlaw myth press accusing Billy Bonney of counterfeiting with William Brockway and murdering freighter Sam Smith**)

(SEE: Historical Organizations: Secret Service, Operatives: Azariah F. Wild, A.L. Drummond, Wallace Hall, Patrick Tyrell,)

FOR DEBUNKING HOAXING OF MAIL CONTRACTOR MIKE COSGROVE IN A MAIL THEFT-COUNTERFEITING CONSPIRACY WITH BILLY

Wilcox, Lucius "Lute" M. (city editor, owner, J.H. Koogler). "The Kid. Interview with Billy Bonney The Best Known Man in New Mexico." *Las Vegas Gazette.* **December 27, 1880. (Source of misread "mail contractor" as "mail carrier" to fabricate Billy in a conspiracy with carrier to read Wild's mail)**

No Author. "Cosgrave's Contract." *The Las Vegas Daily Optic.* **October 19, 1881.** Volume 2, Number 206, Page 4. www.newspaperarchive.com **(Mike Cosgrove as a mail contractor)**

No Author. *Official Register of the United States Containing a List of the Officers and Employees in the Civil, Military, and Naval Service on the First of July, 1881, Volume II.* The Post-Office Department and Postal Service. Washington: Government Printing Office. **1881.** Page 209. Google books. **(Listing Mike Cosgrove's Star Route contract)**

No Author. "Optical Oracles." *The Las Vegas Daily Optic.* **April 26, 1882.** Volume IIL, Number 147, Page 4. www.newspaperarchive.com. **(Mike Cosgrove as a mail contractor having a man named "Dutch" as a mail carrier)**

Michael, W.H. (Clerk). *Miscellaneous Documents of the Senate of the United States for the First Session of the Fiftieth Congress. Volume II.* Washington: Government Printing Office. **1888.** Page 190. Google books. **(About mail contractors)**

FOR DEBUNKING HOAXING OF STINKING SPRINGS'S ROCK HOUSE AS CONNECTED TO COUNTERFEITING

Anaya, Paco. *I Buried Billy.* College Station, Texas: Creative Publishing Company. 1991. **(Using his malarkey about Billy having "spurious" money)**

Rasch, Philip J. *Trailing Billy the Kid.* National Association for Outlaw and Lawman History, Inc. **1995.** Page 108. **(Used for misstating Tom Pickett's malarkey about failure to get *counterfeit money* hidden by Billy in the Stinking Springs rock cabin; when Rasch wrote that it was *real money*; Page 108)**

INDEX

Abbott, E.C. "Teddy Blue" –104
Abbott, George – 114
Abbott, Harold – 114-115, 117, 308
Abreu, Manuel – 42, 163, 168, 195
Abreu, Odelia – 195
Abreu, Stella – 168-169, 188-189, 195, 197, 199-201; **Billy the Kid Museum of:** 168-169, 188, 195-196, 199-201
Acuña, Mark Anthony – 217, 236, 242
Airy, Helen – 204, 208; *Whatever Happened to Billy the Kid?* by: 204
Alamogordo, New Mexico – 114, 129, 339
Alamogordo News – 104, 114
Albuquerque Citizen – 305
Albuquerque Journal – 175-177, 190, 197, 201, 213-214, 218
Albuquerque Museum of Art and History – 189
Albuquerque, New Mexico – 188, 195, 215
Analla, Pablo – 67, 89, 343
Anaya, A.P. "Paco" – 2170-171, 308, 420-423, 426; *I Buried Billy* by: 171, 308, 420-423
Angel, Frank Warner – 53, 55, 69-70, 101, 139, 151, 265-266, 268-269, 277, 355, 460
Anton Chico, New Mexico Territory – 344
Antrim, Catherine McCarty – 126-127, 130, 156, 173, 188, 193, 204, 208, 214, 216-218, 223-226, 230-232, 234, 239, 241-242, 329, 445, 458-460; **attempted exhumation of:** 127, 173, 188, 193, 204, 216-218, 223-226, 231-232, 239, 445, 458-460 (See "Billy the Kid Case" hoax)
Antrim, Henry - (see William H. Bonney)

Antrim, William Henry (see William H. Bonney)
Antrim, Joseph "Josie" – 48
Antrim, William Henry Harrison – 48
Appel, Daniel – 266-270, 276, 278-281, 460-461; **Tunstall autopsy by:** 460-461
Arizona Pioneers' Home Cemetery – 207
Avant, Bundy – 195, 304-306
Axtell, Samuel Beach – 52-53, 55, 70, 185, 187, 269, 271, 278
Baca, Saturnino – 54, 96, 278-280
Baker, Frank – 52, 60, 64, 68-71, 80-81, 268, 270-271
Banks, Leo W. – 190, 208, 211-213
Barlow Billy – 123-125, 129, 136, 140, 143, 148, 185, 195, 203, 290
Barnes, Sidney – 60, 286, 321, 325, 345-351, 353-357, 360, 381, 415-416
Barrier, Adolph – 51, 273
Bean, Frederick – 123-124, 135, 137, 141, 146, 328; *The Return of the Outlaw Billy the Kid* by: 123, 135-142, 284, 328, 330; **transcribing Morrison's "Brushy" tapes by:** 137, 141
Beaver Smith's Saloon – 58
Beckwith family – 81
Beckwith, Robert W. "Bob" – 69, 81, 84-86, 284, 422
Bell, James W. – 26-27, 48, 64-65, 102, 129, 132, 148, 150, 154-155, 174-185, 214-216, 219, 331, 229-230, 236, 247, 257, 318, 323-324, 365, 424, 444, 456; **"Billy the Kid Case" "Probable Cause Statement" sub-investigation for:** 150, 154-155, 174-185, 214-216, 229-230, 257, 444; **Dr. Henry Lee's fake forensics for shooting of:** 176-179, 318, 456 (See "Billy the Kid Case" hoax)

"Big Casino" – 58
Bill Kurtis Productions (See Bill Kurtis)
Billy-Dolan peace meeting (see William H. Bonney)
Billy the Kid (see William H. Bonney)
BillytheKidCase.com website (See Steve Sederwall)
"Billy the Kid Case" (see "Billy the Kid Case" hoax)
"Billy the Kid Case" hoax (Lincoln County Sheriff's Department Case No. 2003-274, De Baca County Sheriff's Department Case No. 03-06-136-01) – 121, 124-135, 139-140, 143-147, 149-173, 175-176, 179, 184-185, 188-189, 191-194, 196, 202, 204-205, 209, 214, 271, 282, 287-288, 290, 300, 302, 307, 311, 315-318, 320-325, 327-328, 330, 333, 337, 375, 379, 420-421, 435; **:Probable Cause Statement" for:** 150-173, 176, 179-181, 188, 197, 214, 228, 232, 266, 291, 307, 315-317, 319-321, 324-325; **"U.S. Marshals Service and Billy the Kid" addendum for:** 320-325; **open records litigation against:** 133, 174-175, 178-179, 190, 192-193, 201-203, 211, 217-218, 226, 247, 263, 320, 333, 337, 375, 379 (See Henry Lee for fake forensics for) (See hoaxers: Bill Richardson, Bill Robins III, Paul Hutton, Henry Lee, Tom Sullivan, Gary Graves, Steve Sederwall, David Turk, Alan Morel, Sherry Tippett, Henry Quintero, Ted Hartley, Rick Staub, Randi McGinn) (See Orchid Cellmark Laboratory) (See John Miller, William Hudspeth)
Billy the Kid Museum in Canton, Texas – 129

Billy the Kid Outlaw Gang – 170, 243, 422
Blakely's Mills, Colorado – 342
Blazer, A.N. – 275-276
Blazer, Joseph – 275, 277
Blazer's Mill – 6, 63, 275, 279, 358
"blood" of Billy the Kid (see "Billy the Kid Case" hoax)
Bonita, Arizona – 45, 48-49
Bonito River – 55
Bonney, William H. "Billy" (William Henry McCarty, Henry Antrim, Billy Bonney, Billy the Kid) – 3, 5-43, 45-117, 121-125, 128, 131, 136-137, 148, 153-156, 158, 164-168, 170-171, 173, 180-181, 190, 193, 197, 204, 215, 217-219, 221, 223-224, 229, 231, 235, 238, 242, 247, 257, 268, 273, 276, 290, 296, 300, 302-304, 307-308, 314, 322, 325, 331-333, 335, 337-370, 374-381, 383, 385-386, 391, 397, 400-401, 404-406, 412-414, 416-420, 422, 425, 429-431, 435, 437, 458; **history of:** 45-66; **words of:** 67-98; **Robin Hood self image of:** 67; **contemporary champions of:** 99-104; **federal indictment of:** 6-9, 357, 425; **Lew Wallace pardon bargain of:** 10, 47, 57, 61, 82, 97, 103, 128, 148, 153, 343, 345, 352-353, 387; **Secret Service pursuit of:** 11, 60, 62, 344-370; **Secret Service pardon bargain for:** 61, 341, 381, 414-416; **Coroner's Jury Report of:** 105-117; **Santa Fe Ring outlaw myth of:** 5-19, 44, 46, 59-61, 66-67, 98-99, 340, 346, 383, 435; **Lew Wallace outlaw myth of:** 20-40, 44, 362; **Pat Garrett outlaw myth of:** 41-43; **exhumation attempts on:** 126, 156, 167, 173, 176, 188, 193, 204, 217, 223-226, 231-232, 235, 239,

242-245; OMI blockade of: 223-226
Bommersbach, Jana – 329
Bordley, William – 318
Bosque Grande – 15-16, 56, 344, 346, 352, 356-357, 360, 365, 373, 377, 387-389, 419
Bosque Redondo – 58, 295
Bowdre, Charles "Charlie" – 6, 11-12, 41, 48, 52-53, 55, 59-63, 65, 74, 88-89, 95, 103, 154, 224, 226, 245-246, 275-276, 287, 316, 344, 346, 349, 357, 359-360, 369, 387, 415, 423-424
Bowdre, Manuela – 56, 344
Bowlin, Joe – 170, 422
Bowlin, Marlyn – 170, 243, 246, 422
Boyle, Andrew "Andy" – 283
Boze Bell, Bob – 121, 125, 147, 300, 327-333, 337, 379; *Illustrated Life and Times of Billy the Kid* by: 327; *True West* magazine of: 134, 252, 266, 296, 299, 318, 373, 389-390, 393, 396, 573, 621, 631, 647, 649-650, 691, 696; **backing the "Billy the Kid Case" hoax by:** 329-330; **backing the "Brushy Bill" hoax by:** 330; **hoaxing, with Steve Sederwall, no outside door in Peter Maxwell's bedroom by:** 331-332; **hoaxing, with Steve Sederwall and David Turk, Billy Bonney as a counterfeiter: by:** 333, 379-381
Brady, William – 10, 32, 50-56, 60, 63-64, 68-69, 73, 75-76, 92, 96, 101, 103, 128, 151, 187, 266-267, 269-274, 279, 284, 343, 359, 379, 406, 424
Bradford, Illinois – 369, 372, 386, 429
Branch, Tom – 131
Breeden, William – 105, 108-112, 114-117, 171

Brewer, Richard "Dick" – 52-53, 65, 68-69, 71-73, 101, 186, 276-277, 357
Brininstool, E.A. – 159
Briscoe, Joe – 58
Bristol, Warren H. – 51, 57-58, 63, 92, 272-273, 364, 404, 406
British Royal Society – 207
Brockway, William E. "Long Bill" alias Edward W. Spencer – 4, 14, 17, 333, 338-343, 345-346, 369-381, 383-388, 390-391, 395-400, 402, 413-415, 427-431; **biography of:** 371-372; **major bill pushers of:** 372-374 (see James B. Doyle, Frank Doyle, Nate Foster, John W. Hays, W.H. West)
Brooklyn, New York – 371, 385
Brooks, James J. – 60-61, 154, 285-286, 345-348, 360, 366, 368-371, 380, 391, 399, 429 (See Secret Service, Azariah Wild)
Brown, Henry Newton – 6-9, 63, 71, 101, 276, 360
Brown, Kevin – 215, 218, 247, 249-250, 252, 254
"Brushy Bill" Roberts - (see Oliver Pleasant Roberts)
Budd, William (See William H. West)
Bugliosi, Vincent – 174; *The Five Reasons Why O.J. Simpson Got Away With Murder* by: 174
Burnam, George P. – 371; *American Counterfeiters by*: 371
Burns, Walter Noble – 43-44, 136; *The Saga of Billy the Kid* by: 43-44, 13643-44, 13643-44, 13643-44, 13643-44, 13643-44, 136
Burt, Billy – 102, 185
Cahill, Frank "Windy" – 49, 52-53, 60, 64, 350
Camp, Ralph – 426

Campbell, Billy – 56-57, 78, 82, 103, 310, 355, 403
Canton, Texas – 127, 129
Capitan Mountains – 65, 79, 270, 368
Capitan, New Mexico – 128, 131, 148, 214, 237, 240, 250, 253, 304, 322, 329
"Capitan Village Hall News" – 148
Caplan, Sara – 174
Carlyle, Jim – 17, 62, 65, 88-89, 365-366, 368
carpenter's bench (See "Billy the Kid Case" hoax, , Henry Lee fake forensics on, Steve Sederwall forgery of forensic report on)
Carter, Julie – 133, 188-190, 201, 206, 214, 318, 337, 375
Casey, Robert – 50
Catron, Thomas Benton – 5-6, 9-10, 47, 49-51, 53-57, 59-60, 63-64, 74-75, 103, 110, 274, 276, 278-279, 281-282, 343-345, 349-350, 353, 355, 357-358, 360-362, 377, 404, 415-416, 420, 425, 430; **Federal indictment No. 411 of Regulators by:** 6-9, 63, 357, 425
Caypless, Edgar – 64, 92
Cedric, Nikki – 189, 318, 320
Chapman, Huston – 10, 20-21, 23, 30, 34, 36, 56-58, 67, 76-77, 82, 103, 153, 355, 357, 403
Charles Fritz Ranch – 274, 343
Chávez, Florencio – 54
Chávez y Chávez, José – 54, 83, 86-87
Cherry, Doris – 175, 178, 189-191
Chisum, John Simpson – 21, 23, 30, 40, 46, 50-53, 81, 89, 95, 273, 305, 339, 343-344, 350, 358, 361, 374, 380, 383, 386-387, 391-396, 400, 421
Clarkson, Lana – 174
Cleveland, Grover – 406, 411-413; **pardon of Billy Wilson by:** 411-413

Cline, Donald – 331; *Brushy Bill Roberts: I Wasn't Billy the Kid* **by:** 331
Coe, Frank – 52, 99, 267, 276, 278
Coe, George – 6-9, 52-53, 63, 99-100, 275-276, 304; *Frontier Fighter* **by:** 100, 275
Coghlan, Pat – 56, 344
Colfax County War – 5
Colorado Springs, Colorado – 372
Cook, David – 310-312, 314
Cook, Eliza Jane (See Eliza Jane McKinney Cook)
Cook, Eliza Jane McKinney – 310, 312, 314
Cook, Jim (Lane) – 314, 380, 391, 393; *Lane of the Llano: Being the Story of Jim (Lane) Cook as Told to T.M. Pearce* **by:** 380, 393
Cook, John (author) – 393
Cook, John – 310-312
Cook, John Enoch – 314
Cook, Margaret Jane – 311-312
Cook, Sarah – 310-312
Cook, Thalis – 311-312
Cooper, Thomas "Tom" – 347-349, 351-352, 355-356, 358, 361, 367, 370, 374, 415, 419
Copeland, John – 53, 185, 278-279
Corbett, Sam – 79, 184
Coroner's Jury Report (see William H. Bonney)
Cosgrove, Cornelius – 418
Cosgrove, Michael "Mike" – 93, 381, 414, 417-419
Coyote Spring – 16, 62, 366, 405
Crawford, Charles "Charlie" – 281
Crawfordsville, Indiana – 20-21, 29
Crawfordsville Saturday Evening Journal – 20, 403
Davis, George – 68-69, 81
Darwin, Charles – 207
Dawson, Charles – 207-208
De Baca County, New Mexico – 130-131, 133, 215-217, 223, 243, 245, 322

De Baca County Sheriff's Department Case No. 03-06-136-01 (See "Billy the Kid Case" hoax)

Dedrick, Dan – 56, 60-62, 340-341, 344, 346-347, 351-352, 355, 360-362, 365-367, 370, 377, 388-390, 396, 405, 415, 419-420; **counterfeit money cattle deal of:** 365, 388-390, 396; **fled to California:** 366 (See Barney Mason, W.H. West)

Dedrick, Mose – 61, 344, 351, 362

Dedrick, Sam – 61, 344, 351, 362

Deer Trail, Colorado – 373, 386, 392-393, 395

Deherra, Toby Jr. – 206

Delaney, John C. – 428, 430 (See Dowlin & Delaney)

Devours, James – 359-361, 366, 377, 420, 431

DeZulovich, Marvis – 319

"DNA of Billy the Kid" (see Billy the Kid Case hoax)

Dobbs, Garrett H. "Kid" – 298, 332

Dolan, James –49, 51, 54, 56-58, 60-61, 63, 68-69, 71, 76, 78, 81-82, 96, 103, 152, 268-270, 278-279, 281-282, 310, 342, 345-350, 355, 360, 374, 377, 380-381, 383, 404-411, 413, 415-416, 419, 427-430

Doña Ana County, New Mexico – 57, 407

Dowlin, M. J. – 380, 428-429

Dowlin, William "Will" – 355, 377, 380, 428-429 (See Dowlin & Delaney)

Dowlin & Delaney – 374, 430

Doyle, Frank W. – 339, 341, 369-374, 381, 386, 388, 390-393, 395-397, 399, 413, 415, 429; **aka "Kibby" (Kibbey):** 370, 397-399; **aka Murphy:** 397; **aka "Duncan":** 370

Doyle, James Brace – 17, 339, 341-342, 369-374, 378, 384-386, 390-391, 395-397, 414-415, 429

Doyle, William "young Doyle" – 373, 386

Drummond, Arthur L. – 342, 371, 385

Dudley, Nathan Augustus Monroe – 10-11, 22, 24, 54-58, 67, 82-87, 103, 277-284, 309, 355, 362 (See William H. Bonney prosecution testimony)

Ealy, Taylor – 267, 281-282

Eanthropus dawsoni – 208 (See Piltdown Man hoax)

Easton, David – 279-280, 350, 404-405

Eichwald, George – 247, 249, 257-258, 263, 379, 444-450; **"Findings of Fact and Conclusions of Law" by:** 257-258, 263, 379, 444-450

Ellis, Benjamin J. "Ben" – 281

Ellis, Isaac – 96

Evans, Jessie – 20, 30, 36, 49, 51, 56-57, 68-69, 82, 103, 129, 151, 268, 280, 355, 403

Farmington, New Mexico Territory – 99, 298

Feliz River – 49, 51, 101, 187

Ferguson, N.M. – 377, 380, 385-386, 427-430

Fidler, Larry Paul – 174

Fisher, Linda – 206

floorboards (See "Billy the Kid Case" hoax, Cold Case Billy the Kid megahoax, Henry Lee fake forensics on, Steve Sederwall forgery of forensic report on)

Flynn, Pat – 298

Forensitec – 209, 451-453

Fortenberry, Terry – 241

Fort Grant, Arizona – 49

Fort Stanton, New Mexico Territory – 50, 54, 77-80, 82, 266, 273, 278, 281-282, 344-345, 348-349, 352, 354-356, 358, 361-362, 416, 419, 427-430, 460

Fort Sumner, New Mexico Territory – 3, 11-12, 14-15, 17,

28, 39, 41, 47-48, 56, 58-62, 65, 88, 105-108, 111, 113, 115, 122, 125-126, 128, 130-133, 136, 138-139, 143, 145, 149, 153-157, 159-160, 164-167, 169, 171, 173, 176, 180-181, 183, 188-189, 195, 198-200, 214, 218, 223-227, 229-236, 240-246, 285, 288, 290-292, 294-295, 298-299, 304-307, 315-317, 332, 344-346, 349, 352, 355-365, 367-369, 378, 387-389, 394, 401, 415-415, 419, 421-422, 425-426

Fort Sumner State Monument – 294-295, 298, 332

Foster, Nathan B. "Nate" – 339, 341, 371-374, 381, 386, 390-393, 395-396, 413, 429-430

Fountain, Albert Jennings – 63, 305

Fountain, Henry – 305

French, Jim "Frenchie" – 11, 52, 54, 61, 278, 309, 344, 359-360

Fritz, Charles "Charlie" – 274, 278, 343

Fritz, Emil – 49-50, 137, 269

Fulginiti, Laura – 205-206, 208-211, 213-214, 451-453; **"Hip Man" of:** 209, 213; **"Scapula Man" of:** 208, 213; **forensic report on exhumations of John Miller and William Hudspeth of:** 209-211, 451-453

Fulton, Maurice Garland – 74, 101, 189, 275, 296

Garrett, Apolinaria (see Apolinaria Gutierrez)

Garrett, Juanita (see Juanita Gutierrez)

Garrett, Patrick Floyd "Pat" – 3, 11, 16, 22-23, 26, 28, 32-33, 38-39, 41-43, 46, 48, 58-59, 61-62, 64-66, 88-89, 92, 104-115, 117, 122-131, 133-134, 136, 138, 140-165, 167-173, 176-188, 190, 193-198, 201-205, 207-208, 213-218, 223, 229-233, 235, 240-241, 243, 246, 256-257, 270, 275, 284-293, 295, 298-304, 306-308, 310-312, 314-317, 319-325, 327-333, 337, 339-341, 345-346, 359, 363-369, 378, 381, 386-387, 389-390, 395-396, 399-400, 402-408, 411, 413-414, 418, 420-426, 435, 444-445, 447, 458; **Coroner's Jury Report absolving of murder:** 105-106; **Statute of Limitations blocking murder prosecution after 1891:** 125-126, 129-130, 149; **letter to Acting-Governor William Ritch by:** 107-109; **collecting Billy the Kid reward by:** 109-114; *The Authentic Life of Billy the Kid* **by:** 41, 43, 123, 152, 160, 179, 181, 232, 275, 287-290, 310, 312, 320, 339-340, 386-387, 389, 395-396, 414, 420, 423-424 (See Coroner's Jury Report for William H. Bonney)

Gates, Susan – 281-282

Gauss, Gottfried – 64, 71-72, 101, 152, 176, 179, 182-183, 186-187, 422

Godfroy, Frederick – 266, 374

Gonzales, Florencio – 265, 268-269

Gonzales, Ignacio – 54

Grant County Herald – 82

Grant County, New Mexico – 131, 133, 216-217, 223, 231, 241

Grant County Rebellion of 1876 – 5

Grant, Joe – 60, 64

Graves, Gary Wayne –130, 134, 217, 231, 238, 243, 245, 322; **De Baca County Case No. 03-06-136-01 for exhumation of Billy the Kid by:** 133, 215 (See "Billy the Kid Case" hoax)

Greathouse, Jim "Whiskey Jim" – 15-17, 62, 88-89, 365-368, 405

Greenham, Walter B. – 342, 369-370, 391, 397-398

Gricus, Greg – 206
Griffin, Willie E. – 225, 245
Grzelachowski, Alexander – 339, 387, 396
Guadalupe Mountains – 80
Gutierrez, Apolinaria – 59
Gutierrez, Celsa – 59, 65, 139, 144, 157
Gutierrez, Juanita – 59
Gutierrez, Saval (Sabal) – 59, 65, 105-106, 108, 164, 171, 307
Haag, Mike – 202, 250, 255
Hadley, Russ – 206
Hall, Wallace W. – 342, 371-372, 377, 381, 385, 390-392, 395-396, 402, 413, 427-430
Hamilton, Texas – 130, 219, 225, 236, 238
Hargrove's Saloon – 58-59
Harnett, Kristen – 209
Hartley, Ted – 133
Haws, Roy L. – 122; *Brushy Bill: Proof That His Claim to be Billy the Kid Was a Hoax* by: 122
Hayes, Rutherford B. – 5, 26, 53, 55
Hays, John W. – 339, 341, 371-374, 380-381, 385-386, 390-392, 395-400, 402, 413-415, 429
headboard (See "Billy the Kid Case" hoax, Cold Case Billy the Kid megahoax, Henry Lee fake forensics on, Steve Sederwall forgery of forensic report on)
Herrera, Fernando - 281
Hico, Texas – 129-130
Hill, Thomas "Tom" – 69-71, 81, 151
Hindman, George – 10, 32, 52, 56, 60, 63-64, 68-70, 76, 268, 271, 274, 406, 424
"Hip Man"(See John Miller, Laura Fulginiti)
Howard, George J. – 75
Hoyt, Henry F. – 56, 67, 75, 103-104, 274, 340, 400-401; **W.H. Bonney's bill of sale to:** 56, 67, 75, 274, 343; *A Frontier Doctor* by: 104, 400; **seeing Billy Bonney and Jesse James eating a meal:** 400-401
Hudspeth, William (illegal exhumation of) – 205-213, 237, 435, 445, 451-452, 454-456 (See "Billy the Kid Case" hoax, Laura Fulginiti)
Hurley, John – 70, 72, 84, 154, 284-286, 316
Hutton, Paul – 121, 124, 130-132, 135, 149-150, 174, 176, 189, 240, 318, 328, 330; **official historian for "Billy the Kid Case" as:** 121, 124, 130-132, 174, 189, 240, 328; **"Investigating History: Billy the Kid" History Channel TV by:** 121, 124-125, 135, 149-150, 328; **bringing in Dr. Henry Lee and Bill Kurtis Productions by:** 174, 189; **fake authentication of carpenter's bench and "blood" by:** 189, 318; **contributing editor to** *True West* **magazine:** 330 (See "Billy the Kid Case" hoax)
Jackson, Calvin – 397
Jacobsen, Joel – 45, 309; *Such Men as Billy the Kid: The Lincoln County War Revisited* by: 45, 309
James, Frank – 122, 399, 402
James, Jesse – 4, 20-21, 30, 36, 104, 122, 338, 340-342, 379-380, 383, 399-403, 431
Jameson, William Carl "W.C." – 121, 123-124, 134-147, 149, 154, 161-162, 166, 168, 171, 179-180, 182, 184, 187, 195, 201-203, 212, 214, 225-227, 234, 240, 263, 265, 270-271, 275, 277-280, 282, 284, 287, 290, 293, 303, 307-310, 315, 328, 330, 332-333, 337-338, 383, 414, 421, 431, 435; **forging "Brushy Bill" Roberts transcript by:** 135-

146; narrating Steve Sederwall's Billy the Kid history hoaxes by: 134, 180, 195, 203, 240, 265, 284, 338, 383, 431; *The Return of the Outlaw Billy the Kid* by: 123, 135-142, 328, 330; *Billy the Kid: Beyond the Grave* by: 139-140; *Billy the Kid: The Lost Interviews* by: 124, 136-137, 140-142, 145-146, 309; *Pat Garrett: The Man Behind the Badge* by: 140, 146-147, 201, 293; *Cold Case Billy the Kid: Investigating History's Mysteries* by: 121, 124, 134, 139-140, 144, 146-147, 154, 161-162, 166, 168, 171, 175, 179, 185, 195, 202, 212, 225-227, 234, 240, 263, 265, 299, 309-310, 312, 315, 332-333, 337-338, 375, 378, 383, 385, 404, 411, 435 (See Frederick Bean, Steve Sederwall, "Billy the Kid Case" hoax, Cold Case Billy the Kid megahoax)

Janofsky, Michael – 127, 129-130

Jaramillo, Lorenzo – 105-106, 108, 164, 307

John S. Dye's Government Counterfeit Detector – 372

Kahn, A. – 399

Kansas City, Missouri – 380, 391

Keleher, William – 45, 308; *Violence in Lincoln County 1869-1881* by: 45, 308

Kimbrell, George – 56, 61, 78, 284, 354, 358-359, 361, 363

King, Frank M. – 114, 117, 312; *Wranglin' the Past: Reminiscences of Frank M. King*: 114, 117, 312

Kinney, John – 6, 54, 74, 98, 274, 277-278, 280-282, 343, 364

Klasner, Lilly – 287; *My Girlhood Among Outlaws* by: 287

Komar, Debra – 223-228, 230, 233-235, 244-245, 458-460; opposing exhumations of Catherine Antrim and Billy Bonney by: 223-226, 228, 230, 233, 244-245, 458-460 (See "Billy the Kid Case" hoax)

Kurtis, Bill – 125, 174-177, 214, 248, 250; **Bill Kurtis Productions of**: 125, 175, 177, 190-192, 205-207, 211, 248, 250-251, 253-255; **funding of Dr. Henry Lee by**: 175

Kyle, Thomas G. – 331

Las Cruces, New Mexico – 39, 80, 96, 107, 303, 418

Las Vegas Daily Gazette – 62, 93, 109, 303, 381, 417

Las Vegas Daily Optic – 157, 288, 418

Las Vegas, New Mexico Territory – 14, 51, 104, 340, 379, 400

Lea, Frank – 399-400

Lea, Joseph – 399-400

Lee, Henry C. – 125-126, 133-134, 147, 150, 155, 174-181, 189-193, 196-202, 204-205, 220-221, 237, 247, 250, 254-255, 257, 259-262, 268, 290, 300, 302, 315, 318, 331-333, 375, 445; **bad reputation of**: 174-175; **brought in by Paul Hutton**: 174, 189; **paid for by Bill Kurtis**: 175; **fake forensics of "blood" of Deputy Bell by**: 150, 155, 174-179, 318; **fake forensics for carpenter's workbench by**: 189-193; no DNA recovered from his specimens of: 126, 133, 192-194, 196, 205, 440-441; **faking the Pat Garrett shooting scene with a washstand and headboard by**: 196-201 (See "Billy the Kid Case" hoax, Orchid Cellmark Lab)

Legislature Revolt of 1872 – 5

Leonard, Ira – 6, 23, 57-58, 61, 63, 88, 91, 96, 102-103, 349, 351-357, 363, 381, 404, 415

Lincoln Bank – 50, 387
Lincoln County courthouse-jail –
   11, 21, 26, 28, 37-38, 48, 64,
   101, 128, 132, 150, 177-178,
   180, 182, 247, 254, 259-260,
   318, 421; **outhouse of:** 64, 129,
   150, 179, 184, 186-187
Lincoln County Heritage Trust –
   330
Lincoln County Leader – 101
Lincoln County, New Mexico – 10-
   11, 13, 16, 18, 21-23, 26, 32, 36,
   48, 50, 52-53, 55-56, 58-62, 64,
   68-70, 77, 82, 93, 96, 101, 104,
   107, 111, 113, 121, 127-128,
   130-131, 143, 147-153, 155-156,
   167, 172-173, 177, 179-180,
   183, 187-189, 191, 193, 202,
   205-207, 212-221, 226, 229,
   235, 237, 239-240, 243, 247,
   249-251, 254-255, 257-258, 262-
   263, 267, 269, 279, 284-286,
   288, 303, 315-317, 319, 321-
   323, 329, 330, 333, 343, 345-
   346, 348-351, 354, 358-359,
   362, 368, 375, 381, 384-385,
   400, 405, 408, 410, 413, 424,
   430, 442, 444-446, 449, 460
Lincoln County Sheriff's
   Department Case No. 2003-274
   (see "Billy the Kid Case" hoax)
Lincoln County Sheriff's
   Department Supplemental
   Report for Case No. 2003-274
   (See John Miller)
Lincoln County War – 3, 5, 10, 13,
   20, 24, 30-32, 40, 43, 46-47, 49,
   51, 57, 59, 61, 63-65, 70, 74-76,
   78, 81, 99-101, 128, 143, 145,
   151, 153, 214, 271, 274, 279,
   282, 320-321, 323, 343-346,
   348, 353, 363, 380, 383-384,
   386-387, 393, 401, 406; **Battle
   in:** 10, 24, 54, 74, 82, 99-101,
   103, 187, 277-284, 298, 343-
   344, 364, 422-424
Lincoln Museum – 18, 105, 107-
   108, 145, 151-152, 206-207, 263
Lincoln, New Mexico – 5, 10, 18,
   24, 30-31, 49-52, 54-57, 60, 64,
   68-73, 76, 78, 82-83, 88-89, 92,
   97-98, 100-101, 103, 127-128,
   132, 148, 152-154, 172, 176,
   181, 185-186, 246, 248, 267,
   271-273, 275, 277, 279-382,
   286, 288, 304, 316-317, 324,
   330, 343, 347-349, 351-352,
   356-365, 368, 384, 387-388,
   393, 403, 408, 417, 419, 422,
   424-425, 427-428, 430
Lincoln pit jail – 52, 69-70
"Little Casino" – 58
Loboto, Frank – 144-145
Long, Jack – 84, 279-280
"Long Rail Brand" – 305
"Long S Brand" – 305
Lopez, Raymond – 315, 401, 487-
   488, 492, 495, 497, 711-712, 714
Los Alamos Laboratory – 132
Lucero, Pedro Antonio – 105-106,
   108, 164, 307
Luminol – 190, 251
Mabry, Thomas Jewett – 115, 122,
   136
Mackie, John – 49
MacNab, Frank – 52-53, 65, 270,
   276, 278, 357
Markland, Absalom – 10
Martin, Billie – 206
Martinez, Atanacio – 51, 69
Martinez, Leo – 235-236, 243
Mason, Barney – 59, 65, 286, 340,
   365, 367, 370, 373, 377, 388-
   390, 396, 399, 413; **as Secret
   Service spy:** 65, 286, 365, 367,
   388; **as exposing Dedrick
   counterfeiting-cattle deal:**
   340, 365, 367, 370, 373, 377,
   388-390, 396, 399, 413
Master Bank of Kansas City –
   394, 396
Mastin Bank of Kansas City –
   392-394, 396
Matthews, Jacob Basil "Billy" –
   52, 58, 69-72, 96, 279, 288
Maxwell bedroom (Peter Maxwell)
   (See Maxwell house)

Maxwell cemetery – 59, 159, 226, 327
Maxwell, Deluvina – 47, 158, 168-170, 197
Maxwell family – 48, 167, 189, 195, 344
Maxwell house (mansion) – 11, 41, 47, 167-168, 188, 295-297; **floor plan of:** 295-297; **Peter Maxwell bedroom in:** 41, 47, 65-66, 67-70, 188, 197-198, 201-204, 218, 268, 290-293, 295-300, 302-303, 320, 327, 331-332; **sale of:** 167-168, 188
Maxwell Land Grant – 5, 47, 59, 305
Maxwell, Lucien Bonaparte – 47, 58-59, 168, 197, 246, 295, 299-300, 305, 332
Maxwell, Luz Trotier de Beaubien – 59, 164, 166, 300, 305, 307
Maxwell, Paulita – 47-48, 59, 65, 300-301, 331-332, 344, 401, 425
Maxwell, Peter "Pete" – 28, 41-42, 47, 59, 65, 105, 125, 136, 157, 168, 188, 195, 198, 202-203, 291, 293, 296-297, 301-302, 304-306, 308, 328, 331-332, 365; **as Coroner's Jury witness to William Bonney's killing:** 42, 105, 125, 302, 328
McCarty, Catherine (see Catherine Antrim)
McCarty, John L. – 298
McCarty, Joseph "Josie" (See Joseph Antrim)
McCarty, William Henry (see William H. Bonney)
McCloskey, William – 270
McCoy, Dave – 442
McDaniels, Jim – 80
McGinn, Randi – 271
McKinney, Collin – 314
McKinney, Elizabeth Francis – 314
McKinney, Thomas Christopher "Kip" – 41, 59, 65, 162, 310-312, 314

McMasters, James E. – 75
McSween, Alexander – 50-55, 57, 64, 71, 75, 79, 81-87, 266-267, 269, 271-273, 277-281, 284, 343, 357, 393, 422
McSween, Susan – 10, 54, 56-58, 282-283, 309, 393
Meadows, John – 65, 104, 425
Memory Lane Cemetery – 223-224, 458-459
Mescalero Indian Reservation – 6, 50, 53, 78, 226, 276, 344, 350
Mesilla, New Mexico Territory – 6, 37, 51, 54, 58, 63-64, 89, 91, 93, 96-97, 132, 272, 280, 321, 325, 404-406
Mesilla Thirty Four – 82
Metz, Leon – 46, 285, 330, 400; ***Pat Garrett: The Story of a Western Lawman* by:** 46, 285, 400
Middleton, John – 6-9, 52-53, 63, 68, 71-73, 101, 276
Miller, Jay – 237-238, 247, 318-320
Miller, John – 121, 130, 133, 147, 204, 206-207, 211-214, 223, 237, 241-242, 244-245, 328, 331, 345, 442-443, 445, 451-457; **birth date of:** 204; **no match with Billy the Kid tintype for:** 331; **Lincoln County Sheriff's Department Supplemental Report for exhumation of:** 206-207, 442-443; **illegal exhumation of:** 133, 147, 204-207, 435, 451-454; **grave-robbed remains of:** 211, 455; **possible faked DNA of:** 211-212, 456; **criminal investigation for exhumation of:** 207 (See Helen Airy, "Billy the Kid Case" hoax, Laura Fulginiti)
Miller, Kenneth – 168
Miller, Kenneth "Kenny" – 195
Miller, Manuel "Mannie" –168, 170, 188, 195, 251

Miller, Stella Abreu (See Stella Abreu)
Monclova, Coahuila, Mexico – 310
Montaño, Jose – 352, 404-405, 408
moon (dark night) error (See Oliver Pleasant "Brushy Bill" Roberts)
Moore Scott – 92, 401
Moore's Hotsprings Hotel – 340, 400-401
Moore, William – 68
Morel, Alan –215, 226 (See "Billy the Kid Case" hoax)
Morrison, William Vincent "Bill" – 122-124, 135-137, 139, 141-143, 146, 148, 185, 203, 277, 309, 337
Morton, William "Buck" – 52, 60, 64, 68-69, 151, 268, 270-271
Moundville, Missouri – 373, 385-386, 402
Mullin, Robert N. – 189, 195, 235, 295-297, 306, 311
Murphy, Lawrence G. – 49-50, 266; **L.G. Murphy & Co. of:** 269, 430
Napolitano, Janet – 133
Nevada, Missouri – 373, 392, 402, 414, 429
Newcomb, John – 265, 267
Newman, Simon – 97
Newman's Semi-Weekly – 97
New York Sun – 13, 61, 340, 343, 381, 383, 416
New York Times – 126, 229, 371, 385
New York World Magazine – 34, 403
Nicholi, Bill – 72, 317
Nolan, Frederick – 45, 218, 232-233, 236, 240, 243, 268, 301, 311, 314, 328, 332; *The Life and Death of John Henry Tunstall* **by:** 45; *The Lincoln County War: A Documentary History* **by:** 45; *The West of Billy the Kid* **by:** 45
Oakley, Kenneth – 208

Office of the Medical Investigator (OMI), Albuquerque, New Mexico – 223-226, 230, 233-234, 243-244, 457-460; **exhumation permits refused by:** 223-226, 234, 457-460 (See Debra Komar, Ross Zumwalt)
O'Folliard, Tom – 11, 41, 48, 54-56, 59-60, 62, 88, 103, 154, 224, 226, 245-246, 298, 309-314, 316, 344, 346, 349, 357, 360-361, 369, 380, 387, 391, 393-394, 415, 423
Oklahoma Indian Territory – 398
Olinger, Robert "Bob" – 26-27, 48, 64-65, 81, 98, 101-102, 129, 132, 152, 155, 180-181, 184, 215-216, 219, 222, 229, 236, 287, 319, 322-324, 364-365, 367, 424, 444
Orchid Cellmark Laboratory – 178, 182, 191-194, 196, 205-206, 209, 211-213, 215, 220, 222, 237, 251-252, 257-258, 440-441, 445-449, 455-457; **DNA faking scandal of:** 192; **no testing for blood done by:** 191-192, 194; **no DNA on carpenter's bench found by:** 196, 440-441; **subpoenaed records from:** 178, 192, 194, 211; **no DNA from John Miller claimed by:** 209; **later possibly fake claim of DNA from John Miller claimed by:** 211-213, 251, 456-457
Ostler, Calvin – 176-177, 190-191, 198, 201-202, 215, 248, 250, 252-253, 255, 258, 445-446, 449
Ostler, Kim – 250, 255
Otero, Miguel – 303-304, 401; *The Real Billy the Kid* **by:** 303
Ortho-tolidine (O-tolidine) – 177, 181, 248, 251
Owens, Jasper – 385
Patrón, Juan – 50, 57, 78, 387
Pecos River – 16, 58, 418
Pecos River Coe Camp – 50, 358
Peñasco River – 49, 58, 70

Pennington, William – 399, 402
Peppin, George – 10-11, 54-56, 79, 81-83, 85, 277-281, 283, 309, 364, 422
Picacho, New Mexico – 46, 54, 278
Pickett, Tom – 62, 93, 423-424, 426
Piltdown Man hoax – 207-208
Pittmon, Geneva Roberts – 122
Poe, John William – 41-42, 58, 65-66, 107, 123, 136, 145, 156-169, 172-173, 183, 197, 201, 203-204, 288-293, 295, 298, 300-304, 306, 317, 324, 331-332; *The Death of Billy the Kid* **by:** 136, 156, 158-159, 163, 197, 290
Poe, Sophie – 183; *Buckboard Days* **by:** 183
Poling, Mike – 206, 452, 454
Polk, Shiela – 207
Posse Comitatus Act – 54-55, 58, 82, 280-282, 284, 360, 364
Prescott, Arizona – 130, 205-206, 209, 213, 451
Prescott Police Department – 209
Purington, George – 281
Quantrill, William – 399, 402
Quintero, Henry – 133, 235, 242-243
Ramsey, JonBenet – 174-175
Ramsey, Burke – 174-175
Rasch, Philip J. – 45, 156, 158-159, 312, 405-406, 411-413, 426; **Tom O'Folliard genealogy by:** 312; **biography Billy Wilson by:** 405-406; **quoting counterfeiting pardon of Billy Wilson by:** 411-413; **Tom Pickett's tall tale on Stinking Springs given by:** 426; *Trailing Billy the Kid* **by:** 159, 312, 411
Regulators – 5-6, 10-11, 20, 47, 52-57, 59-60, 63-64, 70, 74-75, 82, 92, 99-100, 103, 137, 187, 270-272, 274-279, 339, 343-344, 346, 348, 352, 357, 359-361, 370, 378, 380, 404-405, 415
Richardson, William Blaine III "Bill" – 121, 124, 126-128, 130-131, 133-134, 148-150, 176, 193, 205, 214, 228-230, 232, 240-241, 243-244, 257, 271, 238-239, 435 (See "Billy the Kid Case" hoax)
Riley, John – 49-50, 58, 78, 80-81, 152, 269, 282, 349
Rio Grande Republican – 107, 303
Ritch, William – 107-112, 114, 117, 303, 308
Rivers, Frank – 68, 70
Roberts, Andrew "Buckshot" – 6, 10, 53, 60, 63-64, 69, 76, 275-276, 287, 353, 358, 360, 406, 424-425; **federal indictment for killing of:** 6-9, 63, 357, 425
Roberts, Oliver Pleasant "Brushy Bill" –115, 122-127, 129-130, 134-139, 169, 171, 180, 184-187, 193, 196, 203, 205, 207-208, 212, 219, 223-225, 227, 231-232, 234, 236, 242, 245, 265, 268, 270-271, 274-275, 277-278, 282-284, 287, 290, 303, 308-310, 312, 320, 327-328, 330-331, 333, 337-338, 414, 420-421, 431, 435, 445, 460; **Billy the Kid imposter hoax of:** 122-124, 134-136, 171, 287, 320, 327, 420; **failed pardon attempt by:** 115, 122; **fatal moon error by:** 123-124, 135-146; **failed tintype match of:** 330-331; **family debunking of:** 122; **attempted exhumation of:** 219 (See William V. Morrison, C.L. Sonnichsen, W.C. Jameson, Frederick Bean, "Billy the Kid Case" hoax)
Robins, Bill III – 121, 124, 127, 225, 227-228, 233-236, 241-242, 244-245 (see "Billy the Kid Case" hoax)
Robinson, Berry – 54-55, 280-281
Rodarte, Anthony – 206

Rodarte, Misty – 206
Romero, Vincente – 54-55, 57, 82-83, 284, 357
Romney, Pearl Tenney – 206
Romo, Rene – 175-177, 190, 197, 201, 214, 217
Roswell, New Mexico Territory – 59, 80, 104, 304, 306, 345, 366-368, 399-400, 418
Rudabaugh, Dave "Dirty Dave" – 14, 16, 19, 60, 62, 93, 423-424
Rudulph, Milnor – 65-66, 105-105, 108, 145, 156, 158-160, 164-166, 171, 288, 307, 327; **as member of Santa Fe Ring:** 66 (see Coroner's Jury Report for William H. Bonney)
Ruidoso News – 233, 337, 375, 379, 384, 427
RuidosoNews.com – 133, 188-189, 206, 218, 318
Ruidoso River – 73, 430
Rumsey, Roy – 219
Rynerson, William – 51, 57-58, 103, 152, 337
Salazar, Yginio – 101, 186
Sampson, Michael – 376, 380, 385, 413
Sams, Dale – 206
San Andres Mountains – 195, 305-306
Sandia Laboratory – 132, 231
Sandoval, David – 242
San Miguel County, New Mexico Territory – 12-13, 62, 93, 105, 108, 111, 115, 117, 285, 308, 361
San Patricio, New Mexico Territory – 5, 52, 54, 74, 77-78, 269, 278, 364; **massacre at:** 5, 54, 278, 364 (See George Peppin, John Kinney)
Santa Fe Daily New Mexican – 93, 96, 109-110, 157, 288, 416
Santa Fe, New Mexico – 23, 25-26, 28-29, 31, 33-34, 89-91, 94-95, 114, 131-132, 145, 238, 240, 282, 308, 346-351, 356, 367, 369, 372, 380, 386, 399, 405, 407-410, 418, 429
Santa Fe Ring (the Ring) – 5-20, 24, 43-63, 65-67, 74, 78, 82-83, 96, 99-100, 103, 187, 267, 269, 271, 274, 277, 280, 282, 339-340, 344-346, 348, 352, 354-355, 362-363, 368-369; **outlaw myth of Billy the Kid by:** 5-19, 44, 46, 59-61, 66-67, 98-99, 340, 346, 383, 435
Sapatori, Joel – 206
"Scapula Man" (See William Hudspeth, Laura Fulginiti)
Schenk, Jamie – 250, 254
Scurlock, Josiah "Doc" – 6-9, 53, 56, 60, 63, 276, 344, 346, 357, 359-360, 387, 415
Secret Service – 11, 13, 25, 29, 60, 65, 67, 88, 103, 154, 284-285, 316, 321, 323, 338-342, 344-348, 352, 360, 370-372, 376-378, 380-381, 385, 390, 392, 395-396, 402-404, 413-414, 424, 427-428 (See Azariah F. Wild, Wallace W. Hall, Arthur L. Drummond, Patrick D. Tyrrell)
Secret Service Currency Reference Information: 1860's-1880's – 372
Sederwall, Steven M. "Steve" – 121, 127-131, 133-135, 139, 141, 144-316, 319-320, 322, 325, 328-333, 337-338, 375-381, 383-384, 386-388, 390-392, 394-406, 412-429, 431, 442, 444-446, 448-449; **LINCOLN COUNTY SHERIFF'S DEPARTMENT CASE 2003-274, "BILLY THE KID CASE" HOAX IN: "Brushy Bill"-backing "Mayor's Report" of:** 148-149; **deputized for:** 296, 301, 314, 398, 408, 423-424, 468, 472, 481, 514, 518; commissioned deputy card of: 219; **authorship of "Case 2003-274 Probable Cause Statement" claimed by:** 150-

173; Deputy Bell hoaxed killing sub-investigation in: 150, 154-155, 174-185, 214-216, 229-230, 257, 444; hoaxing Bell sub-investigation as his private hobby by: 180-187; hoaxing Bell sub-investigation as entire Case 2003-274 by: 214-216; **participating in carpenter's bench "Billy the Kid blood DNA" hoax by:** 133, 188-190; hoaxing "bench blood DNA" by: 188-190, 192-193; hoaxing carpenter's bench forensics as his private hobby: 195-196, 448; **participating in washstand and headboard forensic hoax against Pat Garrett by:** 197, 201; hoaxing washstand-headboard "investigation" as his private hobby by: 201-204; **hoaxing exhumed John Miller as Billy the Kid by:** 133, 205, 207-209; writing "Lincoln County Sheriff's Department Supplemental Report" for exhumation: 206-207; hoaxing John Miller exhumation as his private hobby by: 212-214; BillytheKidCase.com website selling records of: 175, 222, 379, 448; **open records litigation against:** 133-134, 193-194, 216-222, 226-246, 263; hiding records as his private property by: 133, 216-222; denying being a deputy for Case 2003-274 by: 133; hoaxing of carpenter's bench "blood" by: 193-194; hoaxing of OMI denying Billy the Kid's burial in Fort Sumner by: 226-228; co-authoring the "Memorandum" as a tourism conspiracy against the case by: 228-239; hoaxing the "Memorandum" as a conspiracy against himself: 240-246; hoaxing the litigation as an attack against himself: 263; forging forensic reports of Dr. Henry Lee by: 247-262, 333, 337, 375, 445-447, 449; **"COLD CASE BILLY THE KID" HOAXES BY:** 133, 265-287, 289-314, 331-332; meeting future hoax narrator W.C. Jameson by: 135, 139; **hoaxing the Tunstall murder scene by:** 265-270; **hoaxing the Morton and Baker killing by:** 270; **hoaxing the Sheriff Brady killing by:** 271-274; **hoaxing the "Buckshot" Roberts killing by:** 275-277; hoaxing the Lincoln County War Battle by: 277-284; **hoaxing Pat Garrett as lacking lawman authority by:** 284-287; **hoaxing Pat Garrett as dishonest by:** 287, 289-308; **hoaxing death scene doubts by:** 290-306, 331-332; hoaxing death scene discrepancies by: 290-293; hoaxing no outside door to Peter Maxwell's bedroom by: 293-300, 303, 331-332; hoaxing shooting scene doubts by: 301-302; hoaxing removal of the body by: 302-303; hoaxing a pseudo-Pete Maxwell witness by: 304-306; **hoaxing no Coroner's Jury Report by:** 307-308; **hoaxing discovery of the "Billy the Kid" moniker by:** 308-309; **hoaxing that Tom O'Folliard was "Folliard" by:** 309-314; **THE "BILLY THE KID'S BAD BUCKS" HOAX OF:** 121, 135, 332; **overview of:** 338-342; **articles on:** 375-381; **narrated in W.C. Jameson's** *Cold Case Billy the Kid*: 383-431; **hoaxing a link of a counterfeit bill to Billy the** Kid: 384-385; **hoaxing**

Brockway sources as linked to Billy the Kid: 385-386; hoaxing Billy Bonney's rustling to counterfeiting: 386-390; hoaxing Billy Bonney as in the Brockway gang: 390-400; hoaxing Billy Bonney in league with Jesse James for counterfeiting: 400-403; hoaxing a link between Billy Bonney and Billy Wilson for counterfeiting: 404-414; hoaxing Billy Bonney as murdering Sam Smith: 414-417; hoaxing Billy Bonney as in mail-reading conspiracy with Mike Cosgrove: 417-419; hoaxing Billy Bonney's Secret Service pardon bargain as meaning he was a counterfeiter: 419-420; hoaxing Billy Bonney as doing witness intimidation: 420; hoaxing Billy Bonney as using counterfeit money: 420-421; hoaxing Billy Bonney as hiding counterfeit money in the Stinking Springs cabin: 421-426; hoaxing James Dolan as a Brockway counterfeiter: 427-430

Segale, Blandina – 4

Segura, Alejandro – 105-106, 158, 164-165, 171, 307, 327

Seven Rivers boys (rustlers) – 277-288

Sherman, John – 154, 285, 347-348

Sherman, Texas – 341-342, 369, 386, 390-391, 397

Shield, David – 282

Shield, Elizabeth – 282

Shield family – 282

Shipman, Jack – 311

Shipman, O.L. – 311

Silva, Jesus – 136, 144, 159, 246, 303-304

Silver City, New Mexico Territory – 21, 41, 45, 48, 79-80, 125, 130, 132, 224, 226, 228, 230-232, 234-236, 238-239, 241-244, 329, 458

Simpson, Nicole – 174

Simpson, O.J. – 174

Smith, Charles H. – 371-372, 376-378, 385

Smith, Gregory Scott – 298, 331-332

Smith, Sam – 17, 378, 383-384, 416-417, 431; **as killed by Apaches:** 416-417

Snead, William – 226

Snow, Clyde – 331

Sonnichsen, Charles Leland – 122-124, 135-139, 141-142, 144-146, 203; **forging "Brushy Bill" transcripts by:** 123-124, 136-139, 142; *Alias Billy the Kid* **by:** 123, 135-136, 141, 203

Sparks, Billy – 127, 131, 230, 235, 240-241, 243

Spector, Phil – 174

Spencer, Edward W. (See William E. Brockway)

Spencerian handwriting – 48, 57

Spitz, Werner – 175

Star Route scandals – 418

State Land Office, Santa Fe, New Mexico – 114-116

Statute of Limitations for murder in New Mexico Territory – 125, 129-130, 149

Staub, Rick – 192-194, 205-206, 209, 211-213, 237, 453-454 (See Orchid Cellmark Lab, "Billy the Kid Case" hoax)

Stewart, Frank – 16, 64, 92, 367

Stinking Springs – 11, 41, 48, 62, 64, 88, 92-93, 153, 316, 381, 403, 405-406, 417, 421-422, 424-426

Stockton, Ike – 79, 274

Stolorow, Mark – 192

Sullivan, Pat – 206

Sullivan, Thomas T. "Tom" – 27, 128-131, 133, 148-151, 173,

175, 177-178, 190-192, 198, 202, 205-209, 214-219, 221-222, 226, 228-230, 233-235, 238-240, 243, 248, 250-252, 255, 263, 315, 319, 322, 328-329, 379, 444-445, 448 (See "Billy the Kid Case" hoax)

Struckman, Robert – 425-427

Sunnyside, New Mexico – 49, 206, 260, 329, 332-333, 338, 679, 699

Taeger, Mary Nell – 186, 197

TalkLeft.com – 410, 432

Tascosa, Texas – 40, 54, 65, 177, 597-598, 640

Taylor, Daniel – 340

Taylor, Manuel – 196

Telfer, Lois – 306, 378, 387, 492, 716, 725-726; **denied Billy the Kid exhumation petition of:** 725-726

Texas Ranger Museum (Hall of Fame) – 355

"The House" – 24, 34, 162, 164, 237, 451, 455, 528, 587, 590, 603, 646, 676

The Albuquerque Citizen – 697

The Indianapolis Press – 276, 642

The New Southwest – 258, 262

Thomas, Andrew – 439

Thompson, George – 428

Thornton, William T. – Thunderer (Colt .41) – 559

Tippett, Sherry – 292, 307-308, 310, 312-313, 378, 468, 475, 740

Totty, Frances E. – 345, 397

Traylor, Leslie – 184, 695, 717

Trinidad, Colorado – 154

True West magazine (See Bob Boze Bell)

Trujillo, Francisco – 400, 595

Tucson, Arizona – 98

Tucson Weekly – 407-408, 430, 432, 436

Tularosa Ditch War – 184, 571, 676

Tularosa, New Mexico Territory – 622, 645-646

Tunnell, Dale – 296, 300, 425-431, 433-434, 436-440, 583, 747, 761, 764

Tunstall, John Henry – 5-6, 45, 49-53, 55-58, 60, 64-65, 67-74, 79, 82-83, 85-86, 99-101, 151-152, 184, 187, 265-273, 277-278, 283, 305, 339, 343, 355, 357, 387, 422, 460-461; **Daniel Appel autopsy report to Frank Warner Angel of:** 266-267, 460-461; **Coroner's Jury Report of:** 267-268

Turk, David S. – 121, 134, 153, 172, 176-177, 189, 191, 202, 248, 250, 255, 266, 282, 315-317, 321-325, 333, 337, 375-377, 380, 431; **input for "Probable Cause Statement by:** 153, 172, 315-317; **"The U.S. Marshals Service and Billy the Kid" by:** 321-325; **vouching for Dr. Henry Lee by:** 176; **fake authentication of carpenter's bench by:** 189; **in "Billy the Kid's Bad Bucks" hoax:** 337, 375-377, 380, 431 (See "Billy the Kid Case" hoax, "Billy the Kid's Bad Bucks" hoax)

Turner, Marion F. – 80

Tyrrell, Patrick D. – 402

Upson, Ashmun "Ash" – 41, 43, 59, 152, 232, 387

Utley, Robert M. – 45, 152, 218, 232-233, 271; *Billy the Kid: A Short and Violent Life* **by:** 45, 152

Valdez, Jannay P. – 127, 129-130

Virden, Rick E. – 205-208, 215, 218-219, 221-222, 226, 228-229, 249, 252, 263, 320, 379, 444-448; **deputizing Tom Sullivan and Steve Sederwall for "Billy the Kid Case" by:** 207, 218, 221; **exhumations of John Miller/William Hudspeth under:** 205-207; **attempted exhumation of "Brushy Bill" Roberts by:** 219; **open**

records violation case against: 215, 222, 226, 228-229, 249, 252, 263, 320, 379, 444-448 (See "Billy the Kid Case" hoax)
Waite, Fred Tecumseh – 6-9, 49, 51-52, 63, 69-70, 72-73, 101, 276
Waldo, Henry – 10, 57
Wallace, Lew – 3, 10, 12, 18, 20-40, 44, 47, 55-58, 60-63, 67, 75-78, 81-82, 87-91, 97, 100, 103, 109-114, 122, 127-128, 132, 148, 153, 303, 309, 343, 345, 352-353, 365, 368, 378, 384, 387, 403, 415, 437; **Amnesty Proclamation by:** 56, 76, 352-353; **Billy Bonney pardon bargain by:** 10, 47, 57, 61, 82, 97, 103, 128, 148, 153, 343, 345, 352-353, 387; **testifying against N.A.M. Dudley by:** 57-58; **Billy the Kid reward notices by:** 109-114, 303; **Billy the Kid outlaw myth articles by:** 20-40, 44, 362; **fake switching Jessie Evans to Jesse James by:** 403
Walz, Edgar – 50, 60-61, 74, 103, 274, 278, 345-346, 349-350, 355, 358-361, 415, 420
washstand (See "Billy the Kid Case" hoax, Henry Lee fake forensics on, Steve Sederwall forgery of forensic report on)
Weddle, Jerry (Richard) – 45, 168, 188; *Antrim is my Stepfather's Name* by: 45; **consultation on carpenter's bench by:** 168, 188
West, William H. aka William Budd – 339, 341-342, 346, 355, 357, 361-362, 365-367, 370, 373, 383, 385, 388-389, 391, 399, 405, 413-415, 420
Whitehill, Harvey – 48
White Oaks livery – 56, 61-62, 109, 339, 341, 344, 346, 351, 357, 361, 365-366, 388, 405, 407-410, 419
White Oaks, New Mexico – 13, 16, 19, 56, 61-62, 64-65, 88, 98, 152, 181, 186, 304, 339, 341, 345, 348, 351-352, 355-357, 360-363, 365-367, 369-370, 372-373, 378, 386, 388-389, 391, 393, 396, 399, 405, 407-409, 413, 415-416, 419, 423, 429
White Oaks posse – 62, 65, 88, 366
"White Oaks Rangers" – 16
Widenmann, Robert – 70-73, 101
Wilcox-Brazil Ranch – 423
Wilcox, Lucius "Lute" – 93, 381, 417
Wild, Azariah F. – 11-13, 25, 29, 60, 65, 67, 154, 284-288, 312, 316-317, 321, 339-342, 344-370, 373-374, 376-377, 379-380, 383-386, 388, 390-391, 396-399, 402-406, 414, 417, 420, 424, 430-431; **New Mexico investigation by:** 339-340, 344-370, Billy Bonney pardon offer by: 61, 341, 381, 414-416; Barney Mason as spy in counterfeit money-cattle deal for: 65, 286, 340, 365, 365, 367, 370, 373, 388-390, 396, 399, 413; appointing Pat Garrett as Deputy U.S. Marshal by: 11, 62, 284-287, 323, 363; **Sherman, Texas, investigation of Walter Greenham by:** 341-342, 369, 386, 390-391, 397-399
Wild World Magazine – 159
Will Dowlin & Company – 428-429
Wilson, Gorgonio – 86
Wilson, John B. "Squire" – 51-52, 55, 57, 68, 70, 77, 270, 280
Wilson, William "Billy" alias D.L. Anderson – 14-15, 18-19, 60, 62, 93, 96, 339, 341-341, 346, 349-350, 355, 357, 360, 363, 369-370, 380, 383, 389, 404-415, 418-421, 427;

counterfeiting trial of: 404-406; **counterfeiting pardon of:** 406-412; by President Grover Cleveland: 411-412
Winchester '73 carbine – 18, 29, 35, 52053, 69, 95, 384
Wortley Hotel – 64, 85, 148
Yavapi County, Arizona – 206-207, 452, 454
Yerby Ranch – 89, 344, 369, 387
Yerby, Thomas – 89, 344, 369
Zamora, Francisco – 54-55, 57, 82-83, 86-87, 294, 357
Zuber, Hugo – 67, 89, 343
Zumwalt, Ross – 223, 458-459

www.ingramcontent.com/pod-product-compliance
Lightning Source LLC
Chambersburg PA
CBHW020726160426
43192CB00006B/131